FOURTH

# CONVENIENCE FOOD FACTS

## A Quick Guide
## For Choosing
## Healthy Brand-Name Foods
## In Every Aisle of the Supermarket

**ARLENE MONK, RD, LD, CDE** • **NANCY COOPER, RD, LD, CDE**

**IDC Publishing**
Minneapolis

**Note:** Although this book contains up-to-date information as of 1997, the information on labels does change as products are reformulated. Therefore, if the label information is different from the information you find in this book, use the label information when evaluating nutrition information.

All brand-name products cited in this book are the registered trademark properties of their respective companies.

All Kraft® trademarks are used with permission.

All General Mills® trademarks are used with permission.

© 1997 International Diabetes Center, Institute for Research and Education HealthSystem Minnesota

All rights reserved. No part of this publication may be reproduced, stored in a retrieval system or transmitted, in any form or by any means, electronic, photocopying, recording, or otherwise, without prior permission of

IDC Publishing
3800 Park Nicollet Boulevard
Minneapolis, Minnesota 55416-2699
(612) 993-3393

**Library of Congress Cataloging-in-Publication Data**
Monk, Arlene.
Convenience food facts: a quick guide for choosing healthy brand-name foods in every aisle of the supermarket / Arlene Monk, Nancy Cooper. — 4th ed.
p. cm.
Includes index.
ISBN 1-885115-36-9
1. Food—Composition—Tables. 2. Convenience foods—Composition— Tables. 3. Brand name products—Composition—Tables. 4. Diabetes—Nutritional aspects. I. Cooper, Nancy.
TX551.M56 1997
613.2—dc21                                                                96-49307
                                                                                    CIP

Printed in the United States of America

Publisher: Karol Carstensen
Editor: Sara Frueh
Production Manager: Gail Devery
Cover Design: Circus Design
Text Design: MacLean & Tuminelly

Distributed to bookstores by Chronimed Publishing, Minneapolis, Minnesota

# Acknowledgements

We would like to thank the following for their help in writing and publishing this book: the food companies, who provided us with nutrition information about their products; Karla Gruman, Lauren Tobey, and Jennifer Sarych, dietetic students who gave their willing and capable assistance; Sara Frueh, Gail Devery, and Karol Carstensen, who provided editorial direction and support and managed the production of this book; and Shirley Upham, who assisted in entering the nutrition data.

We would also like to thank the entire IDC staff for their support and encouragement, in particular Donnell D. Etzwiler, MD, Richard Bergenstal, MD, Marion Franz, MS, RD, CDE, and all the IDC dietitians. Lastly, we are grateful to the readers of this book, who continue to strive to combine convenience and good nutrition.

Arlene Monk, RD, LD, CDE
Nancy Cooper, RD, LD, CDE

# Table of Contents

# Introduction

**convenience** *adj* (1917): designed for quick and easy preparation or use.

Time is precious in our hectic world as we struggle to balance the demands of work, family, community, and other areas of our busy lives. The need to save time, or at least to use the hours in a day differently, has affected many of our habits, including what we eat and how we prepare meals. Not only are we eating more food away from home, especially fast food, but we are demanding more convenience in the foods we do prepare at home. It's not surprising, then, that we are consuming more convenience foods than ever.

Convenience foods are simply those foods that require little or no preparation before eating—frozen pizzas, canned spaghetti sauce, and microwave popcorn, for example. Today grocery store shelves are filled with convenience foods of every description, as food companies try to meet the demands of consumers looking for quick, easy, time-saving food options. With all the emphasis on convenience, however, we can sometimes forget about healthful eating. Many convenience foods are loaded with calories, fat, and salt. But when a meal is prepackaged and ready for the microwave, we can often overlook its nutritional content, even if we are otherwise health conscious. Fortunately there are many healthful convenience food choices available, and convenience foods can be a great addition to your mealtime arsenal. The challenge is selecting products that meet your nutrition and health needs as well as your energy and time constraints.

That's what *Convenience Food Facts* will help you do. By providing complete nutrition information about thousands of brand-name foods in one extensive resource, this book lets you find and compare products and gives you helpful hints and guidelines for choosing those that meet your needs. Maybe you're trying to eat a well-balanced, low-fat diet in order to maintain a healthy weight or to help lower your risk of developing a chronic disease. Or perhaps you're watching your sodium intake to control hypertension (high blood pressure), or you have diabetes and you're controlling your blood glucose (sugar) by counting carbohydrates. Whatever your nutrition and health goals are, the information in this book will help you choose convenience foods that will support rather than work against them. *Convenience Food Facts* is a resource you won't want to be without.

## About This Edition

Many new food products have been introduced to the market since the last edition of this book was published. New food companies and brands have also been established. To prepare this new edition, we contacted over two hundred food companies and received up-to-date nutrition information on over three thousand products. We also spent hundreds of hours scanning grocery store shelves, looking for the newest products and the most current labeling information. The result is a comprehensive collection of convenience foods with the most current nutrition information available.

One of our primary objectives in this edition was to make the wealth of information in the book as accessible as possible. We determined very early on that the basic organization of foods in the nutrition tables would be alphabetical. Then, as we compiled and organized the entries and subentries, we continually asked the question: What would I look under to find this product? We tackled the obvious questions fairly quickly and made some editorial decisions. For example, do you look under "Chips, potato" or "Potato Chips"? (We chose "Chips, potato.") Under "Chips, potato" you will find subentries like "Barbeque," "Cheese," etc., with the individual products listed below.

Another of our objectives in this edition was to present the information so that similar products could be compared easily. Creating subentries to organize products by flavor or variety, as in the potato chip example above, worked well for this purpose, allowing readers to see all the brands of similar products in one listing. We realized, however, that we sometimes know and think of foods by brand and that readers might sometimes expect to be able to look up foods by brand. In such cases—as long as we felt the value of comparison would not be compromised—we created brand subentries to enable you to find specific products quickly and easily.

Frozen meals and entrees presented another organizational challenge. We felt the comparison factor was very important to readers, yet we recognized that most people are brand conscious with regard to these foods. In addition, we were dealing with a very large number of products. Our solution was to create entries featuring the main ingredient or ethnic style: Beef Meals/Entrees, Chicken Meals/Entrees, Mexican Meals/Entrees, etc., with subentries by flavor. For quick reference, we also created the Brand-Name Guide to Frozen Meals/Entrees. We also created brand-name guides for frozen pizzas and ready-to-eat cereals. The guides begin on page 409.

## Low-Fat Guidelines

Many health-conscious consumers are trying to eat foods that are low in fat, and with good reason. Not only can choosing low-fat foods help you maintain or lose weight; studies have shown that lowering your fat intake lowers your risk of developing heart disease, diabetes, and certain forms of cancer.

To help you quickly locate products that are low in fat, we have identified these products with this icon: ❶. In order to be considered low-fat, foods must meet certain guidelines that we established for fat and saturated fat content, which are listed below. These guidelines also can help you make good choices when you go shopping and can help you evaluate foods that may not be included in this book.

| FOOD CATEGORY | LOW-FAT GUIDELINE |
|---|---|
| Frozen meals and entrees, and other foods that make up most of a meal | 3 grams of fat or less per 100 calories, and no more than ⅓ of total fat from saturated fat |
| Cheese | 5 grams of fat or less per serving |
| Side dishes, snacks, cereals, and other foods | 3 grams of fat or less per serving |

Foods not marked ❶ do not meet the low-fat guidelines, but that doesn't mean you should never eat them. It's probably unrealistic to expect to avoid entirely foods you really like just because they may have more fat than is recommended. However, you do need to be aware and make conscious choices. You can fit almost any food into a healthful diet, if you are guided by one simple principle: moderation. Consider eating foods not marked ❶ less often or in smaller portions than foods that do meet the low-fat guidelines.

## Nutrition Information

Each product listed in this book includes values for calories and for important nutrients. These values are provided for one serving of the food, and this information was obtained directly from the manufacturer or from the food label.

For products that require the addition of other ingredients, the nutrition information listed is for the product as prepared according to the regular directions. Some products—many brownie and cake mixes, for example—also give low-cholesterol or low-fat preparation directions on the box, which you may find helpful.

In cases where the nutrition information for all of the flavors or varieties of a product was similar or identical, we averaged it. For example, the various flavors of Pillsbury® Cookie Dough are very similar nutritionally, so under the category "Cookie Dough" you'll find one listing for all of them: "Pillsbury® Cookie Dough, all varieties (avg)." In cases where we found no significant nutritional difference among different brands of a food—applesauce or pickles, for example—we averaged the information across brands.

We also calculated the exchange value and the carbohydrate choices for each product, which is information not commonly found on food labels. (See pages 12–15 for information about exchanges and carbohydrate choices.) Each piece of information that is included in the nutrition tables is explained below.

- **Serving size.** All of the nutrition information about the product is based on the portion size given. If you eat double the serving size, you will consume double the calories, fat, carbohydrate, and other nutrients.

- **Total calories.** The calories in food are provided by the protein, carbohydrate, and fat in the food. In order for the caloric value of a food item to be helpful, you need to know the total number of calories that you need to consume in a day. Most people need about ten to fifteen calories per pound of body weight. The table below can help you determine how many calories you need each day to maintain your current weight. If you want to lose weight, you can cut your daily calories by 250 to 500. When followed consistently this calorie reduction should result in a weight loss of one-half to one pound per week. Also, studies have shown that people who include regular physical activity as part of a weight program are more successful in staying with their program and in maintaining weight loss.

| WEIGHT (POUNDS) | CALORIE RANGE |
|---|---|
| 125 | 1600–1900 |
| 150 | 1900–2300 |
| 175 | 2100–2600 |
| 200 | 2200–2600 |
| 225 | 2250–2700 |
| 250 | 2500–2700 |
| 275 | 2500–3000 |
| 300 | 3000–3600 |
| 325 | 3250–3900 |
| 350 | 3500–4200 |

- **Calories from fat.** Controlling the amount of fat in your diet can help you lose or maintain weight and can lower your risk of heart disease and other chronic diseases. It is recommended that 30 percent or less of total daily calories should be from fat.

- **Grams of fat.** This number also helps you evaluate the amount of fat in a product. The chart below explains the maximum number of calories from fat, fat grams, and saturated fat grams you should eat for the number of total calories you consume each day. Each gram of fat provides 9 calories.

- **Grams of saturated fat.** High blood cholesterol levels can increase your risk of heart disease, and saturated fat has the greatest effect on blood cholesterol levels of all the different types of fat in food. Of the total fat consumed in a day, no more than one-third should be saturated fat.

**MAXIMUM RECOMMENDED DAILY FAT INTAKE**

| Total Calories Eaten Per Day | Calories From Fat | Fat Grams | Saturated Fat Grams (approximate) |
|---|---|---|---|
| 3000 | 900 | 100 | 33 |
| 2700 | 810 | 90 | 30 |
| 2400 | 720 | 80 | 26 |
| 2100 | 630 | 70 | 23 |
| 1800 | 540 | 60 | 20 |
| 1500 | 450 | 50 | 16 |
| 1200 | 360 | 40 | 13 |

- **Milligrams of sodium.** For most people, sodium intake should be no more than 3,000 milligrams a day. People with hypertension need to decrease their daily consumption of sodium to no more than 2,400 milligrams. Look for meals and entrees with no more than 800 milligrams of sodium, and look for side dishes, snacks, and other foods with no more than 400 milligrams.

- **Grams of protein.** Protein helps us repair damaged tissue and maintain healthy muscle, skin, and blood cells. Eating two to three servings of lean meat, seafood, eggs, or cheese each day provides most people with adequate protein. Other good sources of protein are tofu and dried beans, peas, and lentils. Each gram of protein provides 4 calories. In a healthful diet, 10 to 15 percent of the total daily calories should be from protein.

- **Grams of carbohydrate.** Carbohydrate is the main nutrient that provides the body with energy, and a healthy diet is based on a strong foundation of carbohydrate foods such as grains, bread, pasta, potatoes, fruit, and vegetables. Each gram of carbohydrate provides 4 calories. In a healthful diet, up to 60 percent of the total daily calories should be from carbohydrate.

- **Food exchanges and carbohydrate choices.** These values are useful for people who follow a meal plan that includes a certain number of carbohydrate choices and/or food exchanges per day. Food exchanges are used by many people who are following a meal plan for weight control or weight loss, or for helping to control a health condition such as diabetes. People with diabetes also use carbohydrate choices to plan and monitor their carbohydrate intake. This practice, along with activity and sometimes medication, helps control blood glucose levels because carbohydrate is the nutrient that affects blood glucose the most.

## The Exchange System

The nutrition tables in this book include exchange information for each food product. This information is not found regularly on food labels, but is essential for people who follow a food or meal plan that is based on the exchange system. The exchange system was established in the 1950s and has been revised several times as more has been learned about nutrition and how the body uses food. The American Diabetes Association and The American Dietetic Association developed the exchange lists.

Exchange lists group foods based on nutritional content. The lists fall into three main groups: carbohydrate, protein, and fat. Carbohydrate foods (Starch List, Fruit List, Milk List, Vegetable List) provide energy; protein foods (Meat and Meat Substitutes List) provide for growth; and fats (Fat List) provide energy and carry the fat-soluble vitamins A, D, E, and K. Together foods from these groups give us the calories and nutrients we need to live, grow, and stay healthy.

Each exchange list gives food choices and the amount of each food that equals one exchange. Each exchange, or serving, from a list is a measured amount of food that has approximately the same carbohydrate, protein, fat, and caloric content as other foods on the same list. Any food on a list can be "exchanged," or traded, in a meal plan for any other food on the same list *in the amounts given*, because each serving provides the same nutritional value and the same number of calories.

To use this meal planning system, you need an individualized meal plan that tells you how many servings or exchanges you should select from each list for meals and snacks. If you would like more information about meal planning and the exchange system, contact a registered dietitian. To locate a registered dietitian in your area, ask your doctor, call your local hospital or public health department, or call The American Dietetic Association's Nutrition Hotline at 1-800-366-1655.

## Carbohydrate Counting

Carbohydrate counting is a relatively new method of food planning used by people with diabetes. Carbohydrate is a nutrient found in grains and starchy vegetables, fruits and fruit juices, and milk and milk products. It is the main nutrient in food that raises blood glucose (sugar) levels. Carbohydrate counting helps people with diabetes easily plan their intake of carbohydrate foods and keep their blood glucose levels from going too high or too low.

To help people who want to count carbohydrates, we have included the number of carbohydrate choices for each food included in the book. We calculated the carbohydrate choices using the "15-Gram Equation." This states that one carbohydrate choice is the amount of a food that contains about 15 grams of carbohydrate. If you are familiar with the exchange lists, think of one carbohydrate choice as equal to one serving from the starch, fruit, or milk list.

### THE 15-GRAM EQUATION
15 grams of carbohydrate = one carbohydrate choice

You can determine the number of carbohydrate choices provided by most food products from the Nutrition Facts label. For example, if the label states that one serving is two oatmeal cookies and contains 30 grams of carbohydrate, those two cookies are counted as two carbohydrate choices ($30 \div 15 = 2$). If you eat four oatmeal cookies (two servings; 60 grams of carbohydrate), you need to count them as four carbohydrate choices ($60 \div 15 = 4$).

Of course, the number of grams of carbohydrate in foods is not always neatly divisible by 15, and carbohydrate counting is not an exact science. We have developed a simple chart to help solve this problem and to make it easier for you to calculate the carbohydrate choices for foods you buy. The chart below, which is based on the 15-Gram Equation, shows the relationship of carbohydrate grams to carbohydrate choices. Use it when you shop to determine quickly how to include the foods you like in your meal plan.

| CARBOHYDRATE GRAMS | CARBOHYDRATE CHOICES |
|:---:|:---:|
| 0–5 | 0 |
| 6–10 | ½ |
| 11–20 | 1 |
| 21–25 | 1½ |
| 26–35 | 2 |
| 36–40 | 2½ |
| 41–50 | 3 |
| 51–55 | 3½ |
| 56–65 | 4 |
| 66–70 | 4½ |
| 71–80 | 5 |

The number of carbohydrate choices for high-fiber foods such as beans and some cereals will not follow the 15-Gram Equation. This is because fiber is not digested or absorbed by the body, but simply "passes through" without affecting blood glucose levels. This can be tricky when reading food labels because carbohydrate from fiber is included in the total carbohydrate listed. To determine the number of carbohydrate choices in fiber-containing foods, you must first subtract the grams of fiber from the total grams of carbohydrate, then divide by 15. In our calculations for this book, we made the appropriate adjustments for fiber before determining the number of carbohydrate choices.

If you have diabetes, carbohydrate counting is a great way to add flexibility and variety to your diet. You can learn more about carbohydrate counting from a registered dietitian. (See page 13 for information about locating a dietitian in your area.)

## Reading Food Labels

Along with this book, you have another tool to help you fit convenience foods into your diet: the food label that manufacturers put on food products. You can use the information on food labels and the guidelines discussed in this book to help you choose healthful food products, and to evaluate foods that may not be included in this book. You also may want to compare information on the label of a product that you have in your cupboard, or that you regularly purchase, to information on similar products listed in this book.

Information displayed on food labels is regulated by two agencies of the government, the United States Department of Agriculture (USDA) and the Food and Drug Administration (FDA). The USDA regulates the labeling of meat and poultry products, while the FDA regulates the labeling of virtually all other food products and the ingredients that are added to food.

One important feature of food labels is the Nutrition Facts label, which lists the type and amount of nutrients found in foods. An example is shown below. Almost all packaged foods in grocery stores and supermarkets are required to have Nutrition Facts labels. Some exceptions are foods that have no nutritional significance to the diet (such as plain coffee, tea, and spices); foods sold in very small packages; and food prepared on-site and intended for immediate consumption, such as deli and bakery items.

As you read Nutrition Facts labels on products, keep in mind that some convenience foods require the addition of ingredients during preparation, such as oil, butter, or eggs. In this case, the label may provide nutrition information for the product as packaged, but not necessarily for the food as it is prepared. Look closely at the label. Products that give nutrition information for the food "as prepared" will state this plainly on the label.

# Nutrition Facts

Serving Size 1 cup (228g)
Servings Per Container 2

**Amount Per Serving**

**Calories** 260   Calories from Fat 120

| | % Daily Value* |
|---|---|
| **Total Fat** 13g | **20%** |
| Saturated Fat 5g | **25%** |
| **Cholesterol** 30mg | **10%** |
| **Sodium** 660mg | **28%** |
| **Total Carbohydrate** 31g | **10%** |
| Dietary Fiber 0g | **0%** |
| **Sugar** 5g | |
| **Protein** 5g | |

| Vitamin A 4% | • | Vitamin C 2% |
|---|---|---|
| Calcium 15% | • | Iron 4% |

* Percent daily values are based on a 2,000 calorie diet. Your daily values may be higher or lower depending on your calorie needs:

| | Calories: | 2,000 | 2,500 |
|---|---|---|---|
| Total Fat | Less than | 65g | 80g |
| Sat Fat | Less than | 20g | 25g |
| Cholesterol | Less than | 300mg | 300mg |
| Sodium | Less than | 2400mg | 2400mg |
| Total Carbohydrate | | 300g | 375g |
| Dietary Fiber | | 25g | 30g |

Calories per gram:
Fat 9   •   Carbohydrate 4   •   Protein 4

If this is not the case and the information is provided for the packaged contents only, you will need to make allowances for ingredients that you add during preparation.

The USDA and FDA also regulate which health terms food manufacturers can put on a food label. In order to be considered "light," or "low calorie," for example, a product must meet certain criteria. This ensures that if you buy a product with a label that reads "low sodium," then it really *is* low sodium. Common food label terms and their meanings are listed below.

| If a label reads . . . | then the product has . . . |
|---|---|
| Calorie Free | less than 5 calories per serving |
| Low Calorie | 40 calories or less per serving |
| Light *or* Lite | ⅓ less calories or 50% less fat than the regular product; if the product has more than half the calories from fat, the fat content *must* be reduced by 50% or more from the regular product |
| Fat Free | less than ½ gram of fat per serving |
| Low Fat | 3 grams or less fat per serving |
| Cholesterol Free | less than 2 milligrams cholesterol and 2 grams or less saturated fat per serving |
| Low Cholesterol | 20 milligrams or less cholesterol and 2 grams or less saturated fat per serving |
| Sodium Free | less than 5 milligrams of sodium per serving |
| Very Low Sodium | 35 milligrams or less sodium per serving |
| Low Sodium | 140 milligrams or less sodium per serving |
| Reduced Sugar *or* Less Sugar | at least 25% less sugar than the regular product |
| High Fiber | 5 grams or more fiber per serving |

A food label is also required to show the list of ingredients used to make the food. All ingredients are listed in descending order by weight. The amount of each ingredient is weighed, and the ingredient that weighs the most is listed first. The ingredient that weighs the least is listed last. Ingredients that make up two percent or less of a food are listed at the end of the list in no particular order. If you have a food allergy or if you are trying to control your intake of sugar, fat, or food additives, ingredient lists are very helpful in making appropriate food choices.

## Decoding the Ingredients List

Many convenience foods contain lengthy lists of mysterious-sounding ingredients called food additives. A food additive is any substance that becomes part of a food product when added during production or processing. Most additives are added to maintain or improve nutritional quality, to maintain freshness, to help process or prepare food, or to make food taste or look more appealing. Some of the more common food additives are sugar and artificial sweeteners, fat and fat substitutes, salt, vitamins, flavorings, colors, and preservatives.

• **Sugar and artificial sweeteners.** Sugars are a type of carbohydrate, and carbohydrates provide the body with energy. However, sugary foods are often high in calories and low in nutrients, and they can contribute to tooth decay, so it still makes good sense to use them in moderation. The Nutrition Facts label lists the grams of carbohydrate that come from sugars and the ingredients list lets you know what type of sugar is in the food. Some of the sugars commonly found in convenience foods are listed below.

### SUGARS

| | | |
|---|---|---|
| Brown sugar | High fructose corn syrup | Maple syrup |
| Corn syrup | Honey | Molasses |
| Dextrin | Hydrogenated starch hydrolysates (HSH) | Polyols |
| Dextrose | | Raw sugar |
| Fructose | Invert sugar | Sorbitol |
| Fruit juice concentrate | Lactose | Sorghum |
| Galactose | Maltose | Sucrose |
| Glucose | Mannitol | Turbinado sugar |
| | | Xylitol |

In response to consumer demand for low-calorie, low-sugar foods, many products have been formulated with artificial sweeteners that contain few or no calories. The low-calorie sweeteners below have been tested for safety by the Food and Drug Administration and are currently approved for use in the United States. However, some people are sensitive to particular artificial sweeteners and may wish to avoid them.

*Acesulfame K (Sunette®, Swiss Sweet™, or Sweet One™):* A synthetic sweetener that is 200 times sweeter than table sugar. It has no nutritional value. Found in sugar-free gum and candy.

*Aspartame (NutraSweet® or Equal®):* A compound of two amino acids that when combined is intensely sweet. It has no nutritional value and is about 200 times sweeter than table sugar.

*Saccharin:* A coal-tar derivative that is 400 times as sweet as sugar. It has no nutritional value. Saccharin has been found to cause cancer in rats at extremely high doses, but no evidence has shown it to cause cancer in humans.

- **Fat and fat substitutes.** Fats are usually pretty easy to spot on an ingredient list—ingredients that mean fat usually have "oil," " lard," or "fat" in their names. However, if you are trying to limit your intake of saturated fat it is helpful to know which fats are saturated. Butter, chicken fat, beef fat, hardened shortenings, hydrogenated shortenings, lard, palm oil, palm kernel oil, and coconut oil are saturated fats often found in convenience foods.

Consumer desire to cut down on fat has triggered a flood of fat-free and low-fat foods from manufacturers, many of which contain substances that attempt to duplicate the taste and texture of fat. The following are some common fat substitutes.

*Carrageenan:* Extracted from particular mosses, seaweeds, and red algae. Commonly found in cheese foods, canned whipped cream, chocolate, and frozen desserts.

*Guar gum:* A vegetable gum made from the seed of the guar plant, found in Pakistan and India. Commonly found in pickled items, frozen dinners, soft drinks, cheese, Mexican foods, cereal, and frozen whipped cream.

*Olestra®:* A relatively new substance made from sucrose and edible fats and oils. It is not absorbed by the body and may cause gastrointestinal discomfort in some people. Used in snack foods.

*Simplesse®:* Made from the proteins of milk and egg.

*Xantham gum:* A gum made from the fermentation of carbohydrates by a microorganism. Commonly found in salad dressing, frozen dinners, Mexican foods, and frozen whipped cream.

Other fat substitutes include dextrins, hydrolized corn starch, modified food starch, polydextrose, and vegetable protein.

- **Other Food Additives.** Other additives that frequently show up on ingredient lists are vitamins, flavorings, and preservatives. Vitamins, which are often listed by names such as ascorbic acid (Vitamin C) or beta carotene (which the body converts to Vitamin A) are added to enhance the nutritional value of a food. Ready-to-eat cereals, for example, are usually fortified with vitamins. Common flavorings are sugars, salt and MSG (monosodium glutamate, a type of salt to which some people are sensitive). Common preservatives include BHA, ascorbic acid, palmitic acid, and benzoic acid.

## How to Use This Book

*Convenience Food Facts* is designed to be a versatile, handy reference for you as you incorporate convenience foods into your lifestyle. Food products are listed alphabetically and you can use the word in the upper corner of each page as a guide—like a dictionary. You can use the book to:

1. Look up a particular food to learn about its nutritional content. For example, if you often use Kraft® Caesar salad dressing and are wondering about its nutritional content, look up "Salad Dressing." The salad dressings are subgrouped by flavor or variety—French, Ranch, Thousand Island, etc.—so you would look under "Caesar" and scan down the list until you arrived at "Caesar, Kraft®." (The Brand-Name Guides and the Index are also helpful for locating specific items.)

2. Look up and compare the nutritional content of various brands of the same food. Suppose you want to find out which tartar sauce contains the lowest amount of fat. Simply look under the entry "Tartar Sauce." There, you will find tartar sauce products from many manufacturers listed next to one another. You can compare the nutritional information for the various products, and see which contains the least amount of fat.

3. Scan the products under an entry you are interested in to see what is available and which product best fits your nutrition and health needs.

4. Look up foods you have already purchased to find out how they compare to other foods.

5. Look up foods to find food exchange information and carbohydrate choices, which are not usually listed on the food label.

As you use *Convenience Food Facts* to help you shop and plan meals, you'll find that it's not hard to choose foods that both fit your busy lifestyle and provide good nutrition. We hope you'll use the information in this book to help you become a more informed consumer, and to help you meet your nutrition goals for a healthier life.

# Convenience Food Nutrition Tables

**KEY**

NA = Not Available. Check the actual package for this information.

~ = Approximately

## PRODUCTS

| | | SERVING SIZE | CALORIES | CALORIES FROM FAT |
|---|---|---|---|---|
| **APPLESAUCE** | | | | |
| ❶ | Applesauce, natural (unsweetened), all brands (avg) | ½ cup | 50 | 0 |
| ❶ | Applesauce, regular, all brands (avg) | ½ cup | 90 | 0 |
| ❶ | Applesauce with cinnamon, all brands (avg) | ½ cup | 105 | 0 |
| **BACON** | | | | |
| | Bacon, Corn King® | 2 slices | 80 | 60 |
| | Bacon, Hillshire Farm® Country Smoked Brand | 1 slice | 60 | 45 |
| | Bacon, Hormel Original Black Label® | 1 oz | 142 | 126 |
| | Bacon, Oscar Meyer® | 2 slices | 60 | 45 |
| | Beef & Turkey Sizzling Breakfast, Lunch and Dinner Strips, Swift Premium® | 1 slice | 70 | 60 |
| | Hickory Smoked Sliced Bacon, Jones Dairy Farm® | 2 slices | 90 | 70 |
| | Smoked Bacon, Elliot's® Up North | 1 slice | 50 | 40 |
| | Smoked Beef Bacon, John Morrell® | 1 slice | 100 | 90 |
| | Smokey Maple Bacon, John Morrell® | 2 slices | 100 | 80 |
| | Thick Sliced Bacon, Farmstead® | 2 slices | 100 | 70 |
| | Thick Sliced Bacon, West Virginia Brand | 1 slice | 80 | 60 |
| ❶ | Turkey Bacon, Jennie-O® Extra Lean | 1 slice | 20 | 5 |
| ❶ | Turkey Bacon, Louis Rich® | 1 slice | 30 | 20 |
| **BACON BITS** | | | | |
| ❶ | Bacon bits (avg) | 1 Tb | 30 | 15 |
| **BAGELS** | | | | |
| ❶ | Bagel, small (2 oz, avg) | 1 bagel | 160 | 10 |
| ❶ | Bagel, medium (3 oz, avg) | 1 bagel | 230 | 10–20 |
| ❶ | Bagel, large (4 oz, avg) | 1 bagel | 280 | 15 |
| **BARBECUE SAUCE** | | | | |
| ❶ | Healthy Choice®, all varieties (avg) | 2 Tb | 25 | 0 |

❶ Meets Low-Fat Guidelines

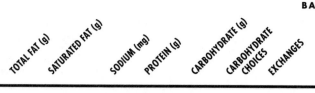

| TOTAL FAT (g) | SATURATED FAT (g) | SODIUM (mg) | PROTEIN (g) | CARBOHYDRATE (g) | CARBOHYDRATE CHOICES | EXCHANGES |
|---|---|---|---|---|---|---|
| 0 | 0 | 10 | 0 | 13 | 1 | 1 fruit |
| 0 | 0 | 10 | 0 | 23 | 1½ | 1½ fruit |
| 0 | 0 | 5 | 0 | 27 | 2 | 2 fruit |
| 7 | 2.5 | 135 | 4 | 0 | 0 | 1 meat |
| 5 | 2.5 | 150 | 3 | 0 | 0 | 1 fat |
| 14 | 6 | 192 | 3 | 0 | 0 | 3 fat |
| 5 | 1.5 | 250 | 4 | 0 | 0 | 1 high fat meat |
| 6 | 2.5 | 230 | 3 | 0 | 0 | 1 fat |
| 8 | 3 | 350 | 4 | 0 | 0 | 1 high fat meat |
| 4 | 1.5 | 240 | 3 | 0 | 0 | 1 fat |
| 10 | 4 | 260 | 3 | 0 | 0 | 2 fat |
| 9 | 3 | 300 | 4 | 1 | 0 | 1 high fat meat |
| 8 | 3 | 370 | 5 | 1 | 0 | 1 high fat meat |
| 7 | 2.5 | 260 | 3 | 0 | 0 | 1½ fat |
| 0.5 | 0 | 130 | 3 | 0 | 0 | free (2 slices = 1 very lean meat) |
| 2.5 | 0.5 | 190 | 2 | 0 | 0 | ½ fat |
| 1.5 | 0 | 130–240 | 3 | 0–2 | 0 | free |
| 1 | 0 | 240–320 | 6 | 26–35 | 2 | 2 starch |
| 1–2 | 0 | 330–460 | 9 | 41–50 | 3 | 3 starch |
| 2 | 1 | 490–550 | 11 | 56–65 | 4 | 4 starch |
| 0 | 0 | 229 | 0 | 6 | ½ | ½ fruit |

1 Carbohydrate Choice = 1 starch or 1 fruit or 1 milk exchange

## PRODUCTS

| | SERVING SIZE | CALORIES | CALORIES FROM FAT |
|---|---|---|---|
| ❶ Hunt's®, all regular varieties (avg) | 2 Tb | 45 | 0 |
| ❶ KC Masterpiece®, all varieties (avg) | 2 Tb | 60 | 0 |
| ❶ Kraft®, all varieties (avg) | 2 Tb | 50 | 5 |

### BEANS (CANNED)

| | | | |
|---|---|---|---|
| ❶ Baked beans (avg) | ½ cup | 150 | 10 |
| ❶ Black beans, butter beans, great northern beans, kidney beans, pinto beans, pinquito beans, white beans (avg) | ½ cup | 80 | 5 |
| ❶ Chili beans (avg) | ½ cup | 100 | 10 |
| ❶ Pork and beans (avg) | ½ cup | 130 | 20 |

### BEANS, REFRIED (CANNED)

| | | | |
|---|---|---|---|
| ❶ Refried beans (avg) | ½ cup | 130 | 27 |
| ❶ Refried beans, fat-free (avg) | ½ cup | 105 | 0 |

### BEEF MEALS/ENTREES (FROZEN);
*see also* Mexican Meals/Entrees; Oriental Meals/Entrees

#### *Beef and Gravy Meals/Entrees*

| | | | |
|---|---|---|---|
| Chopped Sirloin Beef with Gravy, Swanson® | 1 pkg | 350 | 153 |
| Creamed Chipped Beef, Banquet® Toppers | 1 bag | 100 | 35 |
| Creamed Chipped Beef, Stouffer's® | 1 pkg | 160 | 100 |
| Creamed Sauce, Croutons, & Shaved, Cured Beef, Michelina's® | 1 pkg | 360 | 180 |
| Gravy & Beef Patty Meal, Banquet® Homestyle Menu | 1 meal | 300 | 180 |
| Gravy and Charbroiled Beef Patty, Morton® | 1 meal | 290 | 140 |
| Gravy and Sliced Beef, Banquet® Family Size | 2 slices | 100 | 30 |
| ❶ Gravy and Sliced Beef, Banquet® Toppers | 1 bag | 70 | 20 |
| Mushroom Gravy and 6 Charboiled Beef Patties, Banquet® Family Size | 1 patty | 180 | 120 |
| Noodles and Beef with Gravy, Banquet® Family Size | 1 cup | 140 | 30 |

 Meets Low-Fat Guidelines

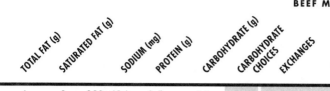

| TOTAL FAT (g) | SATURATED FAT (g) | SODIUM (mg) | PROTEIN (g) | CARBOHYDRATE (g) | CARBOHYDRATE CHOICES | EXCHANGES |
|---|---|---|---|---|---|---|
| <1 | 0 | 283–496 | 0.5 | 11 | 1 | 1 fruit |
| 0.5 | 0 | 40–720 | 0 | 12 | 1 | 1 fruit |
| 0.5 | 0 | 280–540 | 0 | 11 | 1 | 1 fruit |
| | | | | | | |
| 1 | 0 | 500–620 | 7 | 31 | 1½ | 1½ starch, 1 very lean meat |
| <1 | 0 | 370–630 | 6 | 17 | 1 | 1 starch, 1 very lean meat |
| | | | | | | |
| 1 | 0 | 360–600 | 7 | 24 | 1 | 1 starch, 1 very lean meat |
| 2 | <1 | 500–620 | 6 | 27 | 2 | 2 starch |
| | | | | | | |
| 3 | 1.5 | 270–720 | 7 | 20 | 1 | 1 starch, 1 very lean meat |
| 0 | 0 | 350–570 | 7 | 22 | 1 | 1 starch, 1 very lean meat |
| | | | | | | |
| 17 | NA | NA | 19 | 30 | 2 | 1½ starch, 1 veg, 2 meat, 1 fat |
| 3 | 1.5 | 700 | 9 | 8 | ½ | ½ starch, 1 lean meat |
| 11 | 3 | 690 | 10 | 6 | ½ | ½ starch, 1 meat, 1 fat |
| 20 | 6 | 810 | 15 | 29 | 2 | 2 starch, 1 meat, 3 fat |
| 20 | 8 | 1060 | 11 | 21 | 1½ | 1 starch, 1 veg, 1 meat, 3 fat |
| 16 | 7 | 1210 | 11 | 26 | 2 | 2 starch, 1 lean meat, 2 fat |
| 3 | 1.5 | 850 | 13 | 7 | ½ | ½ starch, 2 very lean meat |
| 2 | 1 | 440 | 8 | 5 | 0 | 1 lean meat |
| 13 | 6 | 640 | 8 | 7 | ½ | ½ starch, 1 meat, 1 fat |
| 4 | 2 | 1120 | 11 | 16 | 1 | 1 starch, 1 lean meat |

1 Carbohydrate Choice = 1 starch or 1 fruit or 1 milk exchange

## PRODUCTS

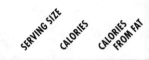

| PRODUCTS | SERVING SIZE | CALORIES | CALORIES FROM FAT |
|---|---|---|---|
| Onion Gravy and  Beef Patties, Banquet® Family Size | 1 patty | 180 | 130 |
| **Beef Stroganoff Meals/Entrees** | | | |
| Beef Stroganoff, Budget Gourmet® Light | 1 entree | 290 | 60 |
| ❶ Beef Stroganoff, Healthy Choice® | 1 meal | 310 | 50 |
| Beef Stroganoff, Stouffer's® | 1 pkg | 390 | 180 |
| Beef Stroganoff and Noodles, Marie Callender's® | 1 cup | 440 | 250 |
| **Beef Tips Meals/Entrees** | | | |
| ❶ Beef Tips Français, Healthy Choice® | 1 meal | 280 | 40 |
| ❶ Beef Tips with Sauce, Healthy Choice® | 1 meal | 290 | 50 |
| Sirloin Beef Tips, Swanson® Hungry-Man® | 1 pkg | 450 | 144 |
| ❶ Traditional Beef Tips, Healthy Choice® | 1 meal | 260 | 50 |
| **Chicken Fried Beef Steak Meals/Entrees** | | | |
| Chicken Fried Beef Steak, Banquet® Country Menu | 1 meal | 400 | 180 |
| Chicken Fried Beef Steak Dinner, Banquet® Extra Helping | 1 meal | 800 | 400 |
| Chicken Fried Steak and Gravy, Marie Callender's® | 1 meal | 650 | 280 |
| **Macaroni and Beef Meals/Entrees** | | | |
| ❶ Beef Macaroni Casserole, Healthy Choice® | 1 meal | 200 | 10 |
| Macaroni & Beef, Banquet® Bake At Home | 1 cup | 230 | 60 |
| Macaroni & Beef, Marie Callender's® | 1 cup | 310 | 100 |
| ❶ Macaroni and Beef, Stouffer's® Lean Cuisine® | 1 pkg | 280 | 70 |
| **Meat Loaf Meals/Entrees** | | | |
| Meat Loaf Dinner, Banquet® Extra Helping | 1 meal | 650 | 340 |
| Meat Loaf Meal, Banquet® Homestyle Menu | 1 meal | 280 | 150 |
| Meatloaf & Gravy with Mashed Potatoes, Marie Callender's® | 1 meal | 540 | 270 |

❶  Meets Low-Fat Guidelines

| TOTAL FAT (g) | SATURATED FAT (g) | SODIUM (mg) | PROTEIN (g) | CARBOHYDRATE (g) | CARBOHYDRATE CHOICES | EXCHANGES |
|---|---|---|---|---|---|---|
| 14 | 6 | 630 | 8 | 7 | ½ | ½ starch, 1 high fat meat, 1 fat |
| 7 | 4 | 580 | 20 | 32 | 2 | 2 starch, 2 lean meat |
| 6 | 2.5 | 440 | 21 | 44 | 3 | 3 starch, 2 very lean meat |
| 20 | 7 | 1100 | 23 | 30 | 2 | 2 starch, 2 meat, 2 fat |
| 27 | 11 | 780 | 24 | 23 | 1½ | 1 starch, 1 veg, 3 meat, 2 fat |
| 5 | 1.5 | 520 | 20 | 40 | 2½ | 2 starch, 1 veg, 2 lean meat |
| 6 | 2.5 | 270 | 19 | 40 | 2½ | 2 starch, 1 veg, 2 lean meat |
| 16 | NA | NA | 28 | 49 | 3 | 3 starch, 1 veg, 2 meat, 1 fat |
| 5 | 2 | 390 | 20 | 32 | 2 | 2 starch, 2 lean meat |
| 20 | 6 | 1180 | 15 | 39 | 2½ | 2 starch, 1 veg, 1 meat, 3 fat |
| 44 | 14 | 2050 | 29 | 73 | 5 | 4½ starch, 1 veg, 2 meat, 6 fat |
| 31 | 10 | 2260 | 23 | 69 | 4½ | 4 starch, 1 veg, 2 meat, 3 fat |
| 1 | 0.5 | 450 | 14 | 34 | 2 | 2 starch, 1 lean meat |
| 7 | 3 | 810 | 13 | 31 | 2 | 2 starch, 1 meat |
| 11 | 4 | 680 | 12 | 40 | 2½ | 2 starch, 1 veg, 1 meat, 1 fat |
| 8 | 2 | 550 | 13 | 40 | 2½ | 2 starch, 1 veg, 1 meat |
| 38 | 16 | 2140 | 29 | 49 | 3 | 3 starch, 1 veg, 3 meat, 4 fat |
| 17 | 7 | 1100 | 12 | 23 | 1½ | 1 starch, 1 veg, 1 meat, 2 fat |
| 30 | 11 | 1230 | 23 | 44 | 3 | 2½ starch, 1 veg, 2 meat, 3 fat |

1 Carbohydrate Choice = 1 starch *or* 1 fruit *or* 1 milk exchange

## PRODUCTS

| PRODUCTS | SERVING SIZE | CALORIES | CALORIES FROM FAT |
|---|---|---|---|
| Meatloaf and Whipped Potatoes, Stouffer's® Homestyle | 1 pkg | 390 | 210 |
| ❶ Meatloaf and Whipped Potatoes, Stouffer's® Lean Cuisine® | 1 pkg | 250 | 60 |
| Meatloaf, Swanson® | 1 pkg | 410 | 162 |
| Meatloaf, Swanson® Hungry-Man® | 1 pkg | 620 | 279 |
| Traditional Meatloaf, Healthy Choice® | 1 meal | 320 | 80 |
| Tomato Sauce with Meat Loaf, Morton® | 1 meal | 250 | 110 |
| **Mesquite Beef Meals/Entrees** | | | |
| ❶ Mesquite Beef Barbecue, Healthy Choice® | 1 meal | 310 | 40 |
| ❶ Mesquite Beef with Rice, Stouffer's® Lean Cuisine® Cafe Classics | 1 pkg | 280 | 60 |
| **Pepper Steak Meals/Entrees** | | | |
| ❶ Green Pepper Steak, Stouffer's® | 1 pkg | 330 | 80 |
| ❶ Pepper Steak, Weight Watchers® | 1 entree | 240 | 40 |
| ❶ Pepper Steak with Rice, Budget Gourmet® | 1 entree | 290 | 70 |
| **Pot Roast Meals/Entrees** | | | |
| Beef Pot Roast and Browned Potatoes, Stouffer's® Homestyle | 1 pkg | 270 | 90 |
| ❶ Beef Pot Roast & Gravy, Marie Callender's® Old Fashioned | 1 cup | 180 | 40 |
| Beef Pot Roast and Whipped Potatoes, Stouffer's® Lean Cuisine® | 1 pkg | 210 | 60 |
| ❶ Yankee Pot Roast, Healthy Choice® | 1 meal | 280 | 50 |
| Yankee Pot Roast, Swanson® Hungry-Man® | 1 pkg | 400 | 99 |
| **Salisbury Steak Meals/Entrees** | | | |
| ❶ Beef Sirloin Salisbury Steak, Budget Gourmet® Light | 1 entree | 240 | 45 |

❶  Meets Low-Fat Guidelines

| TOTAL FAT (g) | SATURATED FAT (g) | SODIUM (mg) | PROTEIN (g) | CARBOHYDRATE (g) | CARBOHYDRATE CHOICES | EXCHANGES |
|---|---|---|---|---|---|---|
| 24 | 8 | 910 | 20 | 24 | 1½ | 1½ starch, 2 meat, 3 fat |
| 7 | 2 | 570 | 22 | 25 | 1½ | 1½ starch, 2 lean meat |
| 18 | NA | NA | 16 | 44 | 3 | 2½ starch, 1 veg, 1 meat, 2 fat |
| 31 | NA | NA | 28 | 57 | 4 | 3½ starch, 1 veg, 2 meat, 4 fat |
| 8 | 4 | 460 | 16 | 46 | 3 | 3 starch, 1 meat |
| 13 | 4 | 1110 | 9 | 24 | 1½ | 1½ starch, 1 meat, 1 fat |
| 4 | 1.5 | 490 | 23 | 45 | 3 | 3 starch, 2 very lean meat |
| 7 | 2 | 470 | 16 | 38 | 2½ | 2½ starch, 1 meat |
| 9 | 3 | 650 | 17 | 45 | 3 | 3 starch, 2 lean meat |
| 4.5 | 1.5 | 690 | 18 | 33 | 2 | 2 starch, 1 veg, 2 very lean meat |
| 8 | 3 | 930 | 16 | 39 | 2½ | 2 starch, 1 veg, 1 meat |
| 10 | 3 | 640 | 19 | 25 | 1½ | 1½ starch, 2 meat |
| 5 | 1 | 660 | 14 | 21 | 1½ | 1½ starch, 1 meat |
| 7 | 1.5 | 570 | 16 | 21 | 1½ | 1 starch, 1 veg, 2 lean meat |
| 5 | 2 | 460 | 19 | 38 | 2½ | 2 starch, 1 veg, 2 lean meat |
| 11 | NA | NA | 28 | 47 | 3 | 3 starch, 1 veg, 2 meat |
| 5 | 2 | 550 | 21 | 28 | 2 | 2 starch, 2 very lean meat |

1 Carbohydrate Choice = 1 starch or 1 fruit or 1 milk exchange

## PRODUCTS

| PRODUCTS | SERVING SIZE | CALORIES | CALORIES FROM FAT |
|---|---|---|---|
| Gravy and 6 Salisbury Steaks, Banquet® Family Size | 1 patty | 200 | 120 |
| Gravy and Salisbury Steak, Banquet® Toppers | 1 bag | 220 | 140 |
| Gravy and Salisbury Steak, Morton® | 1 meal | 210 | 80 |
| Grilled Salisbury Steak, Weight Watchers® | 1 entree | 250 | 80 |
| Salisbury Steak and Gravy and Macaroni & Cheese, Stouffer's® Homestyle | 1 pkg | 370 | 170 |
| Salisbury Steak Dinner, Banquet® Extra Helping | 1 meal | 740 | 410 |
| ❶ Salisbury Steak, Healthy Choice® | 1 meal | 260 | 60 |
| Salisbury Steak in Gravy with Dressing, Swanson® Homestyle Entrees | 1 pkg | 350 | 180 |
| Salisbury Steak Meal, Banquet® Homestyle Menu | 1 meal | 310 | 150 |
| Salisbury Steak with Macaroni & Cheese, Stouffer's® Lean Cuisine® | 1 pkg | 270 | 70 |
| Salisbury Steak, Swanson® | 1 pkg | 390 | 162 |
| Salisbury Steak, Swanson® Hungry-Man® | 1 pkg | 610 | 306 |
| ❶ Traditional Salisbury Steak, Healthy Choice® | 1 meal | 320 | 60 |
| **Swedish Meatballs Meals/Entrees** | | | |
| Gravy with Egg Noodles & Swedish Meatballs, Michelina's® | 1 pkg | 320 | 100 |
| Swedish Meatballs with Pasta, Stouffer's® Lunch Express® | 1 pkg | 530 | 280 |
| Swedish Meatballs, Budget Gourmet® | 1 entree | 550 | 300 |
| Swedish Meatballs, Stouffer's® | 1 pkg | 440 | 200 |
| Swedish Meatballs, Weight Watchers® | 1 entree | 280 | 70 |
| ❶ Swedish Meatballs with Pasta, Stouffer's® Lean Cuisine® | 1 pkg | 290 | 80 |
| ❶ Traditional Swedish Meatballs, Healthy Choice® | 1 meal | 320 | 90 |

❶  Meets Low-Fat Guidelines

| TOTAL FAT (g) | SATURATED FAT (g) | SODIUM (mg) | PROTEIN (g) | CARBOHYDRATE (g) | CARBOHYDRATE CHOICES | EXCHANGES |
|---|---|---|---|---|---|---|
| 14 | 6 | 610 | 12 | 7 | ½ | ½ starch, 2 meat, 1 fat |
| 16 | 7 | 790 | 9 | 8 | ½ | ½ starch, 1 meat, 2 fat |
| 9 | 4 | 950 | 9 | 23 | 1½ | 1½ starch, 1 meat, ½ fat |
| 9 | 3.5 | 590 | 19 | 24 | 1½ | 1½ starch, 1 veg, 2 lean meat |
| 19 | 6 | 1220 | 24 | 26 | 2 | 2 starch, 3 meat |
| 46 | 19 | 1860 | 31 | 52 | 3½ | 3 starch, 1 veg, 3 high fat meat, 4 fat |
| 6 | 2.5 | 500 | 18 | 32 | 2 | 2 starch, 2 lean meat |
| 20 | NA | NA | 19 | 23 | 1½ | 1 starch, 1 veg, 2 meat, 2 fat |
| 16 | 7 | 910 | 14 | 28 | 2 | 1½ starch, 1 veg, 1 meat, 2 fat |
| 8 | 3.5 | 590 | 23 | 27 | 2 | 2 starch, 2 lean meat |
| 18 | NA | NA | 17 | 42 | 3 | 2½ starch, 1 veg, 1 meat, 2 fat |
| 34 | NA | NA | 30 | 45 | 3 | 2½ starch, 1 veg, 3 meat, 3 fat |
| 6 | 3 | 470 | 18 | 48 | 3 | 3 starch, 1 lean meat |
| 12 | 4.5 | 1060 | 14 | 39 | 2½ | 2½ starch, 1 meat, 1 fat |
| 32 | 11 | 1010 | 19 | 41 | 3 | 3 starch, 1 meat, 5 fat |
| 34 | 16 | 1050 | 22 | 40 | 2½ | 2½ starch, 2 meat, 5 fat |
| 23 | 8 | 840 | 23 | 36 | 2½ | 2½ starch, 2 meat, 2 fat |
| 8 | 3.5 | 510 | 18 | 34 | 2 | 2 starch, 1 veg, 2 lean meat |
| 8 | 3 | 590 | 22 | 32 | 2 | 2 starch, 2 lean meat |
| 9 | 3 | 600 | 22 | 37 | 2½ | 2 starch, 1 veg, 2 lean meat |

1 Carbohydrate Choice = 1 starch or 1 fruit or 1 milk exchange

## PRODUCTS

| | SERVING SIZE | CALORIES | CALORIES FROM FAT |
|---|---|---|---|
| **Other Beef Meals/Entrees** | | | |
| Beef Stew, Banquet® Family Size | 1 cup | 160 | 35 |
| ❶ Country Vegetables and Beef, Stouffer's® Lean Cuisine® | 1 pkg | 220 | 35 |
| Sirloin Beef Peppercorn, Stouffer's® Lean Cuisine® Cafe Classics | 1 pkg | 210 | 60 |
| Sirloin Cheddar Melt, Budget Gourmet® | 1 entree | 370 | 190 |
| Sliced Beef Meal, Banquet® Country Menu | 1 meal | 240 | 60 |
| Western Style Meal, Banquet® Country Menu | 1 meal | 350 | 180 |
| **BISCUIT MIX (AS PREPARED)** | | | |
| All Purpose Baking Mix, Bisquick® Original | ⅓ cup | 170 | 50 |
| ❶ All Purpose Baking Mix, Bisquick® Reduced Fat | ⅓ cup | 150 | 25 |
| Baking Mix, Jiffy® | ¼ cup | 190 | 60 |
| ❶ Biscuit and Baking Mix, Pioneer® Low Fat | ¼ cup | 150 | 4.5 |
| Biscuit Mix, Gold Medal® | 2 biscuits | 180 | 50 |
| **BISCUITS (REFRIGERATED)** | | | |
| ❶ Pillsbury® Ballard® Extra Lights® Oven Ready® Biscuits | 3 biscuits | 150 | 20 |
| Pillsbury® Big Country® Biscuits, all varieties (avg) | 1 biscuit | 100 | 35 |
| ❶ Pillsbury® Butter or Buttermilk biscuits, all varieties (avg) | 3 biscuits | 150 | 25 |
| ❶ Pillsbury® Country Biscuits | 3 biscuits | 150 | 25 |
| Pillsbury® Grands!® Biscuits, all varieties (avg) | 1 biscuit | 200 | 90 |
| Pillsbury® Hungry Jack® Flaky Biscuits, all varieties (avg) | 2 biscuits | 170 | 60 |
| Pillsbury® Hungry Jack® Fluffy Biscuits | 2 biscuits | 180 | 70 |
| Pillsbury® Hungry Jack® Honey Tastin'® Biscuits | 2 biscuits | 180 | 60 |

❶  Meets Low-Fat Guidelines

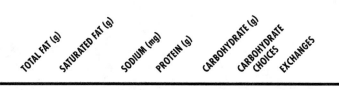

| TOTAL FAT (g) | SATURATED FAT (g) | SODIUM (mg) | PROTEIN (g) | CARBOHYDRATE (g) | CARBOHYDRATE CHOICES | EXCHANGES |
|---|---|---|---|---|---|---|
| 4 | 2 | 1120 | 14 | 17 | 1 | 1 starch, 1 very lean meat |
| 4 | 1 | 579 | 13 | 32 | 2 | 2 starch, 1 lean meat |
| 7 | 1.5 | 480 | 13 | 24 | 1½ | 1½ starch, 1 meat |
| 21 | 10 | 840 | 18 | 29 | 2 | 2 starch, 2 medium meat, 2 fat |
| 7 | 3 | 660 | 26 | 19 | 1 | 1 starch, 1 veg, 3 very lean meat, ½ fat |
| 20 | 9 | 1400 | 14 | 28 | 2 | 1½ starch, 1 veg, 1 meat, 3 fat |
| 6 | 1.5 | 490 | 3 | 25 | 1½ | 1½ starch, 1 fat |
| 2.5 | 0.5 | 460 | 3 | 28 | 2 | 2 starch |
| 4.5 | 1 | 320 | 2 | 22 | 1½ | 1½ starch, ½ fat |
| 0.5 | 0 | 510 | 3 | 40 | 2½ | 2½ starch |
| 6 | 2.5 | 480 | 4 | 27 | 2 | 2 starch, 1 fat |
| 2 | 0 | 490 | 4 | 29 | 2 | 2 starch |
| 4 | 1 | 300 | 2 | 14 | 1 | 1 starch, ½ fat |
| 2.5 | 0 | 490 | 4 | 29 | 2 | 2 starch |
| 2.5 | 0 | 490 | 4 | 29 | 2 | 2 starch |
| 10 | 2.5 | 570–600 | 4 | 23 | 1½ | 1½ starch, 2 fat |
| 7 | 1.5 | 580–600 | 3 | 23 | 1½ | 1½ starch, 1 fat |
| 8 | 2 | 570 | 3 | 23 | 1½ | 1½ starch, 1 fat |
| 7 | 1.5 | 680 | 3 | 25 | 1½ | 1½ starch, 1 fat |

1 Carbohydrate Choice = 1 starch *or* 1 fruit *or* 1 milk exchange

## PRODUCTS

| | SERVING SIZE | CALORIES | CALORIES FROM FAT |
|---|---|---|---|
| Pillsbury® 1869® Biscuits, all varieties (avg) | 1 biscuit | 100 | 45 |

### BRAUNSCHWEIGER
*see* Lunch Meats

### BREAD DOUGH (FROZEN)

| | | | |
|---|---|---|---|
| ❶ White Bread Dough, Rich's® | 1" slice | 150 | 15 |

### BREAD MIX (AS PREPARED)

| | | | |
|---|---|---|---|
| Apple Cinnamon, Pillsbury® Quick Bread | ¹⁄₁₂ loaf | 180 | 50 |
| Banana, Pillsbury® Quick Bread | ¹⁄₁₂ loaf | 170 | 50 |
| Blueberry, Pillsbury® Quick Bread | ¹⁄₁₂ loaf | 180 | 50 |
| Carrot, Pillsbury® Quick Bread | ¹⁄₁₆ loaf | 140 | 45 |
| ❶ Cinnamon Raisin, Krusteaz® | ¹⁄₁₂ loaf | 180 | 25 |
| ❶ Corn Bread, Pillsbury® Ballard® | ¹⁄₁₈ loaf | 130 | 25 |
| ❶ Country White, Krusteaz® | ¹⁄₁₀ loaf | 150 | 20 |
| ❶ Cracked Wheat, Krusteaz® | ¹⁄₁₀ loaf | 150 | 20 |
| ❶ Cracked Wheat, Pillsbury® Bread Machine | ¹⁄₁₂ loaf | 130 | 20 |
| Cranberry, Pillsbury® Quick Bread | ¹⁄₁₂ loaf | 160 | 35 |
| ❶ Crusty White, Pillsbury® Bread Machine | ¹⁄₁₂ loaf | 130 | 20 |
| Date, Pillsbury® Quick Bread | ¹⁄₁₂ loaf | 180 | 35 |
| ❶ Dill Rye, Krusteaz® | ¹⁄₁₀ loaf | 150 | 20 |
| Gingerbread, Pillsbury® | ¹⁄₈ loaf | 220 | 45 |
| ❶ Honey Wheat Berry, Krusteaz® | ¹⁄₁₀ loaf | 150 | 20 |
| ❶ Hot Roll Mix, Pillsbury® | ¼ cup | 130 | 25 |
| ❶ Italian Herb, Krusteaz® | ¹⁄₁₀ loaf | 150 | 20 |
| Nut, Pillsbury® Quick Bread | ¹⁄₁₂ loaf | 170 | 50 |
| ❶ Pumpkin, Pillsbury® Quick Bread | ¹⁄₁₂ loaf | 130 | 15 |
| ❶ Sourdough, Krusteaz® | ¹⁄₁₀ loaf | 150 | 20 |

### BREADSTICKS (REFRIGERATED)

| | | | |
|---|---|---|---|
| ❶ Breadsticks, Pillsbury® | 1 breadstick | 110 | 25 |

❶  Meets Low-Fat Guidelines

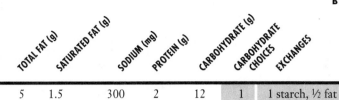

| TOTAL FAT (g) | SATURATED FAT (g) | SODIUM (mg) | PROTEIN (g) | CARBOHYDRATE (g) | CARBOHYDRATE CHOICES | EXCHANGES |
|---|---|---|---|---|---|---|
| 5 | 1.5 | 300 | 2 | 12 | 1 | 1 starch, ½ fat |
| 2 | 0 | 320 | 5 | 29 | 2 | 2 starch |
| 6 | 1 | 170 | 2 | 30 | 2 | 2 starch, 1 fat |
| 6 | 1 | 200 | 3 | 26 | 2 | 2 starch, 1 fat |
| 6 | 1 | 160 | 2 | 29 | 2 | 2 starch, 1 fat |
| 5 | 1 | 150 | 2 | 22 | 1½ | 1½ starch, 1 fat |
| 2.5 | 0 | 200 | 5 | 35 | 2 | 2 starch |
| 2.5 | 1 | 520 | 4 | 23 | 1½ | 1½ starch |
| 2 | 0 | 280 | 5 | 28 | 2 | 2 starch |
| 2 | 0 | 270 | 5 | 27 | 2 | 2 starch |
| 2 | 0 | 260 | 4 | 25 | 1½ | 1½ starch |
| 4 | 1 | 150 | 2 | 30 | 2 | 2 starch, 1 fat |
| 2 | 0 | 250 | 4 | 25 | 1½ | 1½ starch |
| 4 | 1 | 160 | 3 | 32 | 2 | 2 starch, 1 fat |
| 2 | 0 | 170 | 5 | 29 | 2 | 2 starch |
| 5 | 1.5 | 340 | 3 | 40 | 2½ | 2½ starch, ½ fat |
| 2 | 0 | 260 | 5 | 28 | 2 | 2 starch |
| 3 | 0.5 | 220 | 4 | 21 | 1½ | 1½ starch |
| 2 | 0 | 250 | 5 | 28 | 2 | 2 starch |
| 6 | 1 | 190 | 3 | 27 | 2 | 2 starch, 1 fat |
| 1.5 | 0 | 190 | 2 | 26 | 2 | 2 starch |
| 2 | 0 | 290 | 5 | 28 | 2 | 2 starch |
| 2.5 | 0.5 | 290 | 3 | 18 | 1 | 1 starch, ½ fat |

1 Carbohydrate Choice = 1 starch or 1 fruit or 1 milk exchange

# PRODUCTS

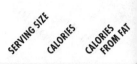

| | SERVING SIZE | CALORIES | CALORIES FROM FAT |
|---|---|---|---|
| **BREAKFAST DRINKS (AS PREPARED)** | | | |
| ❶ Instant Breakfast, Pillsbury®, all varieties (avg) | 1 envelope | 220 | 15 |
| **BREAKFAST MEALS/ENTREES (FROZEN)** *see also* Egg Products, Pancakes, Waffles | | | |
| Classic Omelet Sandwich, Weight Watchers® | 1 sandwich | 220 | 50 |
| Easy Omelets™, Cheddar | 1 container | 160 | 70 |
| Easy Omelets™, Cheddar and Real Ham Bits | 1 container | 150 | 70 |
| Easy Omelets™, Cheddar with Bell Peppers & Onions | 1 container | 150 | 70 |
| English Muffin Sandwich, Weight Watchers® | 1 sandwich | 210 | 50 |
| ❶ Ham & Cheese Frozen Breakfast in a Biscuit, Krusteaz® | 1 biscuit | 260 | 70 |
| Handy Ham and Cheese Omelet, Weight Watchers® | 1 omelet | 220 | 45 |
| Pancakes with Sausage, Swanson® Great Starts® | 1 pkg | 490 | 225 |
| Sausage Biscuit, Weight Watchers® | 1 sandwich | 230 | 100 |
| Sausage Burrito, Swanson® Great Starts® | 1 pkg | 240 | 108 |
| Sausage, Egg & Cheese on a Biscuit, Swanson® | 1 pkg | 490 | 270 |
| Sausage Frozen Breakfast in a Biscuit, Krusteaz® | 1 biscuit | 290 | 120 |
| Scrambled Eggs with Sausage & Hash Browns, | 1 pkg | 360 | 234 |
| ❶ Veggie Frozen Breakfast in a Biscuit, Krusteaz® | 1 biscuit | 240 | 60 |
| **BROTH** *see also* Soup | | | |
| ❶ Beef Broth, Health Valley® Fat-Free No Salt | 1 cup | 30 | 0 |
| ❶ Beef Broth, Health Valley® Fat-Free | 1 cup | 30 | 0 |
| ❶ Bouillon, Knorr®, all varieties (avg) | 1 cup | 15 | 10 |
| ❶ Broth, Knorr®, all varieties (avg) | 1 cup | 15 | 0 |

❶ Meets Low-Fat Guidelines

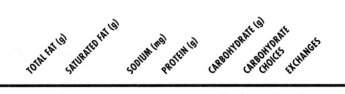

| TOTAL FAT (g) | SATURATED FAT (g) | SODIUM (mg) | PROTEIN (g) | CARBOHYDRATE (g) | CARBOHYDRATE CHOICES | EXCHANGES |
|---|---|---|---|---|---|---|
| 1.5 | 1 | 320 | 13 | 40 | 2½ | 2 starch, 1 milk |
| | | | | | | |
| 6 | 2.5 | 410 | 15 | 26 | 2 | 2 starch, 1 lean meat |
| 8 | 5 | 560 | 17 | 3 | 0 | 2 meat |
| 8 | 4.5 | 620 | 18 | 2 | 0 | 2 meat |
| 8 | 5 | 520 | 17 | 3 | 0 | 2 meat |
| 5 | 3 | 420 | 13 | 26 | 2 | 2 starch, 1 lean meat |
| 8 | 2.5 | 720 | 11 | 35 | 2 | 2 starch, 1 high fat meat |
| 5 | 2.5 | 440 | 13 | 30 | 2 | 2 starch, 1 meat |
| 25 | NA | NA | 14 | 52 | 3½ | 3½ starch, 1 high fat meat, 2 fat |
| 11 | 3.5 | 660 | 11 | 20 | 1 | 1 starch, 1 meat, 1 fat |
| 12 | NA | NA | 9 | 24 | 1½ | 1½ starch, 1 high fat meat |
| 30 | NA | NA | 18 | 36 | 2½ | 2½ starch, 2 high fat meat, 2 fat |
| 13 | 4 | 630 | 10 | 34 | 2 | 2 starch, 1 high fat meat, ½ fat |
| 26 | NA | NA | 12 | 21 | 1½ | 1½ starch, 1 high fat meat, 3 fat |
| 7 | 2.5 | 640 | 10 | 35 | 2 | 2 starch, 1 veg, 1 fat |
| | | | | | | |
| 0 | 0 | 70 | 5 | 2 | 0 | 1 very lean meat (½ cup = free) |
| 0 | 0 | 160 | 5 | 2 | 0 | 1 very lean meat (½ cup = free) |
| 1 | NA | 1090 | 1 | 1 | 0 | free |
| 0 | NA | 773 | 1 | 3 | 0 | free |

1 Carbohydrate Choice = 1 starch or 1 fruit or 1 milk exchange

## PRODUCTS

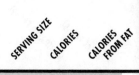

| | SERVING SIZE | CALORIES | CALORIES FROM FAT |
|---|---|---|---|
| ❶ Chicken Broth, Campbell's® Healthy Request | 1 cup | 20 | 0 |
| ❶ Chicken Broth, Campbell's® Low Sodium Ready-to-Serve | 1 can | 30 | 25 |
| ❶ Chicken Broth, Health Valley®, Fat-Free No Salt | 1 cup | 35 | 0 |
| ❶ Chicken Broth, Health Valley® | 1 cup | 35 | 0 |
| ❶ Chicken Broth, Health Valley® Fat-Free | 1 cup | 30 | 0 |
| ❶ Chicken Broth, Progresso® | 1 cup | 20 | 5 |
| ❶ Clear Chicken Broth, Swanson® | 1 cup | 30 | 18 |
| ❶ Instant Beef Broth, Weight Watchers® | 1 pkt | 10 | 0 |
| ❶ Instant Chicken Broth, Weight Watchers® | 1 pkt | 10 | 0 |

### BROWNIE MIX (AS PREPARED)

| | SERVING SIZE | CALORIES | CALORIES FROM FAT |
|---|---|---|---|
| Caramel Brownie Mix, Betty Crocker® | 1 brownie | 190 | 80 |
| Chewy Fudge Brownie Mix, Duncan Hines® | ⅛ pkg | 160 | 60 |
| Chocolate Brownie Mix, Pillsbury® Deluxe | ⅟₂₀ pkg | 180 | 60 |
| Chocolate Chip Brownie Mix, Betty Crocker® | 1 brownie | 200 | 90 |
| Chocolate Chunk Brownie Mix, Betty Crocker® | 1 brownie | 190 | 80 |
| Cookies & Cream Brownie Mix, Betty Crocker® | 1 brownie | 200 | 90 |
| Cream Cheese Brownie Mix, Pillsbury® Swirl Deluxe | ⅟₂₀ pkg | 180 | 80 |
| Dark Chocolate Fudge Brownie Mix, Betty Crocker® | 1 brownie | 190 | 80 |
| Dark Chocolate with Hershey's® Syrup Brownies, Betty Crocker® | 1 brownie | 190 | 70 |
| Double Fudge Brownie Mix, Duncan Hines® | ⅟₂₀ pkg | 170 | 60 |
| Frosted Brownie Mix, Betty Crocker® | 1 brownie | 210 | 80 |
| Frosted Premium Brownie Mix, Betty Crocker® | ⅟₂₀ pkg | 210 | 80 |
| Fudge Brownie Mix, Betty Crocker® (regular size) | 1 brownie | 190 | 70 |
| ❶ Fudge Brownie Mix, Betty Crocker® Low Fat | ⅛ pkg | 130 | 20 |
| Fudge Brownie Mix, Krusteaz® | 1 (2") brownie | 190 | 60 |

❶  Meets Low-Fat Guidelines

| TOTAL FAT (g) | SATURATED FAT (g) | SODIUM (mg) | PROTEIN (g) | CARBOHYDRATE (g) | CARBOHYDRATE CHOICES | EXCHANGES |
|---|---|---|---|---|---|---|
| 0 | 0 | 480 | 3 | 1 | 0 | free |
| 3 | 1 | 140 | 4 | 2 | 0 | 1 lean meat |
| 0 | 0 | 75 | 8 | 0 | 0 | 1 very lean meat (½ cup = free) |
| 0 | 0 | 250 | 8 | 0 | 0 | 1 very lean meat (½ cup = free) |
| 0 | 0 | 170 | 6 | 0 | 0 | 1 very lean meat |
| 0.5 | NA | 860 | 2 | 1 | 0 | free |
| 2 | NA | NA | 2 | 1 | 0 | free |
| 0 | 0 | 800 | 0 | 2 | 0 | free |
| 0 | 0 | 830 | 0 | 2 | 0 | free |
| | | | | | | |
| 9 | 1.5 | 150 | 2 | 27 | 2 | 2 starch, 1 fat |
| 7 | 1.5 | 120 | 2 | 25 | 1½ | 1½ starch, 1 fat |
| 7 | 1.5 | 110 | 2 | 28 | 2 | 2 starch, 1 fat |
| 10 | 3 | 100 | 2 | 26 | 2 | 2 starch, 1½ fat |
| 9 | 2.5 | 100 | 2 | 24 | 1½ | 1½ starch, 1 fat |
| 10 | 2 | 140 | 2 | 27 | 2 | 2 starch, 1½ fat |
| 9 | 2.5 | 95 | 2 | 22 | 1½ | 1½ starch, 1 fat |
| 8 | 1.5 | 140 | 2 | 27 | 2 | 2 starch, 1 fat |
| 8 | 1.5 | 135 | 2 | 28 | 2 | 2 starch, 1 fat |
| 7 | 1.5 | 130 | 2 | 29 | 2 | 2 starch, 1 fat |
| 9 | 2 | 130 | 2 | 31 | 2 | 2 starch, 1 fat |
| 9 | 2 | 130 | 2 | 31 | 2 | 2 starch, 1 fat |
| 8 | 1.5 | 130 | 2 | 29 | 2 | 2 starch, 1 fat |
| 2.5 | 0.5 | 110 | 2 | 26 | 2 | 2 starch |
| 7 | 1.5 | 160 | 2 | 30 | 2 | 2 starch, 1 fat |

1 Carbohydrate Choice = 1 starch or 1 fruit or 1 milk exchange

# PRODUCTS

| | SERVING SIZE | CALORIES | CALORIES FROM FAT |
|---|---|---|---|
| ❶ Fudge Brownie Mix, Krusteaz® Fat Free | 1 (2") brownie | 120 | 0 |
| Fudge Brownie Mix, Pillsbury® Deluxe | 1/16 pkg | 150 | 50 |
| Fudge Brownie Mix, Pillsbury® Lovin' Lites® Deluxe | 1/16 pkg | 160 | 30 |
| Fudge Brownie Mix, Robin Hood®/Gold Medal® | 1 brownie | 170 | 60 |
| German Chocolate Brownie Mix, Betty Crocker® | 1 brownie | 220 | 80 |
| Hot Fudge Brownie Mix, Betty Crocker® | 1 brownie | 190 | 80 |
| Hot Fudge Brownie Mix, Pillsbury® Deluxe | 1/24 pkg | 160 | 60 |
| Mississippi Mud Brownie Mix, Duncan Hines® | 1/20 pkg | 160 | 60 |
| Original Brownie Mix, Betty Crocker® | 1 brownie | 180 | 70 |
| Peanut Butter Candies with Reese's® Pieces Brownie Mix, Betty Crocker® | 1 brownie | 200 | 90 |
| Raspberry Fudge Brownie Mix, Duncan Hines® | 1/20 pkg | 160 | 60 |
| Supreme Brownie Mix, Betty Crocker® Sweet Rewards™ Reduced Fat | 1 brownie | 150 | 40 |
| Walnut Brownie Mix, Betty Crocker® | 1 brownie | 200 | 100 |
| Walnut Brownie Mix, Pillsbury® Deluxe | 1/18 pkg | 180 | 80 |
| Walnut Premium Brownie Mix, Betty Crocker® | 1/18 pkg | 200 | 100 |

## BROWNIES (READY-TO-EAT)

| | SERVING SIZE | CALORIES | CALORIES FROM FAT |
|---|---|---|---|
| ❶ Brownie, Betty Crocker® Sweet Rewards™ | 1 bar | 100 | 0 |
| ❶ Brownie Lights™ Brownies, Little Debbie® | 1 ind. pkg | 190 | 30 |
| ❶ Brownies with Fudge Filling, Health Valley® Fat-Free | 1 brownie | 110 | 0 |
| ❶ Fudge Brownies, Delicious Frookie® Fat-Free | 1 brownie | 110 | 0 |
| ❶ Fudge Brownies, Entenmann's® Fat Free Cholesterol Free | 1/10 strip | 110 | 0 |
| Fudge Brownies, Little Debbie® | 1 ind. pkg | 270 | 120 |
| ❶ Peanut Butter Brownies, Delicious Frookie® Fat-Free | 1 brownie | 110 | 0 |

❶  Meets Low-Fat Guidelines

| TOTAL FAT (g) | SATURATED FAT (g) | SODIUM (mg) | PROTEIN (g) | CARBOHYDRATE (g) | CARBOHYDRATE CHOICES | EXCHANGES |
|---|---|---|---|---|---|---|
| 0 | 0 | 180 | 1 | 28 | 2 | 2 starch |
| 6 | 1 | 95 | 1 | 22 | 1½ | 1½ starch, 1 fat |
| 3.5 | 1 | 125 | 2 | 29 | 2 | 2 starch |
| 7 | 1.5 | 105 | 2 | 24 | 1½ | 1½ starch, 1 fat |
| 9 | 2.5 | 130 | 2 | 33 | 2 | 2 starch, 1 fat |
| 9 | 2.5 | 110 | 2 | 25 | 1½ | 1½ starch, 1 fat |
| 7 | 2 | 100 | 1 | 24 | 1½ | 1½ starch, 1 fat |
| 6 | 1 | 100 | 1 | 26 | 2 | 2 starch, 1 fat |
| 7 | 1.5 | 110 | 2 | 27 | 2 | 2 starch, 1 fat |
| 10 | 2.5 | 120 | 3 | 27 | 2 | 2 starch, 1½ fat |
| 7 | 1 | 100 | 1 | 23 | 1½ | 1½ starch, 1 fat |
| 4 | 1 | 110 | 2 | 27 | 2 | 2 starch |
| 11 | 2 | 105 | 2 | 24 | 1½ | 1½ starch, 2 fat |
| 9 | 1.5 | 90 | 2 | 22 | 1½ | 1½ starch, 1 fat |
| 11 | 2 | 105 | 2 | 24 | 1½ | 1½ starch, 2 fat |
| 0 | 0 | 90 | 2 | 21 | 1½ | 1½ starch |
| 3 | 0.5 | 200 | 3 | 39 | 2½ | 2½ starch |
| 0 | 0 | 30 | 3 | 26 | 2 | 2 starch |
| 0 | 0 | 160 | 1 | 26 | 2 | 2 starch |
| 0 | 0 | 140 | 2 | 27 | 2 | 2 starch |
| 13 | 2.5 | 170 | 2 | 39 | 2½ | 2½ starch, 2 fat |
| 0 | 0 | 160 | 2 | 26 | 2 | 2 starch |

1 Carbohydrate Choice = 1 starch or 1 fruit or 1 milk exchange

## PRODUCTS

| | SERVING SIZE | CALORIES | CALORIES FROM FAT |
|---|---|---|---|

### BUNS, SANDWICH

| | | | |
|---|---|---|---|
| ❶ Hamburger bun, all varieties (avg) | 1 bun | 160 | 25 |
| ❶ Hot dog bun, all varieties (avg) | 1 bun | 125 | 23 |

### BUTTER

| | | | |
|---|---|---|---|
| ❶ Honey Butter, Downey's® | 1 Tb | 60 | 10 |
| Light butter, all brands (avg) | 1 Tb | 50 | 50 |
| Light unsalted butter, all brands (avg) | 1 Tb | 50 | 50 |
| Light whipped butter, salted, all brands (avg) | 1 Tb | 35 | 30 |
| Regular butter, all brands (avg) | 1 Tb | 100 | 100 |
| Regular unsalted butter, all brands (avg) | 1 Tb | 100 | 100 |
| Whipped butter, salted, all brands (avg) | 1 Tb | 35 | 30 |
| Whipped butter, unsalted, all brands (avg) | 1 Tb | 60 | 60 |

### CAKE (FROZEN)

| | | | |
|---|---|---|---|
| Boston Creme Special Recipe Cake, Pepperidge Farm® | ⅛ cake | 260 | 80 |
| Carrot Cake, Oregon Farms® | ⅙ cake | 280 | 130 |
| Chocolate Mousse Special Recipe Cake, Pepperidge Farm® | ⅛ cake | 250 | 100 |
| Deluxe Carrot Special Recipe Cake, Pepperidge Farm® | ⅛ cake | 310 | 150 |
| Divine Devil's Food Cake, Oregon Farms® | ⅙ cake | 260 | 80 |
| Large Layer Cakes, Pepperidge Farm®, all varieties (avg) | ⅙ cake | 300 | 130 |
| Lemon Mousse Special Recipe Cake, Pepperidge Farm® | ⅛ cake | 250 | 110 |
| Pineapple Cream Special Recipe Cake, Pepperidge Farm® | ⅑ cake | 240 | 90 |
| Pound Cake, Pepperidge Farm®, All Butter | ⅕ cake | 290 | 110 |
| Pound Cake, Sara Lee®, All Butter | ¼ cake | 320 | 150 |
| Pound Cake, Sara Lee®, Reduced Fat | ¼ cake | 280 | 100 |
| Strawberry Cream with Coconut Special Recipe Cake, Pepperidge Farm® | ⅑ cake | 230 | 80 |

❶  Meets Low-Fat Guidelines

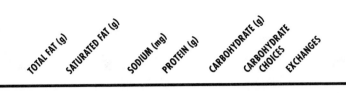

| TOTAL FAT (g) | SATURATED FAT (g) | SODIUM (mg) | PROTEIN (g) | CARBOHYDRATE (g) | CARBOHYDRATE CHOICES | EXCHANGES |
|---|---|---|---|---|---|---|
| 3 | 1–2 | 200–389 | 6 | 26–35 | 2 | 2 starch |
| 2–3 | 0–1 | 160–270 | 4–6 | 22 | 1½ | 1½ starch |
| | | | | | | |
| 1 | 0.5 | 10 | 0 | 11 | 1 | 1 fruit |
| 6 | 4 | 70 | <1 | 0 | 0 | 1 fat |
| 6 | 4 | 0 | <1 | 0 | 0 | 1 fat |
| 4 | 2.5 | 45 | 0 | 0 | 0 | 1 fat |
| 11 | 7 | 90 | 0 | 0 | 0 | 2 fat |
| 11 | 8 | 0 | 0 | 0 | 0 | 2 fat |
| 4 | 2.5 | 45 | 0 | 0 | 0 | 1 fat |
| 7 | 5 | 0 | 0 | 0 | 0 | 1 fat |
| | | | | | | |
| 9 | 2.5 | 120 | 3 | 42 | 3 | 3 starch, 1 fat |
| 15 | 2.5 | 370 | 4 | 38 | 2½ | 2½ starch, 2 fat |
| 10 | 3 | 120 | 2 | 35 | 2 | 2 starch, 2 fat |
| 16 | 4 | 320 | 2 | 39 | 2½ | 2½ starch, 3 fat |
| 9 | 2 | 410 | 3 | 43 | 3 | 3 starch, 1 fat |
| 14 | 4 | 150–280 | 2 | 40 | 2½ | 2½ starch, 2 fat |
| 12 | 4 | 100 | 2 | 34 | 2 | 2 starch, 2 fat |
| 10 | 3 | 120 | 2 | 38 | 2½ | 2½ starch, 1½ fat |
| 13 | 7 | 280 | 5 | 39 | 2½ | 2½ starch, 2 fat |
| 16 | 9 | 280 | 4 | 38 | 2½ | 2½ starch, 3 fat |
| 11 | 3 | 350 | 4 | 42 | 3 | 3 starch, 2 fat |
| 9 | 3 | 115 | 2 | 38 | 2½ | 2½ starch, 1 fat |

1 Carbohydrate Choice = 1 starch *or* 1 fruit *or* 1 milk exchange

| PRODUCTS | SERVING SIZE | CALORIES | CALORIES FROM FAT |
|---|---|---|---|
| **CAKE (READY-TO-EAT)** *see also* Coffee Cake | | | |
| All Butter French Crumb Cake, Entenmann's® | ⅛ cake | 210 | 90 |
| ❶ Apple Spice Crumb Cake, Entenmann's® Fat Free Cholesterol Free | ⅛ cake | 130 | 0 |
| Banana Crunch Cake, Entenmann's® | ⅛ cake | 220 | 90 |
| ❶ Banana Crunch Cake, Entenmann's® Fat Free Cholesterol Free | ⅛ cake | 140 | 0 |
| ❶ Blueberry Crunch Cake, Entenmann's® Fat Free Cholesterol Free | ⅛ cake | 140 | 0 |
| Carrot Cake, Entenmann's® | ⅛ cake | 290 | 140 |
| ❶ Carrot Cake, Entenmann's® Fat Free Cholesterol Free | ⅛ cake | 170 | 0 |
| ❶ Chocolate Crunch Cake, Entenmann's® Fat Free Cholesterol Free | ⅛ cake | 130 | 0 |
| Chocolate Fudge Cake, Entenmann's® | ⅙ cake | 310 | 130 |
| ❶ Fudge Iced Chocolate Cake, Entenmann's® Fat Free Cholesterol Free | ⅙ cake | 210 | 0 |
| ❶ Fudge Iced Golden Cake, Entenmann's® Fat Free Cholesterol Free | ⅙ cake | 220 | 0 |
| ❶ Golden French Crumb Cake, Entenmann's® Fat Free Cholesterol Free | ⅛ cake | 140 | 0 |
| Louisiana Crunch Cake, Entenmann's® | ⅑ cake | 310 | 120 |
| ❶ Louisiana Crunch Cake, Entenmann's® Fat Free Cholesterol Free | ⅙ cake | 220 | 0 |
| Marshmallow Iced Devil's Food Cake, Entenmann's® | ⅙ cake | 350 | 170 |
| ❶ Mocha Iced Chocolate Cake, Entenmann's® Fat Free Cholesterol Free | ⅙ cake | 200 | 0 |
| Thick Fudge Golden Cake, Entenmann's® | ⅙ cake | 330 | 140 |
| **CAKE MIX (AS PREPARED)** | | | |
| ***Angel Food Cake Mix*** | | | |
| ❶ Angel Food, Pillsbury® Moist Supreme™ | ¹⁄₁₂ cake | 140 | 0 |

❶ Meets Low-Fat Guidelines

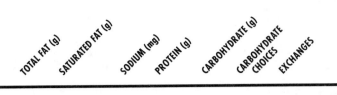

| TOTAL FAT (g) | SATURATED FAT (g) | SODIUM (mg) | PROTEIN (g) | CARBOHYDRATE (g) | CARBOHYDRATE CHOICES | EXCHANGES |
|---|---|---|---|---|---|---|
| 10 | 6 | 240 | 3 | 29 | 2 | 2 starch, 2 fat |
| 0 | 0 | 140 | 2 | 30 | 2 | 2 starch |
| 9 | 2 | 280 | 2 | 32 | 2 | 2 starch, 1 fat |
| 0 | 0 | 150 | 2 | 33 | 2 | 2 starch |
| 0 | 0 | 200 | 2 | 32 | 2 | 2 starch |
| 16 | 3.5 | 240 | 3 | 35 | 2 | 2 starch, 3 fat |
| 0 | 0 | 230 | 3 | 40 | 2½ | 2½ starch |
| 0 | 0 | 170 | 2 | 32 | 2 | 2 starch |
| 14 | 5 | 260 | 3 | 47 | 3 | 3 starch, 2 fat |
| 0 | 0 | 270 | 3 | 51 | 3½ | 3½ starch |
| 0 | 0 | 200 | 3 | 52 | 3½ | 3½ starch |
| 0 | 0 | 150 | 2 | 35 | 2 | 2 starch |
| 13 | 3.5 | 290 | 3 | 45 | 3 | 3 starch, 2 fat |
| 0 | 0 | 220 | 3 | 51 | 3½ | 3½ starch |
| 18 | 5 | 290 | 3 | 45 | 3 | 3 starch, 3 fat |
| 0 | 0 | 270 | 3 | 46 | 3 | 3 starch |
| 16 | 4 | 270 | 3 | 48 | 3 | 3 starch, 3 fat |
| 0 | 0 | 330 | 3 | 31 | 2 | 2 starch |

1 Carbohydrate Choice = 1 starch or 1 fruit or 1 milk exchange

## PRODUCTS

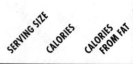

| | SERVING SIZE | CALORIES | CALORIES FROM FAT |
|---|---|---|---|
| ❶ Angel Food, Pillsbury® Plus | ¹⁄₁₀ cake | 150 | 0 |

### Chocolate/Devil's Food Cake Mix

| | SERVING SIZE | CALORIES | CALORIES FROM FAT |
|---|---|---|---|
| Butter Chocolate, Betty Crocker® SuperMoist® | ¹⁄₁₂ cake | 270 | 120 |
| Butter Recipe Chocolate, Pillsbury Plus® | ¹⁄₁₂ cake | 270 | 120 |
| Butter Recipe Chocolate, Pillsbury® Moist Supreme™ | ¹⁄₁₂ cake | 270 | 120 |
| Chocolate Caramel Nut, Pillsbury® Bundt™ | ¹⁄₁₆ cake | 290 | 160 |
| Chocolate Fudge, Betty Crocker® SuperMoist® | ¹⁄₁₂ cake | 180 | 35 |
| ❶ Chocolate, Betty Crocker® Sweet Rewards™ Snack Cake Mix | ¹⁄₈ cake | 170 | 0 |
| Chocolate, Pillsbury Plus® | ¹⁄₁₂ cake | 260 | 110 |
| Chocolate, Pillsbury® Moist Supreme™ | ¹⁄₁₂ cake | 250 | 100 |
| Dark Chocolate, Pillsbury Plus® | ¹⁄₁₂ cake | 250 | 110 |
| Dark Chocolate, Pillsbury® Moist Supreme™ | ¹⁄₁₂ cake | 250 | 100 |
| Devil's Food, Betty Crocker® SuperMoist® Light | ¹⁄₁₀ cake | 230 | 40 |
| Devil's Food, Betty Crocker® Sweet Rewards™ | ¹⁄₁₂ cake | 220 | 70 |
| Devil's Food, Pillsbury Plus® | ¹⁄₁₂ cake | 270 | 130 |
| Devil's Food, Pillsbury Plus® Lovin' Lites® | ¹⁄₁₀ cake | 210 | 40 |
| Devil's Food, Pillsbury® Moist Supreme™ | ¹⁄₁₂ cake | 270 | 130 |
| Devil's Food, Robin Hood® | ¹⁄₅ cake | 310 | 150 |
| Devil's Food, Betty Crocker® SuperMoist® | ¹⁄₁₂ cake | 240 | 100 |
| Devil's Food, Pillsbury® Moist Supreme™ Lovin' Lites® | ¹⁄₁₀ cake | 230 | 45 |
| Double Chocolate Swirl, Betty Crocker® SuperMoist® | ¹⁄₁₂ cake | 250 | 100 |
| Double Hot Fudge, Pillsbury® Bundt™ | ¹⁄₁₆ cake | 280 | 140 |
| German Chocolate, Betty Crocker® SuperMoist® | ¹⁄₁₂ cake | 250 | 100 |
| German Chocolate, Pillsbury Plus® | ¹⁄₁₂ cake | 250 | 100 |
| German Chocolate, Pillsbury® Moist Supreme™ | ¹⁄₁₂ cake | 250 | 100 |
| Milk Chocolate, Betty Crocker® SuperMoist® | ¹⁄₁₂ cake | 250 | 110 |

❶ Meets Low-Fat Guidelines

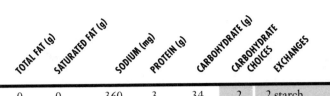

| TOTAL FAT (g) | SATURATED FAT (g) | SODIUM (mg) | PROTEIN (g) | CARBOHYDRATE (g) | CARBOHYDRATE CHOICES | EXCHANGES |
|---|---|---|---|---|---|---|
| 0 | 0 | 360 | 3 | 34 | 2 | 2 starch |
| 13 | 7 | 380 | 4 | 34 | 2 | 2 starch, 2 fat |
| 13 | 7 | 430 | 4 | 33 | 2 | 2 starch, 2 fat |
| 12 | 7 | 420 | 4 | 33 | 2 | 2 starch, 2 fat |
| 18 | 3.5 | 210 | 3 | 28 | 2 | 2 starch, 3 fat |
| 4 | 1.5 | 410 | 2 | 34 | 2 | 2 starch, ½ fat |
| 0 | 0 | 390 | 3 | 38 | 2½ | 2½ starch |
| 12 | 3 | 330 | 3 | 34 | 2 | 2 starch, 2 fat |
| 11 | 2.5 | 280 | 3 | 35 | 2 | 2 starch, 2 fat |
| 12 | 3 | 340 | 3 | 33 | 2 | 2 starch, 2 fat |
| 11 | 2.5 | 340 | 3 | 34 | 2 | 2 starch, 2 fat |
| 4.5 | 2 | 400 | 4 | 43 | 3 | 3 starch |
| 7 | 2 | 370 | 4 | 35 | 2 | 2 starch, 1 fat |
| 14 | 3 | 340 | 4 | 33 | 2 | 2 starch, 2 fat |
| 4.5 | 1.5 | 410 | 2 | 41 | 3 | 3 starch |
| 14 | 3 | 340 | 4 | 33 | 2 | 2 starch, 2 fat |
| 17 | 4 | 430 | 4 | 36 | 2½ | 2½ starch, 3 fat |
| 11 | 3 | 390 | 4 | 35 | 2 | 2 starch, 2 fat |
| 5 | 2 | 420 | 4 | 41 | 3 | 3 starch |
| 11 | 3 | 390 | 4 | 35 | 2 | 2 starch, 2 fat |
| 16 | 5 | 220 | 3 | 32 | 2 | 2 starch, 3 fat |
| 11 | 3 | 410 | 3 | 34 | 2 | 2 starch, 2 fat |
| 11 | 2.5 | 280 | 3 | 34 | 2 | 2 starch, 2 fat |
| 11 | 2.5 | 280 | 3 | 34 | 2 | 2 starch, 2 fat |
| 12 | 3 | 320 | 3 | 33 | 2 | 2 starch, 2 fat |

1 Carbohydrate Choice = 1 starch or 1 fruit or 1 milk exchange

## PRODUCTS

| | SERVING SIZE | CALORIES | CALORIES FROM FAT |
|---|---|---|---|
| **White Cake Mix** | | | |
| Sour Cream White, Betty Crocker® SuperMoist® | ¹⁄₁₀ cake | 280 | 110 |
| White, Betty Crocker® SuperMoist® | ¹⁄₁₂ cake | 230 | 80 |
| White, Betty Crocker® SuperMoist® Light | ¹⁄₁₀ cake | 210 | 30 |
| White, Betty Crocker® Sweet Rewards™ | ¹⁄₁₂ cake | 210 | 50 |
| White, Pillsbury Plus® | ¹⁄₁₀ cake | 280 | 100 |
| White, Pillsbury® Moist Supreme™ | ¹⁄₁₀ cake | 280 | 100 |
| White, Pillsbury® Moist Supreme™ Lovin' Lites® | ¹⁄₁₀ cake | 230 | 45 |
| White, Pillsbury Plus® Lovin' Lites® | ¹⁄₁₀ cake | 230 | 45 |
| **Yellow Cake Mix** | | | |
| Butter Yellow, Betty Crocker® SuperMoist® | ¹⁄₁₂ cake | 260 | 100 |
| Yellow, Betty Crocker® SuperMoist® | ¹⁄₁₂ cake | 240 | 90 |
| Yellow, Betty Crocker® SuperMoist® Light | ¹⁄₁₀ cake | 230 | 40 |
| Yellow, Betty Crocker® Sweet Rewards™ | ¹⁄₁₂ cake | 220 | 60 |
| Yellow, Pillsbury Plus® | ¹⁄₁₂ cake | 250 | 100 |
| Yellow, Pillsbury Plus® Lovin' Lites® | ¹⁄₁₀ cake | 230 | 45 |
| Yellow, Pillsbury® Moist Supreme™ | ¹⁄₁₂ cake | 240 | 90 |
| Yellow, Pillsbury® Moist Supreme™ Lovin' Lites® | ¹⁄₁₀ cake | 230 | 45 |
| Yellow, Robin Hood® | ¹⁄₅ cake | 280 | 120 |
| **Other Cake Mixes** | | | |
| ❶ Apple Cinnamon, Betty Crocker® Sweet Rewards™ Snack Cake | ¹⁄₈ cake | 170 | 0 |
| ❶ Banana, Betty Crocker® Sweet Rewards™ Snack Cake | ¹⁄₈ cake | 170 | 0 |
| Banana, Pillsbury® Plus® | ¹⁄₁₂ cake | 260 | 100 |
| Banana, Pillsbury® Moist Supreme™ | ¹⁄₁₂ cake | 260 | 100 |
| Butter Pecan, Betty Crocker® SuperMoist® | ¹⁄₁₂ cake | 250 | 100 |
| Butter Recipe, Pillsbury Plus® | ¹⁄₁₂ cake | 260 | 110 |

❶   Meets Low-Fat Guidelines

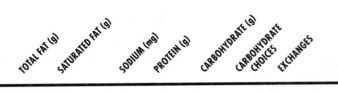

| TOTAL FAT (g) | SATURATED FAT (g) | SODIUM (mg) | PROTEIN (g) | CARBOHYDRATE (g) | CARBOHYDRATE CHOICES | EXCHANGES |
|---|---|---|---|---|---|---|
| 12 | 3 | 380 | 4 | 39 | 2½ | 2½ starch, 2 fat |
| 9 | 2.5 | 290 | 3 | 35 | 2 | 2 starch, 1½ fat |
| 3.5 | 1.5 | 390 | 3 | 43 | 3 | 3 starch |
| 6 | 1.5 | 300 | 3 | 35 | 2 | 2 starch, 1fat |
| 11 | 2.5 | 350 | 3 | 41 | 3 | 3 starch, 1½ fat |
| 11 | 2.5 | 350 | 3 | 41 | 3 | 3 starch, 1½ fat |
| 5 | 1.5 | 350 | 3 | 45 | 3 | 3 starch |
| 5 | 1.5 | 350 | 3 | 42 | 3 | 3 starch |
| 11 | 6 | 330 | 3 | 37 | 2½ | 2½ starch, 1½ fat |
| 10 | 2.5 | 290 | 4 | 34 | 2 | 2 starch, 2 fat |
| 4.5 | 2 | 350 | 4 | 43 | 3 | 3 starch |
| 6 | 1.5 | 300 | 3 | 36 | 2½ | 2½ starch, 1 fat |
| 11 | 2.5 | 300 | 3 | 35 | 2 | 2 starch, 2 fat |
| 5 | 1.5 | 380 | 3 | 43 | 3 | 3 starch |
| 10 | 2.5 | 290 | 3 | 35 | 2 | 2 starch, 2 fat |
| 5 | 1.5 | 380 | 3 | 43 | 3 | 3 starch |
| 13 | 3 | 310 | 3 | 37 | 2½ | 2½ starch, 2 fat |
| 0 | 0 | 250 | 2 | 39 | 2½ | 2½ starch |
| 0 | 0 | 280 | 3 | 39 | 2½ | 2½ starch |
| 11 | 2.5 | 280 | 3 | 36 | 2½ | 2½ starch, 2 fat |
| 11 | 2.5 | 280 | 3 | 36 | 2½ | 2½ starch, 2 fat |
| 11 | 2.5 | 300 | 3 | 34 | 2 | 2 starch, 2 fat |
| 12 | 6 | 370 | 3 | 36 | 2½ | 2½ starch, 2 fat |

1 Carbohydrate Choice = 1 starch *or* 1 fruit *or* 1 milk exchange

## PRODUCTS

| | SERVING SIZE | CALORIES | CALORIES FROM FAT |
|---|---|---|---|
| Butter Recipe, Pillsbury® Moist Supreme™ | 1/12 cake | 260 | 110 |
| Carrot Cake, Betty Crocker® SuperMoist® | 1/10 cake | 300 | 120 |
| Carrot Cake, Pillsbury Plus® | 1/12 cake | 260 | 110 |
| Carrot Cake, Pillsbury® Moist Supreme™ | 1/12 cake | 280 | 110 |
| Cherry Chip, Betty Crocker® SuperMoist® | 1/10 cake | 280 | 110 |
| Chocolate Chip, Betty Crocker® SuperMoist® | 1/12 cake | 280 | 130 |
| Chocolate Chip, Pillsbury Plus® | 1/12 cake | 240 | 90 |
| Chocolate Chip, Pillsbury® Moist Supreme™ | 1/12 cake | 240 | 90 |
| Cinnamon Streusel, Pillsbury® Streusel Swirl® | 1/12 cake | 260 | 100 |
| French Vanilla, Betty Crocker® SuperMoist® | 1/12 cake | 250 | 90 |
| French Vanilla, Pillsbury Plus® | 1/10 cake | 320 | 140 |
| French Vanilla, Pillsbury® Moist Supreme™ | 1/10 cake | 300 | 120 |
| Fudge Marble, Betty Crocker® SuperMoist® | 1/12 cake | 250 | 100 |
| Fudge Swirl, Pillsbury Plus® | 1/12 cake | 270 | 110 |
| Fudge Swirl, Pillsbury® Moist Supreme™ | 1/12 cake | 250 | 90 |
| Funfetti®, Pillsbury Plus® | 1/12 cake | 240 | 80 |
| Golden Vanilla, Betty Crocker® SuperMoist® | 1/12 cake | 280 | 130 |
| Lemon, Betty Crocker® SuperMoist® | 1/12 cake | 250 | 100 |
| ❶ Lemon, Betty Crocker® Sweet Rewards™ Snack Cake | 1/8 cake | 170 | 0 |
| Lemon, Pillsbury Plus® | 1/10 cake | 310 | 120 |
| Lemon, Pillsbury® Moist Supreme™ | 1/10 cake | 300 | 120 |
| Party Swirl, Betty Crocker® SuperMoist® | 1/12 cake | 250 | 100 |
| Peanut Butter Chocolate Swirl, Betty Crocker® SuperMoist® | 1/12 cake | 240 | 90 |
| Rainbow Chip, Betty Crocker® SuperMoist® | 1/12 cake | 250 | 100 |
| Spice, Betty Crocker® SuperMoist® | 1/12 cake | 250 | 100 |
| Strawberry Cream Cheese, Pillsbury® Bundt™ Cake | 1/16 cake | 300 | 150 |
| Strawberry Swirl, Betty Crocker® SuperMoist® | 1/10 cake | 290 | 110 |
| Strawberry, Pillsbury Plus® | 1/10 cake | 260 | 100 |
| Strawberry, Pillsbury® Moist Supreme™ | 1/12 cake | 260 | 100 |

❶ Meets Low-Fat Guidelines

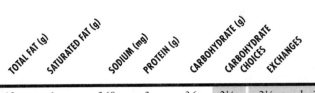

| TOTAL FAT (g) | SATURATED FAT (g) | SODIUM (mg) | PROTEIN (g) | CARBOHYDRATE (g) | CARBOHYDRATE CHOICES | EXCHANGES |
|---|---|---|---|---|---|---|
| 12 | 6 | 360 | 3 | 36 | 2½ | 2½ starch, 2 fat |
| 13 | 3 | 360 | 4 | 41 | 3 | 3 starch, 2 fat |
| 12 | 3 | 300 | 3 | 35 | 2 | 2 starch, 2 fat |
| 12 | 2.5 | 290 | 3 | 35 | 2 | 2 starch, 2 fat |
| 12 | 3 | 350 | 3 | 40 | 2½ | 2½ starch, 2 fat |
| 14 | 3 | 290 | 3 | 35 | 2 | 2 starch, 2½ fat |
| 10 | 3 | 280 | 3 | 35 | 2 | 2 starch, 2 fat |
| 10 | 3 | 280 | 3 | 35 | 2 | 2 starch, 2 fat |
| 11 | 2.5 | 220 | 3 | 38 | 2½ | 2½ starch, 2 fat |
| 10 | 2.5 | 280 | 3 | 35 | 2 | 2 starch, 2 fat |
| 15 | 3.5 | 360 | 4 | 41 | 3 | 3 starch, 2 fat |
| 13 | 3 | 350 | 3 | 42 | 3 | 3 starch, 2 fat |
| 11 | 2.5 | 270 | 3 | 35 | 2 | 2 starch, 2 fat |
| 12 | 3 | 300 | 3 | 37 | 2½ | 2½ starch, 2 fat |
| 10 | 2.5 | 290 | 3 | 37 | 2½ | 2½ starch, 1 fat |
| 9 | 2 | 290 | 3 | 36 | 2½ | 2½ starch, 1 fat |
| 14 | 3 | 260 | 3 | 35 | 2 | 2 starch, 2½ fat |
| 11 | 2.5 | 260 | 3 | 36 | 2½ | 2½ starch, 1½ fat |
| 0 | 0 | 270 | 2 | 39 | 2½ | 2½ starch |
| 13 | 3 | 340 | 4 | 43 | 3 | 3 starch, 2 fat |
| 13 | 3 | 350 | 4 | 42 | 3 | 3 starch, 2 fat |
| 11 | 2.5 | 280 | 3 | 35 | 2 | 2 starch, 2 fat |
| 10 | 2.5 | 320 | 4 | 34 | 2 | 2 starch, 2 fat |
| 11 | 3 | 310 | 3 | 34 | 2 | 2 starch, 2 fat |
| 11 | 2.5 | 310 | 3 | 35 | 2 | 2 starch, 2 fat |
| 17 | 4.5 | 200 | 3 | 34 | 2 | 2 starch, 3 fat |
| 12 | 3 | 330 | 4 | 42 | 3 | 3 starch, 2 fat |
| 11 | 2.5 | 310 | 3 | 36 | 2½ | 2½ starch, 2 fat |
| 11 | 2.5 | 300 | 3 | 36 | 2½ | 2½ starch, 2 fat |

1 Carbohydrate Choice = 1 starch or 1 fruit or 1 milk exchange

## PRODUCTS

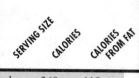

| PRODUCTS | SERVING SIZE | CALORIES | CALORIES FROM FAT |
|---|---|---|---|
| Sunshine Vanilla, Pillsbury Plus® | ¹⁄₁₂ cake | 260 | 110 |
| Sunshine Vanilla, Pillsbury® Moist Supreme™ | ¹⁄₁₂ cake | 260 | 110 |
| White 'N Fudge Swirl, Pillsbury Plus® | ¹⁄₁₂ cake | 200 | 40 |
| White 'N Fudge Swirl, Pillsbury® Moist Supreme™ | ¹⁄₁₂ cake | 250 | 90 |
| White Chocolate Swirl, Betty Crocker® SuperMoist® | ¹⁄₁₂ cake | 250 | 100 |

### CEREAL, HOT

| | | | |
|---|---|---|---|
| ❶ Coco Wheats® | ¹⁄₃ cup | 200 | 10 |
| ❶ Cream of Rice®, Nabisco® | ¹⁄₄ cup | 170 | 0 |
| ❶ Cream of Rye, Roman Meal® | ¹⁄₃ cup | 110 | 10 |
| ❶ Cream of Wheat®, regular or instant, Nabisco® | 1 oz | 100 | 0 |
| ❶ Malt-O-Meal® Chocolate | 3 Tb dry | 120 | 0 |
| ❶ Malt-O-Meal® Maple & Brown Sugar | 3 Tb dry | 120 | 0 |
| ❶ Malt-O-Meal® Quick | 3 Tb dry | 120 | 0 |
| ❶ Malt-O-Meal® Quick, flavored (avg) | ¹⁄₃ cup | 220 | 0 |
| ❶ Malt-O-Meal® Quick, regular | 3 Tb dry | 120 | 0 |
| ❶ Quaker® Old Fashioned Oats | ¹⁄₂ cup dry | 150 | 25 |
| ❶ Quick Quaker® Oats | ¹⁄₂ cup dry | 150 | 25 |
| ❶ Roman Meal® Apple Cinnamon | ¹⁄₃ cup | 110 | 20 |
| ❶ Roman Meal® Oats, Wheat, Dates, Raisins & Almonds | ¹⁄₃ cup | 130 | 15 |
| ❶ Roman Meal® Oats, Wheat, Rye, Bran & Flax | ¹⁄₃ cup | 110 | 15 |
| Roman Meal® Oats, Wheat, Coconut, Rye, Almonds & Honey | ¹⁄₃ cup | 160 | 50 |
| ❶ Roman Meal® Wheat, Rye, Bran & Flax | ¹⁄₃ cup | 90 | 5 |
| ❶ Wheat Hearts®, Nature Valley® | ¹⁄₄ cup | 130 | 10 |

### CEREAL, HOT SINGLE-SERVING

| | | | |
|---|---|---|---|
| ❶ Apple Cinnamon, Fantastic Foods® | 1 container | 210 | 25 |
| ❶ Banana Nut, Fantastic Foods® | 1 container | 180 | 20 |

❶   Meets Low-Fat Guidelines

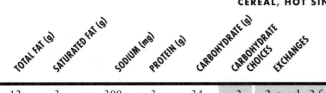

| TOTAL FAT (g) | SATURATED FAT (g) | SODIUM (mg) | PROTEIN (g) | CARBOHYDRATE (g) | CARBOHYDRATE CHOICES | EXCHANGES |
|---|---|---|---|---|---|---|
| 12 | 3 | 300 | 3 | 34 | 2 | 2 starch, 2 fat |
| 12 | 3 | 300 | 3 | 34 | 2 | 2 starch, 2 fat |
| 4.5 | 1.5 | 270 | 2 | 37 | 2½ | 2½ starch |
| 10 | 2.5 | 290 | 2 | 37 | 2½ | 2½ starch, 1 fat |
| 11 | 2.5 | 290 | 4 | 36 | 2½ | 2½ starch, 1½ fat |
| 1 | 0 | 15 | 7 | 41 | 3 | 3 starch |
| 0 | 0 | 0 | 3 | 38 | 2½ | 2½ starch |
| 1 | 0 | 0 | 5 | 20 | 1 | 1 starch |
| 0 | 0 | 0 | 3 | 22 | 1½ | 1½ starch |
| 0 | 0 | 0 | 3 | 28 | 2 | 2 starch |
| 0 | 0 | 0 | 3 | 28 | 2 | 2 starch |
| 0 | 0 | 0 | 4 | 26 | 2 | 2 starch |
| 0 | 0 | 10 | 4 | 50 | 3 | 3 starch |
| 0 | 0 | 0 | 4 | 26 | 2 | 2 starch |
| 3 | 0.5 | 0 | 5 | 27 | 2 | 2 starch |
| 3 | 0.5 | 0 | 5 | 27 | 2 | 2 starch |
| 2 | 0 | 5 | 3 | 18 | 1 | 1 starch |
| 1.5 | 0 | 0 | 5 | 24 | 1½ | 1½ starch |
| 1.5 | 0 | 0 | 5 | 19 | 1 | 1 starch |
| 6 | 3 | 10 | 4 | 22 | 1½ | 1½ starch, 1 fat |
| 0.5 | 0 | 0 | 4 | 15 | 1 | 1 starch |
| 1 | 0 | 0 | 5 | 26 | 2 | 2 starch |
| 3 | 0.5 | 240 | 4 | 42 | 3 | 3 starch |
| 2.5 | 0 | 230 | 4 | 35 | 2 | 2 starch |

1 Carbohydrate Choice = 1 starch or 1 fruit or 1 milk exchange

## PRODUCTS

| | SERVING SIZE | CALORIES | CALORIES FROM FAT |
|---|---|---|---|
| ❶ Coco Wheats® Microwave | 1 pkt | 130 | 5 |
| ❶ Cranberry Orange, Fantastic Foods® | 1 container | 210 | 25 |
| ❶ Instant Cream of Wheat®, Apple & Cinnamon, Nabisco® | 1 pkt | 130 | 0 |
| ❶ Instant Cream of Wheat®, Brown Sugar Cinnamon, Nabisco® | 1 pkt | 130 | 0 |
| ❶ Instant Cream of Wheat®, Maple & Brown Sugar, Nabisco® | 1 pkt | 130 | 0 |
| ❶ Quaker® Instant Oatmeal, Fruit & Cream, all varieties (avg) | 1 pkt | 130 | 25 |
| ❶ Quaker® Instant Oatmeal, regular flavor | 1 pkt | 100 | 20 |
| ❶ Quaker® Quick 'n Hearty™, Brown Sugar Cinnamon Microwave Oatmeal | 1 pkt | 150 | 20 |
| ❶ Quaker® Quick 'n Hearty™ Regular Microwave Oatmeal | 1 pkt | 110 | 20 |
| ❶ Wheat 'N Berries, Fantastic Foods® | 1 container | 210 | 10 |

### CEREAL, READY-TO-EAT

| | SERVING SIZE | CALORIES | CALORIES FROM FAT |
|---|---|---|---|
| ❶ 10 Bran, Apple Cinnamon, Health Valley®, all varieties (avg) | ¾ cup | 100 | 0 |
| ❶ 100% Bran, Nabisco® | ⅓ cup | 80 | 5 |
| 100% Natural Oat Cinnamon & Raisin, Nature Valley® | ¾ cup | 240 | 70 |
| 100% Natural Oat Fruit & Nut, Nature Valley® | ⅔ cup | 250 | 100 |
| 100% Natural Oat Toasted Oats & Honey, Nature Valley® | ¾ cup | 250 | 90 |
| ❶ All-Bran® with Extra Fiber™, Kellogg's® | ½ cup | 50 | 10 |
| ❶ All-Bran®, Kellogg's® | ½ cup | 80 | 10 |
| ❶ Alpha-Bits, Post® | 1 cup | 130 | 5 |
| ❶ Apple Cinnamon Squares®, Kellogg's® | ¾ cup | 180 | 10 |
| ❶ Apple Cinnamon Toasted Oats, Krusteaz® | ¾ cup | 130 | 15 |
| ❶ Apple Cinnamon Toasty O's®, Malt-O-Meal® | ¾ cup | 120 | 15 |
| ❶ Apple Jacks®, Kellogg's® | 1 cup | 110 | 0 |
| ❶ Apple Raisin Crisp®, Kellogg's® | 1 cup | 180 | 0 |

❶ Meets Low-Fat Guidelines

| TOTAL FAT (g) | SATURATED FAT (g) | SODIUM (mg) | PROTEIN (g) | CARBOHYDRATE (g) | CARBOHYDRATE CHOICES | EXCHANGES |
|---|---|---|---|---|---|---|
| 0.5 | 0 | 110 | 3 | 28 | 2 | 2 starch |
| 3 | 0.5 | 220 | 4 | 42 | 3 | 3 starch |
| 0 | 0 | 300 | 2 | 29 | 2 | 2 starch |
| 0 | 0 | 220 | 2 | 29 | 2 | 2 starch |
| 0 | 0 | 180 | 2 | 29 | 2 | 2 starch |
| 2.5 | 0.5 | 170 | 3 | 26 | 2 | 2 starch |
| 2 | 0 | 80 | 4 | 19 | 1 | 1 starch |
| 2 | 0.5 | 260 | 4 | 31 | 2 | 2 starch |
| 2 | 0.5 | 150 | 4 | 19 | 1 | 1 starch |
| 1 | 0 | 290 | 6 | 44 | 3 | 3 starch |
| 0 | 0 | 10 | 3 | 23 | 1½ | 1½ starch |
| 0.5 | 0 | 120 | 4 | 23 | 1 | 1 starch |
| 8 | 1 | 90 | 5 | 38 | 2½ | 2½ starch, 1 fat |
| 11 | 2 | 75 | 6 | 34 | 2 | 2 starch, 2 fat |
| 10 | 1.5 | 90 | 6 | 36 | 2 | 2 starch, 2 fat |
| 1 | 0 | 150 | 4 | 22 | ½ | ½ starch |
| 1 | 0 | 280 | 4 | 22 | 1 | 1 starch |
| 1 | 0 | 210 | 3 | 27 | 2 | 2 starch |
| 1 | 0 | 15 | 4 | 44 | 2½ | 2½ starch |
| 2 | 0 | 150 | 2 | 25 | 1½ | 1½ starch |
| 1.5 | 0 | 190 | 2 | 24 | 1½ | 1½ starch |
| 0 | 0 | 135 | 2 | 27 | 2 | 2 starch |
| 0 | 0 | 340 | 3 | 46 | 3 | 3 starch |

1 Carbohydrate Choice = 1 starch or 1 fruit or 1 milk exchange

| PRODUCTS | SERVING SIZE | CALORIES | CALORIES FROM FAT |
|---|---|---|---|
| ❶ Apple Zaps™, Quaker® | 1 cup | 120 | 10 |
| Banana Nut Crunch, Post® | 1 cup | 250 | 50 |
| ❶ Basic 4®, General Mills® | 1 cup | 210 | 30 |
| Blueberry Morning, Post® | 1¼ cups | 230 | 30 |
| ❶ Blueberry Squares™, Kellogg's® | ¾ cup | 180 | 10 |
| ❶ Body Buddies® Natural Fruit, General Mills® | 1 cup | 120 | 10 |
| ❶ Boo Berry®, General Mills® | 1 cup | 120 | 5 |
| ❶ Bran'nola, Original, Post® | ½ cup | 200 | 25 |
| ❶ Bran'nola, Raisin, Post® | ½ cup | 200 | 25 |
| ❶ Bran Buds®, Kellogg's® | ⅓ cup | 70 | 10 |
| ❶ Bran Flakes, Malt-O-Meal® | ¾ cup | 100 | 5 |
| ❶ Bran Flakes, Post® | ⅔ cup | 90 | 5 |
| ❶ Cap'n Crunch®, Quaker® | ¾ cup | 110 | 15 |
| ❶ Cap'n Crunch's Peanut Butter Crunch®, Quaker® | ¾ cup | 110 | 25 |
| ❶ Cap'n Crunch's Crunch Berries®, Quaker® | ¾ cup | 100 | 15 |
| ❶ Cheerios®, General Mills® | 1 cup | 110 | 15 |
| ❶ Cheerios®, Apple Cinnamon, General Mills® | ¾ cup | 120 | 15 |
| ❶ Cheerios®, Frosted, General Mills® | 1 cup | 120 | 10 |
| ❶ Cheerios®, Honey Nut, General Mills® | 1 cup | 120 | 10 |
| ❶ Cheerios®, Multi-Grain, General Mills® | 1 cup | 110 | 10 |
| ❶ Chewy Blueberry, Outrageous Fruit & Grains® Low Fat | ½ cup | 180 | 10 |
| ❶ Chewy Cherry, Outrageous Fruit & Grains® Low Fat | ½ cup | 180 | 10 |
| ❶ Chewy Raisin, Outrageous Fruit & Grains® Low Fat | ½ cup | 160 | 10 |
| ❶ Cinnamon Mini Buns, Kellogg's® | ¾ cup | 120 | 5 |
| ❶ Cinnamon Toast Crunch®, General Mills® | ¾ cup | 130 | 30 |
| Clusters®, General Mills® | 1 cup | 210 | 30 |
| ❶ Coco-Roos™, Malt-O-Meal® | ¾ cup | 120 | 10 |
| ❶ Cocoa Blasts®, Quaker® | 1 cup | 130 | 10 |

❶ Meets Low-Fat Guidelines

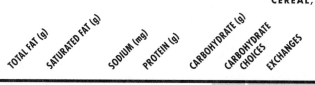

| TOTAL FAT (g) | SATURATED FAT (g) | SODIUM (mg) | PROTEIN (g) | CARBOHYDRATE (g) | CARBOHYDRATE CHOICES | EXCHANGES |
|---|---|---|---|---|---|---|
| 1 | 0.5 | 130 | 1 | 27 | 2 | 2 starch |
| 6 | 1 | 200 | 5 | 43 | 3 | 3 starch |
| 3 | 0 | 320 | 4 | 42 | 3 | 3 starch |
| 3.5 | 0.5 | 250 | 4 | 45 | 3 | 3 starch |
| 1 | 0 | 15 | 4 | 44 | 2½ | 2½ starch |
| 1 | 0 | 290 | 2 | 26 | 2 | 2 starch |
| 0.5 | 0 | 210 | 1 | 27 | 2 | 2 starch |
| 3 | 0.5 | 240 | 4 | 43 | 3 | 3 starch |
| 3 | 0.5 | 220 | 4 | 44 | 3 | 3 starch |
| 1 | 0 | 210 | 3 | 24 | 1 | 1 starch |
| 0.5 | 0 | 210 | 3 | 24 | 1 | 1 starch |
| 0.5 | 0 | 210 | 3 | 22 | 1½ | 1½ starch |
| 1.5 | 0.5 | 210 | 1 | 23 | 1½ | 1½ starch |
| 2.5 | 0.5 | 200 | 2 | 22 | 1½ | 1½ starch |
| 1.5 | 0.5 | 190 | 1 | 22 | 1½ | 1½ starch |
| 2 | 0 | 280 | 3 | 23 | 1½ | 1½ starch |
| 2 | 0 | 160 | 2 | 25 | 1½ | 1½ starch |
| 1 | 0 | 200 | 2 | 25 | 1½ | 1½ starch |
| 1.5 | 0 | 270 | 3 | 24 | 1½ | 1½ starch |
| 1 | 0 | 240 | 3 | 24 | 1½ | 1½ starch |
| 1.5 | 0 | 0 | 5 | 40 | 2½ | 2½ starch |
| 1.5 | 0 | 0 | 5 | 39 | 2½ | 2½ starch |
| 1.5 | 0 | 0 | 5 | 40 | 2½ | 2½ starch |
| 0.5 | 0 | 210 | 1 | 27 | 2 | 2 starch |
| 3 | 0.5 | 210 | 1 | 24 | 1½ | 1½ starch |
| 3.5 | 0 | 270 | 5 | 44 | 3 | 3 starch |
| 1 | 0 | 190 | 1 | 27 | 2 | 2 starch |
| 1 | 0.5 | 135 | 1 | 29 | 2 | 2 starch |

1 Carbohydrate Choice = 1 starch or 1 fruit or 1 milk exchange

## PRODUCTS

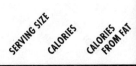

| | PRODUCTS | SERVING SIZE | CALORIES | CALORIES FROM FAT |
|---|---|---|---|---|
| ❶ | Cocoa Comets®, Malt-O-Meal® | ¾ cup | 120 | 10 |
| ❶ | Cocoa Crispies®, Kellogg's® | ¾ cup | 120 | 5 |
| ❶ | Cocoa Pebbles®, Post® | ¾ cup | 120 | 10 |
| ❶ | Cocoa Puffs®, General Mills® | 1 cup | 120 | 10 |
| ❶ | Colossal Crunch™, Malt-O-Meal® | ¾ cup | 120 | 10 |
| ❶ | Common Sense® Oat Bran, Kellogg's® | ¾ cup | 110 | 10 |
| ❶ | Complete® Bran Flakes, Kellogg's® | ¾ cup | 100 | 5 |
| ❶ | Corn Bursts™, Malt-O-Meal® | 1 cup | 110 | 0 |
| ❶ | Corn Flakes, Estee® | 1 box | 90 | 0 |
| ❶ | Corn Flakes, General Mills® Country® | 1 cup | 120 | 5 |
| ❶ | Corn Flakes, Kellogg's® | 1 cup | 110 | 0 |
| ❶ | Corn Flakes, Krusteaz® | 1 cup | 130 | 0 |
| ❶ | Corn Flakes, Malt-O-Meal® | 1 cup | 110 | 0 |
| ❶ | Corn Pops®, Kellogg's® | 1 cup | 110 | 0 |
| ❶ | Count Chocula®, General Mills® | 1 cup | 120 | 10 |
| | Cracklin' Oat Bran®, Kellogg's® | ¾ cup | 230 | 70 |
| ❶ | Crisp Rice Cereal, Krusteaz® | 1 cup | 130 | 0 |
| ❶ | Crispix®, Kellogg's® | 1 cup | 110 | 0 |
| ❶ | Crispy Brown Rice Cereal, Health Valley® | 1 cup | 110 | 0 |
| ❶ | Crispy Rice™, Malt-O-Meal® | 1 cup | 110 | 0 |
| ❶ | Crispy Wheaties® 'n Raisins, General Mills® | 1 cup | 190 | 10 |
| ❶ | Crunchy Corn Bran, Quaker® | ¾ cup | 90 | 10 |
| | C.W. Post® Hearty Granola, Post® | ⅔ cup | 280 | 80 |
| ❶ | Double Dip Crunch®, Kellogg's® | ¾ cup | 110 | 0 |
| ❶ | Fiber One®, General Mills® | ½ cup | 60 | 10 |
| ❶ | Frankenberry®, General Mills® | 1 cup | 120 | 5 |
| ❶ | Froot Loops®, Kellogg's® | 1 cup | 120 | 10 |
| ❶ | Frosted Bran®, Kellogg's® | ¾ cup | 100 | 0 |
| ❶ | Frosted Flakes Cereal, Krusteaz® | ¾ cup | 110 | 0 |
| ❶ | Frosted Flakes®, Kellogg's® | ¾ cup | 120 | 0 |
| ❶ | Frosted Flakes™, Malt-O-Meal® | ¾ cup | 110 | 0 |

❶ Meets Low-Fat Guidelines

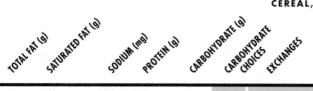

| TOTAL FAT (g) | SATURATED FAT (g) | SODIUM (mg) | PROTEIN (g) | CARBOHYDRATE (g) | CARBOHYDRATE CHOICES | EXCHANGES |
|---|---|---|---|---|---|---|
| 1 | 0 | 190 | 1 | 27 | 2 | 2 starch |
| 0.5 | 0 | 190 | 2 | 27 | 2 | 2 starch |
| 1 | 1 | 160 | 1 | 25 | 1½ | 1½ starch |
| 1 | 0 | 190 | 1 | 27 | 2 | 2 starch |
| 1 | 0 | 230 | 2 | 26 | 2 | 2 starch |
| 1 | 0 | 270 | 4 | 23 | 1½ | 1½ starch |
| 0.5 | 0 | 230 | 3 | 25 | 1 | 1 starch |
| 0 | 0 | 95 | 1 | 27 | 2 | 2 starch |
| 0 | 0 | 50 | 2 | 24 | 1½ | 1½ starch |
| 0.5 | 0 | 290 | 2 | 26 | 2 | 2 starch |
| 0 | 0 | 330 | 2 | 26 | 2 | 2 starch |
| 0 | 0 | 270 | 2 | 28 | 2 | 2 starch |
| 0 | 0 | 310 | 2 | 26 | 2 | 2 starch |
| 0 | 0 | 95 | 1 | 27 | 2 | 2 starch |
| 1 | 0 | 180 | 1 | 27 | 2 | 2 starch |
| 8 | 3 | 180 | 4 | 40 | 2 | 2 starch, 1½ fat |
| 0 | 0 | 260 | 3 | 27 | 2 | 2 starch |
| 0 | 0 | 230 | 2 | 26 | 2 | 2 starch |
| 0 | 0 | 0 | 1 | 30 | 2 | 2 starch |
| 0 | 0 | 250 | 2 | 26 | 2 | 2 starch |
| 1 | 0 | 270 | 4 | 44 | 3 | 3 starch |
| 1 | 0 | 250 | 2 | 23 | 1 | 1 starch |
| 9 | 1 | 150 | 5 | 45 | 3 | 3 starch, 1 fat |
| 0 | 0 | 160 | 2 | 27 | 2 | 2 starch |
| 1 | 0 | 125 | 2 | 24 | 1 | 1 starch |
| 1 | 0 | 210 | 1 | 27 | 2 | 2 starch |
| 1 | 0.5 | 150 | 1 | 26 | 2 | 2 starch |
| 0 | 0 | 200 | 2 | 26 | 2 | 2 starch |
| 0 | 0 | 170 | 1 | 25 | 1½ | 1½ starch |
| 0 | 0 | 200 | 1 | 28 | 2 | 2 starch |
| 0 | 0 | 200 | 1 | 27 | 2 | 2 starch |

1 Carbohydrate Choice = 1 starch or 1 fruit or 1 milk exchange

## PRODUCTS

| | PRODUCTS | SERVING SIZE | CALORIES | CALORIES FROM FAT |
|---|---|---|---|---|
| ❶ | Frosted Krispies®, Kellogg's® | ¾ cup | 110 | 0 |
| ❶ | Frosted Mini-Wheats®, bite size and regular, Kellogg's® | 1 cup | 190 | 10 |
| ❶ | Frosted Wheat Bites, Nabisco® | 1 cup | 190 | 10 |
| ❶ | Frosted Wheat Puffs, Malt-O-Meal® | ¾ cup | 120 | 0 |
| ❶ | Fruit & Fibre®, Dates, Raisins & Walnuts, Post® | 1 cup | 210 | 25 |
| ❶ | Fruit & Fibre®, Peaches, Raisins & Almonds, Post® | 1 cup | 210 | 25 |
| ❶ | Fruit & Frosted O's®, Malt-O-Meal® | 1 cup | 110 | 10 |
| ❶ | Fruit Granola, Nature Valley® Low Fat | ⅔ cup | 210 | 25 |
| ❶ | Fruit Wheats, Blueberry and Strawberry, Nabisco® | ¾ cup | 170 | 5 |
| ❶ | Fruit Wheats, Raspberry, Nabisco® | ¾ cup | 160 | 5 |
| ❶ | Fruit Whirls, Krusteaz® | ¾ cup | 120 | 10 |
| ❶ | Fruitangy Oh's™, Quaker® | 1 cup | 120 | 10 |
| ❶ | Fruitful Bran®, Kellogg's® | 1¼ cups | 170 | 10 |
| ❶ | Fruity Marshmallow Krispies®, Kellogg's® | ¾ cup | 110 | 0 |
| ❶ | Fruity Pebbles®, Post® | ¾ cup | 110 | 10 |
| ❶ | Golden Corn Nuggets™, Malt-O-Meal® | 1 cup | 110 | 0 |
| ❶ | Golden Crisp®, Post® | ¾ cup | 110 | 0 |
| ❶ | Golden Flax Cereal, Health Valley® | 1 cup | 190 | 30 |
| ❶ | Golden Puffs®, Malt-O-Meal® | ¾ cup | 120 | 0 |
| ❶ | Golden Grahams®, General Mills® | ¾ cup | 120 | 10 |
| ❶ | Granola, Health Valley® 98% Fat-Free, all varieties (avg) | ⅔ cup | 180 | 10 |
| ❶ | Granola, Heartland® Lowfat | ½ cup | 210 | 30 |
| ❶ | Granola, Kellogg's® Low Fat | ½ cup | 210 | 30 |
| | Granola, Original, Heartland® | ½ cup | 290 | 100 |
| ❶ | Granola O's, Health Valley® Fat-Free, all varieties (avg) | ¾ cup | 120 | 0 |
| | Granola, Raisin, Heartland® | ½ cup | 290 | 90 |
| ❶ | Granola with Raisins, Kellogg's® Low Fat | ⅔ cup | 210 | 30 |

❶  Meets Low-Fat Guidelines

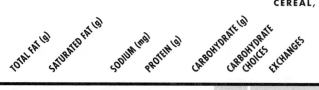

| TOTAL FAT (g) | SATURATED FAT (g) | SODIUM (mg) | PROTEIN (g) | CARBOHYDRATE (g) | CARBOHYDRATE CHOICES | EXCHANGES |
|---|---|---|---|---|---|---|
| 0 | 0 | 230 | 1 | 27 | 2 | 2 starch |
| 1 | 0 | 0 | 5 | 45 | 2½ | 2½ starch |
| 1 | 0 | 10 | 4 | 44 | 3 | 3 starch |
| 0 | 0 | 40 | 2 | 26 | 2 | 2 starch |
| 3 | 0.5 | 260 | 4 | 46 | 3 | 3 starch |
| 3 | 0.5 | 270 | 4 | 46 | 3 | 3 starch |
| 1 | 0 | 150 | 2 | 26 | 2 | 2½ starch |
| 2.5 | 0 | 230 | 4 | 44 | 3 | 3 starch |
| 0.5 | 0 | 15 | 4 | 41 | 3 | 3 starch |
| 0.5 | 0 | 15 | 4 | 40 | 2½ | 2 starch |
| 1 | 0 | 120 | 2 | 25 | 1½ | 1½ starch |
| 1 | 0 | 160 | 2 | 27 | 2 | 2 starch |
| 1 | 0 | 330 | 4 | 44 | 2½ | 2½ starch |
| 0 | 0 | 180 | 1 | 27 | 2 | 2 starch |
| 1 | 0.5 | 150 | 1 | 24 | 1½ | 1½ starch |
| 0 | 0 | 95 | 1 | 27 | 2 | 2 starch |
| 0 | 0 | 40 | 1 | 25 | 1½ | 1½ starch |
| 3 | 0 | 30 | 6 | 38 | 2 | 2 starch |
| 0 | 0 | 40 | 2 | 26 | 2 | 2 starch |
| 1 | 0 | 280 | 1 | 25 | 1½ | 1½ starch |
| 1 | 0 | 25 | 5 | 43 | 2½ | 2½ starch |
| 3 | 1 | 50 | 5 | 40 | 2½ | 2½ starch |
| 3 | 0.5 | 120 | 5 | 43 | 3 | 3 starch |
| 11 | 1.5 | 160 | 9 | 41 | 3 | 3 starch, 2 fat |
| 0 | 0 | 10 | 3 | 26 | 2 | 2 starch |
| 10 | 1.5 | 140 | 8 | 42 | 3 | 3 starch, 1 fat |
| 3 | 1 | 135 | 5 | 43 | 3 | 3 starch |

1 Carbohydrate Choice = 1 starch or 1 fruit or 1 milk exchange

## PRODUCTS

| | PRODUCTS | SERVING SIZE | CALORIES | CALORIES FROM FAT |
|---|---|---|---|---|
| ❶ | Grape-Nuts Flakes, Post® | ¾ cup | 100 | 10 |
| ❶ | Grape-Nuts, Post® | ½ cup | 200 | 10 |
| | Great Grains, Crunchy Pecan, Post® | ⅔ cup | 220 | 60 |
| | Great Grains with Raisins, Dates & Pecans, Post® | ⅔ cup | 210 | 45 |
| ❶ | Healthy Choice™, Multi-Grain Flakes, Kellogg's® | 1 cup | 100 | 0 |
| ❶ | Healthy Choice™, Multi-Grain Squares, Kellogg's® | 1¼ cups | 190 | 10 |
| ❶ | Healthy Choice™, Multi-Grains Raisins & Almonds, Kellogg's® | 1¼ cups | 200 | 20 |
| ❶ | Healthy Choice™, Multi-Grains Raisins, Crunchy Oat Clusters & Almonds, Kellogg's® | 1 cup | 200 | 20 |
| ❶ | Healthy Fiber Flakes, Health Valley® Fat-Free | ¾ cup | 100 | 0 |
| ❶ | Honey Bunches of Oats® with Almonds, Post® | ¾ cup | 130 | 30 |
| ❶ | Honey Bunches of Oats®, Post® | ¾ cup | 120 | 15 |
| ❶ | Honey Clusters & Flakes, Health Valley® Fat-Free, all varieties (avg) | ¾ cup | 130 | 0 |
| ❶ | Honey Frosted Wheaties®, General Mills® | ¾ cup | 110 | 0 |
| ❶ | Honey Graham Oh's, Quaker® | ¾ cup | 110 | 20 |
| ❶ | Honey Nut Toasted Oats, Krusteaz® | ¾ cup | 120 | 15 |
| ❶ | Honey & Nut Toasty O's®, Malt-O-Meal® | 1 cup | 110 | 10 |
| ❶ | Honeycomb®, Post® | 1⅓ cups | 110 | 0 |
| ❶ | Just Right® Fruit & Nut, Kellogg's® | 1 cup | 210 | 15 |
| ❶ | Just Right® with Crunchy Nuggets, Kellogg's® | 1 cup | 200 | 15 |
| ❶ | Kaboom®, General Mills® | 1¼ cups | 120 | 10 |
| ❶ | Kix®, Berry Berry, General Mills® | ¾ cup | 120 | 10 |
| ❶ | Kix®, General Mills® | 1⅓ cups | 120 | 5 |
| ❶ | Life®, Quaker® | ¾ cup | 120 | 15 |
| ❶ | Lucky Charms®, General Mills® | 1 cup | 120 | 10 |
| ❶ | Marshmallow Alpha-Bits®, Post® | 1 cup | 120 | 10 |
| ❶ | Marshmallow Mateys®, Malt-O-Meal® | 1 cup | 120 | 10 |
| ❶ | Marshmallow Treasures®, Malt-O-Meal® | 1 cup | 120 | 10 |

❶  Meets Low-Fat Guidelines

| TOTAL FAT (g) | SATURATED FAT (g) | SODIUM (mg) | PROTEIN (g) | CARBOHYDRATE (g) | CARBOHYDRATE CHOICES | EXCHANGES |
|---|---|---|---|---|---|---|
| 1 | 0 | 140 | 3 | 24 | 1½ | 1½ starch |
| 1 | 0 | 350 | 6 | 47 | 3 | 3 starch |
| 6 | 1 | 150 | 5 | 38 | 2½ | 2½ starch, ½ fat |
| 5 | 0.5 | 150 | 4 | 39 | 2½ | 2½ starch |
| 0 | 0 | 210 | 3 | 25 | 1½ | 1½ starch |
| 1 | 0 | 0 | 5 | 45 | 3 | 3 starch |
| 2 | 0 | 240 | 4 | 44 | 3 | 3 starch |
| 2 | 0 | 240 | 4 | 45 | 3 | 3 starch |
| 0 | 0 | 10 | 3 | 23 | 1½ | 1½ starch |
| 3 | 0.5 | 180 | 3 | 24 | 1½ | 1½ starch |
| 1.5 | 0.5 | 190 | 2 | 25 | 1½ | 1½ starch |
| 0 | 0 | 20 | 3 | 31 | 2 | 2 starch |
| 0 | 0 | 200 | 1 | 27 | 2 | 2 starch |
| 2 | 0.5 | 180 | 1 | 23 | 1½ | 1½ starch |
| 2 | 0 | 220 | 3 | 23 | 1½ | 1½ starch |
| 1 | 0 | 270 | 3 | 24 | 1½ | 1½ starch |
| 0 | 0 | 190 | 2 | 26 | 2 | 2 starch |
| 1.5 | 0 | 260 | 4 | 46 | 3 | 3 starch |
| 1.5 | 0 | 340 | 4 | 46 | 3 | 3 starch |
| 1.5 | 0 | 280 | 3 | 24 | 1½ | 1½ starch |
| 1 | 0 | 170 | 1 | 26 | 2 | 2 starch |
| 0.5 | 0 | 270 | 2 | 26 | 2 | 2 starch |
| 1.5 | 0 | 170 | 3 | 25 | 1½ | 1½ starch |
| 1 | 0 | 210 | 2 | 25 | 1½ | 1½ starch |
| 1 | 0 | 160 | 2 | 25 | 1½ | 1½ starch |
| 1 | 0 | 210 | 2 | 25 | 1½ | 1½ starch |
| 1 | 0 | 210 | 2 | 25 | 1½ | 1½ starch |

1 Carbohydrate Choice = 1 starch or 1 fruit or 1 milk exchange

## PRODUCTS

| PRODUCTS | SERVING SIZE | CALORIES | CALORIES FROM FAT |
|---|---|---|---|
| Mueslix® Crispy Blend, Kellogg's® | ⅔ cup | 200 | 30 |
| Mueslix® Golden Crunch, Kellogg's® | ¾ cup | 210 | 50 |
| ❶ Nut & Honey Crunch O's®, Kellogg's® | ¾ cup | 120 | 25 |
| Nut & Honey Crunch®, Kellogg's® | 1¼ cups | 220 | 30 |
| ❶ Nutri-Grain®, Almond Raisin, Kellogg's® | 1¼ cups | 200 | 25 |
| ❶ Nutri-Grain®, Golden Wheat & Raisin, Kellogg's® | 1¼ cups | 180 | 10 |
| ❶ Nutri-Grain®, Golden Wheat, Kellogg's® | ¾ cup | 100 | 5 |
| ❶ Oat Bran O's, Health Valley® | ¾ cup | 100 | 0 |
| Oatmeal Crisp™, Almond, General Mills® | 1 cup | 220 | 45 |
| ❶ Oatmeal Crisp™, Apple Cinnamon, General Mills® | 1 cup | 210 | 20 |
| ❶ Oatmeal Crisp™, Raisin, General Mills® | 1 cup | 210 | 25 |
| ❶ Oatmeal Squares™, Quaker® | 1 cup | 220 | 25 |
| ❶ Organic Amaranth Flakes, Health Valley® | ¾ cup | 100 | 0 |
| ❶ Organic Blue Corn Flakes, Health Valley® | ¾ cup | 100 | 0 |
| ❶ Organic Bran with Apples and Cinnamon, Health Valley® | ¾ cup | 170 | 0 |
| ❶ Organic Bran with Raisin, Health Valley® | ¾ cup | 190 | 0 |
| ❶ Organic Fiber 7 Flakes, Health Valley® | ¾ cup | 100 | 0 |
| ❶ Organic Oat Bran Flakes with Raisins, Health Valley® | ¾ cup | 110 | 0 |
| ❶ Organic Oat Bran Flakes, Health Valley® | ¾ cup | 100 | 0 |
| Outrageous Original, Outrageous Fruit & Grains® | ¼ cup | 130 | 54 |
| ❶ Peanut Butter Puffs™, Reese's™ | ¾ cup | 130 | 25 |
| ❶ Pop-Tarts Crunch™ Frosted Brown Sugar Cinnamon, Kellogg's® | ¾ cup | 120 | 10 |
| ❶ Pop-Tarts Crunch™ Frosted Strawberry, Kellogg's® | ¾ cup | 120 | 5 |
| ❶ Product 19®, Kellogg's® | 1 cup | 110 | 0 |
| ❶ Puffed Corn Cereal, Health Valley® | 1 cup | 80 | 0 |
| ❶ Puffed Rice, Malt-O-Meal® | 1 cup | 60 | 0 |

❶  Meets Low-Fat Guidelines

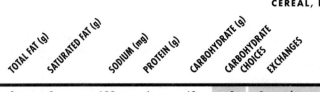

| TOTAL FAT (g) | SATURATED FAT (g) | SODIUM (mg) | PROTEIN (g) | CARBOHYDRATE (g) | CARBOHYDRATE CHOICES | EXCHANGES |
|---|---|---|---|---|---|---|
| 3 | 0 | 190 | 4 | 42 | 3 | 3 starch |
| 5 | 1 | 280 | 6 | 40 | 2 | 2 starch, 1 fat |
| 2.5 | 0 | 200 | 3 | 23 | 1½ | 1½ starch |
| 4 | 1 | 370 | 4 | 45 | 3 | 3 starch |
| 3 | 0 | 330 | 4 | 44 | 3 | 3 starch |
| 1 | 0 | 310 | 4 | 45 | 2½ | 2½ starch |
| 0.5 | 0 | 240 | 3 | 24 | 1½ | 1½ starch |
| 0 | 0 | 10 | 3 | 23 | 1½ | 1½ starch |
| 5 | 0.5 | 250 | 6 | 42 | 3 | 3 starch |
| 2 | 0 | 280 | 4 | 46 | 3 | 3 starch |
| 2.5 | 0 | 210 | 4 | 44 | 3 | 3 starch |
| 2.5 | 0.5 | 260 | 7 | 43 | 3 | 3 starch |
| 0 | 0 | 10 | 3 | 24 | 1½ | 1½ starch |
| 0 | 0 | 10 | 3 | 24 | 1½ | 1½ starch |
| 0 | 0 | 10 | 6 | 39 | 2 | 2 starch |
| 0 | 0 | 10 | 6 | 43 | 2½ | 2½ starch |
| 0 | 0 | 10 | 3 | 24 | 1½ | 1½ starch |
| 0 | 0 | 10 | 3 | 26 | 2 | 2 starch |
| 0 | 0 | 10 | 3 | 24 | 1½ | 1½ starch |
| 6 | 1 | <5 | 4 | 16 | 1 | 1 starch, 1 fat |
| 3 | 0.5 | 210 | 2 | 23 | 1½ | 1½ starch |
| 1 | 0 | 160 | 1 | 26 | 2 | 2 starch |
| 1 | 0 | 125 | 1 | 27 | 2 | 2 starch |
| 0 | 0 | 280 | 3 | 25 | 1½ | 1½ starch |
| 0 | 0 | 0 | 2 | 20 | 1 | 1 starch |
| 0 | 0 | 0 | 1 | 13 | 1 | 1 starch |

1 Carbohydrate Choice = 1 starch or 1 fruit or 1 milk exchange

| PRODUCTS | SERVING SIZE | CALORIES | CALORIES FROM FAT |
|---|---|---|---|
| ❶ Puffed Rice, Quaker® | 1 cup | 50 | 0 |
| ❶ Puffed Wheat, Malt-O-Meal® | 1 cup | 50 | 0 |
| ❶ Raisin Bran, Estee® | 1 box | 90 | 5 |
| ❶ Raisin Bran, Health Valley® | 1¼ cups | 200 | 0 |
| ❶ Raisin Bran, Kellogg's® | 1 cup | 170 | 10 |
| ❶ Raisin Bran, Krusteaz® | ¾ cup | 210 | 15 |
| ❶ Raisin Bran, Malt-O-Meal® | 1 cup | 180 | 10 |
| ❶ Raisin Bran, Post® | 1 cup | 190 | 10 |
| Raisin Nut Bran, General Mills® | ¾ cup | 210 | 40 |
| ❶ Raisin Squares®, Kellogg's® | ¾ cup | 180 | 5 |
| Real Oat Bran, Almond Crunch, Health Valley® | ½ cup | 200 | 35 |
| ❶ Rice Krispies Treats® Cereal, Kellogg's® | ¾ cup | 120 | 15 |
| ❶ Rice Krispies®, Kellogg's® | 1¼ cups | 110 | 0 |
| ❶ Rice Krispies™ Apple Cinnamon, Kellogg's® | ¾ cup | 110 | 0 |
| ❶ S'mores Grahams®, General Mills® | ¾ cup | 120 | 10 |
| ❶ Shredded Wheat 'N Bran, Nabisco® | 1¼ cups | 200 | 5 |
| ❶ Shredded Wheat, Spoon Size, Nabisco® | 1 cup | 170 | 5 |
| ❶ Shredded Wheat, Nabisco® | 2 biscuits | 160 | 5 |
| ❶ Smacks®, Kellogg's® | ¾ cup | 110 | 5 |
| ❶ Special K®, Kellogg's® | 1 cup | 110 | 0 |
| ❶ Strawberry Squares®, Kellogg's® | ¾ cup | 180 | 10 |
| ❶ Sugar Frosted Flakes, Malt-O-Meal® | ¾ cup | 110 | 0 |
| ❶ Sun Crunchers™, General Mills® | 1 cup | 220 | 30 |
| ❶ Sweet Crunch, Quaker® | 1 cup | 110 | 15 |
| ❶ Sweet Puffs, Quaker® | 1 cup | 130 | 5 |
| ❶ Team Flakes, Nabisco® | 1¼ cups | 220 | 0 |
| ❶ Temptations®, French Vanilla Almond, Kellogg's® | ¾ cup | 120 | 15 |
| ❶ Temptations®, Honey Roasted Pecan, Kellogg's® | 1 cup | 120 | 25 |
| ❶ Toasted Oatmeal®, Honey Nut, Quaker® | 1 cup | 190 | 25 |
| ❶ Toasted Oatmeal®, Original, Quaker® | 1¼ cups | 210 | 20 |

❶ Meets Low-Fat Guidelines

| TOTAL FAT (g) | SATURATED FAT (g) | SODIUM (mg) | PROTEIN (g) | CARBOHYDRATE (g) | CARBOHYDRATE CHOICES | EXCHANGES |
|---|---|---|---|---|---|---|
| 0 | 0 | 0 | 1 | 12 | 1 | 1 starch |
| 0 | 0 | 0 | 2 | 11 | 1 | 1 starch |
| 0.5 | 0 | 100 | 4 | 21 | 1½ | 1½ starch |
| 0 | 0 | 20 | 5 | 46 | 2½ | 2½ starch |
| 1 | 0 | 310 | 5 | 43 | 2½ | 2½ starch |
| 1.5 | 0 | 320 | 4 | 45 | 3 | 3 starch |
| 1 | 0 | 260 | 5 | 43 | 2½ | 2½ starch |
| 1 | 0 | 300 | 4 | 46 | 3 | 3 starch |
| 4.5 | 1 | 260 | 5 | 41 | 3 | 3 starch |
| 1 | 0 | 0 | 4 | 44 | 2½ | 2½ starch |
| 4 | 0 | 60 | 6 | 34 | 2 | 2 starch |
| 1.5 | 0 | 170 | 1 | 25 | 1½ | 1½ starch |
| 0 | 0 | 320 | 2 | 26 | 2 | 2 starch |
| 0 | 0 | 220 | 2 | 27 | 2 | 2 starch |
| 1 | 0 | 220 | 1 | 26 | 2 | 2 starch |
| 1 | 0 | 0 | 7 | 47 | 3 | 2½ starch |
| 0.5 | 0 | 0 | 7 | 47 | 3 | 2½ starch |
| 0.5 | 0 | 0 | 5 | 41 | 3 | 2 starch |
| 0.5 | 0 | 75 | 2 | 26 | 1½ | 1½ starch |
| 0 | 0 | 250 | 6 | 21 | 1½ | 1½ starch |
| 1 | 0 | 10 | 4 | 44 | 2½ | 2½ starch |
| 0 | 0 | 200 | 1 | 27 | 2 | 2 starch |
| 3 | 0 | 370 | 5 | 45 | 3 | 3 starch |
| 1.5 | 0.5 | 190 | 1 | 23 | 1½ | 1½ starch |
| 0.5 | 0 | 80 | 2 | 30 | 2 | 2 starch |
| 0 | 0 | 360 | 4 | 49 | 3 | 3 starch |
| 2 | 1 | 210 | 4 | 24 | 1½ | 1½ starch |
| 2.5 | 0 | 240 | 2 | 24 | 1½ | 1½ starch |
| 2.5 | 0.5 | 170 | 5 | 39 | 2½ | 2½ starch |
| 2 | 0 | 360 | 5 | 44 | 3 | 3 starch |

1 Carbohydrate Choice = 1 starch or 1 fruit or 1 milk exchange

| PRODUCTS | SERVING SIZE | CALORIES | CALORIES FROM FAT |
|---|---|---|---|
| ❶ Toasted Oats, Apple & Cinnamon, Malt-O-Meal® | ¾ cup | 120 | 15 |
| ❶ Toasted Oats, Honey & Nut, Malt-O-Meal® | 1 cup | 110 | 10 |
| ❶ Toasted Oats, Krusteaz® | 1 cup | 120 | 15 |
| ❶ Toasted Oats, Malt-O-Meal® | 1 cup | 110 | 15 |
| ❶ Toasties, Post® | 1 cup | 100 | 0 |
| ❶ Toasty O's®, Malt-O-Meal® | 1 cup | 110 | 15 |
| ❶ Tootie Fruities®, Malt-O-Meal® | 1 cup | 110 | 10 |
| ❶ Total® Corn Flakes, General Mills® | 1⅓ cups | 110 | 5 |
| ❶ Total® Raisin Bran, General Mills® | 1 cup | 180 | 10 |
| ❶ Total® Whole Grain, General Mills® | ¾ cup | 110 | 10 |
| ❶ Triples®, General Mills® | 1 cup | 120 | 10 |
| ❶ Trix®, General Mills® | 1 cup | 120 | 15 |
| ❶ Wheaties®, General Mills® | 1 cup | 110 | 10 |

### CEREAL BARS
*see also* Granola Bars

| | | | |
|---|---|---|---|
| ❶ Healthy Cereal Bars, Health Valley® Fat-Free, all varieties (avg) | 1 bar | 110 | 0 |
| ❶ Healthy Energy Bars, Health Valley®, all varieties (avg) | 1 bar | 180 | 15 |
| ❶ Nutri-Grain® Cereal Bars, Kellogg's®, all varieties (avg) | 1 bar | 140 | 25 |
| ❶ Omega-3 Bars, Health Valley®, all varieties (avg) | 1 bar | 140 | 20 |

### CHEESE, NATURAL
*see also* Cottage Cheese, Ricotta Cheese

| | | | |
|---|---|---|---|
| Blue cheese | 1 oz | 100 | 80 |
| Brie cheese | 1 oz | 100 | 70 |
| Feta cheese | ¼ cup (1 oz) | 90 | 60 |
| Goat cheese | ¼ cup (1 oz) | 80 | 60 |
| ❶ Grated cheese (parmesan, romano, Italian blend, avg) | 2 tsp | 25 | 15 |
| Havarti cheese | 1 oz | 120 | 90 |

❶  Meets Low-Fat Guidelines

| TOTAL FAT (g) | SATURATED FAT (g) | SODIUM (mg) | PROTEIN (g) | CARBOHYDRATE (g) | CARBOHYDRATE CHOICES | EXCHANGES |
|---|---|---|---|---|---|---|
| 1.5 | 0 | 190 | 2 | 24 | 1½ | 1½ starch |
| 1 | 0 | 270 | 3 | 24 | 1½ | 1½ starch |
| 2 | 0 | 210 | 3 | 23 | 1½ | 1½ starch |
| 2 | 0 | 280 | 3 | 22 | 1½ | 1½ starch |
| 0 | 0 | 270 | 2 | 24 | 1½ | 1½ starch |
| 2 | 0 | 280 | 3 | 22 | 1½ | 1½ starch |
| 1 | 0 | 150 | 2 | 26 | 2 | 2 starch |
| 0.5 | 0 | 210 | 2 | 25 | 1½ | 1½ starch |
| 1 | 0 | 240 | 4 | 43 | 3 | 3 starch |
| 1 | 0 | 200 | 3 | 24 | 1½ | 1½ starch |
| 1 | 0 | 190 | 2 | 25 | 1½ | 1½ starch |
| 1.5 | 0 | 200 | 1 | 26 | 2 | 2 starch |
| 1 | 0 | 220 | 3 | 24 | 1½ | 1½ starch |
| | | | | | | |
| 0 | 0 | 25 | 2 | 26 | 2 | 2 starch |
| 1.5 | 0 | 10 | 3 | 40 | 2½ | 2½ starch |
| 3 | 0.5 | 60 | 2 | 27 | 2 | 2 starch |
| 2 | 0 | 5 | 3 | 31 | 2 | 2 starch |
| | | | | | | |
| 8 | 6 | 390 | 6 | 0 | 0 | 1 high fat meat |
| 8 | 5 | 180 | 5 | 2 | 0 | 1 high fat meat |
| 7 | 5 | 360 | 5 | <1 | 0 | 1 high fat meat |
| 6 | 4 | 150 | 5 | <1 | 0 | 1 high fat meat |
| 1.5 | 1 | 55–95 | 2.5 | 0 | 0 | free |
| 11 | 7 | 240 | 6 | 0 | 0 | 1 meat, 1 fat |

1 Carbohydrate Choice = 1 starch or 1 fruit or 1 milk exchange

## PRODUCTS

| | SERVING SIZE | CALORIES | CALORIES FROM FAT |
|---|---|---|---|
| Mozzarella cheese, part-skim shredded | ¼ cup | 90 | 50 |
| Natural cheeses (brick, cheddar, colby, Monterey Jack, muenster, provolone, swiss, baby swiss, gouda, avg) | 1 oz or ¼ cup shredded | 105 | 75 |
| ❶ Natural cheeses, ⅓ less fat (cheddar, colby, Monterey Jack, part-skim mozzarella, avg) | 1 oz | 80 | 45 |
| ❶ Natural cheeses, 50% less fat (light swiss, light cheddar, avg) | 1 oz | 75 | 35 |
| ❶ Natural Cheeses, fat-free (avg) | 1 oz | 40 | 0 |
| ❶ String Cheese, Moo Town Snackers®, light (avg) | 1 piece | 60 | 30 |
| String Cheese, Moo Town Snackers®, regular (avg) | 1 piece | 95 | 70 |
| ❶ String Cheese, Mozzarella, Healthy Choice® | 1 stick | 45 | 0 |
| String Cheese, Mozzarella, Kraft Handi-Snacks® | 1 stick | 80 | 50 |
| ❶ String Cheese, Pizza, Healthy Choice® | 1 stick | 45 | 0 |

### CHEESE, NON-DAIRY SUBSTITUTES

| | SERVING SIZE | CALORIES | CALORIES FROM FAT |
|---|---|---|---|
| ❶ AlmondRella™, all varieties (avg) | 1 oz | 60 | 30 |
| ❶ Hard Cheese, Soya Kaas® | 1 oz | 70 | 45 |
| ❶ HempRella™ | 1 oz | 70 | 27 |
| ❶ Soy A Melt, White Wave® Fat Free, all varieties (avg) | 1 oz | 40 | 0 |
| ❶ Soy A Melt, White Wave®, all varieties (avg) | 1 oz | 70 | 45 |
| Soya Kaas® Cream Cheese Spreads (avg) | 1 oz | 100 | 80 |
| ❶ Soya Kaas® Fat Free | 1 oz | 40 | 0 |
| ❶ TofuRella®, all varieties (avg) | 1 oz | 80 | 45 |
| ❶ VeganRella™, all varieties (avg) | 1 oz | 60 | 27 |
| ❶ Zero-FatRella™, all varieties (avg) | 1 oz | 40 | 0 |

### CHEESE, PROCESS

#### Loaf, process cheese

| | SERVING SIZE | CALORIES | CALORIES FROM FAT |
|---|---|---|---|
| ❶ American Flavor Imitation Cheese Food, Golden Image® | ¾ oz | 70 | 45 |
| ❶ American Flavor, Harvest Moon® | ⅔ oz | 50 | 25 |

❶ Meets Low-Fat Guidelines

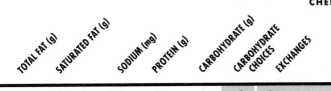

| TOTAL FAT (g) | SATURATED FAT (g) | SODIUM (mg) | PROTEIN (g) | CARBOHYDRATE (g) | CARBOHYDRATE CHOICES | EXCHANGES |
|---|---|---|---|---|---|---|
| 6 | 4 | 210 | 8 | <1 | 0 | 1 meat |
| 8.5 | 5.5 | 160–240 | 6.5 | 0 | 0 | 1 high fat meat |
| 5 | 3.5 | 215 | 9 | <1 | 0 | 1 meat |
| 4 | 2.5 | 50–240 | 8.5 | <1 | 0 | 1 meat |
| 0 | 0 | 200–290 | 9 | 1.5 | 0 | 1 very lean meat |
| 3.5 | 2.5 | 185 | 7 | <1 | 0 | 1 lean meat |
| 8 | 5 | 145 | 5 | 0.5 | 0 | 1 high fat meat |
| 0 | 0 | 200 | 9 | 1 | 0 | 1 very lean meat |
| 6 | 4 | 240 | 7 | <1 | 0 | 1 meat |
| 0 | 0 | 200 | 10 | 1 | 0 | 1 very lean meat |
| 3 | 0.5 | 250 | 5 | 3 | 0 | 1 lean meat |
| 5 | 0.5 | 190–270 | 6 | 1 | 0 | 1 meat |
| 3 | 0 | 170 | 7 | 1 | 0 | 1 lean meat |
| 0 | 0 | 245 | 7 | 2 | 0 | 1 very lean meat |
| 5 | 0.5 | 190–250 | 6 | 1 | 0 | 1 meat |
| 9 | 1.5 | 115 | 3 | 1 | 0 | 2 fat |
| 0 | 0 | 245 | 7 | 2 | 0 | 1 very lean meat |
| 5 | 1 | 290 | 5 | 2 | 0 | 1 meat |
| 3 | 0 | 160 | 1 | 9 | ½ | ½ starch, ½ fat |
| 0 | 0 | 250 | 7 | 3 | 0 | 1 very lean meat |
| 5 | 1.5 | 270 | 5 | 1 | 0 | 1 meat |
| 3 | 2 | 280 | 4 | 1 | 0 | 1 lean meat |

1 Carbohydrate Choice = 1 starch or 1 fruit or 1 milk exchange

| PRODUCTS | SERVING SIZE | CALORIES | CALORIES FROM FAT |
|---|---|---|---|
| American, Imitation, Harvest Moon® | ¼ cup | 120 | 80 |
| ❶ American, Kraft® Deluxe 25% Less Fat | ¾ oz | 70 | 45 |
| American, Kraft® Deluxe | 1 oz | 100 | 80 |
| American, Kraft® | ¼ cup | 110 | 80 |
| ❶ American, Velveeta Light® | 1 oz | 60 | 25 |
| American, Velveeta® | ¼ cup | 130 | 80 |
| Cheddar, Imitation, Harvest Moon® | ¼ cup | 120 | 80 |
| Cheese Food with Garlic, Kraft® | 1 oz | 90 | 60 |
| Cheese Food with Jalapeno Peppers, Kraft® | 1 oz | 90 | 60 |
| Extra Sharp Cheddar, Cracker Barrel® | 2 Tb | 100 | 70 |
| Hot Mexican with Jalapeno Peppers, Velveeta® | ¼ cup | 130 | 80 |
| Jalapeno Pepper Loaf, Kraft® | 1 oz | 80 | 60 |
| Mild Mexican with Jalapeno Peppers, Velveeta® | ¼ cup | 130 | 80 |
| Part-Skim Mozzarella, Imitation, Harvest Moon® | ¼ cup | 110 | 80 |
| ❶ Process Cheese Loaf, Healthy Choice® | 1" cube | 35 | 0 |
| Sharp Cheddar, Cracker Barrel® | 2 Tb | 100 | 70 |
| White American, Kraft® Deluxe | 1 oz | 100 | 80 |

### Slices, process cheese

| | | | |
|---|---|---|---|
| ❶ American Flavor, Kraft® Singles ⅓ Less Fat | ¾ oz slice | 50 | 30 |
| ❶ American Flavor Imitation Cheese Food, Lunchwagon® | ¾ oz slice | 70 | 50 |
| ❶ American Flavor, Light 'N Lively® 50% Less Fat | ¾ oz slice | 50 | 20 |
| American, Harvest Moon® | ⅔ oz slice | 70 | 50 |
| American, Kraft® Deluxe | 1.2 oz slice | 110 | 70 |
| ❶ American, Kraft® Free™ Nonfat | ¾ oz slice | 30 | 0 |
| ❶ American Singles, Healthy Choice® (avg) | 1 slice | 30 | 0 |
| ❶ American, Velveeta® Slices | ¾ oz slice | 60 | 40 |
| ❶ Mexican with Jalapeno Peppers, Kraft® Singles | ¾ oz slice | 70 | 45 |
| ❶ Monterey, Kraft® Singles | ¾ oz slice | 70 | 45 |
| Pimento, Kraft® Deluxe | 1 oz slice | 100 | 70 |

❶  Meets Low-Fat Guidelines

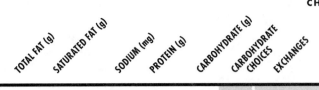

| TOTAL FAT (g) | SATURATED FAT (g) | SODIUM (mg) | PROTEIN (g) | CARBOHYDRATE (g) | CARBOHYDRATE CHOICES | EXCHANGES |
|---|---|---|---|---|---|---|
| 9 | 2 | 500 | 6 | 3 | 0 | 1 meat, 1 fat |
| 5 | 3 | 350 | 4 | 1 | 0 | 1 meat |
| 9 | 6 | 430 | 6 | <1 | 0 | 1 meat, 1 fat |
| 9 | 6 | 440 | 6 | <1 | 0 | 1 meat, 1 fat |
| 3 | 2 | 420 | 6 | 3 | 0 | 1 meat |
| 9 | 6 | 500 | 8 | 3 | 0 | 1 meat, 1 fat |
| 9 | 2 | 480 | 6 | 3 | 0 | 1 meat, 1 fat |
| 7 | 5 | 370 | 5 | 2 | 0 | 1 meat |
| 7 | 5 | 370 | 5 | 2 | 0 | 1 meat |
| 8 | 5 | 290 | 5 | 3 | 0 | 1 meat, ½ fat |
| 9 | 6 | 540 | 8 | 3 | 0 | 1 meat, 1 fat |
| 6 | 4 | 470 | 5 | 2 | 0 | 1 meat |
| 9 | 6 | 520 | 8 | 3 | 0 | 1 meat, 1 fat |
| 8 | 1.5 | 430 | 8 | 1 | 0 | 1 meat, ½ fat |
| 0 | 0 | 390 | 8 | 3 | 0 | 1 very lean meat |
| 8 | 5 | 290 | 5 | 4 | 0 | 1 meat, ½ fat |
| 9 | 6 | 430 | 6 | <1 | 0 | 1 meat, 1 fat |
| 3 | 2 | 330 | 5 | 2 | 0 | 1 lean meat |
| 5 | 1 | 230 | 4 | 1 | 0 | 1 meat |
| 2.5 | 1.5 | 280 | 5 | 2 | 0 | 1 lean meat |
| 6 | 4 | 320 | 4 | 0 | 0 | 1 meat |
| 8 | 6 | 460 | 6 | 3 | 0 | 1 meat, ½ fat |
| 0 | 0 | 320 | 5 | 3 | 0 | 1 very lean meat |
| 0 | 0 | 280 | 5 | 2 | 0 | 1 very lean meat |
| 4.5 | 3 | 300 | 4 | 2 | 0 | 1 meat |
| 5 | 3.5 | 330 | 4 | 2 | 0 | 1 meat |
| 5 | 3.5 | 290 | 4 | 2 | 0 | 1 meat |
| 8 | 6 | 430 | 6 | <1 | 0 | 1 meat, ½ fat |

1 Carbohydrate Choice = 1 starch or 1 fruit or 1 milk exchange

## PRODUCTS

| PRODUCTS | SERVING SIZE | CALORIES | CALORIES FROM FAT |
|---|---|---|---|
| Sharp American, Kraft® Singles | ¾ oz slice | 70 | 50 |
| Sharp American, Old English® | 1 oz slice | 110 | 80 |
| ❶ Sharp Cheddar Artificially Flavored, Kraft Free® | ¾ oz slice | 30 | 0 |
| ❶ Sharp Cheddar Flavor, Kraft® Singles ⅓ Less Fat | ¾ oz slice | 50 | 30 |
| ❶ Swiss Artificially Flavored, Kraft® Free™ | ¾ oz slice | 30 | 0 |
| ❶ Swiss Flavor, Kraft® Singles ⅓ Less Fat | ¾ oz slice | 50 | 25 |
| ❶ Swiss with Pimento, Kraft® Singles | ¾ oz slice | 70 | 45 |
| Swiss, Kraft® Deluxe | 1 oz slice | 90 | 60 |
| ❶ Swiss, Kraft® Singles | ¾ oz slice | 70 | 45 |
| White American, Kraft® Deluxe | 1 oz slice | 110 | 80 |
| ❶ White American, Kraft® Free™ Nonfat | ¾ oz slice | 30 | 0 |
| ❶ White American, Kraft® Singles | ¾ oz slice | 70 | 45 |
| ❶ White American Flavor, Kraft® Singles ⅓ Less Fat | ¾ oz slice | 50 | 30 |
| ❶ White American Flavor, Light 'N Lively® 50% Less Fat | ¾ oz slice | 50 | 20 |
| ❶ White American Singles, Healthy Choice® | 1 slice | 30 | 0 |

### CHEESE PUFFS/CURLS

| PRODUCTS | SERVING SIZE | CALORIES | CALORIES FROM FAT |
|---|---|---|---|
| Baked Cheez Flavored Curls, Old Dutch® | 2 cups | 180 | 126 |
| Cheegles Cheese Balls, Eagle® | 2½ cups | 160 | 90 |
| Cheegles Cheese Balls, Eagle® Reduced Fat | 1½ cups | 150 | 60 |
| Cheegles Cheese Crunch, Eagle® | 1 cup | 160 | 90 |
| ❶ Cheese Curls, Smart Snackers® | 1 bag | 70 | 25 |
| ❶ Cheese Puffs, Health Valley Fat-Free® | 1½ cups | 110 | 0 |
| Cheetos® Crunchy | 15 puffs | 150 | 80 |
| Cheetos® Flamin' Hot | 21 puffs | 160 | 90 |
| Cheetos® Jumbo Puffs | 13 puffs | 160 | 90 |
| Cheetos® Puffs | 29 puffs | 160 | 90 |
| Cheez Balls, Planters® | 1 oz | 150 | 90 |
| Cheez Curls, Planters® | 1 oz | 150 | 80 |
| Crunchy Curls, Old Dutch® | 1⅓ cups | 130 | 50 |

❶  Meets Low-Fat Guidelines

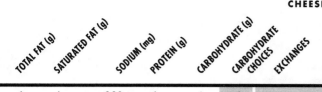

| TOTAL FAT (g) | SATURATED FAT (g) | SODIUM (mg) | PROTEIN (g) | CARBOHYDRATE (g) | CARBOHYDRATE CHOICES | EXCHANGES |
|---|---|---|---|---|---|---|
| 6 | 4 | 300 | 4 | <1 | 0 | 1 meat |
| 9 | 6 | 460 | 6 | <1 | 0 | 1 meat, 1 fat |
| 0 | 0 | 290 | 5 | 3 | 0 | 1 very lean meat |
| 3 | 2 | 300 | 5 | 2 | 0 | 1 lean meat |
| 0 | 0 | 290 | 5 | 3 | 0 | 1 very lean meat |
| 2.5 | 1.5 | 270 | 5 | 2 | 0 | 1 lean meat |
| 5 | 3.5 | 290 | 4 | 2 | 0 | 1 meat |
| 7 | 5 | 420 | 7 | <1 | 0 | 1 meat |
| 5 | 3.5 | 320 | 4 | 1 | 0 | 1 meat |
| 9 | 6 | 460 | 6 | <1 | 0 | 1 meat, 1 fat |
| 0 | 0 | 290 | 4 | 3 | 0 | 1 very lean meat |
| 5 | 3.5 | 290 | 4 | 2 | 0 | 1 meat |
| 3 | 2 | 330 | 5 | 2 | 0 | 1 lean meat |
| 2.5 | 1.5 | 300 | 5 | 2 | 0 | 1 lean meat |
| 0 | 0 | 290 | 5 | 2 | 0 | 1 very lean meat |
| 14 | 2.5 | 460 | 2 | 13 | 1 | 1 starch, 3 fat |
| 10 | 2 | 260 | 2 | 15 | 1 | 1 starch, 2 fat |
| 6 | 1.5 | 200 | 2 | 18 | 1 | 1 starch, 1 fat |
| 10 | 2 | 240 | 2 | 15 | 1 | 1 starch, 2 fat |
| 2.5 | 1 | 85 | 1 | 10 | ½ | ½ starch, ½ fat |
| 0 | 0 | 260 | 3 | 23 | 1½ | 1½ starch |
| 9 | 2.5 | 280 | 2 | 16 | 1 | 1 starch, 2 fat |
| 9 | 2 | 240 | 2 | 16 | 1 | 1 starch, 2 fat |
| 10 | 2.5 | 330 | 2 | 15 | 1 | 1 starch, 2 fat |
| 10 | 2.5 | 370 | 2 | 15 | 1 | 1 starch, 2 fat |
| 10 | 2 | 300 | 2 | 15 | 1 | 1 starch, 2 fat |
| 10 | 2 | 310 | 2 | 15 | 1 | 1 starch, 2 fat |
| 6 | 1 | 230 | 2 | 19 | 1 | 1 starch, 1 fat |

1 Carbohydrate Choice = 1 starch or 1 fruit or 1 milk exchange

## PRODUCTS

| | SERVING SIZE | CALORIES | CALORIES FROM FAT |
|---|---|---|---|
| Puffcorn Curls, Old Dutch® | 2½ cups | 180 | 130 |
| Puffed Balls, Cheetos® | 38 puffs | 160 | 90 |

### CHEESE SAUCE

| | | | |
|---|---|---|---|
| ❶ Mild Cheese Sauce, Zapata® | ¼ cup | 60 | 25 |
| Nacho Cheese Sauce, Kaukauna® | 1 oz | 80 | 54 |
| ❶ Spicy Jalapeno Cheese Sauce, Zapata® | ¼ cup | 70 | 45 |
| Squeezable Cheese, Kaukauna® MicroMelt®, all varieties (avg) | 1 oz | 80 | 54 |
| Squeezable Cheese Sauce, Cheez Whiz® | 2 Tb | 100 | 70 |

### CHEESE SPREAD

#### *Gourmet Cheese Spread*

| | | | |
|---|---|---|---|
| Cheese Spread, Alouette® Elegante™, all varieties (avg) | 2 Tb | 100 | 80 |
| ❶ Cheese Spread, Alouette® Lite, all varieties (avg) | 2 Tb | 50 | 35 |
| Cheese Spread, Alouette®, all varieties (avg) | 2 Tb | 70 | 60 |
| ❶ Cold Pack Cheese Spread, Kaukauna® Lite 50 | 1 oz | 70 | 27 |
| Cold Pack Cheese Spread, Kaukauna® Premium Blend, all varieties (avg) | 1 oz | 100 | 63 |
| Cold Pack Cheese Spread, Kaukauna®, all varieties (avg) | 1 oz | 90 | 63 |
| Creme De Bleu® | 2 Tb | 90 | 70 |
| Creme De Brie®, all varieties (avg) | 2 Tb | 90 | 80 |
| Neufchatel Cheese Snack, Spreadery®, all varieties (avg) | 2 Tb | 80 | 60 |
| Neufchatel, Fleur de Lait®, all varieties (avg) | 2 Tb | 90 | 70 |
| Neufchatel, Kaukauna®, all varieties (avg) | 1 oz | 80 | 63 |
| ❶ Raisin Walnut, Fleur de Lait® Gourmet Light | 2 Tb | 70 | 40 |

#### *Process Cheese Spread*

| | | | |
|---|---|---|---|
| ❶ American Flavor, Harvest Moon® | ¾ oz | 60 | 40 |
| Blue Spread, Kraft® Roka® | 2 Tb | 80 | 60 |
| ❶ Cheese Snack, Spreadery®, all varieties (avg) | 2 Tb | 80 | 40 |

❶ Meets Low-Fat Guidelines

| TOTAL FAT (g) | SATURATED FAT (g) | SODIUM (mg) | PROTEIN (g) | CARBOHYDRATE (g) | CARBOHYDRATE CHOICES | EXCHANGES |
|---|---|---|---|---|---|---|
| 14 | 2 | 240 | 1 | 14 | 1 | 1 starch, 2 fat |
| 10 | 2.5 | 370 | 2 | 13 | 1 | 1 starch, 2 fat |
| 2.5 | 2.5 | 490 | 2 | 7 | ½ | ½ starch |
| 6 | NA | 330 | 3 | 4 | 0 | 1 fat |
| 5 | 3 | 540 | 2 | 5 | 0 | 1 fat |
| 6 | NA | 380 | 4 | 2 | 0 | 1 high fat meat |
| 8 | 4 | 470 | 2 | 4 | 0 | 2 fat |
| 9 | 6 | 150 | 2 | 2 | 0 | 2 fat |
| 4 | 2.5 | 125 | 2 | 2 | 0 | 1 fat |
| 7 | 4 | 80–135 | 1 | 1.5 | 0 | 1 fat |
| 3 | NA | 190 | 5 | 5 | 0 | 1 meat |
| 7 | NA | 160 | 5 | 2 | 0 | 1 high fat meat |
| 7 | NA | 140–210 | 5 | 3 | 0 | 1 high fat meat |
| 7 | 5 | 260 | 4 | 1 | 0 | 1 meat |
| 8 | 5 | 220 | 4 | <1 | 0 | 1 high fat meat |
| 7 | 5 | 180–230 | 3 | 1 | 0 | 1 fat |
| 8 | 5 | 90–200 | 2 | 2 | 0 | 2 fat |
| 7 | NA | 160–200 | 3 | 1 | 0 | 1½ fat |
| 4.5 | 2.5 | 50 | 2 | 5 | 0 | 1 fat |
| 4.5 | 3 | 300 | 3 | 2 | 0 | 1 fat |
| 7 | 4.5 | 340 | 3 | 2 | 0 | 1 fat |
| 4.5 | 3 | 290 | 5 | 3 | 0 | 1 meat |

1 Carbohydrate Choice = 1 starch *or* 1 fruit *or* 1 milk exchange

## PRODUCTS

| | SERVING SIZE | CALORIES | CALORIES FROM FAT |
|---|---|---|---|
| Cheez Whiz®, all varieties (avg) | 2 Tb | 90 | 70 |
| ❶ Cheez Whiz Light® | 2 Tb | 80 | 30 |
| Hot Mexican Spread, Velveeta® | 1 oz | 80 | 50 |
| Italiana Spread, Velveeta® | 1 oz | 80 | 60 |
| Limburger, Mohawk Valley® | 2 Tb | 80 | 60 |
| Mild Mexican Spread, Velveeta® | 1 oz | 80 | 50 |
| ❶ Mozzarella Ball, Healthy Choice® | 1 oz | 45 | 0 |
| Nabisco® Easy Cheese®, all varieties (avg) | 2 Tb | 100 | 60 |
| Olive & Pimento Spread, Kraft® | 2 Tb | 70 | 60 |
| Pasteurized Processed Cheese Spread with Bacon, Kraft® | 2 Tb | 90 | 70 |
| Pimento Spread, Kraft® | 2 Tb | 80 | 60 |
| Pimento Spread, Spreadery® | 2 Tb | 100 | 70 |
| ❶ Pineapple Spread, Kraft® | 2 Tb | 70 | 50 |
| Sharp, Old English® | 2 Tb | 90 | 70 |
| Sharp, Squeez-A-Snak® | 2 Tb | 90 | 70 |

### CHEESECAKE (FROZEN)

| | | | |
|---|---|---|---|
| Cherry, Sara Lee® | ¼ cake | 350 | 100 |
| Original, Eli's® | ⅛ cake | 320 | 200 |
| Original Cream, Sara Lee® | ¼ cake | 350 | 160 |
| Original Cream, Sara Lee® Reduced Fat | ¼ cake | 310 | 120 |
| Strawberry, Sara Lee® | ¼ cake | 330 | 110 |

### CHICKEN (CANNED)

| | | | |
|---|---|---|---|
| Chunk Chicken, Swanson® | ¼ cup | 90 | 27 |

### CHICKEN (FRESH REFRIGERATED)

| | | | |
|---|---|---|---|
| Caribbean Grill, Chicken By George® | 5 oz | 200 | 54 |
| Italian Bleu Cheese, Chicken By George® | 5 oz | 180 | 63 |
| Lemon Oregano, Chicken By George® | 5 oz | 160 | 36 |
| ❶ Mesquite Barbecue, Chicken By George® | 1 breast | 130 | 25 |
| Mustard Dill, Chicken By George® | 5 oz | 180 | 63 |

❶  Meets Low-Fat Guidelines

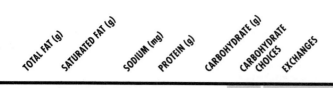

| TOTAL FAT (g) | SATURATED FAT (g) | SODIUM (mg) | PROTEIN (g) | CARBOHYDRATE (g) | CARBOHYDRATE CHOICES | EXCHANGES |
|---|---|---|---|---|---|---|
| 7.5 | 5 | 550 | 4 | 2 | 0 | 1 meat |
| 3 | 2 | 540 | 6 | 6 | ½ | ½ starch, 1 lean meat |
| 6 | 4 | 520 | 5 | 2 | 0 | 1 meat |
| 6 | 4 | 430 | 5 | 2 | 0 | 1 meat |
| 7 | 4.5 | 500 | 4 | 0 | 0 | 1 meat |
| 6 | 4 | 440 | 5 | 3 | 0 | 1 meat |
| 0 | 0 | 200 | 10 | 1 | 0 | 1 very lean meat |
| 7 | 4 | 410 | 5 | 3 | 0 | 1 high fat meat |
| 6 | 4 | 220 | 2 | 3 | 0 | 1 fat |
| 8 | 5 | 570 | 5 | <1 | 0 | 1 high fat meat |
| 6 | 4 | 170 | 2 | 3 | 0 | 1 fat |
| 8 | 5 | 320 | 4 | 3 | 0 | 1 meat, ½ fat |
| 5 | 3.5 | 120 | 2 | 4 | 0 | 1 fat |
| 8 | 5 | 520 | 5 | <1 | 0 | 1 meat, ½ fat |
| 8 | 5 | 440 | 5 | <1 | 0 | 1 meat, ½ fat |
| 12 | 5 | 310 | 6 | 55 | 3½ | 2 starch, 1½ fruit, 2 fat |
| 22 | 14 | 230 | 5 | 23 | 1½ | 1½ starch, 4 fat |
| 18 | 9 | 320 | 7 | 39 | 2½ | 2½ starch, 3 fat |
| 13 | 8 | 310 | 9 | 40 | 3 | 3 starch, 2 fat |
| 12 | 5 | 310 | 6 | 49 | 3 | 3 starch, 2 fat |
| 3 | NA | NA | 16 | 2 | 0 | 2 very lean meat |
| 6 | NA | 610 | 25 | 10 | ½ | ½ starch, 4 very lean meat |
| 8 | NA | 890 | 26 | 2 | 0 | 4 very lean meat, 1 fat |
| 4 | NA | 580 | 26 | 4 | 0 | 4 very lean meat |
| 3 | 1 | 700 | 21 | 5 | 0 | 3 very lean meat |
| 7 | NA | 640 | 26 | 3 | 0 | 4 very lean meat, 1 fat |

1 Carbohydrate Choice = 1 starch *or* 1 fruit *or* 1 milk exchange

## PRODUCTS

| | SERVING SIZE | CALORIES | CALORIES FROM FAT |
|---|---|---|---|
| Roasted, Chicken By George® | 5 oz | 150 | 36 |
| Tomato Herb with Basil, Chicken By George® | 5 oz | 190 | 63 |

### CHICKEN PIECES (FROZEN)

#### Chicken Nuggets and Chunks

| | SERVING SIZE | CALORIES | CALORIES FROM FAT |
|---|---|---|---|
| Breaded Chicken Breast Tenders, Tyson® | 5 pieces | 220 | 130 |
| Chick'n Chunks, Tyson® | 6 pieces | 280 | 180 |
| Chicken & Cheddar Chunks, Banquet® | 4 chunks | 280 | 180 |
| Chicken Breast Tenders, Banquet® | 3 tenders | 260 | 150 |
| Chicken Chunks, Country Skillet® | 5 pieces | 270 | 150 |
| Chicken Nuggets, Banquet® (3 oz) | 6 nuggets | 240 | 130 |
| Chicken Nuggets, Banquet® (4.5 oz) | 6 nuggets | 320 | 160 |
| Chicken Nuggets, Country Skillet® | 10 pieces | 280 | 160 |
| Chicken Nuggets, Morton® | 1 meal | 320 | 150 |
| Mozzarella Cheese Nuggets, Banquet® | 6 pieces | 250 | 130 |
| Southern Chicken Breast Tenders, Banquet® | 3 tenders | 260 | 140 |
| Southern Chicken Chunks, Banquet® | 5 chunks | 270 | 160 |
| Southern Fried Chicken Chunks, Country Skillet® | 5 pieces | 250 | 140 |
| Southern Fried Chicken Nuggets, Banquet® | 6 nuggets | 340 | 180 |

#### Chicken Patties

| | SERVING SIZE | CALORIES | CALORIES FROM FAT |
|---|---|---|---|
| Breaded Chicken Southern Fried Breast Patties, Tyson® | 1 patty | 180 | 110 |
| Chick'n Quick Chick'n Cheddar, Tyson® | 1 patty | 220 | 130 |
| Chicken Parmigiana Patties (6), Banquet® Family Size | 1 patty | 240 | 120 |
| Chicken Patties, Banquet® | 1 patty | 180 | 100 |
| Chicken Patties, Country Skillet® | 1 patty | 190 | 110 |
| Italian-Style Chicken Parmigiana, Banquet® | 1 patty | 250 | 140 |
| Southern Chicken Patties, Banquet® | 1 patty | 170 | 90 |
| Southern Fried Chicken Patties, Country Skillet® | 1 patty | 190 | 110 |

 Meets Low-Fat Guidelines

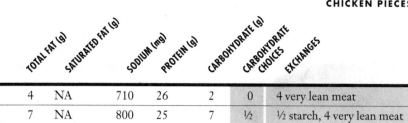

| TOTAL FAT (g) | SATURATED FAT (g) | SODIUM (mg) | PROTEIN (g) | CARBOHYDRATE (g) | CARBOHYDRATE CHOICES | EXCHANGES |
|---|---|---|---|---|---|---|
| 4 | NA | 710 | 26 | 2 | 0 | 4 very lean meat |
| 7 | NA | 800 | 25 | 7 | ½ | ½ starch, 4 very lean meat |
| 15 | 3 | 290 | 14 | 8 | ½ | ½ starch, 2 meat, 1 fat |
| 20 | 4.5 | 490 | 11 | 14 | 1 | 1 starch, 1 meat, 3 fat |
| 19 | 6 | 560 | 12 | 13 | 1 | 1 starch, 1 meat, 3 fat |
| 16 | 4 | 490 | 12 | 16 | 1 | 1 starch, 1 meat, 2 fat |
| 17 | 3 | 720 | 12 | 18 | 1 | 1 starch, 1 meat, 1 fat |
| 15 | 3 | 540 | 14 | 12 | 1 | 1 starch, 2 meat, 1 fat |
| 18 | 4 | 670 | 16 | 25 | 1½ | 1½ starch, 2 meat, 1 fat |
| 18 | 4 | 620 | 14 | 16 | 1 | 1 starch, 2 meat, 1 fat |
| 17 | 4 | 460 | 13 | 30 | 2 | 2 starch, 1 meat, 2 fat |
| 14 | 6 | 460 | 13 | 18 | 1 | 1 starch, 1 meat, 2 fat |
| 16 | 4 | 460 | 12 | 16 | 1 | 1 starch, 1 meat, 2 fat |
| 18 | 4 | 570 | 12 | 16 | 1 | 1 starch, 1 meat, 1 fat |
| 15 | 3 | 550 | 12 | 16 | 1 | 1 starch, 1 meat, 2 fat |
| 20 | 4 | 840 | 16 | 22 | 1½ | 1½ starch, 2 meat, 2 fat |
| 12 | 2 | 360 | 11 | 8 | ½ | ½ starch, 1 meat, 1 fat |
| 14 | 4 | 270 | 11 | 12 | 1 | 1 starch, 1 meat, 2 fat |
| 13 | 3 | 690 | 11 | 18 | 1 | 1 starch, 1 meat, 2 fat |
| 11 | 2.5 | 360 | 10 | 10 | ½ | ½ starch, 1 meat, 1 fat |
| 12 | 2.5 | 500 | 9 | 12 | 1 | 1 starch, 1 meat, 1 fat |
| 15 | 4.5 | 630 | 12 | 17 | 1 | 1 starch, 1 meat, 2 fat |
| 10 | 2 | 430 | 10 | 10 | ½ | ½ starch, 1 meat, 2 fat |
| 12 | 2.5 | 450 | 9 | 12 | 1 | 1 starch, 1 meat, 1 fat |

1 Carbohydrate Choice = 1 starch or 1 fruit or 1 milk exchange

## PRODUCTS

| | SERVING SIZE | CALORIES | CALORIES FROM FAT |
|---|---|---|---|
| **Chicken Wings** | | | |
| BBQ Chicken Wings, Tyson® | 4 pieces | 210 | 120 |
| Hot 'n Spicy Breaded Chicken Wing Sections, Banquet® | 4 pieces | 230 | 140 |
| Wings of Fire, Tyson® | 4 pieces | 220 | 130 |
| **Fried Chicken** | | | |
| Breast Rondelet, Weaver® | 1 piece | 170 | 90 |
| Fried Chicken (Drums & Thighs), Banquet® | 3 oz | 260 | 160 |
| Fried Chicken Breasts, Banquet® Original | 1 piece | 410 | 240 |
| Fried Chicken Pieces, Banquet®, all varieties (avg) | 3 oz | 265 | 160 |
| Fried Chicken, Country Skillet® | 3 oz | 270 | 160 |
| Skinless Fried Chicken, Banquet®, all varieties (avg) | 3 oz | 210 | 120 |
| **Roasted Chicken** | | | |
| Roasted Chicken Breast Halves, Tyson® | ½ breast | 250 | 120 |
| ❶ Roasted Chicken Breast Quarter (without skin), Tyson® | 1 piece | 250 | 70 |
| Roasted Chicken Drumsticks, Tyson® | 3 drumsticks | 330 | 170 |
| Roasted Chicken Leg Quarter (with skin), Tyson® | 1 piece | 480 | 290 |
| Roasted Chicken Thighs (without skin), Tyson® | 1 thigh | 160 | 90 |
| Roasted Half Chicken, Tyson® | 3 oz | 170 | 90 |

### CHICKEN MEALS/ENTREES (FROZEN)
see also Mexican Meals/Entrees, Oriental Meals/Entrees

### Baked Chicken Meals/Entrees

| | SERVING SIZE | CALORIES | CALORIES FROM FAT |
|---|---|---|---|
| Baked Chicken & Gravy and Whipped Potatoes, Stouffer's® Homestyle | 1 pkg | 270 | 110 |
| ❶ Baked Chicken and Whipped Potatoes and Stuffing, Stouffer's® Lean Cuisine® | 1 pkg | 250 | 50 |

 Meets Low-Fat Guidelines

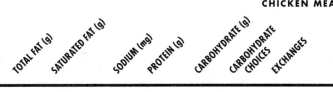

| TOTAL FAT (g) | SATURATED FAT (g) | SODIUM (mg) | PROTEIN (g) | CARBOHYDRATE (g) | CARBOHYDRATE CHOICES | EXCHANGES |
|---|---|---|---|---|---|---|
| 13 | 3.5 | 250 | 19 | 2 | 0 | 3 meat |
| 16 | 5 | 280 | 15 | 5 | 0 | 2 meat, 1 fat |
| 15 | 3.5 | 560 | 20 | 1 | 0 | 3 meat |
| 10 | 2.5 | 410 | 10 | 10 | ½ | ½ starch, 1 meat, 1 fat |
| 18 | 5 | 540 | 15 | 10 | ½ | ½ starch, 2 meat, 2 fat |
| 26 | 13 | 600 | 23 | 18 | 1 | 1 starch, 3 meat, 2 fat |
| 18 | 5 | 605 | 14 | 13 | 1 | 1 starch, 2 meat, 1 fat |
| 18 | 5 | 620 | 14 | 13 | 1 | 1 starch, 2 meat, 1 fat |
| 13 | 3 | 480 | 18 | 7 | ½ | ½ starch, 2 meat |
| 13 | 4 | 670 | 34 | 0 | 0 | 5 lean meat |
| 8 | 2.5 | 1190 | 43 | 1 | 0 | 6 very lean meat |
| 18 | 5 | 870 | 40 | 1 | 0 | 6 lean meat |
| 32 | 10 | 1240 | 44 | 4 | 0 | 6 meat |
| 10 | 3 | 470 | 18 | 0 | 0 | 3 lean meat |
| 10 | 3 | 610 | 19 | 2 | 0 | 3 lean meat |
| 12 | 3 | 750 | 22 | 19 | 1 | 1 starch, 1 veg, 1 lean meat |
| 6 | 0.5 | 590 | 19 | 30 | 2 | 2 starch, 2 lean meat |

1 Carbohydrate Choice = 1 starch or 1 fruit or 1 milk exchange

## PRODUCTS

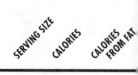

| Products | SERVING SIZE | CALORIES | CALORIES FROM FAT |
|---|---|---|---|
| **Barbecued Chicken Meals/Entrees** | | | |
| ❶ Barbecue Glazed Chicken, Weight Watchers® | 1 entree | 230 | 25 |
| Barbecue Style Chicken Meal, Banquet® Country Menu | 1 meal | 320 | 110 |
| ❶ BBQ Healthy Portion, Tyson® | 1 meal | 360 | 90 |
| ❶ Chicken Mesquite, Tyson® | 1 meal | 310 | 60 |
| ❶ Mesquite Chicken Barbecue, Healthy Choice® | 1 meal | 320 | 20 |
| **Chicken à la King Meals/Entrees** | | | |
| ❶ Chicken à la King, Stouffer's® | 1 pkg | 320 | 90 |
| Chicken à la King, Banquet® Toppers | 1 bag | 100 | 40 |
| ❶ Chicken à la King with Noodles, Michelina's® | 1 pkg | 260 | 70 |
| **Chicken and Noodles Meals/Entrees** | | | |
| Chicken & Noodles, Stouffer's® Homestyle | 1 pkg | 300 | 110 |
| Escalloped Chicken & Noodles, Stouffer's® | 1 pkg | 450 | 240 |
| Escalloped Noodles & Chicken, Marie Callender's® | 1 cup | 270 | 140 |
| Noodles & Chicken, Banquet® Bake At Home | 1 cup | 210 | 80 |
| **Chicken and Pasta Meals/Entrees** | | | |
| ❶ Bow Tie Pasta and Chicken, Stouffer's® Lean Cuisine® Cafe Classics | 1 pkg | 270 | 50 |
| Chicken Alfredo, Stouffer's® Lunch Express® | 1 pkg | 360 | 150 |
| ❶ Chicken Broccoli Alfredo, Healthy Choice® | 1 meal | 370 | 70 |
| Chicken Fettucini, Stouffer's® Homestyle | 1 pkg | 390 | 140 |
| ❶ Chicken Fettucini, Stouffer's® Lean Cuisine® | 1 pkg | 270 | 60 |
| ❶ Chicken Fettuccini Alfredo, Healthy Choice® | 1 meal | 260 | 40 |
| Chicken Fettucini with Broccoli, Stouffer's® Lean Cuisine® Lunch Express® | 1 pkg | 290 | 70 |
| Chicken Pasta Primavera, Banquet® | 1 meal | 330 | 120 |
| Chicken with Linguini, Stouffer's® Lunch Express® | 1 pkg | 300 | 100 |

❶  Meets Low-Fat Guidelines

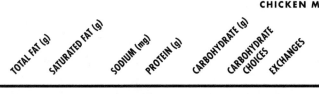

| TOTAL FAT (g) | SATURATED FAT (g) | SODIUM (mg) | PROTEIN (g) | CARBOHYDRATE (g) | CARBOHYDRATE CHOICES | EXCHANGES |
|---|---|---|---|---|---|---|
| 2.5 | 0.5 | 440 | 20 | 33 | 2 | 2 starch, 1 veg, 2 very lean meat |
| 12 | 2.5 | 800 | 18 | 36 | 2½ | 2 starch, 1 veg, 1 meat, 1 fat |
| 10 | 2.5 | 590 | 18 | 49 | 3 | 3 starch, 1 lean meat, 1 fat |
| 7 | 2 | 590 | 23 | 38 | 2½ | 2½ starch, 2 lean meat |
| 2 | 0.5 | 290 | 19 | 55 | 3½ | 3 starch, 1 veg, 1 lean meat |
| 10 | 3 | 750 | 15 | 43 | 3 | 3 starch, 1 meat |
| 4 | 1.5 | 480 | 9 | 7 | ½ | ½ starch, 1 meat |
| 7 | 2.5 | 850 | 13 | 34 | 2 | 2 starch, 1 veg, 1 meat |
| 13 | 3 | 950 | 20 | 25 | 1½ | 1½ starch, 2 meat, ½ fat |
| 28 | 6 | 1170 | 17 | 32 | 2 | 2 starch, 2 meat, 3 fat |
| 16 | 6 | 670 | 10 | 22 | 1½ | 1½ starch, 1 meat, 2 fat |
| 9 | 3 | 810 | 10 | 24 | 1½ | 1½ starch, 1 meat |
| 6 | 1.5 | 550 | 19 | 34 | 2 | 2 starch, 2 lean meat |
| 17 | 6 | 620 | 18 | 34 | 2 | 2 starch, 2 meat, 1 fat |
| 8 | 3 | 470 | 23 | 53 | 3½ | 3 starch, 1 veg, 2 lean meat |
| 15 | 4 | 1250 | 31 | 32 | 2 | 2 starch, 4 lean meat |
| 6 | 2.5 | 580 | 22 | 33 | 2 | 2 starch, 2 lean meat |
| 4.5 | 2 | 410 | 22 | 35 | 2 | 2 starch, 2 lean meat |
| 8 | 3.5 | 570 | 16 | 38 | 2½ | 2½ starch, 1 meat |
| 13 | 5 | 930 | 13 | 40 | 2½ | 2 starch, 1 veg, 1 meat, 1 fat |
| 11 | 2 | 680 | 15 | 36 | 2½ | 2½ starch, 1 meat, 1 fat |

1 Carbohydrate Choice = 1 starch or 1 fruit or 1 milk exchange

## PRODUCTS

| PRODUCTS | SERVING SIZE | CALORIES | CALORIES FROM FAT |
|---|---|---|---|
| Fettucini with Broccoli & Chicken, Marie Callender's® | 1 cup | 420 | 230 |
| Grilled Chicken and Angel Hair Pasta, Stouffer's® Lunch Express® | 1 pkg | 340 | 120 |
| ❶ Pasta and Chicken Marinara, Stouffer's® Lean Cuisine® Lunch Express® | 1 pkg | 270 | 50 |
| Pasta Primavera with Chicken, Marie Callender's® | 1 cup | 310 | 170 |
| ❶ Penne Pollo, Weight Watchers® | 1 entree | 290 | 50 |

### Chicken Parmigiana Meals/Entrees

| | SERVING SIZE | CALORIES | CALORIES FROM FAT |
|---|---|---|---|
| Breaded Chicken Parmigiana, Marie Callender's® | 1 meal | 620 | 250 |
| Chicken Parmigiana, Banquet® fat | 1 meal | 290 | 130 |
| ❶ Chicken Parmigiana, Healthy Choice® lean meat | 1 meal | 300 | 35 |
| ❶ Chicken Parmesan, Stouffer's® Lean Cuisine® Cafe Classics | 1 pkg | 240 | 60 |
| Chicken Parmigiana, Tyson® | 1 meal | 290 | 100 |
| ❶ Chicken Parmigiana, Weight Watchers® | 1 entree | 310 | 70 |
| Chicken Parmigiana Dinner, Banquet® Extra Helping | 1 meal | 650 | 300 |
| Chicken Parmigiana Patties (6), Banquet® Family Size | 1 patty | 240 | 120 |
| ❶ Chicken Parmigiana with Spaghetti, Stouffer's® Homestyle | 1 pkg | 320 | 100 |

### Fried Chicken Meals/Entrees

| | SERVING SIZE | CALORIES | CALORIES FROM FAT |
|---|---|---|---|
| All White Meat Fried Chicken Dinner, Banquet® Extra Helping | 1 meal | 820 | 370 |
| Breaded Chicken Patty, Morton® | 1 meal | 280 | 140 |
| Breaded Chicken Patty Meal, Banquet® Country Menu | 1 meal | 380 | 190 |
| Chicken Nugget Meal, Banquet® Homestyle Menu | 1 meal | 410 | 190 |

❶ Meets Low-Fat Guidelines

| TOTAL FAT (g) | SATURATED FAT (g) | SODIUM (mg) | PROTEIN (g) | CARBOHYDRATE (g) | CARBOHYDRATE CHOICES | EXCHANGES |
|---|---|---|---|---|---|---|
| 26 | 11 | 530 | 18 | 30 | 2 | 1½ starch, 1 veg, 2 meat, 3 fat |
| 13 | 3 | 650 | 21 | 35 | 2 | 2 starch, 1 veg, 2 meat |
| 6 | 1.5 | 540 | 15 | 38 | 2½ | 2 starch, 1 veg, 1 meat |
| 19 | 8 | 450 | 12 | 22 | 1½ | 1½ starch, 1 meat, 2 fat |
| 5 | 2 | 620 | 22 | 40 | 2½ | 2 starch, 1 veg, 2 lean meat |
| 27 | 8 | 730 | 31 | 63 | 4 | 4 starch, 1 veg, 2 meat, 3 fat |
| 15 | 4 | 900 | 14 | 27 | 2 | 1½ starch, 1 veg, 1 meat, 2 |
| 4 | 2 | 490 | 20 | 47 | 3 | 2½ starch, 1 veg, 2 very |
| 7 | 2.5 | 580 | 20 | 25 | 1½ | 1½ starch, 2 lean meat |
| 11 | 2.5 | 680 | 17 | 31 | 2 | 2 starch, 2 meat |
| 7 | 2 | 500 | 21 | 39 | 2½ | 2 starch, 1 veg, 2 lean meat |
| 33 | 8 | 1770 | 24 | 64 | 4 | 4 starch, 1 veg, 2 meat, 4 fat |
| 13 | 3 | 690 | 11 | 18 | 1 | 1 starch, 1 lean meat, 2 fat |
| 10 | 2 | 890 | 27 | 30 | 2 | 2 starch, 3 lean meat |
| 41 | 9 | 1890 | 40 | 72 | 5 | 4½ starch, 1 veg, 4 meat, 3 fat |
| 15 | 3 | 840 | 11 | 24 | 1½ | 1½ starch, 1 meat, 2 fat |
| 21 | 5 | 1270 | 17 | 31 | 2 | 2 starch, 1 veg, 1 meat, 3 fat |
| 21 | 5 | 650 | 18 | 38 | 2½ | 2 starch, 1 veg, 1 meat, 3 fat |

1 Carbohydrate Choice = 1 starch or 1 fruit or 1 milk exchange

## PRODUCTS

| PRODUCTS | SERVING SIZE | CALORIES | CALORIES FROM FAT |
|---|---|---|---|
| Chicken Nuggets, Swanson® | 1 pkg | 500 | 216 |
| ❶ Country Breaded Chicken, Healthy Choice® | 1 meal | 350 | 60 |
| Country Fried Chicken and Gravy, Marie Callender's® | 1 meal | 610 | 240 |
| Fried Chicken, Morton® | 1 meal | 420 | 220 |
| Fried Chicken (Dark Portions), Swanson® | 1 pkg | 560 | 252 |
| Fried Chicken (Dark Portions), Swanson® Hungry-Man® | 1 pkg | 810 | 369 |
| Fried Chicken (White Portions), Swanson® | 1 pkg | 550 | 234 |
| Fried Chicken (White Portions), Swanson® Hungry-Man® | 1 pkg | 810 | 360 |
| Fried Chicken and Whipped Potatoes, Stouffer's® Homestyle | 1 pkg | 330 | 150 |
| Fried Chicken Dinner, Banquet® Extra Helping | 1 meal | 790 | 350 |
| Fried Chicken Meal, Banquet® Country Menu Our Original | 1 meal | 470 | 240 |
| Southern Fried Chicken Dinner, Banquet® Extra Helping | 1 meal | 750 | 330 |
| Southern Fried Chicken Meal, Banquet® Country Menu | 1 meal | 530 | 270 |
| White Meat Fried Chicken Meal, Banquet® Country Menu | 1 meal | 470 | 250 |

### Glazed Chicken Meals/Entrees

| PRODUCTS | SERVING SIZE | CALORIES | CALORIES FROM FAT |
|---|---|---|---|
| ❶ Country Glazed Chicken, Healthy Choice® | 1 meal | 200 | 15 |
| ❶ Glazed Chicken Tenders with Rice Pilaf, Tyson® | 1 meal | 240 | 50 |
| ❶ Glazed Chicken with Vegetable Rice, Stouffer's® Lean Cuisine® | 1 pkg | 240 | 60 |
| ❶ Roast Glazed Chicken, Weight Watchers® | 1 entree | 240 | 50 |
| ❶ Southwestern Glazed Chicken, Healthy Choice® | 1 meal | 300 | 30 |

❶  Meets Low-Fat Guidelines

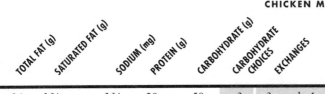

| TOTAL FAT (g) | SATURATED FAT (g) | SODIUM (mg) | PROTEIN (g) | CARBOHYDRATE (g) | CARBOHYDRATE CHOICES | EXCHANGES |
|---|---|---|---|---|---|---|
| 24 | NA | NA | 20 | 50 | 3 | 3 starch, 1 veg, 1 meat, 3 fat |
| 7 | 1.5 | 500 | 18 | 55 | 3½ | 3 starch, 1 veg, 2 very lean meat |
| 27 | 8 | 1680 | 25 | 67 | 4½ | 4 starch, 1 veg, 2 meat, 3 fat |
| 25 | 8 | 1000 | 20 | 30 | 2 | 2 starch, 2 meat, 3 fat |
| 28 | NA | NA | 21 | 56 | 4 | 3½ starch, 1 veg, 1 meat, 3 fat |
| 41 | NA | NA | 34 | 76 | 5 | 5 starch, 1 veg, 2 meat, 5 fat |
| 26 | NA | NA | 23 | 60 | 4 | 3½ starch, 1 veg, 2 meat, 2 fat |
| 40 | NA | NA | 35 | 77 | 5 | 5 starch, 1 veg, 3 meat, 4 fat |
| 16 | 4 | 780 | 18 | 29 | 2 | 2 starch, 2 meat, 1 fat |
| 39 | 9 | 1820 | 37 | 72 | 5 | 4½ starch, 1 veg, 3 meat, 4 fat |
| 27 | 9 | 980 | 21 | 35 | 2 | 2 starch, 1 veg, 2 meat, 3 fat |
| 37 | 9 | 2140 | 38 | 67 | 4½ | 4 starch, 1 veg, 3 meat, 4 fat |
| 30 | 8 | 1610 | 22 | 44 | 3 | 2½ starch, 1 veg, 2 meat, 3 fat |
| 28 | 11 | 1100 | 22 | 33 | 2 | 2 starch, 1 veg, 2 meat, 3 fat |
| 1.5 | 0.5 | 480 | 17 | 30 | 2 | 2 starch, 2 very lean meat |
| 6 | 1.5 | 450 | 16 | 30 | 2 | 2 starch, 1 meat |
| 6 | 1 | 460 | 22 | 24 | 1½ | 1½ starch, 3 very lean meat |
| 6 | 1 | 550 | 18 | 29 | 2 | 1½ starch, 1 veg, 2 lean meat |
| 3 | 1 | 430 | 20 | 48 | 3 | 3 starch, 2 very lean meat |

1 Carbohydrate Choice = 1 starch or 1 fruit or 1 milk exchange

## PRODUCTS

| | SERVING SIZE | CALORIES | CALORIES FROM FAT |
|---|---|---|---|
| **Herb Roasted Chicken Meals/Entrees** | | | |
| ❶ Country Herb Chicken, Healthy Choice® | 1 meal | 270 | 35 |
| ❶ Herb Roasted Chicken, Stouffer's® Lean Cuisine® Cafe Classics | 1 pkg | 210 | 40 |
| ❶ Herb Roasted Chicken, Tyson® | 1 meal | 320 | 50 |
| Herb Roasted Chicken & Mashed Potatoes, Marie Callender's® | 1 meal | 670 | 380 |
| ❶ Roasted Chicken with Herb Sauce, Tyson® | 1 meal | 220 | 30 |
| **Honey Mustard Chicken Meals/Entrees** | | | |
| ❶ Chicken Dijon, Healthy Choice® | 1 meal | 280 | 35 |
| ❶ Honey Mustard Chicken, Healthy Choice® | 1 meal | 260 | 20 |
| ❶ Honey Mustard Chicken, Stouffer's® Lean Cuisine® Cafe Classics | 1 pkg | 270 | 45 |
| ❶ Honey Mustard Chicken, Tyson® | 1 meal | 330 | 50 |
| ❶ Honey Mustard Chicken, Weight Watchers® Smart Ones® | 1 entree | 200 | 15 |
| ❶ Honey Roasted Chicken with Honey Mustard Sauce, Tyson® | 1 meal | 190 | 25 |
| **Italian Chicken Meals/Entrees** | | | |
| ❶ Cacciatore Chicken, Healthy Choice® | 1 meal | 260 | 25 |
| ❶ Chicken and Vegetables Marsala, Healthy Choice® | 1 meal | 220 | 10 |
| ❶ Chicken Carbonara, Stouffer's® Lean Cuisine® Cafe Classics | 1 pkg | 290 | 70 |
| ❶ Chicken Italiano with Fettucini and Vegetables, Stouffer's® Lean Cuisine® | 1 pkg | 270 | 60 |
| ❶ Chicken Marinara, Tyson® | 1 meal | 430 | 80 |
| ❶ Chicken Marsala, Tyson® | 1 meal | 180 | 45 |
| ❶ Chicken Marsala, Weight Watchers® Smart Ones® | 1 entree | 150 | 15 |
| ❶ Chicken Picatta, Tyson® | 1 meal | 180 | 45 |

❶  Meets Low-Fat Guidelines

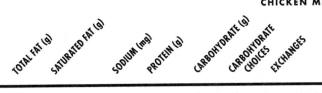

| TOTAL FAT (g) | SATURATED FAT (g) | SODIUM (mg) | PROTEIN (g) | CARBOHYDRATE (g) | CARBOHYDRATE CHOICES | EXCHANGES |
|---|---|---|---|---|---|---|
| 4 | 1.5 | 340 | 20 | 40 | 2½ | 2 starch, 1 veg, 2 very lean meat |
| 5 | 1 | 430 | 17 | 25 | 1½ | 1½ starch, 2 lean meat |
| 6 | 1.5 | 610 | 22 | 44 | 3 | 3 starch, 2 very lean meat |
| 42 | 15 | 2100 | 43 | 32 | 2 | 2 starch, 1 veg, 5 meat, 3 fat |
| 3.5 | 1 | 460 | 19 | 27 | 2 | 2 starch, 2 very lean meat |
| 4 | 1.5 | 410 | 21 | 41 | 3 | 2½ starch, 1 veg, 2 very lean meat |
| 2 | 0 | 550 | 21 | 40 | 2½ | 2½ starch, 2 very lean meat |
| 5 | 2 | 580 | 16 | 39 | 2½ | 2½ starch, 1 lean meat |
| 6 | 1.5 | 620 | 22 | 49 | 3 | 3 starch, 2 very lean meat |
| 2 | 0.5 | 340 | 13 | 33 | 2 | 2 starch, 1 veg, 1 very lean meat |
| 3 | 0.5 | 460 | 21 | 20 | 1 | 1 starch, 3 very lean meat |
| 3 | 0.5 | 510 | 22 | 36 | 2½ | 2 starch, 1 veg, 2 lean meat |
| 1 | 0 | 440 | 22 | 32 | 2 | 1½ starch, 1 veg, 2 very lean meat |
| 8 | 2 | 540 | 22 | 32 | 2 | 2 starch, 2 lean meat |
| 6 | 1.5 | 560 | 22 | 31 | 2 | 2 starch, 2 lean meat |
| 9 | 2.5 | 660 | 27 | 59 | 4 | 4 starch, 2 lean meat |
| 5 | 1.5 | 520 | 15 | 19 | 1 | 1 starch, 2 lean meat |
| 2 | 0.5 | 500 | 10 | 22 | 1½ | 1 starch, 1 veg, 1 very lean meat |
| 5 | 1.5 | 470 | 15 | 19 | 1 | 1 starch, 2 meat |

1 Carbohydrate Choice = 1 starch or 1 fruit or 1 milk exchange

## PRODUCTS

| PRODUCTS | SERVING SIZE | CALORIES | CALORIES FROM FAT |
|---|---|---|---|
| ❶ Chicken Piccata, Stouffer's® Lean Cuisine® Cafe Classics | 1 pkg | 290 | 50 |
| ❶ Garlic Chicken Milano, Healthy Choice® | 1 meal | 240 | 40 |
| ❶ Italian Chicken with Herb Glaze, Tyson® | 1 meal | 190 | 35 |
| ❶ Italian Healthy Portion, Tyson® | 1 meal | 390 | 70 |
| ❶ Italian Style Vegetables & Chicken, Budget Gourmet® Light | 1 entree | 240 | 50 |
| ❶ Lemon Herb Chicken Piccata, Weight Watchers® Smart Ones® | 1 entree | 190 | 15 |
| Potatoes Mozzarella with Chicken, Budget Gourmet® | 1 entree | 390 | 170 |

### Other Chicken Meals/Entrees

| | | | |
|---|---|---|---|
| Broccoli & Cheese Chicken Meal, Tyson® | 1 meal | 260 | 100 |
| ❶ Cajun Chicken, Tyson® | 1 meal | 260 | 35 |
| ❶ Calypso Chicken, Stouffer's® Lean Cuisine® Cafe Classics | 1 pkg | 280 | 60 |
| ❶ Chicken & Dumplings with Gravy Meal, Banquet® Homestyle Menu | 1 meal | 260 | 70 |
| Chicken and Dumplings, Banquet® Family Size | 1 cup | 290 | 120 |
| ❶ Chicken à l'Orange, Stouffer's® Lean Cuisine® | 1 pkg | 260 | 20 |
| ❶ Chicken and Vegetables, Stouffer's® Lean Cuisine® | 1 pkg | 240 | 45 |
| ❶ Chicken Breast in Wine Sauce, Stouffer's® Lean Cuisine® Cafe Classics | 1 pkg | 220 | 50 |
| ❶ Chicken Cordon Bleu, Weight Watchers® | 1 entree | 230 | 40 |
| Chicken Français, Tyson® | 1 meal | 260 | 90 |
| ❶ Chicken Francesca, Healthy Choice® | 1 meal | 360 | 50 |
| ❶ Chicken Imperial, Healthy Choice® | 1 meal | 230 | 40 |
| ❶ Chicken in Peanut Sauce, Stouffer's® Lean Cuisine® | 1 pkg | 280 | 60 |
| Chicken Kiev, Tyson® | 1 meal | 440 | 230 |
| ❶ Chicken Mediterranean, Stouffer's® Lean Cuisine® Cafe Classics | 1 pkg | 250 | 35 |

❶ Meets Low-Fat Guidelines

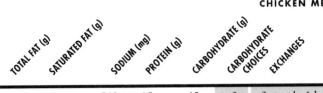

| TOTAL FAT (g) | SATURATED FAT (g) | SODIUM (mg) | PROTEIN (g) | CARBOHYDRATE (g) | CARBOHYDRATE CHOICES | EXCHANGES |
|---|---|---|---|---|---|---|
| 6 | 1.5 | 540 | 15 | 45 | 3 | 3 starch, 1 lean meat |
| 4 | 2 | 510 | 18 | 34 | 2 | 2 starch, 2 very lean meat |
| 3.5 | 1.5 | 440 | 21 | 19 | 1 | 1 starch, 3 very lean meat |
| 8 | 2.5 | 790 | 29 | 52 | 3½ | 3½ starch, 3 very lean meat |
| 6 | 2 | 560 | 10 | 37 | 2½ | 2 starch, 1 veg, 1 lean meat, ½ fat |
| 2 | 0.5 | 460 | 10 | 34 | 2 | 2 starch, 1 veg, 1 very lean meat |
| 19 | 12 | 810 | 15 | 40 | 2½ | 2½ starch, 1 meat, 2 fat |
| 11 | 5 | 630 | 19 | 21 | 1½ | 1 starch, 1 veg, 2 meat |
| 4 | 1 | 370 | 17 | 38 | 2½ | 2½ starch, 1 lean meat |
| 6 | 2 | 590 | 15 | 42 | 3 | 3 starch, 1 lean meat |
| 8 | 2.5 | 780 | 13 | 35 | 2 | 2 starch, 1 veg, 1 meat |
| 14 | 5 | 1270 | 12 | 30 | 2 | 2 starch, 1 meat, 1 fat |
| 2.5 | 0.5 | 260 | 19 | 40 | 2½ | 2½ starch, 2 very lean meat |
| 5 | 1 | 520 | 19 | 30 | 2 | 1½ starch, 1 veg, 2 lean meat |
| 6 | 2 | 560 | 16 | 25 | 1½ | 1½ starch, 2 lean meat |
| 4.5 | 1.5 | 650 | 15 | 21 | 1½ | 1 starch, 1 veg, 2 lean meat |
| 10 | 3 | 790 | 19 | 23 | 1½ | 1½ starch, 2 meat |
| 5 | 2 | 500 | 27 | 51 | 3½ | 3½ starch, 2 very lean meat |
| 4 | 1 | 470 | 17 | 31 | 2 | 2 starch, 2 very lean meat |
| 6 | 1 | 590 | 23 | 33 | 2 | 2 starch, 2 lean meat |
| 25 | 11 | 680 | 18 | 36 | 2½ | 2½ starch, 2 meat, 3 fat |
| 4 | 1 | 570 | 19 | 35 | 2 | 2 starch, 2 lean meat |

1 Carbohydrate Choice = 1 starch or 1 fruit or 1 milk exchange

## PRODUCTS

| | SERVING SIZE | CALORIES | CALORIES FROM FAT |
|---|---|---|---|
| ❶ Chicken Mirabella, Smart Ones® | 1 entree | 170 | 15 |
| Chicken Monterey with Mexican-Style Rice, Stouffer's® Homestyle | 1 pkg | 410 | 180 |
| Chicken Supreme, Tyson® | 1 meal | 230 | 80 |
| Chicken with Garden Vegetables and Rice, Stouffer's® Lunch Express® | 1 pkg | 340 | 100 |
| Creamed Chicken, Stouffer's® | 1 pkg | 280 | 180 |
| Creamy Chicken & Broccoli, Stouffer's® | 1 pkg | 320 | 140 |
| French Recipe Chicken, Budget Gourmet® Light | 1 entree | 180 | 60 |
| ❶ Grilled Chicken Meal, Tyson® | 1 meal | 220 | 35 |
| ❶ Grilled Chicken Salsa, Stouffer's® Lean Cuisine® Cafe Classics | 1 pkg | 240 | 60 |
| ❶ Microwave Grilled Chicken Sandwich, Tyson® | 1 sandwich | 210 | 50 |
| Potatoes Mozzarella with Chicken, Budget Gourmet® | 1 entree | 390 | 170 |

### CHILDREN'S MEALS/ENTREES (FROZEN)

| | SERVING SIZE | CALORIES | CALORIES FROM FAT |
|---|---|---|---|
| ❶ Big League Hamburger Pizza, Kid Cuisine® | 1 meal | 400 | 100 |
| Buckaroo Beef Patty Sandwich with Cheese, Kid Cuisine® | 1 meal | 410 | 130 |
| Chillin' Cheese Pizza, Swanson® Fun Feast® | 1 pkg | 350 | 81 |
| Chompin' Chicken Drumlets, Swanson® Fun Feast® | 1 pkg | 500 | 216 |
| Cosmic Chicken Nuggets, Kid Cuisine® | 1 meal | 440 | 150 |
| Frazzlin' Fried Chicken, Swanson® Fun Feast® | 1 pkg | 660 | 324 |
| Frenzied Fish Sticks, Swanson® Fun Feast® | 1 pkg | 360 | 126 |
| Funtastic Fish Sticks, Kid Cuisine® | 1 meal | 370 | 110 |
| Growlin' Grilled Cheese, Swanson® Fun Feast® | 1 pkg | 470 | 180 |
| High Flying Fried Chicken, Kid Cuisine® | 1 meal | 440 | 170 |

❶ Meets Low-Fat Guidelines

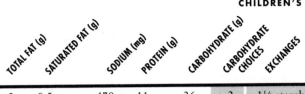

| TOTAL FAT (g) | SATURATED FAT (g) | SODIUM (mg) | PROTEIN (g) | CARBOHYDRATE (g) | CARBOHYDRATE CHOICES | EXCHANGES |
|---|---|---|---|---|---|---|
| 2 | 0.5 | 470 | 11 | 26 | 2 | 1½ starch, 1 veg, 1 very lean meat |
| 20 | 9 | 700 | 23 | 35 | 2 | 2 starch, 2 meat, 2 fat |
| 8 | 2 | 310 | 15 | 24 | 1½ | 1½ starch, 2 lean meat |
| 11 | 3 | 750 | 15 | 45 | 3 | 2½ starch, 1 veg, 1 meat, 1 fat |
| 20 | 7 | 720 | 17 | 8 | ½ | ½ starch, 2 meat, 2 fat |
| 15 | 5 | 820 | 19 | 26 | 2 | 1½ starch, 1 veg, 2 meat, 1 fat |
| 7 | 2.5 | 910 | 13 | 19 | 1 | 1 starch, 1 lean meat, 1 fat |
| 4 | 1 | 480 | 18 | 28 | 2 | 2 starch, 2 very lean meat |
| 6 | 1.5 | 550 | 15 | 32 | 2 | 2 starch, 1 meat |
| 6 | 1.5 | 460 | 13 | 25 | 1½ | 1½ starch, 2 lean meat |
| 19 | 12 | 810 | 15 | 40 | 2½ | 2½ starch, 1 meat, 2 fat |
| 11 | 3.5 | 530 | 14 | 61 | 4 | 4 starch, 1 meat |
| 15 | 5 | 540 | 12 | 58 | 4 | 4 starch, 1 meat, 1 fat |
| 9 | NA | NA | 10 | 57 | 4 | 3½ starch, 1 veg, 1 meat |
| 24 | NA | NA | 16 | 55 | 3½ | 3½ starch, 1 veg, 1 meat, 3 fat |
| 16 | 4.5 | 1070 | 18 | 54 | 3½ | 3½ starch, 1 meat, 2 fat |
| 36 | NA | NA | 26 | 58 | 4 | 3½ starch, 1 veg, 2 meat, 4 fat |
| 14 | NA | NA | 11 | 47 | 3 | 3 starch, 1 veg, 1 meat, 1 fat |
| 12 | 2.5 | 550 | 11 | 55 | 3½ | 3½ starch, 1 lean meat, 1 fat |
| 20 | NA | NA | 17 | 56 | 4 | 3½ starch, 1 veg, 1 meat, 2 fat |
| 19 | 4.5 | 940 | 18 | 49 | 3 | 3 starch, 2 meat, 1 fat |

1 Carbohydrate Choice = 1 starch *or* 1 fruit *or* 1 milk exchange

## PRODUCTS

| | SERVING SIZE | CALORIES | CALORIES FROM FAT |
|---|---|---|---|
| ❶ Magical Macaroni & Cheese, Kid Cuisine® | 1 meal | 420 | 110 |
| ❶ Pirate Pizza with Cheese, Kid Cuisine® | 1 meal | 430 | 100 |
| ❶ Raptor Ravioli with Cheese, Kid Cuisine® | 1 meal | 320 | 40 |
| Rip-Roaring Macaroni & Beef, Kid Cuisine® | 1 meal | 370 | 90 |
| Roarin' Ravioli, Swanson® Fun Feast® | 1 pkg | 420 | 99 |
| ❶ Super Charging Chicken Sandwich, Kid Cuisine® | 1 meal | 480 | 130 |

### CHILI (CANNED)
see also Soup

| | SERVING SIZE | CALORIES | CALORIES FROM FAT |
|---|---|---|---|
| ❶ Chili, Health Valley® Fat-Free, all varieties (avg) | ½ cup | 80 | 0 |
| Chili, Open Range® | 1 cup | 353 | 234 |
| ❶ Chili Beef, Healthy Choice® | 1 cup | 170 | 15 |
| Chili with Beans, Gephardt® | 1 cup | 322 | 135 |
| Chili with Beans, Just Rite® | 1 cup | 379 | 239 |
| Chili with Beans, Old El Paso® | 1 cup | 200 | 70 |
| Chili with Beans, Open Range® | 1 cup | 281 | 144 |
| ❶ Mild Vegetarian Chili with Lentils, Health Valley® | ½ cup | 80 | 0 |
| ❶ Vegetarian Chili with Beans, Health Valley® No Salt, all varieties (avg) | ½ cup | 80 | 0 |
| ❶ Vegetarian Chili with Beans, Health Valley®, all regular varieties (avg) | ½ cup | 80 | 0 |

### CHILI (FROZEN)

| | SERVING SIZE | CALORIES | CALORIES FROM FAT |
|---|---|---|---|
| Chicken Chunk Chili with Beans, Howlin' Coyote® | 1 bowl | 250 | 100 |
| Chili & Cornbread, Marie Callender's® | 1 dinner | 350 | 120 |
| Chili with Beans & Cornbread, Marie Callender's® | 1 dinner | 350 | 120 |
| Chili with Beans, Stouffer's® | 1 pkg | 270 | 90 |
| ❶ Chili-Mac, Michelina's® | 1 pkg | 290 | 80 |
| Green Chile Chili, Howlin' Coyote® | 1 bowl | 240 | 110 |
| ❶ Homestyle Chili with Beans, Howlin' Coyote® | 1 bowl | 280 | 80 |

❶ Meets Low-Fat Guidelines

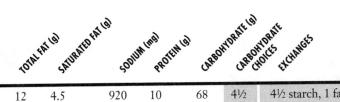

| TOTAL FAT (g) | SATURATED FAT (g) | SODIUM (mg) | PROTEIN (g) | CARBOHYDRATE (g) | CARBOHYDRATE CHOICES | EXCHANGES |
|---|---|---|---|---|---|---|
| 12 | 4.5 | 920 | 10 | 68 | 4½ | 4½ starch, 1 fat |
| 11 | 3 | 440 | 12 | 71 | 5 | 5 starch, 1 fat |
| 4.5 | 1.5 | 780 | 7 | 63 | 4 | 4 starch |
| 9 | 4 | 900 | 12 | 58 | 4 | 4 starch, 1 fat |
| 11 | NA | NA | 12 | 69 | 4½ | 4 starch, 1 veg, 1 meat |
| 15 | 4 | 770 | 17 | 71 | 5 | 4½ starch, 1 veg, 1 meat, 1 fat |
| | | | | | | |
| 0 | 0 | 170 | 7 | 15 | 1 | 1 starch, 1 very lean meat |
| 26 | 11.5 | 1216 | 17.5 | 19 | 1 | 1 starch, 2 meat, 3 fat |
| 1.5 | 0.5 | 380 | 14 | 30 | 2 | 2 starch, 1 very lean meat |
| 15 | 5.5 | 673 | 15 | 32 | 2 | 2 starch, 2 meat, ½ fat |
| 27 | 13 | 1233 | 18 | 31 | 2 | 2 starch, 2 meat, 3 fat |
| 7 | 1.5 | 420 | 19 | 15 | 1 | 1 starch, 2 lean meat |
| 16 | 7.5 | 1291 | 17 | 25 | 1½ | 1½ starch, 2 meat, 1 fat |
| 0 | 0 | 100 | 7 | 14 | 1 | 1 starch, 1 very lean meat |
| 0 | 0 | 35 | 7 | 15 | 1 | 1 starch, 1 very lean meat |
| 0 | 0 | 100 | 7 | 15 | 1 | 1 starch, 1 very lean meat |
| | | | | | | |
| 11 | 2.5 | 670 | 20 | 20 | 1 | 1 starch, 2½ meat |
| 13 | 6 | 1380 | 14 | 45 | 3 | 3 starch, 1 meat, 1 fat |
| 13 | 6 | 1380 | 14 | 45 | 3 | 3 starch, 1 meat, 1 fat |
| 10 | 4 | 1130 | 15 | 29 | 2 | 2 starch, 1 meat, 1 fat |
| 8 | 3 | 830 | 14 | 38 | 2½ | 2½ starch, 1 meat |
| 12 | 3 | 710 | 24 | 9 | ½ | ½ starch, 3 meat |
| 9 | 3 | 690 | 30 | 18 | 1 | 1 starch, 4 meat |

1 Carbohydrate Choice = 1 starch or 1 fruit or 1 milk exchange

## PRODUCTS

| | SERVING SIZE | CALORIES | CALORIES FROM FAT |
|---|---|---|---|
| ❶ Mean Bean Chili, Howlin' Coyote® | 1 cup | 180 | 45 |
| ❶ Three Bean Chili with Rice, Stouffer's® Lean Cuisine® | 1 pkg | 210 | 60 |

### CHILI MIX (CANNED)

| | | | |
|---|---|---|---|
| ❶ Chili Fixings, Hunt's® Homestyle Separates | ½ cup | 84 | 9 |
| ❶ Chili Makin's, S&W®, all varieties (avg) | ½ cup | 80 | 0 |

### CHIPS, CORN

#### *Doritos® Corn Chips*

| | | | |
|---|---|---|---|
| Cooler Ranch | 15 chips | 140 | 60 |
| Nacho Cheesier | 15 chips | 140 | 60 |
| Original Thins | 9 chips | 140 | 70 |
| Salsa 'N Cheese Thins | 9 chips | 150 | 70 |
| Taco Supreme | 15 chips | 140 | 70 |
| Toasted Corn | 18 chips | 140 | 60 |
| Zesty Salsa | 15 chips | 140 | 60 |

#### *Fritos® Corn Chips*

| | | | |
|---|---|---|---|
| B-B-Q | 29 chips | 150 | 90 |
| Cheddar & Sour Cream | 29 chips | 160 | 90 |
| Choice | 17 chips | 160 | 90 |
| Mesquite Grille B-B-Q | 12 chips | 160 | 90 |
| Original | 32 chips | 160 | 90 |
| Ranch | 10 chips | 150 | 80 |
| Sour Cream & Onion | 28 chips | 160 | 90 |

#### *Old Dutch® Corn Chips*

| | | | |
|---|---|---|---|
| Bar-B-Q | ¾ cup | 165 | 90 |
| Original | ¾ cup | 170 | 90 |
| Restaurante Style White Corn Tortilla Chips | 7 chips | 140 | 54 |
| Tostados | 11 chips | 150 | 63 |
| White Corn Tostados | 11 chips | 150 | 60 |

❶  Meets Low-Fat Guidelines

| TOTAL FAT (g) | SATURATED FAT (g) | SODIUM (mg) | PROTEIN (g) | CARBOHYDRATE (g) | CARBOHYDRATE CHOICES | EXCHANGES |
|---|---|---|---|---|---|---|
| 5 | 0.5 | 580 | 8 | 25 | 1½ | 1½ starch, 1 meat |
| 6 | 2 | 460 | 8 | 32 | 2 | 2 starch, 1 lean meat |
| | | | | | | |
| 1 | 0 | 858 | 5.5 | 19 | 1 | 1 starch |
| 0 | 0 | 630–870 | 6 | 19 | 1 | 1 starch, 1 very lean meat |
| | | | | | | |
| 7 | 1 | 160 | 2 | 18 | 1 | 1 starch, 1 fat |
| 7 | 1 | 170 | 2 | 18 | 1 | 1 starch, 1 fat |
| 7 | 1 | 135 | 2 | 18 | 1 | 1 starch, 1 fat |
| 8 | 1.5 | 180 | 2 | 17 | 1 | 1 starch, 1 fat |
| 7 | 1.5 | 200 | 2 | 18 | 1 | 1 starch, 1 fat |
| 6 | 1 | 65 | 2 | 19 | 1 | 1 starch, 1 fat |
| 7 | 1.5 | 170 | 2 | 18 | 1 | 1 starch, 1 fat |
| | | | | | | |
| 10 | 1.5 | 300 | 2 | 15 | 1 | 1 starch, 2 fat |
| 10 | 1.5 | 260 | 2 | 15 | 1 | 1 starch, 2 fat |
| 10 | 2 | 200 | 2 | 15 | 1 | 1 starch, 2 fat |
| 10 | 1.5 | 150 | 2 | 15 | 1 | 1 starch, 2 fat |
| 10 | 1.5 | 160 | 2 | 15 | 1 | 1 starch, 2 fat |
| 9 | 1.5 | 135 | 2 | 16 | 1 | 1 starch, 2 fat |
| 10 | 1.5 | 170 | 2 | 15 | 1 | 1 starch, 2 fat |
| | | | | | | |
| 10 | 1.5 | 200 | 3 | 16 | 1 | 1 starch, 2 fat |
| 10 | 1.5 | 180 | 2 | 16 | 1 | 1 starch, 2 fat |
| 6 | 1 | 123 | 2 | 18 | 1 | 1 starch, 1 fat |
| 7 | 1 | 200 | 3 | 19 | 1 | 1 starch, 1 fat |
| 7 | 1 | 135 | 3 | 20 | 1 | 1 starch, 1 fat |

1 Carbohydrate Choice = 1 starch or 1 fruit or 1 milk exchange

## PRODUCTS

| | SERVING SIZE | CALORIES | CALORIES FROM FAT |
|---|---|---|---|
| **Santitas® Corn Chips** | | | |
| 100% White Corn Chips | 6 chips | 140 | 60 |
| Restaurant Style Chips | 7 chips | 140 | 60 |
| Restaurant Style Strips | 12 chips | 140 | 60 |
| **Tostitos® Corn Chips** | | | |
| ❶ Baked Cool Ranch | 11 chips | 120 | 30 |
| ❶ Baked Original | 13 chips | 110 | 5 |
| ❶ Baked Unsalted | 13 chips | 110 | 10 |
| Bite Size 100% White Corn | 24 chips | 140 | 70 |
| Lime N' Chili | 6 chips | 150 | 70 |
| Round 100% White Corn | 13 chips | 150 | 70 |
| Restaurant Style | 6 chips | 130 | 50 |
| **Other Corn Chips** | | | |
| ❶ Chili Corn Chips, Rubschlager® | 9 chips | 110 | 5 |
| Corn Chips, Planters® | 1 oz | 160 | 90 |
| ❶ Corn Chips, Guiltless Gourmet® Baked Not Fried, all varieties (avg) | 20 chips | 110 | 10 |
| King Size Corn Chips, Planters® | 1 oz | 160 | 90 |
| Nachips, Old El Paso® | 9 chips | 150 | 70 |
| Nacho Cheese Yellow Corn Tortilla Chips, Tyson® Mexican Original® | 13 chips | 140 | 60 |
| Restaurant Style Blue Corn Chips, Zapata® | 10 chips | 140 | 63 |
| Tortilla Chips, Tyson® Mexican Original® | 12 chips | 170 | 60 |
| White Corn Tortilla, Old El Paso® | 11 chips | 140 | 70 |
| Yellow Corn Tortilla Chips, Tyson® Mexican Original® | 12 chips | 150 | 60 |

## CHIPS, POTATO

### Barbecue Potato Chips

| | SERVING SIZE | CALORIES | CALORIES FROM FAT |
|---|---|---|---|
| Barbecue Flavor, Ripplin's® | 12 chips | 150 | 80 |
| BBQ, Lay's® | 15 chips | 150 | 90 |

❶ Meets Low-Fat Guidelines

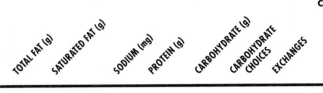

| TOTAL FAT (g) | SATURATED FAT (g) | SODIUM (mg) | PROTEIN (g) | CARBOHYDRATE (g) | CARBOHYDRATE CHOICES | EXCHANGES |
|---|---|---|---|---|---|---|
| 6 | 1 | 75 | 2 | 19 | 1 | 1 starch, 1 fat |
| 6 | 1 | 75 | 2 | 19 | 1 | 1 starch, 1 fat |
| 6 | 1 | 40 | 2 | 19 | 1 | 1 starch, 1 fat |
| | | | | | | |
| 3 | 0.5 | 170 | 2 | 21 | 1½ | 1½ starch |
| 1 | 0 | 140 | 3 | 24 | 1½ | 1½ starch |
| 1 | 0 | 0 | 3 | 24 | 1½ | 1½ starch |
| 8 | 1 | 110 | 2 | 17 | 1 | 1 starch, 1 fat |
| 7 | 1 | 180 | 2 | 17 | 1 | 1 starch, 1 fat |
| 8 | 1 | 85 | 2 | 17 | 1 | 1 starch, 1 fat |
| 6 | 1 | 80 | 2 | 19 | 1 | 1 starch, 1 fat |
| | | | | | | |
| 0.5 | 0 | 240 | 5 | 20 | 1 | 1 starch |
| 10 | 1.5 | 170 | 2 | 16 | 1 | 1 starch, 2 fat |
| 1 | 0 | 160 | 2.5 | 22 | 1½ | 1½ starch |
| | | | | | | |
| 10 | 1.5 | 170 | 2 | 16 | 1 | 1 starch, 2 fat |
| 8 | 1.5 | 85 | 3 | 17 | 1 | 1 starch, 1 fat |
| 6 | 1 | 180 | 2 | 19 | 1 | 1 starch, 1 fat |
| | | | | | | |
| 7 | 3 | 85 | 2 | 18 | 1 | 1 starch, 1 fat |
| 7 | 1 | 75 | 2 | 22 | 1½ | 1½ starch, 1 fat |
| 8 | 1 | 60 | 2 | 16 | 1 | 1 starch, 1 fat |
| 7 | 1 | 5 | 2 | 21 | 1½ | 1½ starch, 1 fat |
| | | | | | | |
| 9 | 2 | 240 | 2 | 16 | 1 | 1 starch, 2 fat |
| 10 | 2 | 220 | 1 | 15 | 1 | 1 starch, 2 fat |

1 Carbohydrate Choice = 1 starch *or* 1 fruit *or* 1 milk exchange

| PRODUCTS | SERVING SIZE | CALORIES | CALORIES FROM FAT |
|---|---|---|---|
| BBQ, Lay's® KC Masterpiece | 15 chips | 150 | 90 |
| BBQ, Old Dutch® | 12 chips | 150 | 80 |
| Louisiana BBQ Thins, Eagle® | 18 chips | 150 | 70 |
| Mesquite BBQ Kettle Chips, Old Dutch® | 15 chips | 130 | 50 |
| Mesquite BBQ Ripples, Eagle® | 19 chips | 160 | 90 |
| Mesquite Grille B-B-Q, Ruffles® | 15 chips | 150 | 90 |
| Mesquite Thins, Eagle® | 19 chips | 160 | 90 |

### Cheese Potato Chips

| | | | |
|---|---|---|---|
| Cheddar & Sour Cream Flavored, Old Dutch® | 12 chips | 160 | 90 |
| Cheddar & Sour Cream Ripples, Eagle® | 16 chips | 160 | 100 |
| Cheddar & Sour Cream, Ruffles® | 13 chips | 160 | 90 |
| Cheddar Flavor, O'Boisies® | 16 chips | 150 | 90 |
| Cheese 'n Bacon, Tato Skins® | 18 chips | 150 | 80 |

### Plain Potato Chips

| | | | |
|---|---|---|---|
| Baked Potato Flavor, Tato Skins® | 18 chips | 150 | 70 |
| Cape Cod Selects, Eagle® | 19 chips | 130 | 50 |
| Crispy Cooked Thins, Eagle® | 19 chips | 150 | 80 |
| Hawaiian Kettle, Eagle® | 19 chips | 150 | 70 |
| Idaho Russet Dark & Crunchy, Eagle® | 22 chips | 140 | 70 |
| No Salt Thins, Eagle® | 20 chips | 150 | 90 |
| No Salt, Cape Cod® | 20 chips | 150 | 90 |
| Original Flavor, Ripplin's® | 13 chips | 160 | 100 |
| Original Kettle Chips, Old Dutch® | 15 chips | 130 | 50 |
| Original, Lay's® | 18 chips | 150 | 90 |
| Original, O'Boisies® | 16 chips | 150 | 80 |
| Original, Ruffles® | 12 chips | 150 | 90 |
| Potato Chips, Cape Cod® | 19 chips | 150 | 70 |
| Potato Chips, Critic's Choice® | 1 oz | 150 | 80 |
| Potato Chips, Eagle® | 1 oz | 160 | 90 |
| Potato Chips, Old Dutch® | 12–15 chips | 150 | 80 |

❶  Meets Low-Fat Guidelines

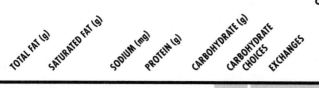

| TOTAL FAT (g) | SATURATED FAT (g) | SODIUM (mg) | PROTEIN (g) | CARBOHYDRATE (g) | CARBOHYDRATE CHOICES | EXCHANGES |
|---|---|---|---|---|---|---|
| 9 | 2.5 | 270 | 2 | 15 | 1 | 1 starch, 2 fat |
| 9 | 1 | 300 | 2 | 15 | 1 | 1 starch, 2 fat |
| 8 | 2 | 160 | 2 | 17 | 1 | 1 starch, 1 fat |
| 6 | 1 | 230 | 2 | 19 | 1 | 1 starch, 1 fat |
| 10 | 2 | 170 | 2 | 15 | 1 | 1 starch, 2 fat |
| 9 | 3 | 120 | 1 | 15 | 1 | 1 starch, 2 fat |
| 10 | 2 | 170 | 2 | 15 | 1 | 1 starch, 2 fat |
| | | | | | | |
| 9 | 1.5 | 190 | 2 | 16 | 1 | 1 starch, 2 fat |
| 11 | 1 | 200 | 2 | 14 | 1 | 1 starch, 2 fat |
| 10 | 2.5 | 230 | 1 | 15 | 1 | 1 starch, 2 fat |
| 10 | 2 | 135 | 2 | 15 | 1 | 1 starch, 2 fat |
| 9 | 1.5 | 170 | <1 | 17 | 1 | 1 starch, 2 fat |
| | | | | | | |
| 8 | 1.5 | 150 | 1 | 17 | 1 | 1 starch, 1 fat |
| 6 | 0.5 | 110 | 2 | 18 | 1 | 1 starch, 1 fat |
| 8 | 2 | 110 | 2 | 15 | 1 | 1 starch, 1 fat |
| 8 | 2 | 150 | 2 | 17 | 1 | 1 starch, 1 fat |
| 7 | 1.5 | 150 | 2 | 17 | 1 | 1 starch, 1 fat |
| 10 | 2.5 | 0 | 2 | 14 | 1 | 1 starch, 2 fat |
| 10 | 2.5 | 0 | 2 | 14 | 1 | 1 starch, 2 fat |
| 11 | 2 | 210 | 2 | 15 | 1 | 1 starch, 2 fat |
| 6 | 1 | 140 | 2 | 18 | 1 | 1 starch, 1 fat |
| 10 | 2.5 | 120 | 2 | 15 | 1 | 1 starch, 2 fat |
| 9 | 2 | 180 | 1 | 15 | 1 | 1 starch, 2 fat |
| 10 | 3 | 125 | 2 | 14 | 1 | 1 starch, 2 fat |
| 8 | 2 | 110 | 2 | 17 | 1 | 1 starch, 1 fat |
| 9 | 2 | 250 | 2 | 15 | 1 | 1 starch, 2 fat |
| 10 | 2 | 180 | 2 | 14 | 1 | 1 starch, 2 fat |
| 9 | 1 | 160 | 2 | 16 | 1 | 1 starch, 2 fat |

1 Carbohydrate Choice = 1 starch or 1 fruit or 1 milk exchange

| PRODUCTS | SERVING SIZE | CALORIES | CALORIES FROM FAT |
|---|---|---|---|
| Rachel's® Made from the Heart | 1 oz | 140 | 80 |
| Reduced Fat, Ruffles® | 16 chips | 130 | 60 |
| Ripple Potato Chips, Eagle® | 17 chips | 150 | 90 |
| Ripl® Potato Chips, Old Dutch® | 12 chips | 150 | 80 |
| Thins, Eagle® | 20 chips | 150 | 90 |
| Unsalted, Lay's® | 19 chips | 160 | 90 |
| Wavy Original, Lay's® | 11 chips | 160 | 90 |
| **Sour Cream and Onion Potato Chips** | | | |
| Artificially Flavored Sour Cream and Onion, O'Boisie® | 15 chips | 150 | 80 |
| Artificially Flavored Sour Cream 'n Onion, Tato Skins® | 18 chips | 150 | 90 |
| Sour Cream & Chive, Cape Cod® | 18 chips | 150 | 80 |
| Sour Cream & Onion Flavored, Old Dutch® | 12 chips | 150 | 80 |
| Sour Cream & Onion Ripples, Eagle® | 16 chips | 160 | 90 |
| Sour Cream & Onion Thins, Eagle® | 19 chips | 160 | 90 |
| Sour Cream & Onion, Lay's® | 22 chips | 160 | 90 |
| Sour Cream & Onion, Ruffles® | 13 chips | 150 | 90 |
| **Other Potato Chip Flavors** | | | |
| Dill Flavored, Old Dutch® | 12 chips | 140 | 70 |
| Jalapeno & Cheddar Kettle Chips, Old Dutch® | 15 chips | 130 | 60 |
| Onion & Garlic Flavored, Old Dutch® | 12 chips | 140 | 70 |
| Ranch, Ruffles® | 13 chips | 150 | 80 |
| Salt & Vinegar Kettle Chips, Old Dutch® | 15 chips | 130 | 50 |
| Salt & Vinegar, Lay's® | 19 chips | 160 | 90 |
| Sea Salt & Vinegar Potato Chips, Cape Cod® | 18 chips | 150 | 70 |
| Spicy Fiesta Thins, Eagle® | 19 chips | 160 | 90 |
| Tangy Ranch, Lay's® | 17 chips | 160 | 90 |

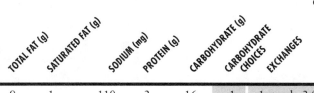

| TOTAL FAT (g) | SATURATED FAT (g) | SODIUM (mg) | PROTEIN (g) | CARBOHYDRATE (g) | CARBOHYDRATE CHOICES | EXCHANGES |
|---|---|---|---|---|---|---|
| 9 | 1 | 110 | 2 | 16 | 1 | 1 starch, 2 fat |
| 6 | 1 | 130 | 2 | 18 | 1 | 1 starch, 1 fat |
| 10 | 2 | 180 | 2 | 14 | 1 | 1 starch, 2 fat |
| 9 | 1 | 150 | 2 | 16 | 1 | 1 starch, 2 fat |
| 10 | 2.5 | 180 | 2 | 14 | 1 | 1 starch, 2 fat |
| 10 | 2.5 | 10 | 2 | 15 | 1 | 1 starch, 2 fat |
| 10 | 2.5 | 120 | 2 | 15 | 1 | 1 starch, 2 fat |
| 9 | 2 | 190 | 2 | 15 | 1 | 1 starch, 2 fat |
| 10 | 1.5 | 160 | <1 | 17 | 1 | 1 starch, 2 fat |
| 9 | 2 | 160 | 2 | 15 | 1 | 1 starch, 2 fat |
| 9 | 1 | 220 | 2 | 17 | 1 | 1 starch, 2 fat |
| 10 | 2 | 180 | 2 | 14 | 1 | 1 starch, 2 fat |
| 10 | 2 | 180 | 2 | 14 | 1 | 1 starch, 2 fat |
| 9 | 2.5 | 180 | 2 | 15 | 1 | 1 starch, 2 fat |
| 10 | 3 | 170 | 2 | 16 | 1 | 1 starch, 2 fat |
| 8 | 1 | 330 | 2 | 16 | 1 | 1 starch, 1 fat |
| 6 | 1.5 | 190 | 2 | 17 | 1 | 1 starch, 1 fat |
| 8 | 1 | 420 | 2 | 16 | 1 | 1 starch, 1 fat |
| 9 | 2.5 | 280 | 2 | 15 | 1 | 1 starch, 2 fat |
| 6 | 1 | 360 | 1 | 18 | 1 | 1 starch, 1 fat |
| 10 | 2.5 | 340 | 2 | 15 | 1 | 1 starch, 2 fat |
| 8 | 2 | 130 | 2 | 17 | 1 | 1 starch, 1 fat |
| 9 | 2.5 | 220 | 2 | 15 | 1 | 1 starch, 2 fat |
| 9 | 2.5 | 220 | 2 | 15 | 1 | 1 starch, 2 fat |

1 Carbohydrate Choice = 1 starch or 1 fruit or 1 milk exchange

## PRODUCTS

| | SERVING SIZE | CALORIES | CALORIES FROM FAT |
|---|---|---|---|

### CHIPS, SNACK
*see also* Cheese Puffs/Curls

| Product | | | |
|---|---|---|---|
| Bagel Chips, Onion Multigrain, Pepperidge Farm® | 1 oz | 120 | 35 |
| Bagel Chips, Three Cheese, Pepperidge Farm® | 1 oz | 140 | 60 |
| Bagel Chips, Toasted Onion & Garlic, Pepperidge Farm® | 1 oz | 110 | 40 |
| Bugles®, all varieties (avg) | 1⅓ cups | 160 | 80 |
| ❶ Bugles® Light, all varieties (avg) | 1½ cups | 125 | 25 |
| ❶ Caraway Rye Cocktail Chips, Rubschlager® | 9 chips | 100 | 5 |
| Cheese Pizza Flavor, Pizzarias® | 14 chips | 150 | 60 |
| Cheesy Quesadilla, Chacho's™ | 14 chips | 150 | 70 |
| Chili Cheese Tortilla Crisps, Pepperidge Farm® | 36 pieces | 130 | 60 |
| Cinnamon Crispana, Chacho's™ | 13 chips | 150 | 60 |
| French Onion, Sunchips® | 13 chips | 140 | 60 |
| Funyuns, Frito-Lay® | 13 pieces | 140 | 60 |
| ❶ Garlic Cocktail Chips, Rubschlager® | 9 chips | 100 | 5 |
| Golden Crisps™, Cheddar Cheese, Old Dutch® | 18 chips | 130 | 42 |
| Golden Crisps™, French Onion, Old Dutch® | 18 chips | 128 | 36 |
| Harvest Cheddar, Sunchips® | 13 chips | 140 | 60 |
| Nacho Cheese, Old Dutch® | 17 chips | 155 | 72 |
| Original Tortilla Crisps, Pepperidge Farm® | 36 pieces | 130 | 60 |
| Original, Sunchips® | 14 chips | 140 | 60 |
| ❶ Pizza Chips, Rubschlager® | 9 chips | 100 | 5 |
| Pizza Supreme Flavor, Pizzarias® | 14 chips | 150 | 70 |
| Restaurant Style Original, Chacho's™ | 15 chips | 150 | 70 |
| Salsa Tortilla Crisps, Pepperidge Farm® | 36 pieces | 130 | 60 |
| ❶ Snack Crisps, Estee®, all varieties (avg) | 30 crisps | 130 | 30 |
| Zesty Pepperoni Flavor, Pizzarias® | 14 chips | 150 | 60 |
| Zings® Snack Chips, Nabisco® | 1 bag | 240 | 100 |

❶  Meets Low-Fat Guidelines

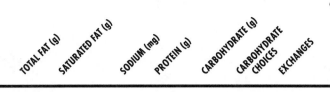

| TOTAL FAT (g) | SATURATED FAT (g) | SODIUM (mg) | PROTEIN (g) | CARBOHYDRATE (g) | CARBOHYDRATE CHOICES | EXCHANGES |
|---|---|---|---|---|---|---|
| 3.5 | 0 | 200 | 3 | 19 | 1 | 1 starch, ½ fat |
| 7 | 1 | 240 | 4 | 16 | 1 | 1 starch, 1 fat |
| 4.5 | 1 | 280 | 3 | 18 | 1 | 1 starch, ½ fat |
| 9 | 8 | 295 | 2 | 18 | 1 | 1 starch, 1½ fat |
| 2.5 | 0.5 | 385 | 2 | 23 | 1½ | 1½ starch |
| 0.5 | 0 | 240 | 5 | 20 | 1 | 1 starch |
| 7 | 1.5 | 210 | 3 | 19 | 1 | 1 starch, 1 fat |
| 8 | 1.5 | 270 | 3 | 18 | 1 | 1 starch, 1 fat |
| 7 | 1 | 340 | 4 | 18 | 1 | 1 starch, 1 fat |
| 7 | 1 | 75 | 2 | 20 | 1 | 1 starch, 1 fat |
| 6 | 1 | 115 | 2 | 19 | 1 | 1 starch, 1 fat |
| 7 | 1.5 | 250 | 2 | 18 | 1 | 1 starch, 1 fat |
| 0.5 | 0 | 240 | 5 | 20 | 1 | 1 starch |
| 4.6 | 0.8 | 179 | 2.1 | 20 | 1 | 1 starch, 1 fat |
| 4 | 0.7 | 190 | 2.1 | 21 | 1½ | 1½ starch, ½ fat |
| 6 | 1 | 115 | 2 | 18 | 1 | 1 starch, 1 fat |
| 8 | 1.5 | 250 | 3 | 19 | 1 | 1 starch, 1 fat |
| 6 | 1 | 290 | 4 | 18 | 1 | 1 starch, 1 fat |
| 7 | 1 | 115 | 2 | 18 | 1 | 1 starch, 1 fat |
| 0.5 | 0 | 240 | 5 | 20 | 1 | 1 starch |
| 7 | 1.5 | 200 | 3 | 19 | 1 | 1 starch, 1 fat |
| 8 | 1 | 210 | 2 | 18 | 1 | 1 starch, 1 fat |
| 7 | 1 | 350 | 3 | 18 | 1 | 1 starch, 1 fat |
| 3 | 0.5 | 145 | 2 | 23 | 1½ | 1½ starch |
| 7 | 1.5 | 210 | 3 | 20 | 1 | 1 starch, 1 fat |
| 11 | 2 | 420 | 3 | 34 | 2 | 2 starch, 2 fat |

1 Carbohydrate Choice = 1 starch *or* 1 fruit *or* 1 milk exchange

| PRODUCTS | SERVING SIZE | CALORIES | CALORIES FROM FAT |
|---|---|---|---|
| **CHOCOLATE CHIPS** | | | |
| Chocolate Chips, real milk chocolate, all varieties (avg) | 27 chips | 70 | 35 |
| Chocolate Chips, real semisweet chocolate, all varieties (avg) | 27 chips | 60 | 30 |
| **CINNAMON ROLLS**<br>*see* Sweet Rolls | | | |
| **CLAMS (CANNED)** | | | |
| ● Minced Clams, Progresso® | ¼ cup | 25 | 0 |
| **COBBLER (FROZEN)** | | | |
| Apple Crumb, Pet-Ritz® | ⅙ pkg | 280 | 80 |
| Apple, Marie Callender's® | 4.25 oz | 350 | 160 |
| Apple, Pet-Ritz® | ⅙ pkg | 280 | 110 |
| Berry, Marie Callender's® | 4.25 oz | 390 | 170 |
| Berry, Marie Callender's® Personal Dessert Size | 10 oz | 350 | 170 |
| Blackberry Crumb, Pet-Ritz® | ⅙ pkg | 260 | 70 |
| Blackberry, Pet-Ritz® | ⅙ pkg | 260 | 100 |
| Blueberry, Marie Callender's® | 4 oz | 340 | 160 |
| Blueberry, Pet-Ritz® | ⅙ pkg | 280 | 100 |
| Cherry, Marie Callender's® | 4.25 oz | 390 | 170 |
| Cherry, Pet-Ritz® | ⅙ pkg | 300 | 90 |
| Cherry Crumb, Pet-Ritz® | ⅙ pkg | 280 | 50 |
| Peach, Marie Callender's® | 4.25 oz | 370 | 160 |
| Peach, Marie Callender's® Personal Dessert Size | 10 oz | 340 | 150 |
| Peach, Pet-Ritz® | ⅙ pkg | 230 | 80 |
| Peach Crumb, Pet-Ritz® | ⅙ pkg | 230 | 60 |
| Strawberry, Pet-Ritz® | ⅙ pkg | 260 | 90 |
| **COCKTAIL SAUCE** | | | |
| ● Cocktail Sauce, Heinz® | ¼ cup | 60 | 0 |
| ● Cocktail Sauce, Kraft® SauceWorks® | ¼ cup | 60 | 5 |

 Meets Low-Fat Guidelines

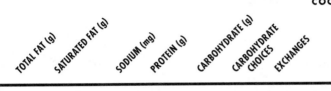

| TOTAL FAT (g) | SATURATED FAT (g) | SODIUM (mg) | PROTEIN (g) | CARBOHYDRATE (g) | CARBOHYDRATE CHOICES | EXCHANGES |
|---|---|---|---|---|---|---|
| 4 | 2 | 10 | 1 | 9 | ½ | ½ starch, ½ fat |
| 3.5 | 2 | 0 | 1 | 8 | ½ | ½ starch, ½ fat |
| 0 | 0 | 250 | 4 | 2 | 0 | 1 very lean meat |
| 9 | 4 | 270 | 2 | 49 | 3 | 2 starch, 1 fruit, 1 fat |
| 18 | 4 | 170 | 2 | 45 | 3 | 1 starch, 2 fruit, 3 fat |
| 12 | 5 | 380 | 2 | 41 | 3 | 2 starch, 1 fruit, 2 fat |
| 19 | 5 | 170 | 3 | 41 | 3 | 1 starch, 2 fruit, 3 fat |
| 19 | 4 | 225 | 3 | 40 | 2½ | 1½ starch, 1 fruit, 4 fat |
| 8 | 3 | 170 | 3 | 45 | 3 | 2 starch, 1 fruit, 1 fat |
| 11 | 4 | 230 | 2 | 38 | 2½ | 1½ starch, 1 fruit, 2 fat |
| 18 | 4 | 220 | 3 | 42 | 3 | 1 starch, 2 fruit, 3 fat |
| 11 | 5 | 240 | 4 | 42 | 3 | 2 starch, 1 fruit, 2 fat |
| 19 | 5 | 100 | 3 | 50 | 3 | 1 starch, 2 fruit, 4 fat |
| 11 | 4 | 300 | 2 | 48 | 3 | 2 starch, 1 fruit, 2 fat |
| 6 | 2.5 | 330 | 2 | 54 | 3½ | 2½ starch, 1 fruit, 1 fat |
| 18 | 3 | 170 | 3 | 47 | 3 | 2 starch, 1 fruit, 3 fat |
| 16 | 4 | 140 | 3 | 44 | 3 | 2 starch, 1 fruit, 3 fat |
| 9 | 3 | 220 | 1 | 37 | 2½ | 1½ starch, 1 fruit, 1 fat |
| 7 | 3 | 170 | 2 | 38 | 2½ | 1½ starch, 1 fruit, 1 fat |
| 9 | 3 | 330 | 2 | 41 | 3 | 2 starch, 1 fruit, 1 fat |
| 0 | 0 | 680 | 1 | 14 | 1 | 1 fruit |
| 0.5 | 0 | 800 | 1 | 13 | 1 | 1 fruit |

1 Carbohydrate Choice = 1 starch or 1 fruit or 1 milk exchange

## PRODUCTS

| | SERVING SIZE | CALORIES | CALORIES FROM FAT |
|---|---|---|---|
| ❶ Cocktail Sauce, Reese® | ¼ cup | 90 | 5 |

### COFFEE BEVERAGES, INSTANT

| | SERVING SIZE | CALORIES | CALORIES FROM FAT |
|---|---|---|---|
| ❶ Cappio Cappucino, Maxwell House® | 8 oz | 95 | 20 |
| ❶ Cappio Iced Cappucino, Maxwell House® | 8 oz | 135 | 20 |
| ❶ Flavored Instant Coffee, General Foods International Coffees®, all regular varieties (avg) | 1⅓ Tb | 60 | 25 |
| ❶ Flavored Instant Coffee, General Foods International Coffees®, all sugar-free, low-calorie varieties (avg) | 1⅓ Tb | 30 | 18 |

### COFFEE CAKE

| | SERVING SIZE | CALORIES | CALORIES FROM FAT |
|---|---|---|---|
| Cheese, Entenmann's® | ⅙ cake | 190 | 70 |
| Cheese Filled Crumb, Entenmann's® | ⅛ cake | 210 | 90 |
| ❶ Cinnamon Apple, Entenmann's® Fat Free Cholesterol Free | ⅑ cake | 130 | 0 |
| Crumb, Entenmann's® | ¹⁄₁₀ cake | 250 | 110 |

### COFFEE CREAMER

| | SERVING SIZE | CALORIES | CALORIES FROM FAT |
|---|---|---|---|
| ❶ Coffee Rich Non-Dairy Creamer, Rich's®, all varieties (avg) | 1 Tb | 10 | 5 |
| ❶ Farm Rich Non-Dairy Creamer, Rich's®, all varieties (avg) | 1 Tb | 10 | 0 |
| ❶ International Delight®, all regular varieties (avg) | 1 Tb | 30–45 | 0–15 |

### COLD CUTS
see Lunch Meats

### COOKIE DOUGH

| | SERVING SIZE | CALORIES | CALORIES FROM FAT |
|---|---|---|---|
| Pillsbury® Cookie Dough, all varieties (avg) (refrigerated) | 1 oz or 2 cookies | 130 | 50 |
| Mrs. Field's® Chocolate Chip Cookie Dough (frozen) | 1 cookie | 270 | 130 |

### COOKIE MIX (AS PREPARED)

| | SERVING SIZE | CALORIES | CALORIES FROM FAT |
|---|---|---|---|
| Chocolate Chip Cookie Mix, Robin Hood®/Gold Medal® | 2 cookies | 170 | 80 |

❶  Meets Low-Fat Guidelines

| TOTAL FAT (g) | SATURATED FAT (g) | SODIUM (mg) | PROTEIN (g) | CARBOHYDRATE (g) | CARBOHYDRATE CHOICES | EXCHANGES |
|---|---|---|---|---|---|---|
| 0.5 | 0 | 830 | 0 | 22 | 1½ | 1½ fruit |
| 2 | 0.5 | 70 | 1.5 | 18 | 1 | 1 starch |
| 2.5 | 1.5 | 115 | 2 | 27 | 2 | 2 starch |
| 2.5 | 0.5 | 25–110 | <1 | 8 | ½ | ½ starch |
| 2 | 0.5 | 30–75 | <1 | 3.5 | 0 | free |
| 8 | 3.5 | 160 | 4 | 24 | 1½ | 1½ starch, 1 fat |
| 10 | 4 | 190 | 4 | 25 | 1½ | 1½ starch, 2 fat |
| 0 | 0 | 110 | 2 | 29 | 2 | 2 starch |
| 12 | 3 | 210 | 4 | 33 | 2 | 2 starch, 2 fat |
| 1 | 0 | 0 | 0 | 1 | 0 | free |
| 0 | 0 | 5 | 0 | 1 | 0 | free |
| 0–1.5 | 0 | 8 | 0 | 7 | ½ | ½ starch |
| 6 | 1.5 | 65–135 | 1 | 17 | 1 | 1 starch, 1 fat |
| 14 | 7 | 135 | 3 | 34 | 2 | 2 starch, 2 fat |
| 8 | 2.5 | 120 | 2 | 21 | 1½ | 1½ starch, 1 fat |

1 Carbohydrate Choice = 1 starch or 1 fruit or 1 milk exchange

## PRODUCTS

| PRODUCTS | SERVING SIZE | CALORIES | CALORIES FROM FAT |
|---|---|---|---|
| ❶ Chocolate Chip Cookie Mix, Sweet 'N Low® | 3 cookies | 120 | 20 |
| Double Chocolate Chunk Cookie Mix, Robin Hood®/Gold Medal® | 2 cookies | 150 | 60 |
| Gingerbread Mix Fun Kit, Betty Crocker® | 2 cookies | 150 | 40 |
| Oatmeal Chocolate Chip Cookie Mix, Robin Hood®/Gold Medal® | 2 cookies | 160 | 70 |
| Peanut Butter Cookie Mix, Robin Hood®/Gold Medal® | 2 cookies | 160 | 70 |

## COOKIES

### Animal Cookies

| | | | |
|---|---|---|---|
| Animal Crackers, Sunshine® | 14 crackers | 140 | 35 |
| Barnum's Animals® Crackers, Nabisco® | 12 crackers | 140 | 35 |
| Iced Animal Cookies, Keebler® | 6 cookies | 140 | 40 |

### Chocolate/Fudge Cookies

| | | | |
|---|---|---|---|
| ❶ American Chocolate Delight, Delicious Frookie® Fat Free | 2 cookies | 100 | 0 |
| Beacon Hill (Chocolate Walnut), Pepperidge Farm® American Collection | 1 cookie | 130 | 60 |
| Brownie Chocolate Nut, Pepperidge Farm® Old Fashioned | 3 cookies | 160 | 80 |
| ❶ Chocolate Brownie, Entenmann's® Fat Free, Cholesterol Free | 2 cookies | 80 | 0 |
| Chocolate Chocolate Walnut, Pepperidge Farm® Soft Baked | 1 cookie | 130 | 50 |
| Chocolate Cookie Bits, Grandma's® | 9 cookies | 170 | 70 |
| ❶ Chocolate, Health Valley® Fat-Free, all varieties (avg) | 2 cookies | 70 | 0 |
| Chocolate Funky Monkeys, Delicious Frookie® | 16 cookies | 120 | 35 |
| Chocolate Snaps, Nabisco® | 7 cookies | 140 | 45 |
| ❶ Chocolate Truffle, SnackWell's® | 1 cookie | 60 | 0 |
| Chocolate Wafers, Fifty 50® Foods | 5 wafers | 180 | 99 |
| ❶ Devil's Food Cookie Cakes, SnackWell's® | 1 cookie | 50 | 0 |

❶ Meets Low-Fat Guidelines

| TOTAL FAT (g) | SATURATED FAT (g) | SODIUM (mg) | PROTEIN (g) | CARBOHYDRATE (g) | CARBOHYDRATE CHOICES | EXCHANGES |
|---|---|---|---|---|---|---|
| 2.5 | <1 | 30 | 2 | 22 | 1½ | 1½ starch |
| 6 | 2 | 95 | 2 | 21 | 1½ | 1½ starch, 1 fat |
| 4.5 | 1 | 170 | 1 | 25 | 1½ | 1½ starch ½ fat |
| 7 | 2 | 130 | 2 | 20 | 1 | 1 starch, 1 fat |
| 8 | 1.5 | 150 | 3 | 19 | 1 | 1 starch, 1 fat |
| 4 | 1 | 125 | 2 | 24 | 1½ | 1½ starch, ½ fat |
| 4 | 0.5 | 160 | 2 | 23 | 1½ | 1½ starch, ½ fat |
| 4.5 | 2 | 130 | 2 | 24 | 1½ | 1½ starch, ½ fat |
| 0 | 0 | 140 | 2 | 24 | 1½ | 1½ starch |
| 7 | 2 | 100 | 2 | 16 | 1 | 1 starch, 1 fat |
| 9 | 3 | 115 | 2 | 18 | 1 | 1 starch, 2 fat |
| 0 | 0 | 90 | 1 | 20 | 1 | 1 starch |
| 6 | 2 | 45 | 2 | 16 | 1 | 1 starch, 1 fat |
| 8 | 2 | 230 | 2 | 24 | 1½ | 1½ starch, 1 fat |
| 0 | 0 | 25 | 2 | 17 | 1 | 1 starch |
| 4 | 0.5 | NA | 2 | 20 | 1 | 1 starch, ½ fat |
| 5 | 2 | 180 | 2 | 23 | 1½ | 1½ starch, ½ fat |
| 0 | 0 | 55 | 1 | 13 | 1 | 1 starch |
| 11 | 2.5 | 45 | 2 | 17 | 1 | 1 starch, 2 fat |
| 0 | 0 | 25 | 1 | 13 | 1 | 1 starch |

1 Carbohydrate Choice = 1 starch or 1 fruit or 1 milk exchange

## PRODUCTS

| PRODUCTS | SERVING SIZE | CALORIES | CALORIES FROM FAT |
|---|---|---|---|
| ❶ Double Fudge Cookie Cakes, SnackWell's® | 1 cookie | 50 | 0 |
| ❶ Elfin Delights® Fat Free Devils Food, Keebler® | 1 cookie | 70 | 0 |
| E.L. Fudge®, Keebler®, all varieties (avg) | 3 cookies | 165 | 70 |
| Family Fudge Covered Grahams, Nabisco® | 3 cookies | 140 | 60 |
| Famous Chocolate Wafers, Nabisco® | 5 cookies | 140 | 35 |
| Fudge 'N Caramel®, Keebler® | 2 cookies | 120 | 50 |
| Fudge Brownie, Fifty 50® Foods | 4 cookies | 160 | 72 |
| Fudge Cookies, Estee® | 4 cookies | 150 | 60 |
| Fudge Dipped Grahams, Sunshine® | 4 cookies | 170 | 80 |
| Fudge Mint Patties, Sunshine® | 2 cookies | 130 | 60 |
| Fudge Sticks®, Keebler® | 3 cookies | 150 | 70 |
| Pure Chocolate Grahams, Nabisco® | 3 cookies | 160 | 70 |
| Vienna Fingers™, Chocolate, Sunshine® | 2 cookies | 120 | 30 |

### Chocolate Chip Cookies

| | | | |
|---|---|---|---|
| Bite-Size Chocolate Chip, SnackWell's® | 13 cookies | 130 | 30 |
| Charleston (Milk Chocolate Toffee), Pepperidge Farm® American Collection | 1 cookie | 130 | 60 |
| Chesapeake (Chocolate Chunk), Pepperidge Farm® American Collection | 1 cookie | 140 | 70 |
| Chewy Chips Ahoy!®, Nabisco® | 3 cookies | 170 | 70 |
| Chips Ahoy!® Chunky, Nabisco® | 1 cookie | 80 | 40 |
| Chips Ahoy!® Mini, Nabisco® | 14 cookies | 150 | 70 |
| Chips Ahoy!®, Nabisco® | 3 cookies | 160 | 70 |
| Chips Ahoy!®, Nabisco® Reduced Fat | 3 cookies | 150 | 50 |
| Chip-A-Roos™, Sunshine® | 3 cookies | 190 | 90 |
| Chips Deluxe®, Bakery Crisp, Keebler® | 3 cookies | 180 | 80 |
| Chips Deluxe®, Bite Size, Keebler® | 8 cookies | 160 | 80 |
| Chips Deluxe®, Chocolate Lovers, Keebler® | 1 cookie | 90 | 40 |
| Chips Deluxe®, Keebler® | 1 cookie | 80 | 40 |
| ❶ Chips Deluxe®, Keebler® 25% Reduced Fat | 1 cookie | 70 | 30 |
| Chocolate Chip Cookies, SnackWell's® Reduced Fat | 13 cookies | 130 | 30 |

❶  Meets Low-Fat Guidelines

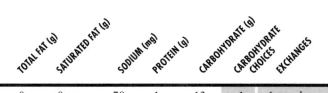

| TOTAL FAT (g) | SATURATED FAT (g) | SODIUM (mg) | PROTEIN (g) | CARBOHYDRATE (g) | CARBOHYDRATE CHOICES | EXCHANGES |
|---|---|---|---|---|---|---|
| 0 | 0 | 70 | 1 | 12 | 1 | 1 starch |
| 0 | 0 | 80 | 1 | 14 | 1 | 1 starch |
| 8 | 2 | 110 | 2 | 23 | 1½ | 1½ starch, 1 fat |
| 7 | 1.5 | 125 | 2 | 19 | 1 | 1 starch, 1 fat |
| 4 | 1.5 | 230 | 2 | 23 | 1½ | 1½ starch, 1 fat |
| 6 | 4 | 55 | <1 | 16 | 1 | 1 starch, 1 fat |
| 8 | 1.5 | 20 | 3 | 19 | 1 | 1 starch, 1 fat |
| 7 | 1.5 | 45 | 2 | 19 | 1 | 1 starch, 1 fat |
| 9 | 6 | 75 | 2 | 21 | 1½ | 1½ starch, 1 fat |
| 7 | 3.5 | 60 | 1 | 16 | 1 | 1 starch, 1 fat |
| 8 | 4.5 | 55 | 1 | 20 | 1 | 1 starch, 1 fat |
| 8 | 5 | 90 | 2 | 21 | 1½ | 1½ starch, 1 fat |
| 3.5 | 1 | 115 | 2 | 22 | 1½ | 1½ starch |
| 3.5 | 1.5 | 170 | 2 | 22 | 1½ | 1½ starch |
| 7 | 2.5 | 110 | 1 | 16 | 1 | 1 starch, 1 fat |
| 8 | 1.5 | 100 | 2 | 15 | 1 | 1 starch, 1 fat |
| 8 | 2.5 | 125 | 1 | 23 | 1½ | 1½ starch, 1 fat |
| 4 | 3 | 60 | 1 | 11 | 1 | 1 starch, ½ fat |
| 7 | 2.5 | 105 | 2 | 21 | 1½ | 1½ starch, 1 fat |
| 8 | 2.5 | 105 | 2 | 21 | 1½ | 1½ starch, 1 fat |
| 6 | 1.5 | 150 | 2 | 23 | 1½ | 1½ starch, 1 fat |
| 10 | 3.5 | 150 | 2 | 23 | 1½ | 1½ starch, 2 fat |
| 9 | 3 | 135 | 2 | 23 | 1½ | 1½ starch, 2 fat |
| 9 | 3 | 110 | 2 | 20 | 1 | 1 starch, 2 fat |
| 5 | 2.5 | 75 | <1 | 11 | 1 | 1 starch, 1 fat |
| 4.5 | 1.5 | 60 | 1 | 9 | ½ | ½ starch, 1 fat |
| 3 | 1 | 70 | 1 | 11 | 1 | 1 starch |
| 3.5 | 1.5 | 170 | 2 | 22 | 1½ | 1½ starch |

1 Carbohydrate Choice = 1 starch or 1 fruit or 1 milk exchange

## PRODUCTS

| | SERVING SIZE | CALORIES | CALORIES FROM FAT |
|---|---|---|---|
| Chocolate Chip Snaps, Nabisco® | 7 cookies | 150 | 45 |
| Chocolate Chip, Delicious Frookie® | 3 cookies | 140 | 60 |
| Chocolate Chip, Entenmann's® | 3 cookies | 140 | 60 |
| Chocolate Chip, Estee® | 4 cookies | 150 | 60 |
| Chocolate Chip, Fifty 50® Foods | 4 cookies | 170 | 90 |
| Chocolate Chip, Keebler® Soft Batch® | 1 cookie | 80 | 35 |
| Chocolate Chip, Pepperidge Farm® Old Fashioned | 3 cookies | 140 | 60 |
| Chocolate Chip, Rippin' Good® | 3 cookies | 150 | 60 |
| Chocolate Chip, Smart Snackers® | 2 cookies | 140 | 45 |
| Chocolate Chunk, Pepperidge Farm® Soft Baked | 1 cookie | 130 | 50 |
| Fudge Chocolate Chip, Grandma's Big® | 1 cookie | 170 | 60 |
| ❶ Healthy Chips, Health Valley® Fat-Free, all varieties (avg) | 3 cookies | 100 | 0 |
| Milk Chocolate Macadamia, Pepperidge Farm® Soft Baked | 1 cookie | 130 | 60 |
| Mini Chocolate Chip, Sunshine® | 5 cookies | 160 | 70 |
| Mint Chocolate Chip, Delicious Frookie® | 3 cookies | 140 | 60 |
| Nantucket (Chocolate Chunk) Pepperidge Farm® American Collection | 1 cookie | 130 | 60 |
| Nutty Fudge, Grandma's Big® | 1 cookie | 190 | 70 |
| ❶ Oatmeal Chocolatey Chip, Entenmann's® Fat Free Cholesterol Free | 2 cookies | 80 | 0 |
| Peanut Butter Chocolate Chip, Grandma's Big® | 1 cookie | 190 | 90 |
| Sausalito (Milk Chocolate Macadamia) Pepperidge Farm® American Collection | 1 cookie | 140 | 70 |

### Chocolate Sandwich Cookies

| | | | |
|---|---|---|---|
| ❶ Chocolate Creme Sandwich, SnackWell's® | 2 cookies | 110 | 20 |
| Chocolate Frookwich, Delicious Frookie® | 2 crackers | 100 | 35 |
| Chocolate Sandwich, Fifty 50® Foods | 3 cookies | 160 | 63 |
| Chocolate Sandwich, Smart Snackers® | 2 cookies | 140 | 35 |
| Chocolate Sandwich, Estee® | 3 cookies | 160 | 50 |

❶   Meets Low-Fat Guidelines

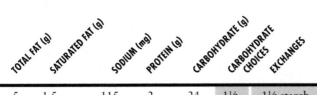

| TOTAL FAT (g) | SATURATED FAT (g) | SODIUM (mg) | PROTEIN (g) | CARBOHYDRATE (g) | CARBOHYDRATE CHOICES | EXCHANGES |
|---|---|---|---|---|---|---|
| 5 | 1.5 | 115 | 2 | 24 | 1½ | 1½ starch, 1 fat |
| 7 | 1 | 120 | 2 | 17 | 1 | 1 starch, 1 fat |
| 7 | 2 | 90 | 1 | 20 | 1 | 1 starch, 1 fat |
| 7 | 2 | 30 | 2 | 21 | 1½ | 1½ starch, 1 fat |
| 10 | 3 | 50 | 2 | 17 | 1 | 1 starch, 2 fat |
| 3.5 | 1 | 70 | <1 | 10 | ½ | ½ starch, ½ fat |
| 7 | 2.5 | 65 | 2 | 18 | 1 | 1 starch, 1 fat |
| 7 | 2 | 150 | 2 | 22 | 1½ | 1½ starch, 1 fat |
| 5 | 2 | 90 | 2 | 22 | 1½ | 1½ starch, ½ fat |
| 6 | 2.5 | 35 | 1 | 16 | 1 | 1 starch, 1 fat |
| 6 | 2 | 160 | 2 | 27 | 2 | 2 starch, 1 fat |
| 0 | 0 | 40 | 3 | 24 | 1½ | 1½ starch |
| 6 | 2.5 | 55 | 1 | 16 | 1 | 1 starch, 1 fat |
| 8 | 3 | 120 | 2 | 20 | 1 | 1 starch, 1½ fat |
| 7 | 1 | 120 | 2 | 17 | 1 | 1 starch, 1 fat |
| 7 | 3 | 75 | 1 | 16 | 1 | 1 starch, 1 fat |
| 8 | 1.5 | 150 | 3 | 25 | 1½ | 1½ starch, 1 fat |
| 0 | 0 | 110 | 1 | 19 | 1 | 1 starch |
| 10 | 3 | 170 | 4 | 23 | 1½ | 1½ starch, 2 fat |
| 7 | 2 | 110 | 2 | 16 | 1 | 1 starch, 1 fat |
| 2.5 | 0.5 | 220 | 1 | 20 | 1 | 1 starch |
| 4 | 0 | 60 | 1 | 14 | 1 | 1 starch, ½ fat |
| 7 | 2 | 35 | 2 | 26 | 2 | 2 starch, 1 fat |
| 3.5 | 1 | 160 | 2 | 23 | 1½ | 1½ starch |
| 6 | 1.5 | 60 | 2 | 24 | 1½ | 1½ starch, 1 fat |

1 Carbohydrate Choice = 1 starch or 1 fruit or 1 milk exchange

## PRODUCTS

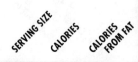

| PRODUCTS | SERVING SIZE | CALORIES | CALORIES FROM FAT |
|---|---|---|---|
| Chocolate Sandwich, Grandma's Value Line® | 3 cookies | 180 | 50 |
| Chocolate Sandwich, Rippin' Good® | 3 cookies | 170 | 60 |
| ❶ Chocolate Sandwich Cookies with Chocolate Creme, SnackWell's® Reduced Fat | 2 cookies | 100 | 20 |
| ❶ Elfin Delights® 50% Reduced Fat Chocolate Sandwich, Keebler®, all varieties (avg) | 2 cookies | 110 | 25 |
| Hydrox™, Sunshine® | 3 cookies | 150 | 60 |
| Hydrox™, Sunshine® Reduced Fat | 3 cookies | 130 | 35 |
| Oreo® Double Stuf® Chocolate Sandwich, Nabisco® | 2 cookies | 140 | 60 |
| Oreo® Fudge Covered Chocolate Sandwich, Nabisco® | 1 cookie | 110 | 50 |
| Oreo® Chocolate Sandwich, Nabisco® | 3 cookies | 160 | 60 |
| Oreo® Sandwich, Nabisco® Reduced Fat | 3 cookies | 140 | 45 |
| Oreo® White Fudge Covered Chocolate Sandwich, Nabisco® | 1 cookie | 110 | 50 |

### Fruit-Filled Cookies

| PRODUCTS | SERVING SIZE | CALORIES | CALORIES FROM FAT |
|---|---|---|---|
| ❶ American Cran-Orange Cookies, Delicious Frookie® Fat-Free | 2 cookies | 90 | 0 |
| ❶ Apple Fig Bars, Estee® | 2 bars | 100 | 10 |
| ❶ Apple Fruitins, Delicious Frookie® | 2 cookies | 110 | 18 |
| ❶ Apple Newtons®, Nabisco® Fat Free | 2 cookies | 110 | 20 |
| ❶ Apple Raisin Bars, Smart Snackers® | 1 bar | 70 | 20 |
| ❶ Apple, Sunshine® Golden Fruit™ | 1 cookie | 80 | 15 |
| ❶ Apricot Tart Cookies, Healthy Choice® | 2 tarts | 110 | 15 |
| Apricot Raspberry Cookies, Pepperidge Farm® | 3 cookies | 140 | 50 |
| ❶ Cherry Cobbler Cookies, Pepperidge Farm® | 1 cookie | 70 | 25 |
| ❶ Cranberry Fig Bars, Estee® | 2 bars | 100 | 10 |
| ❶ Cranberry Newtons®, Nabisco® | 2 cookies | 100 | 0 |
| ❶ Fig Bars, Estee® Low Fat | 2 bars | 100 | 10 |
| ❶ Fig Bars, Rippin' Good® Fat Free Mini Bits | 4 bars | 100 | 0 |
| ❶ Fig Bars, Sunshine® | 2 cookies | 110 | 25 |

❶  Meets Low-Fat Guidelines

| TOTAL FAT (g) | SATURATED FAT (g) | SODIUM (mg) | PROTEIN (g) | CARBOHYDRATE (g) | CARBOHYDRATE CHOICES | EXCHANGES |
|---|---|---|---|---|---|---|
| 5 | 1.5 | 200 | 2 | 31 | 2 | 2 starch, ½ fat |
| 7 | 1.5 | 150 | 2 | 24 | 1½ | 1½ starch, 1 fat |
| 2.5 | .5 | 190 | 1 | 20 | 1 | 1 starch |
| 2.5 | 0.5 | 110 | 1 | 19 | 1 | 1 starch |
| 7 | 2 | 125 | 2 | 21 | 1½ | 1½ starch, 1 fat |
| 4 | 1 | 140 | 1 | 24 | 1½ | 1½ starch |
| 7 | 1.5 | 150 | 1 | 19 | 1 | 1 starch, 1 fat |
| 6 | 1.5 | 85 | 1 | 14 | 1 | 1 starch, 1 fat |
| 7 | 1.5 | 220 | 2 | 23 | 1½ | 1½ starch, 1 fat |
| 5 | 1 | 190 | 2 | 24 | 1½ | 1½ starch, ½ fat |
| 6 | 1.5 | 85 | 1 | 14 | 1 | 1 starch, 1 fat |
| 0 | 0 | 110 | 2 | 21 | 1½ | 1½ starch |
| 1 | 0 | 25 | 1 | 22 | 1½ | 1½ starch |
| 2 | 0 | 40 | 1 | 22 | 1½ | 1½ starch |
| 2.5 | 1 | 120 | 1 | 20 | 1 | 1 starch |
| 2 | 0.5 | 60 | 1 | 14 | 1 | 1 starch |
| 1.5 | 0 | 55 | 1 | 15 | 1 | 1starch |
| 1.5 | 0 | 80 | 2 | 22 | 1½ | 1½ starch |
| 6 | 2 | 110 | 2 | 22 | 1½ | 1½ starch, 1 fat |
| 2.5 | 1 | 45 | <1 | 11 | 1 | 1 starch |
| 1 | 0 | 20 | 1 | 22 | 1½ | 1½ starch |
| 0 | 0 | 95 | 1 | 23 | 1½ | 1½ starch |
| 1 | 0 | 20 | 1 | 23 | 1½ | 1½ starch |
| 0 | 0 | 45 | 1 | 22 | 1½ | 1½ starch |
| 2.5 | 0.5 | 60 | 1 | 20 | 1 | 1 starch |

1 Carbohydrate Choice = 1 starch or 1 fruit or 1 milk exchange

| PRODUCTS | SERVING SIZE | CALORIES | CALORIES FROM FAT |
|---|---|---|---|
| ❶ Fig Fruit Filled Cookies, Smart Snackers® | 1 bar | 70 | 0 |
| ❶ Fig Fruitins, Delicious Frookie® | 2 cookies | 110 | 18 |
| ❶ Fig Fruitins, Delicious Frookie® Fat Free | 2 cookies | 90 | 0 |
| ❶ Fig Newtons®, Nabisco® Fat Free | 2 cookies | 100 | 0 |
| ❶ Peach Tart Cookies, Pepperidge Farm® | 2 cookies | 120 | 25 |
| Raspberry Filled Linzer Distinctive Cookies, Pepperidge Farm® | 1 cookie | 100 | 35 |
| ❶ Raisin Cookies, Sunshine® Golden Fruit™ | 1 cookie | 80 | 15 |
| ❶ Raspberry Fruit Center Cookies, Health Valley® Fat-Free | 1 cookie | 70 | 0 |
| ❶ Raspberry Fruit Filled Cookies, Smart Snackers® | 1 bar | 70 | 0 |
| ❶ Raspberry Fruitins, Delicious Frookie® Fat Free | 2 cookies | 90 | 0 |
| ❶ Raspberry Newtons®, Nabisco® | 2 cookies | 100 | 0 |
| ❶ Raspberry Tart Cookies, Healthy Choice® | 2 tarts | 110 | 15 |
| ❶ Strawberry Newtons®, Nabisco® | 2 cookies | 100 | 0 |
| ❶ Vanilla Raspberry Tart Cookies, Pepperidge Farm® Wholesome Choice | 2 cookies | 120 | 25 |

### Ginger/Molasses Cookies

| | | | |
|---|---|---|---|
| Ginger, Eagle® Gourmet | 1 cookie | 240 | 30 |
| Gingerman, Pepperidge Farm® Old Fashioned | 4 cookies | 120 | 35 |
| ❶ Ginger Snaps, Nabisco® Old Fashion | 4 cookies | 120 | 25 |
| Ginger Snaps, Sunshine® | 7 cookies | 130 | 40 |
| Ginger Spice, Delicious Frookie® | 3 cookies | 130 | 45 |
| Iced Gingerbread, Sunshine® | 5 cookies | 130 | 50 |
| ❶ Ice Spice, Rippin' Good® | 3 cookies | 130 | 25 |
| Molasses Crisps, Pepperidge Farm® Old Fashioned | 5 cookies | 150 | 60 |
| Molasses, Grandma's Big® | 1 cookie | 160 | 35 |

### Graham Cookies

| | | | |
|---|---|---|---|
| Bugs Bunny® Chocolate Graham, Nabisco® | 13 pieces | 140 | 40 |
| Bugs Bunny® Graham, Nabisco® | 10 cookies | 140 | 40 |

❶ Meets Low-Fat Guidelines

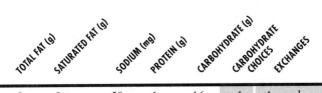

| TOTAL FAT (g) | SATURATED FAT (g) | SODIUM (mg) | PROTEIN (g) | CARBOHYDRATE (g) | CARBOHYDRATE CHOICES | EXCHANGES |
|---|---|---|---|---|---|---|
| 0 | 0 | 50 | 1 | 16 | 1 | 1 starch |
| 2 | 0 | 40 | 1 | 22 | 1½ | 1½ starch |
| 0 | 0 | 75 | 1 | 20 | 1 | 1 starch |
| 0 | 0 | 115 | 1 | 22 | 1½ | 1½ starch |
| 3 | 1 | 115 | 1 | 23 | 1½ | 1½ starch |
| 4 | 1 | 65 | 1 | 15 | 1 | 1 starch, ½ fat |
| 1.5 | 0 | 40 | 1 | 15 | 1 | 1 starch |
| 0 | 0 | 20 | 2 | 18 | 1 | 1 starch |
| 0 | 0 | 45 | 1 | 16 | 1 | 1 starch |
| 0 | 0 | 75 | 1 | 21 | 1½ | 1½ starch |
| 0 | 0 | 115 | 1 | 23 | 1½ | 1½ starch |
| 1.5 | 0 | 80 | 2 | 22 | 1½ | 1½ starch |
| 0 | 0 | 115 | 1 | 23 | 1½ | 1½ starch |
| 3 | 1 | 115 | 1 | 23 | 1½ | 1½ starch |
| 3.5 | 1 | 180 | 4 | 49 | 3 | 3 starch |
| 3.5 | 1 | 95 | 5 | 21 | 1½ | 1½ starch |
| 2.5 | 0.5 | 170 | 1 | 22 | 1½ | 1½ starch |
| 4.5 | 1 | 150 | 2 | 22 | 1½ | 1½ starch, ½ fat |
| 5 | 0.5 | 135 | 2 | 21 | 1½ | 1½ starch, ½ fat |
| 6 | 1.5 | 135 | 2 | 19 | 1 | 1 starch, 1 fat |
| 3 | 0.5 | 190 | 2 | 24 | 1½ | 1½ starch |
| 6 | 1.5 | 140 | 2 | 20 | 1 | 1 starch, 1 fat |
| 4 | 1 | 260 | 2 | 29 | 2 | 2 starch |
| 5 | 1 | 180 | 2 | 22 | 1½ | 1½ starch, ½ fat |
| 5 | 1 | 160 | 2 | 23 | 1½ | 1½ starch, 1 fat |

1 Carbohydrate Choice = 1 starch *or* 1 fruit *or* 1 milk exchange

## PRODUCTS

| PRODUCTS | SERVING SIZE | CALORIES | CALORIES FROM FAT |
|---|---|---|---|
| Cinnamon Graham Tiny Goldfish, Pepperidge Farm® | 19 pieces | 150 | 60 |
| Deluxe® Grahams, Keebler® | 3 cookies | 140 | 60 |
| Graham Tiny Goldfish Cookies, Pepperidge Farm® | 19 pieces | 150 | 70 |
| Pure Chocolate Grahams, Nabisco® | 3 cookies | 160 | 70 |
| **Lemon Cookies** | | | |
| Double Decker Lemon Creme Wafers, Estee® | 5 wafers | 170 | 70 |
| Lemon Cookie Bits, Grandma's® | 9 cookies | 150 | 60 |
| Lemon Coolers™, Sunshine® | 5 cookies | 140 | 50 |
| Lemon Creme, Eagle® | 6 cookies | 260 | 100 |
| Lemon Frookwich, Delicious Frookie® | 2 crackers | 100 | 35 |
| Lemon Nut Crunch, Pepperidge Farm® Old Fashioned | 3 cookies | 170 | 80 |
| **Macaroon Cookies** | | | |
| ❶ Frookaroons, Delicious Frookie® | 2 cookies | 80 | 5 |
| Macaroon, Rippin' Good® | 3 cookies | 150 | 70 |
| **Marshmallow Cookies** | | | |
| ❶ Daisies Marshmallow, Rippin' Good® Fat Free | 3 cookies | 110 | 0 |
| Mallomars® Chocolate, Nabisco® | 2 cookies | 120 | 45 |
| Marshmallow Puffs Fudge, Nabisco® | 1 cookie | 90 | 35 |
| Marshmallow Twirls Fudge Cakes, Nabisco® | 1 cookie | 130 | 50 |
| Pinwheels® Pure Chocolate and Marshmallow, Nabisco® | 1 cookie | 130 | 45 |
| Toasted Coconut Marshmallow, Rippin' Good® | 3 cookies | 140 | 35 |
| **Oatmeal Cookies** | | | |
| Country Style Oatmeal, Sunshine® | 3 cookies | 170 | 60 |
| Iced Oatmeal, Sunshine® | 2 cookies | 120 | 45 |
| Irish Oatmeal, Pepperidge Farm® Old Fashioned | 3 cookies | 130 | 50 |
| Oatmeal, Fifty 50® Foods | 4 cookies | 140 | 54 |

❶ Meets Low-Fat Guidelines

| TOTAL FAT (g) | SATURATED FAT (g) | SODIUM (mg) | PROTEIN (g) | CARBOHYDRATE (g) | CARBOHYDRATE CHOICES | EXCHANGES |
|---|---|---|---|---|---|---|
| 7 | 2.5 | 140 | 2 | 20 | 1 | 1 starch, 1 fat |
| 7 | 4.5 | 105 | 1 | 19 | 1 | 1 starch, 1 fat |
| 7 | 0.5 | 150 | 2 | 20 | 1 | 1 starch, 1 fat |
| 8 | 5 | 90 | 2 | 21 | 1½ | 1½ starch, 1 fat |
| 8 | 1.5 | 0 | 1 | 23 | 1½ | 1½ starch, 1 fat |
| 6 | 2.5 | 90 | 2 | 21 | 1½ | 1½ starch, 1 fat |
| 6 | 1.5 | 100 | 1 | 21 | 1½ | 1½ starch, 1 fat |
| 11 | 2.5 | 190 | 3 | 37 | 2½ | 2½ starch, 2 fat |
| 4 | 0 | 60 | 1 | 14 | 1 | 1 starch, ½ fat |
| 9 | 2 | 60 | 2 | 18 | 1 | 1 starch, 2 fat |
| 0 | 0 | 160 | 1 | 26 | 2 | 2 starch |
| 7 | 3 | 150 | 2 | 20 | 1 | 1 starch, 1 fat |
| 0 | 0 | 80 | 1 | 27 | 2 | 2 starch |
| 5 | 3 | 35 | 1 | 17 | 1 | 1 starch, 1 fat |
| 4 | 1 | 45 | 1 | 14 | 1 | 1 starch, ½ fat |
| 6 | 1.5 | 75 | 1 | 20 | 1 | 1 starch, 1 fat |
| 5 | 2.5 | 35 | 1 | 21 | 1½ | 1½ starch, ½ fat |
| 4 | 1 | 115 | 2 | 24 | 1½ | 1½ starch |
| 7 | 1.5 | 160 | 2 | 24 | 1½ | 1½ starch, 1 fat |
| 5 | 1 | 90 | 2 | 18 | 1 | 1 starch, 1 fat |
| 6 | 1.5 | 70 | 2 | 19 | 1 | 1 starch, 1 fat |
| 6 | 1.5 | 55 | 3 | 20 | 1 | 1 starch, 1 fat |

1 Carbohydrate Choice = 1 starch or 1 fruit or 1 milk exchange

## PRODUCTS

| | SERVING SIZE | CALORIES | CALORIES FROM FAT |
|---|---|---|---|
| ❶ Oatmeal, Nabisco® Family Favorites | 1 cookie | 80 | 30 |
| Oatmeal, Rippin' Good® | 3 cookies | 150 | 50 |
| Oatmeal Chocolate Chip, Sunshine® | 3 cookies | 170 | 70 |
| ❶ Oatmeal Raisin, Delicious Frookie® Fat Free | 2 cookies | 90 | 0 |
| ❶ Oatmeal Raisin, Entenmann's® Fat Free Cholesterol Free | 2 cookies | 80 | 0 |
| Oatmeal Raisin, Estee® | 4 cookies | 130 | 40 |
| Oatmeal Raisin, Pepperidge Farm® Old Fashioned | 3 cookies | 160 | 60 |
| Oatmeal Raisin, Pepperidge Farm® Soft Baked | 1 cookie | 110 | 40 |
| ❶ Oatmeal Raisin, Smart Snackers® | 2 cookies | 120 | 15 |
| ❶ Oatmeal Raisin, SnackWell's® | 2 cookies | 110 | 25 |
| Santa Fe (Oatmeal Raisin), Pepperidge Farm® American Collection | 1 cookie | 120 | 40 |
| ❶ Soft Batch® Oatmeal Raisin, Keebler® | 1 cookie | 70 | 30 |

### Peanut Butter Cookies

| | SERVING SIZE | CALORIES | CALORIES FROM FAT |
|---|---|---|---|
| Granola Peanut Butter Sandwich, Rippin' Good® | 2 cookies | 150 | 50 |
| Nutter Butter® Bites Peanut Butter Sandwich, Nabisco® | 10 cookies | 150 | 60 |
| Nutter Butter® Peanut Butter Sandwich, Nabisco® | 2 cookies | 130 | 50 |
| Nutter Butter® Peanut Creme Patties, Nabisco® | 5 patties | 160 | 80 |
| P.B. Fudgebutters®, Keebler® | 2 cookies | 130 | 70 |
| Peanut Butter, Fifty 50® Foods | 4 cookies | 160 | 63 |
| Peanut Butter Cookie Bits, Grandma's® | 9 cookies | 150 | 60 |
| Peanut Butter Frookwich, Delicious Frookie® | 2 crackers | 100 | 35 |
| Peanut Butter Sandwich, Estee® | 3 cookies | 160 | 60 |
| Peanut Butter Sandwich, Grandma's® | 5 cookies | 210 | 80 |
| Pitter Patter®, Keebler® | 1 cookie | 90 | 35 |

### Sugar Cookies

| | SERVING SIZE | CALORIES | CALORIES FROM FAT |
|---|---|---|---|
| Sugar Cookie, Pepperidge Farm® Old Fashioned | 3 cookies | 140 | 60 |

❶  Meets Low-Fat Guidelines

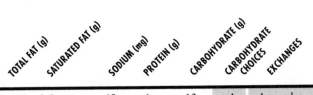

| TOTAL FAT (g) | SATURATED FAT (g) | SODIUM (mg) | PROTEIN (g) | CARBOHYDRATE (g) | CARBOHYDRATE CHOICES | EXCHANGES |
|---|---|---|---|---|---|---|
| 3 | 0.5 | 65 | 1 | 12 | 1 | 1 starch |
| 6 | 1.5 | 135 | 2 | 21 | 1½ | 1½ starch, 1 fat |
| 8 | 3 | 130 | 3 | 23 | 1½ | 1½ starch, 1 fat |
| 0 | 0 | 110 | 2 | 21 | 1½ | 1½ starch |
| 0 | 0 | 120 | 1 | 18 | 1 | 1 starch |
| 5 | 1 | 25 | 2 | 19 | 1 | 1 starch, 1 fat |
| 6 | 1.5 | 150 | 2 | 23 | 1½ | 1½ starch, 1 fat |
| 4 | 1 | 60 | 1 | 17 | 1 | 1 starch, ½ fat |
| 2 | 0 | 90 | 2 | 22 | 1½ | 1½ starch |
| 2.5 | 0 | 135 | 2 | 20 | 1 | 1 starch |
| 4.5 | 1 | 110 | 2 | 18 | 1 | 1 starch, 1 fat |
| 3 | 1 | 65 | <1 | 10 | ½ | ½ starch, ½ fat |
| 6 | 1.5 | 100 | 3 | 20 | 1 | 1 starch, 1 fat |
| 7 | 1.5 | 125 | 3 | 20 | 1 | 1 starch, 1 fat |
| 6 | 1 | 110 | 3 | 19 | 1 | 1 starch, 1 fat |
| 9 | 1.5 | 80 | 4 | 17 | 1 | 1 starch, 2 fat |
| 7 | 4 | 90 | 2 | 14 | 1 | 1 starch, 1 fat |
| 7 | 1.5 | 25 | 3 | 19 | 1 | 1 starch, 1 fat |
| 6 | 1.5 | 135 | 3 | 21 | 1½ | 1½ starch, 1 fat |
| 4 | 0 | 60 | 1 | 14 | 1 | 1 starch, ½ fat |
| 7 | 1 | 55 | 4 | 22 | 1½ | 1½ starch, 1 fat |
| 9 | 2 | 190 | 4 | 29 | 2 | 2 starch, 1 fat |
| 4 | 1 | 115 | 2 | 12 | 1 | 1 starch, ½ fat |
| 6 | 1.5 | 90 | 2 | 20 | 1 | 1 starch, 1 fat |

1 Carbohydrate Choice = 1 starch or 1 fruit or 1 milk exchange

## PRODUCTS

| | SERVING SIZE | CALORIES | CALORIES FROM FAT |
|---|---|---|---|
| Sugar Cookie, Rippin' Good® | 3 cookies | 150 | 60 |
| **Sugar Wafers** | | | |
| Biscos® Sugar Wafers, Nabisco® | 8 cookies | 140 | 60 |
| Chocolate Creme Wafers, Estee® | 7 wafers | 160 | 70 |
| Chocolate Sugar Wafers, Sunshine® | 3 wafers | 130 | 60 |
| Krisp Kreem® Sugar Wafers, Keebler® | 5 pieces | 140 | 60 |
| Peanut Butter Sugar Wafers, Sunshine® | 4 wafers | 170 | 80 |
| Sandwich Wafer, Grandma's Value Line®, all varieties (avg) | 1 pkg | 230 | 70 |
| Triple Decker Banana/Chocolate/Strawberry Wafers, Estee® | 3 wafers | 140 | 60 |
| Vanilla Sugar Wafers, Sunshine® | 3 wafers | 130 | 60 |
| **Shortbread** | | | |
| Fudge Striped Shortbread, Nabisco® Family Favorites | 3 cookies | 160 | 70 |
| Fudge Striped Shortbread, Sunshine® | 3 cookies | 160 | 80 |
| Lorna Doone® Shortbread, Nabisco® | 4 cookies | 140 | 60 |
| Pecan Passion® Pecan Shortbread, Nabisco® | 1 cookie | 90 | 45 |
| Pecan Sandies® Shortbread, Keebler® | 1 cookie | 80 | 45 |
| Pecan Shortbread, Pepperidge Farm® Old Fashioned | 2 cookies | 140 | 80 |
| Shortbread, Estee® | 4 cookies | 130 | 40 |
| Shortbread, Pepperidge Farm® Old Fashioned | 2 cookies | 140 | 70 |
| **Vanilla Cookies** | | | |
| French Vanilla Creme, Keebler® | 1 cookie | 80 | 30 |
| Golden Vanilla Wafers, Keebler® | 8 cookies | 150 | 6 |
| Golden Vanilla Wafers, Keebler® 30% Reduced Fat | 8 cookies | 130 | 30 |
| Nilla® Wafers, Nabisco® | 8 cookies | 140 | 40 |
| Vanilla & Strawberry Creme Wafers, Estee® | 5 wafers | 170 | 70 |
| Vanilla Cookie Bits, Grandma's® | 9 cookies | 150 | 60 |

❶ Meets Low-Fat Guidelines

| TOTAL FAT (g) | SATURATED FAT (g) | SODIUM (mg) | PROTEIN (g) | CARBOHYDRATE (g) | CARBOHYDRATE CHOICES | EXCHANGES |
|---|---|---|---|---|---|---|
| 6 | 1.5 | 125 | 2 | 22 | 1½ | 1½ starch, 1 fat |
| 6 | 1.5 | 40 | <1 | 21 | 1½ | 1½ starch, 1 fat |
| 8 | 1.5 | 0 | <1 | 21 | 1½ | 1½ starch, 1 fat |
| 7 | 2 | 30 | 2 | 17 | 1 | 1 starch, 1 fat |
| 7 | 1.5 | 50 | 1 | 19 | 1 | 1 starch, 1 fat |
| 9 | 2 | 75 | 3 | 19 | 1 | 1 starch, 2 fat |
| 8 | 2 | 70 | 2 | 39 | 2½ | 2½ starch, 1 fat |
| 7 | 1 | 0 | 1 | 18 | 1 | 1 starch, 1 fat |
| 6 | 1.5 | 20 | 1 | 18 | 1 | 1 starch, 1 fat |
| 8 | 1.5 | 140 | 2 | 22 | 1½ | 1½ starch, 1 fat |
| 9 | 5 | 85 | 2 | 20 | 1 | 1 starch, 2 fat |
| 7 | 1 | 130 | 2 | 19 | 1 | 1 starch, 1 fat |
| 5 | 1 | 35 | <1 | 9 | ½ | ½ starch, 1 fat |
| 5 | 1 | 75 | <1 | 9 | ½ | ½ starch, 1 fat |
| 9 | 2.5 | 85 | 1 | 14 | 1 | 1 starch, 2 fat |
| 4 | 1 | 150 | 2 | 22 | 1½ | 1½ starch, ½ fat |
| 7 | 2.5 | 105 | 2 | 16 | 1 | 1 starch, 1 fat |
| 3.5 | 1 | 85 | <1 | 12 | 1 | 1 starch |
| 7 | 2 | 120 | 1 | 20 | 1 | 1 starch, 1 fat |
| 3.5 | 0.5 | 140 | 2 | 25 | 1½ | 1½ starch |
| 5 | 1 | 105 | 2 | 24 | 1½ | 1½ starch, 1 fat |
| 8 | 1 | 0 | 1 | 23 | 1½ | 1½ starch, 1 fat |
| 7 | 1.5 | 80 | 2 | 21 | 1½ | 1½ starch, 1 fat |

1 Carbohydrate Choice = 1 starch *or* 1 fruit *or* 1 milk exchange

## PRODUCTS

| | SERVING SIZE | CALORIES | CALORIES FROM FAT |
|---|---|---|---|
| Vanilla Creme Wafers, Estee® | 7 wafers | 160 | 70 |
| Vanilla Funky Monkeys, Delicious Frookie® | 16 cookies | 120 | 36 |
| Vanilla Tiny Goldfish, Pepperidge Farm® | 19 pieces | 150 | 60 |
| Vanilla Wafers, Fifty 50® Foods | 5 wafers | 180 | 117 |
| Vanilla Wafers, Sunshine® | 7 cookies | 150 | 60 |

### Vanilla Sandwich Cookies

| | SERVING SIZE | CALORIES | CALORIES FROM FAT |
|---|---|---|---|
| Cookie Break® Vanilla Creme Sandwich, Nabisco® | 3 cookies | 160 | 60 |
| ❶ Vanilla Creme Sandwich, SnackWell's® | 2 cookies | 110 | 20 |
| Vanilla Frookwich, Delicious Frookie® | 2 crackers | 100 | 35 |
| Vanilla Sandwich, Estee® | 3 cookies | 160 | 50 |
| Vanilla Sandwich, Fifty 50® Foods | 3 cookies | 170 | 63 |
| Vanilla Sandwich, Grandma's® | 5 cookies | 210 | 90 |
| Vanilla Sandwich, Nabisco® Family Favorites | 3 cookies | 170 | 70 |
| Vanilla Sandwich, Rippin' Good® | 3 cookies | 160 | 50 |
| ❶ Vanilla Sandwich, Smart Snackers® | 2 cookies | 140 | 25 |

### Other Cookies

| | SERVING SIZE | CALORIES | CALORIES FROM FAT |
|---|---|---|---|
| Bordeaux, Milk Chocolate, Pepperidge Farm® Distinctive Cookies | 3 cookies | 160 | 80 |
| Bordeaux, Pepperidge Farm® Distinctive Cookies | 4 cookies | 130 | 50 |
| Brussels, Mint, Pepperidge Farm® Distinctive Cookies | 3 cookies | 190 | 90 |
| Brussels, Pepperidge Farm® Distinctive Cookies | 3 cookies | 150 | 60 |
| Butter, Fifty 50® Foods | 4 cookies | 160 | 72 |
| Butter Chessman, Pepperidge Farm® Distinctive Cookies | 3 cookies | 120 | 45 |
| Butter Flavored, Sunshine® | 5 cookies | 140 | 50 |
| Chocolate Covered Ritz®, Nabisco® | 3 cookies | 150 | 80 |
| Coconut, Estee® | 4 cookies | 140 | 60 |

❶  Meets Low-Fat Guidelines

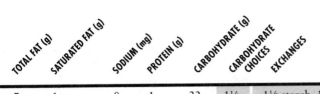

| TOTAL FAT (g) | SATURATED FAT (g) | SODIUM (mg) | PROTEIN (g) | CARBOHYDRATE (g) | CARBOHYDRATE CHOICES | EXCHANGES |
|---|---|---|---|---|---|---|
| 7 | 1 | 0 | <1 | 22 | 1½ | 1½ starch, 1 fat |
| 4 | 0.5 | 130 | 2 | 20 | 1 | 1 starch, ½ fat |
| 7 | 2.5 | 50 | 2 | 21 | 1½ | 1½ starch, 1 fat |
| 13 | 2.5 | 50 | 2 | 18 | 1 | 1 starch, 2 fat |
| 7 | 1.5 | 110 | 2 | 20 | 1 | 1 starch, 1 fat |
| 6 | 1.5 | 115 | 1 | 23 | 1½ | 1½ starch, 1 fat |
| 2.5 | 0.5 | 100 | 1 | 21 | 1½ | 1½ starch |
| 4 | 0 | 60 | 1 | 14 | 1 | 1 starch, ½ fat |
| 5 | 1 | 35 | 2 | 25 | 1½ | 1½ starch, 1 fat |
| 7 | 1.5 | 20 | 2 | 27 | 2 | 2 starch, 1 fat |
| 9 | 2.5 | 110 | 3 | 30 | 2 | 2 starch, 1 fat |
| 8 | 1.5 | 120 | 2 | 25 | 1½ | 1½ starch, 1 fat |
| 6 | 1.5 | 105 | 2 | 25 | 1½ | 1½ starch, 1 fat |
| 3 | 1 | 80 | 1 | 25 | 1½ | 1½ starch |
| 9 | 3.5 | 95 | 2 | 19 | 1 | 1 starch, 2 fat |
| 5 | 2.5 | 95 | 2 | 20 | 1 | 1 starch, 1 fat |
| 10 | 3.5 | 100 | 2 | 22 | 1½ | 1½ starch, 2 fat |
| 7 | 3 | 80 | 2 | 20 | 1 | 1 starch, 1 fat |
| 8 | 5 | 65 | 2 | 20 | 1 | 1 starch, 1 fat |
| 5 | 3 | 80 | 2 | 18 | 1 | 1 starch, 1 fat |
| 6 | 1.5 | 135 | 2 | 21 | 1½ | 1½ starch, 1 fat |
| 9 | 5 | 95 | 2 | 17 | 1 | 1 starch, 2 fat |
| 6 | 2 | 25 | 2 | 19 | 1 | 1 starch, 1 fat |

1 Carbohydrate Choice = 1 starch or 1 fruit or 1 milk exchange

| PRODUCTS | SERVING SIZE | CALORIES | CALORIES FROM FAT |
|---|---|---|---|
| Coconut, Fifty 50® Foods | 4 cookies | 160 | 90 |
| Duplex Sandwich, Fifty 50® Foods | 3 cookies | 160 | 63 |
| Dutch Windmill, Rippin' Good® | 3 cookies | 150 | 60 |
| ❶ Elfin Delights® Creme Sandwich, Keebler® 50% Reduced Fat | 2 cookies | 110 | 25 |
| ❶ Fat-Free Jumbo Cookies, Health Valley®, all varieties (avg) | 1 cookie | 80 | 0 |
| ❶ Fudge Creme, Healthy Choice® | 3 cookies | 130 | 15 |
| Fudge Stripes®, Keebler® | 3 cookies | 160 | 70 |
| Geneva, Pepperidge Farm® Distinctive Cookies | 3 cookies | 160 | 80 |
| Grasshopper®, Keebler® | 4 cookies | 150 | 60 |
| Hazelnut, Pepperidge Farm® Old Fashioned | 3 cookies | 160 | 70 |
| Heyday® Fudge, Caramel and Peanut Bars, Nabisco® | 1 bar | 110 | 45 |
| Lido, Pepperidge Farm® Distinctive Cookies | 1 cookie | 90 | 40 |
| Milano, Double Chocolate, Pepperidge Farm® Distinctive Cookies | 2 cookies | 150 | 70 |
| Milano, Hazelnut, Pepperidge Farm® Distinctive Cookies | 2 cookies | 130 | 70 |
| Milano, Milk Chocolate, Pepperidge Farm® Distinctive Cookies | 3 cookies | 180 | 90 |
| Milano, Mint, Pepperidge Farm® Distinctive Cookies | 2 cookies | 140 | 70 |
| Milano, Orange, Pepperidge Farm® Distinctive Cookies | 2 cookies | 140 | 70 |
| Milano, Pepperidge Farm® Distinctive Cookies | 3 cookies | 180 | 90 |
| Mystic Mint® Sandwich, Nabisco® | 1 cookie | 90 | 35 |
| Pecan Sandies®, Bite Size, Keebler® | 8 cookies | 170 | 90 |
| ❶ Pecan Sandies®, Keebler® 25% Reduced Fat | 1 cookie | 70 | 30 |
| Pecan Sandies® Sandwich with Praline Creme, Keebler® | 1 cookie | 80 | 50 |
| Sweet Spots®, Keebler® | 1 pkg | 120 | 50 |
| Tahoe (White Chunk Macadamia), Pepperidge Farm® American Collection | 1 cookie | 130 | 70 |

❶ Meets Low-Fat Guidelines

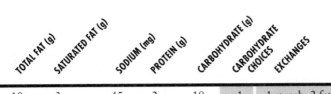

| TOTAL FAT (g) | SATURATED FAT (g) | SODIUM (mg) | PROTEIN (g) | CARBOHYDRATE (g) | CARBOHYDRATE CHOICES | EXCHANGES |
|---|---|---|---|---|---|---|
| 10 | 3 | 45 | 2 | 18 | 1 | 1 starch, 2 fat |
| 7 | 1.5 | 25 | 2 | 26 | 2 | 2 starch, 1 fat |
| 6 | 1.5 | 120 | 2 | 21 | 1½ | 1½ starch, 1 fat |
| 2.5 | 0.5 | 90 | 1 | 19 | 1 | 1 starch |
| 0 | 0 | 35 | 2 | 19 | 1 | 1 starch |
| 2 | 1 | 60 | 1 | 28 | 2 | 2 starch |
| 8 | 4.5 | 140 | 1 | 21 | 1½ | 1½ starch, 1 fat |
| 9 | 3.5 | 95 | 2 | 19 | 1 | 1 starch, 2 fat |
| 7 | 5 | 70 | 1 | 20 | 1 | 1 starch, 1 fat |
| 8 | 2 | 135 | 2 | 21 | 1½ | 1½ starch, 1 fat |
| 5 | 1 | 40 | 2 | 13 | 1 | 1 starch, 1 fat |
| 4.5 | 1.5 | 45 | <1 | 11 | 1 | 1 starch, ½ fat |
| 8 | 3 | 70 | 2 | 17 | 1 | 1 starch, 1 fat |
| 7 | 2 | 65 | 2 | 15 | 1 | 1 starch, 1 fat |
| 10 | 3.5 | 80 | 2 | 21 | 1½ | 1½ starch, 2 fat |
| 8 | 3.5 | 70 | 1 | 16 | 1 | 1 starch, 1 fat |
| 8 | 2.5 | 70 | 1 | 16 | 1 | 1 starch, 1 fat |
| 10 | 3.5 | 80 | 2 | 21 | 1½ | 1½ starch, 2 fat |
| 4 | 1 | 65 | 1 | 11 | 1 | 1 starch, ½ fat |
| 10 | 2 | 95 | 2 | 18 | 1 | 1 starch, 2 fat |
| 3 | 0.5 | 50 | 1 | 10 | ½ | ½ starch, ½ fat |
| 6 | 1.5 | 35 | 1 | 9 | ½ | ½ starch, 1 fat |
| 6 | 3 | 80 | 1 | 17 | 1 | 1 starch, 1 fat |
| 7 | 3 | 110 | 2 | 16 | 1 | 1 starch, 1 fat |

1 Carbohydrate Choice = 1 starch *or* 1 fruit *or* 1 milk exchange

## PRODUCTS

| PRODUCTS | SERVING SIZE | CALORIES | CALORIES FROM FAT |
|---|---|---|---|
| Toffee Sandies®, Keebler® | 1 cookie | 80 | 40 |
| Vienna Fingers™, Sunshine® | 2 cookies | 140 | 50 |
| Vienna Fingers™, Sunshine® Low Fat | 2 cookies | 130 | 30 |
| **COOKING SPRAY** | | | |
| ❶ All brands (avg) | ⅓ second spray | 0 | 0 |
| **CORNBREAD (FROZEN)** | | | |
| ❶ Cornbread, Marie Callender's® and Honey Butter (included in package) | 1 piece 1 Tb | 150 50 | 30 45 |
| **CORNBREAD MIX** | | | |
| ❶ Honey Cornbread & Muffin Mix, Krusteaz®, Fat Free | ¼ cup mix | 120 | 0 |
| ❶ Miracle Maize | ⅓ cup | 170 | 25 |
| **CORN CHIPS** *see* Chips, corn | | | |
| **COTTAGE CHEESE** | | | |
| ❶ Cottage Cheese, all creamed varieties (avg) | ½ cup | 110 | 45 |
| ❶ Cottage Cheese, all dry curd varieties (avg) | ¼ cup | 45 | 0 |
| ❶ Cottage Cheese, all lowfat varieties (avg) | ½ cup | 95 | 20 |
| ❶ Cottage Cheese, all nonfat varieties (avg) | ½ cup | 80 | 0 |
| **CRACKERS** | | | |
| ***Butter Crackers*** | | | |
| ❶ Butter Flavored Thins, Pepperidge Farm® Distinctive Crackers | 4 crackers | 70 | 25 |
| ❶ Classic Golden, SnackWell's® | 6 crackers | 60 | 10 |
| Club, Red Oval Farms® | 4 crackers | 117 | 41 |
| Hi Ho™, Sunshine® | 9 crackers | 160 | 80 |
| Hi Ho™, Sunshine® Reduced Fat | 10 crackers | 140 | 50 |

❶  Meets Low-Fat Guidelines

| TOTAL FAT (g) | SATURATED FAT (g) | SODIUM (mg) | PROTEIN (g) | CARBOHYDRATE (g) | CARBOHYDRATE CHOICES | EXCHANGES |
|---|---|---|---|---|---|---|
| 4.5 | 1 | 55 | <1 | 10 | ½ | ½ starch, 1 fat |
| 6 | 1.5 | 105 | 2 | 21 | 1½ | 1½ starch, 1 fat |
| 3.5 | 0.5 | 95 | 1 | 23 | 1½ | 1½ starch |
| 0 | 0 | 0 | 0 | 0 | 0 | free |
| 3 | 1 | 310 | 2 | 27 | 2 | 2 starch |
| 5 | 2 | 30 | 0 | 2 | 0 | 1 fat |
| 0 | 0 | 410 | 2 | 27 | 2 | 2 starch |
| 2.5 | 0 | 300 | 3 | 32 | 2 | 2 starch |
| 4.5 | 3.5 | 340–440 | 14 | 3.5 | 0 | 2 lean meat |
| 0 | 0 | 25 | 8 | 3 | 0 | 1 very lean meat |
| 2.5 | 1.5 | 380 | 16 | 4 | 0 | 2 lean meat |
| 0 | 0 | 350–440 | 14 | 5 | 0 | 2 very lean meat |
| 3 | 1 | 95 | 1 | 10 | ½ | ½ starch, ½ fat |
| 1 | 0 | 140 | 1 | 11 | 1 | 1 starch |
| 4.5 | NA | 236 | 2 | 15 | 1 | 1 starch, ½ fat |
| 9 | 1.5 | 280 | 2 | 18 | 1 | 1 starch, 2 fat |
| 5 | 1 | 280 | 2 | 21 | 1½ | 1½ starch, ½ fat |

1 Carbohydrate Choice = 1 starch or 1 fruit or 1 milk exchange

## PRODUCTS

| | SERVING SIZE | CALORIES | CALORIES FROM FAT |
|---|---|---|---|
| Ritz Bitz® Mini Ritz Crackers, Nabisco® | 48 crackers | 170 | 80 |
| Ritz®, Nabisco® | 5 crackers | 80 | 35 |
| Ritz®, Nabisco® Low Sodium | 5 crackers | 80 | 35 |

### Cheese Crackers

| | | | |
|---|---|---|---|
| Better Cheddars®, Nabisco® | 22 crackers | 150 | 70 |
| Better Cheddars®, Nabisco® Low Sodium | 22 crackers | 150 | 70 |
| Better Cheddars®, Nabisco® Reduced Fat | 24 crackers | 140 | 50 |
| Cheddar Cheese, Pepperidge Farm® Reduced Sodium | 60 pieces | 150 | 60 |
| Cheddar Cheese Tiny Goldfish Crackers, Pepperidge Farm® | 55 pieces | 140 | 50 |
| ❶ Cheddar Lights, Health Valley®, all varieties (avg) | 1½ cups | 120 | 20 |
| ❶ Cheese, SnackWell's® Reduced Fat | 38 crackers | 130 | 20 |
| Cheese Nips® Snack Crackers, Nabisco® | 29 crackers | 150 | 60 |
| Cheese Tid-Bit® Baked Snack Crackers, Nabisco® | 32 crackers | 150 | 70 |
| Cheez-It™, Sunshine® | 27 crackers | 160 | 80 |
| Cheez-It™, Sunshine® Low Sodium | 27 crackers | 160 | 80 |
| Cheez-It™, Sunshine® Reduced Fat | 30 crackers | 130 | 40 |
| ❶ Krispy™ Mild Cheddar, Sunshine® | 5 crackers | 60 | 20 |
| Nabs® Cheese Peanut Butter Sandwich, Nabisco® | 6 crackers | 190 | 80 |
| Nacho Tortilla Crisps, Nabisco® | 28 crisps | 130 | 35 |
| Parmesan Cheese Tiny Goldfish Crackers, Pepperidge Farm® | 60 pieces | 140 | 50 |
| Ritz Bits® Sandwiches Made with Real Cheese, Nabisco® | 14 pieces | 160 | 80 |
| Swiss Cheese Snack Crackers, Nabisco® | 15 crackers | 140 | 60 |
| ❶ Zesty Cheese, SnackWell's® | 32 crackers | 120 | 20 |

### Graham Crackers

| | | | |
|---|---|---|---|
| ❶ Cinnamon Grahams, Nabisco® Honey Maid® | 10 crackers | 140 | 25 |

❶  Meets Low-Fat Guidelines

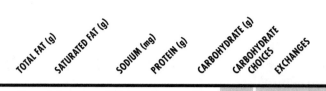

| TOTAL FAT (g) | SATURATED FAT (g) | SODIUM (mg) | PROTEIN (g) | CARBOHYDRATE (g) | CARBOHYDRATE CHOICES | EXCHANGES |
|---|---|---|---|---|---|---|
| 9 | 1.5 | 250 | 2 | 18 | 1 | 1 starch, 2 fat |
| 4 | 0.5 | 135 | 1 | 10 | ½ | ½ starch, ½ fat |
| 4 | 0.5 | 35 | 1 | 10 | ½ | ½ starch, ½ fat |
| | | | | | | |
| 8 | 2 | 290 | 4 | 17 | 1 | 1 starch, 1 fat |
| 7 | 1.5 | 75 | 3 | 18 | 1 | 1 starch, 1 fat |
| 6 | 1.5 | 350 | 3 | 19 | 1 | 1 starch, 1 fat |
| 6 | 1.5 | 140 | 3 | 18 | 1 | 1 starch, 1 fat |
| | | | | | | |
| 6 | 1.5 | 200 | 4 | 19 | 1 | 1 starch, 1 fat |
| | | | | | | |
| 2 | 1 | 280 | 4 | 21 | 1½ | 1½ starch |
| | | | | | | |
| 2 | 0.5 | 340 | 4 | 23 | 1½ | 1½ starch |
| 6 | 1.5 | 310 | 3 | 18 | 1 | 1 starch, 1 fat |
| 8 | 1.5 | 420 | 2 | 17 | 1 | 1 starch, 1 fat |
| | | | | | | |
| 8 | 2 | 240 | 4 | 16 | 1 | 1 starch, 2 fat |
| 8 | 2 | 70 | 4 | 16 | 1 | 1 starch, 2 fat |
| 4.5 | 1 | 280 | 4 | 19 | 1 | 1 starch, 1 fat |
| 2 | 0.5 | 180 | 2 | 10 | ½ | ½ starch |
| 10 | 2 | 390 | 4 | 24 | 1½ | 1½ starch, 2 fat |
| | | | | | | |
| 4 | 0.5 | 150 | 2 | 20 | 1 | 1 starch, ½ fat |
| 5 | 1.5 | 300 | 4 | 19 | 1 | 1 starch, 1 fat |
| | | | | | | |
| 10 | 2.5 | 300 | 3 | 17 | 1 | 1 starch, 2 fat |
| | | | | | | |
| 7 | 1.5 | 350 | 2 | 18 | 1 | 1 starch, 1 fat |
| 2 | 0.5 | 350 | 3 | 23 | 1½ | 1½ starch |
| | | | | | | |
| 3 | 0.5 | 210 | 2 | 26 | 2 | 2 starch |

1 Carbohydrate Choice = 1 starch or 1 fruit or 1 milk exchange

| PRODUCTS | SERVING SIZE | CALORIES | CALORIES FROM FAT |
|---|---|---|---|
| ❶ Cinnamon Grahams, SnackWell's® | 20 pieces | 110 | 0 |
| Cinnamon Grahams, Sunshine® | 2 crackers | 140 | 50 |
| ❶ Graham, Health Valley® Fat-Free, all varieties (avg) | 11 crackers | 100 | 0 |
| ❶ Honey Grahams, Delicious Frookie® | 2 cookies | 130 | 25 |
| ❶ Honey Grahams, Nabisco® Honey Maid® | 8 crackers | 120 | 25 |
| Honey Grahams, Sunshine® | 2 crackers | 120 | 40 |

**Sandwich Crackers**

| | | | |
|---|---|---|---|
| Nabs® Peanut Butter Toast Sandwich, Nabisco® | 6 crackers | 190 | 80 |
| Peanut Butter & Cheese Crackers, Eagle® | 6 crackers | 230 | 110 |
| Peanut Butter on Toast Crackers, Eagle® | 6 crackers | 210 | 90 |
| Ritz Bits® Sandwiches with Real Peanut Butter, Nabisco® | 13 crackers | 150 | 70 |

**Saltine Crackers**

| | | | |
|---|---|---|---|
| ❶ Krispy™, Sunshine® | 5 crackers | 60 | 10 |
| ❶ Krispy™, Sunshine® Fat Free | 5 crackers | 60 | 0 |
| ❶ Krispy™ Soup & Oyster, Sunshine® | 17 crackers | 60 | 15 |
| ❶ Krispy™ Unsalted Tops, Sunshine® | 5 crackers | 60 | 10 |
| ❶ Oysterettes® Soup and Oyster Crackers, Nabisco® | 19 crackers | 60 | 20 |
| Premium Bits, Nabisco® | 34 crackers | 150 | 60 |
| ❶ Premium, Nabisco®, Fat Free | 5 crackers | 50 | 0 |
| ❶ Premium, Nabisco®, Low Sodium | 5 crackers | 60 | 10 |
| ❶ Premium, Nabisco®, Original | 5 crackers | 60 | 15 |
| ❶ Premium, Nabisco®, Unsalted Tops | 5 crackers | 60 | 15 |
| ❶ Premium Soup and Oyster Crackers, Nabisco® | 23 crackers | 60 | 15 |
| ❶ Soup and Oyster Crackers, Keebler® Zesta | 42 crackers | 70 | 25 |
| ❶ Zesta®, Keebler® 50% Reduced Sodium | 5 crackers | 60 | 20 |
| ❶ Zesta®, Keebler® Fat Free | 5 crackers | 50 | 0 |
| ❶ Zesta® Original, Keebler® | 5 crackers | 60 | 20 |

❶ Meets Low-Fat Guidelines

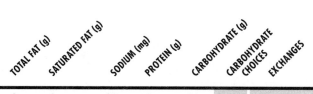

| TOTAL FAT (g) | SATURATED FAT (g) | SODIUM (mg) | PROTEIN (g) | CARBOHYDRATE (g) | CARBOHYDRATE CHOICES | EXCHANGES |
|---|---|---|---|---|---|---|
| 0 | 0 | 90 | 2 | 26 | 2 | 2 starch |
| 6 | 1.5 | 150 | 2 | 22 | 1½ | 1½ starch, 1 fat |
| 0 | 0 | 30 | 4 | 23 | 1½ | 1½ starch |
| 2 | 0.5 | 120 | 2 | 21 | 1½ | 1½ starch |
| 3 | 0.5 | 180 | 2 | 22 | 1½ | 1½ starch |
| 4 | 1 | 130 | 2 | 20 | 1 | 1 starch, ½ fat |
| 10 | 2 | 380 | 4 | 24 | 1½ | 1½ starch, 2 fat |
| 12 | 2 | 320 | 6 | 25 | 1½ | 1½ starch, 2 fat |
| 10 | 2.5 | 430 | 5 | 23 | 1½ | 1½ starch, 2 fat |
| 8 | 1.5 | 130 | 4 | 17 | 1 | 1 starch, 1 fat |
| 1.5 | 0 | 180 | 2 | 10 | ½ | ½ starch |
| 0 | 0 | 135 | 2 | 12 | 1 | 1 starch |
| 1.5 | 0 | 200 | 2 | 11 | 1 | 1 starch |
| 1.5 | 0 | 120 | 2 | 10 | ½ | ½ starch |
| 2.5 | 0.5 | 150 | 1 | 10 | ½ | ½ starch |
| 7 | 1 | 340 | 2 | 19 | 1 | 1 starch, 1 fat |
| 0 | 0 | 130 | 1 | 11 | 1 | 1 starch |
| 1 | 0 | 35 | 1 | 10 | ½ | ½ starch |
| 1.5 | 0 | 180 | 1 | 10 | ½ | ½ starch |
| 1.5 | 0 | 135 | 1 | 10 | ½ | ½ starch |
| 1.5 | 0 | 230 | 1 | 11 | 1 | 1 starch |
| 2.5 | 1 | 160 | 1 | 10 | ½ | ½ starch, ½ fat |
| 2 | 0.5 | 95 | 1 | 11 | 1 | 1 starch |
| 0 | 0 | 90 | 1 | 11 | 1 | 1 starch |
| 2 | 0.5 | 190 | 1 | 10 | ½ | ½ starch |

1 Carbohydrate Choice = 1 starch or 1 fruit or 1 milk exchange

## PRODUCTS

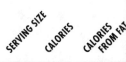

| PRODUCTS | SERVING SIZE | CALORIES | CALORIES FROM FAT |
|---|---|---|---|
| ● Zesta® Unsalted Tops, Keebler® | 5 crackers | 70 | 20 |
| **Wheat Crackers** | | | |
| ● Cracked Wheat, Pepperidge Farm® Distinctive Crackers | 2 crackers | 70 | 25 |
| ● Frookwheats, Delicious Frookie®, all varieties (avg) | 10 crackers | 60 | 0 |
| Hearty Wheat, Pepperidge Farm® Distinctive Crackers | 3 crackers | 80 | 30 |
| Hi Ho™ Whole Wheat, Sunshine® | 9 crackers | 150 | 70 |
| ● Krispy™ Whole Wheat, Sunshine® | 5 crackers | 60 | 10 |
| ● Mini Stoned Wheat Thins, Red Oval Farms® | 16 crackers | 105 | 22.5 |
| ● Stoned Wheat Thins, Red Oval Farms® | 4 crackers | 107 | 22.5 |
| ● Stoned Wheat Thins, Red Oval Farms® Low Salt | 4 crackers | 108 | 22.5 |
| Triscuit® Wafers, Garden Herb, Nabisco® | 6 wafers | 130 | 40 |
| Triscuit® Wafers, Nabisco® | 7 wafers | 140 | 45 |
| Triscuit® Wafers, Nabisco®, Low Sodium | 7 wafers | 150 | 50 |
| ● Triscuit® Wafers, Nabisco®, Reduced Fat | 8 wafers | 130 | 25 |
| Triscuit® Wafers, Whole Wheat 'n Bran, Nabisco® | 7 wafers | 140 | 45 |
| Triscuit® Wafers, Whole Wheat 'n Rye, Nabisco® | 7 wafers | 140 | 45 |
| ● Wheat, SnackWell's® | 5 crackers | 60 | 0 |
| ● Wheat, SnackWell's® Fat Free | 5 crackers | 60 | 0 |
| Wheatables, Keebler®, all regular varieties (avg) | 25 crackers | 150 | 63 |
| Wheatables, Keebler®, 50% Reduced Sodium | 25 crackers | 150 | 70 |
| Wheatables, Keebler®, Reduced Fat | 29 crackers | 130 | 30 |
| ● Wheatsworth® Stoned Ground Wheat Crackers, Nabisco® | 5 crackers | 80 | 30 |
| Wheat Thins®, Nabisco® Low Salt | 16 crackers | 140 | 50 |
| Wheat Thins®, Nabisco® Multi-Grain | 17 crackers | 130 | 35 |
| Wheat Thins®, Nabisco® Original | 16 crackers | 140 | 50 |
| Wheat Thins®, Nabisco® Reduced Fat | 18 crackers | 120 | 35 |

● Meets Low-Fat Guidelines

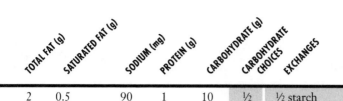

| TOTAL FAT (g) | SATURATED FAT (g) | SODIUM (mg) | PROTEIN (g) | CARBOHYDRATE (g) | CARBOHYDRATE CHOICES | EXCHANGES |
|---|---|---|---|---|---|---|
| 2 | 0.5 | 90 | 1 | 10 | ½ | ½ starch |
| 2.5 | 1 | 150 | 1 | 9 | ½ | ½ starch |
| 0 | 0 | 65 | 1 | 13 | 1 | 1 starch |
| 3.5 | 0 | 100 | 2 | 10 | ½ | ½ starch, ½ fat |
| 8 | 1.5 | 280 | 3 | 18 | 1 | 1 starch, 2 fat |
| 1.5 | 0 | 130 | 2 | 10 | ½ | ½ starch |
| 2.5 | NA | 217 | 3 | 18 | 1 | 1 starch |
| 2.5 | NA | 217 | 3 | 18 | 1 | 1 starch |
| 2.5 | NA | 125 | 3 | 18 | 1 | 1 starch |
| 4.5 | 1 | 130 | 3 | 28 | 2 | 2 starch |
| 5 | 1 | 170 | 3 | 21 | 1½ | 1½ starch, ½ fat |
| 6 | 1 | 50 | 3 | 21 | 1½ | 1½ starch, 1 fat |
| 3 | 0.5 | 180 | 3 | 24 | 1½ | 1½ starch |
| 5 | 1 | 170 | 3 | 22 | 1½ | 1½ starch, ½ fat |
| 5 | 1 | 180 | 3 | 22 | 1½ | 1½ starch, 1 fat |
| 0 | 0 | 170 | 2 | 12 | 1 | 1 starch |
| 0 | 0 | 170 | 2 | 12 | 1 | 1 starch |
| 7 | 2 | 325 | 3 | 18 | 1 | 1 starch, 1½ fat |
| 7 | 2 | 160 | 3 | 18 | 1 | 1 starch, 1½ fat |
| 3.5 | 1 | 320 | 3 | 21 | 1½ | 1½ starch |
| 2.5 | 0.5 | 170 | 2 | 10 | ½ | ½ starch |
| 6 | 1 | 75 | 2 | 20 | 1 | 1 starch, 1 fat |
| 4 | 0.5 | 290 | 2 | 21 | 1½ | 1½ starch, ½ fat |
| 6 | 1 | 170 | 2 | 19 | 1 | 1 starch, 1 fat |
| 4 | 0.5 | 220 | 2 | 21 | 1½ | 1½ starch, ½ fat |

1 Carbohydrate Choice = 1 starch or 1 fruit or 1 milk exchange

## PRODUCTS

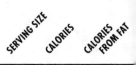

| | SERVING SIZE | CALORIES | CALORIES FROM FAT |
|---|---|---|---|
| **Other Crackers** | | | |
| Chicken in a Biskit®, Nabisco® | 14 crackers | 160 | 80 |
| ❶ Cracked Pepper Water Biscuit, Pepperidge Farm® International Collection | 5 crackers | 60 | 10 |
| ❶ Cracked Pepper, SnackWell's® | 7 crackers | 60 | 0 |
| ❶ Cracked Pepper, Sunshine® Krispy™ | 5 crackers | 60 | 10 |
| ❶ Crackers, Health Valley® Fat-Free, all regular varieties (avg) | 6 crackers | 50 | 0 |
| ❶ French Onion, SnackWell's® | 32 crackers | 120 | 15 |
| Garden Crisps® Vegetable, Nabisco® | 15 crackers | 130 | 30 |
| ❶ Garlic & Herb, Delicious Frookie® | 4 crackers | 35 | 0 |
| Harvest Crisps® Five Grain, Nabisco® | 13 crackers | 130 | 30 |
| Harvest Crisps® Oat, Nabisco® | 13 crackers | 140 | 40 |
| Original Tiny Goldfish Crackers, Pepperidge Farm® | 55 pieces | 140 | 60 |
| Pizza Tiny Goldfish Crackers, Pepperidge Farm® | 55 pieces | 140 | 60 |
| ❶ Sesame, Pepperidge Farm® Distinctive Crackers | 3 crackers | 70 | 25 |
| Sociables®, Nabisco® | 7 crackers | 80 | 35 |
| ❶ Stoned Rye Crackers, Red Oval Farms® | 4 crackers | 105 | 23 |
| Vegetable Thins® Snack Crackers, Nabisco® | 14 crackers | 160 | 80 |
| ❶ Water Biscuit, Pepperidge Farm® International Collection Original | 5 crackers | 60 | 10 |
| ❶ Water Crackers, Delicious Frookie® | 4 crackers | 35 | 0 |
| Waverly® Crackers, Nabisco® | 5 crackers | 70 | 30 |
| **CRANBERRY SAUCE** | | | |
| ❶ Jellied, Festal® | ¼ cup | 100 | 0 |
| ❶ Jellied, Ocean Spray® | ¼ cup | 110 | 0 |
| ❶ Whole, Festal® | ¼ cup | 100 | 0 |
| ❶ Whole Berry, Ocean Spray® | ¼ cup | 110 | 0 |

❶  Meets Low-Fat Guidelines

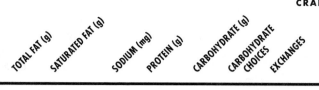

| TOTAL FAT (g) | SATURATED FAT (g) | SODIUM (mg) | PROTEIN (g) | CARBOHYDRATE (g) | CARBOHYDRATE CHOICES | EXCHANGES |
|---|---|---|---|---|---|---|
| 9 | 1.5 | 270 | 2 | 17 | 1 | 1 starch, 2 fat |
| 1 | 0.5 | 90 | 2 | 12 | 1 | 1 starch |
| 0 | 0 | 150 | 2 | 13 | 1 | 1 starch |
| 1.5 | 0 | 180 | 2 | 10 | ½ | ½ starch |
| 0 | 0 | 80 | 2 | 11 | 1 | 1 starch |
| 2 | 0 | 290 | 2 | 23 | 1½ | 1½ starch |
| 3.5 | 0.5 | 290 | 2 | 22 | 1½ | 1½ starch |
| 0 | 0 | 120 | 1 | 7 | ½ | ½ starch |
| 3.5 | 0.5 | 300 | 3 | 23 | 1½ | 1½ starch |
| 4.5 | 1 | 300 | 3 | 22 | 1½ | 1½ starch, ½ fat |
| 6 | 2 | 230 | 3 | 19 | 1 | 1 starch, 1 fat |
| 6 | 1.5 | 160 | 3 | 19 | 1 | 1 starch, 1 fat |
| 2.5 | 0 | 95 | 1 | 9 | ½ | ½ starch |
| 4 | 0.5 | 150 | 1 | 9 | ½ | ½ starch, 1 fat |
| 2.5 | NA | 179 | 3 | 18 | 1 | 1 starch |
| 9 | 1.5 | 310 | 2 | 19 | 1 | 1 starch, 2 fat |
| 1 | 0.5 | 100 | 2 | 11 | 1 | 1 starch |
| 0 | 0 | 40 | 1 | 7 | ½ | ½ starch |
| 3.5 | 1 | 135 | 1 | 10 | ½ | ½ starch, ½ fat |
| 0 | 0 | 15 | 0 | 26 | 2 | 2 fruit |
| 0 | 0 | 35 | 0 | 27 | 2 | 2 fruit |
| 0 | 0 | 15 | 0 | 26 | 2 | 2 fruit |
| 0 | 0 | 35 | 0 | 28 | 2 | 2 fruit |

1 Carbohydrate Choice = 1 starch *or* 1 fruit *or* 1 milk exchange

| PRODUCTS | SERVING SIZE | CALORIES | CALORIES FROM FAT |
|---|---|---|---|
| **CREAM CHEESE** | | | |
| Cream Cheese, brick or soft, plain or flavored, all varieties (avg) | 2 Tb | 105 | 85 |
| ❶ Fat Free Cream Cheese, all varieties (avg) | 2 Tb | 30 | 0 |
| Light Cream Cheese, all varieties (avg) | 2 Tb | 70 | 50 |
| Whipped Cream Cheese, all varieties (avg) | 3 Tb | 105 | 85 |
| **CROUTONS** | | | |
| ❶ Homestyle, Pepperidge Farm®, all varieties (avg) | 6–9 croutons | 30 | 10 |
| ❶ Regular, Pepperidge Farm®, all varieties (avg) | 9 croutons | 35 | 10 |
| ❶ Salad Toppers, Pepperidge Farm®, all varieties (avg) | 1 Tb | 35 | 15 |
| ❶ Salad Crispins®, all varieties (avg) | 1 Tb | 35 | 9 |
| **DESSERT BAR MIX (AS PREPARED)** | | | |
| Apple Streusel, Pillsbury® Deluxe Bar Mix | ¹⁄₂₄ pkg | 150 | 50 |
| Caramel Oatmeal Dessert Bar, Betty Crocker® | 1 bar | 180 | 70 |
| Chips Ahoy™, Pillsbury® Deluxe Bar Mix | ¹⁄₁₈ pkg | 180 | 60 |
| Chocolate Chunk Dessert Bar, Betty Crocker® | 1 bar | 120 | 40 |
| Chocolate Peanut Butter Dessert Bar, Betty Crocker® | 1 bar | 200 | 80 |
| Easy Layer Dessert Bar, Betty Crocker® | 1 bar | 140 | 50 |
| Fudge Swirl Cookie, Pillsbury® Deluxe Bar Mix | ¹⁄₂₀ pkg | 180 | 70 |
| Hershey® Cookie Bars, Betty Crocker® | 1 bar | 140 | 50 |
| Lemon Cheesecake, Pillsbury® Deluxe Bar Mix | ¹⁄₂₄ pkg | 180 | 90 |
| M&M's Cookie Bars, Betty Crocker® | 1 bar | 170 | 60 |
| Nutter Butter™, Pillsbury® Deluxe Bar Mix | ¹⁄₁₈ pkg | 180 | 60 |
| Oreo™, Pillsbury® Deluxe Bar Mix | ¹⁄₂₄ pkg | 150 | 50 |
| Raspberry Dessert Bar, Betty Crocker® | 1 bar | 170 | 50 |
| S'mores Dessert Bar, Betty Crocker® | 1 bar | 180 | 70 |
| Strawberry Swirl Cheese Cake Bars, Betty Crocker® | 1 bar | 210 | 110 |

❶  Meets Low-Fat Guidelines

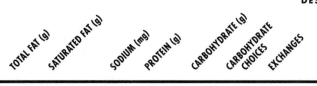

| TOTAL FAT (g) | SATURATED FAT (g) | SODIUM (mg) | PROTEIN (g) | CARBOHYDRATE (g) | CARBOHYDRATE CHOICES | EXCHANGES |
|---|---|---|---|---|---|---|
| 9.5 | 6.5 | 90–200 | 1.5 | 2.5 | 0 | 2 fat |
| 0 | 0 | 135–200 | 4.5 | 2 | 0 | 1 very lean meat |
| 5 | 3.5 | 80–150 | 3 | 2 | 0 | 1 fat |
| 10 | 6.5 | 95–200 | 2 | 1.5 | 0 | 2 fat |
| 1 | 0 | 65–90 | 1 | 4 | 0 | free |
| 1.5 | 0 | 65–95 | 1 | 4 | 0 | free |
| 2 | 0 | 25–85 | 1 | 4 | 0 | free |
| 1 | NA | 115 | <1 | 4 | 0 | free |
| 6 | 1.5 | 55 | 1 | 23 | 1½ | 1½ starch, 1 fat |
| 8 | 2 | 115 | 2 | 24 | 1½ | 1½ starch, 1 fat |
| 7 | 2 | 125 | 2 | 26 | 2 | 2 starch, 1 fat |
| 4.5 | 1.5 | 85 | 1 | 17 | 1 | 1 starch, ½ fat |
| 9 | 2.5 | 190 | 3 | 25 | 1½ | 1½ starch, 1½ fat |
| 6 | 3 | 105 | 1 | 21 | 1½ | 1½ starch, 1 fat |
| 8 | 1.5 | 110 | 1 | 25 | 1½ | 1½ starch, 1 fat |
| 6 | 1.5 | 130 | 1 | 21 | 1½ | 1½ starch, 1 fat |
| 10 | 3.5 | 50 | 2 | 20 | 1 | 1 starch, 2 fat |
| 7 | 2 | 140 | 1 | 24 | 1½ | 1½ starch, 1 fat |
| 7 | 1.5 | 170 | 3 | 26 | 2 | 2 starch, 1 fat |
| 6 | 1.5 | 130 | 1 | 22 | 1½ | 1½ starch, 1 fat |
| 6 | 1.5 | 160 | 2 | 26 | 2 | 2 starch, ½ fat |
| 7 | 1.5 | 140 | 2 | 26 | 2 | 2 starch, 1 fat |
| 12 | 3.5 | 80 | 2 | 23 | 1½ | 1½ starch, 2 fat |

1 Carbohydrate Choice = 1 starch or 1 fruit or 1 milk exchange

## PRODUCTS

| | SERVING SIZE | CALORIES | CALORIES FROM FAT |
|---|---|---|---|
| Sunkist® Lemon Dessert Bar, Betty Crocker® | 1 bar | 140 | 40 |
| **DESSERT BARS (FROZEN)** | | | |
| Brownie à la Mode, Weight Watchers® | 1 brownie | 190 | 40 |
| ❶ Chocolate Frosted Brownie, Weight Watchers® | 1 brownie | 100 | 20 |
| ❶ Double Fudge Brownie Parfait, Weight Watchers® | 1 parfait | 190 | 25 |
| Figurines, Pillsbury®, all varieties (avg) | 2 bars | 220 | 100 |
| ❶ Peanut Butter Fudge Brownie, Weight Watchers® | 1 brownie | 110 | 20 |
| **DESSERT BARS (READY-TO-EAT)** | | | |
| Apple Oatmeal Spice Bar, Grandma's® | 1 bar | 170 | 50 |
| ❶ Blueberry Dessert Bar, Betty Crocker® Sweet Rewards™ | 1 bar | 120 | 0 |
| Chocolate Fudge Bar, Grandma's® | 1 bar | 190 | 60 |
| ❶ Chocolate Sandwich Bars, Health Valley®, all varieties (avg) | 1 bar | 150 | 0 |
| Classic Munchie, Campfire® (1.7 oz) | 1 bar | 180 | 30 |
| ❶ Crisp Rice Bars, Health Valley® Fat-Free, all varieties (avg) | 1 bar | 110 | 0 |
| ❶ Fruit Bars, Health Valley® Fat-Free, all varieties (avg) | 1 bar | 140 | 0 |
| ❶ Healthy Cheesecake Bars, Health Valley® No Fat Added, all varieties (avg) | 1 bar | 160 | 15 |
| ❶ Lemon Dessert Bar, Betty Crocker® Sweet Rewards™ | 1 bar | 120 | 0 |
| ❶ Low Fat Munchie, Campfire® (1.7 oz) | 1 bar | 170 | 25 |
| ❶ Marshmallow Bars, Health Valley® Fat-Free, all varieties (avg) | 1 bar | 90 | 0 |
| ❶ Rice Krispies Treats Squares, Kellogg's® | 1 bar | 90 | 20 |
| ❶ Strawberry Dessert Bar, Betty Crocker® Sweet Rewards™ | 1 bar | 120 | 0 |
| **DESSERT BARS (REFRIGERATED)** | | | |
| Fudge Brownies, Pillsbury® | ½₀ pkg | 160 | 50 |

❶ Meets Low-Fat Guidelines

| TOTAL FAT (g) | SATURATED FAT (g) | SODIUM (mg) | PROTEIN (g) | CARBOHYDRATE (g) | CARBOHYDRATE CHOICES | EXCHANGES |
|---|---|---|---|---|---|---|
| 4.5 | 1 | 90 | 2 | 24 | 1½ | 1½ starch, ½ fat |
| | | | | | | |
| 4 | 1.5 | 170 | 5 | 34 | 2 | 2 starch, ½ fat |
| 2.5 | 1 | 135 | 2 | 22 | 1½ | 1½ starch |
| 2.5 | 2 | 170 | 6 | 39 | 2½ | 2½ starch |
| 11 | 2.5 | 110 | 5 | 24 | 1½ | 1½ starch, 2 fat |
| 2.5 | 0.5 | 140 | 2 | 21 | 1½ | 1½ starch |
| | | | | | | |
| 5 | 1.5 | 270 | 2 | 28 | 2 | 2 starch, ½ fat |
| 0 | 0 | 70 | 1 | 29 | 2 | 2 starch |
| 7 | 2.5 | 160 | 2 | 29 | 2 | 2 starch, 1 fat |
| 0 | 0 | 30 | 3 | 35 | 2 | 2 starch |
| 3.5 | 0.5 | 210 | 2 | 35 | 2 | 2 starch |
| 0 | 0 | 5 | 1 | 26 | 2 | 2 starch |
| 0 | 0 | 4 | 3 | 35 | 2 | 2 starch |
| 1.5 | 0 | 30 | 3 | 34 | 2 | 2 starch |
| 0 | 0 | 65 | 1 | 29 | 2 | 2 starch |
| 3 | 0 | 180 | 2 | 36 | 2½ | 2½ starch |
| 0 | 0 | 10 | 1 | 22 | 1½ | 1½ starch |
| 2 | 0 | 75 | 1 | 18 | 1 | 1 starch |
| 0 | 0 | 70 | 1 | 29 | 2 | 2 starch |
| | | | | | | |
| 6 | 1.5 | 110 | 2 | 24 | 1½ | 1½ starch, 1fat |

1 Carbohydrate Choice = 1 starch or 1 fruit or 1 milk exchange

## PRODUCTS

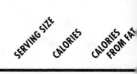

### DESSERT MIX (AS PREPARED)

| | SERVING SIZE | CALORIES | CALORIES FROM FAT |
|---|---|---|---|
| Banana Cream Chilled Dessert Mix, Betty Crocker® | ⅑ dessert | 250 | 90 |
| ❶ Blueberry Fruit Dessert, Sans Sucre® | ¼ cup | 60 | 0 |
| Boston Cream Pie, Betty Crocker® | ⅒ pie | 200 | 35 |
| ❶ Cake Mix, Sweet 'N Low®, all varieties (avg) | ⅙ cake | 140 | 30 |
| Cheesecake Jell-O® No Bake Dessert (Blueberry, Cherry, Strawberry, avg) | ⅙ cake | 330 | 110 |
| Cheesecake Jell-O® No Bake Dessert (Real, Homestyle, avg) | ⅙ cake | 355 | 140 |
| ❶ Cheesecake Mousse, Sans Sucre® | ½ cup | 75 | 15 |
| ❶ Chocolate Cheesecake Mousse, Sans Sucre® | ½ cup | 75 | 15 |
| Chocolate French Silk Chilled Dessert Mix, Betty Crocker® | ⅛ dessert | 270 | 100 |
| ❶ Chocolate Mousse, Sans Sucre® | ½ cup | 70 | 25 |
| Chocolate Pudding Cake, Betty Crocker® | ⅛ cake | 170 | 30 |
| Chocolate Silk Pie, Jell-O® No Bake Dessert | ⅙ pie | 310 | 140 |
| ❶ Cinnamon Apple Fruit Dessert, Sans Sucre® | ¼ cup | 60 | 0 |
| Coconut Cream Dessert Mix, Betty Crocker® | ⅑ dessert | 290 | 120 |
| Coconut Cream Pie, Jell-O® No Bake Dessert | ⅙ pie | 330 | 170 |
| Cookies & Cream Dessert Mix, Betty Crocker® | ⅙ dessert | 360 | 130 |
| ❶ French Vanilla Mousse, Sans Sucre® | ½ cup | 70 | 20 |
| Gingerbread Cake and Cookie Mix, Betty Crocker® | ⅛ pkg | 230 | 60 |
| ❶ Gingerbread Mix, Sweet 'N Low® Lite | ⅙ cake | 150 | 30 |
| Golden Pound Cake, Betty Crocker® | ⅛ cake | 290 | 110 |
| ❶ Key Lime Pie Filling and Mousse, Sans Sucre® | ½ cup | 75 | 25 |
| ❶ Lemon Chiffon Cake, Betty Crocker® | 1/16 cake | 140 | 30 |
| ❶ Lemon Mousse, Sans Sucre® | ½ cup | 70 | 20 |
| Lemon Pudding Cake, Betty Crocker® | ⅛ cake | 180 | 35 |
| ❶ Mocha Cappuccino Mousse, Sans Sucre® | ½ cup | 70 | 25 |
| ❶ Pina Colada Fruit Dessert, Sans Sucre® | ¼ cup | 70 | 15 |

❶  Meets Low-Fat Guidelines

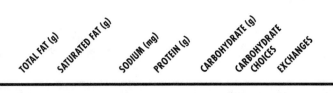

| TOTAL FAT (g) | SATURATED FAT (g) | SODIUM (mg) | PROTEIN (g) | CARBOHYDRATE (g) | CARBOHYDRATE CHOICES | EXCHANGES |
|---|---|---|---|---|---|---|
| 11 | 3 | 430 | 4 | 35 | 2 | 2 starch, 2 fat |
| 0 | 0 | 10 | 0 | 14 | 1 | 1 fruit |
| 4 | 1.5 | 300 | 3 | 38 | 2½ | 2½ starch |
| 3 | 1 | 30 | 2 | 30 | 2 | 2 starch |
| 12 | 4 | 395 | 5 | 50 | 3 | 3 starch, 2 fat |
| 15 | 5 | 510–550 | 6 | 47 | 3 | 3 starch, 2½ fat |
| 1.5 | <1 | 80 | 4 | 7 | ½ | ½ starch or ½ milk |
| 1.5 | <1 | 80 | 4 | 7 | ½ | ½ starch or ½ milk |
| 11 | 4 | 250 | 5 | 39 | 2½ | 2½ starch, 2 fat |
| 2.5 | 1 | 25 | 1 | 6 | ½ | ½ starch |
| 3.5 | 1 | 180 | 2 | 33 | 2 | 2 starch |
| 16 | 6 | 490 | 5 | 38 | 2½ | 2½ starch, 3 fat |
| 0 | 0 | 10 | 0 | 14 | 1 | 1 fruit |
| 13 | 6 | 480 | 5 | 38 | 2½ | 2½ starch, 2 fat |
| 19 | 9 | 410 | 4 | 37 | 2½ | 2½ starch, 3 fat |
| 15 | 4.5 | 460 | 5 | 52 | 3½ | 3½ starch, 2 fat |
| 2 | 1 | 25 | 1 | 7 | ½ | ½ starch |
| 7 | 2 | 370 | 3 | 38 | 2½ | 2½ starch, 1 fat |
| 3 | 1 | 30 | 2 | 30 | 2 | 2 starch |
| 12 | 3.5 | 240 | 4 | 41 | 3 | 3 starch, 2 fat |
| 3 | 1.5 | 40 | 1 | 7 | ½ | ½ starch, ½ fat |
| 3 | 0.5 | 140 | 3 | 26 | 2 | 2 starch |
| 2 | 1 | 25 | 1 | 7 | ½ | ½ starch |
| 4 | 1 | 210 | 2 | 33 | 2 | 2 starch |
| 2.5 | 1 | 25 | 1 | 6 | ½ | ½ starch |
| 1.5 | 1 | 10 | 0 | 12 | 1 | 1 fruit |

1 Carbohydrate Choice = 1 starch *or* 1 fruit *or* 1 milk exchange

## PRODUCTS

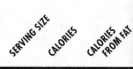

| PRODUCTS | SERVING SIZE | CALORIES | CALORIES FROM FAT |
|---|---|---|---|
| Pineapple Upside Down Cake, Betty Crocker® | ⅙ cake | 400 | 130 |
| ❶ Strawberry Fruit Dessert, Sans Sucre® | ¼ cup | 60 | 0 |
| ❶ Strawberry Mousse, Sans Sucre® | ½ cup | 70 | 20 |
| Sunkist® Lemon Supreme, Betty Crocker® | ⅑ dessert | 320 | 110 |

### DESSERTS, INDIVIDUAL (FROZEN)

| | SERVING SIZE | CALORIES | CALORIES FROM FAT |
|---|---|---|---|
| Blueberry Cheesecake, Cafe Classics | 5 oz | 230 | 100 |
| Brownie Cheesecake, Weight Watchers® | 1 cake | 200 | 50 |
| ❶ Caramel Fudge à la Mode, Weight Watchers® | 1 cake | 160 | 30 |
| Caramel Nut Bars, Weight Watchers® | 1 bar | 130 | 70 |
| Chocolate Cappuccino, Cafe Classics | 5 oz | 270 | 110 |
| Chocolate Chip Cookie Dough Sundae, Weight Watchers® | 1 sundae | 180 | 40 |
| Chocolate Eclair, Weight Watchers® | 1 eclair | 150 | 35 |
| Chocolate Mousse, Weight Watchers® | 1 mousse | 190 | 45 |
| ❶ Chocolate Mousse Bar, Weight Watchers® | 1 bar | 70 | 10 |
| ❶ Chocolate Raspberry Royale, Weight Watchers® | 1 cake | 190 | 30 |
| Creme Caramel, Cafe Classics | 5 oz | 260 | 110 |
| Crispy Pralines 'n Creme Bars, Weight Watchers® | 1 bar | 130 | 60 |
| Double Fudge Cake, Weight Watchers® | 1 cake | 190 | 40 |
| English Toffee Crunch Bars, Weight Watchers® | 1 bar | 120 | 60 |
| French Style Cheesecake, Weight Watchers® | 1 cake | 180 | 45 |
| New York Style Cheesecake, Weight Watchers® | 1 cake | 150 | 45 |
| Praline Pecan Mousse, Weight Watchers® | 1 mousse | 170 | 35 |
| ❶ Praline Toffee Crunch Parfait, Weight Watchers® | 1 parfait | 190 | 25 |
| Raspberry Peach Melba, Cafe Classics | 5 oz | 220 | 90 |
| ❶ Strawberry Parfait Royale, Weight Watchers® | 1 parfait | 180 | 20 |
| Triple Chocolate Caramel Mousse, Weight Watchers® | 1 mousse | 200 | 40 |
| Triple Chocolate Cheesecake, Weight Watchers® | 1 cake | 200 | 45 |

❶  Meets Low-Fat Guidelines

| TOTAL FAT (g) | SATURATED FAT (g) | SODIUM (mg) | PROTEIN (g) | CARBOHYDRATE (g) | CARBOHYDRATE CHOICES | EXCHANGES |
|---|---|---|---|---|---|---|
| 15 | 4 | 350 | 3 | 63 | 4 | 3 starch, 1 fruit, 2 fat |
| 0 | 0 | 10 | 0 | 14 | 1 | 1 fruit |
| 2 | 1 | 25 | 1 | 7 | ½ | ½ starch |
| 13 | 3.5 | 140 | 2 | 52 | 3½ | 3½ starch, 2 fat |
| 11 | 7 | 210 | 5 | 30 | 2 | 2 starch, 2 fat |
| 6 | 2 | 220 | 9 | 33 | 2 | 2 starch, 1 fat |
| 3 | 1 | 180 | 4 | 29 | 2 | 2 starch |
| 8 | 3.5 | 25 | 2 | 14 | 1 | 1 starch, 1 fat |
| 12 | 7 | 230 | 4 | 37 | 2½ | 2½ starch, 2 fat |
| 4 | 1.5 | 115 | 3 | 33 | 2 | 2 starch, ½ fat |
| 4 | 1 | 160 | 2 | 25 | 1½ | 1½ starch, ½ fat |
| 5 | 1.5 | 150 | 6 | 31 | 2 | 2 starch, ½ fat |
| 1 | 0.5 | 80 | 4 | 18 | 1 | 1 starch |
| 3 | 1 | 190 | 5 | 39 | 2½ | 2½ starch |
| 12 | 7 | 190 | 5 | 33 | 2 | 2 starch, 2 fat |
| 7 | 3.5 | 40 | 2 | 15 | 1 | 1 starch, 1 fat |
| 4.5 | 1 | 200 | 4 | 36 | 2½ | 2½ starch |
| 7 | 3.5 | 25 | 1 | 12 | 1 | 1 starch, 1 fat |
| 5 | 2 | 230 | 7 | 28 | 2 | 2 starch, ½ fat |
| 5 | 2 | 140 | 6 | 21 | 1½ | 1½ starch, ½ fat |
| 3.5 | 1 | 140 | 4 | 31 | 2 | 2 starch |
| 3 | 2 | 140 | 5 | 40 | 2½ | 2½ starch |
| 11 | 6 | 190 | 4 | 27 | 2 | 1 starch, 1 fruit, 2 fat |
| 2 | 1 | 100 | 5 | 35 | 2 | 2 starch |
| 4 | 1 | 120 | 5 | 34 | 2 | 2 starch, ½ fat |
| 5 | 2.5 | 200 | 7 | 32 | 2 | 2 starch, ½ fat |

1 Carbohydrate Choice = 1 starch or 1 fruit or 1 milk exchange

## PRODUCTS

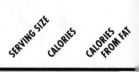

| PRODUCTS | SERVING SIZE | CALORIES | CALORIES FROM FAT |
|---|---|---|---|
| Triple Chocolate Eclair, Weight Watchers® | 1 eclair | 160 | 45 |
| Vanilla Sandwich Bar, Weight Watchers® | 1 bar | 160 | 35 |

### DIP (CAN OR JAR)

| PRODUCTS | SERVING SIZE | CALORIES | CALORIES FROM FAT |
|---|---|---|---|
| ❶ Bean Dip, Old Dutch® | 2 Tb | 30 | 5 |
| ❶ Black Bean Dip, Eagle® | 2 Tb | 35 | 10 |
| ❶ Black Bean Dip, Old El Paso® | 2 Tb | 20 | 0 |
| ❶ Cheese 'n Salsa Dip, Old El Paso®, all varieties (avg) | 2 Tb | 40 | 25 |
| ❶ Cheese and Salsa Dip, Eagle® | 2 Tb | 40 | 25 |
| French Onion Dip, Old Dutch® | 2 Tb | 50 | 40 |
| ❶ Jalapeno Dip, Old El Paso® | 2 Tb | 30 | 10 |
| ❶ Mild Bean Dip, Eagle® | 2 Tb | 40 | 15 |
| ❶ Mild Cheddar Dip, Old Dutch® | 2 Tb | 45 | 30 |
| Nacho Cheese Dip, Old Dutch® | 2 Tb | 50 | 35 |
| Ranch Dip, Old Dutch® | 2 Tb | 50 | 40 |
| ❶ Spicy BBQ Black Bean Dip, Guiltless Gourmet® | 2 Tb | 35 | 0 |
| ❶ Spicy BBQ Pinto Bean Dip, Guiltless Gourmet® | 2 Tb | 40 | 0 |
| ❶ Spicy Black Bean Dip, Guiltless Gourmet® | 2 Tb | 30 | 0 |
| ❶ Spicy Nacho Dip, Guiltless Gourmet® | 2 Tb | 25 | 0 |
| ❶ Spicy Pinto Bean Dip, Guiltless Gourmet® | 2 Tb | 35 | 0 |

### DIP (REFRIGERATED)

| PRODUCTS | SERVING SIZE | CALORIES | CALORIES FROM FAT |
|---|---|---|---|
| ❶ Bacon Horseradish Dip, Land O' Lakes® No-Fat | 2 Tb | 30 | 0 |
| ❶ Cucumber Dill Dip, Land O' Lakes® No-Fat | 2 Tb | 30 | 0 |
| ❶ Dill Dip, Old Home® Light | 2 Tb | 40 | 20 |
| ❶ French Onion Dip, Land O' Lakes® No-Fat | 2 Tb | 30 | 0 |
| Mild Guacamole Dip, Old Home® | 2 Tb | 60 | 45 |
| ❶ Ranch Dip, Land O' Lakes® No-Fat | 2 Tb | 30 | 0 |
| Ranch Snack Dip, Old Home® | 2 Tb | 50 | 35 |
| ❶ Salsa Dip, Land O' Lakes® No-Fat | 2 Tb | 25 | 0 |
| ❶ Southwestern Dip, Old Home® Light | 2 Tb | 45 | 20 |

❶ Meets Low-Fat Guidelines

| TOTAL FAT (g) | SATURATED FAT (g) | SODIUM (mg) | PROTEIN (g) | CARBOHYDRATE (g) | CARBOHYDRATE CHOICES | EXCHANGES |
|---|---|---|---|---|---|---|
| 5 | 1 | 190 | 3 | 25 | 1½ | 1½ starch, ½ fat |
| 3.5 | 2 | 180 | 4 | 30 | 2 | 2 starch |
| | | | | | | |
| 0.5 | 0 | 90 | 1 | 5 | 0 | free |
| 1 | 0 | 220 | 2 | 5 | 0 | free |
| 0 | 0 | 150 | 1 | 4 | 0 | free |
| 3 | 1 | 300 | <1 | 3 | 0 | ½ fat |
| | | | | | | |
| 3 | 1 | 300 | 1 | 3 | 0 | ½ fat |
| 4 | 2 | 150 | 1 | 3 | 0 | 1 fat |
| 1 | 0 | 125 | 1 | 4 | 0 | free |
| 1.5 | 0 | 160 | 2 | 5 | 0 | free |
| 3 | 1 | 170 | <1 | 3 | 0 | ½ fat |
| 4 | 1 | 260 | <1 | 3 | 0 | 1 fat |
| 4.5 | 2.5 | 260 | 1 | 3 | 0 | 1 fat |
| 0 | 0 | 125 | 2 | 6 | ½ | ½ starch |
| 0 | 0 | 110 | 2 | 7 | ½ | ½ starch |
| 0 | 0 | 100 | 2 | 5 | 0 | free |
| 0 | 0 | 150 | 1 | 5 | 0 | free |
| 0 | 0 | 100 | 2 | 6 | ½ | ½ starch |
| | | | | | | |
| 0 | 0 | 175 | 2 | 5 | 0 | free |
| | | | | | | |
| 0 | 0 | 130 | 1 | 6 | ½ | ½ starch |
| 2.5 | 0 | 160 | 1 | 3 | 0 | ½ fat |
| 0 | 0 | 320 | 1 | 5 | 0 | free |
| 5 | 1 | 140 | <1 | 3 | 0 | 1 fat |
| 0 | 0 | 180 | 1 | 6 | ½ | ½ starch |
| 4 | 1.5 | 105 | 1 | 3 | 0 | 1 fat |
| 0 | 0 | 290 | 1 | 5 | 0 | free |
| 2.5 | 0 | 160 | 2 | 3 | 0 | ½ fat |

1 Carbohydrate Choice = 1 starch or 1 fruit or 1 milk exchange

## PRODUCTS

| | SERVING SIZE | CALORIES | CALORIES FROM FAT |
|---|---|---|---|
| Spicy Guacamole Dip, Old Home® | 2 Tb | 60 | 40 |
| ❶ Spinach Dip, Old Home® Light | 2 Tb | 45 | 20 |
| Spinach Dip, Old Home® Pride | 2 Tb | 90 | 80 |

### DRINK MIX (AS PREPARED)

| | | | |
|---|---|---|---|
| ❶ Country Time®, all varieties (avg) | 8 fl oz | 70 | 0 |
| ❶ Country Time® Sugar Free, all varieties (avg) | 8 fl oz | 5 | 0 |
| ❶ Crystal Light® Soft Drink, all varieties (avg) | 8 fl oz | 5 | 0 |
| ❶ Kool-Aid® Sugar Free Low Calorie Drink, all varieties (avg) | 8 fl oz | 5 | 0 |
| ❶ Kool-Aid® Sugar Sweetened Drink, all varieties (avg) | 8 fl oz | 65 | 0 |
| ❶ Kool-Aid® Unsweetened Soft Drink all varieties (avg) | 8 fl oz | 100 | 0 |
| ❶ Tang® Drink, all varieties (avg) | 8 fl oz | 100 | 0 |
| ❶ Tang® Sugar Free Low-Calorie Drink | 8 fl oz | 5 | 0 |

### EGG PRODUCTS, LOW-CHOLESTEROL

| | | | |
|---|---|---|---|
| ❶ Better'n Eggs™, Morningstar Farms® | ¼ cup | 20 | 0 |
| ❶ Egg Beaters® | ¼ cup | 30 | 0 |
| ❶ Scramblers, Morningstar Farms® | ¼ cup | 35 | 0 |
| ❶ Second Nature® No Fat Real Egg Product | ¼ cup | 40 | 0 |

### EGG ROLLS (FROZEN)

#### Mini Egg Rolls

| | | | |
|---|---|---|---|
| BBQ-Flavored Beef & Pork Egg Rolls, Yu Sing® | 10 rolls | 340 | 130 |
| BBQ-Flavored Chicken Egg Rolls, Yu Sing® | 10 rolls | 280 | 70 |
| Chicken Egg Rolls, Chun King® | 12 rolls | 400 | 120 |
| Chicken Egg Rolls, La Choy® | 14 rolls | 430 | 100 |
| Chicken Egg Rolls, Yu Sing® | 10 rolls | 290 | 90 |
| Chinese Style Vegetables with Lobster Egg Rolls, La Choy® | 14 rolls | 410 | 100 |
| Pork & Shrimp Bite Size Egg Rolls, La Choy® | 15 rolls | 240 | 80 |

❶ Meets Low-Fat Guidelines

| TOTAL FAT (g) | SATURATED FAT (g) | SODIUM (mg) | PROTEIN (g) | CARBOHYDRATE (g) | CARBOHYDRATE CHOICES | EXCHANGES |
|---|---|---|---|---|---|---|
| 4.5 | 1 | 170 | <1 | 3 | 0 | 1 fat |
| 2.5 | 0 | 135 | 1 | 3 | 0 | ½ fat |
| 9 | 3 | 135 | 1 | 2 | 0 | 2 fat |
| | | | | | | |
| 0 | 0 | 10 | 0 | 17 | 1 | 1 fruit |
| 0 | 0 | 40 | 0 | 0 | 0 | free |
| 0 | 0 | 5–60 | 0 | 0 | 0 | free |
| 0 | 0 | 0 | 0 | 0 | 0 | free |
| | | | | | | |
| 0 | 0 | 0 | 0 | 16 | 1 | 1 fruit |
| 0 | 0 | 20 | 0 | 25 | 1½ | 1½ fruit |
| 0 | 0 | 0 | 0 | 25 | 1½ | 1½ fruit |
| 0 | 0 | 0 | 0 | 1 | 0 | free |
| | | | | | | |
| 0 | 0 | 90 | 5 | 0 | 0 | 1 very lean meat |
| 0 | 0 | 100 | 6 | 1 | 0 | 1 very lean meat |
| 0 | 0 | 95 | 6 | 2 | 0 | 1 very lean meat |
| 0 | 0 | 115 | 6 | 3 | 0 | 1 very lean meat |
| | | | | | | |
| 14 | 3 | 430 | 8 | 45 | 3 | 3 starch, 1 meat, 1 fat |
| 8 | 2 | 290 | 13 | 40 | 2½ | 2½ starch, 1 meat |
| 14 | 3 | 510 | 11 | 58 | 4 | 4 starch, 2 fat |
| 11 | 2.5 | 900 | 15 | 67 | 4½ | 4½ starch, 1 meat |
| 10 | 6 | 420 | 10 | 40 | 2½ | 2½ starch, 1 meat, ½ fat |
| 11 | 2.5 | 690 | 13 | 65 | 4 | 4 starch, 1 meat |
| 9 | 2 | 350 | 8 | 31 | 2 | 2 starch, 1 meat |

1 Carbohydrate Choice = 1 starch or 1 fruit or 1 milk exchange

## PRODUCTS

| | SERVING SIZE | CALORIES | CALORIES FROM FAT |
|---|---|---|---|
| Pork & Shrimp Egg Rolls, Chun King® | 12 rolls | 420 | 150 |
| Pork & Shrimp Egg Rolls, La Choy® | 14 rolls | 430 | 110 |
| Pork & Shrimp Egg Rolls, Yu Sing® | 10 rolls | 280 | 60 |
| Shrimp Egg Rolls, Chun King® | 12 rolls | 370 | 100 |
| Shrimp Egg Rolls, La Choy® | 14 rolls | 410 | 80 |
| Shrimp Egg Rolls, Yu Sing® | 10 rolls | 290 | 80 |
| Sweet & Sour Chicken Egg Rolls, Yu Sing® | 10 rolls | 330 | 90 |
| Sweet & Sour Pork Egg Rolls, Yu Sing® | 10 rolls | 300 | 70 |
| ***Regular Egg Rolls*** | | | |
| Chicken Egg Rolls, Chun King® | 1 roll | 170 | 50 |
| Chicken Egg Rolls, La Choy® | 1 roll | 170 | 50 |
| Moo Shu Pork Egg Rolls, La Choy® | 1 roll | 190 | 60 |
| Pork Egg Rolls, Chun King® | 1 roll | 170 | 50 |
| Pork Egg Rolls, La Choy® | 1 roll | 170 | 50 |
| Shrimp Egg Rolls, Chun King® | 1 roll | 150 | 35 |
| Shrimp Egg Rolls, La Choy® | 1 roll | 150 | 35 |
| Sweet & Sour Chicken Egg Rolls, La Choy® | 1 roll | 180 | 40 |
| Vegetarian Egg Rolls, Worthington® | 1 roll | 180 | 80 |

### ENGLISH MUFFINS

| | SERVING SIZE | CALORIES | CALORIES FROM FAT |
|---|---|---|---|
| ❶ English muffin, small (avg) | 1 muffin | 120 | 10 |
| ❶ English muffin, medium (avg) | 1 muffin | 140 | 10 |
| ❶ English muffin, large (avg) | 1 muffin | 220 | 10 |

### FISH (FROZEN)
*see also* Seafood

| | SERVING SIZE | CALORIES | CALORIES FROM FAT |
|---|---|---|---|
| Battered Fish Fillets, Van de Kamp's® | 1 fillet | 180 | 100 |
| Battered Fish Sticks, Van de Kamp's® | 6 sticks | 260 | 140 |
| Breaded Fish Fillets, Van de Kamp's® | 2 fillets | 280 | 170 |
| Breaded Fish Sticks, Van de Kamp's® | 6 sticks | 290 | 150 |
| ❶ Crisp & Healthy™ Baked Breaded Fish Fillets, Van de Kamp's® | 2 fillets | 150 | 25 |

❶ Meets Low-Fat Guidelines

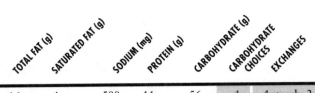

| TOTAL FAT (g) | SATURATED FAT (g) | SODIUM (mg) | PROTEIN (g) | CARBOHYDRATE (g) | CARBOHYDRATE CHOICES | EXCHANGES |
|---|---|---|---|---|---|---|
| 16 | 4 | 500 | 11 | 56 | 4 | 4 starch, 2 fat |
| 12 | 3 | 890 | 15 | 65 | 4 | 4 starch, 1 meat, ½ fat |
| 7 | 2.5 | 630 | 12 | 42 | 3 | 3 starch, 1 lean meat |
| 11 | 2 | 700 | 10 | 57 | 4 | 4 starch, 1 fat |
| 9 | 2 | 990 | 14 | 68 | 4½ | 4½ starch, 1 meat |
| 9 | 2.5 | 380 | 19 | 32 | 2 | 2 starch, 2 lean meat |
| 10 | 3 | 380 | 11 | 49 | 3 | 3 starch, 1 meat |
| 8 | 2 | 220 | 10 | 47 | 3 | 3 starch, 1 meat |
| | | | | | | |
| 5 | 2.5 | 450 | 7 | 25 | 1½ | 1½ starch, 1 lean meat |
| 5 | 2.5 | 450 | 7 | 25 | 1½ | 1½ starch, 1 lean meat |
| 7 | 1.5 | 330 | 6 | 25 | 1½ | 1½ starch, 1½ fat |
| 6 | 1.5 | 390 | 6 | 23 | 1½ | 1½ starch, 1 fat |
| 6 | 1.5 | 390 | 6 | 23 | 1½ | 1½ starch, 1 fat |
| 4 | 0.5 | 420 | 6 | 24 | 1½ | 1½ starch, ½ fat |
| 4 | 0.5 | 420 | 6 | 24 | 1½ | 1½ starch, ½ fat |
| 4 | 1 | 300 | 6 | 29 | 2 | 2 starch |
| 8 | 1.5 | 380 | 6 | 20 | 1 | 1 starch, 1 meat, ½ fat |
| | | | | | | |
| 1 | 0 | 190 | 4 | 21–25 | 1½ | 1½ starch |
| 1 | 0 | 170–320 | 6 | 26–35 | 2 | 2 starch |
| 1 | 0 | 290–540 | 8 | 41–50 | 3 | 3 starch |
| | | | | | | |
| 11 | 1.5 | 340 | 8 | 12 | 1 | 1 starch, 1 meat, 1 fat |
| 16 | 3 | 540 | 11 | 18 | 1 | 1 starch, 1 meat, 2 fat |
| 19 | 3 | 270 | 11 | 17 | 1 | 1 starch, 1 meat, 2½ fat |
| 17 | 2.5 | 390 | 13 | 23 | 1½ | 1½ starch, 1 meat, 2 fat |
| 2.5 | 0.5 | 380 | 12 | 20 | 1 | 1 starch, 1 lean meat |

1 Carbohydrate Choice = 1 starch *or* 1 fruit *or* 1 milk exchange

## PRODUCTS

| PRODUCTS | SERVING SIZE | CALORIES | CALORIES FROM FAT |
|---|---|---|---|
| Crispy Crunch Breaded Fish Fillets, Mrs. Paul's® | 2 fillets | 230 | 90 |
| Crunch Breaded Fish Sticks, Mrs. Paul's® | 5 sticks | 210 | 81 |
| Crunchy Golden Fish Fillets, Gorton's® | 2 fillets | 250 | 130 |
| Garlic and Herb Crunchy Fish Fillets, Gorton's® | 2 fillets | 250 | 120 |
| Golden Fish Sticks, Gorton's® | 6 sticks | 260 | 130 |
| Grilled Fish Fillets, Gorton's®, all varieties (avg) | 1 fillet | 120 | 50 |
| Grilled Fish Fillets, Mrs. Paul's®, all varieties (avg) | 1 fillet | 130 | 50 |
| Haddock Fillets in Batter, Van de Kamp's® | 2 fillets | 260 | 140 |
| Lemon Pepper Battered Fish Fillets, Gorton's® | 2 fillets | 250 | 120 |
| Lightly Breaded Flounder Fillets, Van de Kamp's® | 1 fillet | 230 | 100 |
| Ocean Perch Fillets in Batter, Van de Kamp's® | 2 fillets | 300 | 180 |
| Southern Fried Country Style Crunchy Breaded Fish Fillets, Gorton's® | 2 fillets | 270 | 150 |

### FISH MEALS/ENTREES (FROZEN)
see also Seafood Meals/Entrees

| | | | |
|---|---|---|---|
| Fish Fillet with Macaroni & Cheese, Stouffer's® Homestyle | 1 pkg | 430 | 190 |
| Fish 'n Chips, Swanson® | 1 pkg | 500 | 180 |
| Fish 'n Chips, Swanson® Homestyle Entrees | 1 pkg | 310 | 108 |
| ❶ Grilled Fish with Vegetables, Stouffer's® Lean Cuisine® Cafe Classics | 1 pkg | 170 | 45 |
| ❶ Lemon Pepper Fish, Healthy Choice® | 1 meal | 290 | 45 |

### FRENCH FRIES (FROZEN)
see also Hash Browns/Home Fries, Potato Side Dishes

| | | | |
|---|---|---|---|
| ❶ Country Style Dinner Fries®, Ore-Ida | 84 g | 110 | 27 |
| Crispers!®, Ore-Ida® | ~17 fries | 220 | 117 |
| Crispy Crowns!®, Ore-Ida® | 84 g | 190 | 99 |
| Crispy Crunchies!®, Ore-Ida® | 84 g | 160 | 81 |
| Deep Fries Crinkle Cuts, Ore-Ida® | 84 g | 160 | 63 |

❶ Meets Low-Fat Guidelines

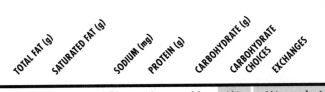

| TOTAL FAT (g) | SATURATED FAT (g) | SODIUM (mg) | PROTEIN (g) | CARBOHYDRATE (g) | CARBOHYDRATE CHOICES | EXCHANGES |
|---|---|---|---|---|---|---|
| 10 | NA | NA | 13 | 22 | 1½ | 1½ starch, 1 lean meat, 1 fat |
| 9 | NA | NA | 10 | 20 | 1 | 1 starch, 1 lean meat, 1 fat |
| 14 | 4 | 480 | 11 | 21 | 1½ | 1½ starch, 1 meat, 1 fat |
| 13 | 4 | 700 | 11 | 21 | 1½ | 1½ starch, 1 meat, 1 fat |
| 14 | 3.5 | 480 | 11 | 22 | 1½ | 1½ starch, 1 meat, 1 fat |
| 6 | 1 | 160–370 | 16 | 1 | 0 | 2 lean meat |
| 6 | 1 | 230 | 18 | 0 | 0 | 2½ lean meat |
| 16 | 2.5 | 530 | 13 | 18 | 1 | 1 starch, 2 meat, 1 fat |
| 13 | 4 | 700 | 11 | 21 | 1½ | 1½ starch, 1 meat, 2 fat |
| 11 | 1.5 | 400 | 15 | 19 | 1 | 1 starch, 2 meat |
| 20 | 2.5 | 480 | 12 | 19 | 1 | 1 starch, 2 meat, 2 fat |
| 16 | 4 | 660 | 11 | 20 | 1 | 1 starch, 1 meat, 2 fat |
| 21 | 5 | 930 | 24 | 37 | 2½ | 2½ starch, 2 lean meat, 3 fat |
| 20 | NA | NA | 19 | 59 | 4 | 3½ starch, 1 veg, 1 meat, 3 fat |
| 12 | NA | NA | 12 | 38 | 2½ | 2 starch, 1 veg, 1 meat, 1 fat |
| 5 | 1 | 520 | 16 | 14 | 1 | ½ starch, 1 veg, 2 lean meat |
| 5 | 1 | 360 | 14 | 47 | 3 | 3 starch, 1 lean meat |
| 3 | NA | NA | 2 | 19 | 1 | 1 starch |
| 13 | NA | NA | 2 | 24 | 1½ | 1½ starch, 2 fat |
| 11 | NA | NA | 2 | 21 | 1½ | 1½ starch, 2 fat |
| 9 | NA | NA | 2 | 18 | 1 | 1 starch, 2 fat |
| 7 | NA | NA | 2 | 23 | 1½ | 1½ starch, 1 fat |

1 Carbohydrate Choice = 1 starch *or* 1 fruit *or* 1 milk exchange

## PRODUCTS

| | SERVING SIZE | CALORIES | CALORIES FROM FAT |
|---|---|---|---|
| Deep Fries French Fries, Ore-Ida® | 84 g | 160 | 63 |
| Extra Zesty Snackin' Fries™, Ore-Ida® | 140 g | 340 | 180 |
| Fast Fries™, Ore-Ida® | ~23 pieces | 140 | 54 |
| ● French Fry Style Potatoes, Basic Country Goodness™ Fat Free | 20 pieces | 70 | 0 |
| French Fries, Inland Valley® Fries-To-Go™ | 1 box | 260 | 130 |
| French Fries, Micro Magic® | 1 box | 220 | 90 |
| Golden Crinkles®, Ore-Ida® | ~14 fries | 120 | 32 |
| Golden Fries®, Ore-Ida® | ~16 fries | 120 | 36 |
| Golden Twirls™, Ore-Ida® | ~10 pieces | 160 | 63 |
| Nacho Crispers™, Ore-Ida® | ~17 fries | 170 | 81 |
| Pixie Crinkles®, Ore-Ida® | ~33 fries | 140 | 45 |
| Ranch Flavor Fast Fries™, Ore-Ida® | ~23 pieces | 150 | 63 |
| Shoestrings, Ore-Ida® | ~38 fries | 150 | 45 |
| Snackin' Fries™, Ore-Ida® | 140 g | 340 | 180 |
| Tater ABC's™, Ore-Ida® | 84 g | 190 | 99 |
| Texas Crispers™, Ore-Ida® | ~7 wedges | 170 | 90 |
| Waffle Fries, Ore-Ida® | ~9 pieces | 140 | 45 |
| Zesties!®, Ore-Ida® | ~12 fries | 160 | 81 |

### FRENCH TOAST (FROZEN)

| | | | |
|---|---|---|---|
| Cinnamon, Aunt Jemima® | 2 pieces | 240 | 50 |
| Cinnamon Swirl, Krusteaz® | 2 slices | 230 | 50 |
| Classic Style, Krusteaz® | 2 slices | 230 | 50 |
| Original, Aunt Jemima® | 2 pieces | 240 | 50 |
| ● Sourdough, Krusteaz® | 1 slice | 140 | 20 |

### FROSTING (READY-TO-SPREAD)

| | | | |
|---|---|---|---|
| ● Betty Crocker® Creamy Deluxe® Low Fat, all varieties (avg) | 2 Tb | 120 | 10 |
| Betty Crocker® Creamy Deluxe®, all varieties (avg) | 2 Tb | 150 | 50 |

● Meets Low-Fat Guidelines

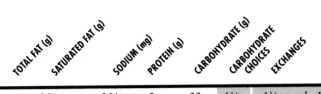

| TOTAL FAT (g) | SATURATED FAT (g) | SODIUM (mg) | PROTEIN (g) | CARBOHYDRATE (g) | CARBOHYDRATE CHOICES | EXCHANGES |
|---|---|---|---|---|---|---|
| 7 | NA | NA | 2 | 22 | 1½ | 1½ starch, 1 fat |
| 20 | NA | NA | 4 | 35 | 2 | 2 starch, 4 fat |
| 6 | NA | NA | 2 | 18 | 1 | 1 starch, 1 fat |
| 0 | 0 | 5 | 2 | 15 | 1 | 1 starch |
| 14 | 6 | 75 | 3 | 30 | 2 | 2 starch, 2 fat |
| 10 | 2.5 | 45 | 3 | 27 | 2 | 2 starch, 1½ fat |
| 3.5 | NA | NA | 2 | 20 | 1 | 1 starch |
| 4 | NA | NA | 2 | 20 | 1 | 1 starch, ½ fat |
| 7 | NA | NA | 2 | 22 | 1½ | 1½ starch, 1 fat |
| 9 | NA | NA | 2 | 21 | 1½ | 1½ starch, 1 fat |
| 5 | NA | NA | 3 | 21 | 1½ | 1½ starch, ½ fat |
| 7 | NA | NA | 2 | 21 | 1½ | 1½ starch, 1 fat |
| 5 | NA | NA | 2 | 22 | 1½ | 1½ starch, ½ fat |
| 20 | NA | NA | 4 | 35 | 2 | 2 starch, 4 fat |
| 11 | NA | NA | 2 | 20 | 1 | 1 starch, 2 fat |
| 10 | NA | NA | 2 | 19 | 1 | 1 starch, 2 fat |
| 5 | NA | NA | 2 | 22 | 1½ | 1½ starch, ½ fat |
| 9 | NA | NA | 2 | 19 | 1 | 1 starch, 2 fat |
| 6 | 2 | 330 | 9 | 37 | 2½ | 2½ starch, 1 fat |
| 5 | 1 | 540 | 9 | 36 | 2½ | 2½ starch, ½ fat |
| 5 | 1 | 540 | 9 | 36 | 2½ | 2½ starch, ½ fat |
| 6 | 1.5 | 360 | 9 | 38 | 2½ | 2½ starch, 1 fat |
| 2 | 0.5 | 280 | 6 | 24 | 1½ | 1½ starch |
| 1 | 0.5 | 25–55 | 0 | 27 | 2 | 2 fruit |
| 6 | 1.5 | 35–85 | 0 | 24 | 1½ | 1½ fruit, 1 fat |

1 Carbohydrate Choice = 1 starch *or* 1 fruit *or* 1 milk exchange

## PRODUCTS

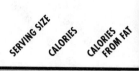

| | SERVING SIZE | CALORIES | CALORIES FROM FAT |
|---|---|---|---|
| Pillsbury Creamy Supreme®, all varieties except Coconut Pecan (avg) | 2 Tb | 145 | 55 |
| Pillsbury® Frosting Supreme®, all varieties with nuts or coconut (avg) | 2 Tb | 160 | 80 |
| Pillsbury Frosting Supreme®, all varieties without nuts or coconut (avg) | 2 Tb | 145 | 55 |
| ❶ Pillsbury Frosting Supreme® Lovin Lites®, all varieties (avg) | 2 Tb | 135 | 25 |

### FROZEN YOGURT
*see* Yogurt, frozen

### FRUIT (CANNED)

| | SERVING SIZE | CALORIES | CALORIES FROM FAT |
|---|---|---|---|
| ❶ Fruit (peaches, pears, pineapple, fruit cocktail) in heavy syrup, all brands (avg) | ½ cup | 95 | 0 |
| ❶ Fruit (peaches, pears, pineapple, fruit cocktail) in light syrup/juice, all brands (avg) | ½ cup | 60 | 0 |

### FRUIT SNACKS

| | SERVING SIZE | CALORIES | CALORIES FROM FAT |
|---|---|---|---|
| ❶ Apple Chips, Smart Snackers® | 1 bag | 70 | 0 |
| ❶ Fruit by the Foot® (cherry, grape or strawberry, avg) | 1 roll | 80 | 15 |
| ❶ Fruit Leather, Stretch Island Fruit®, all varieties (avg) | 2 pieces | 90 | 0 |
| ❶ Fruit Roll-Ups®, all varieties (avg) | 2 rolls | 110 | 10 |
| ❶ Fruit Roll-Ups® Pouch, all varieties (avg) | 1 roll | 50 | 5 |
| ❶ Fruit Snacks, Smart Snackers® | 1 pouch | 50 | 0 |
| ❶ Fruit String Thing™, all varieties (avg) | 1 pouch | 80 | 10 |
| ❶ Fun Snacks, Betty Crocker®, all shapes (avg) | 1 pouch | 90 | 10 |
| ❶ Gushers®, all varieties (avg) | 1 pouch | 90 | 10 |

### GARLIC BREAD (FROZEN)

| | SERVING SIZE | CALORIES | CALORIES FROM FAT |
|---|---|---|---|
| 5 Cheese Garlic Bread, Joseph Campione | ⅙ loaf | 170 | 90 |
| Garlic & Olive Oil Loaves, Pepperidge Farm® Reduced Fat | 2½" | 170 | 60 |
| Hearth Baked Garlic Bread, Joseph Campione | 2 oz | 180 | 80 |

❶ Meets Low-Fat Guidelines

| TOTAL FAT (g) | SATURATED FAT (g) | SODIUM (mg) | PROTEIN (g) | CARBOHYDRATE (g) | CARBOHYDRATE CHOICES | EXCHANGES |
|---|---|---|---|---|---|---|
| 6 | 1.5 | 45–95 | 0 | 22 | 1½ | 1½ fruit, 1 fat |
| 9 | 4 | 60 | 0 | 18 | 1 | 1 fruit, 2 fat |
| 6 | 1.5 | 45–95 | 0 | 23 | 1½ | 1½ fruit, 1 fat |
| 3 | 1 | 80 | 0 | 27 | 2 | 2 fruit, ½ fat |
| 0 | 0 | 15 | 0 | 24 | 1½ | 1½ fruit |
| 0 | 0 | 10 | 0 | 15 | 1 | 1 fruit |
| 0 | 0 | 125 | 0 | 18 | 1 | 1 fruit |
| 1.5 | 0.5 | 40 | 0 | 17 | 1 | 1 fruit |
| 0 | 0 | 3 | 0 | 24 | 1½ | 1½ fruit |
| 1 | 0.5 | 105 | 0 | 24 | 1½ | 1½ fruit |
| 0.5 | 0 | 50 | 0 | 12 | 1 | 1 fruit |
| 0 | 0 | 125 | 0 | 13 | 1 | 1 fruit |
| 1 | 0 | 40 | 0 | 17 | 1 | 1 fruit |
| 1 | 0 | 25 | 0 | 21 | 1½ | 1½ fruit |
| 1 | 0 | 45 | 0 | 20 | 1 | 1 fruit |
| 10 | 4 | 270 | 7 | 14 | 1 | 1 starch, 1 high fat meat |
| 7 | 1.5 | 290 | 4 | 23 | 1½ | 1½ starch, 1 fat |
| 9 | 2 | 370 | 5 | 21 | 1½ | 1½ starch, 1 fat |

1 Carbohydrate Choice = 1 starch or 1 fruit or 1 milk exchange

## PRODUCTS

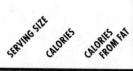

| | SERVING SIZE | CALORIES | CALORIES FROM FAT |
|---|---|---|---|
| ❶ Hearth Baked Light Garlic Bread, Joseph Campione | 2 oz | 100 | 10 |
| Mozzarella Garlic Cheese Bread, Pepperidge Farm® | ⅙ loaf | 200 | 90 |
| Original Garlic Bread, Cole's® | ⅛ loaf | 180 | 90 |
| Parmesan Garlic Crusty Italian Bread, Pepperidge Farm® | 2½" | 170 | 70 |
| Two Cheddar Cheese Bread, Pepperidge Farm® | ⅙ loaf | 210 | 100 |
| Zesty Italian Garlic Loaves, Pepperidge Farm® Reduced Fat | 2½" | 160 | 60 |

### GELATIN

| | SERVING SIZE | CALORIES | CALORIES FROM FAT |
|---|---|---|---|
| ❶ Gelatin Snacks, all regular varieties (avg) | 1 snack | 80 | 0 |
| ❶ Gelatin Snacks, all sugar-free, low-calorie varieties (avg) | 1 snack | 10 | 0 |

### GRAHAM CRACKERS
*see* Crackers

### GRANOLA BARS

#### Grandma's® Granola Bars

| | SERVING SIZE | CALORIES | CALORIES FROM FAT |
|---|---|---|---|
| Soft Granola Bar | 1 bar | 180 | 50 |

#### Health Valley® Granola Bars

| | SERVING SIZE | CALORIES | CALORIES FROM FAT |
|---|---|---|---|
| ❶ Granola Fruit Bars, Fat-Free | 1 bar | 140 | 0 |
| ❶ Granola Bar Variety Pack | 1 bar | 140 | 0 |

#### Kellogg's® Granola Bars

| | SERVING SIZE | CALORIES | CALORIES FROM FAT |
|---|---|---|---|
| ❶ Crunchy Almond & Brown Sugar Granola Bars, Low Fat | 1 bar | 80 | 15 |
| Rice Krispies® Chewy Granola Bar with Chocolate Chips | 1 bar | 120 | 35 |

#### Nature Valley® Granola Bars

| | SERVING SIZE | CALORIES | CALORIES FROM FAT |
|---|---|---|---|
| ❶ Chewy Granola Bars, Low Fat, all varieties (avg) | 1 bar | 110 | 15 |
| Chocolate Chip Granola Bars | 2 bars | 220 | 80 |

❶  Meets Low-Fat Guidelines

| TOTAL FAT (g) | SATURATED FAT (g) | SODIUM (mg) | PROTEIN (g) | CARBOHYDRATE (g) | CARBOHYDRATE CHOICES | EXCHANGES |
|---|---|---|---|---|---|---|
| 1 | 0 | 180 | 4 | 19 | 1 | 1 starch |
| 10 | 5 | 280 | 6 | 21 | 1½ | 1½ starch, 1½ fat |
| 9 | 2 | 260 | 3 | 20 | 1 | 1 starch, 2 fat |
| 7 | 2.5 | 280 | 6 | 20 | 1 | 1 starch, 1 fat |
| 11 | 5 | 280 | 5 | 21 | 1½ | 1½ starch, 2 fat |
| 6 | 2 | 320 | 4 | 24 | 1½ | 1½ starch, 1 fat |
| 0 | 0 | 45 | 0 | 20 | 1 | 1 fruit |
| 0 | 0 | 50 | 0 | 0 | 0 | free |
| 6 | 1.5 | 260 | 3 | 29 | 2 | 2 starch, 1 fat |
| 0 | 0 | 5 | 2 | 35 | 2 | 2 starch |
| 0 | 0 | 5 | 2 | 35 | 2 | 2 starch |
| 1.5 | 0 | 60 | 2 | 16 | 1 | 1 starch |
| 4 | 1.5 | 60 | 1 | 20 | 1 | 1 starch, 1 fat |
| 2 | 0 | 70 | 2 | 21 | 1½ | 1½ starch |
| 9 | 2 | 110 | 3 | 33 | 2 | 2 starch, 1 fat |

1 Carbohydrate Choice = 1 starch or 1 fruit or 1 milk exchange

| PRODUCTS | SERVING SIZE | CALORIES | CALORIES FROM FAT |
|---|---|---|---|
| Cinnamon Graham Granola Bars | 2 bars | 170 | 50 |
| Cinnamon Granola Bars | 2 bars | 210 | 70 |
| Oat Bran Granola Bars | 2 bars | 210 | 70 |
| Oats 'n Honey Granola Bars | 2 bars | 200 | 60 |
| Peanut Butter Granola Bars | 2 bars | 220 | 90 |
| **Quaker® Granola Bars** | | | |
| Chewy® Chocolate Chip Granola Bars | 1 bar | 120 | 35 |
| ❶ Chewy® Granola Bars, Low-Fat, all varieties (avg) | 1 bar | 110 | 20 |
| Chewy® Peanut Butter & Chocolate Chip Granola Bars | 1 bar | 120 | 40 |
| **Sunbelt® Granola Bars** | | | |
| Almond Chewy Granola Bar | 1 pkg | 200 | 30 |
| Chocolate Chip Granola Bar | 1 pkg | 220 | 90 |
| Fudge Dipped Chewy Granola Bar with Peanuts | 1 pkg | 270 | 140 |
| Fudge Dipped Macaroon Chewy Granola Bar | 1 pkg | 280 | 150 |
| Oats and Honey Granola Bar | 1 pkg | 210 | 80 |
| **GRAVY (CAN OR JAR)** | | | |
| ❶ Beef Gravy, Franco-American® | ¼ cup | 30 | 18 |
| ❶ Beef Gravy, Franco-American® Fat Free | ¼ cup | 20 | 0 |
| ❶ Beef Gravy, Heinz® Fat Free | ¼ cup | 10 | 0 |
| ❶ Bistro au Jus, Heinz® Home Style | ¼ cup | 15 | 0 |
| Chicken Gravy, Franco-American® | ¼ cup | 45 | 36 |
| ❶ Chicken Gravy, Franco-American® Fat Free | ¼ cup | 15 | 0 |
| ❶ Chicken Gravy, Heinz® Fat Free | ¼ cup | 15 | 0 |
| ❶ Classic Chicken Gravy, Heinz® Home Style | ¼ cup | 25 | 10 |
| ❶ Cream of Chicken Gravy, Pepperidge Farm® | ¼ cup | 30 | 9 |
| ❶ Hearty Beef Gravy with Pieces of Beef, Pepperidge Farm® | ¼ cup | 25 | 9 |
| ❶ Pork Gravy, Heinz® Home Style | ¼ cup | 25 | 10 |
| ❶ Rich Mushroom Gravy, Heinz® Home Style | ¼ cup | 20 | 5 |

❶  Meets Low-Fat Guidelines

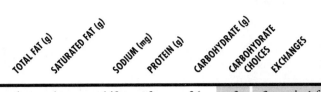

| TOTAL FAT (g) | SATURATED FAT (g) | SODIUM (mg) | PROTEIN (g) | CARBOHYDRATE (g) | CARBOHYDRATE CHOICES | EXCHANGES |
|---|---|---|---|---|---|---|
| 6 | 1 | 140 | 3 | 26 | 2 | 2 starch, 1 fat |
| 8 | 1 | 140 | 4 | 33 | 2 | 2 starch, 1 fat |
| 8 | 1 | 170 | 5 | 32 | 2 | 2 starch, 1 fat |
| 6 | 1 | 170 | 4 | 35 | 2 | 2 starch, 1 fat |
| 10 | 1.5 | 150 | 5 | 30 | 2 | 2 starch, 1½ fat |
| | | | | | | |
| 4 | 1.5 | 70 | 2 | 21 | 1½ | 1½ starch |
| 2 | 0.5 | 95 | 1.5 | 22 | 1½ | 1½ starch |
| | | | | | | |
| 4.5 | 1.5 | 105 | 3 | 19 | 1 | 1 starch, 1 fat |
| | | | | | | |
| 10 | 2.5 | 95 | 3 | 25 | 1½ | 1½ starch, 2 fat |
| 10 | 4 | 95 | 3 | 33 | 2 | 2 starch, 2 fat |
| 15 | 4 | 95 | 4 | 33 | 2 | 2 starch, 3 fat |
| 16 | 8 | 100 | 3 | 34 | 2 | 2 starch, 3 fat |
| 9 | 3 | 105 | 3 | 32 | 2 | 2 starch, 1 fat |
| | | | | | | |
| 2 | NA | NA | 1 | 4 | 0 | free |
| 0 | 0 | 310 | 0 | 5 | 0 | free |
| 0 | 0 | 350 | 1 | 3 | 0 | free |
| 0.5 | 0 | 350 | 1 | 2 | 0 | free |
| 4 | NA | NA | 1 | 3 | 0 | 1 fat |
| 0 | 0 | 320 | <1 | 3 | 0 | free |
| 0 | 0 | 330 | 1 | 3 | 0 | free |
| 1 | 0 | 360 | 1 | 3 | 0 | free |
| 1 | NA | NA | 1 | 3 | 0 | free |
| 1 | NA | NA | 1 | 4 | 0 | free |
| | | | | | | |
| 1 | 0 | 340 | 1 | 3 | 0 | free |
| 0.5 | 0 | 370 | 1 | 3 | 0 | free |

1 Carbohydrate Choice = 1 starch or 1 fruit or 1 milk exchange

| PRODUCTS | SERVING SIZE | CALORIES | CALORIES FROM FAT |
|---|---|---|---|
| ❶ Roasted Turkey Gravy, Heinz® Home Style | ¼ cup | 30 | 15 |
| ❶ Savory Beef Gravy, Heinz® Home Style | ¼ cup | 25 | 10 |
| ❶ Seasoned Turkey Gravy with Pieces of Turkey, Pepperidge Farm® | ¼ cup | 30 | 9 |
| ❶ Turkey Gravy, Franco-American® | ¼ cup | 25 | 9 |
| ❶ Turkey Gravy, Heinz® Fat Free | ¼ cup | 15 | 0 |

### HASH BROWNS/HOME FRIES (FROZEN)
*see also* French Fries

| | | | |
|---|---|---|---|
| ❶ Cheddar Browns!™, Ore-Ida® | 1 patty | 90 | 22.5 |
| Cottage Fries, Ore-Ida® | ~14 fries | 130 | 36 |
| ❶ Country Style Hash Browns, Ore-Ida® | 1 cup | 60 | 0 |
| Golden Patties®, Ore-Ida® | 1 patty | 140 | 63 |
| Hash Browns, Ore-Ida®, Microwave | 1 patty | 110 | 54 |
| ❶ Potatoes O'Brien, Ore-Ida® | ~¾ cup | 60 | 0 |
| ❶ Potato Wedges with Skins™, Ore-Ida® | ~7 wedges | 110 | 23 |
| ❶ Real Hash Brown Potatoes, Idahoan® | ⅔ cup | 120 | 5 |
| ❶ Shredded Hash Browns, Ore-Ida® | ~¾ cup | 70 | 0 |
| ❶ Southern Style Hash Browns, Ore-Ida® | ~¾ cup | 70 | 0 |
| Toaster Hash Browns, Ore-Ida® | 2 patties | 190 | 108 |

### HASH BROWNS/HOME FRIES (REFRIGERATED)

| | | | |
|---|---|---|---|
| ❶ Diced Potatoes with Onions, Simply Potatoes® | ½ cup | 80 | 0 |
| ❶ Shredded Hash Browns, Simply Potatoes® | ½ cup | 70 | 0 |
| ❶ Sliced Home Fries, Simply Potatoes® | ½ cup | 70 | 0 |
| ❶ Southwest Style Hash Browns, Simply Potatoes® | ½ cup | 80 | 5 |

### HORSERADISH SAUCE

| | | | |
|---|---|---|---|
| ❶ Cream Style Horseradish Sauce, Kraft® | 1 tsp | 5 | 0 |
| ❶ Horseradish Sauce, Kraft® | 1 tsp | 0 | 0 |
| ❶ Horseradish Sauce, Kraft® SauceWorks® | 1 tsp | 20 | 15 |
| ❶ Horseradish Sauce, Western® | 2 Tb | 15 | 13.5 |

❶  Meets Low-Fat Guidelines

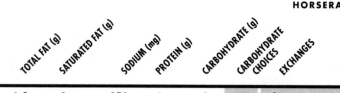

| TOTAL FAT (g) | SATURATED FAT (g) | SODIUM (mg) | PROTEIN (g) | CARBOHYDRATE (g) | CARBOHYDRATE CHOICES | EXCHANGES |
|---|---|---|---|---|---|---|
| 1.5 | 0 | 370 | 1 | 3 | 0 | free |
| 1 | 0 | 350 | 2 | 2 | 0 | free |
| 1 | NA | NA | 2 | 4 | 0 | free |
| 1 | NA | NA | <1 | 3 | 0 | free |
| 0 | 0 | 310 | 1 | 3 | 0 | free |
| 2.5 | NA | NA | 3 | 14 | 1 | 1 starch |
| 4 | NA | NA | 2 | 21 | 1½ | 1½ starch |
| 0 | NA | NA | 2 | 13 | 1 | 1 starch |
| 7 | NA | NA | 1 | 16 | 1 | 1 starch, 1 fat |
| 6 | NA | NA | 1 | 13 | 1 | 1 starch, 1 fat |
| 0 | NA | NA | 1 | 13 | 1 | 1 starch |
| 2.5 | NA | NA | 2 | 22 | 1½ | 1½ starch |
| 0.5 | 0 | 150 | 3 | 26 | 2 | 2 starch |
| 0 | NA | NA | 2 | 15 | 1 | 1 starch |
| 0 | NA | NA | 2 | 17 | 1 | 1 starch |
| 12 | NA | NA | 2 | 24 | 1½ | 1½ starch, 2 fat |
| 0 | 0 | 290 | 2 | 18 | 1 | 1 starch |
| 0 | 0 | 70 | 2 | 17 | 1 | 1 starch |
| 0 | 0 | 70 | 2 | 17 | 1 | 1 starch |
| 0.5 | 0 | 320 | 2 | 18 | 1 | 1 starch |
| 0 | 0 | 50 | 0 | 0 | 0 | free |
| 0 | 0 | 50 | 0 | 0 | 0 | free |
| 1.5 | 0 | 35 | 0 | <1 | 0 | free |
| 1.5 | 0 | 50 | 0 | 0 | 0 | free |

1 Carbohydrate Choice = 1 starch or 1 fruit or 1 milk exchange

## PRODUCTS

| | SERVING SIZE | CALORIES | CALORIES FROM FAT |
|---|---|---|---|

### HOT COCOA MIX

| | | | |
|---|---|---|---|
| ❶ Carnation®, all regular varieties (avg) | 3 Tb | 110 | 10 |
| ❶ Carnation® Fat Free | 2 Tb | 25 | 0 |
| ❶ Carnation® No Sugar Added Reduced Calorie | 2 Tb | 50 | 0 |
| ❶ Ghirardelli®, all varieties (avg) | 2.5 Tb | 80 | 15 |
| ❶ Hershey's®, all varieties (avg) | 1 pkt | 150 | 25 |
| ❶ Swiss Miss®, all varieties (avg) | 1 pkt | 110 | 10 |
| Swiss Miss® Chocolate Sensations | 1 pkt | 150 | 35 |
| ❶ Swiss Miss® Lite, all varieties (avg) | 1 pkt | 75 | <5 |
| ❶ Swiss Miss® Premiere, all varieties (avg) | 1 pkt | 145 | 25 |
| ❶ Swiss Miss® Sugar Free | 1 pkt | 50 | 10 |
| ❶ Weight Watchers® | 1 pkt | 70 | 0 |

### HOT DOGS

| | | | |
|---|---|---|---|
| Ballpark® Beef Franks | 1 frank | 180 | 150 |
| Ballpark® Franks | 1 frank | 180 | 150 |
| ❶ Ballpark® Franks, Fat Free | 1 frank | 45 | 0 |
| Ballpark® Lite Franks | 1 frank | 110 | 70 |
| ❶ Healthy Choice® Franks (Beef, Bunsize, or Jumbo, avg) | 1 frank | 70 | 15 |
| ❶ Healthy Choice® Franks, Low-Fat | 1 frank | 50 | 10 |
| ❶ Hormel® Light & Lean® 97 Franks | 1.6 oz | 45 | 10 |
| Hormel® Wranglers® Franks, all varieties (avg) | 2 oz | 180 | 144 |
| Louis Rich® Chicken or Turkey Franks, all varieties (avg) | 1 link | 85 | 55 |
| Oscar Meyer Franks and Hot Dogs, all varieties except Light and Bun Length® (avg) | 1 link | 140 | 120 |
| Oscar Meyer® Bun Length® Wieners (avg) | 1 link | 180 | 150 |
| Oscar Meyer® Big & Juicy® Franks and Weiners (avg) | 1 link | 230 | 190 |
| Oscar Meyer® Light Franks and Wieners (avg) | 1 link | 110 | 80 |
| Oscar Meyer® Little Wieners, all varieties (avg) | 6 links | 170 | 140 |

❶ Meets Low-Fat Guidelines

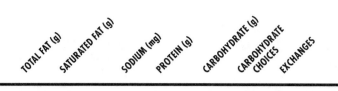

| TOTAL FAT (g) | SATURATED FAT (g) | SODIUM (mg) | PROTEIN (g) | CARBOHYDRATE (g) | CARBOHYDRATE CHOICES | EXCHANGES |
|---|---|---|---|---|---|---|
| 1 | 0 | 100 | 1 | 24 | 1½ | 1½ starch |
| 0 | 0 | 135 | 2 | 4 | 0 | free |
| 0 | 0 | 140 | 4 | 8 | 0 | ½ milk or ½ starch |
| 1.5 | 1 | 30 | 1 | 19 | 1 | 1 starch |
| 3 | 0.5 | 145 | 3 | 27 | 2 | 2 starch, ½ fat |
| 1 | <1 | 139 | 2 | 23 | 1½ | 1½ starch |
| 4 | 2 | 171 | 2 | 27 | 2 | 2 starch |
| <1 | 0 | 197 | 2 | 17 | 1 | 1 starch |
| 3 | 1 | 216 | 2 | 28 | 2 | 2 starch |
| 1 | 0 | 162 | 3 | 10 | ½ | ½ starch |
| 0 | 0 | 160 | 6 | 10 | ½ | 1 milk |
| | | | | | | |
| 16 | 7 | 670 | 6 | 2 | 0 | 1 meat, 2 fat |
| 16 | 6 | 660 | 6 | 2 | 0 | 1 meat, 2 fat |
| 0 | 0 | 560 | 6 | 4 | 0 | 1 very lean meat |
| 8 | 2 | 730 | 7 | 4 | 0 | 1 meat, 1 fat |
| 1.5 | 0.5 | 480 | 9 | 5 | 0 | 1 lean meat |
| 1.5 | 0.5 | 380 | 5 | 5 | 0 | 1 lean meat |
| 1 | NA | 390 | 6 | 2 | 0 | 1 very lean meat |
| 16 | 6 | 515 | 7 | 1 | 0 | 1 meat, 2 fat |
| 6.5 | 2 | 420–500 | 5 | 2 | 0 | 1 high fat meat |
| 13 | 5 | 450–520 | 5 | 1 | 0 | 1 meat, 1½ fat |
| 17 | 6 | 570 | 6 | 1 | 0 | 1 meat, 2 fat |
| 22 | 10 | 690–770 | 10 | 1 | 0 | 1 meat, 3 fat |
| 8 | 3 | 590–620 | 6 | 2 | 0 | 1 meat, ½ fat |
| 16 | 6 | 570–610 | 7 | 1 | 0 | 1 meat, 2 fat |

1 Carbohydrate Choice = 1 starch or 1 fruit or 1 milk exchange

## PRODUCTS

| | SERVING SIZE | CALORIES | CALORIES FROM FAT |
|---|---|---|---|

## ICE CREAM

### Butter Pecan Ice Cream

| | | | |
|---|---|---|---|
| Butter Pecan, Breyers® Light | ½ cup | 120 | 35 |
| Butter Pecan, Edy's Grand | ½ cup | 160 | 90 |
| Butter Pecan, Edy's Grand Light | ½ cup | 120 | 45 |
| Butter Pecan, Haagen-Daz® | ½ cup | 310 | 210 |
| Butter Pecan, Kemp's® Old Fashioned | ½ cup | 170 | 100 |
| ❶ Butter Pecan Crunch, Healthy Choice® | ½ cup | 120 | 20 |

### Chocolate Ice Cream

| | | | |
|---|---|---|---|
| Chocolate, Breyers® | ½ cup | 160 | 80 |
| Chocolate, Edy's Grand | ½ cup | 140 | 80 |
| Chocolate, Edy's Grand No Sugar Added | ½ cup | 100 | 40 |
| Chocolate, Haagen-Daz® | ½ cup | 270 | 160 |
| Chocolate Chocolate Chip, Edy's Grand | ½ cup | 160 | 90 |
| Chocolate Chocolate Chip, Haagen-Daz® | ½ cup | 300 | 180 |
| ❶ Chocolate Fudge, Edy's Fat Free No Sugar Added | ½ cup | 80 | 0 |
| Chocolate Fudge Mousse, Edy's Grand Light | ½ cup | 110 | 35 |
| ❶ Chocolate Fudge Mousse, Healthy Choice® | ½ cup | 120 | 20 |
| French Silk, Edy's Grand Light | ½ cup | 120 | 45 |
| ❶ French Silk Chocolate, Kemp's® Fat Free | ½ cup | 100 | 0 |
| ❶ Triple Chocolate Chunk, Healthy Choice® | ½ cup | 140 | 20 |
| Triple Chocolate Tornado™, Weight Watchers® | ½ cup | 150 | 30 |

### Chocolate Chip Ice Cream

| | | | |
|---|---|---|---|
| Cherry Chocolate Chip, Edy's Grand | ½ cup | 150 | 70 |
| ❶ Cherry Chocolate Chunk, Healthy Choice® Special Creations | ½ cup | 110 | 20 |
| Chocolate Chip, Edy's Grand No Sugar Added | ½ cup | 100 | 45 |
| Chocolate Chip, Kemp's® Old Fashioned | ½ cup | 170 | 80 |
| Vanilla Chocolate Chip, Haagen-Daz® | ½ cup | 310 | 180 |

❶　Meets Low-Fat Guidelines

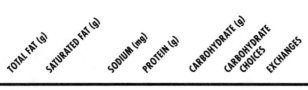

| TOTAL FAT (g) | SATURATED FAT (g) | SODIUM (mg) | PROTEIN (g) | CARBOHYDRATE (g) | CARBOHYDRATE CHOICES | EXCHANGES |
|---|---|---|---|---|---|---|
| 4 | 0 | 115 | 3 | 19 | 1 | 1 starch, 1 fat |
| 9 | 5 | 50 | 3 | 16 | 1 | 1 starch, 2 fat |
| 5 | 2 | 45 | 3 | 16 | 1 | 1 starch, 1 fat |
| 23 | 11 | 160 | 5 | 20 | 1 | 1 starch, 4½ fat |
| 11 | 5 | 80 | 3 | 17 | 1 | 1 starch, 2 fat |
| 2 | 1 | 60 | 3 | 22 | 1½ | 1½ starch |
| 8 | 6 | 30 | 3 | 19 | 1 | 1 starch, 2 fat |
| 9 | 5 | 30 | 3 | 15 | 1 | 1 starch, 2 fat |
| 4 | 2.5 | 45 | 3 | 13 | 1 | 1 starch, ½ fat |
| 18 | 11 | 75 | 5 | 22 | 1½ | 1½ starch, 3 fat |
| 10 | 6 | 25 | 2 | 17 | 1 | 1 starch, 2 fat |
| 20 | 12 | 70 | 5 | 26 | 2 | 2 starch, 3½ fat |
| 0 | 0 | 55 | 4 | 21 | 1½ | 1½ starch |
| 4 | 2.5 | 40 | 3 | 17 | 1 | 1 starch, ½ fat |
| 2 | 1 | 50 | 3 | 21 | 1½ | 1½ starch |
| 5 | 3 | 40 | 3 | 18 | 1 | 1 starch, ½ fat |
| 0 | 0 | 60 | 3 | 24 | 1½ | 1½ starch |
| 2 | 1 | 60 | 3 | 21 | 1½ | 1½ starch |
| 3.5 | 1.5 | 80 | 4 | 26 | 2 | 2 starch |
| 8 | 4 | 35 | 3 | 18 | 1 | 1 starch, 1 fat |
| 2 | 1 | 55 | 3 | 19 | 1 | 1 starch |
| 5 | 2.5 | 50 | 3 | 14 | 1 | 1 starch, 1 fat |
| 9 | 6 | 55 | 3 | 20 | 1 | 1 starch, 2 fat |
| 20 | 12 | 90 | 5 | 26 | 2 | 2 starch, 3½ fat |

1 Carbohydrate Choice = 1 starch or 1 fruit or 1 milk exchange

| PRODUCTS | SERVING SIZE | CALORIES | CALORIES FROM FAT |
|---|---|---|---|
| **Coffee Ice Cream** | | | |
| Caffe Almond Fudge, Starbuck's Coffee® | ½ cup | 250 | 117 |
| ❶ Cappuccino Mocha Fudge, Healthy Choice® Special Creations | ½ cup | 120 | 20 |
| ❶ Chocolate Fudge Chunk, Edy's Low Fat | ½ cup | 110 | 20 |
| Coffee, Edy's Grand | ½ cup | 140 | 70 |
| Coffee, Haagen-Daz® | ½ cup | 270 | 160 |
| ❶ Coffee Fudge, Edy's Fat Free No Sugar Added | ½ cup | 80 | 0 |
| Coffee with Heath® Toffee Crunch, Ben & Jerry's® | ½ cup | 280 | 170 |
| Dark Roast Espresso Swirl, Starbuck's Coffee® | ½ cup | 220 | 90 |
| Espresso Chip, Edy's Grand | ½ cup | 150 | 80 |
| ❶ Espresso Chip, Edy's Low Fat | ½ cup | 100 | 20 |
| Italian Roast Coffee, Starbuck's Coffee® | ½ cup | 230 | 108 |
| Javachip, Starbuck's Coffee® | ½ cup | 250 | 117 |
| **Cookies and Cream Ice Cream** | | | |
| Cookies 'N Cream, Edy's Grand | ½ cup | 150 | 70 |
| ❶ Cookies 'N Cream, Edy's Low Fat | ½ cup | 110 | 20 |
| Cookies & Cream, Haagen-Daz® | ½ cup | 270 | 160 |
| ❶ Cookies 'N Cream, Healthy Choice® | ½ cup | 120 | 20 |
| ❶ Cookies 'N Cream, Kemp's® Fat Free | ½ cup | 110 | 0 |
| Cookies 'N Cream, Kemp's® Old Fashioned | ½ cup | 160 | 80 |
| Midnight Cookies & Cream, Haagen-Daz® | ½ cup | 300 | 160 |
| Mint Cookies 'N Cream, Edy's Grand Light | ½ cup | 110 | 40 |
| **Cookie Dough Ice Cream** | | | |
| Chocolate Chip Cookie Dough, Ben & Jerry's® | ½ cup | 270 | 150 |
| ❶ Cookie Chunk, Edy's Fat Free | ½ cup | 110 | 0 |
| Cookie Dough, Edy's Grand | ½ cup | 170 | 80 |
| Cookie Dough, Edy's Grand Light | ½ cup | 120 | 40 |
| Cookie Dough Craze™, Weight Watchers® | ½ cup | 140 | 35 |

❶  Meets Low-Fat Guidelines

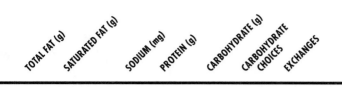

| TOTAL FAT (g) | SATURATED FAT (g) | SODIUM (mg) | PROTEIN (g) | CARBOHYDRATE (g) | CARBOHYDRATE CHOICES | EXCHANGES |
|---|---|---|---|---|---|---|
| 13 | 10 | 45 | 5 | 30 | 2 | 2 starch, 2 fat |
| 2 | 1 | 60 | 3 | 22 | 1½ | 1½ starch |
| 2 | 1.5 | 50 | 3 | 22 | 1½ | 1½ starch |
| 8 | 5 | 35 | 3 | 15 | 1 | 1 starch, 1 fat |
| 18 | 11 | 85 | 5 | 21 | 1½ | 1½ starch, 3 fat |
| 0 | 0 | 55 | 3 | 20 | 1 | 1 starch |
| 19 | 10 | 120 | 4 | 28 | 2 | 2 starch, 3 fat |
| 10 | 5 | 70 | 4 | 29 | 2 | 2 starch, 1½ fat |
| 8 | 6 | 30 | 3 | 16 | 1 | 1 starch, 1 fat |
| 2 | 1.5 | 40 | 3 | 20 | 1 | 1 starch |
| 12 | 6 | 5 | 5 | 27 | 2 | 2 starch, 2 fat |
| 13 | 8 | 15 | 4 | 30 | 2 | 2 starch, 2 fat |
| 8 | 5 | 75 | 3 | 18 | 1 | 1 starch, 1 fat |
| 2 | 1 | 55 | 3 | 21 | 1½ | 1½ starch |
| 17 | 11 | 115 | 5 | 23 | 1½ | 1½ starch, 3 fat |
| 2 | 1 | 90 | 3 | 21 | 1½ | 1½ starch |
| 0 | 0 | 85 | 4 | 26 | 2 | 2 starch |
| 9 | 5 | 80 | 3 | 21 | 1½ | 1½ starch, 1 fat |
| 18 | 11 | 140 | 5 | 29 | 2 | 2 starch, 3 fat |
| 4 | 2.5 | 55 | 3 | 15 | 1 | 1 starch, ½ fat |
| 17 | 9 | 95 | 4 | 30 | 2 | 2 starch, 3 fat |
| 0 | 0 | 105 | 4 | 23 | 1½ | 1½ starch |
| 9 | 5 | 65 | 3 | 20 | 1 | 1 starch, 2 fat |
| 5 | 2.5 | 60 | 3 | 18 | 1 | 1 starch, 1 fat |
| 3.5 | 2 | 85 | 3 | 24 | 1½ | 1½ starch, ½ fat |

1 Carbohydrate Choice = 1 starch or 1 fruit or 1 milk exchange

## PRODUCTS

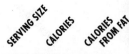

| PRODUCTS | SERVING SIZE | CALORIES | CALORIES FROM FAT |
|---|---|---|---|
| ❶ Peanut Butter Cookie Dough 'N Fudge, Healthy Choice® | ½ cup | 120 | 20 |
| **Fudge Brownie Ice Cream** | | | |
| Brownie Batter, Edy's Grand | ½ cup | 150 | 70 |
| Brownies 'N Fudge, Edy's Grand Light | ½ cup | 110 | 35 |
| ❶ Brownie Sundae, Wells' Blue Bunny® Health Smart | ½ cup | 90 | 0 |
| Double Fudge Brownie, Edy's Grand | ½ cup | 160 | 80 |
| ❶ Fudge Brownie, Healthy Choice® | ½ cup | 120 | 20 |
| ❶ Fudge Brownie A La Mode, Healthy Choice® Special Creations | ½ cup | 120 | 20 |
| **Fudge Ice Cream** | | | |
| ❶ Caramel Nutty Fudge, Kemp's® Fat Free | ½ cup | 120 | 0 |
| Chocolate Fudge Sundae, Edy's Grand | ½ cup | 170 | 90 |
| ❶ Marble Fudge, Edy's Fat Free | ½ cup | 100 | 0 |
| Mocha Almond Fudge, Edy's Grand Light | ½ cup | 110 | 40 |
| Toasted Almond Fudge, Kemp's® Old Fashioned | ½ cup | 170 | 90 |
| ❶ Toffee Fudge Swirl, Kemp's® Fat Free | ½ cup | 120 | 0 |
| ❶ Turtle Fudge Cake, Healthy Choice® Special Creations | ½ cup | 130 | 20 |
| Vanilla Caramel Fudge, Ben & Jerry's® | ½ cup | 280 | 150 |
| ❶ Vanilla Fudge Swirl, Kemp's® Fat Free No Sugar Added | ½ cup | 60 | 0 |
| **Mint Chocolate Ice Cream** | | | |
| ❶ After Dinner Mint, Kemp's® Fat Free | ½ cup | 110 | 0 |
| ❶ Mint Chocolate Chip, Healthy Choice® | ½ cup | 120 | 20 |
| Mint Chocolate Chip, Breyers® Light | ½ cup | 100 | 45 |
| Mint Chocolate Chip, Edy's Grand | ½ cup | 160 | 80 |
| Mint Chocolate Cookie, Ben & Jerry's® | ½ cup | 260 | 160 |
| ❶ Mint Fudge, Edy's Fat Free | ½ cup | 100 | 0 |
| ❶ Mint Fudge Brownie, Kemp's® Fat Free | ½ cup | 110 | 0 |

❶   Meets Low-Fat Guidelines

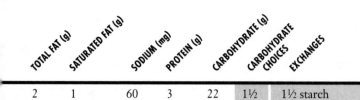

| TOTAL FAT (g) | SATURATED FAT (g) | SODIUM (mg) | PROTEIN (g) | CARBOHYDRATE (g) | CARBOHYDRATE CHOICES | EXCHANGES |
|---|---|---|---|---|---|---|
| 2 | 1 | 60 | 3 | 22 | 1½ | 1½ starch |
| | | | | | | |
| 8 | 4 | 55 | 3 | 18 | 1 | 1 starch, 1 fat |
| 4 | 2 | 45 | 3 | 18 | 1 | 1 starch, ½ fat |
| 0 | 0 | 75 | 4 | 21 | 1½ | 1½ starch |
| 9 | 5 | 40 | 2 | 19 | 1 | 1 starch, 2 fat |
| 2 | 1 | 55 | 3 | 22 | 1½ | 1½ starch |
| 2 | 1 | 55 | 3 | 19 | 1 | 1 starch |
| | | | | | | |
| 0 | 0 | 85 | 3 | 28 | 2 | 2 starch |
| 10 | 5 | 55 | 3 | 18 | 1 | 1 starch, 2 fat |
| 0 | 0 | 75 | 3 | 23 | 1½ | 1½ starch |
| 4 | 2 | 35 | 3 | 16 | 1 | 1 starch, ½ fat |
| 10 | 4.5 | 65 | 4 | 19 | 1 | 1 starch, 2 fat |
| 0 | 0 | 90 | 3 | 28 | 2 | 2 starch |
| 2 | 1 | 60 | 3 | 25 | 1½ | 1½ starch |
| 17 | 10 | 75 | 4 | 33 | 2 | 2 starch, 3 fat |
| 0 | 0 | 70 | 3 | 19 | 1 | 1 starch |
| | | | | | | |
| 0 | 0 | 75 | 4 | 24 | 1½ | 1½ starch |
| 2 | 1 | 50 | 3 | 21 | 1½ | 1½ starch |
| 5 | 3 | 40 | 3 | 13 | 1 | 1 starch, 1 fat |
| 9 | 5 | 35 | 3 | 17 | 1 | 1 starch, 2 fat |
| 17 | 10 | 120 | 4 | 27 | 2 | 2 starch, 3 fat |
| 0 | 0 | 75 | 3 | 23 | 1½ | 1½ starch |
| 0 | 0 | 100 | 4 | 27 | 2 | 2 starch |

1 Carbohydrate Choice = 1 starch or 1 fruit or 1 milk exchange

## PRODUCTS

| | SERVING SIZE | CALORIES | CALORIES FROM FAT |
|---|---|---|---|
| Peppermint Bon Bon, Kemp's® Old Fashioned | ½ cup | 160 | 80 |
| **Rocky Road Ice Cream** | | | |
| ❶ Reckless Rocky Road™, Weight Watchers® | ½ cup | 140 | 30 |
| ❶ Rocky Road, Edy's Low Fat | ½ cup | 110 | 20 |
| Rocky Road, Edy's Grand | ½ cup | 170 | 90 |
| Rocky Road, Edy's Grand Light | ½ cup | 120 | 40 |
| ❶ Rocky Road, Healthy Choice® | ½ cup | 140 | 20 |
| ❶ Rockie Road Brownie, Kemp's® Fat Free | ½ cup | 120 | 0 |
| **Strawberry Ice Cream** | | | |
| Real Strawberry, Edy's Grand | ½ cup | 130 | 50 |
| Real Strawberry, Kemp's® Old Fashioned | ½ cup | 140 | 60 |
| Strawberry, Haagen-Daz® | ½ cup | 250 | 150 |
| ❶ Strawberry Shortcake, Edy's Fat Free | ½ cup | 100 | 0 |
| **Toffee/Praline Ice Cream** | | | |
| Almond Praline, Edy's Grand | ½ cup | 160 | 70 |
| Butter Brickle, Kemp's® Old Fashioned | ½ cup | 160 | 70 |
| ❶ Caramel Praline Crunch, Edy's Fat Free | ½ cup | 110 | 0 |
| ❶ Heath® Toffee and Caramel, Edy's Low Fat | ½ cup | 120 | 20 |
| Macadamia Brittle, Haagen-Daz® | ½ cup | 300 | 180 |
| Positively Praline Crunch™, Weight Watchers® | ½ cup | 140 | 25 |
| ❶ Praline & Caramel, Healthy Choice® | ½ cup | 130 | 20 |
| ❶ Praline Caramel Cluster, Healthy Choice® Special Creations | ½ cup | 130 | 20 |
| Pralines 'N Caramel, Edy's Grand Light | ½ cup | 120 | 35 |
| Rainforest Crunch™, Ben & Jerry's® | ½ cup | 300 | 200 |
| Vanilla with Heath™ Toffee Crunch, Ben & Jerry's® | ½ cup | 280 | 170 |
| **Vanilla Ice Cream** | | | |
| ❶ French Vanilla, Breyers® Low Fat | ½ cup | 90 | 15 |
| French Vanilla, Edy's Grand | ½ cup | 160 | 90 |

❶  Meets Low-Fat Guidelines

| TOTAL FAT (g) | SATURATED FAT (g) | SODIUM (mg) | PROTEIN (g) | CARBOHYDRATE (g) | CARBOHYDRATE CHOICES | EXCHANGES |
|---|---|---|---|---|---|---|
| 9 | 6 | 55 | 2 | 19 | 1 | 1 starch, 2 fat |
| 3 | 1.5 | 75 | 4 | 23 | 1½ | 1½ starch, ½ fat |
| 2 | 0.5 | 35 | 3 | 21 | 1½ | 1½ starch |
| 10 | 5 | 30 | 3 | 17 | 1 | 1 starch, 2 fat |
| 4 | 2.5 | 35 | 3 | 16 | 1 | 1 starch, ½ fat |
| 2 | 1 | 60 | 3 | 28 | 2 | 2 starch |
| 0 | 0 | 80 | 3 | 29 | 2 | 2 starch |
| 6 | 4 | 25 | 2 | 17 | 1 | 1 starch, 1 fat |
| 6 | 4 | 50 | 2 | 18 | 1 | 1 starch, 1 fat |
| 16 | 10 | 80 | 4 | 23 | 1½ | 1½ starch, 3 fat |
| 0 | 0 | 85 | 3 | 22 | 1½ | 1½ starch |
| 8 | 4 | 85 | 3 | 20 | 1 | 1 starch, 2 fat |
| 8 | 5 | 65 | 2 | 20 | 1 | 1 starch, 1½ fat |
| 0 | 0 | 85 | 3 | 24 | 1½ | 1½ starch |
| 2 | 1 | 40 | 2 | 23 | 1½ | 1½ starch |
| 20 | 11 | 120 | 4 | 25 | 1½ | 1½ starch, 4 fat |
| 3 | 1.5 | 105 | 3 | 25 | 1½ | 1½ starch |
| 2 | 0.5 | 70 | 3 | 25 | 1½ | 1½ starch |
| 2 | 0.5 | 70 | 3 | 25 | 1½ | 1½ starch |
| 4 | 2 | 60 | 3 | 18 | 1 | 1 starch, ½ fat |
| 23 | 11 | 140 | 5 | 24 | 1½ | 1½ starch, 4 fat |
| 19 | 11 | 115 | 3 | 28 | 2 | 2 starch, 3 fat |
| 1.5 | 0.5 | 45 | 3 | 17 | 1 | 1 starch |
| 10 | 6 | 30 | 2 | 16 | 1 | 1 starch, 2 fat |

1 Carbohydrate Choice = 1 starch or 1 fruit or 1 milk exchange

## PRODUCTS

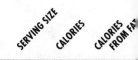

| PRODUCTS | SERVING SIZE | CALORIES | CALORIES FROM FAT |
|---|---|---|---|
| ❶ Oh! So Very Vanilla™, Weight Watchers® | ½ cup | 120 | 25 |
| Vanilla, Ben & Jerry's® | ½ cup | 230 | 150 |
| ❶ Vanilla, Edy's Fat Free | ½ cup | 90 | 0 |
| Vanilla, Edy's Grand | ½ cup | 150 | 90 |
| Vanilla, Edy's Grand Light | ½ cup | 100 | 35 |
| ❶ Vanilla, Edy's Low Fat | ½ cup | 100 | 20 |
| ❶ Vanilla, Good Humor-Breyers® Fat Free | ½ cup | 100 | 0 |
| Vanilla, Haagen-Daz® | ½ cup | 270 | 160 |
| ❶ Vanilla, Healthy Choice® | ½ cup | 100 | 20 |
| ❶ Vanilla, Kemp's® Fat Free | ½ cup | 100 | 0 |
| ❶ Vanilla, Kemp's® Fat Free No Sugar Added | ½ cup | 60 | 0 |
| Vanilla, Kemp's® Old Fashioned | ½ cup | 150 | 70 |
| Vanilla Bean, Edy's Grand | ½ cup | 150 | 80 |
| **_Other Ice Cream Flavors_** | | | |
| Banana Split, Edy's Grand | ½ cup | 170 | 90 |
| ❶ Bananas Foster, Healthy Choice® Special Creations | ½ cup | 110 | 15 |
| ❶ Black Cherry Vanilla Swirl, Edy's Fat Free | ½ cup | 100 | 0 |
| ❶ Black Forest, Healthy Choice® Special Creations | ½ cup | 120 | 20 |
| Cheesecake Chunk, Edy's Grand Light | ½ cup | 120 | 40 |
| Cherry Garcia®, Ben & Jerry's® | ½ cup | 240 | 140 |
| Cherry Vanilla, Haagen-Daz® | ½ cup | 240 | 140 |
| Dreamy Caramel Cream, Edy's Grand Light | ½ cup | 110 | 35 |
| Maple Nut, Kemp's® Old Fashioned | ½ cup | 170 | 80 |
| Peanut Butter Cup, Ben & Jerry's® | ½ cup | 370 | 240 |
| Peanut Butter Cups, Edy's Grand Light | ½ cup | 120 | 40 |
| ❶ Sorbet & Cream, Healthy Choice®, all varieties (avg) | ½ cup | 90 | 15 |
| Strawberry Cheesecake Chunk, Edy's Grand | ½ cup | 150 | 70 |
| ❶ Vanilla 'N Caramel, Edy's Fat Free No Sugar Added | ½ cup | 80 | 0 |

❶  Meets Low-Fat Guidelines

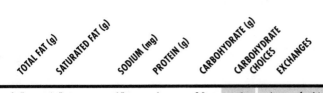

| TOTAL FAT (g) | SATURATED FAT (g) | SODIUM (mg) | PROTEIN (g) | CARBOHYDRATE (g) | CARBOHYDRATE CHOICES | EXCHANGES |
|---|---|---|---|---|---|---|
| 2.5 | 1.5 | 65 | 4 | 20 | 1 | 1 starch, ½ fat |
| 17 | 10 | 55 | 4 | 21 | 1½ | 1½ starch, 3 fat |
| 0 | 0 | 70 | 4 | 20 | 1 | 1 starch |
| 10 | 6 | 30 | 2 | 14 | 1 | 1 starch, 2 fat |
| 4 | 2.5 | 35 | 3 | 14 | 1 | 1 starch, ½ fat |
| 2 | 1 | 40 | 3 | 19 | 1 | 1 starch |
| 0 | 0 | 50 | 3 | 21 | 1½ | 1½ starch |
| 18 | 11 | 85 | 5 | 21 | 1½ | 1½ starch, 3 fat |
| 2 | 1 | 50 | 3 | 18 | 1 | 1 starch |
| 0 | 0 | 65 | 4 | 23 | 1½ | 1½ starch |
| 0 | 0 | 70 | 3 | 19 | 1 | 1 starch |
| 8 | 5 | 55 | 2 | 18 | 1 | 1 starch, 1 fat |
| 9 | 6 | 30 | 2 | 15 | 1 | 1 starch, 2 fat |
| 10 | 4 | 50 | 3 | 19 | 1 | 1 starch, 2 fat |
| 1.5 | 1 | 60 | 3 | 21 | 1½ | 1½ starch |
| 0 | 0 | 70 | 4 | 21 | 1½ | 1½ starch |
| 2 | 1 | 50 | 3 | 23 | 1½ | 1½ starch |
| 5 | 3 | 35 | 3 | 16 | 1 | 1 starch, 1 fat |
| 16 | 10 | 60 | 4 | 25 | 1½ | 1½ starch, 3 fat |
| 15 | 9 | 75 | 4 | 23 | 1½ | 1½ starch, 3 fat |
| 4 | 2 | 50 | 3 | 16 | 1 | 1 starch, ½ fat |
| 9 | 4.5 | 60 | 3 | 17 | 1 | 1 starch, 2 fat |
| 26 | 12 | 140 | 8 | 30 | 2 | 2 starch, 5 fat |
| 5 | 3 | 45 | 3 | 17 | 1 | 1 starch, 1 fat |
| 2 | 1 | 50 | 2 | 17 | 1 | 1 starch |
| 8 | 5 | 30 | 3 | 18 | 1 | 1 starch, 2 fat |
| 0 | 0 | 55 | 3 | 20 | 1 | 1 starch |

1 Carbohydrate Choice = 1 starch *or* 1 fruit *or* 1 milk exchange

## PRODUCTS

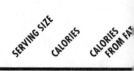

| PRODUCTS | SERVING SIZE | CALORIES | CALORIES FROM FAT |
|---|---|---|---|
| Vanilla Chocolate Strawberry, Edy's Grand | ½ cup | 130 | 70 |
| Vanilla Swiss Almond, Haagen-Daz® | ½ cup | 310 | 190 |
| Wavy Gravy, Ben & Jerry's® | ½ cup | 330 | 210 |
| **ICE CREAM, NON-DAIRY SUBSTITUTES** | | | |
| Plain 6 oz, White Wave® Organic | 1 container | 140 | 45 |
| Plain quarts, White Wave® Organic | 1 cup | 180 | 60 |
| Rice Dream®, all varieties (avg) | ½ cup | 138 | 50 |
| ❶ White Wave®, all varieties (avg) | 1 container | 155 | 15 |
| **ICE CREAM CONES** | | | |
| ❶ Chocolate Cones, Nabisco® Oreo® | 1 cone | 50 | 10 |
| ❶ Cinnamon Cones, Nabisco® Teddy Grahams® | 1 cone | 60 | 5 |
| ❶ Cups, Nabisco® Comet® | 1 cone | 20 | 0 |
| ❶ Frones, Delicious Frookie® | 1 cone | 50 | 9 |
| ❶ Sugar Cones, Nabisco® Comet® | 1 cone | 50 | 0 |
| ❶ Waffle Cones, Nabisco® Comet® | 1 cone | 70 | 5 |
| **ICE CREAM TOPPINGS** | | | |
| ❶ Apple Pie à la Mode, Hershey's® Chocolate Shoppe Sundae Syrup™ | 2 Tb | 100 | 0 |
| ❶ Butterscotch, Kraft® | 2 Tb | 130 | 15 |
| ❶ Butterscotch, Mrs. Richardson's® | 2 Tb | 130 | 10 |
| ❶ Butterscotch, Smucker's® Fat Free | 2 Tb | 130 | 0 |
| ❶ Butterscotch, Smucker's® Sundae Syrup™ | 2 Tb | 110 | 0 |
| ❶ Butterscotch Caramel Fudge, Mrs. Richardson's® | 2 Tb | 130 | 15 |
| ❶ Caramel, Hershey's® Chocolate Shoppe Sundae Syrup™ | 2 Tb | 100 | 0 |
| ❶ Caramel, Kraft® | 2 Tb | 120 | 0 |
| ❶ Caramel, Mrs. Richardson's® Fat Free | 2 Tb | 130 | 0 |
| ❶ Caramel, Smucker's® Fat Free | 2 Tb | 130 | 0 |
| ❶ Caramel, Smucker's® Sundae Syrup™ | 2 Tb | 110 | 0 |
| ❶ Chocolate, Smucker's® Sundae Syrup™ | 2 Tb | 110 | 0 |

 Meets Low-Fat Guidelines

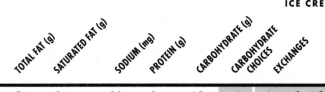

| TOTAL FAT (g) | SATURATED FAT (g) | SODIUM (mg) | PROTEIN (g) | CARBOHYDRATE (g) | CARBOHYDRATE CHOICES | EXCHANGES |
|---|---|---|---|---|---|---|
| 7 | 5 | 30 | 3 | 15 | 1 | 1 starch, 1 fat |
| 21 | 11 | 90 | 6 | 23 | 1½ | 1½ starch, 4 fat |
| 24 | 10 | 95 | 6 | 29 | 2 | 2 starch, 4 fat |
| 5 | 1 | 55 | 9 | 13 | 1 | 1 starch, 1 meat |
| 7 | 1.5 | 70 | 12 | 18 | 1 | 1 starch, 1 meat |
| 5.5 | NA | 80 | 1 | 19 | 1 | 1 starch, 1 fat |
| 1.5 | 0 | 45 | 5 | 23–33 | 1½–2 | 1½–2 starch |
| 1 | 0 | 110 | 1 | 10 | ½ | ½ starch |
| 0.5 | 0 | 55 | 1 | 13 | 1 | 1 starch |
| 0 | 0 | 20 | 0 | 4 | 0 | free |
| 1 | NA | 30 | 1 | 9 | ½ | ½ starch |
| 0 | 0 | 40 | <1 | 11 | 1 | 1 starch |
| 0.5 | 0 | 30 | 1 | 14 | 1 | 1 starch |
| 0 | 0 | 90 | 0 | 25 | 1½ | 1½ fruit |
| 1.5 | 1 | 150 | <1 | 28 | 2 | 2 fruit |
| 1 | 0.5 | 200 | <1 | 30 | 2 | 2 fruit |
| 0 | 0 | 110 | 0 | 31 | 2 | 2 fruit |
| 0 | 0 | 70 | 0 | 27 | 2 | 2 fruit |
| 1.5 | 1.5 | 60 | <1 | 30 | 2 | 2 fruit |
| 0 | 0 | 95 | <1 | 25 | 1½ | 1½ fruit |
| 0 | 0 | 90 | 2 | 28 | 2 | 2 fruit |
| 0 | 0 | 55 | <1 | 32 | 2 | 2 fruit |
| 0 | 0 | 110 | 0 | 31 | 2 | 2 fruit |
| 0 | 0 | 70 | 0 | 27 | 2 | 2 fruit |
| 0 | 0 | 70 | 0 | 27 | 2 | 2 fruit |

1 Carbohydrate Choice = 1 starch or 1 fruit or 1 milk exchange

## PRODUCTS

| PRODUCTS | SERVING SIZE | CALORIES | CALORIES FROM FAT |
|---|---|---|---|
| ❶ Chocolate Flavored, Kraft® | 2 Tb | 110 | 0 |
| Dark Chocolate Fudge, Mrs. Richardson's® | 2 Tb | 140 | 50 |
| ❶ Double Chocolate, Hershey's® Chocolate Shoppe Sundae Syrup™ | 2 Tb | 110 | 0 |
| Hot Fudge, Kraft® | 2 Tb | 140 | 40 |
| Hot Fudge, Mrs. Richardson's® | 2 Tb | 140 | 60 |
| ❶ Hot Fudge, Mrs. Richardon's® Fat Free | 2 Tb | 110 | 0 |
| Hot Fudge, Smucker's® | 2 Tb | 140 | 35 |
| ❶ Hot Fudge, Smucker's® Light Toppings | 2 Tb | 90 | 0 |
| ❶ Pineapple, Kraft® | 2 Tb | 110 | 0 |
| ❶ Strawberry, Kraft® | 2 Tb | 110 | 0 |
| ❶ Strawberry, Mrs. Richardson's® | 2 Tb | 70 | 0 |

### ICE CREAM TREATS/FRUIT POPS

| | SERVING SIZE | CALORIES | CALORIES FROM FAT |
|---|---|---|---|
| ❶ All Natural Juice Bars, Good Humor-Breyers® Minute Maid® | 1 bar | 50 | 0 |
| Arctic D'Lites™, Weight Watchers® | 1 bar | 130 | 60 |
| ❶ Berries 'n Creme Mousse, Weight Watchers® | 1 bar | 70 | 10 |
| Caramel Nut Bars, Weight Watchers® | 1 bar | 130 | 70 |
| Chocolate Dip, Weight Watchers® | 1 bar | 100 | 50 |
| ❶ Chocolate Mousse Bar, Weight Watchers® | 1 bar | 70 | 10 |
| ❶ Chocolate Treat®, Weight Watchers® | 1 bar | 100 | 5 |
| Classic Vanilla, Dove® Bite Size Ice Creams | 5 bars | 320 | 190 |
| ❶ Cool Fruits, Pink Lemonade, Delicious Frookie® | 2 pops | 70 | 0 |
| ❶ Creamsicle, Good Humor-Breyers® No Sugar Added | 1 piece | 25 | 0 |
| Crispy Pralines 'n Creme Bars, Weight Watchers® | 1 bar | 130 | 60 |
| Dove® Bars, all varieties (avg) | 1 bar | 265 | 150 |
| English Toffee Crunch Bars, Weight Watchers® | 1 bar | 120 | 60 |
| ❶ Freezer Bars, Mr. Freeze® (1 oz or 1.5 oz) | 3 (1 oz) or 2 (1.5 oz) bars | 50 | 0 |
| ❶ Freezer Bars, Mr. Freeze® (2 oz) | 1 bar | 35 | 0 |

❶ Meets Low-Fat Guidelines

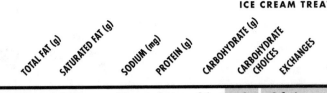

| TOTAL FAT (g) | SATURATED FAT (g) | SODIUM (mg) | PROTEIN (g) | CARBOHYDRATE (g) | CARBOHYDRATE CHOICES | EXCHANGES |
|---|---|---|---|---|---|---|
| 0 | 0 | 30 | 2 | 26 | 2 | 2 fruit |
| 6 | 5 | 75 | 1 | 20 | 1 | 1 fruit, 1 fat |
| 0 | 0 | 25 | <1 | 26 | 2 | 2 fruit |
| 4 | 2 | 100 | 1 | 24 | 1½ | 1½ fruit, 1 fat |
| 6 | 6 | 75 | 1 | 20 | 1 | 1 fruit, 1 fat |
| 0 | 0 | 60 | 1 | 25 | 1½ | 1½ fruit |
| 4 | 1 | 60 | 2 | 24 | 1½ | 1½ fruit, 1 fat |
| 0 | 0 | 92 | 2 | 23 | 1½ | 1½ fruit |
| 0 | 0 | 15 | 0 | 28 | 2 | 2 fruit |
| 0 | 0 | 15 | 0 | 29 | 2 | 2 fruit |
| 0 | 0 | 15 | 0 | 18 | 1 | 1 fruit |
| 0 | 0 | 0 | 0 | 12 | 1 | 1 fruit |
| 7 | 3.5 | 20 | 3 | 14 | 1 | 1 starch, 1 fat |
| 1.5 | 0 | 75 | 3 | 17 | 1 | 1 starch |
| 8 | 3.5 | 25 | 2 | 14 | 1 | 1 starch, 1 fat |
| 6 | 3 | 15 | 2 | 11 | 1 | 1 starch, 1 fat |
| 1 | 0.5 | 80 | 4 | 18 | 1 | 1 starch |
| 1 | 0 | 150 | 3 | 21 | 1½ | 1½ starch |
| 21 | 14 | 50 | 4 | 31 | 2 | 2 starch, 4 fat |
| 0 | 0.5 | 0 | 0 | 18 | 1 | 1 starch |
| 0 | 0 | 10 | 0 | 5 | 0 | free |
| 7 | 3.5 | 40 | 2 | 15 | 1 | 1 starch, 1 fat |
| 17 | 11 | 30–90 | 3 | 26–31 | 2 | 2 starch, 3 fat |
| 7 | 3.5 | 25 | 1 | 12 | 1 | 1 starch, 1 fat |
| 0 | 0 | 20 | 0 | 14 | 1 | 1 fruit |
| 0 | 0 | 15 | 0 | 9 | ½ | ½ fruit |

1 Carbohydrate Choice = 1 starch or 1 fruit or 1 milk exchange

## PRODUCTS

| | SERVING SIZE | CALORIES | CALORIES FROM FAT |
|---|---|---|---|
| ❶ Freezer Bars, Sugar-Free, Mr. Freeze® (1 oz or 1.5 oz) | 3 (1 oz) or 2 (1.5) oz bars | 20 | 0 |
| French Vanilla, Dove® Bite Size Ice Creams | 5 bars | 330 | 190 |
| ❶ Frozen Yogurt Creamsicle, Breyers® Fat Free | 1 piece | 60 | 0 |
| ❶ Fudgsicle, Good Humor-Breyers® | 1 piece | 120 | 10 |
| ❶ Fudgsicle, Good Humor-Breyers® Fat Free | 1 piece | 60 | 0 |
| ❶ Fudgsicle, Good Humor-Breyers® Sugar Free | 1 piece | 40 | 5 |
| ❶ Fruit Juicee, Good Humor-Breyers® Minute Maid® | 1 bar | 60 | 0 |
| ❶ Ice Cream Sandwiches, SnackWell's™ | 1 sandwich | 90 | 15 |
| ❶ Junior Juice Pops, Good Humor-Breyers® | 2 pieces | 120 | 10 |
| Klondike Dark Chocolate Ice Cream Bar, Good Humor-Breyers® | 1 piece | 290 | 180 |
| Klondike Ice Cream Bar, Good Humor-Breyers® Reduced Fat | 1 piece | 190 | 90 |
| Klondike Premium Big Bear Ice Cream Sandwich, Good Humor-Breyers® | 1 piece | 200 | 70 |
| ❶ Orange Vanilla Treat®, Weight Watchers® | 1 bar | 70 | 10 |
| ❶ Popsicle, Good Humor-Breyers® Sugar Free | 1 piece | 15 | 0 |
| ❶ Popsicle Rainbow Juice Jets, Good Humor-Breyers® | 1 piece | 45 | 0 |
| ❶ Popsicle Tingle Twister, Good Humor-Breyers® | 1 piece | 45 | 0 |
| ❶ Sherbet Cyclone, Good Humor-Breyers® | 1 piece | 50 | 0 |
| Vanilla Sandwich Bar, Weight Watchers® | 1 bar | 160 | 35 |
| Vanilla Viennetta, Good Humor-Breyers® | 1 slice | 190 | 100 |
| ❶ Yog-A-Bar® Swirl, TCBY® | 1 bar | 80 | 5 |
| Yog-A-Bar® Vanilla with No Sugar Added, TCBY® | 1 bar | 120 | 70 |
| Yog-A-Bar® Vanilla with Pieces of Heath® Toffee, TCBY® | 1 bar | 190 | 100 |
| Yog-A-Bar® Vanilla with Toasted Almonds, TCBY® | 1 bar | 190 | 100 |

❶  Meets Low-Fat Guidelines

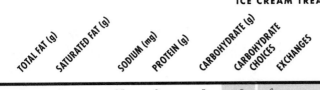

| TOTAL FAT (g) | SATURATED FAT (g) | SODIUM (mg) | PROTEIN (g) | CARBOHYDRATE (g) | CARBOHYDRATE CHOICES | EXCHANGES |
|---|---|---|---|---|---|---|
| 0 | 0 | 45 | 0 | 5 | 0 | free |
| 21 | 13 | 35 | 3 | 33 | 2 | 2 starch, 4 fat |
| 0 | 0 | 50 | 3 | 13 | 1 | 1 starch |
| 1 | <0 | 75 | 4 | 24 | 1½ | 1½ starch |
| 0 | 0 | 50 | <1 | 13 | 1 | 1 starch |
| 0 | 0.5 | 35 | 2 | 8 | ½ | ½ starch |
| 0 | 0.5 | 45 | 0 | 15 | 1 | 1 fruit |
| 1.5 | 1 | 85 | 2 | 18 | 1 | 1 starch |
| 1.5 | 0.5 | 20 | <1 | 26 | 2 | 2 fruit |
| 20 | 14 | 75 | 3 | 24 | 1½ | 1½ starch, 4 fat |
| 10 | 7 | 65 | 4 | 19 | 1 | 1 starch, 2 fat |
| 7 | 3 | 130 | 3 | 31 | 2 | 2 starch, 1 fat |
| 1 | 0.5 | 80 | 4 | 17 | 1 | 1 starch |
| 0 | 0 | 0 | 0 | 3 | 0 | free |
| 0 | 0 | 0 | 0 | 12 | 1 | 1 fruit |
| 0 | 0 | 0 | 0 | 11 | 1 | 1 fruit |
| 0.5 | 0 | 15 | 1 | 11 | 1 | 1 starch |
| 3.5 | 2 | 180 | 4 | 30 | 2 | 2 starch |
| 11 | 7 | 40 | 3 | 19 | 1 | 1 starch, 2 fat |
| 0.5 | 0.5 | 30 | 2 | 18 | 1 | 1 starch |
| 8 | 7 | 25 | 3 | 13 | 1 | 1 starch, 1 fat |
| 11 | 7 | 45 | 2 | 22 | 1½ | 1½ starch, 2 fat |
| 11 | 7 | 30 | 3 | 19 | 1 | 1 starch, 2 fat |

1 Carbohydrate Choice = 1 starch *or* 1 fruit *or* 1 milk exchange

## PRODUCTS

| | SERVING SIZE | CALORIES | CALORIES FROM FAT |
|---|---|---|---|
| **JAM/JELLY/FRUIT SPREADS** | | | |
| ❶ Fruit Spread, Kraft® Reduced Calorie, all varieties (avg) | 1 Tb | 20 | 0 |
| ❶ Jam, Kraft®, all varieties (avg) | 1 Tb | 55 | 0 |
| ❶ Jam, Smucker's®, all varieties (avg) | 1 Tb | 50 | 0 |
| ❶ Jelly, Kraft®, all varieties (avg) | 1 Tb | 55 | 0 |
| ❶ Jelly, Smucker's®, all regular varieties (avg) | 1 Tb | 50 | 0 |
| ❶ Jelly, Smucker's® Low Sugar, all varieties (avg) | 1 Tb | 25 | 0 |
| ❶ Preserves, Knott's Berry Farm®, all regular varieties (avg) | 1 Tb | 50 | 0 |
| ❶ Preserves, Kraft®, all varieties (avg) | 1 Tb | 50 | 0 |
| ❶ Preserves, Smucker's®, all varieties (avg) | 1 Tb | 50 | 0 |
| ❶ Preserves, Smucker's® Light, all varieties (avg) | 1 Tb | 10 | 0 |
| ❶ Preserves, Smucker's® Low Sugar, all varieties (avg) | 1 Tb | 25 | 0 |
| ❶ Spreadable Fruit, Polaner® All Fruit, all varieties (avg) | 1 Tb | 40 | 0 |
| ❶ Spreadable Fruit, Smucker's® Simply Fruit®, all varieties (avg) | 1 Tb | 40 | 0 |
| ❶ Strawberry Preserves, Knott's Berry Farm® Light® | 1 Tb | 20 | 0 |

### JELLO
*see* Gelatin

### JUICE DRINKS

| | | | |
|---|---|---|---|
| ❶ All Sport®, all light varieties (avg) | 8 oz | 0 | 0 |
| ❶ All Sport®, all regular varieties (avg) | 8 oz | 75 | 0 |
| ❶ Capri Sun® juice drink, all varieties (avg) | 6.75 oz | 105 | 0 |
| ❶ Fruitopia® (Apple Raspberry Embrace, Tropical Consideration, avg) | 8 oz | 75 | 0 |
| ❶ Fruitopia® (Fruit Integration, Strawberry Passion Awareness, Tangerine Wavelength, The Grape Beyond, avg) | 8 oz | 125 | 0 |
| ❶ Fruitopia® Lemonades, all varieties (avg) | 8 oz | 120 | 0 |

❶ Meets Low-Fat Guidelines

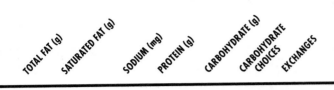

| TOTAL FAT (g) | SATURATED FAT (g) | SODIUM (mg) | PROTEIN (g) | CARBOHYDRATE (g) | CARBOHYDRATE CHOICES | EXCHANGES |
|---|---|---|---|---|---|---|
| 0 | 0 | 20 | 0 | 5 | 0 | free |
| 0 | 0 | 10 | 0 | 13 | 1 | 1 fruit |
| 0 | 0 | 0 | 0 | 13 | 1 | 1 fruit |
| 0 | 0 | 10 | 0 | 13 | 1 | 1 fruit |
| 0 | 0 | 0 | 0 | 13 | 1 | 1 fruit |
| 0 | 0 | 0 | 0 | 6 | ½ | ½ fruit |
| 0 | 0 | 10 | 0 | 13 | 1 | 1 fruit |
| 0 | 0 | 10 | 0 | 13 | 1 | 1 fruit |
| 0 | 0 | 0 | 0 | 13 | 1 | 1 fruit |
| 0 | 0 | 0 | 0 | 5 | 0 | free |
| 0 | 0 | 0 | 0 | 6 | ½ | ½ fruit |
| 0 | 0 | 0 | 0 | 10 | ½ | ½ fruit |
| 0 | 0 | 0 | 0 | 10 | ½ | ½ fruit |
| 0 | 0 | 0 | 0 | 5 | 0 | free |
| 0 | 0 | 55 | 0 | 0.5 | 0 | free |
| 0 | 0 | 55 | 0 | 21 | 1½ | 1½ fruit |
| 0 | 0 | 20 | 0 | 28 | 2 | 2 fruit |
| 0 | 0 | 24 | 0 | 19 | 1 | 1 fruit |
| 0 | 0 | 28 | 0 | 30 | 2 | 2 fruit |
| 0 | 0 | 26 | 0 | 28 | 2 | 2 fruit |

1 Carbohydrate Choice = 1 starch or 1 fruit or 1 milk exchange

## PRODUCTS

| | SERVING SIZE | CALORIES | CALORIES FROM FAT |
|---|---|---|---|
| ❶ Hi-C®, all varieties (avg) | 8 oz | 120 | 0 |
| ❶ Minute Maid® 5 Alive®, all varieties (avg) | 8 oz | 120 | 0 |
| ❶ Minute Maid® Cranberry Apple Cocktail | 8 oz | 165 | 0 |
| ❶ Minute Maid® Drink Box Punch | 8.45 oz | 120 | 0 |
| ❶ Minute Maid® fruit juices and punches, all varieties (avg) | 8 oz | 120 | 0 |
| ❶ Minute Maid® Hi-C® can, all varieties (avg) | 7.7 oz | 115 | 0 |
| ❶ Minute Maid® Hi-C® Drink Box, all varieties (avg) | 8.45 oz | 125 | 0 |
| ❶ Minute Maid® Punch, frozen or chilled, all varieties (avg) | 8 oz | 125 | 0 |
| ❶ Powerade®, all varieties (avg) | 8 oz | 75 | 0 |
| ❶ Snapple® Diet Drinks, all varieties (avg) | 8 oz | 20 | 0 |
| ❶ Snapple® Drinks (11.5 oz cans), sweetened, all varieties (avg) | 1 can | 165 | 0 |
| ❶ Snapple® Drinks, sweetened, all varieties (avg) | 8 oz | 120 | 0 |
| ❶ Squeezit® 100, all varieties (avg) | 1 bottle | 95 | 0 |
| ❶ Squeezit®, all varieties except orange (avg) | 1 bottle | 110 | 0 |
| ❶ Squeezit®, orange | 1 bottle | 110 | 0 |
| ❶ Tropicana Twister Light, bottled, all varieties (avg) | 8 oz | 40 | 0 |
| ❶ Tropicana Twister, bottled, all varieties (avg) | 8 oz | 125 | 0 |

### JUICE, FRUIT

| | SERVING SIZE | CALORIES | CALORIES FROM FAT |
|---|---|---|---|
| ❶ Apple juice, all brands (avg) | 8 oz | 115 | 0 |
| ❶ Cranberry Juice, W. Knudsen® | 8 oz | 60 | 0 |
| ❶ Grape juice, all brands (avg) | 8 oz | 160 | 0 |
| ❶ Grapefruit juice, all brands (avg) | 8 oz | 95 | 0 |
| ❶ Lemonade, all brands (avg) | 8 oz | 120 | 0 |
| ❶ Nectar, W. Knudsen®, all varieties (avg) | 8 oz | 120 | 0 |
| ❶ Orange juice, all brands (avg) | 8 oz | 110 | 0 |
| ❶ Prune Juice, Sunsweet® | 8 oz | 180 | 0 |

❶  Meets Low-Fat Guidelines

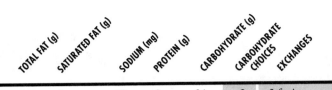

| TOTAL FAT (g) | SATURATED FAT (g) | SODIUM (mg) | PROTEIN (g) | CARBOHYDRATE (g) | CARBOHYDRATE CHOICES | EXCHANGES |
|---|---|---|---|---|---|---|
| 0 | 0 | 30 | 0 | 31 | 2 | 2 fruit |
| 0 | 0 | 25 | 0 | 30 | 2 | 2 fruit |
| 0 | 0 | 26 | 0 | 42 | 3 | 3 fruit |
| 0 | 0 | 30 | 0 | 33 | 2 | 2 fruit |
| 0 | 0 | 29 | 0 | 29 | 2 | 2 fruit |
| 0 | 0 | 30 | 0 | 31 | 2 | 2 fruit |
| 0 | 0 | 30 | 0 | 34 | 2 | 2 fruit |
| 0 | 0 | 15 | 0 | 31 | 2 | 2 fruit |
| 0 | 0 | 28 | 0 | 19 | 1 | 1 fruit |
| 0 | 0 | 10 | 0 | 4.5 | 0 | free |
| 0 | 0 | 15 | 0 | 40 | 2½ | 2½ fruit |
| 0 | 0 | 10 | 0 | 30 | 2 | 2 fruit |
| 0 | 0 | 20 | 0 | 23 | 1½ | 1½ fruit |
| 0 | 0 | 0 | 0 | 28 | 2 | 2 fruit |
| 0 | 0 | 45 | 0 | 28 | 2 | 2 fruit |
| 0 | 0 | 20 | 0 | 9 | ½ | ½ fruit |
| 0 | 0 | 20 | 0 | 31 | 2 | 2 fruit |
| 0 | 0 | 20 | 0 | 29 | 2 | 2 fruit |
| 0 | 0 | 25 | <1 | 14 | 1 | 1 fruit |
| 0 | 0 | 25 | 0 | 40 | 2½ | 2½ fruit |
| 0 | 0 | 5 | 0 | 24 | 1½ | 1½ fruit |
| 0 | 0 | 25 | 0 | 29 | 2 | 2 fruit |
| 0 | 0 | 35 | <1 | 30 | 2 | 2 fruit |
| 0 | 0 | 15 | 0 | 27 | 2 | 2 fruit |
| 0 | 0 | 75 | 1 | 43 | 3 | 3 fruit |

1 Carbohydrate Choice = 1 starch or 1 fruit or 1 milk exchange

## PRODUCTS

| | SERVING SIZE | CALORIES | CALORIES FROM FAT |
|---|---|---|---|

### JUICE, VEGETABLE

| | | | |
|---|---|---|---|
| ❶ Carrot juice, all brands (avg) | 12 oz | 120 | 10 |
| ❶ Tomato juice, all brands (avg) | 8 oz | 50 | 0 |
| ❶ Tomato juice, low sodium (avg) | 8 oz | 50 | 0 |
| ❶ Tomato juice, no salt added, all brands (avg) | 8 oz | 35 | 0 |
| ❶ V8® Low Sodium | 8 oz | 60 | 0 |
| ❶ Vegetable juice blend, all brands (avg) | 8 oz | 70 | 0 |

### LASAGNA
*see* Pasta Meals/Entrees

### LUNCH KITS

*Hillshire Farm® Lunch 'n Munch*

| | | | |
|---|---|---|---|
| Bologna/American | 4.5 oz | 480 | 335 |
| Bologna/American/Snickers® | 4.25 oz | 490 | 305 |
| Bologna/American/Snickers®/Hi-C® | 4.25 oz | 590 | 305 |
| Cooked Ham/Swiss | 4.5 oz | 360 | 200 |
| Cooked Ham/Swiss/Oreo® | 4.125 oz | 370 | 190 |
| Cooked Ham/Swiss/Snickers®/Hi-C® | 4.125 oz | 470 | 190 |
| Honey Ham/Cheddar/Snickers®/Hi-C® | 4.25 oz | 500 | 205 |
| Pepperoni/American | 4.5 oz | 570 | 415 |
| Smoked Chicken/Monterey Jack | 4.5 oz | 350 | 180 |
| Smoked Chicken/Monterey Jack/Snickers® | 4.25 oz | 400 | 200 |
| Smoked Cotto Salami/Monterey Jack | 4.5 oz | 440 | 290 |
| Smoked Turkey/Cheddar | 4.5 oz | 350 | 190 |
| Smoked Turkey/Cheddar/Brownie | 4.5 oz | 400 | 200 |
| Smoked Turkey/Cheddar/Brownie/Hi-C® | 4.5 oz | 500 | 200 |

❶ Meets Low-Fat Guidelines

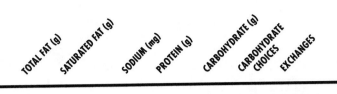

| TOTAL FAT (g) | SATURATED FAT (g) | SODIUM (mg) | PROTEIN (g) | CARBOHYDRATE (g) | CARBOHYDRATE CHOICES | EXCHANGES |
|---|---|---|---|---|---|---|
| 1 | 0 | 250 | 2 | 27 | 2 | 2 fruit |
| 0 | 0 | 530–720 | 2 | 7 | ½ | ½ starch or 1 veg |
| 0 | 0 | 140 | 2 | 10 | ½ | ½ starch or 2 veg |
| 0 | 0 | 15 | 2 | 7 | ½ | ½ starch or 1 veg |
| 0 | 0 | 140 | 2 | 11 | 1 | 1 starch or 2 veg |
| 0 | 0 | 340–640 | 2 | 11 | 1 | 1 starch or 2 veg |
| 37 | NA | 1390 | 17 | 20 | 1 | 1 starch, 2 meat, 5 fat |
| 34 | NA | 1110 | 15 | 31 | 2 | 2 starch, 2 meat, 4 fat |
| 34 | NA | 1130 | 15 | 55 | 3½ | 2 starch, 1½ fruit, 2 meat, 4 fat |
| 22 | NA | 1380 | 20 | 19 | 1 | 1 starch, 3 meat, 1 fat |
| 21 | NA | 1160 | 19 | 30 | 2 | 2 starch, 2 meat, 2 fat |
| 21 | NA | 1180 | 16 | 54 | 3½ | 2 starch, 1½ fruit, 2 meat, 2 fat |
| 23 | NA | 1030 | 17 | 56 | 4 | 2½ starch, 1½ fruit, 2 meat, 2 fat |
| 46 | NA | 1670 | 22 | 20 | 1 | 1 starch, 3 meat, 6 fat |
| 20 | NA | 1260 | 22 | 19 | 1 | 1 starch, 3 meat, 1 fat |
| 23 | NA | 1080 | 19 | 31 | 2 | 2 starch, 2 meat, 2 fat |
| 32 | NA | 1270 | 18 | 21 | 1½ | 1½ starch, 2 meat, 4 fat |
| 21 | NA | 1130 | 21 | 20 | 1 | 1 starch, 3 meat, 1 fat |
| 22 | NA | 1240 | 17 | 34 | 2 | 2 starch, 2 meat, 2 fat |
| 22 | NA | 1260 | 17 | 58 | 4 | 2½ starch, 1½ fruit, 2 meat, 2 fat |

1 Carbohydrate Choice = 1 starch *or* 1 fruit *or* 1 milk exchange

## PRODUCTS

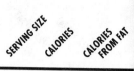

### Oscar Meyer® Lunchables

| | SERVING SIZE | CALORIES | CALORIES FROM FAT |
|---|---|---|---|
| Bologna/American | 1 pkg | 470 | 320 |
| Bologna/Wild Cherry Fun Pack | 1 pkg | 530 | 250 |
| Chicken/Turkey Deluxe | 1 pkg | 390 | 210 |
| Ham/Cheddar | 1 pkg | 360 | 200 |
| Ham/Fruit Punch Low Fat | 1 pkg | 360 | 90 |
| Ham/Fruit Punch Fun Pack | 1 pkg | 440 | 180 |
| Ham/Surfer Cooler™ Low Fat | 1 pkg | 390 | 100 |
| Ham/Swiss | 1 pkg | 340 | 180 |
| Pizza—Mozzarella/Fruit Punch Fun Pack | 1 pkg | 450 | 140 |
| Pizza—Pepperoni/Mozzarella | 1 pkg | 330 | 140 |
| Pizza—Pepperoni/Orange Fun Pack | 1 pkg | 480 | 150 |
| Pizza—Two Cheese | 1 pkg | 330 | 110 |
| Salami/American | 1 pkg | 430 | 270 |
| Turkey/Cheddar | 1 pkg | 350 | 180 |
| Turkey/Ham Deluxe | 1 pkg | 370 | 190 |
| Turkey/Monterey Jack | 1 pkg | 350 | 190 |
| Turkey/Pacific Cooler™ Low Fat | 1 pkg | 360 | 80 |
| Turkey/Pacific Cooler™ Fun Pack | 1 pkg | 450 | 180 |
| Turkey/Surfer Cooler™ Fun Pack | 1 pkg | 430 | 140 |

## LUNCH MEATS

### Alpine Lace® Lunch Meats

| | SERVING SIZE | CALORIES | CALORIES FROM FAT |
|---|---|---|---|
| ❶ Cooked Ham | 2 oz | 60 | 20 |
| ❶ Fat-Free Turkey Breast | 2 oz | 50 | 0 |

❶  Meets Low-Fat Guidelines

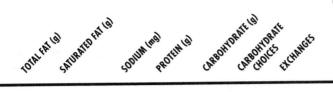

| TOTAL FAT (g) | SATURATED FAT (g) | SODIUM (mg) | PROTEIN (g) | CARBOHYDRATE (g) | CARBOHYDRATE CHOICES | EXCHANGES |
|---|---|---|---|---|---|---|
| 35 | 17 | 1640 | 17 | 22 | 1½ | 1½ starch, 2 meat, 5½ fat |
| 28 | 13 | 1120 | 13 | 60 | 4 | 2 starch, 2 fruit, 1 meat, 4 fat |
| 23 | 12 | 1820 | 21 | 24 | 1½ | 1½ starch, 2 meat, 2 fat |
| 22 | 11 | 1750 | 20 | 21 | 1½ | 1½ starch, 2 meat, 2 fat |
| 10 | 4.5 | 1150 | 17 | 52 | 3½ | 1½ starch, 2 fruit, 2 meat |
| 20 | 9 | 1270 | 15 | 54 | 3½ | 1½ starch, 2 fruit, 2 meat, 2 fat |
| 11 | 5 | 1350 | 17 | 58 | 4 | 2 starch, 2 fruit, 1 meat, 1 fat |
| 20 | 10 | 1790 | 21 | 20 | 1 | 1 starch, 2 meat, 2 fat |
| 15 | 9 | 740 | 17 | 61 | 4 | 2 starch, 2 fruit, 2 meat, ½ fat |
| 15 | 7 | 850 | 17 | 32 | 2 | 2 starch, 2 meat, ½ fat |
| 17 | 8 | 900 | 18 | 65 | 4 | 2 starch, 2 fruit, 2 meat, 1 fat |
| 13 | 7 | 710 | 17 | 29 | 2 | 2 starch, 2 meat |
| 30 | 15 | 1610 | 18 | 21 | 1½ | 1½ starch, 2 meat, 4 fat |
| 20 | 11 | 1760 | 20 | 22 | 1½ | 1½ starch, 2 meat, 2 fat |
| 21 | 10 | 1930 | 21 | 25 | 1½ | 1½ starch, 2 meat, 2 fat |
| 21 | 11 | 1690 | 20 | 20 | 1 | 1 starch, 1 meat, 3 fat |
| 9 | 4.5 | 1190 | 15 | 56 | 4 | 2 starch, 2 fruit, 1 meat |
| 20 | 10 | 1340 | 16 | 54 | 3½ | 1½ starch, 2 fruit, 2 meat, 2 fat |
| 15 | 8 | 1240 | 13 | 61 | 4 | 2 starch, 2 fruit, 1 meat, 2 fat |
| 2 | 1 | 440 | 10 | 2 | 0 | 1 lean meat |
| 0 | 0 | 290 | 12 | 0 | 0 | 2 very lean meat |

1 Carbohydrate Choice = 1 starch *or* 1 fruit *or* 1 milk exchange

| PRODUCTS | SERVING SIZE | CALORIES | CALORIES FROM FAT |
|---|---|---|---|
| **Land O' Frost® Lunch Meats** | | | |
| Premium Meats (ham, turkey, chicken, avg) | 2 oz | 80 | 40 |
| ❶ Sandwich Shop Meats, all varieties (avg) | 2 oz | 60 | 15 |
| Thin Sliced Meats, all varieties (avg) | 1 pkg | 120 | 60 |
| **Oscar Meyer® Lunch Meats** | | | |
| Braunschweiger | 2 slices | 170 | 140 |
| Braunschweiger Spread | 2 oz | 190 | 160 |
| ❶ Free™ Cold Cuts, all varieties (avg) | 2 oz | 35 | 0 |
| ❶ Deli-Thin® Cold Cuts, all varieties (avg) | 4 slices | 60 | 15 |
| ❶ Healthy Favorites® Cold Cuts, all varieties (avg) | 4 slices | 55 | 15 |
| ❶ Lean Ham Cold Cuts, all varieties (avg) | 3 slices | 65 | 20 |
| ❶ Lean Turkey Cold Cuts, all varieties (avg) | 1 slice | 30 | 10 |
| Light Bologna, all varieties (avg) | 1 oz | 60 | 35 |
| Regular Bologna, all varieties (avg) | 1 oz | 90 | 70 |
| Salami, all varieties (avg) | 2 slices | 110 | 90 |
| **Healthy Choice® Lunch Meats** | | | |
| ❶ Cold Cuts, all varieties (avg) | 1 slice | 30 | 5 |
| ❶ Deli-Thin Sliced Meats, all varieties (avg) | 6 slices | 55 | 10 |
| **Hillshire Farm® Lunch Meats** | | | |
| ❶ 10 oz Lunch Meats, all varieties (avg) | 1 oz | 35 | 10 |
| ❶ Deli Select products, all varieties (avg) | 1 slice | 10 | NA |
| ❶ Flavor Pack Lunch Meats, all varieties (avg) | 1 slice | 20 | 0 |
| Hard Salami | 1 oz | 100 | 81 |
| Light Summer Sausage | 2 oz | 150 | 108 |
| Summer Sausage, all varieties except Light | 2 oz | 180 | 144 |
| **Hormel® Lunch Meats** | | | |
| ❶ Ham (Cure 81®, Curemaster®, and Light & Lean® 97, and Deli Cooked brands, avg) | 2 oz | 60 | 20 |
| Homeland® Hard Salami | 1 oz | 117 | 90 |

❶　Meets Low-Fat Guidelines

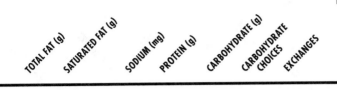

| TOTAL FAT (g) | SATURATED FAT (g) | SODIUM (mg) | PROTEIN (g) | CARBOHYDRATE (g) | CARBOHYDRATE CHOICES | EXCHANGES |
|---|---|---|---|---|---|---|
| 5 | 1 | 660–740 | 9 | 3 | 0 | 1 meat |
| 1.5 | 0 | 810–1020 | 9.5 | 1 | 0 | 1 lean meat |
| 7 | 3 | 930–1090 | 12 | 1 | 0 | 2 lean meat |
|  |  |  |  |  |  |  |
| 16 | 6 | 590 | 7 | 1 | 0 | 1 meat, 2 fat |
| 17 | 6 | 630 | 8 | 2 | 0 | 1 meat, 2 fat |
| 0 | 0 | 280–650 | 4–9 | 2 | 0 | 1 very lean meat |
| 1.5 | <1 | 500–740 | 9.5 | 1 | 0 | 1 lean meat |
| 1.5 | <1 | 430 | 9 | 2 | 0 | 1 lean meat |
| 2.5 | 1 | 520–820 | 10 | 1 | 0 | 1 lean meat |
| 1 | 0 | 320 | 5 | 1 | 0 | 1 very lean meat |
| 4 | 1.5 | 310 | 3 | 2 | 0 | ½ high fat meat |
| 8 | 4 | 285 | 3 | 1 | 0 | ½ high fat meat, 1 fat |
| 9 | 3 | 490–650 | 6 | 1 | 0 | 1 meat, 1 fat |
|  |  |  |  |  |  |  |
| 1 | 0.5 | 240 | 5 | 1 | 0 | 1 very lean meat |
| 1 | 0.5 | 420–480 | 10 | 2 | 0 | 2 very lean meat |
|  |  |  |  |  |  |  |
| 1 | NA | 340–470 | 5 | 1 | 0 | 1 very lean meat |
| <1 | NA | 80–135 | 2 | <1 | 0 | free (4 slices = 1 very lean meat) |
| <1 | NA | 170–230 | 4 | 1 | 0 | 1 very lean meat |
| 9 | NA | 450 | 5 | 0 | 0 | 1 high fat meat |
| 12 | NA | 630 | 10 | 1 | 0 | 1 meat, 1½ fat |
| 16 | NA | 605–670 | 9 | 1 | 0 | 1 meat, 2 fat |
|  |  |  |  |  |  |  |
| 2 | 1 | 344–627 | 10 | 1 | 0 | 1 lean meat |
|  |  |  |  |  |  |  |
| 10 | 4 | 448 | 6 | NA | 0 | 1 meat, 1 fat |

1 Carbohydrate Choice = 1 starch or 1 fruit or 1 milk exchange

# PRODUCTS

| | SERVING SIZE | CALORIES | CALORIES FROM FAT |
|---|---|---|---|
| **Louis Rich® Lunch Meats** | | | |
| ❶ Deli-Thin® cold cuts, all varieties (avg) | 4 slices | 55 | 15 |
| ❶ Carving Board™ meats, all varieties (avg) | 2 slices | 45 | 10 |
| ❶ Chicken Breast | 1 slice | 35 | 20 |
| ❶ Fat Free Turkey Breast | 2 oz | 55 | 0 |
| Turkey Bologna | 1 slice | 50 | 30 |
| ❶ Turkey Salami | 1 slice | 40 | 25 |
| ❶ Turkey Ham | 1 slice | 35 | 10 |
| **Tyson Holly Farms® Lunch Meats** | | | |
| ❶ Fat-Free Sliced Meats, all varieties (avg) | 2 slices | 35 | 0 |
| ❶ Sliced Chicken Breast | 3 slices | 50 | 0 |
| **MACARONI AND CHEESE (DRY, AS PREPARED)** | | | |
| Deluxe Original, Kraft® | ~1 cup | 320 | 90 |
| Macaroni & Cheese, Golden Grain® | 1 cup | 340 | 150 |
| Mild White Cheddar, Kraft® | ~1 cup | 390 | 150 |
| Original, Kraft®, all varieties (avg) | ~1 cup | 390 | 150 |
| Rotini & Cheese, Broccoli, Kraft® Velveeta® | ~1 cup | 400 | 140 |
| Shells & Cheese, Kraft® Velveeta®, all varieties (avg) | ~1 cup | 365 | 120 |
| Thick 'N Creamy®, Kraft® | ~1 cup | 320 | 90 |
| Whole Wheat Macaroni & Cheese Dinner, Hodgeson Mill® | 1 cup | 387 | 182 |
| **MACARONI AND CHEESE (FROZEN)** *see also* Pasta Meals/Entrees | | | |
| Homestyle Macaroni & Cheese, Budget Gourmet® | 1 entree | 360 | 160 |
| Macaroni & Cheese, Banquet® | 1 meal | 350 | 110 |
| ❶ Macaroni and Cheese, Banquet® | 1 pkg | 200 | 30 |
| ❶ Macaroni and Cheese, Banquet® Family Size | 1 cup | 210 | 40 |
| Macaroni & Cheese, Banquet® Bake At Home | 1 cup | 300 | 100 |
| ❶ Macaroni & Cheese, Budget Gourmet® Light | 1 entree | 310 | 60 |

❶ Meets Low-Fat Guidelines

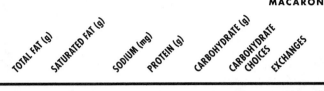

| TOTAL FAT (g) | SATURATED FAT (g) | SODIUM (mg) | PROTEIN (g) | CARBOHYDRATE (g) | CARBOHYDRATE CHOICES | EXCHANGES |
|---|---|---|---|---|---|---|
| 1.5 | <1 | 480–620 | 9 | 1 | 0 | 1 lean meat |
| <1.5 | <1 | 530–570 | 9 | 1 | 0 | 1 lean meat |
| 2 | <1 | 340 | 5 | 1 | 0 | 1 lean meat |
| 0 | 0 | 600–730 | 10 | 1.5 | 0 | 2 very lean meat |
| 3.5 | 1 | 270 | 3 | 1 | 0 | ½ high fat meat |
| 2.5 | 1 | 280 | 5 | 0 | 0 | 1 lean meat |
| 1 | 0 | 300 | 5 | 1 | 0 | 1 very lean meat |
| 0 | 0 | 450 | 7 | 2 | 0 | 1 very lean meat |
| 0 | 0 | 680–720 | 11 | 2 | 0 | 2 very lean meat |
| 10 | 6 | 730 | 14 | 44 | 3 | 3 starch, 1 meat |
| 17 | 3.5 | 680 | 8 | 40 | 2½ | 2½ starch, 3 fat |
| 17 | 4 | 730 | 11 | 48 | 3 | 3 starch, 1 meat, 2 fat |
| 17 | 4.5 | 760 | 12 | 48 | 3 | 3 starch, 1 meat, 2 fat |
| 16 | 10 | 1240 | 18 | 46 | 3 | 3 starch, 1 meat, 2 fat |
| 14 | 8 | 1115 | 17 | 45 | 3 | 3 starch, 1 meat, 3 fat |
| 10 | 6 | 730 | 12 | 50 | 3 | 3 starch, 1 meat |
| 18 | 4 | 677 | 11 | 50 | 3 | 3 starch, 1 meat, 2 fat |
| 18 | 10 | 1190 | 15 | 34 | 2 | 2 starch, 1 high fat meat, 2 fat |
| 12 | 3.5 | 960 | 13 | 47 | 3 | 3 starch, 1 meat, 1 fat |
| 3 | 1.5 | 600 | 7 | 35 | 2 | 2 starch, 1 lean meat |
| 5 | 2 | 1290 | 8 | 33 | 2 | 2 starch, 1 meat |
| 10 | 5 | 1190 | 14 | 39 | 2½ | 2½ starch, 1 meat, ½ fat |
| 7 | 3 | 570 | 12 | 50 | 3 | 3 starch, 2 lean meat |

1 Carbohydrate Choice = 1 starch or 1 fruit or 1 milk exchange

## PRODUCTS

| PRODUCTS | SERVING SIZE | CALORIES | CALORIES FROM FAT |
|---|---|---|---|
| ❶ Macaroni & Cheese, Healthy Choice® | 1 meal | 290 | 45 |
| Macaroni & Cheese, Michelina's® | 1 pkg | 380 | 120 |
| Macaroni & Cheese, Michelina's® Double Serving | 1 cup | 360 | 110 |
| ❶ Macaroni & Cheese, Morton® (6.5 oz) | 1 pkg | 200 | 30 |
| ❶ Macaroni & Cheese, Morton® Multi-Serving | 1 cup | 230 | 35 |
| Macaroni & Cheese, Stouffer's® Family Size | 1 cup | 320 | 140 |
| Macaroni & Cheese, Stouffer's® Lean Cuisine® | 1 pkg | 270 | 60 |
| Macaroni and Cheese, Marie Callender's® | 1 cup | 420 | 150 |
| Macaroni and Cheese, Weight Watchers® | 1 entree | 280 | 60 |
| Macaroni & Cheese and Broccoli, Stouffer's® Lean Cuisine® Lunch Express® | 1 pkg | 240 | 50 |
| Macaroni & Cheese with Broccoli, Stouffer's® Lunch Express® | 1 pkg | 360 | 170 |

### MARGARINE

| | | | |
|---|---|---|---|
| ❶ Extra light, all varieties (avg) | 1 Tb | 20 | 20 |
| ❶ Fat Free, all varieties (avg) | 1 Tb | 10 | 0 |
| Light, all varieties (avg) | 1 Tb | 50 | 50 |
| Regular, stick or tub, all varieties (avg) | 1 Tb | 100 | 100 |
| Whipped, all varieties (avg) | 1 Tb | 70 | 70 |

### MAYONNAISE

| | | | |
|---|---|---|---|
| ❶ Mayonnaise, all fat-free varieties (avg) | 1 Tb | 10 | 0 |
| Mayonnaise, all light varieties (avg) | 1 Tb | 50 | 45 |
| Mayonnaise, all regular varieties (avg) | 1 Tb | 100 | 100 |
| ❶ Miracle Whip® Free®, Kraft® | 1 Tb | 15 | 0 |
| Miracle Whip®, Kraft® | 1 Tb | 70 | 60 |
| Sandwich Spread, Hellmann's® or Best Foods® | 1 Tb | 50 | 45 |

### MEAL MIXES (AS PREPARED)

#### Beef Meal Mixes

| | | | |
|---|---|---|---|
| Beef Pasta, Hamburger Helper® | 1 cup | 250 | 80 |

❶ Meets Low-Fat Guidelines

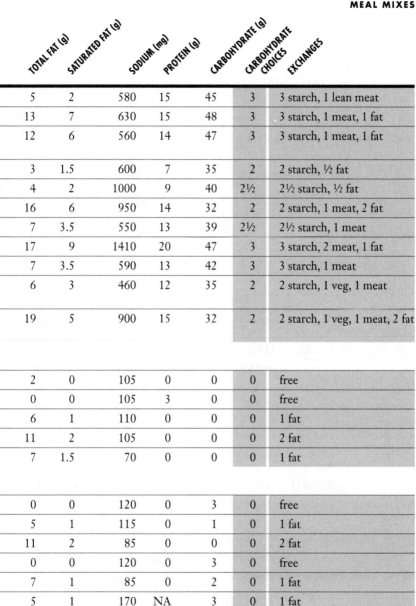

| TOTAL FAT (g) | SATURATED FAT (g) | SODIUM (mg) | PROTEIN (g) | CARBOHYDRATE (g) | CARBOHYDRATE CHOICES | EXCHANGES |
|---|---|---|---|---|---|---|
| 5 | 2 | 580 | 15 | 45 | 3 | 3 starch, 1 lean meat |
| 13 | 7 | 630 | 15 | 48 | 3 | 3 starch, 1 meat, 1 fat |
| 12 | 6 | 560 | 14 | 47 | 3 | 3 starch, 1 meat, 1 fat |
| 3 | 1.5 | 600 | 7 | 35 | 2 | 2 starch, ½ fat |
| 4 | 2 | 1000 | 9 | 40 | 2½ | 2½ starch, ½ fat |
| 16 | 6 | 950 | 14 | 32 | 2 | 2 starch, 1 meat, 2 fat |
| 7 | 3.5 | 550 | 13 | 39 | 2½ | 2½ starch, 1 meat |
| 17 | 9 | 1410 | 20 | 47 | 3 | 3 starch, 2 meat, 1 fat |
| 7 | 3.5 | 590 | 13 | 42 | 3 | 3 starch, 1 meat |
| 6 | 3 | 460 | 12 | 35 | 2 | 2 starch, 1 veg, 1 meat |
| 19 | 5 | 900 | 15 | 32 | 2 | 2 starch, 1 veg, 1 meat, 2 fat |
| 2 | 0 | 105 | 0 | 0 | 0 | free |
| 0 | 0 | 105 | 3 | 0 | 0 | free |
| 6 | 1 | 110 | 0 | 0 | 0 | 1 fat |
| 11 | 2 | 105 | 0 | 0 | 0 | 2 fat |
| 7 | 1.5 | 70 | 0 | 0 | 0 | 1 fat |
| 0 | 0 | 120 | 0 | 3 | 0 | free |
| 5 | 1 | 115 | 0 | 1 | 0 | 1 fat |
| 11 | 2 | 85 | 0 | 0 | 0 | 2 fat |
| 0 | 0 | 120 | 0 | 3 | 0 | free |
| 7 | 1 | 85 | 0 | 2 | 0 | 1 fat |
| 5 | 1 | 170 | NA | 3 | 0 | 1 fat |
| 9 | 3.5 | 900 | 18 | 23 | 1½ | 1½ starch, 2 meat |

1 Carbohydrate Choice = 1 starch or 1 fruit or 1 milk exchange

## PRODUCTS

| PRODUCTS | SERVING SIZE | CALORIES | CALORIES FROM FAT |
|---|---|---|---|
| Beef Romanoff, Hamburger Helper® | 1 cup | 290 | 100 |
| Beef Stew, Hamburger Helper Homestyle® | 1 cup | 250 | 90 |
| Beef Stroganoff, Dinner Sensations™ | 1 cup | 320 | 130 |
| Beef Taco, Hamburger Helper® | 1 cup | 310 | 100 |
| ❶ Beef Teriyaki, Dinner Sensations™ | 1 cup | 260 | 40 |
| Beef Teriyaki, Hamburger Helper® | 1 cup | 290 | 90 |
| Beef Vegetable Soup, Hamburger Helper® | 1 cup | 190 | 70 |
| Burrito, Old El Paso® | 1 burrito | 280 | 60 |
| Cheddar Melt, Hamburger Helper® | 1 cup | 310 | 100 |
| Cheddar 'n Bacon, Hamburger Helper® | 1 cup | 350 | 140 |
| Cheeseburger Macaroni, Hamburger Helper® | 1 cup | 360 | 140 |
| Cheesy Italian, Hamburger Helper® | 1 cup | 330 | 120 |
| Cheesy Shells, Hamburger Helper® | 1 cup | 340 | 140 |
| Chili Macaroni, Hamburger Helper® | 1 cup | 290 | 90 |
| Fettuccini Alfredo, Hamburger Helper® | 1 cup | 300 | 120 |
| Hamburger Stew, Hamburger Helper® | 1 cup | 250 | 90 |
| Lasagne, Hamburger Helper® | 1 cup | 280 | 90 |
| Meat Loaf, Hamburger Helper® | ⅙ loaf | 280 | 130 |
| Mushroom & Wild Rice, Hamburger Helper® | 1 cup | 310 | 110 |
| Nacho Cheese, Hamburger Helper® | 1 cup | 320 | 120 |
| Pizzabake, Hamburger Helper® | ⅙ pan | 270 | 90 |
| Pizza Pasta with Cheese Topping, Hamburger Helper® | 1 cup | 290 | 90 |
| Potato Stroganoff, Hamburger Helper® | 1 cup | 270 | 100 |
| Potatoes AuGratin, Hamburger Helper® | 1 cup | 290 | 120 |
| Rice Oriental, Hamburger Helper® | 1 cup | 310 | 90 |
| Salisbury, Hamburger Helper Homestyle® | 1 cup | 270 | 90 |
| Soft Taco, Old El Paso® | 2 tacos | 380 | 100 |
| Spaghetti, Hamburger Helper® | 1 cup | 300 | 100 |
| Stroganoff, Hamburger Helper® | 1 cup | 350 | 130 |
| Swedish Meatballs, Hamburger Helper Homestyle® | 1 cup | 300 | 130 |

❶  Meets Low-Fat Guidelines

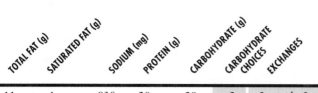

| TOTAL FAT (g) | SATURATED FAT (g) | SODIUM (mg) | PROTEIN (g) | CARBOHYDRATE (g) | CARBOHYDRATE CHOICES | EXCHANGES |
|---|---|---|---|---|---|---|
| 11 | 4 | 930 | 20 | 28 | 2 | 2 starch, 2 meat |
| 10 | 3.5 | 750 | 18 | 26 | 2 | 2 starch, 2 meat |
| 15 | 6 | 660 | 19 | 28 | 2 | 2 starch, 2 meat, ½ fat |
| 11 | 4 | 920 | 20 | 30 | 2 | 2 starch, 2 meat |
| 4.5 | 1 | 600 | 17 | 38 | 2½ | 2½ starch, 2 very lean meat |
| 10 | 3.5 | 990 | 18 | 34 | 2 | 2 starch, 2 meat |
| 8 | 3 | 680 | 14 | 17 | 1 | 1 starch, 2 lean meat |
| 7 | 3 | 840 | 0 | 35 | 2 | 2 starch, 2 lean meat |
| 12 | 4.5 | 900 | 20 | 31 | 2 | 2 starch, 2 meat |
| 16 | 6 | 890 | 24 | 28 | 2 | 2 starch, 3 meat |
| 16 | 6 | 1000 | 23 | 31 | 2 | 2 starch, 3 meat |
| 14 | 5 | 920 | 22 | 29 | 2 | 2 starch, 3 meat |
| 16 | 6 | 850 | 22 | 29 | 2 | 2 starch, 3 meat |
| 10 | 4 | 870 | 19 | 30 | 2 | 2 starch, 2 meat |
| 13 | 5 | 890 | 21 | 26 | 2 | 2 starch, 2 meat |
| 10 | 4 | 920 | 19 | 22 | 1½ | 1½ starch, 2 meat |
| 10 | 4 | 950 | 19 | 30 | 2 | 2 starch, 2 meat |
| 15 | 6 | 600 | 25 | 11 | 1 | 1 starch, 3 meat |
| 12 | 4.5 | 880 | 20 | 30 | 2 | 2 starch, 2 meat |
| 13 | 5 | 930 | 22 | 30 | 2 | 2 starch, 2 meat |
| 10 | 3.5 | 720 | 17 | 28 | 2 | 2 starch, 2 meat |
| 10 | 4 | 670 | 19 | 31 | 2 | 2 starch, 2 meat |
| 12 | 4.5 | 870 | 18 | 25 | 1½ | 1½ starch, 2 meat |
| 14 | 5 | 820 | 18 | 24 | 1½ | 1½ starch, 2 meat |
| 10 | 4 | 1050 | 19 | 35 | 2 | 2 starch, 2 meat |
| 10 | 4 | 790 | 19 | 26 | 2 | 2 starch, 2 meat |
| 10 | 4 | 1340 | 5 | 40 | 2½ | 2½ starch, 2 fat |
| 11 | 4 | 940 | 21 | 29 | 2 | 2 starch, 2 meat |
| 14 | 5 | 960 | 23 | 33 | 2 | 2 starch, 2 meat, ½ fat |
| 14 | 5 | 780 | 19 | 24 | 1½ | 1½ starch, 2 meat, ½ fat |

1 Carbohydrate Choice = 1 starch *or* 1 fruit *or* 1 milk exchange

## PRODUCTS

| | SERVING SIZE | CALORIES | CALORIES FROM FAT |
|---|---|---|---|
| Taco, Old El Paso® | 2 tacos | 270 | 120 |
| Three Cheese, Hamburger Helper® | 1 cup | 340 | 130 |
| Zesty Italian, Hamburger Helper® | 1 cup | 320 | 100 |
| Zesty Mexican, Hamburger Helper® | 1 cup | 300 | 100 |
| **Chicken Meal Mixes** | | | |
| Chicken Alfredo, Dinner Sensations™ | 1 cup | 310 | 110 |
| Stir-Fried Chicken, Skillet Chicken Helper® | 1 cup | 270 | 90 |
| ❶ Sweet & Sour Chicken, Dinner Sensations™ | 1 cup | 330 | 35 |
| **Stir Fry Meal Mixes** | | | |
| Broccoli Stir Fry, Green Giant® Create a Meal!® | 1⅓ cups | 290 | 120 |
| ❶ Lo Mein Stir Fry, Green Giant® Create a Meal!® | 1⅓ cups | 320 | 60 |
| Sechuan Stir Fry, Green Giant® Create a Meal!® | 1¼ cups | 320 | 130 |
| ❶ Sweet & Sour Stir Fry, Green Giant® Create a Meal!® | 1¼ cups | 290 | 60 |
| ❶ Teriyaki Stir Fry, Green Giant® Create a Meal!® | 1¼ cups | 240 | 50 |
| Vegetable Almond Stir Fry, Green Giant® Create a Meal!® | 1⅓ cups | 320 | 100 |
| **Tuna Meal Mixes** | | | |
| Augratin, Tuna Helper® | 1 cup | 310 | 110 |
| Cheesy Pasta, Tuna Helper® | 1 cup | 280 | 100 |
| Classic Tuna Melt, Tuna Helper® | 1 cup | 300 | 120 |
| Creamy Broccoli, Tuna Helper® | 1 cup | 310 | 110 |
| Creamy Pasta, Tuna Helper® | 1 cup | 300 | 120 |
| Fettuccine Alfredo, Tuna Helper® | 1 cup | 310 | 120 |
| Garden Cheddar, Tuna Helper® | 1 cup | 310 | 110 |
| Pasta Salad, Tuna Helper® | ⅔ cup | 380 | 240 |
| Tetrazzini, Tuna Helper® | 1 cup | 310 | 110 |
| Tuna Pot Pie, Tuna Helper® | 1 cup | 440 | 220 |
| ❶ Tuna Romanoff, Tuna Helper® | 1 cup | 280 | 70 |

 Meets Low-Fat Guidelines

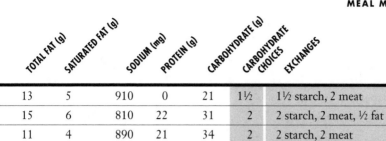

| TOTAL FAT (g) | SATURATED FAT (g) | SODIUM (mg) | PROTEIN (g) | CARBOHYDRATE (g) | CARBOHYDRATE CHOICES | EXCHANGES |
|---|---|---|---|---|---|---|
| 13 | 5 | 910 | 0 | 21 | 1½ | 1½ starch, 2 meat |
| 15 | 6 | 810 | 22 | 31 | 2 | 2 starch, 2 meat, ½ fat |
| 11 | 4 | 890 | 21 | 34 | 2 | 2 starch, 2 meat |
| 11 | 4 | 730 | 19 | 32 | 2 | 2 starch, 2 meat |
| 12 | 4 | 640 | 21 | 29 | 2 | 2 starch, 2 meat |
| 9 | 2 | 810 | 18 | 30 | 2 | 2 starch, 2 lean meat |
| 4 | 1 | 320 | 16 | 57 | 4 | 2 starch, 2 fruit, 2 very lean meat |
| 13 | 3 | 1160 | 27 | 16 | 1 | ½ starch, 1 veg, 3 meat |
| 7 | 1 | 1140 | 32 | 32 | 2 | 2 starch, 3 lean meat |
| 14 | 3 | 1280 | 27 | 21 | 1½ | 1 starch, 1 veg, 3 meat |
| 7 | 1 | 460 | 27 | 29 | 2 | 1½ starch, 1 veg, 3 lean meat |
| 6 | 1 | 930 | 27 | 19 | 1 | 1 starch, 1 veg, 3 lean meat |
| 11 | 1.5 | 1190 | 32 | 22 | 1½ | 1 starch, 1 veg, 4 lean meat |
| 12 | 3 | 930 | 14 | 36 | 2½ | 2½ starch, 1 meat, 1 fat |
| 11 | 2.5 | 890 | 14 | 32 | 2 | 2 starch, 1 meat, 1 fat |
| 13 | 2.5 | 850 | 13 | 31 | 2 | 2 starch, 1 meat, 1 fat |
| 12 | 3 | 880 | 14 | 35 | 2 | 2 starch, 1 veg, 1 meat, 1 fat |
| 13 | 3.5 | 910 | 14 | 31 | 2 | 2 starch, 1 meat, 1 fat |
| 13 | 3.5 | 940 | 14 | 32 | 2 | 2 starch, 1 meat, 1 fat |
| 12 | 3 | 1040 | 16 | 35 | 2 | 2 starch, 1 veg, 1 meat, 1 fat |
| 27 | 3 | 730 | 10 | 26 | 2 | 2 starch, 1 meat, 4 fat |
| 12 | 3 | 1010 | 17 | 33 | 2 | 2 starch, 2 meat |
| 24 | 7 | 1080 | 18 | 40 | 2½ | 2½ starch, 2 meat, 2 fat |
| 8 | 1.5 | 800 | 15 | 38 | 2½ | 2½ starch, 1 meat |

1 Carbohydrate Choice = 1 starch or 1 fruit or 1 milk exchange

## PRODUCTS

| | SERVING SIZE | CALORIES | CALORIES FROM FAT |
|---|---|---|---|
| **MEAT SPREAD (CANNED)** | | | |
| Chunky Chicken, Underwood® | ¼ cup | 120 | 70 |
| Chunky Chicken, Underwood® Red Devil Snackers® | 1 pkg | 270 | 140 |
| Deviled Ham, Underwood® | ¼ cup | 160 | 130 |
| Deviled Ham, Underwood® Red Devil Snackers® | 1 pkg | 310 | 200 |
| Honey Ham, Underwood® | ¼ cup | 180 | 140 |
| Honey Ham, Underwood® Red Devil Snackers® | 1 pkg | 340 | 210 |
| Liverwurst, Underwood® | ¼ cup | 160 | 130 |
| Roast Beef, Underwood® | ¼ cup | 130 | 100 |
| Sandwich, Oscar Meyer® | 2 oz | 130 | 90 |
| Sell's Liver Paté, Underwood® | ¼ cup | 160 | 130 |
| **MEXICAN MEALS/ENTREES (FROZEN)** | | | |
| ***Beef Mexican Meals/Entrees*** | | | |
| Beef & Bean Bite Size Burritos, Patio® | 10 burritos | 420 | 170 |
| ❶ Beef & Two Cheese Enchiladas Chili 'N Beans, Patio® | 2 enchiladas | 250 | 60 |
| Beef and Bean Burrito, Old El Paso®, hot | 1 burrito | 320 | 90 |
| Beef and Bean Burrito, Old El Paso®, medium | 1 burrito | 320 | 90 |
| ❶ Beef and Bean Burrito, Old El Paso®, mild | 1 burrito | 330 | 80 |
| Beef Chimichanga, Old El Paso® | 1 piece | 370 | 180 |
| Beef Enchilada, Banquet® | 1 meal | 380 | 110 |
| Beef Enchilada Dinner, Patio® | 1 meal | 350 | 90 |
| ❶ Beef Enchiladas Chili 'N Beans, Patio® | 2 enchiladas | 250 | 60 |
| Beef Enchiladas, Patio® Family Pack | 2 enchiladas | 200 | 60 |
| ❶ Beef Enchiladas Rio Grande, Healthy Choice® | 1 meal | 410 | 80 |
| Chili Gravy with Beef Enchilada and Tamale, Morton® | 1 meal | 260 | 70 |
| ❶ Chili Sauce with Beef and 6 Beef Enchiladas, Banquet® Family Size | 1 enchilada | 130 | 40 |

❶  Meets Low-Fat Guidelines

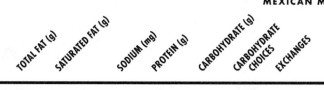

| TOTAL FAT (g) | SATURATED FAT (g) | SODIUM (mg) | PROTEIN (g) | CARBOHYDRATE (g) | CARBOHYDRATE CHOICES | EXCHANGES |
|---|---|---|---|---|---|---|
| 8 | 2.5 | 470 | 9 | 2 | 0 | 1 meat, ½ fat |
| 16 | 3.5 | 720 | 13 | 20 | 1 | 1 starch, 1 meat, 2 fat |
| 14 | 4.5 | 440 | 8 | 0 | 0 | 1 meat, 2 fat |
| 22 | 6 | 680 | 11 | 18 | 1 | 1 starch, 1 meat, 3 fat |
| 16 | 6 | 330 | 8 | 3 | 0 | 1 meat, 2 fat |
| 24 | 7 | 560 | 11 | 20 | 1 | 1 starch, 1 meat, 1 fat |
| 14 | 5 | 380 | 7 | 3 | 0 | 1 meat, 2 fat |
| 11 | 4.5 | 390 | 9 | 0 | 0 | 1 meat, 1 fat |
| 10 | 4 | 460 | 4 | 8 | ½ | ½ starch, 2 fat |
| 14 | 5 | 380 | 7 | 3 | 0 | 1 meat, 2 fat |
| 19 | 7 | 800 | 11 | 51 | 3½ | 3½ starch, 1 meat, 2 fat |
| 6 | 2.5 | 1130 | 12 | 35 | 2 | 2 starch, 1 meat |
| 10 | 4 | 850 | 12 | 45 | 3 | 3 starch, 1 meat |
| 10 | 4 | 800 | 12 | 46 | 3 | 3 starch, 1 meat |
| 9 | 3 | 690 | 12 | 48 | 3 | 3 starch, 1 meat |
| 20 | 5 | 470 | 9 | 37 | 2½ | 2½ starch, 1 meat, 2 fat |
| 12 | 5 | 1330 | 15 | 54 | 3½ | 3 starch, 1 veg, 1 meat, 1 fat |
| 10 | 4 | 1700 | 12 | 52 | 3½ | 3½ starch, 1 meat |
| 7 | 2.5 | 1350 | 12 | 35 | 2 | 2 starch, 1 meat |
| 6 | 3 | 740 | 5 | 31 | 2 | 2 starch, 1 fat |
| 8 | 3 | 480 | 14 | 70 | 4½ | 4½ starch, 1 lean meat |
| 7 | 3 | 1000 | 8 | 40 | 2½ | 2½ starch, 1 fat |
| 4 | 1.5 | 690 | 4 | 19 | 1 | 1 starch, ½ fat |

1 Carbohydrate Choice = 1 starch or 1 fruit or 1 milk exchange

## PRODUCTS

| PRODUCTS | SERVING SIZE | CALORIES | CALORIES FROM FAT |
|---|---|---|---|
| Pizza Burrito, pepperoni, Old El Paso® | 1 burrito | 260 | 90 |
| Pizza Burrito, sausage, Old El Paso® | 1 burrito | 260 | 80 |
| **Chicken Mexican Meals/Entrees** | | | |
| Chicken Chimichanga, Old El Paso® | 1 piece | 350 | 150 |
| ❶ Chicken Con Queso Burrito, Healthy Choice® | 1 burrito | 280 | 60 |
| ❶ Chicken Enchilada, Banquet® | 1 meal | 360 | 90 |
| Chicken Enchilada and Mexican-Style Rice, Stouffer's® | 1 pkg | 370 | 130 |
| ❶ Chicken Enchilada Dinner, Patio® | 1 meal | 380 | 80 |
| ❶ Chicken Enchilada Suiza with Mexican-Style Rice, Stouffer's® Lean Cuisine® | 1 pkg | 290 | 40 |
| Chicken Enchilada Suprema, Healthy Choice® | 1 meal | 390 | 80 |
| ❶ Chicken Enchiladas Suiza, Healthy Choice® | 1 meal | 270 | 40 |
| Chicken Enchiladas Suiza, Weight Watchers® | 1 entree | 270 | 80 |
| ❶ Chicken Picante, Healthy Choice® | 1 meal | 220 | 20 |
| ❶ Fiesta Chicken, Smart Ones® | 1 entree | 220 | 15 |
| ❶ Fiesta Chicken Fajitas, Healthy Choice® | 1 meal | 260 | 35 |
| ❶ Fiesta Chicken with Rice and Vegetables, Stouffer's® Lean Cuisine® | 1 pkg | 260 | 40 |
| ❶ Mexican Style Rice with Chicken, Stouffer's® Lean Cuisine® Lunch Express® | 1 pkg | 270 | 70 |
| ❶ Mexican-Style Chicken and Rice, Stouffer's® Lunch Express® | 1 pkg | 280 | 70 |
| ❶ Nacho Grande Chicken Enchiladas, Weight Watchers® | 1 entree | 290 | 70 |
| Spicy Chicken & Cheese Bite Size Burritos, Patio® | 10 burritos | 400 | 150 |
| **Other Mexican Meals/Entrees** | | | |
| Bean and Cheese Burrito, Old El Paso® | 1 burrito | 290 | 80 |
| ❶ Black Bean Burrito, Life Choice® | 1 meal | 410 | 15 |

❶   Meets Low-Fat Guidelines

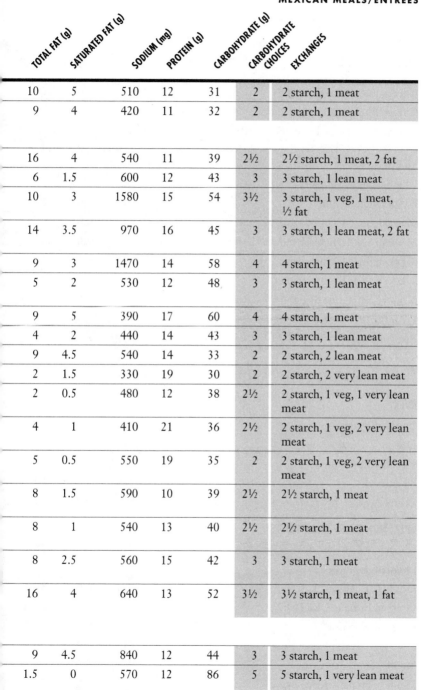

| TOTAL FAT (g) | SATURATED FAT (g) | SODIUM (mg) | PROTEIN (g) | CARBOHYDRATE (g) | CARBOHYDRATE CHOICES | EXCHANGES |
|---|---|---|---|---|---|---|
| 10 | 5 | 510 | 12 | 31 | 2 | 2 starch, 1 meat |
| 9 | 4 | 420 | 11 | 32 | 2 | 2 starch, 1 meat |
| 16 | 4 | 540 | 11 | 39 | 2½ | 2½ starch, 1 meat, 2 fat |
| 6 | 1.5 | 600 | 12 | 43 | 3 | 3 starch, 1 lean meat |
| 10 | 3 | 1580 | 15 | 54 | 3½ | 3 starch, 1 veg, 1 meat, ½ fat |
| 14 | 3.5 | 970 | 16 | 45 | 3 | 3 starch, 1 lean meat, 2 fat |
| 9 | 3 | 1470 | 14 | 58 | 4 | 4 starch, 1 meat |
| 5 | 2 | 530 | 12 | 48 | 3 | 3 starch, 1 lean meat |
| 9 | 5 | 390 | 17 | 60 | 4 | 4 starch, 1 meat |
| 4 | 2 | 440 | 14 | 43 | 3 | 3 starch, 1 lean meat |
| 9 | 4.5 | 540 | 14 | 33 | 2 | 2 starch, 2 lean meat |
| 2 | 1.5 | 330 | 19 | 30 | 2 | 2 starch, 2 very lean meat |
| 2 | 0.5 | 480 | 12 | 38 | 2½ | 2 starch, 1 veg, 1 very lean meat |
| 4 | 1 | 410 | 21 | 36 | 2½ | 2 starch, 1 veg, 2 very lean meat |
| 5 | 0.5 | 550 | 19 | 35 | 2 | 2 starch, 1 veg, 2 very lean meat |
| 8 | 1.5 | 590 | 10 | 39 | 2½ | 2½ starch, 1 meat |
| 8 | 1 | 540 | 13 | 40 | 2½ | 2½ starch, 1 meat |
| 8 | 2.5 | 560 | 15 | 42 | 3 | 3 starch, 1 meat |
| 16 | 4 | 640 | 13 | 52 | 3½ | 3½ starch, 1 meat, 1 fat |
| 9 | 4.5 | 840 | 12 | 44 | 3 | 3 starch, 1 meat |
| 1.5 | 0 | 570 | 12 | 86 | 5 | 5 starch, 1 very lean meat |

1 Carbohydrate Choice = 1 starch or 1 fruit or 1 milk exchange

## PRODUCTS

| PRODUCTS | SERVING SIZE | CALORIES | CALORIES FROM FAT |
|---|---|---|---|
| ❶ Cheese Enchilada, Banquet® | 1 meal | 340 | 60 |
| ❶ Cheese Enchilada Dinner, Patio® | 1 meal | 330 | 70 |
| ❶ Cheese Enchiladas, Patio® Family Pack | 2 enchiladas | 170 | 35 |
| Cheese Enchilada & Mexican-Style Rice, Stouffer's® | 1 pkg | 370 | 130 |
| Chimichanga, Banquet® | 1 meal | 470 | 210 |
| Fiesta Dinner, Patio® | 1 meal | 340 | 80 |
| Mexican Style Combination, Banquet® | 1 meal | 380 | 100 |
| Mexican Style Dinner, Banquet® Extra Helping | 1 meal | 820 | 300 |
| Mexican Style Dinner, Patio® | 1 meal | 430 | 130 |
| Mexican Style Meal, Banquet® | 1 meal | 400 | 120 |
| Nacho Cheese Bite Size Burritos, Patio® | 10 burritos | 360 | 110 |
| Pizza Burrito, cheese, Old El Paso® | 1 burrito | 320 | 80 |
| Ranchera Dinner, Patio® | 1 meal | 410 | 130 |
| Salisbury Con Queso, Patio® | 1 meal | 390 | 180 |
| ❶ Vegetable Enchilada Sonora, Life Choice® | 1 meal | 420 | 10 |

### MILK

| | SERVING SIZE | CALORIES | CALORIES FROM FAT |
|---|---|---|---|
| ❶ Lowfat, 1% (avg) | 8 oz | 105 | 20 |
| Lowfat, 2% (avg) | 8 oz | 120 | 45 |
| ❶ Lowfat, Chocolate (avg) | 8 oz | 150 | 10 |
| ❶ Skim (avg) | 8 oz | 85 | 0 |
| Whole (avg) | 8 oz | 160 | 70 |

### MILK, NON-DAIRY SUBSTITUTES

| | SERVING SIZE | CALORIES | CALORIES FROM FAT |
|---|---|---|---|
| ❶ Chocolate Enriched, Rice Dream® | 8 oz | 160 | 20 |
| ❶ Original, EdenBlend® | 8 oz | 120 | 30 |
| Original, Edensoy® Extra | 8 oz | 130 | 35 |
| ❶ Original Enriched, Rice Dream® | 8 oz | 120 | 20 |
| Original, Edensoy® | 8 oz | 130 | 35 |
| ❶ Soy Moo, Health Valley Fat-Free® | 8 oz | 110 | 0 |
| ❶ Vanilla, Edensoy® Extra | 8 oz | 150 | 30 |
| ❶ Vanilla Enriched, Rice Dream® | 8 oz | 130 | 20 |

❶  Meets Low-Fat Guidelines

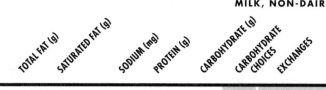

| TOTAL FAT (g) | SATURATED FAT (g) | SODIUM (mg) | PROTEIN (g) | CARBOHYDRATE (g) | CARBOHYDRATE CHOICES | EXCHANGES |
|---|---|---|---|---|---|---|
| 6 | 2.5 | 1500 | 15 | 56 | 4 | 4 starch, 1 lean meat |
| 8 | 3 | 1570 | 13 | 52 | 3½ | 3½ starch, 1 meat |
| 4 | 2 | 880 | 6 | 26 | 2 | 2 starch |
| 14 | 5 | 890 | 12 | 48 | 3 | 3 starch, 1 meat, 1 fat |
| 23 | 7 | 1180 | 13 | 56 | 4 | 4 starch, 1 meat, 3 fat |
| 9 | 4 | 1760 | 13 | 51 | 3½ | 3½ starch, 1 meat |
| 11 | 5 | 1370 | 15 | 55 | 3½ | 3½ starch, 1 meat, ½ fat |
| 34 | 14 | 2060 | 28 | 100 | 6½ | 6½ starch, 1 meat, 5 fat |
| 15 | 6 | 1840 | 15 | 59 | 4 | 4 starch, 1 meat, 1 fat |
| 13 | 5 | 1520 | 14 | 56 | 4 | 4 starch, 1 meat, 1 fat |
| 13 | 4 | 500 | 10 | 52 | 3½ | 3½ starch, 2 fat |
| 9 | 4 | 430 | 13 | 27 | 2 | 2 starch, 1 meat |
| 15 | 6 | 2400 | 13 | 55 | 3½ | 3½ starch, 1 meat, 1 fat |
| 20 | 11 | 1570 | 18 | 33 | 2 | 2 starch, 2 meat, 2 fat |
| 1.5 | 0 | 600 | 12 | 89 | 5 | 5 starch, 1 veg |
| 2.5 | 1.5 | 110–135 | 8 | 11–13 | 1 | 1 milk, ½ fat |
| 5 | 3.5 | 110 | 8 | 11 | 1 | 1 milk, 1 fat |
| 1 | 0.5 | 210 | 8 | 26 | 2 | 1 milk, 1 fruit |
| 0 | 0 | 110–135 | 8 | 11–13 | 1 | 1 milk |
| 8 | 5 | 130 | 8 | 13 | 1 | 1 milk, 1½ fat |
| 2.5 | 0 | 100 | 1 | 35 | 2 | 2 starch |
| 3 | 0.5 | 85 | 7 | 16 | 1 | 1 milk |
| 4 | 0.5 | 105 | 10 | 13 | 1 | 1 milk, ½ fat |
| 2 | 0 | 90 | 1 | 25 | 1½ | 1½ starch |
| 4 | 0.5 | 105 | 10 | 13 | 1 | 1 milk, ½ fat |
| 0 | 0 | 60 | 6 | 22 | 1½ | 1½ starch |
| 3 | 0 | 90 | 6 | 23 | 1½ | 1 starch, 1 milk |
| 2 | 0 | 90 | 1 | 28 | 2 | 2 starch |

1 Carbohydrate Choice = 1 starch or 1 fruit or 1 milk exchange

## PRODUCTS

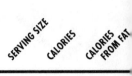

SERVING SIZE    CALORIES    CALORIES FROM FAT

### MUFFIN MIX (AS PREPARED)

| Products | Serving Size | Calories | Calories from Fat |
|---|---|---|---|
| Muffin mix, Betty Crocker®, all varieties (avg) | 1 muffin | 160 | 35–70 |
| ❶ Muffin mix, Betty Crocker® Fat Free, all varieties (avg) | 1 muffin | 120 | 0 |
| Muffin mix, Gold Medal®/Robin Hood®, all varieties (avg) | 1 muffin | 170 | 60 |
| Muffin mix, Krusteaz®, all varieties (avg) | 1 muffin | 170 | 50 |
| ❶ Muffin mix, Krusteaz® Fat Free, all varieties (avg) | 1 muffin | 130 | 0 |
| ❶ Muffin mix, Sweet Rewards®, all varieties (avg) | 1 muffin | 120 | 0 |

### MUFFINS

| Products | Serving Size | Calories | Calories from Fat |
|---|---|---|---|
| Blueberry, Entenmann's® | 1 muffin | 160 | 60 |
| ❶ Blueberry, Entenmann's® Fat Free Cholesterol Free | 1 muffin | 120 | 0 |
| Blueberry, Hostess® Mini | 5 muffins | 240 | 120 |
| ❶ Blueberry, Pepperidge Farm® Wholesome Choice | 1 muffin | 140 | 20 |
| Blueberry, Weight Watchers® | 1 muffin | 180 | 35 |
| ❶ Bran with Raisins, Pepperidge Farm® Wholesome Choice | 1 muffin | 150 | 20 |
| Chocolate Chip, Weight Watchers® | 1 muffin | 200 | 35 |
| Cinnamon Apple, Hostess® Mini Muffins | 5 muffins | 260 | 140 |
| ❶ Corn, Pepperidge Farm® Wholesome Choice | 1 muffin | 150 | 25 |
| Harvest Honey Bran, Weight Watchers® | 1 muffin | 220 | 40 |

### MUSHROOMS (CANNED)

| Products | Serving Size | Calories | Calories from Fat |
|---|---|---|---|
| ❶ Mushrooms, all brands, all regular varieties (avg) | ½ cup with liquid | 25 | 0 |
| ❶ No Salt Added Mushrooms, Giorgio® | ½ cup with liquid | 20 | 0 |

### MUSTARD

| Products | Serving Size | Calories | Calories from Fat |
|---|---|---|---|
| ❶ Mustard, all varieties (avg) | 1 tsp | 2 | 0 |

 Meets Low-Fat Guidelines

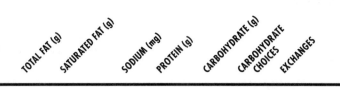

| TOTAL FAT (g) | SATURATED FAT (g) | SODIUM (mg) | PROTEIN (g) | CARBOHYDRATE (g) | CARBOHYDRATE CHOICES | EXCHANGES |
|---|---|---|---|---|---|---|
| 4–7 | 1.5 | 180–220 | 2.5 | 22 | 1½ | 1½ starch, 1 fat |
| 0 | 0 | 200 | 2 | 27 | 2 | 2 starch |
| 7 | 1.5 | 180–270 | 3 | 22–25 | 1½ | 1½ starch, 1 fat |
| 5 | 1.5 | 230–330 | 3.5 | 26–31 | 2 | 2 starch, ½ fat |
| 0 | 0 | 300–400 | 2 | 28–33 | 2 | 2 starch |
| 0 | 0 | 200 | 2 | 28 | 2 | 2 starch |
| 7 | 1.5 | 210 | 2 | 24 | 1½ | 1½ starch, 1 fat |
| 0 | 0 | 220 | 2 | 26 | 2 | 2 starch |
| 13 | 2 | 180 | 3 | 30 | 2 | 2 starch, 2 fat |
| 2.5 | 0 | 190 | 3 | 27 | 2 | 2 starch |
| 4 | 1 | 270 | 3 | 34 | 2 | 2 starch |
| 2.5 | 0.5 | 260 | 4 | 30 | 2 | 2 starch |
| 4 | 1.5 | 250 | 4 | 39 | 2½ | 2½ starch |
| 16 | 2.5 | 180 | 3 | 28 | 2 | 2 starch, 2 fat |
| 3 | 0 | 190 | 4 | 27 | 2 | 2 starch |
| 4.5 | 1 | 180 | 3 | 42 | 3 | 3 starch |
| 0 | 0 | 450 | 2 | 4 | 0 | 1 veg |
| 0 | 0 | 20 | 2 | 3 | 0 | 1 veg |
| 0 | 0 | 65 | 0 | 0 | 0 | free |

1 Carbohydrate Choice = 1 starch *or* 1 fruit *or* 1 milk exchange

## PRODUCTS

| | SERVING SIZE | CALORIES | CALORIES FROM FAT |
|---|---|---|---|

### NOODLES, FLAVORED (DRY, AS PREPARED)
see also Pasta; Soup Mix

| | | | |
|---|---|---|---|
| Beef Cup Noodles, Nissin® | 1 container | 290 | 110 |
| Beef Cup Noodles Twin Pack, Nissin® | 1 container | 160 | 60 |
| Beef Onion Cup Noodles, Nissin® | 1 container | 280 | 100 |
| Beef Top Ramen Noodles, Nissin® | ½ pkg | 200 | 70 |
| ❶ Beef Top Ramen Noodles, Nissin® Low Fat | ½ pkg | 150 | 10 |
| Cheddar Cheese Noodles, Nissin® | 1 container | 330 | 140 |
| Chicken Noodles, Nissin® | 1 container | 330 | 140 |
| Chicken Cup Noodles, Nissin® | 1 container | 300 | 110 |
| Chicken Cup Noodles, Nissin® Twin Pack | 1 container | 160 | 60 |
| Chicken Top Ramen Noodles, Nissin® | ½ pkg | 200 | 70 |
| ❶ Chicken Top Ramen Noodles, Nissin® Low Fat | ½ pkg | 150 | 10 |
| Chicken Mushroom Cup Noodles, Nissin® | 1 container | 300 | 120 |
| Chicken Mushroom Top Ramen Noodles, Nissin® | ½ pkg | 200 | 70 |
| Chicken Sesame Top Ramen Noodles, Nissin® | ½ pkg | 200 | 70 |
| Chow Mein Noodles, La Choy® | ½ cup | 137 | 52 |
| Crab Cup Noodles, Nissin® | 1 container | 290 | 110 |
| Crispy Wide Noodles, La Choy® | ½ cup | 148 | 74 |
| Demae Top Ramen Noodles, Nissin® | ½ pkg | 200 | 70 |
| Garden Vegetable Cup Noodles, Nissin® | 1 container | 290 | 110 |
| Garden Vegetable Top Ramen Noodles, Nissin® | ½ pkg | 200 | 70 |
| Lobster Cup Noodles, Nissin® | 1 container | 300 | 120 |
| ❶ Oriental Noodles, Knorr® | 1 container | 210 | 25 |
| Oriental Top Ramen Noodles, Nissin® | ½ pkg | 200 | 70 |
| ❶ Oriental Top Ramen Noodles, Nissin® Low Fat | ½ pkg | 150 | 10 |
| Pork Cup Noodles, Nissin® | 1 container | 290 | 110 |
| Pork Top Ramen Noodles, Nissin® | ½ pkg | 200 | 70 |
| ❶ Rice Noodles, La Choy® | ½ cup | 121 | 27 |
| Shrimp Cup Noodles, Nissin® | 1 container | 290 | 110 |

 Meets Low-Fat Guidelines

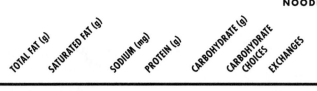

| TOTAL FAT (g) | SATURATED FAT (g) | SODIUM (mg) | PROTEIN (g) | CARBOHYDRATE (g) | CARBOHYDRATE CHOICES | EXCHANGES |
|---|---|---|---|---|---|---|
| 12 | 6 | 1540 | 7 | 39 | 2½ | 2½ starch, 2 fat |
| 7 | 3 | 870 | 4 | 20 | 1 | 1 starch, 1 fat |
| 11 | 6 | 1300 | 6 | 40 | 2½ | 2½ starch, 2 fat |
| 8 | 4 | 1020 | 4 | 27 | 2 | 2 starch, 1 fat |
| 1 | 0 | 1140 | 3 | 31 | 2 | 2 starch |
| 15 | 7 | 940 | 6 | 43 | 3 | 3 starch, 2 fat |
| 15 | 7 | 940 | 7 | 41 | 3 | 3 starch, 2 fat |
| 12 | 6 | 1220 | 6 | 39 | 2½ | 2½ starch, 2 fat |
| 7 | 4 | 940 | 3 | 20 | 1 | 1 starch, 1 fat |
| 8 | 4 | 930 | 4 | 27 | 2 | 2 starch, 1 fat |
| 1 | 0 | 1120 | 3 | 31 | 2 | 2 starch |
| 13 | 6 | 1360 | 6 | 39 | 2½ | 2½ starch, 2 fat |
| 8 | 4 | 720 | 4 | 27 | 2 | 2 starch, 1 fat |
| 8 | 4 | 770 | 4 | 27 | 2 | 2 starch, 1 fat |
| 6 | 1.0 | 217 | 3 | 19 | 1 | 1 starch, 1 fat |
| 12 | 6 | 1310 | 6 | 39 | 2½ | 2½ starch, 2 fat |
| 8 | 1.5 | 289 | 3 | 16 | 1 | 1 starch, 1½ fat |
| 8 | 4 | 830 | 4 | 27 | 2 | 2 starch, 1 fat |
| 12 | 6 | 1310 | 6 | 40 | 2½ | 2½ starch, 2 fat |
| 8 | 4 | 1190 | 4 | 27 | 2 | 2 starch, 1 fat |
| 13 | 7 | 1300 | 6 | 40 | 2½ | 2½ starch, 2 fat |
| 3 | 0.5 | 830 | 7 | 39 | 2½ | 2½ starch |
| 8 | 4 | 900 | 4 | 27 | 2 | 2 starch, 1 fat |
| 1 | 0 | 1220 | 3 | 31 | 2 | 2 starch |
| 12 | 6 | 1510 | 7 | 39 | 2½ | 2½ starch, 2 fat |
| 8 | 4 | 820 | 4 | 27 | 2 | 2 starch, 1 fat |
| 3 | 0.5 | 378 | 2 | 21 | 1½ | 1½ starch |
| 12 | 6 | 1550 | 7 | 39 | 2½ | 2½ starch, 2 fat |

1 Carbohydrate Choice = 1 starch or 1 fruit or 1 milk exchange

## PRODUCTS

| | SERVING SIZE | CALORIES | CALORIES FROM FAT |
|---|---|---|---|
| Shrimp Cup Noodles, Nissin® Twin Pack | 1 container | 150 | 50 |
| Shrimp Picante Cup Noodles, Nissin® | 1 container | 290 | 110 |
| Shrimp Top Ramen Noodles, Nissin® | ½ pkg | 200 | 70 |
| Spicy Beef Top Ramen Noodles, Nissin® | ½ pkg | 200 | 70 |
| Spicy Chicken Cup Noodles, Nissin® | 1 container | 300 | 120 |
| Spicy Chicken Cup Noodles, Nissin® Twin Pack | 1 container | 160 | 60 |

## NUTS

| | SERVING SIZE | CALORIES | CALORIES FROM FAT |
|---|---|---|---|
| Cashews | 1 oz (~¼ cup) | 170 | 130 |
| Mixed nuts | 1 oz (~¼ cup) | 180 | 130 |
| Roasted almonds | 1 oz (3 Tb) | 180 | 150 |
| Roasted peanuts | 1 oz (~¼ cup) | 170 | 120 |
| Spanish peanuts, salted | 3 Tb | 160 | 120 |
| Walnuts | 1 oz | 210 | 180 |

## OATMEAL
*see* Cereal, hot

## OIL

| | SERVING SIZE | CALORIES | CALORIES FROM FAT |
|---|---|---|---|
| Canola, all brands (avg) | 1 Tb | 120 | 120 |
| Coconut, all brands (avg) | 1 Tb | 130 | 130 |
| Corn, all brands (avg) | 1 Tb | 120 | 120 |
| Olive, all brands (avg) | 1 Tb | 120 | 120 |
| Peanut, all brands (avg) | 1 Tb | 120 | 120 |
| Safflower, all brands (avg) | 1 Tb | 120 | 120 |
| Sunflower, all brands (avg) | 1 Tb | 120 | 120 |

## OLIVES

| | SERVING SIZE | CALORIES | CALORIES FROM FAT |
|---|---|---|---|
| ❶ Olives, black with pits, all brands (avg) | 3 olives (½ oz) | 25 | 20 |
| ❶ Olives, green, stuffed, all brands (avg) | 3 olives (½ oz) | 25 | 20 |

 Meets Low-Fat Guidelines

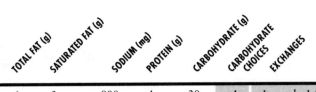

| TOTAL FAT (g) | SATURATED FAT (g) | SODIUM (mg) | PROTEIN (g) | CARBOHYDRATE (g) | CARBOHYDRATE CHOICES | EXCHANGES |
|---|---|---|---|---|---|---|
| 6 | 3 | 900 | 4 | 20 | 1 | 1 starch, 1 fat |
| 12 | 6 | 1290 | 6 | 40 | 2½ | 2½ starch, 2 fat |
| 8 | 4 | 1070 | 4 | 27 | 2 | 2 starch, 1 fat |
| 8 | 4 | 710 | 4 | 27 | 2 | 2 starch, 1 fat |
| 13 | 7 | 1120 | 7 | 38 | 2½ | 2½ starch, 2 fat |
| 7 | 3 | 900 | 4 | 20 | 1 | 1 starch, 1 fat |
| 15 | 2.5 | 120–160 | 5 | 8 | ½ | ½ starch, 1 meat, 1½ fat |
| 15 | 2.5 | 50–140 | 6 | 5 | 0 | 1 meat, 2 fat |
| 17 | 1 | 110 | 6 | 4 | 0 | 1 meat, 2 fat |
| 15 | 2.5 | 130–250 | 7 | 5 | 0 | 1 meat, 2 fat |
| 14 | 2 | 140 | 6 | 6 | ½ | ½ starch, 1 meat, 1½ fat |
| 20 | 1.5 | 0 | 5 | 3 | 0 | 1 meat, 3 fat |
| 14 | 1 | 0 | 0 | 0 | 0 | 3 fat |
| 14 | 12 | 0 | 0 | 0 | 0 | 3 fat |
| 14 | 2 | 0 | 0 | 0 | 0 | 3 fat |
| 14 | 2 | 0 | 0 | 0 | 0 | 3 fat |
| 14 | 2.5 | 0 | 0 | 0 | 0 | 3 fat |
| 14 | 1 | 0 | 0 | 0 | 0 | 3 fat |
| 14 | 1.5 | 0 | 0 | 0 | 0 | 3 fat |
| 2.5 | 0 | 110 | 0 | 1 | 0 | ½ fat |
| 2.0 | 0 | 240 | 0 | 1 | 0 | ½ fat |

1 Carbohydrate Choice = 1 starch or 1 fruit or 1 milk exchange

## PRODUCTS

| | SERVING SIZE | CALORIES | CALORIES FROM FAT |
|---|---|---|---|
| **ONION RINGS (FROZEN)** | | | |
| Onion Ringers®, Ore-Ida® | 88 g | 240 | 126 |
| **ORIENTAL MEALS/ENTREES (FROZEN)** | | | |
| *Beef Oriental Meals/Entrees* | | | |
| ❶ Beef & Peppers Cantonese, Healthy Choice® | 1 meal | 270 | 50 |
| ❶ Beef Broccoli Beijing, Healthy Choice® | 1 meal | 330 | 30 |
| ❶ Beef Pepper Steak Oriental, Healthy Choice® | 1 meal | 250 | 35 |
| ❶ Noodles with Vegetables and Beef, La Choy® | 1 cup | 156 | 31 |
| Oriental Beef, Stouffer's® Lean Cuisine® | 1 pkg | 250 | 70 |
| ❶ Oriental Beef, Stouffer's® Lunch Express® | 1 pkg | 290 | 70 |
| ❶ Oriental Beef & Peppers with Rice, Yu Sing® | 1 pkg | 290 | 70 |
| ❶ Oriental Beef & Peppers with Rice, Yu Sing® Double Serving | 1 cup | 300 | 60 |
| *Chicken Oriental Meals/Entrees* | | | |
| ❶ Chicken & Almonds with Rice, Yu Sing® | 1 pkg | 310 | 50 |
| ❶ Chicken Cantonese, Healthy Choice® | 1 meal | 210 | 5 |
| Chicken Chow Mein, Banquet® | 1 meal | 210 | 60 |
| Chicken Chow Mein, Chun King® | 1 meal | 370 | 130 |
| Chicken Chow Mein, La Choy® | 1 cup | 80 | 31 |
| ❶ Chicken Chow Mein, Weight Watchers® Smart Ones® | 1 entree | 200 | 15 |
| ❶ Chicken Chow Mein with Rice, Stouffer's® Lean Cuisine® | 1 pkg | 210 | 45 |
| ❶ Chicken Chow Mein with Rice, Stouffer's® Lunch Express® | 1 pkg | 260 | 35 |
| ❶ Chicken Chow Mein with Rice, Yu Sing® | 1 pkg | 270 | 45 |
| ❶ Chicken Fried Rice, Yu Sing® | 1 cup | 260 | 50 |
| ❶ Chicken Imperial, Healthy Choice® | 1 meal | 230 | 40 |
| ❶ Chicken Lo Mein, Banquet® | 1 meal | 270 | 60 |

❶ Meets Low-Fat Guidelines

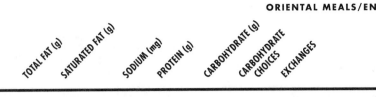

| TOTAL FAT (g) | SATURATED FAT (g) | SODIUM (mg) | PROTEIN (g) | CARBOHYDRATE (g) | CARBOHYDRATE CHOICES | EXCHANGES |
|---|---|---|---|---|---|---|
| 14 | NA | NA | 3 | 26 | 2 | 1½ starch, 1 veg, 2 fat |
| 5 | 2.5 | 560 | 16 | 40 | 2½ | 2 starch, 1 veg, 1 lean meat |
| 3 | 1 | 500 | 20 | 55 | 3½ | 3 starch, 1 veg, 2 very lean meat |
| 4 | 1.5 | 470 | 19 | 34 | 2 | 2 starch, 2 lean meat |
| 3.5 | 1.5 | 1332 | 7 | 27 | 2 | 1½ starch, 1 veg, ½ fat |
| 8 | 3 | 480 | 14 | 30 | 2 | 2 starch, 1 meat |
| 8 | 1 | 880 | 12 | 43 | 3 | 2½ starch, 1 veg, 1 meat |
| 7 | 2.5 | 1160 | 9 | 45 | 3 | 2½ starch, 1 veg, 1 meat |
| 7 | 2.5 | 1130 | 9 | 47 | 3 | 2½ starch, 1 veg, 1 lean meat |
| 6 | 1 | 980 | 13 | 50 | 3 | 3 starch, 1 lean meat |
| 0.5 | 0 | 360 | 19 | 31 | 2 | 2 starch, 2 very lean meat |
| 7 | 2 | 850 | 9 | 28 | 2 | 2 starch, 1 meat |
| 14 | 5 | 2010 | 16 | 45 | 3 | 3 starch, 1 meat, 1 fat |
| 3.5 | 1 | 1352 | 8 | 6 | ½ | 1 veg, 1 lean meat |
| 2 | 0.5 | 490 | 12 | 34 | 2 | 2 starch, 1 veg, 1 very lean meat |
| 5 | 1 | 510 | 13 | 28 | 2 | 2 starch, 1 lean meat |
| 4 | 1 | 940 | 13 | 43 | 3 | 2½ starch, 1 veg, 1 lean meat |
| 5 | 1 | 920 | 9 | 45 | 3 | 3 starch, 1 very lean meat |
| 6 | 2 | 740 | 13 | 39 | 2½ | 2½ starch, 1 lean meat |
| 4 | 1 | 470 | 17 | 31 | 2 | 2 starch, 2 very lean meat |
| 6 | 1 | 1060 | 11 | 43 | 3 | 3 starch, 1 very lean meat |

1 Carbohydrate Choice = 1 starch or 1 fruit or 1 milk exchange

| PRODUCTS | SERVING SIZE | CALORIES | CALORIES FROM FAT |
|---|---|---|---|
| Chicken Oriental, Stouffer's® Lunch Express® | 1 pkg | 370 | 110 |
| ❶ Chicken Oriental with Vegetables and Vermicelli, Stouffer's® Lean Cuisine® | 1 pkg | 260 | 60 |
| ❶ Chicken Teriyaki, Healthy Choice® | 1 meal | 270 | 20 |
| ❶ Chinese Style Vegetables & Chicken, Budget Gourmet® Light | 1 entree | 260 | 60 |
| Crunchy Walnut Chicken, Chun King® | 1 meal | 470 | 180 |
| ❶ Fried Rice with Chicken, Chun King® | 1 meal | 270 | 60 |
| ❶ Ginger Chicken Hunan, Healthy Choice® | 1 meal | 350 | 20 |
| ❶ Kung Pao Chicken, Yu Sing® | 1 pkg | 300 | 60 |
| ❶ Mandarin Chicken, Healthy Choice® | 1 meal | 280 | 20 |
| ❶ Mandarin Chicken, Stouffer's® Lean Cuisine® Lunch Express® | 1 pkg | 270 | 50 |
| ❶ Noodles with Vegetables and Chicken, La Choy® | 1 cup | 163 | 30 |
| Oriental Style Chicken, Banquet® | 1 meal | 260 | 80 |
| ❶ Oriental Sweet & Sour Chicken with Rice, Yu Sing® | 1 pkg | 340 | 30 |
| Rice and Chicken Stir-Fry, Stouffer's® Lean Cuisine® Lunch Express® | 1 pkg | 280 | 80 |
| ❶ Sesame Chicken, Healthy Choice® | 1 meal | 240 | 25 |
| ❶ Sesame Chicken Shanghai, Healthy Choice® | 1 meal | 310 | 45 |
| ❶ Spicy Szechuan Style Vegetables and Chicken, Budget Gourmet® | 1 entree | 330 | 90 |
| ❶ Sweet and Sour Chicken, Healthy Choice® | 1 meal | 310 | 45 |
| ❶ Sweet & Sour Chicken with Rice, Yu Sing® Double Serving | 1 cup | 330 | 25 |
| ❶ Sweet & Sour Noodles with Chicken, La Choy® | 1 cup | 256 | 28 |

❶  Meets Low-Fat Guidelines

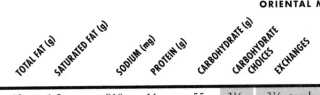

| TOTAL FAT (g) | SATURATED FAT (g) | SODIUM (mg) | PROTEIN (g) | CARBOHYDRATE (g) | CARBOHYDRATE CHOICES | EXCHANGES |
|---|---|---|---|---|---|---|
| 12 | 1.5 | 910 | 11 | 55 | 3½ | 3½ starch, 1 lean meat, 1 fat |
| 6 | 1 | 530 | 21 | 30 | 2 | 1½ starch, 1 veg, 2 lean meat |
| 2 | 0.5 | 420 | 21 | 42 | 3 | 2½ starch, 1 veg, 2 very lean meat |
| 6 | 1 | 750 | 10 | 42 | 3 | 3 starch, 1 lean meat, ½ fat |
| 19 | 5 | 1820 | 19 | 56 | 4 | 4 starch, 2 meat, 1 fat |
| 6 | 1.5 | 1330 | 9 | 44 | 3 | 3 starch, ½ fat |
| 2.5 | 0.5 | 430 | 24 | 59 | 4 | 3½ starch, 1 veg, 2 very lean meat |
| 6 | 1 | 1030 | 13 | 46 | 3 | 3 starch, 1 meat |
| 2.5 | 0 | 520 | 20 | 44 | 3 | 2½ starch, 1 veg, 2 very lean meat |
| 6 | 1 | 520 | 12 | 41 | 3 | 2½ starch, 1 veg, 1 lean meat |
| 3.5 | 1.5 | 858 | 10 | 24 | 1½ | 1½ starch, 1 veg, 1 lean meat |
| 9 | 2.5 | 610 | 12 | 34 | 2 | 2 starch, 1 veg, 1 meat |
| 3 | 0.5 | 980 | 11 | 67 | 4½ | 3 starch, 1 fruit, 1 veg, 1 very lean meat |
| 9 | 1 | 590 | 11 | 39 | 2½ | 2 starch, 1 veg, 1 lean meat, 1 fat |
| 3 | 0.5 | 600 | 16 | 38 | 2½ | 2 starch, 1 veg, 1 lean meat |
| 5 | 1 | 460 | 24 | 42 | 3 | 2½ starch, 1 veg, 2 very lean meat |
| 10 | 2 | 1020 | 15 | 46 | 3 | 3 starch, 1 meat, 1 fat |
| 5 | 1 | 250 | 23 | 42 | 3 | 2½ starch, 1 veg, 2 very lean meat |
| 3 | 0.5 | 920 | 10 | 64 | 4 | 3 starch, 1 fruit, 1 very lean meat |
| 3 | 1.5 | 697 | 7 | 49 | 3 | 1 starch, 2 fruit, 1 lean meat |

1 Carbohydrate Choice = 1 starch or 1 fruit or 1 milk exchange

## PRODUCTS

| | SERVING SIZE | CALORIES | CALORIES FROM FAT |
|---|---|---|---|
| **Pork Oriental Meals/Entrees** | | | |
| ❶ Fried Rice with Pork, Chun King® | 1 meal | 290 | 50 |
| Pork & Shrimp Fried Rice, Yu Sing® Double Serving | 1 cup | 280 | 80 |
| ❶ Pork Chop Suey with Rice, Yu Sing® | 1 pkg | 300 | 60 |
| ❶ Sweet & Sour Pork, Chun King® | 1 meal | 450 | 60 |
| **Shrimp Oriental Meals/Entrees** | | | |
| ❶ Shrimp Lo Mein, Yu Sing® | 1 pkg | 220 | 20 |
| **Vegetable Oriental Meals/Entrees** | | | |
| ❶ Hunan Style Rice and Vegetables, Weight Watchers® International Selections | 1 entree | 250 | 60 |
| Kung Pao Noodles and Vegetables, Weight Watchers® International Selections | 1 entree | 260 | 90 |
| ❶ Noodles with Vegetables, La Choy® | 1 cup | 131 | 12 |
| ❶ Peking Style Rice and Vegetables, Weight Watchers® International Selections | 1 entree | 270 | 50 |
| ❶ Teriyaki Stir-Fry, Stouffer's® Lean Cuisine® Lunch Express® | 1 pkg | 260 | 45 |
| **PANCAKE BATTER (REFRIGERATED)** | | | |
| Blueberry, Bisquick Shake & Pour® | 3 pancakes | 220 | 40 |
| ❶ Buttermilk, Bisquick Shake & Pour® | 3 pancakes | 200 | 30 |
| Buttermilk, Fast Shake® | ½ cup | 230 | 30 |
| Original, Bisquick Shake & Pour® | 3 pancakes | 210 | 30 |
| **PANCAKE MIX (AS PREPARED)** | | | |
| Buckwheat, Krusteaz® | 3 (4") pancakes | 280 | 40 |
| ❶ Buttermilk, Betty Crocker® Complete | 3 pancakes | 200 | 25 |
| ❶ Buttermilk, Krusteaz® | 3 (4") pancakes | 200 | 30 |

❶ Meets Low-Fat Guidelines

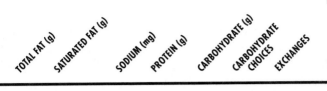

| TOTAL FAT (g) | SATURATED FAT (g) | SODIUM (mg) | PROTEIN (g) | CARBOHYDRATE (g) | CARBOHYDRATE CHOICES | EXCHANGES |
|---|---|---|---|---|---|---|
| 6 | 2 | 1310 | 11 | 48 | 3 | 3 starch, 1 lean meat |
| 9 | 4 | 1300 | 11 | 40 | 2½ | 2½ starch, 1 meat |
| 6 | 2 | 1050 | 9 | 49 | 3 | 2½ starch, 1 veg, 1 lean meat |
| 6 | 2.5 | 1180 | 12 | 86 | 6 | 3 starch, 3 fruit, 1 lean meat |
| 2 | 0 | 950 | 11 | 38 | 2½ | 2½ starch, 1 very lean meat |
| 7 | 3 | 630 | 7 | 39 | 2½ | 2 starch, 1 veg, 1 meat |
| 10 | 1.5 | 690 | 8 | 35 | 2 | 2 starch, 1 veg, 1 meat |
| 1 | 0.5 | 1311 | 5 | 27 | 2 | 1½ starch, 1 veg |
| 6 | 1 | 640 | 7 | 48 | 3 | 3 starch, 1 veg, ½ fat |
| 5 | 1 | 550 | 15 | 39 | 2½ | 2 starch, 1 veg, 1 lean meat |
| 4 | 1 | 640 | 6 | 40 | 2½ | 2½ starch |
| 3 | 1 | 680 | 7 | 38 | 2½ | 2½ starch |
| 4 | 1 | 650 | 6 | 43 | 3 | 3 starch |
| 4 | 1 | 710 | 5 | 39 | 2½ | 2½ starch |
| 4 | 1 | 820 | 9 | 51 | 3½ | 3½ starch |
| 2.5 | 0.5 | 540 | 5 | 39 | 2½ | 2½ starch |
| 3 | 0.5 | 800 | 6 | 38 | 2½ | 2½ starch |

1 Carbohydrate Choice = 1 starch or 1 fruit or 1 milk exchange

## PRODUCTS

| | SERVING SIZE | CALORIES | CALORIES FROM FAT |
|---|---|---|---|
| Buttermilk, Pillsbury® Hungry Jack® | ⅓ cup | 230 | 50 |
| Buttermilk, Robin Hood® | 3 pancakes | 230 | 50 |
| ❶ Crepe Mix, Krusteaz® | 2 crepes | 100 | 30 |
| ❶ Harvest Apple Spice, Krusteaz® | 2 (4") pancakes | 210 | 30 |
| ❶ Imitation Blueberry, Krusteaz® | 3 (4") pancakes | 210 | 30 |
| ❶ Oatbran, Krusteaz® Lite | 3 (4") pancakes | 140 | 10 |
| Original, Pillsbury® Hungry Jack® | ⅓ cup | 220 | 50 |
| Pancake Mix, Krusteaz® Old Fashioned | 3 (4") pancakes | 230 | 80 |
| Pancake Mix, Pillsbury® Hungry Jack® Extra Lights® | ⅓ cup | 230 | 50 |
| ❶ Pancake Mix, Sweet 'N Low® | 5 (3") cakes | 160 | 18 |
| Pre-Measured Packets, Pillsbury® Hungry Jack® | ½ pkt | 200 | 30 |
| ❶ Whole Wheat and Honey, Krusteaz® | 3 (4") pancakes | 230 | 10 |

### PANCAKES (FROZEN)

| | | | |
|---|---|---|---|
| Blueberry, Hungry Jack® | 3 pancakes | 230 | 30 |
| ❶ Blueberry, Krusteaz® | 2 pancakes | 170 | 30 |
| Buttermilk, Hungry Jack® | 3 pancakes | 240 | 35 |
| Buttermilk, Krusteaz® | 3 pancakes | 270 | 45 |
| Buttermilk Minis, Hungry Jack® | 11 pancakes | 230 | 35 |
| ❶ Mini Pancakes, Krusteaz® | 6 pancakes | 120 | 25 |
| Original, Hungry Jack® | 3 pancakes | 240 | 35 |

### PASTA (CANNED)

| | | | |
|---|---|---|---|
| Beef Ravioli, Hunt's® Homestyle Separates | 1 cup | 221 | 67.5 |
| Beef Ravioli, Progresso® | 1 cup | 260 | 45 |
| Beef Ravioli in Tomato and Meat Sauce, Chef Boyardee® | 1 cup | 230 | 45 |
| Beefaroni, Chef Boyardee® | 1 cup | 260 | 60 |

❶  Meets Low-Fat Guidelines

| TOTAL FAT (g) | SATURATED FAT (g) | SODIUM (mg) | PROTEIN (g) | CARBOHYDRATE (g) | CARBOHYDRATE CHOICES | EXCHANGES |
|---|---|---|---|---|---|---|
| 6 | 1 | 710 | 8 | 35 | 2 | 2 starch, 1 fat |
| 6 | 2 | 560 | 8 | 35 | 2 | 2 starch, 1 fat |
| 3 | 1 | 150 | 4 | 15 | 1 | 1 starch |
| 3 | 0 | 640 | 5 | 41 | 3 | 3 starch |
| 3 | 0 | 750 | 6 | 40 | 2½ | 2½ starch |
| 1 | 0 | 390 | 6 | 35 | 2 | 2 starch |
| 6 | 1 | 700 | 5 | 38 | 2½ | 2½ starch, ½ fat |
| 9 | 2 | 570 | 8 | 28 | 2 | 2 starch, 1 fat |
| 6 | 1 | 650 | 7 | 36 | 2½ | 2½ starch, ½ fat |
| 2 | <1 | 280 | 4 | 32 | 2 | 2 starch |
| 3.5 | 1 | 780 | 5 | 38 | 2½ | 2½ starch |
| 1.5 | 0 | 500 | 9 | 45 | 3 | 3 starch |
| 3.5 | 0.5 | 550 | 5 | 45 | 3 | 3 starch |
| 3 | 1 | 430 | 5 | 31 | 2 | 2 starch |
| 4 | 1 | 580 | 5 | 46 | 3 | 3 starch |
| 5 | 1.5 | 700 | 8 | 48 | 3 | 3 starch |
| 4 | 1 | 550 | 5 | 44 | 3 | 3 starch |
| 2.5 | 0.5 | 310 | 3 | 21 | 1½ | 1½ starch |
| 4 | 1 | 550 | 5 | 47 | 3 | 3 starch |
| 7.5 | 3 | 1116 | 10 | 32 | 2 | 2 starch, 1 meat |
| 5 | 2 | 940 | 9 | 45 | 3 | 3 starch, 1 lean meat |
| 5 | 2.5 | 1150 | 9 | 37 | 2½ | 2½ starch, 1 lean meat |
| 7 | 3 | 870 | 10 | 37 | 2½ | 2½ starch, 1 meat |

1 Carbohydrate Choice = 1 starch or 1 fruit or 1 milk exchange

## PRODUCTS

| | SERVING SIZE | CALORIES | CALORIES FROM FAT |
|---|---|---|---|
| ❶ Cheese Ravioli, Progresso® | 1 cup | 220 | 20 |
| ❶ Cheese Ravioli in Tomato Sauce, Chef Boyardee® | 1 cup | 210 | 0 |
| ❶ Cheese Ravioli in Tomato Sauce with Beef, Chef Boyardee® | 1 cup | 220 | 30 |
| ❶ Cheese Tortellini in Hearty Tomato Sauce, Chef Boyardee® | 1 cup | 230 | 10 |
| Chili Mac, Chef Boyardee® | 1 cup | 260 | 100 |
| ❶ Garfield Pizzos, Franco-American® | 1 cup | 210 | 27 |
| ❶ Gargoyles, Franco-American® | 1 cup | 190 | 18 |
| ❶ Homestyle Noodles, Morningstar Farms® | ½ cup | 160 | 0 |
| Lasagna, Chef Boyardee® | 1 cup | 280 | 90 |
| ❶ Macaroni & Cheese, Chef Boyardee® | 1 cup | 180 | 10 |
| ❶ Meat Tortellini in Hearty Tomato and Meat Sauce, Chef Boyardee® | 1 cup | 260 | 30 |
| ❶ Mini Ravioli, Chef Boyardee® | 1 cup | 240 | 50 |
| ❶ Pasta Shapes in Tomato and Cheese Flavored Sauce, Chef Boyardee®, all varieties (avg) | 1 cup | 205 | 0 |
| Pasta with Mini Meatballs in Tomato Sauce, Chef Boyardee® | 1 cup | 263 | 73 |
| ❶ Sir Chompsalot Bite Size Beef Ravioli, Chef Boyardee® | 1 cup | 210 | 30 |
| Sir Chompsalot Bite Size O-Rings with Mini Meatballs, Chef Boyardee® | 1 cup | 260 | 90 |
| Spaghetti and Meat Balls in Tomato Sauce, Chef Boyardee® | 1 cup | 250 | 90 |
| Spaghetti O's® with Meatballs, Franco-American® | 1 can | 220 | 81 |

### PASTA (DRY)

| | | | |
|---|---|---|---|
| ❶ Pasta, all varieties (avg) | 2 oz | 210 | 10 |

### PASTA (REFRIGERATED)

| | | | |
|---|---|---|---|
| ❶ Angel Hair, Trio's® | 1 cup | 320 | 25 |
| ❶ Angel's Hair, Di Giorno® | 2 oz | 160 | 10 |

❶ Meets Low-Fat Guidelines

| TOTAL FAT (g) | SATURATED FAT (g) | SODIUM (mg) | PROTEIN (g) | CARBOHYDRATE (g) | CARBOHYDRATE CHOICES | EXCHANGES |
|---|---|---|---|---|---|---|
| 2 | 1 | 930 | 7 | 43 | 3 | 3 starch |
| 0 | 0 | 860 | 7 | 44 | 3 | 3 starch |
| 3 | 1.5 | 1110 | 9 | 38 | 2½ | 2½ starch, 1 very lean meat |
| 1 | 0 | 770 | 9 | 46 | 3 | 3 starch |
| 11 | 5 | 1480 | 10 | 30 | 2 | 2 starch, 1 meat, 1 fat |
| 3 | NA | NA | 6 | 39 | 2½ | 2½ starch |
| 2 | NA | NA | 5 | 36 | 2½ | 2½ starch |
| 0 | 0 | 10 | 5 | 33 | 2 | 2 starch |
| 10 | 4 | 910 | 10 | 36 | 2½ | 2½ starch, 1 meat, ½ fat |
| 1.5 | 1 | 1090 | 8 | 35 | 2 | 2 starch, 1 very lean meat |
| 3 | 1.5 | 810 | 10 | 48 | 3 | 3 starch, 1 very lean meat |
| 6 | 2.5 | 1180 | 8 | 37 | 2½ | 2½ starch, 1 lean meat |
| 0 | 0 | 840 | 6 | 45 | 3 | 3 starch |
| 8 | 4 | 963 | 9 | 38 | 2½ | 2½ starch, 1 meat |
| 4 | 1.5 | 800 | 8 | 37 | 2½ | 2½ starch, 1 very lean meat |
| 10 | 4 | 780 | 8 | 33 | 2 | 2 starch, 1 meat, ½ fat |
| 10 | 4 | 950 | 9 | 32 | 2 | 2 starch, 1 meat, ½ fat |
| 9 | NA | NA | 10 | 25 | 1½ | 1½ starch, 1 meat, ½ fat |
| 1 | 0 | 10 | 7 | 42 | 3 | 3 starch |
| 3 | 1 | 30 | 13 | 61 | 4 | 4 starch |
| 1 | 0 | 190 | 7 | 31 | 2 | 2 starch |

1 Carbohydrate Choice = 1 starch or 1 fruit or 1 milk exchange

| PRODUCTS | SERVING SIZE | CALORIES | CALORIES FROM FAT |
|---|---|---|---|
| ❶ Cheese and Garlic Ravioli, Di Giorno Light® | 1 cup | 270 | 20 |
| Cheese Tortellini, Di Giorno® | ¾ cup | 260 | 60 |
| Chicken & Prosciutto Tortellini, Contadina® | 1 cup | 350 | 100 |
| Chicken & Rosemary Ravioli, Contadina® | 1¼ cups | 330 | 90 |
| Chicken & Vegetable Tortellini, Contadina® | ¾ cup | 260 | 60 |
| ❶ Fettuccine, Di Giorno®, all varieties (avg) | 2.5 oz | 190 | 15 |
| Fettucine, Contadina® | 1¼ cups | 250 | 30 |
| ❶ Fettucine, Contadina® Cholesterol Free | 1 cup | 240 | 20 |
| ❶ Fettucini, Trio's® | 1 cup | 320 | 25 |
| Four Cheese Ravioli, Contadina® | 1 cup | 290 | 90 |
| Four Cheese Ravioli, Contadina® Light | 1 cup | 240 | 35 |
| Hot Red Pepper Cheese Tortellini, Di Giorno® | 1 cup | 310 | 80 |
| Italian Herb Cheese Ravioli, Di Giorno® | 1 cup | 350 | 120 |
| Linguine, Contadina® | 1¼ cups | 260 | 30 |
| ❶ Linguine, Contadina® Cholesterol Free | 1¼ cups | 250 | 20 |
| ❶ Linguine, Di Giorno®, all varieties (avg) | 2.5 oz | 190 | 15 |
| ❶ Linguini, Trio's® | 1 cup | 320 | 25 |
| Mozzarella Garlic Tortellini, Di Giorno® | 1 cup | 300 | 80 |
| Mushroom Tortellini, Di Giorno® | 1 cup | 290 | 70 |
| Ravioli with Italian Sausage, Di Giorno® | ¾ cup | 340 | 110 |
| Ravioli, Trio's® | 1 cup | 340 | 80 |
| ❶ Ravioli, Trio's® Lowfat | 1 cup | 300 | 40 |
| ❶ Spaghetti, Trio's® Cholesterol Free | 1 cup | 310 | 15 |
| Spinach Fettucine, Contadina® | 1¼ cups | 270 | 35 |
| Spinach Three Cheese Tortellini, Contadina® | ¾ cup | 270 | 50 |
| Sweet Italian Sausage Tortellini, Contadina® | 1 cup | 320 | 80 |
| Three Cheese Tortellini, Contadina® | ¾ cup | 260 | 50 |
| ❶ Tomato and Cheese Ravioli, Di Giorno Light® | 1 cup | 280 | 25 |
| Tortellini, Trio's® | 1 cup | 320 | 70 |
| ❶ Tortellini, Trio's® Lowfat | 1 cup | 270 | 20 |
| ❶ Tortellini with Chicken and Herbs, Di Giorno® | 1 cup | 260 | 45 |

❶  Meets Low-Fat Guidelines

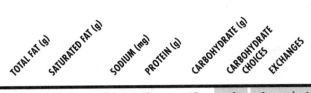

| TOTAL FAT (g) | SATURATED FAT (g) | SODIUM (mg) | PROTEIN (g) | CARBOHYDRATE (g) | CARBOHYDRATE CHOICES | EXCHANGES |
|---|---|---|---|---|---|---|
| 2 | 1 | 580 | 17 | 45 | 3 | 3 starch, 1 very lean meat |
| 6 | 3.5 | 230 | 12 | 37 | 2½ | 2½ starch, 1 meat |
| 12 | 4 | 410 | 14 | 46 | 3 | 3 starch, 1 lean meat, 1 fat |
| 10 | 3 | 490 | 14 | 47 | 3 | 3 starch, 1 lean meat, 1 fat |
| 7 | 2 | 220 | 10 | 39 | 2½ | 2 starch, 1 veg, 1 lean meat |
| 1.5 | 0 | 125 | 7 | 39 | 2½ | 2½ starch |
| 3.5 | 1 | 30 | 10 | 45 | 3 | 3 starch |
| 2.5 | 0 | 16 | 9 | 46 | 3 | 3 starch |
| 3 | 1 | 30 | 13 | 61 | 4 | 4 starch |
| 10 | 5 | 330 | 14 | 35 | 2 | 2 starch, 1 meat, 1 fat |
| 4.5 | 2 | 300 | 12 | 38 | 2½ | 2½ starch, 1 lean meat |
| 9 | 5 | 310 | 16 | 41 | 3 | 3 starch, 1 meat |
| 13 | 8 | 610 | 15 | 44 | 3 | 3 starch, 1 meat, 1 fat |
| 4 | 1 | 30 | 10 | 47 | 3 | 3 starch |
| 2.5 | 0 | 20 | 9 | 49 | 3 | 3 starch |
| 1.5 | 0 | 125 | 7 | 39 | 2½ | 2½ starch |
| 3 | 1 | 30 | 13 | 61 | 4 | 4 starch |
| 9 | 5 | 440 | 15 | 40 | 2½ | 2½ starch, 1 meat |
| 7 | 4.5 | 510 | 14 | 42 | 3 | 3 starch, 1 lean meat |
| 12 | 5 | 630 | 16 | 41 | 3 | 3 starch, 1 meat, 1 fat |
| 10 | 5 | 350 | 16 | 46 | 3 | 3 starch, 1 meat |
| 3 | 2.5 | 450 | 13 | 53 | 3½ | 3½ starch, 1 very lean meat |
| 1.5 | 0 | 15 | 11 | 63 | 4 | 4 starch |
| 4 | 1 | 110 | 12 | 46 | 3 | 3 starch |
| 6 | 3 | 300 | 11 | 42 | 3 | 3 starch, 1 lean meat |
| 9 | 3 | 300 | 12 | 48 | 3 | 3 starch, 1 meat |
| 6 | 3 | 270 | 11 | 41 | 3 | 3 starch, 1 lean meat |
| 3 | 1.5 | 490 | 14 | 49 | 3 | 3 starch, 1 very lean meat |
| 8 | 3 | 400 | 15 | 47 | 3 | 3 starch, 1 meat |
| 3 | 0 | 450 | 13 | 50 | 3 | 3 starch, 1 very lean meat |
| 5 | 2.5 | 290 | 13 | 40 | 2½ | 2½ starch, 1 lean meat |

1 Carbohydrate Choice = 1 starch *or* 1 fruit *or* 1 milk exchange

## PRODUCTS

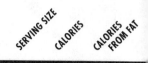

| PRODUCTS | SERVING SIZE | CALORIES | CALORIES FROM FAT |
|---|---|---|---|
| Tortellini with Meat, Di Giorno® | ¾ cup | 290 | 80 |

### PASTA MEALS/ENTREES (FROZEN)
*see also* Macaroni and Cheese

### *Fettuccine Alfredo Meals/Entrees*

| | | | |
|---|---|---|---|
| ❶ Chicken Fettucini, Weight Watchers® | 1 entree | 290 | 60 |
| Fettuccine Alfredo, Banquet® | 1 meal | 370 | 160 |
| ❶ Fettucini Alfredo, Healthy Choice® | 1 meal | 250 | 45 |
| Fettucini Alfredo, Marie Callender's® | 1 cup | 350 | 190 |
| Fettucini Alfredo, Michelina's® | 1 pkg | 430 | 160 |
| Fettucini Alfredo, Stouffer's® | 1 pkg | 580 | 350 |
| Fettucini Alfredo, Stouffer's® Lean Cuisine® | 1 pkg | 270 | 60 |
| Fettucini Alfredo with Broccoli, Michelina's® Double Serving | 1 cup | 350 | 140 |
| Fettuccine Alfredo with Broccoli & Chicken, Michelina's® | 1 pkg | 350 | 110 |
| Fettucini Alfredo with Broccoli, Weight Watchers® | 1 entree | 230 | 50 |
| Fettucini with Broccoli & Chicken, Marie Callender's® | 1 cup | 420 | 230 |

### *Lasagna Meals/Entrees*

| | | | |
|---|---|---|---|
| ❶ Cheese Lasagna Casserole, Stouffer's® Lean Cuisine® Lunch Express® | 1 pkg | 270 | 60 |
| ❶ Cheese Lasagna with Chicken Scaloppini, Stouffer's® Lean Cuisine® Cafe Classics | 1 pkg | 290 | 80 |
| ❶ Classic Cheese Lasagna, Stouffer's® Lean Cuisine® | 1 pkg | 290 | 60 |
| Cheese Manicotti, Stouffer's® | 1 pkg | 340 | 150 |
| Four Cheese Lasagna, Stouffer's® | 1 pkg | 410 | 170 |
| Garden Lasagna, Weight Watchers® | 1 entree | 270 | 60 |
| Italiana Cheese Lasagna, Weight Watchers® | 1 entree | 300 | 70 |
| Lasagna, Marie Callender's® Extra Cheese | 1 cup | 330 | 140 |
| Lasagna Alfredo, Michelina's® | 1 pkg | 390 | 160 |

❶  Meets Low-Fat Guidelines

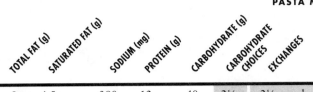

| TOTAL FAT (g) | SATURATED FAT (g) | SODIUM (mg) | PROTEIN (g) | CARBOHYDRATE (g) | CARBOHYDRATE CHOICES | EXCHANGES |
|---|---|---|---|---|---|---|
| 9 | 4.5 | 380 | 12 | 40 | 2½ | 2½ starch, 1 meat |
| 7 | 2 | 590 | 19 | 39 | 2½ | 2½ starch, 2 lean meat |
| 18 | 8 | 940 | 12 | 39 | 2½ | 2 starch, 1 veg, 1 meat, 2 fat |
| 5 | 2 | 480 | 11 | 39 | 2½ | 2½ starch, 1 lean meat |
| 21 | 9 | 400 | 10 | 29 | 2 | 2 starch, 1 meat, 3 fat |
| 18 | 9 | 700 | 15 | 49 | 3 | 3 starch, 1 meat, 2 fat |
| 39 | 21 | 810 | 14 | 42 | 3 | 3 starch, 1 meat, 6 fat |
| 7 | 3 | 590 | 13 | 38 | 2½ | 2½ starch, 1 meat |
| 16 | 8 | 620 | 12 | 37 | 2½ | 2 starch, 1 veg, 1 meat, 2 fat |
| 13 | 7 | 680 | 17 | 42 | 3 | 2½ starch, 1 veg, 1 meat, 1 fat |
| 6 | 3 | 450 | 10 | 34 | 2 | 2 starch, 1 veg, 1 meat |
| 26 | 11 | 530 | 18 | 30 | 2 | 1½ starch, 1 veg, 1 meat, 3 fat |
| 7 | 2.5 | 590 | 14 | 38 | 2½ | 2½ starch, 1 meat |
| 8 | 2.5 | 560 | 20 | 34 | 2 | 2 starch, 2 lean meat |
| 6 | 3 | 560 | 20 | 38 | 2½ | 2½ starch, 2 lean meat |
| 16 | 7 | 810 | 18 | 32 | 2 | 2 starch, 2 meat, 1 fat |
| 19 | 10 | 840 | 22 | 37 | 2½ | 2½ starch, 2 meat, 1 fat |
| 7 | 3.5 | 540 | 14 | 36 | 2½ | 2 starch, 1 veg, 1 meat |
| 8 | 3.5 | 650 | 20 | 38 | 2½ | 2½ starch, 2 lean meat |
| 16 | 8 | 770 | 15 | 32 | 2 | 2 starch, 1 meat, 2 fat |
| 18 | 9 | 640 | 15 | 41 | 3 | 3 starch, 1 meat, 2 fat |

1 Carbohydrate Choice = 1 starch or 1 fruit or 1 milk exchange

## PRODUCTS

| PRODUCTS | SERVING SIZE | CALORIES | CALORIES FROM FAT |
|---|---|---|---|
| Lasagna Alfredo, Michelina's® Double Serving | 1 cup | 350 | 150 |
| ❶ Lasagna Florentine, Smart Ones® | 1 entree | 200 | 15 |
| Lasagna Polo, Michelina's® | 1 pkg | 330 | 110 |
| ❶ Lasagna Roma, Healthy Choice® | 1 meal | 390 | 45 |
| Lasagna with Meat Sauce, Banquet® | 1 meal | 290 | 80 |
| Lasagna with Meat Sauce, Banquet® Bake At Home | 1 cup | 240 | 60 |
| Lasagna with Meat Sauce, Banquet® Family Size | 1 cup | 230 | 70 |
| Lasagna with Meat Sauce, Marie Callender's® | 1 cup | 370 | 170 |
| Lasagna with Meat Sauce, Marie Callender's® Multi-Serves | 1 cup | 350 | 150 |
| Lasagna with Meat Sauce, Michelina's® | 1 pkg | 320 | 90 |
| Lasagna with Meat Sauce, Michelina's® Double Serving | 1 cup | 290 | 80 |
| Lasagna with Meat Sauce, Stouffer's® | 1 pkg | 360 | 120 |
| Lasagna with Meat Sauce, Stouffer's® Family-Size | 1 cup | 270 | 97 |
| Lasagna with Meat Sauce, Stouffer's® Lean Cuisine® | 1 pkg | 290 | 70 |
| Lasagna with Meat Sauce, Stouffer's® Lunch Express® | 1 pkg | 330 | 80 |
| Lasagna with Meat Sauce, Weight Watchers® | 1 entree | 270 | 60 |
| Lasagna with Vegetables, Michelina's® | 1 pkg | 270 | 50 |
| ❶ Vegetable Lasagna, Banquet® | 1 meal | 260 | 50 |
| Vegetable Lasagna, Stouffer's® | 1 pkg | 450 | 210 |
| Vegetable Lasagna, Stouffer's® Family-Size | 1 cup | 340 | 150 |
| ❶ Vegetable Lasagna, Stouffer's® Lean Cuisine® | 1 pkg | 270 | 60 |
| ❶ Vegetable Lasagna Primavera, Life Choice® | 1 meal | 170 | 10 |
| ❶ Zucchini Lasagna, Healthy Choice® | 1 meal | 330 | 15 |

❶ Meets Low-Fat Guidelines

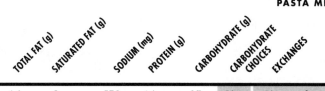

| TOTAL FAT (g) | SATURATED FAT (g) | SODIUM (mg) | PROTEIN (g) | CARBOHYDRATE (g) | CARBOHYDRATE CHOICES | EXCHANGES |
|---|---|---|---|---|---|---|
| 16 | 8 | 570 | 14 | 37 | 2½ | 2½ starch, 1 meat, 2 fat |
| 2 | 0 | 590 | 10 | 34 | 2 | 2 starch |
| 12 | 5 | 730 | 16 | 38 | 2½ | 2½ starch, 1 meat, 1 fat |
| 5 | 2 | 580 | 26 | 60 | 4 | 4 starch, 2 very lean meat |
| 9 | 2 | 900 | 14 | 39 | 2½ | 2½ starch, 1 meat |
| 7 | 3 | 650 | 12 | 32 | 2 | 2 starch, 1 meat |
| 8 | 4 | 530 | 12 | 29 | 2 | 2 starch, 1 meat |
| 18 | 9 | 740 | 17 | 34 | 2 | 2 starch, 2 meat, 1 fat |
| 16 | 8 | 770 | 17 | 32 | 2 | 2 starch, 2 meat, 1 fat |
| 10 | 4 | 700 | 16 | 41 | 3 | 3 starch, 1 lean meat, 1 fat |
| 8 | 3.5 | 600 | 14 | 38 | 2½ | 2½ starch, 1 meat |
| 13 | 5 | 780 | 27 | 34 | 2 | 2 starch, 1 veg, 3 lean meat |
| 10.5 | 4.5 | 610 | 19 | 25 | 1½ | 1½ starch, 2 meat |
| 8 | 4 | 560 | 20 | 35 | 2 | 2 starch, 2 lean meat |
| 10 | 5 | 910 | 18 | 42 | 3 | 3 starch, 2 lean meat |
| 7 | 3 | 570 | 14 | 38 | 2½ | 2½ starch, 1 meat |
| 6 | 3 | 760 | 13 | 41 | 3 | 2½ starch, 1 veg, 1 lean meat |
| 6 | 2 | 850 | 11 | 41 | 3 | 2½ starch, 1 veg, ½ fat |
| 23 | 8 | 980 | 20 | 41 | 3 | 2½ starch, 1 veg, 2 meat, 2 fat |
| 17 | 6 | 760 | 12 | 34 | 2 | 2 starch, 1 veg, 1 meat, 2 fat |
| 7 | 2.5 | 540 | 17 | 35 | 2 | 2 starch, 1 veg, 1 meat |
| 1 | 0.5 | 600 | 10 | 30 | 1½ | 1 starch, 1 veg, 1 very lean meat |
| 1.5 | 1 | 310 | 20 | 58 | 4 | 3½ starch, 1 veg, 1 very lean meat |

1 Carbohydrate Choice = 1 starch *or* 1 fruit *or* 1 milk exchange

## PRODUCTS

| | SERVING SIZE | CALORIES | CALORIES FROM FAT |
|---|---|---|---|
| **Macaroni and Beef Meals/Entrees** | | | |
| Macaroni & Beef, Banquet® Bake At Home | 1 cup | 230 | 60 |
| Macaroni and Beef, Stouffer's® | 1 pkg | 420 | 180 |
| ❶ Macaroni and Beef, Stouffer's® Lean Cuisine® | 1 pkg | 280 | 70 |
| ❶ Macaroni and Beef, Weight Watchers® | 1 entree | 220 | 40 |
| **Pasta Primavera Meals/Entrees** | | | |
| Fettucini Primavera, Stouffer's® Lean Cuisine® | 1 pkg | 260 | 70 |
| ❶ Fettucini Primavera, Stouffer's® Lunch Express® | 1 pkg | 420 | 220 |
| Fettucini Primavera with Tortellini, Marie Callender's® | 1 cup | 310 | 170 |
| Pasta Primavera with Chicken, Marie Callender's® | 1 cup | 310 | 170 |
| Penne Primavera, Michelina's® | 1 pkg | 340 | 100 |
| Spinach Ravioli with Primavera Sauce, Michelina's® | 1 pkg | 370 | 160 |
| **Ravioli Meals/Entrees** | | | |
| Cheese Ravioli, Stouffer's® Lean Cuisine® | 1 pkg | 240 | 60 |
| Cheese Ravioli, Stouffer's® Lunch Express® | 1 pkg | 360 | 130 |
| Cheese Ravioli in Marinara Sauce, Marie Callender's® | 1 cup | 370 | 130 |
| ❶ Cheese Ravioli Parmigiana, Healthy Choice® | 1 meal | 250 | 35 |
| Cheese Ravioli with Alfredo & Broccoli Sauce, Michelina's® | 1 pkg | 420 | 210 |
| ❶ Ravioli Florentine, Smart Ones® | 1 entree | 190 | 15 |
| **Spaghetti Meals/Entrees** | | | |
| ❶ Spaghetti & Pomodoro Sauce with 3 Meatballs, Michelina's® | 1 pkg | 290 | 60 |
| ❶ Spaghetti & Pomodoro Sauce with 6 Meatballs, Michelina's® Double Serving | 1 cup | 230 | 50 |
| Spaghetti and Meat Sauce, Marie Callender's® | 1 cup | 260 | 90 |
| Spaghetti Bolognese, Banquet® | 1 meal | 370 | 150 |

❶  Meets Low-Fat Guidelines

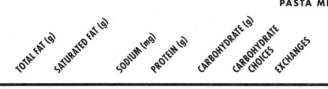

| TOTAL FAT (g) | SATURATED FAT (g) | SODIUM (mg) | PROTEIN (g) | CARBOHYDRATE (g) | CARBOHYDRATE CHOICES | EXCHANGES |
|---|---|---|---|---|---|---|
| 7 | 3 | 810 | 13 | 31 | 2 | 2 starch, 1 meat |
| 20 | 8 | 1530 | 20 | 40 | 2½ | 2½ starch, 2 meat, 2 fat |
| 8 | 2 | 550 | 13 | 40 | 2½ | 2½ starch, 1 meat |
| 4.5 | 1.5 | 560 | 13 | 32 | 2 | 2 starch, 1 meat |
| | | | | | | |
| 8 | 2.5 | 580 | 15 | 33 | 2 | 2 starch, 1 veg, 1 meat |
| 25 | 12 | 690 | 15 | 33 | 2 | 2 starch, 1 veg, 1 meat, 4 fat |
| 19 | 8 | 380 | 10 | 25 | 1½ | 1½ starch, 1 meat, 3 fat |
| 19 | 8 | 450 | 12 | 22 | 1½ | 1½ starch, 1 meat, 2 fat |
| 12 | 5 | 740 | 11 | 47 | 3 | 3 starch, 1 meat, 1 fat |
| 18 | 6 | 810 | 12 | 39 | 2½ | 2 starch, 1 veg, 1 meat, 2 fat |
| | | | | | | |
| 7 | 3 | 590 | 11 | 34 | 2 | 2 starch, 1 meat |
| 14 | 5 | 700 | 15 | 43 | 3 | 3 starch, 1 meat, 1 fat |
| 14 | 5 | 520 | 14 | 47 | 3 | 3 starch, 1 meat, 1 fat |
| 4 | 2 | 290 | 11 | 44 | 3 | 3 starch, 1 lean meat |
| 24 | 10 | 800 | 15 | 37 | 2½ | 2 starch, 1 veg, 1 meat, 3 fat |
| 2 | 0 | 420 | 8 | 37 | 2½ | 2½ starch |
| | | | | | | |
| 6 | 1.5 | 890 | 12 | 46 | 3 | 3 starch, 1 lean meat |
| 5 | 1.5 | 790 | 9 | 35 | 2 | 2 starch, 1 lean meat |
| 10 | 3 | 570 | 11 | 32 | 2 | 2 starch, 1 meat, ½ fat |
| 16 | 5 | 1040 | 14 | 40 | 2½ | 2½ starch, 1 meat, 2 fat |

1 Carbohydrate Choice = 1 starch or 1 fruit or 1 milk exchange

## PRODUCTS

| | PRODUCTS | SERVING SIZE | CALORIES | CALORIES FROM FAT |
|---|---|---|---|---|
| ❶ | Spaghetti Bolognese, Healthy Choice® | 1 meal | 260 | 25 |
| ❶ | Spaghetti Bolognese, Michelina's® | 1 pkg | 270 | 50 |
| ❶ | Spaghetti Bolognese, Michelina's® Double Serving | 1 cup | 240 | 50 |
| | Spaghetti Marinara, Marie Callender's® | 1 cup | 270 | 90 |
| ❶ | Spaghetti Marinara, Michelina's® | 1 pkg | 250 | 25 |
| | Spaghetti with Meatballs, Stouffer's® | 1 pkg | 420 | 130 |
| ❶ | Spaghetti with Meatballs, Stouffer's® Lean Cuisine® | 1 pkg | 290 | 60 |
| ❶ | Spaghetti with Meat Sauce, Morton® | 1 meal | 170 | 25 |
| ❶ | Spaghetti with Meat Sauce, Stouffer's® Lean Cuisine® | 1 pkg | 290 | 60 |
| | Spaghetti with Meat Sauce, Stouffer's® Lunch Express® | 1 pkg | 320 | 90 |
| | Spaghetti with Meat Sauce, Weight Watchers® | 1 entree | 290 | 50 |

### Tuna Noodle Casserole Meals/Entrees

| | | | | |
|---|---|---|---|---|
| ❶ | Pasta and Tuna Casserole, Stouffer's® Lean Cuisine® Lunch Express® | 1 pkg | 280 | 50 |
| | Tuna Noodle Casserole, Stouffer's® | 1 pkg | 320 | 90 |
| | Tuna Noodle Casserole, Weight Watchers® | 1 entree | 270 | 60 |

### Other Pasta Meals/Entrees

| | | | | |
|---|---|---|---|---|
| ❶ | Angel Hair Pasta, Smart Ones® | 1 entree | 170 | 15 |
| ❶ | Angel Hair Pasta, Stouffer's® Lean Cuisine® | 1 pkg | 210 | 35 |
| ❶ | Bow Tie Pasta and Chicken, Stouffer's® Lean Cuisine® Cafe Classics | 1 pkg | 270 | 50 |
| | Bowtie Pasta and Mushrooms Marsala, Weight Watchers® International Selections | 1 entree | 280 | 80 |
| ❶ | Cheddar Bake with Pasta, Stouffer's® Lean Cuisine® | 1 pkg | 220 | 60 |
| | Cheese Cannelloni, Stouffer's® Lean Cuisine® | 1 pkg | 240 | 45 |
| | Cheese Manicotti, Weight Watchers® | 1 entree | 260 | 60 |

 Meets Low-Fat Guidelines

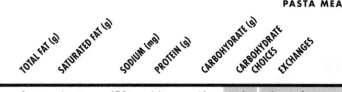

| TOTAL FAT (g) | SATURATED FAT (g) | SODIUM (mg) | PROTEIN (g) | CARBOHYDRATE (g) | CARBOHYDRATE CHOICES | EXCHANGES |
|---|---|---|---|---|---|---|
| 3 | 1 | 470 | 14 | 43 | 3 | 3 starch, 1 very lean meat |
| 6 | 1.5 | 660 | 11 | 43 | 3 | 3 starch, 1 lean meat |
| 5 | 1.5 | 610 | 9 | 38 | 2½ | 2½ starch, 1 lean meat |
| 10 | 3 | 540 | 10 | 35 | 2 | 2 starch, 1 meat, ½ fat |
| 3 | 0 | 760 | 8 | 49 | 3 | 3 starch |
| 15 | 4 | 680 | 19 | 51 | 3½ | 3½ starch, 2 meat |
| 7 | 2 | 520 | 17 | 40 | 2½ | 2½ starch, 2 lean meat |
| 3 | 1 | 600 | 6 | 30 | 2 | 2 starch |
| 6 | 1.5 | 550 | 14 | 45 | 3 | 3 starch, 1 lean meat |
| 10 | 3.5 | 580 | 15 | 43 | 3 | 3 starch, 1 meat |
| 6 | NA | 560 | 14 | 45 | 3 | 3 starch, 1 meat |
| 6 | 2 | 590 | 18 | 39 | 2½ | 2½ starch, 2 very lean meat |
| 10 | 3.5 | 1130 | 20 | 37 | 2½ | 2½ starch, 2 lean meat |
| 7 | 3.5 | 590 | 13 | 39 | 2½ | 2½ starch, 1 meat |
| 2 | 0 | 520 | 8 | 29 | 2 | 2 starch, 1 very lean meat |
| 4 | 1 | 420 | 9 | 35 | 2 | 2 starch, 1 veg, 1 very lean meat |
| 6 | 1.5 | 550 | 19 | 34 | 2 | 2 starch, 1 veg, 2 lean meat |
| 9 | 3.5 | 560 | 13 | 36 | 2½ | 2½ starch, 1 meat |
| 6 | 2 | 560 | 12 | 29 | 2 | 2 starch, 1 meat |
| 5 | 3 | 590 | 19 | 29 | 2 | 2 starch, 2 lean meat |
| 7 | 3.5 | 570 | 17 | 31 | 2 | 2 starch, 2 lean meat |

1 Carbohydrate Choice = 1 starch or 1 fruit or 1 milk exchange

| PRODUCTS | SERVING SIZE | CALORIES | CALORIES FROM FAT |
|---|---|---|---|
| Cheese Tortellini with Parmesano Sauce, Michelina's® | 1 pkg | 360 | 120 |
| Escalloped Noodles & Chicken, Marie Callender's® | 1 cup | 270 | 140 |
| Fettuccini Carbonara, Michelina's® | 1 pkg | 370 | 120 |
| ❶ Lemon Herb Chicken Piccata, Weight Watchers® Smart Ones® | 1 entree | 190 | 15 |
| ❶ Linguini with Clams, Michelina's® | 1 pkg | 310 | 40 |
| ❶ Linguini with Seafood, Michelina's® | 1 pkg | 270 | 45 |
| ❶ Marinara Sauce, Penne Pasta, Italian Sausage & Peppers, Michelina's® Double Serving | 1 cup | 240 | 60 |
| ❶ Marinara Twist, Stouffer's® Lean Cuisine® | 1 pkg | 240 | 25 |
| Meat Ravioli with Pomodoro Sauce, Michelina's® | 1 pkg | 300 | 110 |
| ❶ Mostaccioli Parmesano, Michelina's® | 1 pkg | 280 | 60 |
| Noodles & Chicken, Banquet® Bake At Home | 1 cup | 210 | 80 |
| Noodles and Beef with Gravy, Banquet® Family Size | 1 cup | 140 | 30 |
| Noodles Romanoff, Stouffer's® | 1 pkg | 490 | 230 |
| Noodles Stroganoff, Michelina's® | 1 pkg | 290 | 120 |
| Noodles with Chicken, Peas & Carrots, Michelina's® | 1 pkg | 280 | 90 |
| ❶ Pasta and Chicken Marinara, Stouffer's® Lean Cuisine® Lunch Express® | 1 pkg | 270 | 50 |
| Pasta and Spinach Romano, Weight Watchers® International Selections | 1 entree | 240 | 70 |
| ❶ Pasta and Tuna Casserole, Stouffer's® Lean Cuisine® Lunch Express® | 1 pkg | 280 | 50 |
| ❶ Pasta and Turkey Dijon, Stouffer's® Lean Cuisine® Lunch Express® | 1 pkg | 270 | 60 |
| ❶ Pasta Shells Marinara, Healthy Choice® | 1 meal | 370 | 35 |
| Pasta with Tomato Basil Sauce, Weight Watchers® International Selections | 1 entree | 260 | 80 |

❶   Meets Low-Fat Guidelines

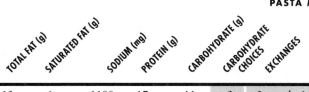

| TOTAL FAT (g) | SATURATED FAT (g) | SODIUM (mg) | PROTEIN (g) | CARBOHYDRATE (g) | CARBOHYDRATE CHOICES | EXCHANGES |
|---|---|---|---|---|---|---|
| 13 | 6 | 1100 | 17 | 44 | 3 | 3 starch, 1 meat, 1 fat |
| 16 | 6 | 670 | 10 | 22 | 1½ | 1½ starch, 1 meat, 2 fat |
| 13 | 6 | 630 | 12 | 48 | 3 | 3 starch, 1 meat, 1 fat |
| 2 | 0.5 | 460 | 10 | 34 | 2 | 2 starch, 1 very lean meat, 1 veg |
| 4.5 | 0.5 | 560 | 20 | 46 | 3 | 3 starch, 2 very lean meat |
| 5 | 0.5 | 750 | 12 | 42 | 3 | 3 starch, 1 lean meat |
| 7 | 2 | 580 | 10 | 33 | 2 | 2 starch, 1 veg, 1 meat |
| 3 | 1 | 440 | 10 | 42 | 3 | 2½ starch, 1 veg, 1 very lean meat |
| 12 | 4 | 1000 | 15 | 34 | 2 | 2 starch, 2 meat |
| 6 | 1.5 | 550 | 10 | 45 | 3 | 3 starch, 1 lean meat |
| 9 | 3 | 810 | 10 | 24 | 1½ | 1½ starch, 1 meat |
| 4 | 2 | 1120 | 11 | 16 | 1 | 1 starch, 1 lean meat |
| 25 | 6 | 1400 | 18 | 48 | 3 | 3 starch, 2 meat, 2 fat |
| 13 | 6 | 630 | 12 | 31 | 2 | 2 starch, 1 meat, 1 fat |
| 10 | 4.5 | 820 | 14 | 32 | 2 | 2 starch, 1 meat, ½ fat |
| 6 | 1.5 | 540 | 15 | 38 | 2½ | 2½ starch, 1 lean meat |
| 8 | 3.5 | 510 | 11 | 32 | 2 | 2 starch, 1 meat |
| 6 | 2 | 590 | 18 | 39 | 2½ | 2½ starch, 2 very lean meat |
| 6 | 1.5 | 570 | 16 | 37 | 2½ | 2½ starch, 1 lean meat |
| 4 | 2 | 390 | 25 | 59 | 4 | 4 starch, 2 very lean meat |
| 9 | 3.5 | 360 | 12 | 33 | 2 | 2 starch, 1 meat |

1 Carbohydrate Choice = 1 starch *or* 1 fruit *or* 1 milk exchange

| PRODUCTS | SERVING SIZE | CALORIES | CALORIES FROM FAT |
|---|---|---|---|
| ❶ Penne Pasta with Marinara Sauce & Italian Sausage, Michelina's® | 1 pkg | 270 | 70 |
| ❶ Penne Pasta with Sun-Dried Tomatoes, Weight Watchers® | 1 entree | 290 | 80 |
| Penne Polo, Michelina's® | 1 pkg | 330 | 100 |
| Penne Polo, Michelina's® Double Serving | 1 cup | 300 | 90 |
| Rigatoni Parmigiana, Marie Callender's® | 1 cup | 300 | 130 |
| Rigatoni Parmigiana, Marie Callender's® Multi-Serves | 1 cup | 320 | 130 |
| ❶ Rigatoni, Stouffer's® Lean Cuisine® | 1 pkg | 180 | 35 |
| ❶ Rigatoni Pomodoro, Michelina's® | 1 pkg | 230 | 25 |
| Shells & Cheese with Jalapeno Peppers, Michelina's® | 1 pkg | 350 | 120 |
| ❶ Spicy Penne Pasta and Ricotta, Weight Watchers® International Selections | 1 entree | 280 | 50 |
| ❶ Sun Dried Tomato Manicotti, Life Choice® | 1 meal | 220 | 20 |
| Three Cheese Manicotti, Healthy Choice® | 1 meal | 310 | 80 |
| ❶ Vegetable Pasta Italiano, Healthy Choice® | 1 meal | 240 | 10 |
| White Cheddar & Broccoli, Banquet® | 1 meal | 350 | 110 |

## PASTA SALAD, BOXED (AS PREPARED)

| | | | |
|---|---|---|---|
| Caesar, Suddenly Salad® | ¾ cup | 220 | 80 |
| Classic Pasta, Suddenly Salad® | ¾ cup | 220 | 60 |
| Classic Ranch with Bacon, Kraft® | ~¾ cup | 360 | 210 |
| Creamy Caesar, Kraft® | ~¾ cup | 350 | 200 |
| ❶ Garden Italian, Suddenly Salad® 94% Fat Free | ¾ cup | 140 | 10 |
| Garden Primavera, Kraft® | ~¾ cup | 280 | 110 |
| Ranch & Bacon, Suddenly Salad® | ¾ cup | 320 | 170 |

## PASTA SAUCE (CAN OR JAR)

### Barilla® Pasta Sauce

| | | | |
|---|---|---|---|
| Green and Black Olive | ½ cup | 100 | 50 |

❶  Meets Low-Fat Guidelines

| TOTAL FAT (g) | SATURATED FAT (g) | SODIUM (mg) | PROTEIN (g) | CARBOHYDRATE (g) | CARBOHYDRATE CHOICES | EXCHANGES |
|---|---|---|---|---|---|---|
| 8 | 2.5 | 620 | 11 | 38 | 2½ | 2½ starch, 1 meat |
| 9 | 3 | 560 | 13 | 40 | 2½ | 2½ starch, 1 meat |
| 11 | 4.5 | 720 | 14 | 41 | 3 | 3 starch, 1 meat, ½ fat |
| 10 | 4.5 | 670 | 13 | 37 | 2½ | 2½ starch, 1 meat, ½ fat |
| 14 | 6 | 650 | 12 | 32 | 2 | 2 starch, 1 meat, 1 fat |
| 14 | 7 | 670 | 15 | 32 | 2 | 2 starch, 2 meat |
| 4 | 1.5 | 560 | 10 | 25 | 1½ | 1½ starch, 1 lean meat |
| 3 | 0 | 550 | 7 | 44 | 3 | 3 starch |
| 13 | 6 | 450 | 14 | 43 | 3 | 3 starch, 1 meat, 1 fat |
| 6 | 2 | 370 | 12 | 45 | 3 | 3 starch, 1 meat |
| 2.5 | 1 | 540 | 11 | 39 | 2 | 2 starch, 1 veg, 1 very lean meat |
| 9 | 5 | 450 | 16 | 41 | 3 | 3 starch, 1 meat |
| 1 | 0 | 480 | 9 | 48 | 3 | 3 starch |
| 12 | 4.5 | 900 | 12 | 48 | 3 | 3 starch, 1 veg, 1 meat, 1 fat |
| 9 | 1.5 | 580 | 5 | 30 | 2 | 2 starch, 1 fat |
| 7 | 1 | 830 | 5 | 34 | 2 | 2 starch, 1 fat |
| 23 | 4 | 500 | 7 | 30 | 2 | 2 starch, 4 fat |
| 22 | 4 | 650 | 7 | 30 | 2 | 2 starch, 4 fat |
| 1 | 0 | 540 | 5 | 29 | 2 | 2 starch |
| 12 | 2.5 | 730 | 8 | 34 | 2 | 2 starch, 2 fat |
| 19 | 3 | 490 | 7 | 31 | 2 | 2 starch, 3½ fat |
| 6 | 1.5 | 710 | 2 | 9 | ½ | ½ starch, 1 fat or 2 veg, 1 fat |

1 Carbohydrate Choice = 1 starch or 1 fruit or 1 milk exchange

## PRODUCTS

| PRODUCTS | SERVING SIZE | CALORIES | CALORIES FROM FAT |
|---|---|---|---|
| Marinara | ½ cup | 80 | 35 |
| Mushroom and Garlic | ½ cup | 80 | 30 |
| Spicy Pepper | ½ cup | 80 | 30 |
| Sweet Pepper and Garlic | ½ cup | 70 | 30 |
| ❶ Tomato Basil | ½ cup | 70 | 20 |

### Contadina® Pasta Sauce

| | | | |
|---|---|---|---|
| ❶ Pasta Ready Tomatoes | ½ cup | 40 | 15 |
| ❶ Pasta Ready Tomatoes Primavera | ½ cup | 50 | 15 |
| ❶ Pasta Ready Tomatoes with Crushed Red Pepper | ½ cup | 60 | 30 |
| ❶ Pasta Ready Tomatoes with Mushrooms | ½ cup | 50 | 15 |
| ❶ Pasta Ready Tomatoes with Olives | ½ cup | 60 | 30 |
| Pasta Ready Tomatoes with Three Cheeses | ½ cup | 70 | 35 |

### Healthy Choice® Pasta Sauce

| | | | |
|---|---|---|---|
| ❶ Extra Chunky, all varieties (avg) | ½ cup | 43 | 0 |
| ❶ Original, all varieties (avg) | ½ cup | 50 | 5 |
| ❶ Super Chunky, all varieties (avg) | ½ cup | 45 | 0 |

### Hunt's® Pasta Sauce

| | | | |
|---|---|---|---|
| ❶ Chunky Italian Style Vegetable Spaghetti Sauce | ½ cup | 61 | 9 |
| ❶ Chunky Marinara Spaghetti Sauce | ½ cup | 63 | 9 |
| ❶ Chunky Spaghetti Sauce | ½ cup | 38 | 4.5 |
| ❶ Chunky Spaghetti Sauce with Italian Sausage | ½ cup | 77 | 23 |
| ❶ Chunky Tomato, Garlic and Onion Spaghetti Sauce | ½ cup | 60 | 9 |
| ❶ Classic Spaghetti Sauce with Garlic & Herb | ½ cup | 60 | 18 |
| ❶ Classic Spaghetti Sauce with Parmesan | ½ cup | 50 | 18 |
| ❶ Classic Spaghetti Sauce with Tomato & Basil | ½ cup | 48 | 18 |

❶  Meets Low-Fat Guidelines

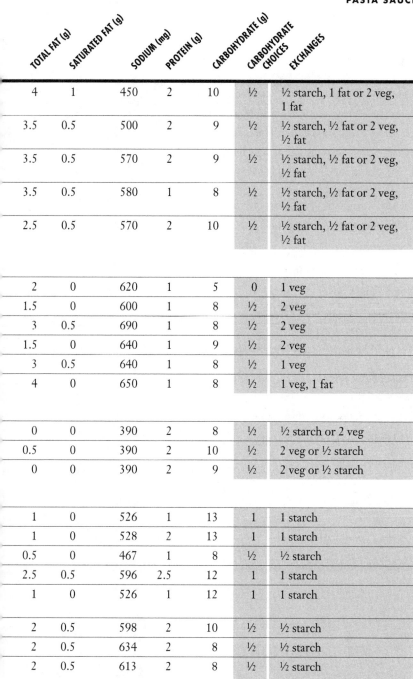

| TOTAL FAT (g) | SATURATED FAT (g) | SODIUM (mg) | PROTEIN (g) | CARBOHYDRATE (g) | CARBOHYDRATE CHOICES | EXCHANGES |
|---|---|---|---|---|---|---|
| 4 | 1 | 450 | 2 | 10 | ½ | ½ starch, 1 fat or 2 veg, 1 fat |
| 3.5 | 0.5 | 500 | 2 | 9 | ½ | ½ starch, ½ fat or 2 veg, ½ fat |
| 3.5 | 0.5 | 570 | 2 | 9 | ½ | ½ starch, ½ fat or 2 veg, ½ fat |
| 3.5 | 0.5 | 580 | 1 | 8 | ½ | ½ starch, ½ fat or 2 veg, ½ fat |
| 2.5 | 0.5 | 570 | 2 | 10 | ½ | ½ starch, ½ fat or 2 veg, ½ fat |
| | | | | | | |
| 2 | 0 | 620 | 1 | 5 | 0 | 1 veg |
| 1.5 | 0 | 600 | 1 | 8 | ½ | 2 veg |
| 3 | 0.5 | 690 | 1 | 8 | ½ | 2 veg |
| 1.5 | 0 | 640 | 1 | 9 | ½ | 2 veg |
| 3 | 0.5 | 640 | 1 | 8 | ½ | 1 veg |
| 4 | 0 | 650 | 1 | 8 | ½ | 1 veg, 1 fat |
| | | | | | | |
| 0 | 0 | 390 | 2 | 8 | ½ | ½ starch or 2 veg |
| 0.5 | 0 | 390 | 2 | 10 | ½ | 2 veg or ½ starch |
| 0 | 0 | 390 | 2 | 9 | ½ | 2 veg or ½ starch |
| | | | | | | |
| 1 | 0 | 526 | 1 | 13 | 1 | 1 starch |
| 1 | 0 | 528 | 2 | 13 | 1 | 1 starch |
| 0.5 | 0 | 467 | 1 | 8 | ½ | ½ starch |
| 2.5 | 0.5 | 596 | 2.5 | 12 | 1 | 1 starch |
| 1 | 0 | 526 | 1 | 12 | 1 | 1 starch |
| | | | | | | |
| 2 | 0.5 | 598 | 2 | 10 | ½ | ½ starch |
| 2 | 0.5 | 634 | 2 | 8 | ½ | ½ starch |
| 2 | 0.5 | 613 | 2 | 8 | ½ | ½ starch |

1 Carbohydrate Choice = 1 starch *or* 1 fruit *or* 1 milk exchange

## PRODUCTS

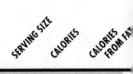

| | SERVING SIZE | CALORIES | CALORIES FROM FAT |
|---|---|---|---|
| ❶ Homestyle Spaghetti Sauce Flavored with Meat | ½ cup | 56 | 23 |
| ❶ Homestyle Spaghetti Sauce with Mushrooms | ½ cup | 56 | 23 |
| ❶ Homestyle Traditional Spaghetti Sauce | ½ cup | 56 | 23 |
| ❶ Italian Style Cheese & Garlic Spaghetti Sauce | ½ cup | 65 | 23 |
| ❶ Light Traditional Spaghetti Sauce, all varieties (avg) | ½ cup | 41 | 9 |
| ❶ Original Spaghetti Sauce Flavored with Meat | ½ cup | 65 | 23 |
| ❶ Original Spaghetti Sauce with Mushrooms | ½ cup | 65 | 23 |
| ❶ Original Traditional Spaghetti Sauce | ½ cup | 65 | 23 |

### Newman's Own® Pasta Sauce

| | | | |
|---|---|---|---|
| Bombolina™ Spaghetti Sauce | ½ cup | 100 | 45 |
| ❶ Sockarooni™ Spaghetti Sauce | ½ cup | 60 | 15 |
| ❶ Venetian Spaghetti Sauce | ½ cup | 60 | 15 |
| ❶ Venetian Spaghetti Sauce with Mushrooms | ½ cup | 60 | 15 |

### Prego® Pasta Sauce

| | | | |
|---|---|---|---|
| Spaghetti Sauce Flavored with Meat | ½ cup | 160 | 54 |
| Spaghetti Sauce with Mushrooms | ½ cup | 150 | 45 |
| Traditional Spaghetti Sauce | ½ cup | 150 | 54 |

### Progresso® Pasta Sauce

| | | | |
|---|---|---|---|
| Alfredo (Authentic) | ½ cup | 310 | 250 |
| Creamy Clam | ½ cup | 100 | 50 |
| Marinara | ½ cup | 90 | 40 |
| Marinara (Authentic) | ½ cup | 100 | 50 |
| Meat-Flavored Sauce | ½ cup | 100 | 40 |
| Mushroom Spaghetti Sauce | ½ cup | 100 | 40 |
| ❶ Red Clam Sauce | ½ cup | 80 | 30 |
| Rock Lobster Sauce | ½ cup | 100 | 70 |
| Spaghetti Sauce | ½ cup | 100 | 40 |
| White Clam (Authentic) | ½ cup | 90 | 60 |
| White Clam Sauce | ½ cup | 120 | 80 |

 Meets Low-Fat Guidelines

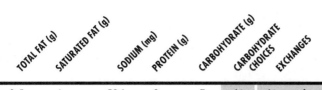

| TOTAL FAT (g) | SATURATED FAT (g) | SODIUM (mg) | PROTEIN (g) | CARBOHYDRATE (g) | CARBOHYDRATE CHOICES | EXCHANGES |
|---|---|---|---|---|---|---|
| 2.5 | 1 | 596 | 2 | 7 | ½ | ½ starch |
| 2.5 | 0.5 | 586 | 2 | 7 | ½ | ½ starch |
| 2.5 | 0.5 | 596 | 2 | 7 | ½ | ½ starch |
| 2.5 | 0.5 | 690 | 3 | 9 | ½ | ½ starch |
| 1 | 0 | 405 | 2 | 7 | ½ | ½ starch |
| 2.5 | 0.5 | 604 | 2 | 11 | 1 | 1 starch |
| 2.5 | .5 | 604 | 2 | 11 | 1 | 1 starch |
| 2.5 | .5 | 621 | 2 | 11 | 1 | 1 starch |
| 5 | 1 | 690 | 2 | 12 | 1 | 1 starch, ½ fat |
| 2 | 0 | 590 | 2 | 9 | ½ | ½ starch |
| 2 | 0 | 590 | 2 | 9 | ½ | ½ starch |
| 2 | 0 | 590 | 2 | 9 | ½ | ½ starch |
| 6 | NA | NA | 3 | 23 | 1½ | 1½ starch, 1 fat |
| 5 | NA | NA | 2 | 20 | 1 | 1 starch, 1 fat |
| 6 | NA | NA | 2 | 22 | 1½ | 1½ starch, 1 fat |
| 27 | 15 | 670 | 10 | 5 | 0 | 1 meat, 4 fat |
| 6 | 1.5 | 560 | 5 | 8 | ½ | ½ starch, 1 meat |
| 4.5 | 0.5 | 480 | 2 | 8 | ½ | ½ starch, 1 fat |
| 5 | 1.5 | 440 | 3 | 9 | ½ | ½ starch, 1 fat |
| 4.5 | 1 | 610 | 4 | 12 | 1 | 1 starch, ½ fat |
| 4.5 | 1 | 580 | 3 | 12 | 1 | 1 starch, ½ fat |
| 3 | 0.5 | 620 | 6 | 8 | ½ | ½ starch, 1 lean meat |
| 7 | 1 | 430 | 3 | 6 | ½ | ½ starch, 1 fat |
| 4.5 | 1 | 620 | 3 | 12 | 1 | 1 starch, ½ fat |
| 7 | 1.5 | 470 | 5 | 2 | 0 | 1 high fat meat |
| 9 | 1.5 | 310 | 10 | 1 | 0 | 1 meat, 1 fat |

1 Carbohydrate Choice = 1 starch or 1 fruit or 1 milk exchange

## PRODUCTS

| | SERVING SIZE | CALORIES | CALORIES FROM FAT |
|---|---|---|---|
| **Ragu® Pasta Sauce** | | | |
| Gardenstyle Chunky Garden Combination | ½ cup | 120 | 40 |
| Gardenstyle Chunky Green & Red Pepper | ½ cup | 120 | 40 |
| Gardenstyle Chunky Mushroom & Green Pepper | ½ cup | 120 | 40 |
| Gardenstyle Chunky Mushroom & Onion | ½ cup | 120 | 40 |
| Gardenstyle Chunky Tomato, Garlic & Onion | ½ cup | 120 | 40 |
| Gardenstyle Super Mushroom | ½ cup | 120 | 40 |
| Gardenstyle Super Vegetable Primavera | ½ cup | 110 | 35 |
| ❶ Light, No Sugar Added | ½ cup | 60 | 15 |
| ❶ Light Chunky Mushroom | ½ cup | 50 | 0 |
| ❶ Light Garden Harvest | ½ cup | 50 | 0 |
| ❶ Light Tomato & Herb | ½ cup | 50 | 0 |
| Old World Mushroom Style Spaghetti Sauce | ½ cup | 80 | 35 |
| Old World Style Marinara | ½ cup | 90 | 50 |
| Old World Style Spaghetti Sauce Flavored with Meat | ½ cup | 90 | 45 |
| Old World Style Traditional Spaghetti Sauce | ½ cup | 80 | 35 |
| **Other Pasta Sauces** | | | |
| ❶ Angelia Mia® Marinara Sauce | ½ cup | 47 | 15 |
| ❶ Angelia Mia® Spaghetti Sauce with Tomato Bits | ½ cup | 49 | 4.5 |
| ❶ Eden® Organic Spaghetti Sauce | ½ cup | 80 | 20 |
| ❶ Weight Watchers® Pasta Sauce with Mushrooms | ¼ cup | 60 | 0 |
| **PASTA SAUCE (REFRIGERATED)** | | | |
| Alfredo, Contadina® | ½ cup | 400 | 340 |
| Alfredo, Contadina® Light | ½ cup | 190 | 120 |
| Alfredo, Di Giorno® | ¼ cup | 230 | 200 |
| Alfredo, Di Giorno Light®, Reduced Fat | ¼ cup | 170 | 90 |
| Alfredo, Trio's® | ½ cup | 300 | 250 |

❶  Meets Low-Fat Guidelines

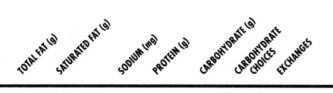

| TOTAL FAT (g) | SATURATED FAT (g) | SODIUM (mg) | PROTEIN (g) | CARBOHYDRATE (g) | CARBOHYDRATE CHOICES | EXCHANGES |
|---|---|---|---|---|---|---|
| 4 | 0..5 | 540 | 2 | 18 | 1 | 1 starch, ½ fat |
| 4 | 0.5 | 570 | 2 | 19 | 1 | 1 starch, ½ fat |
| 4 | 0.5 | 550 | 2 | 19 | 1 | 1 starch, ½ fat |
| 4 | 0.5 | 560 | 2 | 19 | 1 | 1 starch, ½ fat |
| 4 | 0.5 | 550 | 2 | 19 | 1 | 1 starch, ½ fat |
| 4 | 0.5 | 540 | 3 | 19 | 1 | 1 starch, ½ fat |
| 4 | 0.5 | 480 | 2 | 17 | 1 | 1 starch, ½ fat |
| 1.5 | 0 | 390 | 3 | 9 | ½ | ½ starch |
| 0 | 0 | 390 | 3 | 11 | 1 | 2 veg |
| 0 | 0 | 390 | 2 | 11 | 1 | 2 veg |
| 0 | 0 | 390 | 2 | 11 | 1 | 2 veg |
| 3.5 | 0.5 | 820 | 2 | 10 | ½ | ½ starch, ½ fat |
| 5 | 1 | 820 | 2 | 9 | ½ | ½ starch, 1 fat |
| 5 | 1 | 820 | 3 | 9 | ½ | ½ starch, 1 fat |
| 3.5 | 0.5 | 820 | 2 | 10 | ½ | ½ starch, ½ fat |
| 1.5 | 0.5 | 503 | 2 | 9 | ½ | ½ starch |
| 0.5 | 0 | 607 | 1.5 | 11 | 1 | 1 starch |
| 2.5 | 0 | 10 | 3 | 12 | 1 | 1 starch |
| 0 | 0 | 420 | 2 | 11 | 1 | 1 starch or 2 veg |
| 38 | 21 | 510 | 7 | 8 | ½ | ½ starch, 1 meat, 6 fat |
| 13 | 7 | 560 | 8 | 10 | ½ | ½ starch, 1 meat, 1 fat |
| 22 | 10 | 550 | 4 | 2 | 0 | 1 meat, 3 fat |
| 10 | 6 | 600 | 5 | 16 | 1 | 1 starch, 2 fat |
| 28 | 17 | 610 | 9 | 3 | 0 | 1 high fat meat, 4 fat |

1 Carbohydrate Choice = 1 starch or 1 fruit or 1 milk exchange

## PRODUCTS

| PRODUCTS | SERVING SIZE | CALORIES | CALORIES FROM FAT |
|---|---|---|---|
| Alfredo, Trio's® Light | ½ cup | 160 | 80 |
| ❶ Chunky Tomato with Basil, Di Giorno Light® | ½ cup | 70 | 0 |
| Four Cheese, Di Giorno® | ¼ cup | 200 | 170 |
| Marinara, Contadina® | ½ cup | 80 | 30 |
| Marinara, Di Giorno® | ½ cup | 100 | 40 |
| Olive Oil and Garlic with Grated Cheeses, Di Giorno® | ¼ cup | 370 | 320 |
| Pesto, Di Giorno® | ¼ cup | 320 | 280 |
| Pesto, Trio's | ¼ cup | 310 | 300 |
| Pesto with Sun Dried Tomatoes, Contadina® | ¼ cup | 250 | 210 |
| ❶ Plum Tomato & Basil, Contadina® | ½ cup | 70 | 25 |
| ❶ Plum Tomato & Mushroom, Di Giorno® | ½ cup | 70 | 0 |
| Tomato, Trio's® | ½ cup | 90 | 60 |
| ❶ Tomato, Trio's® Lowfat | ½ cup | 70 | 30 |
| Tomato, Trio's® Thick & Chunky | ½ cup | 90 | 60 |
| Traditional Meat, Di Giorno® | ½ cup | 120 | 50 |

## PASTA SIDE DISHES (DRY, AS PREPARED)

### Alfredo Pasta Side Dishes

| | | | |
|---|---|---|---|
| Alfredo, Lipton® Noodles & Sauce | 1 cup | 250 | 60 |
| Alfredo Broccoli, Lipton® Noodles & Sauce | 1 cup | 260 | 70 |
| Alfredo Carbonara, Lipton® Noodles & Sauce | 1 cup | 260 | 70 |
| Alfredo Sauce with Fettuccine Pasta, Pasta Roni® | 1 cup | 470 | 240 |
| Fettucine Pasta with Classic Alfredo Sauce, Knorr® | 1 cup | 330 | 110 |

### Butter Pasta Side Dishes

| | | | |
|---|---|---|---|
| Butter, Lipton® Noodles & Sauce | 1 cup | 260 | 70 |
| Butter & Herb, Lipton® Noodles & Sauce | 1 cup | 250 | 60 |
| Herb & Butter Sauce with Penne Pasta, Pasta Roni® | 1 cup | 430 | 220 |
| Lemon & Butter Sauce with Angel Hair Pasta, Pasta Roni® | 1 cup | 360 | 140 |

❶  Meets Low-Fat Guidelines

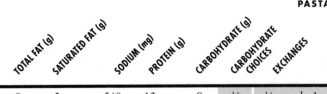

| TOTAL FAT (g) | SATURATED FAT (g) | SODIUM (mg) | PROTEIN (g) | CARBOHYDRATE (g) | CARBOHYDRATE CHOICES | EXCHANGES |
|---|---|---|---|---|---|---|
| 8 | 5 | 560 | 12 | 9 | ½ | ½ starch, 1 meat |
| 0 | 0 | 290 | 2 | 16 | 1 | 1 starch |
| 19 | 11 | 410 | 5 | 2 | 0 | 1 meat, 3 fat |
| 4 | 0.5 | 560 | 2 | 10 | ½ | ½ starch, ½ fat |
| 4.5 | 1 | 530 | 3 | 12 | 1 | 1 starch, ½ fat |
| 36 | 8 | 540 | 9 | 3 | 0 | 1 meat, 6 fat |
| 31 | 7 | 500 | 8 | 3 | 0 | 1 meat, 5 fat |
| 33 | 6 | 380 | 3 | 1 | 0 | 6½ fat |
| 23 | 4.5 | 510 | 3 | 8 | ½ | 1 veg, 5 fat |
| 2.5 | 0.5 | 490 | 2 | 9 | ½ | ½ starch or 2 veg |
| 0 | 0 | 310 | 2 | 15 | 1 | 1 starch |
| 7 | 1 | 370 | 2 | 6 | ½ | ½ starch, 1 fat |
| 3 | 1.5 | 450 | 0 | 11 | 1 | 1 starch |
| 7 | 1 | 370 | 2 | 6 | ½ | ½ starch, 1 fat |
| 6 | 2 | 610 | 6 | 12 | 1 | 1 starch, 1 fat |
| 7 | 3.5 | 940 | 10 | 38 | 2½ | 2½ starch, 1 fat |
| 7 | 3.5 | 940 | 10 | 39 | 2½ | 2½ starch, 1 fat |
| 7 | 3 | 890 | 10 | 38 | 2½ | 2½ starch, 1 fat |
| 26 | 6 | 1110 | 13 | 48 | 3 | 3 starch, 1 meat, 4 fat |
| 12 | 4.5 | 945 | 11 | 44 | 3 | 3 starch, 2 fat |
| 8 | 3.5 | 910 | 8 | 40 | 2½ | 2½ starch, 1 fat |
| 7 | 2.5 | 860 | 9 | 41 | 3 | 3 starch, 1 fat |
| 25 | 6 | 910 | 10 | 43 | 3 | 3 starch, 1 meat, 3 fat |
| 15 | 3.5 | 980 | 9 | 48 | 3 | 3 starch, 2 fat |

1 Carbohydrate Choice = 1 starch or 1 fruit or 1 milk exchange

## PRODUCTS

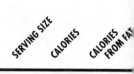

| Products | Serving Size | Calories | Calories from Fat |
|---|---|---|---|
| **Cheese Pasta Side Dishes** | | | |
| Angel Hair Parmesan, Lipton® Golden Sauté | 1 cup | 240 | 40 |
| Broccoli Au Gratin Sauce with Fettuccine Pasta, Pasta Roni® | 1 cup | 280 | 100 |
| Cheddar Bacon, Lipton® Noodles & Sauce | 1 cup | 230 | 40 |
| Cheddar Broccoli, Lipton® Pasta & Sauce | 1 cup | 260 | 35 |
| Cheddar Cheese Egg Noodle Dinner, Kraft® | ~1 cup | 430 | 190 |
| Cheese, Lipton® Noodles & Sauce | 1 cup | 250 | 40 |
| Four Cheese Sauce with Corkscrew Pasta, Pasta Roni® | 1 cup | 410 | 160 |
| Italian Cheese Bow Ties, Lipton® Pasta & Sauce | 1 cup | 230 | 45 |
| Mild Cheddar Sauce with Fettuccine Pasta, Pasta Roni® | 1 cup | 290 | 100 |
| Parmesan, Lipton® Noodles & Sauce | 1 cup | 250 | 70 |
| Parmesan Cheese Sauce with Angel Hair Pasta, Pasta Roni® | 1 cup | 320 | 130 |
| Parmesano Sauce with Tenderthin Pasta, Pasta Roni® | 1 cup | 390 | 150 |
| Penne Pasta with Sun-Dried Tomato Parmesan, Knorr® | 1 cup | 320 | 75 |
| Three Cheese, Lipton® Pasta & Sauce | 1 cup | 240 | 45 |
| White Cheddar & Broccoli Sauce with Rigatoni Pasta, Pasta Roni® | 1 cup | 400 | 170 |
| White Cheddar Sauce with Pasta Shells, Pasta Roni® | 1 cup | 390 | 150 |
| **Chicken Pasta Side Dishes** | | | |
| ❶ Angel Hair Chicken, Lipton® Golden Sauté | 1 cup | 210 | 10 |
| Chicken Broccoli, Lipton® Noodles & Sauce | 1 cup | 220 | 35 |
| Chicken & Broccoli Sauce with Linguine, Pasta Roni® | 1 cup | 370 | 140 |
| Chicken Egg Noodle Dinner, Kraft® | ~1 cup | 330 | 110 |
| Chicken Flavored, Lipton® Noodles & Sauce | 1 cup | 230 | 40 |
| ❶ Chicken Herb Parmesan, Lipton® Golden Sauté | 1 cup | 230 | 20 |

❶  Meets Low-Fat Guidelines

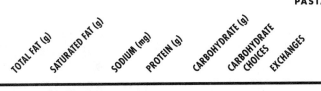

| TOTAL FAT (g) | SATURATED FAT (g) | SODIUM (mg) | PROTEIN (g) | CARBOHYDRATE (g) | CARBOHYDRATE CHOICES | EXCHANGES |
|---|---|---|---|---|---|---|
| 5 | 2 | 890 | 8 | 42 | 3 | 3 starch |
| 10 | 3 | 860 | 10 | 39 | 2½ | 2½ starch, 1 meat, 1 fat |
| 4.5 | 2 | 930 | 9 | 38 | 2½ | 2½ starch |
| 3.5 | 1.5 | 870 | 9 | 46 | 3 | 3 starch |
| 21 | 6 | 780 | 12 | 46 | 3 | 3 starch, 1 meat, 3 fat |
| 4.5 | 2 | 850 | 10 | 44 | 3 | 3 starch |
| 19 | 5 | 1040 | 13 | 49 | 3 | 3 starch, 1 meat, 2 fat |
| 5 | 2.5 | 790 | 8 | 37 | 2½ | 2½ starch |
| 11 | 3.5 | 890 | 10 | 39 | 2½ | 2½ starch, 1 meat, 1 fat |
| 8 | 3.5 | 750 | 10 | 37 | 2½ | 2½ starch, 1 fat |
| 15 | 4 | 890 | 9 | 40 | 2½ | 2½ starch, 1 meat, 1 fat |
| 17 | 4.5 | 940 | 12 | 49 | 3 | 3 starch, 1 meat, 2 fat |
| 9 | 2 | 585 | 9 | 51 | 3½ | 3½ starch, 1 fat |
| 5 | 2.5 | 870 | 9 | 41 | 3 | 3 starch |
| 19 | 5 | 1010 | 12 | 48 | 3 | 3 starch, 1 meat, 2 fat |
| 17 | 5 | 1030 | 12 | 48 | 3 | 3 starch, 1 meat, 2 fat |
| 1.5 | 0.5 | 850 | 8 | 44 | 3 | 3 starch |
| 4 | 1.5 | 750 | 9 | 40 | 2½ | 2½ starch |
| 16 | 3.5 | 950 | 11 | 49 | 3 | 3 starch, 1 meat, 1 fat |
| 12 | 3.5 | 1430 | 10 | 45 | 3 | 3 starch, 1 lean meat, 1 fat |
| 4.5 | 1.5 | 760 | 8 | 41 | 3 | 3 starch |
| 2.5 | 1 | 830 | 8 | 46 | 3 | 3 starch |

1 Carbohydrate Choice = 1 starch or 1 fruit or 1 milk exchange

## PRODUCTS

| PRODUCTS | SERVING SIZE | CALORIES | CALORIES FROM FAT |
|---|---|---|---|
| ❶ Chicken Primavera, Lipton® Pasta & Sauce | 1 cup | 220 | 25 |
| Chicken Sauce with Fettuccine, Pasta Roni® | 1 cup | 320 | 120 |
| Chicken Tetrazzini, Lipton® Noodles & Sauce | 1 cup | 220 | 40 |
| Creamy Chicken Parmesan Sauce with Linguine, Pasta Roni® | 1 cup | 410 | 160 |
| Creamy Chicken, Lipton® Noodles & Sauce | 1 cup | 230 | 50 |

### Garlic Pasta Side Dishes

| | | | |
|---|---|---|---|
| Creamy Garlic, Lipton® Pasta & Sauce | 1 cup | 260 | 50 |
| Creamy Garlic Sauce with Corkscrew Pasta, Pasta Roni® | 1 cup | 420 | 220 |
| Garlic & Olive Oil Sauce with Vermicelli, Pasta Roni® | 1 cup | 360 | 140 |
| ❶ Garlic Butter, Lipton® Golden Sauté | 1 cup | 220 | 30 |
| ❶ Herb & Garlic Penne, Lipton® Golden Sauté | 1 cup | 230 | 30 |

### Tomato Pasta Side Dishes

| | | | |
|---|---|---|---|
| ❶ Herb Tomato, Lipton® Pasta & Sauce | 1 cup | 240 | 15 |
| Tangy Italian Spaghetti Dinner, Kraft® | ~1 cup | 270 | 40 |
| Tomato & Garden Vegetable Sauce with Lasagna, Pasta Roni® | 1 cup | 230 | 70 |
| Tomato Basil Sauce with Rigatoni, Pasta Roni® | 1 cup | 240 | 80 |
| Mild American Spaghetti Dinner, Kraft® | ~1 cup | 270 | 40 |

### Other Pasta Side Dishes

| | | | |
|---|---|---|---|
| Beef, Lipton® Noodles & Sauce | 1 cup | 220 | 30 |
| Bowtie Pasta and Beans with Savory Herb Sauce, Knorr® | 1 cup | 310 | 80 |
| Broccoli & Mushroom with Tenderthin Pasta, Pasta Roni® | 1 cup | 450 | 220 |
| Herb Sauce with Angel Hair Pasta, Pasta Roni® | 1 cup | 320 | 120 |
| Noodles & Beef, Hunt's® Homestyle Separates | 1 cup | 151 | 36 |
| Romanoff, Lipton® Noodles & Sauce | 1 cup | 260 | 70 |
| Romanoff Sauce with Fettuccine, Pasta Roni® | 1 cup | 400 | 180 |

❶ Meets Low-Fat Guidelines

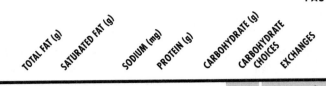

| TOTAL FAT (g) | SATURATED FAT (g) | SODIUM (mg) | PROTEIN (g) | CARBOHYDRATE (g) | CARBOHYDRATE CHOICES | EXCHANGES |
|---|---|---|---|---|---|---|
| 3 | 1.5 | 730 | 7 | 40 | 2½ | 2½ starch |
| 13.5 | 2.5 | 1020 | 10 | 41 | 3 | 3 starch, 1 meat, 1 fat |
| 5 | 2 | 850 | 8 | 37 | 2½ | 2½ starch, ½ fat |
| 18 | 5 | 1090 | 13 | 51 | 3½ | 3½ starch, 1 meat, 2 fat |
| 6 | 2.5 | 710 | 9 | 39 | 2½ | 2½ starch, 1 fat |
| 6 | 2.5 | 840 | 8 | 45 | 3 | 3 starch, ½ fat |
| 25 | 6 | 1010 | 9 | 41 | 3 | 3 starch, 1 meat, 3 fat |
| 16 | 3 | 1010 | 9 | 48 | 3 | 3 starch, 1 meat, 1 fat |
| 3 | 2 | 790 | 7 | 42 | 3 | 3 starch |
| 3 | 2 | 810 | 8 | 44 | 3 | 3 starch |
| 2 | <1 | 690 | 9 | 48 | 3 | 3 starch |
| 4.5 | 1 | 780 | 10 | 46 | 3 | 3 starch, 1 veg |
| 8 | 1.5 | 600 | 7 | 36 | 2½ | 2½ starch, 1 fat |
| 9 | 2 | 690 | 6 | 35 | 2 | 2 starch, 2 fat |
| 4.5 | 1 | 690 | 9 | 48 | 3 | 3 starch, 1 veg |
| 3.5 | 1 | 930 | 8 | 42 | 3 | 3 starch |
| 8 | 1.5 | 845 | 12 | 47 | 3 | 3 starch, 1 fat |
| 24 | 6 | 1130 | 11 | 49 | 3 | 3 starch, 1 meat, 3 fat |
| 13 | 3.5 | 850 | 9 | 42 | 3 | 3 starch, 2 fat |
| 4 | 1.5 | 1241 | 10 | 22 | 1½ | 1½ starch, 1 lean meat |
| 7 | 3.5 | 920 | 9 | 41 | 3 | 3 starch, 1 fat |
| 20 | 5 | 1070 | 11 | 46 | 3 | 3 starch, 1 meat, 2 fat |

1 Carbohydrate Choice = 1 starch *or* 1 fruit *or* 1 milk exchange

| PRODUCTS | SERVING SIZE | CALORIES | CALORIES FROM FAT |
|---|---|---|---|
| Rotini Pasta in a Delicate Mushroom Sauce, Knorr® | 1 cup | 300 | 60 |
| Rotini Primavera, Lipton® Pasta & Sauce | 1 cup | 240 | 45 |
| Sour Cream & Chive, Lipton® Noodles & Sauce | 1 cup | 260 | 70 |
| Spaghetti with Meat Sauce Dinner, Kraft® | ~1 cup | 330 | 100 |
| Stir Fry Sauce with Oriental Style Noodles, Pasta Roni® | 1 cup | 290 | 110 |
| Stroganoff, Lipton® Noodles & Sauce | 1 cup | 210 | 35 |
| Stroganoff Sauce with Fettuccine, Pasta Roni® | 1 cup | 360 | 130 |
| Tri-Color Fusilli Pasta with Creamy Pesto Sauce, Knorr® | 1 cup | 300 | 75 |

### PASTA SIDE DISHES (FROZEN)

| | SERVING SIZE | CALORIES | CALORIES FROM FAT |
|---|---|---|---|
| Alfredo Pasta Accents!®, Green Giant® | 2 cups | 210 | 70 |
| Creamy Cheddar Pasta Accents!®, Green Giant® | 2⅓ cups | 250 | 70 |
| Florentine Pasta Accents!®, Green Giant® | 2 cups | 310 | 80 |
| Garden Herb Seasoning Pasta Accents!®, Green Giant® | 2 cups | 230 | 60 |
| Garlic Seasoning Pasta Accents!®, Green Giant® | 2 cups | 260 | 90 |
| ❶ Linguini with Asparagus, Norpac® | 1 cup | 50 | 0 |
| Primavera Pasta Accents!®, Green Giant® | 2¼ cups | 320 | 110 |
| White Cheddar Sauce Pasta Accents!®, Green Giant® | 1¾ cups | 300 | 110 |

### PASTRIES (FROZEN)
see also Sweet Rolls; Toaster Pastries

| | SERVING SIZE | CALORIES | CALORIES FROM FAT |
|---|---|---|---|
| Apple Danish, Pepperidge Farm® | 1 danish | 210 | 80 |
| Apple Dumplings, Pepperidge Farm® | 1 dumpling | 290 | 100 |
| Apple Fruit Squares, Pepperidge Farm® | 1 square | 210 | 90 |
| Apple Mini Turnovers, Pepperidge Farm® | 1 turnover | 140 | 70 |
| Apple Turnovers, Pillsbury® | 2 turnovers | 350 | 150 |
| Apple Turnovers, Pepperidge Farm® | 1 turnover | 330 | 130 |

❶ Meets Low-Fat Guidelines

| TOTAL FAT (g) | SATURATED FAT (g) | SODIUM (mg) | PROTEIN (g) | CARBOHYDRATE (g) | CARBOHYDRATE CHOICES | EXCHANGES |
|---|---|---|---|---|---|---|
| 7 | 1.5 | 765 | 10 | 50 | 3 | 3 starch, 1 fat |
| 5 | 2 | 880 | 8 | 42 | 3 | 3 starch |
| 8 | 3.5 | 800 | 8 | 41 | 3 | 3 starch, 1 fat |
| 11 | 4 | 830 | 12 | 46 | 3 | 3 starch, 1 meat, 1 fat |
| 12 | 15 | 890 | 7 | 38 | 2½ | 2½ starch, 2 fat |
| 4 | 2 | 850 | 9 | 37 | 2½ | 2½ starch |
| 14 | 4 | 1020 | 12 | 48 | 3 | 3 starch, 1 meat, 1 fat |
| 9 | 2 | 845 | 9 | 47 | 3 | 3 starch, 1 fat |
| 8 | 2.5 | 480 | 9 | 25 | 1½ | 1 starch, 2 veg, 2 fat |
| 8 | 3 | 700 | 9 | 36 | 2½ | 2 starch, 1 veg, 1 fat |
| 9 | 3 | 910 | 13 | 44 | 3 | 2½ starch, 1 veg, 1 meat, ½ fat |
| 7 | 4 | 750 | 9 | 32 | 2 | 2 starch, 1 veg, 1 fat |
| 10 | 5 | 640 | 7 | 36 | 2½ | 2 starch, 1 veg, 2 fat |
| 0 | 0 | 0 | 3 | 10 | ½ | ½ starch or 2 veg |
| 12 | 5 | 500 | 13 | 40 | 2½ | 2 starch, 2 veg, 1 meat, 1 fat |
| 12 | 3.5 | 570 | 10 | 38 | 2½ | 2 starch, 1 veg, 1 meat, 1 fat |
| 9 | 2.5 | 190 | 4 | 29 | 2 | 2 starch, 1 fat |
| 11 | 2.5 | 160 | 3 | 44 | 3 | 2 starch, 1 fruit, 2 fat |
| 10 | 4.5 | 210 | 2 | 27 | 2 | 1 starch, 1 fruit, 2 fat |
| 8 | 2 | 80 | 2 | 15 | 1 | 1 starch, 1 fat |
| 17 | 3.5 | 660 | 4 | 45 | 3 | 2 starch, 1 fruit, 3 fat |
| 14 | 3 | 180 | 4 | 48 | 3 | 2 starch, 1 fruit, 2 fat |

1 Carbohydrate Choice = 1 starch or 1 fruit or 1 milk exchange

## PRODUCTS

| | SERVING SIZE | CALORIES | CALORIES FROM FAT |
|---|---|---|---|
| Apple Turnovers with Vanilla Icing, Pepperidge Farm® | 1 turnover | 360 | 130 |
| Blueberry Turnovers, Pepperidge Farm® | 1 turnover | 340 | 140 |
| Cheese Danish, Pepperidge Farm® | 1 danish | 230 | 100 |
| Cherry Dumplings, Pepperidge Farm® | 1 dumpling | 280 | 800 |
| Cherry Mini Turnovers, Pepperidge Farm® | 1 turnover | 140 | 70 |
| Cherry Turnovers, Pillsbury® | 2 turnovers | 360 | 150 |
| Cherry Turnovers, Pepperidge Farm® | 1 turnover | 320 | 120 |
| Cherry Turnovers with Vanilla, Pepperidge Farm® | 1 turnover | 340 | 120 |
| Dark Chocolate Clouds, Pepperidge Farm® | 2 pastries | 580 | 340 |
| Milk Chocolate Clouds, Pepperidge Farm® | 2 pastries | 580 | 340 |
| Patty Shells, Pepperidge Farm® | 1 shell | 230 | 130 |
| Peach Cobbler Mini Turnovers, Pepperidge Farm® | 1 turnover | 160 | 70 |
| Peach Dumplings, Pepperidge Farm® | 1 dumpling | 300 | 100 |
| Peach Turnovers, Pepperidge Farm® | 1 turnover | 340 | 140 |
| Puff Pastry Dough Sheets, Pepperidge Farm® | ⅙ sheet | 200 | 100 |
| Raspberry Danish, Pepperidge Farm® | 1 danish | 210 | 80 |
| Raspberry Turnovers, Pepperidge Farm® | 1 turnover | 220 | 130 |
| Raspberry Turnovers with Vanilla Icing, Pepperidge Farm® | 1 turnover | 360 | 130 |
| Strawberry Mini Turnovers, Pepperidge Farm® | 1 turnover | 140 | 60 |

### PASTRIES (READY-TO-EAT)

| | SERVING SIZE | CALORIES | CALORIES FROM FAT |
|---|---|---|---|
| All Butter Loaf, Entenmann's® | ⅙ loaf | 220 | 90 |
| ❶ Apricot Danish Twist, Entenmann's® Fat Free Cholesterol Free | ⅛ danish | 150 | 0 |
| Apple Puffs, Entenmann's® | 1 puff | 260 | 110 |
| Apple Strudel, Entenmann's® | ¼ strudel | 310 | 120 |
| ❶ Black Forest Pastry, Entenmann's® Fat Free Cholesterol Free | ⅑ danish | 130 | 0 |
| Chocolate Eclairs, Entenmann's® | 1 eclair | 250 | 80 |

❶  Meets Low-Fat Guidelines

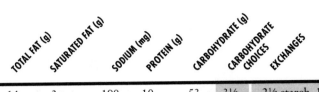

| TOTAL FAT (g) | SATURATED FAT (g) | SODIUM (mg) | PROTEIN (g) | CARBOHYDRATE (g) | CARBOHYDRATE CHOICES | EXCHANGES |
|---|---|---|---|---|---|---|
| 14 | 3 | 190 | 10 | 53 | 3½ | 2½ starch, 1 fruit, 2 fat |
| 16 | 3 | 200 | 4 | 45 | 3 | 2 starch, 1 fruit, 3 fat |
| 11 | 3.5 | 230 | 6 | 25 | 1½ | 1½ starch, 1 meat, 1 fat |
| 9 | 2 | 280 | 3 | 47 | 3 | 2 starch, 1 fruit, 1 fat |
| 8 | 2 | 70 | 2 | 16 | 1 | 1 starch, 1 fat |
| 17 | 3.5 | 650 | 4 | 48 | 3 | 2 starch, 1 fruit, 3 fat |
| 13 | 3 | 190 | 4 | 46 | 3 | 2 starch, 1 fruit, 2 fat |
| 13 | 3 | 200 | 4 | 51 | 3½ | 2½ starch, 1 fruit, 2 fat |
| 38 | 15 | 380 | 6 | 53 | 3½ | 3½ starch, 7 fat |
| 38 | 15 | 400 | 6 | 54 | 3½ | 3½ starch, 7 fat |
| 14 | 3 | 135 | 3 | 23 | 1½ | 1½ starch, 2½ fat |
| 8 | 2 | 45 | 2 | 21 | 1½ | 1½ starch, 1 fat |
| 11 | 2.5 | 150 | 3 | 47 | 3 | 2 starch, 1 fruit, 2 fat |
| 15 | 3 | 180 | 4 | 47 | 3 | 2 starch, 1 fruit, 3 fat |
| 11 | 2.5 | 135 | 3 | 23 | 1½ | 1½ starch, 2 fat |
| 9 | 2.5 | 190 | 4 | 29 | 2 | 1 starch, 1 fruit, 2 fat |
| 14 | 3 | 190 | 4 | 47 | 3 | 2 starch, 1 fruit, 2 fat |
| 14 | 3 | 190 | 4 | 53 | 3½ | 2½ starch, 1 fruit, 2 fat |
| 7 | 1.5 | 100 | 2 | 18 | 1 | 1 starch, 1 fat |
| 10 | 6 | 290 | 3 | 31 | 2 | 2 starch, 2 fat |
| 0 | 0 | 110 | 3 | 34 | 2 | 2 starch |
| 12 | 3 | 220 | 2 | 36 | 2½ | 2½ starch, 2 fat |
| 14 | 3.5 | 230 | 3 | 44 | 3 | 3 starch, 2 fat |
| 0 | 0 | 115 | 3 | 32 | 2 | 2 starch |
| 9 | 2 | 220 | 3 | 44 | 3 | 3 starch, 1 fat |

1 Carbohydrate Choice = 1 starch *or* 1 fruit *or* 1 milk exchange

## PRODUCTS

| | SERVING SIZE | CALORIES | CALORIES FROM FAT |
|---|---|---|---|
| Chocolate Iced Eclair with Bavarian Creme Filling, Rich's® | 1 eclair | 190 | 80 |
| ❶ Cinnamon Apple Twist, Entenmann's® Fat Free Cholesterol Free | ⅛ danish | 150 | 0 |
| Cinnamon Filbert Ring, Entenmann's® | ⅙ danish | 270 | 150 |
| Glazed Chocolate PopEms®, Entenmann's® | 4 pieces | 200 | 90 |
| Glazed PopEms®, Entenmann's® | 6 pieces | 240 | 100 |
| ❶ Lemon Twist, Entenmann's® Fat Free Cholesterol Free | ⅛ danish | 130 | 0 |
| Marble Loaf, Entenmann's® | ⅛ loaf | 200 | 90 |
| ❶ Pastry Loaves, Entenmann's® Fat Free Cholesterol Free, all varieties (avg) | ⅛ loaf | 135 | 0 |
| Pecan Danish Ring, Entenmann's® | ⅛ danish | 230 | 130 |
| ❶ Raspberry Cheese Pastry, Entenmann's® Fat Free Cholesterol Free | ⅑ danish | 140 | 0 |
| Raspberry Danish Twist, Entenmann's® | ⅛ danish | 220 | 100 |
| ❶ Raspberry Twist, Entenmann's® Fat Free Cholesterol Free | ⅛ danish | 140 | 0 |
| Walnut Danish Ring, Entenmann's® | ⅛ danish | 230 | 130 |

### PEANUT BUTTER

| | | | |
|---|---|---|---|
| Chunky, all brands (avg) | 2 Tb | 190 | 140 |
| Creamy, all brands (avg) | 2 Tb | 190 | 140 |
| Low sodium, all brands (avg) | 2 Tb | 190 | 140 |
| Reduced fat, all brands (avg) | 2 Tb | 190 | 100 |
| Whipped, all brands (avg) | 2 Tb | 150 | 100 |

### PICKLE RELISH

| | | | |
|---|---|---|---|
| ❶ Sweet pickle relish, all brands (avg) | 1 Tb | 15 | 0 |

### PICKLES

| | | | |
|---|---|---|---|
| ❶ Dill pickles, all brands (avg) | 1 oz | 5 | 0 |
| ❶ Sweet pickles/ bread and butter pickles, all brands (avg) | 1 oz (28 g) | 30 | 0 |

❶  Meets Low-Fat Guidelines

| TOTAL FAT (g) | SATURATED FAT (g) | SODIUM (mg) | PROTEIN (g) | CARBOHYDRATE (g) | CARBOHYDRATE CHOICES | EXCHANGES |
|---|---|---|---|---|---|---|
| 9 | 7 | 115 | 2 | 24 | 1½ | 1½ starch, 2 fat |
| 0 | 0 | 110 | 3 | 35 | 2 | 2 starch |
| 17 | 3 | 190 | 4 | 27 | 2 | 2 starch, 3 fat |
| 10 | 2.5 | 190 | 2 | 29 | 2 | 2 starch, 2 fat |
| 11 | 2.5 | 210 | 2 | 33 | 2 | 2 starch, 2 fat |
| 0 | 0 | 140 | 3 | 31 | 2 | 2 starch |
| 10 | 6 | 230 | 2 | 25 | 1½ | 1½ starch, 2 fat |
| 0 | 0 | 150–250 | 2.5 | 28–34 | 2 | 2 starch |
| 15 | 3 | 160 | 3 | 23 | 1½ | 1½ starch, 3 fat |
| 0 | 0 | 110 | 3 | 32 | 2 | 2 starch |
| 11 | 3 | 170 | 3 | 28 | 2 | 2 starch, 2 fat |
| 0 | 0 | 125 | 3 | 33 | 2 | 2 starch |
| 14 | 3 | 160 | 4 | 23 | 1½ | 1½ starch, 2 fat |
| 16 | 3 | 130 | 8 | 6 | ½ | ½ starch, 1 meat, 2 fat |
| 16 | 3 | 140 | 7 | 7 | ½ | ½ starch, 1 meat, 2 fat |
| 16 | 3 | 10 | 8 | 6 | ½ | ½ starch, 1 meat, 2 fat |
| 12 | 2.5 | 185 | 7 | 13 | 1 | 1 starch, 1 meat, 1 fat |
| 12 | 3 | 110 | 6 | 5 | 0 | 1 meat, 1½ fat |
| 0 | 0 | 85 | 0 | 3 | 0 | free |
| 0 | 0 | 210–420 | 0 | 1 | 0 | free |
| 0 | 0 | 135–190 | 0 | 7 | ½ | 1 veg |

1 Carbohydrate Choice = 1 starch or 1 fruit or 1 milk exchange

## PRODUCTS

| | SERVING SIZE | CALORIES | CALORIES FROM FAT |
|---|---|---|---|

### PIE (FROZEN)

#### Apple Pie

| Products | Serving Size | Calories | Calories from Fat |
|---|---|---|---|
| Apple, Banquet® | ⅕ pie | 300 | 120 |
| Apple, Mrs. Smith's® (8") | ⅙ pie | 270 | 100 |
| Apple, Mrs. Smith's® (8") Reduced Fat | ⅙ pie | 250 | 70 |
| Apple, Mrs. Smith's® (9") | ⅛ pie | 310 | 130 |
| Apple, Mrs. Smith's® (10") | ¹⁄₁₀ pie | 280 | 110 |
| Apple (no sugar added), Mrs. Smith's® (8") | ⅙ pie | 210 | 70 |
| Apple Cranberry, Mrs. Smith's® (8") | ⅙ pie | 280 | 100 |
| Apple Old Fashioned, Mrs. Smith's® (9") | ⅛ pie | 350 | 140 |
| Dutch Apple, Mrs. Smith's® (8") | ⅙ pie | 320 | 100 |
| Dutch Apple, Mrs. Smith's® (9") | ⅛ pie | 350 | 130 |
| Dutch Apple, Mrs. Smith's® (10") | ¹⁄₁₀ pie | 320 | 110 |
| Dutch Apple Old Fashioned, Mrs. Smith's® (9") | ⅑ pie | 310 | 110 |
| Homestyle Dutch Apple, Sara Lee® (9") | ⅛ pie | 350 | 130 |

#### Berry Pie

| Products | Serving Size | Calories | Calories from Fat |
|---|---|---|---|
| Berry, Mrs. Smith's® (8") | ⅙ pie | 280 | 100 |
| Blackberry, Mrs. Smith's® (8") | ⅙ pie | 280 | 100 |
| Blueberry, Mrs. Smith's® (8") | ⅙ pie | 260 | 100 |
| Red Raspberry, Mrs. Smith's® (8") | ⅙ pie | 280 | 100 |
| Strawberry, Mrs. Smith's® (8") | ⅕ pie | 280 | 100 |

#### Cherry Pie

| Products | Serving Size | Calories | Calories from Fat |
|---|---|---|---|
| Cherry, Banquet® | ⅕ pie | 290 | 120 |
| Cherry, Mrs. Smith's® (8") | ⅙ pie | 270 | 100 |
| Cherry, Mrs. Smith's® (8") Reduced Fat | ⅙ pie | 250 | 70 |
| Cherry, Mrs. Smith's® (9") | ⅛ pie | 310 | 120 |
| Cherry, Mrs. Smith's® (10") | ¹⁄₁₀ pie | 280 | 100 |
| Cherry (no sugar added), Mrs. Smith's® (8") Reduced Fat | ⅙ pie | 220 | 70 |
| Cherry, Sara Lee® (9") | ⅛ pie | 330 | 130 |

❶ Meets Low-Fat Guidelines

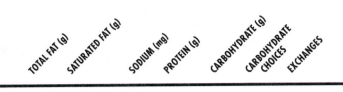

| TOTAL FAT (g) | SATURATED FAT (g) | SODIUM (mg) | PROTEIN (g) | CARBOHYDRATE (g) | CARBOHYDRATE CHOICES | EXCHANGES |
|---|---|---|---|---|---|---|
| 13 | 6 | 370 | 3 | 41 | 3 | 2 starch, 1 fruit, 2 fat |
| 11 | 2 | 300 | 2 | 41 | 3 | 1 starch, 2 fruit, 2 fat |
| 8 | 1.5 | 290 | 2 | 43 | 3 | 1 starch, 2 fruit, 1 fat |
| 14 | 2.5 | 370 | 2 | 44 | 3 | 1 starch, 2 fruit, 3 fat |
| 12 | 2.5 | 310 | 2 | 43 | 3 | 1 starch, 2 fruit, 2 fat |
| 8 | 1.5 | 290 | 2 | 32 | 2 | 1 starch, 1 fruit, 1 fat |
| 11 | 2 | 300 | 2 | 43 | 3 | 1 starch, 2 fruit, 2 fat |
| 16 | 3 | 400 | 2 | 50 | 3 | 1 starch, 2 fruit, 3 fat |
| 13 | 2.5 | 260 | 3 | 48 | 3 | 1 starch, 2 fruit, 2 fat |
| 14 | 3 | 290 | 3 | 52 | 3½ | 1 starch, 2½ fruit, 3 fat |
| 12 | 2.5 | 250 | 3 | 50 | 3 | 1 starch, 2 fruit, 2 fat |
| 12 | 2.5 | 230 | 2 | 49 | 3 | 1 starch, 2 fruit, 2 fat |
| 15 | 3 | 320 | 3 | 53 | 3½ | 1 starch, 2½ fruit, 3 fat |
| | | | | | | |
| 11 | 2 | 340 | 2 | 44 | 3 | 1 starch, 2 fruit, 2 fat |
| 11 | 2 | 320 | 2 | 43 | 3 | 1 starch, 2 fruit, 2 fat |
| 11 | 2 | 320 | 2 | 39 | 2½ | 1 starch, 1½ fruit, 2 fat |
| 11 | 2 | 320 | 2 | 43 | 3 | 1 starch, 2 fruit, 2 fat |
| 11 | 2.5 | 190 | 2 | 45 | 3 | 1 starch, 2 fruit, 2 fat |
| | | | | | | |
| 14 | 6 | 310 | 3 | 39 | 2½ | 1½ starch, 1 fruit, 2 fat |
| 11 | 2 | 320 | 2 | 41 | 3 | 1 starch, 2 fruit, 2 fat |
| 8 | 1.5 | 310 | 2 | 44 | 3 | 1 starch, 2 fruit, 1 fat |
| 13 | 2.5 | 390 | 3 | 45 | 3 | 1 starch, 2 fruit, 2 fat |
| 11 | 2 | 340 | 2 | 44 | 3 | 1 starch, 2 fruit, 2 fat |
| 8 | 1.5 | 310 | 3 | 35 | 2 | 1 starch, 1 fruit, 1 fat |
| | | | | | | |
| 15 | 3.5 | 290 | 3 | 46 | 3 | 1 starch, 2 fruit, 3 fat |

1 Carbohydrate Choice = 1 starch or 1 fruit or 1 milk exchange

## PRODUCTS

| | SERVING SIZE | CALORIES | CALORIES FROM FAT |
|---|---|---|---|
| Cherry Old Fashioned, Mrs. Smith's® (9") | ⅛ pie | 320 | 120 |
| **Chocolate Pie** | | | |
| Chocolate Cream, Banquet® | ⅓ pie | 360 | 180 |
| Chocolate Cream, Mrs. Smith's® (8") | ¼ pie | 330 | 150 |
| Chocolate Cream, Pet-Ritz® | ¼ pie | 290 | 120 |
| Chocolate Mocha, Weight Watchers® | 1 pie | 170 | 35 |
| French Silk Chocolate, Mrs. Smith's® (8") | ⅕ pie | 410 | 190 |
| Homestyle Chocolate Cream, Sara Lee® | ⅕ pie | 500 | 280 |
| Mississippi Mud Pie, Weight Watchers® | 1 pie | 160 | 45 |
| Peanut Butter Chocolate, Pet-Ritz® | ¼ pie | 300 | 140 |
| **Cream Pie** | | | |
| Banana Cream, Banquet® | ⅓ pie | 350 | 190 |
| Banana Cream, Mrs. Smith's® (8") | ¼ pie | 280 | 130 |
| Banana Cream, Pet-Ritz® | ¼ pie | 270 | 110 |
| Boston Cream, Mrs. Smith's® (8") | ⅛ pie | 170 | 50 |
| Coconut Cream, Banquet® | ⅓ pie | 350 | 180 |
| Coconut Cream, Mrs. Smith's® (8") | ¼ pie | 340 | 170 |
| Coconut Cream, Pet-Ritz® | ¼ pie | 270 | 110 |
| Coconut Cream, Sara Lee® Homestyle | ⅕ pie | 480 | 280 |
| Coconut Custard, Mrs. Smith's® (8") | ⅕ pie | 280 | 110 |
| Fudge Vanilla Cream, Pet-Ritz® | ¼ pie | 300 | 130 |
| Key Lime, Pet-Ritz® | ¼ pie | 270 | 110 |
| Lemon Cream, Banquet® | ⅓ pie | 360 | 180 |
| Lemon Cream, Mrs. Smith's® (8") | ¼ pie | 300 | 130 |
| Lemon Cream, Pet-Ritz® | ¼ pie | 270 | 110 |
| Lemon Meringue, Mrs. Smith's® (8") | ⅕ pie | 302 | 74 |
| Lemon Meringue, Sara Lee® Homestyle | ⅙ pie | 350 | 100 |
| **Peach Pie** | | | |
| Peach, Sara Lee® (9") | ⅛ pie | 330 | 120 |

❶ Meets Low-Fat Guidelines

| TOTAL FAT (g) | SATURATED FAT (g) | SODIUM (mg) | PROTEIN (g) | CARBOHYDRATE (g) | CARBOHYDRATE CHOICES | EXCHANGES |
|---|---|---|---|---|---|---|
| 13 | 2.5 | 350 | 3 | 48 | 3 | 1 starch, 2 fruit, 2 fat |
| 20 | 5 | 240 | 3 | 43 | 3 | 3 starch, 3 fat |
| 17 | 4 | 200 | 3 | 42 | 3 | 1 starch, 2 fruit, 3 fat |
| 13 | 8 | 270 | 3 | 39 | 2½ | 2½ starch, 2 fat |
| 4 | 1 | 125 | 6 | 31 | 2 | 2 starch |
| 21 | 6 | 250 | 3 | 55 | 3½ | 1 starch, 2½ fruit, 4 fat |
| 32 | 16 | 440 | 4 | 49 | 3 | 2 starch, 1 fruit, 6 fat |
| 5 | 1.5 | 120 | 4 | 24 | 1½ | 1½ starch, ½ fat |
| 15 | 8 | 250 | 3 | 37 | 2½ | 2½ starch, 2½ fat |
| 21 | 5 | 290 | 3 | 39 | 2½ | 2½ starch, 4 fat |
| 14 | 4 | 170 | 2 | 37 | 2½ | 1 starch, 1½ fruit, 2 fat |
| 13 | 8 | 250 | 3 | 37 | 2½ | 2½ starch, 2 fat |
| 5 | 1.5 | 140 | 2 | 29 | 2 | 1 starch, 1 fruit, ½ fat |
| 20 | 6 | 250 | 3 | 39 | 2½ | 2½ starch, 3 fat |
| 19 | 5 | 260 | 2 | 40 | 2½ | 1 starch, 1½ fruit, 4 fat |
| 13 | 8 | 250 | 3 | 37 | 2½ | 2½ starch, 2 fat |
| 31 | 14 | 430 | 4 | 47 | 3 | 2 starch, 1 fruit, 6 fat |
| 12 | 5 | 190 | 7 | 35 | 2 | 2 starch, 2 fat |
| 15 | 9 | 190 | 3 | 40 | 2½ | 2½ starch, 2½ fat |
| 13 | 8 | 250 | 3 | 37 | 2½ | 2½ starch, 2 fat |
| 20 | 5 | 240 | 3 | 43 | 3 | 3 starch, 3 fat |
| 15 | 4 | 260 | 2 | 40 | 2½ | 1 starch, 1½ fruit, 3 fat |
| 13 | 8 | 250 | 3 | 37 | 2½ | 2½ starch, 2 fat |
| 8.2 | 1.8 | 218 | 2 | 55 | 3½ | 1 starch, 2½ fruit, 1 fat |
| 11 | 2.5 | 460 | 2 | 59 | 4 | 1 starch, 3 fruit, 2 fat |
| 13 | 3 | 250 | 3 | 50 | 3 | 1 starch, 2 fruit, 2 fat |

1 Carbohydrate Choice = 1 starch or 1 fruit or 1 milk exchange

## PRODUCTS

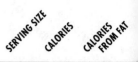

| | SERVING SIZE | CALORIES | CALORIES FROM FAT |
|---|---|---|---|
| **Pecan Pie** | | | |
| Pecan, Sara Lee® (9") | ⅛ pie | 520 | 220 |
| Pecan, Mrs. Smith's® (8") | ⅙ pie | 520 | 210 |
| Pecan, Mrs. Smith's® (10") | ⅒ pie | 500 | 210 |
| **Pumpkin Pie** | | | |
| Pumpkin, Banquet® | ⅕ pie | 250 | 70 |
| Pumpkin, Sara Lee® (9") | ⅛ pie | 260 | 100 |
| Hearty Pumpkin, Mrs. Smith's® (8") | ⅕ pie | 250 | 70 |
| Hearty Pumpkin, Mrs. Smith's® (9") | ⅛ pie | 240 | 60 |
| Pumpkin Cream, Pet-Ritz® | ¼ pie | 270 | 110 |
| Pumpkin Custard, Mrs. Smith's® (8") | ⅕ pie | 270 | 80 |
| Pumpkin Custard, Mrs. Smith's® (9") | ⅛ pie | 240 | 70 |
| Pumpkin Custard, Mrs. Smith's® (10") | ⅒ pie | 250 | 70 |
| **PIE CRUST (FROZEN)** | | | |
| All Vegetable Shortening, Pet-Ritz® (9") | ⅛ crust | 90 | 60 |
| Deep Dish Regular, Pet-Ritz® (9") | ⅛ crust | 100 | 50 |
| Deep Dish Vegetable Shortening, Pet-Ritz® | ⅛ crust | 100 | 60 |
| Extra Large, Pet-Ritz® (9⅝") | ⅛ crust | 120 | 70 |
| Graham Cracker, Pet-Ritz® | ⅛ crust | 110 | 60 |
| Regular, Pet-Ritz® (9") | ⅛ crust | 80 | 45 |
| Tart Crust, Pet-Ritz® (3") | 1 tart | 140 | 80 |
| Tart Crust, Pet-Ritz® (6") | ¼ crust | 110 | 70 |
| **PIE CRUST (READY-TO-USE)** | | | |
| Nilla® Pie Crust, Nabisco® | ⅙ pie crust | 140 | 70 |
| Oreo® Pie Crust, Nabisco® | ⅙ pie crust | 140 | 60 |
| **PIE CRUST (REFRIGERATED)** | | | |
| Pie Crust, Pillsbury® | ⅛ crust | 110 | 60 |

❶ Meets Low-Fat Guidelines

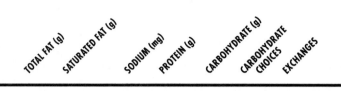

| TOTAL FAT (g) | SATURATED FAT (g) | SODIUM (mg) | PROTEIN (g) | CARBOHYDRATE (g) | CARBOHYDRATE CHOICES | EXCHANGES |
|---|---|---|---|---|---|---|
| 24 | 4.5 | 480 | 5 | 70 | 4½ | 2 starch, 2½ fruit, 4 fat |
| 23 | 4 | 450 | 5 | 73 | 5 | 2 starch, 3 fruit, 4 fat |
| 23 | 4 | 460 | 5 | 68 | 4½ | 2 starch, 2½ fruit, 4 fat |
| | | | | | | |
| 8 | 3 | 340 | 4 | 40 | 2½ | 2½ starch, 1 fat |
| 11 | 2.5 | 460 | 4 | 37 | 2½ | 2½ starch, 1 fat |
| 8 | 1.5 | 320 | 4 | 42 | 3 | 3 starch, 1 fat |
| 7 | 1.5 | 300 | 5 | 39 | 2½ | 2½ starch, 1 fat |
| 13 | 8 | 250 | 3 | 37 | 2½ | 2½ starch, 2 fat |
| 8 | 2 | 350 | 5 | 44 | 3 | 3 starch, 1 fat |
| 8 | 2 | 310 | 5 | 39 | 2½ | 2½ starch, 1 fat |
| 8 | 2 | 330 | 5 | 42 | 3 | 3 starch, 1 fat |
| | | | | | | |
| 6 | 1.5 | 60 | 1 | 8 | ½ | ½ starch, 1 fat |
| 6 | 2 | 70 | 1 | 10 | ½ | ½ starch, 1 fat |
| 7 | 2 | 65 | 1 | 9 | ½ | ½ starch, 1 fat |
| 7 | 3 | 90 | 2 | 13 | 1 | 1 starch, 1 fat |
| 6 | 1.5 | 120 | 1 | 13 | 1 | 1 starch, 1 fat |
| 5 | 2 | 60 | 1 | 9 | ½ | ½ starch, 1 fat |
| 9 | 2 | 130 | 2 | 11 | 1 | 1 starch, 2 fat |
| 7 | 1.5 | 105 | 2 | 9 | ½ | ½ starch, 1 fat |
| | | | | | | |
| 8 | 1.5 | 65 | 1 | 18 | 1 | 1 starch, 1 fat |
| 7 | 1.5 | 180 | 1 | 18 | 1 | 1 starch, 1 fat |
| | | | | | | |
| 7 | 3 | 140 | <1 | 12 | 1 | 1 starch, 1 fat |

1 Carbohydrate Choice = 1 starch or 1 fruit or 1 milk exchange

## PRODUCTS

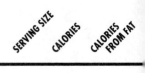

### PIZZA (FROZEN; ALL PIZZAS ARE 12" UNLESS NOTED)

#### *Canadian Bacon Pizza*

| | SERVING SIZE | CALORIES | CALORIES FROM FAT |
|---|---|---|---|
| Canadian Style Bacon, Red Baron® | ¼ pizza | 380 | 160 |
| Candian Style Bacon, Tombstone® Original | ¼ pizza | 360 | 140 |
| Canadian Style Bacon, Totino's® Party® Pizza | ½ pizza | 320 | 140 |
| Two Cheese & Canadian Style Bacon, Totino's® Select | ⅓ pizza | 310 | 130 |

#### *Cheese Pizza*

| | | | |
|---|---|---|---|
| Cheese, Jack's® Naturally Rising | ⅙ pizza | 290 | 90 |
| Cheese, Jack's® Naturally Rising (9") | ⅓ pizza | 300 | 90 |
| Cheese, Totino's® Totino's® Party® Pizza | ½ pizza | 320 | 130 |
| Cheese, Totino's® Party® Pizza, Family Size | ⅓ pizza | 360 | 140 |
| Double Cheese, Jack's® Great Combinations™ (9") | ½ pizza | 430 | 190 |
| Double Cheese, Jack's® Naturally Rising | ¼ pizza | 380 | 170 |
| Extra Cheese, Marie Callender's® | ½ pizza | 410 | 230 |
| Extra Cheese, Tombstone® Original | ¼ pizza | 370 | 150 |
| Extra Cheese, Tombstone® Original (9") | ½ pizza | 420 | 170 |
| 4 Cheese, Red Baron® | ¼ pizza | 430 | 190 |
| Four Cheese, Tombstone Special Order® | ⅕ pizza | 400 | 170 |
| Four Cheese, Wolfgang Puck's® (8") | ½ pizza | 360 | 130 |
| Italian Style Three Cheese, Tombstone® ThinCrust | ¼ pizza | 380 | 200 |
| Three Cheese, Pappalo's® Deep Dish | ⅕ pizza | 370 | 110 |
| Three Cheese, Pappalo's® Pizzeria Style | ¼ pizza | 340 | 110 |
| Three Cheese Pizzeria Style, Pappalo's® (9") | ½ pizza | 400 | 140 |
| Three Cheese, Totino's® Select | ⅓ pizza | 300 | 130 |

#### *Chicken Pizza*

| | | | |
|---|---|---|---|
| Barbecue Chicken, Wolfgang Puck's® (8") | ½ pizza | 340 | 100 |
| Spicy Chicken, Wolfgang Puck's® (8") | ½ pizza | 360 | 140 |

❶ Meets Low-Fat Guidelines

| TOTAL FAT (g) | SATURATED FAT (g) | SODIUM (mg) | PROTEIN (g) | CARBOHYDRATE (g) | CARBOHYDRATE CHOICES | EXCHANGES |
|---|---|---|---|---|---|---|
| 17 | 7 | 930 | 19 | 40 | 2½ | 2½ starch, 2 meat, 1 fat |
| 15 | 7 | 920 | 20 | 36 | 2½ | 2½ starch, 2 meat |
| 15 | 2.5 | 900 | 14 | 33 | 2 | 2 starch, 1 meat, 2 fat |
| 14 | 5 | 790 | 17 | 30 | 2 | 2 starch, 2 meat |
| | | | | | | |
| 10 | 6 | 500 | 15 | 35 | 2 | 2 starch, 1 meat, ½ fat |
| 10 | 6 | 500 | 15 | 38 | 2½ | 2½ starch, 1 meat, ½ fat |
| 14 | 5 | 630 | 15 | 33 | 2 | 2 starch, 1 meat, 2 fat |
| 16 | 6 | 720 | 16 | 38 | 2½ | 2½ starch, 1 meat, 2 fat |
| 21 | 12 | 740 | 23 | 38 | 2½ | 2½ starch, 2 meat, 2 fat |
| | | | | | | |
| 19 | 11 | 670 | 21 | 32 | 2 | 2 starch, 2 meat, 1 fat |
| 25 | 10 | 630 | 15 | 30 | 2 | 2 starch, 1 meat, 4 fat |
| 17 | 9 | 680 | 18 | 36 | 2½ | 2½ starch, 2 meat, 1 fat |
| 19 | 9 | 730 | 20 | 42 | 3 | 3 starch, 2 meat, 1 fat |
| 21 | 10 | 810 | 20 | 41 | 3 | 3 starch, 2 meat, 1½ fat |
| 19 | 10 | 760 | 20 | 37 | 2½ | 2½ starch, 2 meat, 1 fat |
| 15 | 6 | 530 | 17 | 40 | 3 | 3 starch, 1 meat, 1 fat |
| 22 | 12 | 730 | 20 | 25 | 1½ | 1½ starch, 2 meat, 2 fat |
| | | | | | | |
| 12 | 6 | 670 | 19 | 46 | 3 | 3 starch, 2 meat |
| 12 | 6 | 770 | 19 | 39 | 2½ | 2½ starch, 2 meat |
| 15 | 8 | 760 | 21 | 44 | 3 | 3 starch, 2 meat |
| 14 | 6 | 590 | 14 | 29 | 2 | 2 starch, 1 meat, 1½ fat |
| | | | | | | |
| 11 | 5 | 540 | 20 | 39 | 2½ | 2½ starch, 2 meat |
| 16 | 7 | 620 | 19 | 36 | 2½ | 2½ starch, 2 meat, ½ fat |

1 Carbohydrate Choice = 1 starch or 1 fruit or 1 milk exchange

## PRODUCTS

| | SERVING SIZE | CALORIES | CALORIES FROM FAT |
|---|---|---|---|
| **Combination Pizza** | | | |
| Bacon Burger, Totino's® Party® Pizza | ½ pizza | 370 | 180 |
| Bacon Cheeseburger, Jack's® Naturally Rising | ⅙ pizza | 350 | 140 |
| Cheese, Sausage and Mushroom, Tombstone® Original | ⅕ pizza | 320 | 140 |
| Chicken & Broccoli, Marie Callender's® | ½ pizza | 350 | 140 |
| Classic 5 Meat Combo, Marie Callender's® | ½ pizza | 350 | 130 |
| Combination, Jack's® Naturally Rising | ⅙ pizza | 360 | 150 |
| Combination, Totino's® Party® Pizza | ½ pizza | 390 | 190 |
| Combination, Totino's® Party® Pizza, Family Size | ¼ pizza | 300 | 140 |
| Deluxe, Marie Callender's® | ½ pizza | 380 | 210 |
| Deluxe, Tombstone® Original | ⅕ pizza | 320 | 140 |
| Deluxe, Tombstone® Original (9") | ⅓ pizza | 320 | 150 |
| Four Meat, Tombstone Special Order® | ⅙ pizza | 350 | 160 |
| Four Meat, Tombstone Special Order® (9") | ⅓ pizza | 400 | 180 |
| Italian Style Four Meat Combo, Tombstone® ThinCrust | ¼ pizza | 410 | 230 |
| Italian Style Supreme, Tombstone® ThinCrust | ¼ pizza | 400 | 220 |
| Mexican Style, Jack's® SuperCheese® | ⅕ pizza | 320 | 150 |
| Mexican Style Supreme, Red Baron® | ⅕ pizza | 430 | 220 |
| Mexican Style Supreme Taco, Tombstone® ThinCrust | ¼ pizza | 380 | 210 |
| Pepperoni & Mushroom, Jack's® Great Combinations™ | ¼ pizza | 340 | 140 |
| Pepperoni & Mushroom, Wolfgang Puck's® (8") | ½ pizza | 390 | 130 |
| Pepperoni & Sausage, Jack's® Great Combinations™ (9") | ½ pizza | 380 | 170 |
| Pepperoni and Sausage, Tombstone Original® (9") | ⅓ pizza | 360 | 190 |
| Primavera, Marie Callender's® | ½ pizza | 350 | 140 |
| Sausage & Mushroom, Red Baron® | ⅕ pizza | 350 | 160 |

❶  Meets Low-Fat Guidelines

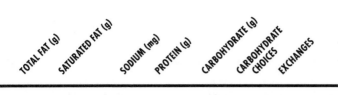

| TOTAL FAT (g) | SATURATED FAT (g) | SODIUM (mg) | PROTEIN (g) | CARBOHYDRATE (g) | CARBOHYDRATE CHOICES | EXCHANGES |
|---|---|---|---|---|---|---|
| 20 | 4.5 | 880 | 15 | 33 | 2 | 2 starch, 1 meat, 3 fat |
| 15 | 7 | 680 | 18 | 35 | 2 | 2 starch, 2 meat, ½ fat |
| 16 | 7 | 630 | 15 | 29 | 2 | 2 starch, 1 meat, 2 fat |
| 15 | 7 | 610 | 19 | 34 | 2 | 2 starch, 1 veg, 2 meat, ½ fat |
| 14 | 7 | 770 | 16 | 36 | 2½ | 2½ starch, 2 meat |
| 17 | 8 | 680 | 17 | 34 | 2 | 2 starch, 2 meat, 1 fat |
| 21 | 4.5 | 910 | 15 | 34 | 2 | 2 starch, 1 meat, 3 fat |
| 16 | 3.5 | 740 | 12 | 28 | 2 | 2 starch, 1 meat, 2 fat |
| 23 | 5 | 690 | 14 | 30 | 2 | 2 starch, 1 meat, 3 fat |
| 16 | 7 | 640 | 15 | 29 | 2 | 2 starch, 1 meat, 2 fat |
| 16 | 7 | 620 | 15 | 28 | 2 | 2 starch, 1 meat, 2 fat |
| 18 | 8 | 810 | 17 | 31 | 2 | 2 starch, 2 meat, 1 fat |
| 20 | 10 | 910 | 19 | 35 | 2 | 2 starch, 2 meat, 2 fat |
| 25 | 12 | 940 | 20 | 25 | 1½ | 1½ starch, 2 meat, 3 fat |
| 24 | 11 | 880 | 18 | 26 | 2 | 2 starch, 2 meat, 2 fat |
| 17 | 9 | 690 | 15 | 27 | 2 | 2 starch, 1 meat, 2 fat |
| 24 | 10 | 730 | 15 | 38 | 2½ | 2½ starch, 1 meat, 3 fat |
| 23 | 11 | 850 | 16 | 26 | 2 | 2 starch, 1 meat, 3 fat |
| 16 | 7 | 740 | 17 | 32 | 2 | 2 starch, 2 meat, 1 fat |
| 15 | 6 | 690 | 21 | 43 | 3 | 3 starch, 2 meat |
| 18 | 8 | 790 | 18 | 36 | 2½ | 2½ starch, 2 meat, 1 fat |
| 21 | 9 | 820 | 16 | 28 | 2 | 2 starch, 2 meat, 2 fat |
| 15 | 6 | 630 | 14 | 40 | 2½ | 2½ starch, 1 meat, 2 fat |
| 18 | 7 | 710 | 15 | 33 | 2 | 2 starch, 1 meat, 2 fat |

1 Carbohydrate Choice = 1 starch *or* 1 fruit *or* 1 milk exchange

## PRODUCTS

| PRODUCTS | SERVING SIZE | CALORIES | CALORIES FROM FAT |
|---|---|---|---|
| Sausage and Pepperoni, Tombstone for One® | 1 pizza | 590 | 330 |
| Sausage and Pepperoni, Tombstone® Original | ⅕ pizza | 340 | 160 |
| Sausage & Pepperoni, Jack's® Great Combinations™ | ¼ pizza | 350 | 170 |
| Sausage & Pepperoni, Jack's® SuperCheese® | ⅕ pizza | 340 | 170 |
| Sausage & Pepperoni, Marie Callender's® | ½ pizza | 430 | 250 |
| Sausage & Pepperoni, Red Baron® | ⅕ pizza | 370 | 180 |
| Sausage & Pepperoni, Pappalo's® Deep Dish | ⅕ pizza | 330 | 130 |
| Sausage & Pepperoni, Pappalo's® Pizzeria Style | ¼ pizza | 380 | 150 |
| Sausage & Pepperoni, Pappalo's® Pizzeria Style (9") | ½ pizza | 430 | 170 |
| Sausage & Pepperoni, Totino's® Select | ⅓ pizza | 360 | 170 |
| Sausage and Pepperoni with Double Cheese, Tombstone Double Top® | ⅙ pizza | 360 | 180 |
| Special Deluxe, Jack's® SuperCheese® | ⅕ pizza | 300 | 150 |
| Special Deluxe, Red Baron® | ⅕ pizza | 340 | 160 |
| Super Supreme, Tombstone Special Order® | ⅙ pizza | 350 | 160 |
| Super Supreme, Tombstone Special Order® (9") | ⅓ pizza | 400 | 180 |
| Supreme, Pappalo's® Deep Dish | ⅕ pizza | 340 | 130 |
| Supreme, Pappalo's® Pizzeria Style | ¼ pizza | 380 | 140 |
| Supreme, Pappalo's® Pizzeria Style (9") | ½ pizza | 290 | 120 |
| Supreme, Red Baron® | ⅕ pizza | 350 | 160 |
| Supreme, Tombstone Light® | ⅕ pizza | 270 | 80 |
| Supreme, Tombstone® Original | ⅕ pizza | 330 | 150 |
| Supreme, Totino's® Party® Pizza | ½ pizza | 380 | 180 |
| Supreme, Totino's® Select | ⅓ pizza | 340 | 160 |
| The Works, Jack's® Naturally Rising | ⅙ pizza | 330 | 130 |
| The Works, Jack's® Naturally Rising (9") | ¼ pizza | 280 | 110 |
| Three Meat, Totino's® Party® Pizza | ½ pizza | 360 | 170 |
| Zesty Italiano, Totino's® Party® Pizza | ½ pizza | 390 | 190 |
| Zesty Mexican Style, Totino's® Party® Pizza | ½ pizza | 370 | 170 |

❶ Meets Low-Fat Guidelines

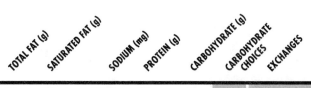

| TOTAL FAT (g) | SATURATED FAT (g) | SODIUM (mg) | PROTEIN (g) | CARBOHYDRATE (g) | CARBOHYDRATE CHOICES | EXCHANGES |
|---|---|---|---|---|---|---|
| 37 | 15 | 1200 | 25 | 40 | 2½ | 2½ starch, 3 meat, 4 fat |
| 18 | 8 | 740 | 16 | 29 | 2 | 2 starch, 1 meat, 2 fat |
| 19 | 8 | 770 | 17 | 29 | 2 | 2 starch, 2 meat, 1 fat |
| 19 | 10 | 750 | 19 | 24 | 1½ | 1½ starch, 2 meat, 1 fat |
| 28 | 11 | 730 | 15 | 29 | 2 | 2 starch, 2 meat, 3 fat |
| 20 | 8 | 770 | 16 | 32 | 2 | 2 starch, 2 meat, 1 fat |
| 14 | 8 | 650 | 16 | 36 | 2½ | 2½ starch, 1 meat, 1 fat |
| 17 | 9 | 780 | 18 | 39 | 2½ | 2½ starch, 2 meat, 1 fat |
| 19 | 11 | 870 | 21 | 44 | 3 | 3 starch, 2 meat, 1 fat |
| 19 | 7 | 760 | 17 | 30 | 2 | 2 starch, 2 meat, 1 fat |
| 20 | 10 | 800 | 20 | 25 | 1½ | 1½ starch, 2 meat, 2 fat |
| 16 | 7 | 660 | 15 | 24 | 1½ | 1½ starch, 2 meat, 1 fat |
| 18 | 7 | 690 | 13 | 32 | 2 | 2 starch, 1 meat, 2 fat |
| 18 | 9 | 800 | 17 | 31 | 2 | 2 starch, 2 meat, 1 fat |
| 21 | 10 | 900 | 19 | 36 | 2½ | 2½ starch, 2 meat, 2 fat |
| 14 | 8 | 680 | 17 | 37 | 2½ | 2½ starch, 2 meat |
| 16 | 9 | 790 | 18 | 40 | 2½ | 2½ starch, 2 meat, 1 fat |
| 13 | 7 | 610 | 14 | 30 | 2 | 2 starch, 1 meat, 1 fat |
| 18 | 7 | 710 | 15 | 32 | 2 | 2 starch, 1 meat, 2 fat |
| 9 | 3.5 | 710 | 25 | 30 | 2 | 2 starch, 3 lean meat, |
| 17 | 8 | 720 | 15 | 29 | 2 | 2 starch, 1 meat, 2 fat |
| 20 | 4.5 | 890 | 15 | 34 | 2 | 2 starch, 1 meat, 3 fat |
| 18 | 7 | 770 | 16 | 29 | 2 | 2 starch, 1 meat, 2 fat |
| 14 | 7 | 580 | 16 | 34 | 2 | 2 starch, 2 meat |
| 12 | 6 | 480 | 13 | 29 | 2 | 2 starch, 1 meat, 1 fat |
| 19 | 4 | 910 | 15 | 33 | 2 | 2 starch, 1 meat, 2½ fat |
| 21 | 4.5 | 900 | 15 | 35 | 2 | 2 starch, 2 meat, 2 fat |
| 19 | 4.5 | 750 | 15 | 34 | 2 | 2 starch, 2 meat, 1½ fat |

1 Carbohydrate Choice = 1 starch *or* 1 fruit *or* 1 milk exchange

## PRODUCTS

| | SERVING SIZE | CALORIES | CALORIES FROM FAT |
|---|---|---|---|
| **Hamburger Pizza** | | | |
| Cheese and Hamburger, Tombstone® Original | ⅕ pizza | 320 | 150 |
| Cheese and Hamburger, Tombstone® Original (9") | ⅓ pizza | 310 | 140 |
| Hamburger, Totino's® Party® Pizza | ½ pizza | 350 | 160 |
| **Pepperoni Pizza** | | | |
| Cheese and Pepperoni, Tombstone® Original | ⅕ pizza | 340 | 160 |
| Cheese and Pepperoni, Tombstone® Original (9") | ⅓ pizza | 340 | 170 |
| Italian Style Pepperoni, Tombstone® Thin Crust | ¼ pizza | 420 | 240 |
| Pepperoni, Jack's® Naturally Rising | ⅙ pizza | 350 | 140 |
| Pepperoni, Marie Callender's® | ½ pizza | 440 | 260 |
| Pepperoni, Red Baron® | ¼ pizza | 450 | 210 |
| Pepperoni, Tombstone Special Order® | ⅙ pizza | 360 | 170 |
| Pepperoni, Tombstone Special Order® (9") | ⅓ pizza | 400 | 190 |
| Pepperoni, Pappalo's® Deep Dish | ⅕ pizza | 340 | 130 |
| Pepperoni, Totino's® Party® Pizza | ½ pizza | 380 | 190 |
| Pepperoni, Totino's® Party® Pizza, Family Size | ⅓ pizza | 410 | 200 |
| Pepperoni, Pappalo's® Pizzeria Style | ¼ pizza | 380 | 150 |
| Pepperoni, Pappalo's® Pizzeria Style (9") | ½ pizza | 440 | 170 |
| Pepperoni with Double Cheese, Tombstone Double Top® | ⅙ pizza | 350 | 180 |
| Two Cheese & Pepperoni, Totino's® Select | ⅓ pizza | 360 | 170 |
| **Sausage Pizza** | | | |
| Cheese and Sausage, Tombstone® Original | ⅕ pizza | 320 | 150 |
| Cheese and Sausage, Tombstone® Original (9") | ⅓ pizza | 310 | 140 |
| Italian Style Italian Sausage, Tombstone® ThinCrust | ¼ pizza | 400 | 220 |
| Sausage, Jack's® Naturally Rising | ⅙ pizza | 340 | 140 |
| Sausage, Jack's® SuperCheese® | ¼ pizza | 380 | 180 |

❶ Meets Low-Fat Guidelines

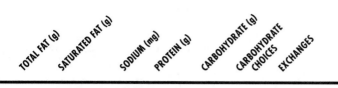

| TOTAL FAT (g) | SATURATED FAT (g) | SODIUM (mg) | PROTEIN (g) | CARBOHYDRATE (g) | CARBOHYDRATE CHOICES | EXCHANGES |
|---|---|---|---|---|---|---|
| 16 | 8 | 660 | 15 | 29 | 2 | 2 starch, 1 meat, 2 fat |
| 16 | 7 | 620 | 14 | 28 | 2 | 2 starch, 1 meat, 2 fat |
| 18 | 4 | 860 | 15 | 33 | 2 | 2 starch, 1 meat, 2½ fat |
| 18 | 8 | 750 | 15 | 29 | 2 | 2 starch, 1 meat, 2 fat |
| 19 | 8 | 740 | 15 | 28 | 2 | 2 starch, 1 meat, 2 fat |
| 27 | 13 | 950 | 20 | 25 | 1½ | 1½ starch, 2 meat, 3 fat |
| 16 | 8 | 710 | 17 | 35 | 2 | 2 starch, 1 meat, 2 fat |
| 29 | 11 | 770 | 14 | 30 | 2 | 2 starch, 1 meat, 4 fat |
| 24 | 9 | 920 | 19 | 40 | 2½ | 2½ starch, 2 meat, 2 fat |
| 19 | 9 | 790 | 16 | 31 | 2 | 2 starch, 2 meat, 1 fat |
| 21 | 10 | 880 | 19 | 35 | 2 | 2 starch, 2 meat, 2 fat |
| 14 | 6 | 720 | 17 | 37 | 2½ | 2½ starch, 1 meat, 1½ fat |
| 21 | 5 | 920 | 14 | 33 | 2 | 2 starch, 1 meat, 3 fat |
| 22 | 5 | 1000 | 15 | 37 | 2½ | 2½ starch, 1 meat, 3 fat |
| 17 | 8 | 840 | 18 | 38 | 2½ | 2½ starch, 2 meat, 1 fat |
| 19 | 9 | 950 | 21 | 45 | 3 | 3 starch, 2 meat, 1 fat |
| 20 | 10 | 850 | 19 | 25 | 1½ | 1½ starch, 2 meat, 2 fat |
| 19 | 7 | 760 | 17 | 31 | 2 | 2 starch, 2 meat, 1 fat |
| 16 | 8 | 650 | 15 | 29 | 2 | 2 starch, 1 meat, 2 fat |
| 16 | 7 | 610 | 14 | 28 | 2 | 2 starch, 1 meat, 2 fat |
| 24 | 11 | 880 | 19 | 25 | 1½ | 1½ starch, 2 meat, 3 fat |
| 15 | 7 | 600 | 17 | 34 | 2 | 2 starch, 2 meat, ½ fat |
| 20 | 10 | 770 | 22 | 29 | 2 | 2 starch, 2 meat, 1½ fat |

1 Carbohydrate Choice = 1 starch or 1 fruit or 1 milk exchange

## PRODUCTS

| | SERVING SIZE | CALORIES | CALORIES FROM FAT |
|---|---|---|---|
| Sausage, Red Baron® | ⅕ pizza | 350 | 160 |
| Sausage & Herb, Wolfgang Puck's® (8") | ½ pizza | 380 | 160 |
| Sausage Deep Dish, Pappalo's® | ⅕ pizza | 330 | 120 |
| Sausage, Totino's® Party® Pizza | ½ pizza | 380 | 180 |
| Sausage, Totino's® Party® Pizza, Family Size | ¼ pizza | 300 | 140 |
| Sausage, Pappalo's® Pizzeria Style | ¼ pizza | 370 | 140 |
| Sausage, Pappalo's® Pizzeria Style (9") | ½ pizza | 420 | 160 |
| Sausage with Double Cheese, Tombstone® Double Top | ⅙ pizza | 350 | 170 |
| Three Sausage, Tombstone Special Order® | ⅙ pizza | 340 | 150 |
| Three Sausage, Tombstone Special Order® (9") | ⅓ pizza | 390 | 170 |
| Turkey Sausage, Wolfgang Puck's® (8") | ½ pizza | 320 | 110 |
| Two Cheese & Sausage, Totino's® Select | ⅓ pizza | 360 | 170 |

### Vegetable Pizza

| | SERVING SIZE | CALORIES | CALORIES FROM FAT |
|---|---|---|---|
| Artichoke Heart, Wolfgang Puck's® (8") | ½ pizza | 340 | 150 |
| ❶ Grilled Vegetable Cheeseless, Wolfgang Puck's® (8") | ½ pizza | 200 | 0 |
| ❶ Mushroom & Spinach, Wolfgang Puck's® | ½ pizza | 270 | 70 |
| Sliced Tomato & Mozzarella, Marie Callender's® | ½ pizza | 350 | 140 |
| ❶ Vegetable, Tombstone Light® | ⅕ pizza | 240 | 60 |
| Vegetable Harvest, Jack's® | ⅕ pizza | 250 | 90 |
| Zucchini & Tomato, Wolfgang Puck's® (8") | ½ pizza | 290 | 100 |

### PIZZA, SINGLE-SERVING (FROZEN)

#### Canadian Bacon Pizza, single-serving

| | SERVING SIZE | CALORIES | CALORIES FROM FAT |
|---|---|---|---|
| Canadian Style Bacon, Jeno's® Crisp 'n Tasty® | 1 pizza | 430 | 160 |

#### Cheese Pizza, single-serving

| | SERVING SIZE | CALORIES | CALORIES FROM FAT |
|---|---|---|---|
| ❶ Cheese, Healthy Choice® French Bread Pizza | 1 pizza | 310 | 35 |
| Cheese, Jeno's® | 1 pizza | 240 | 100 |
| Cheese, Jeno's® Crisp 'n Tasty® | 1 pizza | 450 | 170 |

❶  Meets Low-Fat Guidelines

| TOTAL FAT (g) | SATURATED FAT (g) | SODIUM (mg) | PROTEIN (g) | CARBOHYDRATE (g) | CARBOHYDRATE CHOICES | EXCHANGES |
|---|---|---|---|---|---|---|
| 18 | 7 | 710 | 15 | 33 | 2 | 2 starch, 1 meat, 2 fat |
| 18 | 8 | 650 | 19 | 36 | 2½ | 2½ starch, 2 meat, 1 fat |
| 13 | 8 | 600 | 16 | 36 | 2½ | 2½ starch, 1 meat, 1 fat |
| 20 | 4.5 | 870 | 15 | 34 | 2 | 2 starch, 1 meat, 3 fat |
| 16 | 3.5 | 720 | 12 | 28 | 2 | 2 starch, 1 meat, 1½ fat |
| 16 | 10 | 710 | 18 | 38 | 2½ | 2½ starch, 2 meat, ½ fat |
| 18 | 11 | 800 | 20 | 45 | 3 | 3 starch, 2 meat, 1 fat |
| 19 | 10 | 740 | 20 | 25 | 1½ | 1½ starch, 2 meat, 1 fat |
| 17 | 3.5 | 740 | 16 | 31 | 2 | 2 starch, 2 meat, 2 fat |
| 19 | 9 | 830 | 19 | 35 | 2 | 2 starch, 2 meat, 1 fat |
| 13 | 6 | 500 | 15 | 37 | 2½ | 2½ starch, 1 meat, 1 fat |
| 19 | 7 | 760 | 17 | 31 | 2 | 2 starch, 2 meat, 1 fat |
| 17 | 6 | 450 | 15 | 34 | 2 | 2 starch, 1 meat, 2 fat |
| 0 | 0 | 430 | 6 | 42 | 3 | 3 starch |
| 8 | 3 | 380 | 14 | 36 | 2½ | 2½ starch, 1 meat |
| 15 | 6 | 600 | 14 | 40 | 2½ | 2 starch, 1 veg, 1 meat, 1 fat |
| 7 | 2.5 | 500 | 25 | 31 | 2 | 2 starch, 3 lean meat |
| 10 | 6 | 450 | 14 | 26 | 2 | 2 starch, 1 meat, ½ fat |
| 11 | 5 | 380 | 12 | 37 | 2½ | 2½ starch, 1 meat, ½ fat |
| 18 | 3.5 | 1150 | 17 | 49 | 3 | 3 starch, 2 meat, 1 fat |
| 4 | 2 | 470 | 20 | 49 | 3 | 3 starch, 2 very lean meat |
| 11 | 3.5 | 530 | 10 | 25 | 1½ | 1½ starch, 1 meat, 1 fat |
| 19 | 6 | 870 | 19 | 51 | 3½ | 3½ starch, 2 meat, 1 fat |

1 Carbohydrate Choice = 1 starch or 1 fruit or 1 milk exchange

# PRODUCTS

| PRODUCTS | SERVING SIZE | CALORIES | CALORIES FROM FAT |
|---|---|---|---|
| Cheese, Michelina's® Krisp 'n Flaky™ Crust | 1 pizza | 420 | 190 |
| Cheese, Pepperidge Farm® Croissant Crust | 1 pizza | 390 | 180 |
| Cheese, Stouffer's® French Bread Pizza | 1 pizza | 350 | 120 |
|  Cheese, Stouffer's® Lean Cuisine® French Bread Pizza | 1 pizza | 350 | 70 |
| Cheese, Tombstone for One® ½ Less Fat | 1 pizza | 360 | 90 |
| Cheese, Totino's® | 1 pizza | 240 | 100 |
| Double Cheese, Stouffer's® French Bread Pizza | 1 pizza | 420 | 170 |
| Extra Cheese, Tombstone for One® | 1 pizza | 540 | 270 |
| Extra Cheese, Weight Watchers® | 1 entree | 390 | 100 |
| Three Cheese, Pappalo's® | 1 pizza | 500 | 180 |
| Three Cheese, Pappalo's® Deep Dish | 1 pizza | 540 | 180 |
| White, Stouffer's® French Bread Pizza | 1 pizza | 490 | 250 |

### Combination Pizza, single-serving

| | | | |
|---|---|---|---|
| Bacon Cheddar, Stouffer's® French Bread Pizza | 1 pizza | 440 | 200 |
| Cheeseburger, Stouffer's® French Bread Pizza | 1 pizza | 440 | 230 |
| Combination, Jeno's® | 1 pizza | 310 | 160 |
| Combination, Jeno's® Crisp 'n Tasty® | 1 pizza | 520 | 250 |
| Combination, Michelina's® Krisp 'n Flaky™ Crust | 1 pizza | 430 | 210 |
| Combination, Totino's® | 1 pizza | 310 | 160 |
| Deluxe, Pepperidge Farm® Croissant Crust Pizza | 1 pizza | 450 | 240 |
| Deluxe, Stouffer's® French Bread Pizza | 1 pizza | 440 | 200 |
|  Deluxe, Stouffer's® Lean Cuisine® French Bread Pizza | 1 pizza | 330 | 50 |
|  Deluxe Combo, Weight Watchers® | 1 entree | 380 | 100 |
| Mexican-Style, Michelina's® Krisp 'n Flaky™ Crust | 1 pizza | 400 | 190 |
| Pepperoni & Mushroom, Stouffer's® French Bread Pizza | 1 pizza | 430 | 190 |
| Sausage & Pepperoni, Pappalo's® | 1 pizza | 570 | 240 |

 Meets Low-Fat Guidelines

| TOTAL FAT (g) | SATURATED FAT (g) | SODIUM (mg) | PROTEIN (g) | CARBOHYDRATE (g) | CARBOHYDRATE CHOICES | EXCHANGES |
|---|---|---|---|---|---|---|
| 22 | 12 | 680 | 16 | 41 | 3 | 3 starch, 1 high fat meat, 2 fat |
| 20 | 7 | 770 | 12 | 39 | 2½ | 2½ starch, 1 meat, 3 fat |
| 14 | 5 | 660 | 15 | 42 | 3 | 3 starch, 1 meat, 3 fat |
| 8 | 4 | 400 | 22 | 48 | 3 | 3 starch, 2 lean meat |
| 10 | 4.5 | 920 | 23 | 45 | 3 | 3 starch, 2 lean meat |
| 11 | 3.5 | 530 | 10 | 25 | 1½ | 1½ starch, 1 meat, 1 fat |
| 19 | 7 | 790 | 19 | 44 | 3 | 3 starch, 1 meat, 2 fat |
| 30 | 14 | 910 | 27 | 41 | 3 | 3 starch, 3 meat, 2 fat |
| 12 | 4 | 590 | 23 | 49 | 3 | 3 starch, 2 meat |
| 20 | 10 | 960 | 29 | 50 | 3 | 3 starch, 3 meat, ½ fat |
| 20 | 10 | 1000 | 30 | 61 | 4 | 4 starch, 3 meat |
| 28 | 8 | 760 | 17 | 43 | 3 | 3 starch, 1 meat, 4 fat |
| 22 | 7 | 940 | 16 | 44 | 3 | 3 starch, 1 meat, 3 fat |
| 26 | 9 | 1110 | 21 | 31 | 2 | 2 starch, 2 meat, 3 fat |
| 18 | 4.5 | 720 | 11 | 25 | 1½ | 1½ starch, 1 meat, 2 fat |
| 28 | 7 | 1120 | 17 | 49 | 3 | 3 starch, 2 meat, 3 fat |
| 24 | 12 | 800 | 15 | 40 | 2½ | 2½ starch, 1 meat, 3 fat |
| 18 | 4.5 | 720 | 11 | 25 | 1½ | 1½ starch, 1 meat, 2 fat |
| 27 | 10 | 910 | 14 | 40 | 2½ | 2½ starch, 1 meat, 4 fat |
| 22 | 7 | 980 | 19 | 42 | 3 | 3 starch, 1 meat, 3 fat |
| 6 | 2.5 | 560 | 23 | 45 | 3 | 3 starch, 2 very lean meat |
| 11 | 3.5 | 550 | 23 | 47 | 3 | 3 starch, 2 meat |
| 21 | 11 | 770 | 15 | 38 | 2½ | 2½ starch, 1 meat, 3 fat |
| 21 | 6 | 1000 | 17 | 43 | 3 | 3 starch, 1 meat, 3 fat |
| 27 | 16 | 1170 | 30 | 51 | 3½ | 3½ starch, 3 meat, 2 fat |

1 Carbohydrate Choice = 1 starch or 1 fruit or 1 milk exchange

## PRODUCTS

| | SERVING SIZE | CALORIES | CALORIES FROM FAT |
|---|---|---|---|
| Sausage & Pepperoni, Pappalo's® Deep Dish | 1 pizza | 610 | 240 |
| Sausage & Pepperoni, Stouffer's® French Bread Pizza | 1 pizza | 490 | 220 |
| Sausage and Pepperoni, Tombstone for One® | 1 pizza | 590 | 330 |
| ❶ Supreme, Healthy Choice® French Bread Pizza | 1 pizza | 340 | 50 |
| Supreme, Jeno's® Crisp 'n Tasty® | 1 pizza | 520 | 250 |
| Supreme, Michelina's® Krisp 'n Flaky™ Crust | 1 pizza | 440 | 220 |
| Supreme, Pappalo's® | 1 pizza | 570 | 240 |
| Supreme, Pappalo's® Deep Dish | 1 pizza | 610 | 240 |
| Supreme, Tombstone for One® | 1 pizza | 570 | 310 |
| Supreme, Tombstone for One® ½ Less Fat | 1 pizza | 400 | 110 |
| Supreme, Totino's® | 1 pizza | 290 | 150 |
| Three Meat, Jeno's® Crisp 'n Tasty® | 1 pizza | 500 | 230 |
| Zesty Mexican Style, Totino's® | 1 pizza | 280 | 140 |

### Hamburger Pizza, single-serving
| | | | |
|---|---|---|---|
| Hamburger, Jeno's® Crisp 'N Tasty® | 1 pizza | 480 | 210 |

### Pepperoni Pizza, single-serving
| | | | |
|---|---|---|---|
| Cheese and Pepperoni, Tombstone for One® | 1 pizza | 580 | 320 |
| ❶ Pepperoni, Healthy Choice® French Bread Pizza | 1 pizza | 360 | 80 |
| Pepperoni, Jeno's® | 1 pizza | 280 | 140 |
| Pepperoni, Jeno's® Crisp 'n Tasty® | 1 pizza | 500 | 230 |
| Pepperoni, Michelina's® Krisp 'n Flaky™ Crust | 1 pizza | 440 | 220 |
| Pepperoni, Pappalo's® | 1 pizza | 570 | 240 |
| Pepperoni, Pappalo's® Deep Dish | 1 pizza | 600 | 230 |
| Pepperoni, Pepperidge Farm® Croissant Crust Pizza | 1 pizza | 420 | 200 |
| Pepperoni, Stouffer's® French Bread Pizza | 1 pizza | 420 | 180 |
| ❶ Pepperoni, Stouffer's® Lean Cuisine® French Bread Pizza | 1 pizza | 330 | 70 |
| Pepperoni, Tombstone for One® ½ Less Fat | 1 pizza | 400 | 120 |

❶  Meets Low-Fat Guidelines

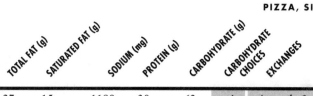

| TOTAL FAT (g) | SATURATED FAT (g) | SODIUM (mg) | PROTEIN (g) | CARBOHYDRATE (g) | CARBOHYDRATE CHOICES | EXCHANGES |
|---|---|---|---|---|---|---|
| 27 | 15 | 1180 | 30 | 62 | 4 | 4 starch, 3 meat, 2 fat |
| 25 | 7 | 1130 | 22 | 45 | 3 | 3 starch, 2 meat, 2 fat |
| 37 | 15 | 1200 | 25 | 40 | 2½ | 2½ starch, 3 meat, 4 fat |
| 6 | 2 | 510 | 22 | 49 | 3 | 3 starch, 2 lean meat |
| 28 | 7 | 1120 | 17 | 49 | 3 | 3 starch, 2 meat, 3 fat |
| 24 | 9 | 740 | 13 | 42 | 3 | 3 starch, 1 meat, 3 fat |
| 27 | 16 | 1170 | 30 | 51 | 3½ | 3½ starch, 3 meat, 2 fat |
| 27 | 16 | 1230 | 30 | 62 | 4 | 4 starch, 3 meat, 2 fat |
| 34 | 14 | 1130 | 24 | 41 | 3 | 3 starch, 2 meat, 4 fat |
| 13 | 5 | 1090 | 27 | 45 | 3 | 3 starch, 3 lean meat |
| 17 | 4 | 680 | 10 | 25 | 1½ | 1½ starch, 1 meat, 2 fat |
| 26 | 6 | 1180 | 18 | 48 | 3 | 3 starch, 2 meat, 2½ fat |
| 16 | 4 | 560 | 10 | 25 | 1½ | 1½ starch, 1 meat, 2 fat |
| 23 | 5 | 1100 | 19 | 49 | 3 | 3 starch, 2 meat, 2 fat |
| 35 | 15 | 1170 | 25 | 41 | 3 | 3 starch, 2 meat, 4 fat |
| 9 | 4 | 580 | 22 | 48 | 3 | 3 starch, 2 lean meat |
| 16 | 3.5 | 710 | 10 | 25 | 1½ | 1½ starch, 1 meat, 2 fat |
| 26 | 6 | 1170 | 17 | 49 | 3 | 3 starch, 2 meat, 2½ fat |
| 24 | 12 | 850 | 15 | 41 | 3 | 3 starch, 1 meat, 3 fat |
| 27 | 13 | 1280 | 30 | 52 | 3½ | 3½ starch, 3 meat, 2 fat |
| 26 | 12 | 1300 | 30 | 62 | 4 | 4 starch, 3 meat, 1 fat |
| 23 | 9 | 810 | 15 | 39 | 2½ | 2½ starch, 1 meat, 3 fat |
| 20 | 6 | 930 | 18 | 42 | 3 | 3 starch, 1 meat, 2 fat |
| 7 | 3 | 590 | 20 | 46 | 3 | 3 starch, 2 lean meat |
| 13 | 5 | 1040 | 26 | 45 | 3 | 3 starch, 2 meat |

1 Carbohydrate Choice = 1 starch or 1 fruit or 1 milk exchange

## PRODUCTS

| | SERVING SIZE | CALORIES | CALORIES FROM FAT |
|---|---|---|---|
| Pepperoni, Totino's® | 1 pizza | 280 | 140 |
| Pepperoni, Weight Watchers® | 1 entree | 390 | 100 |
| **Sausage Pizza, single-serving** | | | |
| Italian Sausage, Tombstone for One® | 1 pizza | 560 | 300 |
| ❶ Sausage, Healthy Choice® French Bread Pizza | 1 pizza | 330 | 35 |
| Sausage, Jeno's | 1 pizza | 280 | 140 |
| Sausage, Jeno's® Crisp 'n Tasty® | 1 pizza | 510 | 240 |
| Sausage, Michelina's® Krisp 'n Flaky™ Crust | 1 pizza | 410 | 180 |
| Sausage, Stouffer's® French Bread Pizza | 1 pizza | 420 | 180 |
| Sausage, Totino's® | 1 pizza | 280 | 140 |
| **Vegetable Pizza, single-serving** | | | |
| Vegetable, Tombstone for One® ½ Less Fat | 1 pizza | 360 | 90 |
| Vegetable Deluxe, Stouffer's® French Bread Pizza | 1 pizza | 400 | 150 |
| **PIZZA CRUST (REFRIGERATED)** | | | |
| ❶ Original Italian Bread Shell, Boboli® (8 oz) | ½ shell | 150 | 25 |
| ❶ Pizza Crust, Pillsbury® | ¼ crust | 180 | 25 |
| Pizza Crusts, Totino's® | ¼ crust | 180 | 60 |
| Thin Crust Italian Bread Shell, Boboli® (10 oz) | ⅕ shell | 160 | 30 |
| **PIZZA SAUCE** | | | |
| ❶ Pizza sauce, all brands (avg) | ¼ cup | 30–50 | 0–15 |
| **PIZZA SNACKS (FROZEN)** | | | |
| Cheese & Sausage, Bagel Bites® | 4 pieces | 200 | 60 |
| Combination, Totino's® Pizza Rolls® | 10 rolls | 370 | 150 |
| Extra Cheese, Bagel Bites® | 4 pieces | 190 | 50 |
| Hamburger & Cheese, Totino's® Pizza Rolls® | 10 rolls | 350 | 130 |
| Nacho Cheese & Beef, Totino's® Pizza Rolls® | 10 rolls | 340 | 140 |
| Pepperoni, Jack's® Pizza Bursts | 6 snacks | 260 | 130 |
| Pepperoni & Cheese, Totino's® Pizza Rolls® | 10 rolls | 360 | 150 |

❶  Meets Low-Fat Guidelines

| TOTAL FAT (g) | SATURATED FAT (g) | SODIUM (mg) | PROTEIN (g) | CARBOHYDRATE (g) | CARBOHYDRATE CHOICES | EXCHANGES |
|---|---|---|---|---|---|---|
| 16 | 3.5 | 710 | 10 | 25 | 1½ | 1½ starch, 1 meat, 2 fat |
| 12 | 4 | 650 | 23 | 48 | 3 | 3 starch, 2 meat |
| | | | | | | |
| 33 | 14 | 1130 | 25 | 40 | 2½ | 2½ starch, 3 meat, 3 fat |
| 4 | 1.5 | 470 | 20 | 52 | 3½ | 3½ starch, 1 very lean meat |
| 16 | 4 | 65 | 10 | 25 | 1½ | 1½ starch, 1 meat, 1 fat |
| 27 | 6 | 1070 | 17 | 49 | 3 | 3 starch, 2 meat, 3 fat |
| 20 | 10 | 820 | 16 | 43 | 3 | 3 starch, 1 meat, 3 fat |
| 20 | 5 | 900 | 19 | 41 | 3 | 3 starch, 1 meat, 2 fat |
| 16 | 4 | 650 | 10 | 25 | 1½ | 1½ starch, 1 meat, 2 fat |
| | | | | | | |
| 10 | 4 | 730 | 22 | 46 | 3 | 3 starch, 2 meat |
| 17 | 6 | 830 | 18 | 43 | 3 | 3 starch, 1 meat, 2 fat |
| | | | | | | |
| 3 | 1 | 290 | 7 | 25 | 1½ | 1½ starch |
| 2.5 | 0.5 | 390 | 6 | 33 | 2 | 2 starch |
| 7 | 1 | 190 | 4 | 25 | 1½ | 1½ starch, 1 fat |
| 3.5 | 1 | 290 | 7 | 24 | 1½ | 1½ starch |
| | | | | | | |
| 0–2 | 0 | 190–420 | 1 | 5 | 0 | 1 veg |
| | | | | | | |
| 7 | 2.5 | 520 | 9 | 26 | 2 | 2 starch, 1 fat |
| 17 | 5 | 410 | 15 | 38 | 2½ | 2½ starch, 1 meat, 2 fat |
| 6 | 2 | 510 | 10 | 25 | 1½ | 1½ starch, 1 meat |
| 14 | 4.5 | 570 | 15 | 40 | 2½ | 2½ starch, 1 meat, 1½ fat |
| 16 | 6 | 730 | 13 | 37 | 2½ | 2½ starch, 1 meat, 1½ fat |
| 14 | 5 | 550 | 9 | 24 | 1½ | 1½ starch, 1 meat, 1 fat |
| 17 | 5 | 580 | 15 | 37 | 2½ | 2½ starch, 1 meat, 2 fat |

1 Carbohydrate Choice = 1 starch or 1 fruit or 1 milk exchange

## PRODUCTS

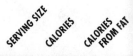

| PRODUCTS | SERVING SIZE | CALORIES | CALORIES FROM FAT |
|---|---|---|---|
| Sausage & Cheese, Totino's® Pizza Rolls® | 10 rolls | 350 | 140 |
| Sausage & Mushroom, Totino's® Pizza Rolls® | 10 rolls | 330 | 130 |
| Sausage & Pepperoni, Jack's® Pizza Bursts | 6 snacks | 240 | 110 |
| Spicy Italian Style, Totino's® Pizza Rolls® | 10 rolls | 370 | 160 |
| SuperCheese, Jack's® Pizza Bursts | 6 snacks | 250 | 120 |
| Supreme, Bagel Bites® | 4 pieces | 190 | 50 |
| Three Cheese, Totino's® Pizza Rolls® | 10 rolls | 360 | 140 |
| Three Meat, Totino's® Pizza Rolls® | 10 rolls | 340 | 140 |

### POCKET SANDWICHES (FROZEN)

#### Croissant Pockets™

| | SERVING SIZE | CALORIES | CALORIES FROM FAT |
|---|---|---|---|
| Chicken, Broccoli & Cheddar | 1 sandwich | 300 | 90 |
| Ham & Cheddar | 1 sandwich | 360 | 160 |
| Pepperoni Pizza | 1 sandwich | 350 | 140 |

#### Healthy Choice™ Hearty Handfuls

| | SERVING SIZE | CALORIES | CALORIES FROM FAT |
|---|---|---|---|
| ❶ Chicken & Broccoli | 1 sandwich | 320 | 50 |
| ❶ Chicken & Mushroom | 1 sandwich | 300 | 35 |
| ❶ Garlic Chicken | 1 sandwich | 330 | 45 |
| ❶ Philly Beef Steak | 1 sandwich | 290 | 45 |
| ❶ Roast Beef | 1 sandwich | 310 | 45 |
| ❶ Turkey & Vegetables | 1 sandwich | 310 | 35 |

#### Hot Pockets™

| | SERVING SIZE | CALORIES | CALORIES FROM FAT |
|---|---|---|---|
| Barbecue | 1 sandwich | 340 | 110 |
| Beef & Cheddar | 1 sandwich | 360 | 160 |
| Beef Fajita | 1 sandwich | 360 | 150 |
| Chicken & Cheddar with Broccoli | 1 sandwich | 300 | 100 |
| Ham & Cheese | 1 sandwich | 340 | 130 |
| Pepperoni & Sausage Pizza | 1 sandwich | 340 | 150 |
| Pepperoni Pizza | 1 sandwich | 350 | 150 |
| Turkey & Ham with Cheese | 1 sandwich | 320 | 110 |

❶  Meets Low-Fat Guidelines

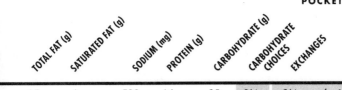

| TOTAL FAT (g) | SATURATED FAT (g) | SODIUM (mg) | PROTEIN (g) | CARBOHYDRATE (g) | CARBOHYDRATE CHOICES | EXCHANGES |
|---|---|---|---|---|---|---|
| 15 | 4 | 580 | 14 | 39 | 2½ | 2½ starch, 1 meat, 2 fat |
| 14 | 4 | 570 | 13 | 38 | 2½ | 2½ starch, 1 meat, 1½ fat |
| 12 | 4 | 500 | 8 | 26 | 2 | 2 starch, 1 meat, 1 fat |
| 18 | 5 | 370 | 15 | 37 | 2½ | 2½ starch, 1 meat, 2 fat |
| 13 | 6 | 500 | 10 | 24 | 1½ | 1½ starch, 1 meat, 1 fat |
| 6 | 2.5 | 560 | 9 | 26 | 2 | 2 starch, 1 meat |
| 15 | 6 | 610 | 15 | 42 | 3 | 3 starch, 1 meat, 1 fat |
| 15 | 4.5 | 630 | 15 | 37 | 2½ | 2½ starch, 1 meat, 1 fat |
| | | | | | | |
| 11 | 3.5 | 640 | 14 | 37 | 2½ | 2½ starch, 1 meat, 1 fat |
| 17 | 7 | 710 | 13 | 39 | 2½ | 2½ starch, 1 meat, 2 fat |
| 15 | 4.5 | 870 | 16 | 39 | 2½ | 2½ starch, 1 meat, 2 fat |
| | | | | | | |
| 5 | 1.5 | 580 | 17 | 51 | 3½ | 3½ starch, 1 lean meat |
| 4 | 1.5 | 560 | 17 | 49 | 3 | 3 starch, 1 lean meat |
| 5 | 1.5 | 600 | 20 | 53 | 3½ | 3½ starch 1 lean meat |
| 5 | 1.5 | 550 | 15 | 47 | 3 | 3 starch, 1 lean meat |
| 4.5 | 1.5 | 550 | 14 | 52 | 3½ | 3½ starch, 1 very lean meat |
| 4.5 | 1.5 | 560 | 18 | 51 | 3½ | 3½ starch, 1 very lean meat |
| | | | | | | |
| 12 | 5 | 850 | 13 | 45 | 3 | 3 starch, 1 meat, 1 fat |
| 18 | 9 | 830 | 14 | 36 | 2½ | 2½ starch, 1 meat, 1 fat |
| 17 | 8 | 780 | 14 | 39 | 2½ | 2½ starch, 1 meat, 2 fat |
| 12 | 5 | 620 | 12 | 37 | 2½ | 2½ starch, 1 meat, 1 fat |
| 15 | 7 | 840 | 14 | 37 | 2½ | 2½ starch, 1 meat, 1 fat |
| 16 | 6 | 630 | 12 | 38 | 2½ | 2½ starch, 1 meat, 1 fat |
| 17 | 8 | 780 | 13 | 38 | 2½ | 2½ starch, 1 meat, 2 fat |
| 13 | 6 | 680 | 14 | 38 | 2½ | 2½ starch, 1 meat, 1 fat |

1 Carbohydrate Choice = 1 starch or 1 fruit or 1 milk exchange

## PRODUCTS

| | SERVING SIZE | CALORIES | CALORIES FROM FAT |
|---|---|---|---|
| **Ken & Robert's® Veggie Pockets** | | | |
| ❶ All varieties (avg) | 1 pocket | 250 | 80 |
| **Lean Pockets™** | | | |
| ❶ Beef & Broccoli | 1 sandwich | 250 | 60 |
| ❶ Chicken Fajita | 1 sandwich | 260 | 70 |
| ❶ Chicken Parmesan | 1 sandwich | 260 | 80 |
| ❶ Glazed Chicken Supreme | 1 sandwich | 240 | 60 |
| ❶ Pizza Deluxe | 1 sandwich | 270 | 70 |
| ❶ Turkey & Ham with Cheddar | 1 sandwich | 260 | 70 |
| ❶ Turkey, Broccoli & Cheese | 1 sandwich | 260 | 70 |
| **Pepperidge Farm® Pocket Sandwiches** | | | |
| Broccoli-with-Cheese Vegetables in Pastry | 1 pastry | 240 | 120 |
| **Red Baron® Pocket Sandwiches** | | | |
| Beef & Cheddar Deli Pouches™ | 1 piece | 310 | 120 |
| Chicken, Broccoli & Cheddar Pastry Pouches™ | 1 piece | 300 | 120 |
| Ham & Cheese Pastry Pouches™ | 1 piece | 320 | 130 |
| Sausage & Pepperoni Pastry Pouches™ | 1 piece | 350 | 160 |
| **Totino's Hearty Pockets™** | | | |
| Chicken Fajita Grande | 1 sandwich | 206 | 68 |
| Mega Meat | 1 sandwich | 251 | 104 |
| Packed with Pepperoni | 1 sandwich | 265 | 116 |
| Piled High Ham and Cheese | 1 sandwich | 237 | 95 |
| **Totino's Pizza Pops®** | | | |
| Italian Sausage® | 1 piece | 271 | 119 |
| Italian Sausage & Pepperoni | 1 piece | 280 | 134 |
| Pepperoni | 1 piece | 283 | 131 |
| Supreme | 1 piece | 265 | 118 |

❶  Meets Low-Fat Guidelines

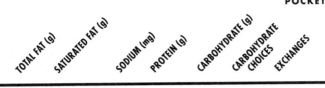

| TOTAL FAT (g) | SATURATED FAT (g) | SODIUM (mg) | PROTEIN (g) | CARBOHYDRATE (g) | CARBOHYDRATE CHOICES | EXCHANGES |
|---|---|---|---|---|---|---|
| 8 | 0.5 | 500 | 8 | 39 | 2½ | 2½ starch, 1 fat |
| 7 | 3 | 710 | 9 | 37 | 2½ | 2 starch, 1 veg, 1 meat |
| 8 | 3 | 770 | 12 | 36 | 2½ | 2½ starch, 1 meat |
| 8 | 3 | 630 | 12 | 34 | 2 | 2 starch, 1 meat, ½ fat |
| 7 | 2.5 | 600 | 10 | 34 | 2 | 2 starch, 1 meat |
| 8 | 3 | 680 | 12 | 37 | 2½ | 2½ starch, 1 meat |
| 7 | 3 | 810 | 15 | 35 | 2 | 2 starch, 2 lean meat |
| 8 | 3 | 710 | 12 | 35 | 2 | 2 starch, 1 veg, 1 meat |
| 14 | 4.5 | 430 | 6 | 24 | 1½ | 1½ starch, 3 fat |
| 14 | 4.5 | 860 | 14 | 33 | 2 | 2 starch, 1 meat, 1 fat |
| 13 | 3.5 | 780 | 12 | 33 | 2 | 2 starch, 1 meat, 1 fat |
| 15 | 5 | 980 | 14 | 33 | 2 | 2 starch, 1 meat, 1 fat |
| 18 | 6 | 850 | 14 | 33 | 2 | 2 starch, 1 meat, 2 fat |
| 7.5 | 2.9 | 705 | 8 | 26 | 2 | 2 starch, 1 meat |
| 11.6 | 4.6 | 551 | 10.8 | 26 | 2 | 2 starch, 1 meat, 1 fat |
| 12.9 | 5 | 556 | 11.3 | 26 | 2 | 2 starch, 1 meat, 1 fat |
| 10.5 | 4.6 | 761 | 10.9 | 25 | 1½ | 1½ starch, 1 meat, 1 fat |
| 13.2 | 5 | 598 | 11.4 | 27 | 2 | 2 starch, 1 meat, 1 fat |
| 14.9 | 4.9 | 600 | 11.3 | 25 | 1½ | 1½ starch, 1 meat, 2 fat |
| 14.5 | 5 | 703 | 11.8 | 26 | 2 | 2 starch, 1 meat, 1 fat |
| 13.2 | 4.2 | 598 | 10.1 | 27 | 2 | 2 starch, 1 meat, 1 fat |

1 Carbohydrate Choice = 1 starch *or* 1 fruit *or* 1 milk exchange

# PRODUCTS

| | SERVING SIZE | CALORIES | CALORIES FROM FAT |
|---|---|---|---|

## POPCORN (READY-TO-EAT)

### Butter Popcorn

| Product | Serving Size | Calories | Calories from Fat |
|---|---|---|---|
| Butter, Vic's Regular® | 2½ cups | 150 | 63 |
| ❶ Butter, Vic's Low-Fat® | 3 cups | 120 | 13.5 |
| ❶ Butter Flavor, Nature's Popcorn® | 1 cup | 70 | 27 |
| ❶ Butter Flavored, Smart Snackers® | 1 bag | 90 | 20 |
| Old Fashioned Butter, Cape Cod® | 3 cups | 170 | 90 |

### Caramel/Toffee Popcorn

| Product | Serving Size | Calories | Calories from Fat |
|---|---|---|---|
| ❶ Butter Toffee, Smart Snackers® | 1 bag | 110 | 25 |
| ❶ Caramel, Estee® | 1 cup | 120 | 15 |
| ❶ Caramel, Smart Snackers® | 1 bag | 100 | 10 |
| ❶ Caramel, Vic's Fat-Free® | 1 cup | 110 | 0 |
| ❶ Caramel, Vic's Lite® | 1 cup | 110 | 18 |
| Caramel, Vic's Regular® (8 oz) | ¾ cup | 130 | 36 |
| ❶ Caramel Corn Puffs, Health Valley Fat-Free® | 1⅓ cups | 110 | 0 |
| ❶ Caramel Corn with Peanuts, Old Dutch® | ⅔ cup | 128 | 30 |
| ❶ Carmel Puffcorn, Old Dutch® | 1 oz | 120 | 20 |

### Cheese Popcorn

| Product | Serving Size | Calories | Calories from Fat |
|---|---|---|---|
| White Cheddar, Cape Cod® | ⅔ cup | 170 | 110 |
| White Cheddar, Smart Snackers® | 1 bag | 90 | 35 |
| ❶ White Cheddar, Nature's Popcorn® | 1 cup | 80 | 27 |
| ❶ White Cheddar, Vic's Low-Fat® | 2½ cups | 110 | 22.5 |
| White Cheese, Vic's Lite® | 2½ cups | 130 | 54 |
| White Cheese, Vic's Regular® (8 oz) | 2 cups | 180 | 117 |
| Yellow Cheddar, Vic's Regular® (8 oz) | 1½ cups | 190 | 126 |
| Yellow Cheese, Vic's Lite® | 2½ cups | 140 | 63 |

❶   Meets Low-Fat Guidelines

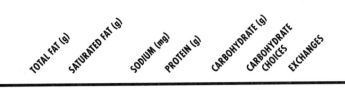

| TOTAL FAT (g) | SATURATED FAT (g) | SODIUM (mg) | PROTEIN (g) | CARBOHYDRATE (g) | CARBOHYDRATE CHOICES | EXCHANGES |
|---|---|---|---|---|---|---|
| 7 | 1 | 190 | 3 | 20 | 1 | 1 starch, 1 fat |
| 1.5 | 0 | 110 | 3 | 23 | 1½ | 1½ starch |
| 3 | 1 | 100 | 2 | 12 | 1 | 1 starch (3 cups = 2½ starch, 1 fat) |
| 2.5 | 1 | 100 | 2 | 14 | 1 | 1 starch |
| 10 | 3 | 220 | 3 | 18 | 1 | 1 starch, 2 fat |
| | | | | | | |
| 2.5 | 1 | 90 | 1 | 21 | 1½ | 1½ starch |
| 1.5 | 0 | 90 | <1 | 26 | 2 | 2 starch |
| 1 | 0 | 45 | 1 | 22 | 1½ | 1½ starch |
| 0 | 0 | 180 | 1 | 24 | 1½ | 1½ starch |
| 2 | 0.5 | 100 | 1 | 22 | 1½ | 1½ starch |
| 4 | 1 | 75 | <1 | 22 | 1½ | 1½ starch |
| 0 | 0 | 60 | 2 | 24 | 1½ | 1½ starch |
| 3 | 1 | 75 | 2 | 23 | 1½ | 1½ starch |
| 2.5 | 0.5 | 100 | 0 | 24 | 1½ | 1½ starch |
| | | | | | | |
| 12 | 2.5 | 270 | 4 | 13 | 1 | 1 starch, 2 fat (3 cups = 4 starch, 10 fat |
| 4 | 1 | 125 | 2 | 12 | 1 | 1 starch |
| 3 | 1 | 120 | 2 | 12 | 1 | 1 starch, ½ fat (3 cups = 2½ starch, 1 fat) |
| 2.5 | 1 | 260 | 4 | 19 | 1 | 1 starch |
| 6 | 1.5 | 200 | 4 | 15 | 1 | 1 starch, 1 fat |
| 13 | 3 | 270 | 3 | 13 | 1 | 1 starch, 2 fat |
| 14 | 4 | 190 | 4 | 10 | ½ | ½ starch, 3 fat (3 cups = 1 starch, 5 fat) |
| 7 | 1.5 | 200 | 4 | 15 | 1 | 1 starch, 1 fat |

1 Carbohydrate Choice = 1 starch *or* 1 fruit *or* 1 milk exchange

## PRODUCTS

| | SERVING SIZE | CALORIES | CALORIES FROM FAT |
|---|---|---|---|
| **Plain Popcorn** | | | |
| All Natural, Cape Cod® | ⅗ cup | 160 | 80 |
| ● White, Vic's Lite® ½ Salt | 2¾ cups | 130 | 27 |
| ● White, Vic's Low-Fat® | 3½ cups | 110 | 9 |
| White, Vic's Regular® | 2½ cups | 150 | 54 |
| White, Vic's Regular® ½ Salt | 2½ cups | 150 | 54 |
| ● White, Vic's Regular Lite® | 2¾ cups | 130 | 27 |
| **Other Popcorn Flavors** | | | |
| ● Sour Cream and Chives, Nature's Popcorn® | 1 cup | 70 | 27 |

### POPCORN, MICROWAVE (AS PREPARED)

| | SERVING SIZE | CALORIES | CALORIES FROM FAT |
|---|---|---|---|
| **Butter Popcorn, microwave** | | | |
| ● Butter, Jolly Time® Light | 1 cup | 20 | 5 |
| Butter, Pop Secret® | 4 cups | 150 | 90 |
| ● Butter, Pop Secret® 94% Fat Free | 6 cups | 110 | 15 |
| Butter, Pop Secret® Light | 6 cups | 130 | 45 |
| Butter, Pop Secret® Light Movie Theater® | 6 cups | 130 | 45 |
| Butter, Pop Secret® Movie Theater® | 4 cups | 150 | 90 |
| Butter Flavor, Act II® | ~⅓ bag | 170 | 100 |
| ● Butter Flavor, Act II® 96% Fat Free | ½ bag | 120 | 10 |
| Butter Flavor, Act II® Light | ½ bag | 130 | 45 |
| ● Butter Flavor, Healthy Choice® | ½ bag | 130 | 20 |
| Butter Flavor, Orville Redenbacher's® Gourmet | 4 cups | 170 | 110 |
| Butter Flavor, Orville Redenbacher's® Gourmet, No Salt Added | 4 cups | 180 | 110 |
| Butter Flavor, Orville Redenbacher's® Gourmet, Snack Size | 1 bag | 250 | 170 |
| Butter Flavor, Orville Redenbacher's® Light | 5½ cups | 120 | 50 |
| ● Butter Flavored, American's Best® | 1 cup | 20 | 0 |

● Meets Low-Fat Guidelines

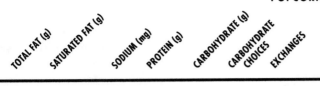

| TOTAL FAT (g) | SATURATED FAT (g) | SODIUM (mg) | PROTEIN (g) | CARBOHYDRATE (g) | CARBOHYDRATE CHOICES | EXCHANGES |
|---|---|---|---|---|---|---|
| 9 | 2 | 200 | 3 | 18 | 1 | 1 starch, 2 fat (3 cups = 6 starch, 8 fat) |
| 3 | 0.5 | 75 | 3 | 22 | 1½ | 1½ starch |
| 1 | 0 | 110 | 3 | 22 | 1½ | 1½ starch |
| 6 | 1 | 150 | 3 | 20 | 1 | 1 starch, 1 fat |
| 6 | 1 | 75 | 3 | 20 | 1 | 1 starch, 1 fat |
| 3 | 0.5 | 150 | 3 | 22 | 1½ | 1½ starch |
| 3 | 1 | 120 | 2 | 12 | 1 | 1 starch (3 cups = 2½ starch, 1 fat) |
| 1 | 0 | 25 | <1 | 4 | 0 | free (3 cups = 1 starch) |
| 10 | 2.5 | 210 | 3 | 16 | 1 | 1 starch, 2 fat |
| 2 | 0 | 230 | 4 | 23 | 1½ | 1½ starch |
| 5 | 1 | 190 | 3 | 20 | 1 | 1 starch, 1 fat |
| 5 | 1 | 250 | 3 | 20 | 1 | 1 starch, 1 fat |
| 10 | 2.5 | 230 | 2 | 16 | 1 | 1 starch, 2 fat |
| 11 | 2.5 | 400 | 3 | 19 | 1 | 1 starch, 2 fat |
| 1.5 | 0 | 550 | 4 | 26 | 2 | 2 starch |
| 5 | 1 | 400 | 3 | 24 | 1½ | 1½ starch, ½ fat |
| 2.5 | 0 | 340 | 4 | 27 | 2 | 2 starch |
| 13 | 2.5 | 390 | 2 | 15 | 1 | 1 starch, 2 fat |
| 12 | 2.5 | 5 | 2 | 19 | 1 | 1 starch, 2 fat |
| 19 | 4 | 570 | 3 | 22 | 1½ | 1½ starch, 3 fat |
| 6 | 1 | 360 | 3 | 20 | 1 | 1 starch, 1 fat |
| 0 | 0 | 10 | <1 | 5 | 0 | free (3 cups = 1 starch) |

1 Carbohydrate Choice = 1 starch or 1 fruit or 1 milk exchange

## PRODUCTS

| | SERVING SIZE | CALORIES | CALORIES FROM FAT |
|---|---|---|---|
| ❶ Butter Flavored, Jolly Time® | 1 cup | 35 | 15 |
| Butter Lover's®, Act II® | ~⅓ bag | 190 | 130 |
| Butter Lover's®, Act II® Light | ½ bag | 150 | 60 |
| ❶ Newman's Own® Old Style Picture Show Popcorn®, light varieties (avg) | 3½ cups | 110 | 30 |
| Newman's Own® Old Style Picture Show Popcorn®, regular varieties (avg) | 3½ cups | 170 | 100 |

### Cheese Popcorn, microwave

| | | | |
|---|---|---|---|
| ❶ Cheddar Cheese Flavored, Jolly Time® | 1 cup | 45 | 30 |
| Cheddar Cheese, Pop Secret® | 5 cups | 150 | 90 |
| Nacho Cheese, Pop Secret® | 5 cups | 150 | 90 |

### Natural Popcorn, microwave

| | | | |
|---|---|---|---|
| Natural, Act II® | ~ ⅓ bag | 180 | 110 |
| Natural, Act II® Light | ½ bag | 130 | 45 |
| ❶ Natural, Healthy Choice® | ½ bag | 130 | 20 |
| ❶ Natural, Jolly Time® Light | 1 cup | 25 | 10 |
| Natural, Pop Secret® | 4 cups | 150 | 90 |
| ❶ Natural, Pop Secret® 94% Fat Free | 6 cups | 110 | 15 |
| Natural, Pop Secret® Light | 6 cups | 130 | 45 |
| ❶ Natural Flavor, Jolly Time® | 1 cup | 40 | 20 |
| Natural Flavor, Orville Redenbacher's® Gourmet | 4 cups | 160 | 100 |
| Natural Flavor Light, Orville Redenbacher's® Gourmet | 5½ cups | 111 | 45 |

### Other Microwave Popcorn Varieties

| | | | |
|---|---|---|---|
| ❶ Popcorn, Healthy Choice® | 6 cups | 130 | 20 |
| ❶ Popcorn, Smart Snackers® | 1 bag | 100 | 10 |
| Redenbudder's Cheddar, Orville Redenbacher's® Gourmet | ⅓ bag | 170 | 120 |

❶  Meets Low-Fat Guidelines

| TOTAL FAT (g) | SATURATED FAT (g) | SODIUM (mg) | PROTEIN (g) | CARBOHYDRATE (g) | CARBOHYDRATE CHOICES | EXCHANGES |
|---|---|---|---|---|---|---|
| 2 | 0 | 40 | <1 | 4 | 0 | free (3 cups = 1 starch, 1 fat) |
| 14 | 3 | 530 | 3 | 17 | 1 | 1 starch, 3 fat |
| 7 | 1.5 | 550 | 4 | 24 | 1½ | 1½ starch, 1 fat |
| 3 | 1 | 90 | 2 | 20 | 1 | 1 starch, ½ fat |
| 11 | 2 | 180 | 2 | 16 | 1 | 1 starch, 2 fat |
| 3 | 0.5 | 45 | <1 | 4 | 0 | free (3 cups = 1 starch, 1½ fat) |
| 10 | 2.5 | 230 | 3 | 16 | 1 | 1 starch, 2 fat |
| 10 | 2.5 | 250 | 3 | 16 | 1 | 1 starch, 2 fat |
| 12 | 2.5 | 260 | 3 | 19 | 1 | 1 starch, 2 fat |
| 5 | 1 | 180 | 3 | 24 | 1½ | 1½ starch, ½ fat |
| 2.5 | 0 | 340 | 4 | 27 | 2 | 2 starch |
| 1 | 0 | 25 | <1 | 4 | 0 | free (3 cups = 1 starch) |
| 10 | 2.5 | 280 | 3 | 16 | 1 | 1 starch, 2 fat |
| 2 | 0 | 230 | 4 | 23 | 1½ | 1½ starch |
| 5 | 1 | 260 | 3 | 20 | 1 | 1 starch, 1 fat |
| 2.5 | .05 | 40 | <1 | 4 | 0 | free (3 cups = 1 starch, 1 fat) |
| 11 | 2.5 | 510 | 2 | 18 | 1 | 1 starch, 2 fat |
| 5 | 1 | 357 | 2.5 | 18 | 1 | 1 starch, 1 fat |
| 2.5 | 0 | 340 | 4 | 27 | 2 | 2 starch |
| 1 | 0 | 0 | 3 | 20 | 1 | 1 starch |
| 13 | 3 | 370 | 2 | 15 | 1 | 1 starch, 2 fat |

1 Carbohydrate Choice = 1 starch *or* 1 fruit *or* 1 milk exchange

## PRODUCTS

| | SERVING SIZE | CALORIES | CALORIES FROM FAT |
|---|---|---|---|
| Redenbudder's Movie Theater, Orville Redenbacher's® Gourmet | ⅓ bag | 180 | 120 |
| Redenbudder's Movie Theater Light, Orville Redenbacher's® Gourmet | ⅓ bag | 110 | 45 |
| ❶ Smart Pop, Orville Redenbacher's® Gourmet | 5 cups | 90 | 20 |

### POPCORN CAKES

| | SERVING SIZE | CALORIES | CALORIES FROM FAT |
|---|---|---|---|
| ❶ Apple Cinnamon (Mini), Orville Redenbacher's® | 11 cakes | 97 | 4.5 |
| ❶ Butter (Mini), Orville Redenbacher's® | 13 cakes | 99 | 18 |
| ❶ Butter, Orville Redenbacher's® | 3 cakes | 113 | 18 |
| ❶ Caramel (Mini), Orville Redenbacher's® | 11 cakes | 97 | 4.5 |
| ❶ Caramel, Orville Redenbacher's® | 2 cakes | 84 | 0 |
| ❶ Honey Nut (Mini), Orville Redenbacher's® | 11 cakes | 97 | 4.5 |
| ❶ Pop Secret® Popcorn Bars, all varieties (avg) | 1 bar | 70 | 10 |
| ❶ White Cheddar Cheese, Orville Redenbacher's® | 3 cakes | 111 | 18 |
| ❶ White Cheddar Cheese (Mini), Orville Redenbacher's® | 13 cakes | 98 | 13.5 |

### POPCORN OIL

| | SERVING SIZE | CALORIES | CALORIES FROM FAT |
|---|---|---|---|
| Popping and Topping Oil, Orville Redenbacher's® | 1 Tb | 120 | 120 |

### POPSICLES
see Ice Cream Treats/Fruit Pops

### POP-TARTS
see Toaster Pastries

### PORK MEALS/ENTREES (FROZEN)
see also Oriental Meals/Entrees

| | SERVING SIZE | CALORIES | CALORIES FROM FAT |
|---|---|---|---|
| Angel Hair Pasta with Sausage, Marie Callender's® | 1 cup | 370 | 140 |
| Ham and Asparagus Bake, Stouffer's® | 1 pkg | 520 | 320 |
| Italian Sausage & Peppers, Banquet® | 1 meal | 340 | 120 |
| Pork Cutlet Meal, Banquet® Country Menu | 1 meal | 410 | 210 |

❶　Meets Low-Fat Guidelines

| TOTAL FAT (g) | SATURATED FAT (g) | SODIUM (mg) | PROTEIN (g) | CARBOHYDRATE (g) | CARBOHYDRATE CHOICES | EXCHANGES |
|---|---|---|---|---|---|---|
| 13 | 3 | 500 | 2 | 16 | 1 | 1 starch, 2 fat |
| 5 | 1 | 320 | 3 | 19 | 1 | 1 starch, 1 fat |
| 3 | 0 | 280 | 3 | 20 | 1 | 1 starch |
| 0.5 | 0 | 4 | 2.5 | 26 | 2 | 2 starch |
| 2 | 0.5 | 170 | 3 | 23 | 1½ | 1½ starch |
| 2 | 0.5 | 192 | 3.5 | 26 | 2 | 2 starch |
| 0.5 | 0 | 34 | 2.5 | 26 | 2 | 2 starch |
| 0 | 0 | 29 | 2 | 23 | 1½ | 1½ starch |
| 0.5 | 0 | 30 | 2.5 | 26 | 2 | 2 starch |
| 1 | 0.5 | 55 | 0 | 16 | 1 | 1 starch |
| 2 | 0 | 111 | 4 | 26 | 2 | 2 starch |
| 1.5 | 0 | 98 | 3.5 | 23 | 1½ | 1½ starch |
| 13 | 2 | 0 | 0 | 0 | 0 | 3 fat |
| 15 | 4 | 630 | 14 | 43 | 3 | 3 starch, 1 meat, 1 fat |
| 36 | 14 | 1040 | 16 | 32 | 2 | 2 starch, 1 veg, 1 meat, 5 fat |
| 13 | 3.5 | 840 | 11 | 43 | 3 | 3 starch, 1 meat, 1 fat |
| 24 | 6 | 940 | 13 | 37 | 2½ | 2 starch, 1 veg, 1 meat, 3 fat |

1 Carbohydrate Choice = 1 starch or 1 fruit or 1 milk exchange

## PRODUCTS

| | SERVING SIZE | CALORIES | CALORIES FROM FAT |
|---|---|---|---|
| **POT PIES (FROZEN)** | | | |
| All-Meat Chicken, Tyson® | 1 pie | 600 | 350 |
| Beef, Banquet® | 1 pie | 330 | 140 |
| Beef, Stouffer's® | 1 pie | 450 | 240 |
| Beef, Swanson® | 1 pkg | 380 | 171 |
| Chicken, Banquet® | 1 pie | 350 | 160 |
| Chicken, Banquet®, Family Size | 1 cup | 480 | 260 |
| Chicken, Stouffer's® | 1 pkg | 560 | 320 |
| Chicken, Stouffer's®, 2-serving size | ½ pkg | 540 | 310 |
| ❶ Chicken, Stouffer's® Lean Cuisine® | 1 pkg | 320 | 90 |
| Chicken, Swanson® | 1 pkg | 390 | 198 |
| Chicken, Swanson® Hungry-Man® | 1 pkg | 650 | 306 |
| Chicken, Tyson® | 1 pie | 550 | 310 |
| Chicken, Marie Callender's® Multi Serves | 1 cup | 520 | 300 |
| Chicken Au Gratin, Marie Callender's® Multi Serves | 1 cup | 740 | 470 |
| Chicken Au Gratin, Marie Callender's® | 1 pie | 720 | 430 |
| Chicken, Broccoli & Cheese, Tyson® | 1 pie | 580 | 310 |
| Turkey, Banquet® | 1 pie | 370 | 180 |
| Turkey, Marie Callender's® | 1 pie | 710 | 420 |
| Turkey, Stouffer's® | 1 pkg | 530 | 300 |
| ❶ Turkey, Stouffer's® Lean Cuisine® | 1 pkg | 300 | 80 |
| Turkey, Swanson® | 1 pkg | 390 | 189 |
| Turkey, Swanson® Hungry-Man® | 1 pkg | 650 | 306 |
| Turkey, Tyson® | 1 pie | 550 | 300 |
| Vegetable Cheese, Banquet® | 1 pie | 390 | 160 |
| Vegetable with Beef, Morton® | 1 pie | 310 | 150 |
| Vegetable with Chicken, Morton® | 1 pie | 320 | 160 |
| Vegetable with Turkey, Morton® | 1 pie | 300 | 160 |

❶  Meets Low-Fat Guidelines

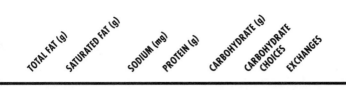

| TOTAL FAT (g) | SATURATED FAT (g) | SODIUM (mg) | PROTEIN (g) | CARBOHYDRATE (g) | CARBOHYDRATE CHOICES | EXCHANGES |
|---|---|---|---|---|---|---|
| 39 | 8 | 790 | 16 | 48 | 3 | 3 starch, 1 meat, 6 fat |
| 15 | 7 | 1000 | 9 | 38 | 2½ | 2½ starch, 1 veg, 1 meat, 1 fat |
| 26 | 9 | 1140 | 19 | 36 | 2½ | 2 starch, 1 veg, 2 meat, 3 fat |
| 19 | NA | NA | 12 | 39 | 2½ | 2 starch, 1 veg, 1 meat, 2 fat |
| 18 | 7 | 950 | 10 | 36 | 2½ | 2 starch, 1 veg, 1 meat, 2 fat |
| 29 | 11 | 1010 | 14 | 39 | 2½ | 2 starch, 1 veg, 1 meat, 4 fat |
| 36 | 10 | 1050 | 20 | 40 | 2½ | 2 starch, 1 veg, 2 meat, 5 fat |
| 35 | 10 | 950 | 16 | 40 | 2½ | 2 starch, 1 veg, 2 meat, 5 fat |
| 10 | 2.5 | 590 | 18 | 39 | 2½ | 2 starch, 1 veg, 2 meat |
| 22 | NA | NA | 9 | 40 | 2½ | 2 starch, 1 veg, 1 meat, 3 fat |
| 34 | NA | NA | 19 | 64 | 4 | 4 starch, 1 veg, 1 meat, 5 fat |
| 35 | 8 | 740 | 15 | 46 | 3 | 3 starch, 1 veg, 1 meat, 5 fat |
| 34 | 7 | 700 | 13 | 41 | 3 | 2½ starch, 1 veg, 1 meat, 5 fat |
| 53 | 14 | 610 | 21 | 46 | 3 | 2½ starch, 1 veg, 2 meat, 8 fat |
| 48 | 13 | 1040 | 19 | 53 | 3½ | 3 starch, 1 veg, 1 meat, 8 fat |
| 35 | 9 | 1150 | 18 | 48 | 3 | 3 starch, 1 veg, 1 meat, 5 fat |
| 20 | 8 | 850 | 10 | 38 | 2½ | 2 starch, 1 veg, 1 meat, 3 fat |
| 46 | 10 | 770 | 17 | 57 | 4 | 3½ starch, 1 veg, 1 meat, 7 fat |
| 33 | 9 | 1040 | 21 | 36 | 2½ | 2 starch, 1 veg, 2 meat, 4 fat |
| 9 | 2 | 590 | 20 | 34 | 2 | 2 starch, 1 veg, 2 lean meat |
| 21 | NA | NA | 10 | 40 | 2½ | 2 starch, 1 veg, 1 meat, 3 fat |
| 34 | NA | NA | 21 | 65 | 4 | 4 starch, 1 veg, 1 meat, 5 fat |
| 33 | 8 | 780 | 15 | 49 | 3 | 3 starch, 1 veg, 1 meat, 5 fat |
| 18 | 8 | 1000 | 8 | 49 | 3 | 3 starch, 1 veg, 3 fat |
| 17 | 8 | 1380 | 7 | 34 | 2 | 2 starch, 1 veg, 3 fat |
| 18 | 7 | 1020 | 8 | 32 | 2 | 2 starch, 1 veg, 3 fat |
| 18 | 9 | 1060 | 8 | 29 | 2 | 1½ starch, 1 veg, 3 fat |

1 Carbohydrate Choice = 1 starch *or* 1 fruit *or* 1 milk exchange

## PRODUCTS

| | SERVING SIZE | CALORIES | CALORIES FROM FAT |
|---|---|---|---|
| Vegetarian Beef, Worthington® | 1 pie | 410 | 210 |
| Vegetarian Chicken, Worthington® | 1 pie | 450 | 240 |
| Yankee, Marie Callender's®, Multi Serves | 1 cup | 640 | 350 |
| Yankee, Marie Callender's® | 1 pie | 690 | 400 |

### POTATO CHIPS
*see* Chips, potato

### POTATO SIDE DISHES (DRY, AS PREPARED)

| | | SERVING SIZE | CALORIES | CALORIES FROM FAT |
|---|---|---|---|---|
| ❶ | Au Gratin, Betty Crocker®, all size boxes (avg) | ½ cup | 130 | 30 |
| ❶ | Au Gratin, Idahoan® | ⅓ cup | 110 | 10 |
| ❶ | Broccoli Au Gratin, Betty Crocker® | ½ cup | 110 | 25 |
| ❶ | Cheddar & Bac'Os®, Betty Crocker® | ½ cup | 120 | 25 |
| ❶ | Cheddar & Sour Cream, Betty Crocker® | ½ cup | 130 | 25 |
| | Cheddar and Bacon Twice Baked, Betty Crocker® | ⅔ cup | 210 | 100 |
| ❶ | Cheddar Cheese, Betty Crocker® | ½ cup | 120 | 20 |
| | Cheddar Cheese Potato Buds®, Betty Crocker® | ⅔ cup | 190 | 90 |
| ❶ | Cheesy Scalloped, Betty Crocker® | ½ cup | 120 | 25 |
| ❶ | Creamy Ranch Potatoes with Sour Cream & Chives, Idahoan® | ¼ cup | 110 | 20 |
| | Hash Brown, Betty Crocker® | ½ cup | 200 | 70 |
| | Garlic, Potato Shakers® | ⅔ cup | 130 | 35 |
| ❶ | Julienne, Betty Crocker® | ½ cup | 110 | 25 |
| ❶ | Mashed, Idaohan® Complete | ⅓ cup | 100 | 15 |
| ❶ | Mashed, Idahoan® Real One Step | ⅓ cup | 80 | 10 |
| ❶ | Mashed, Natural Butter Flavor, Ore-Ida® | ~⅔ cup | 80 | 18 |
| | Original, Potato Shakers® | ⅔ cup | 140 | 35 |
| | Potato Buds® Betty Crocker® | ⅔ cup | 160 | 70 |
| ❶ | Ranch, Betty Crocker® | ½ cup | 130 | 20 |
| ❶ | Scalloped Potatoes 'n Ham, Betty Crocker® | ½ cup | 120 | 25 |
| ❶ | Scalloped, Betty Crocker®, all size boxes (avg) | ½ cup | 130 | 30 |

❶  Meets Low-Fat Guidelines

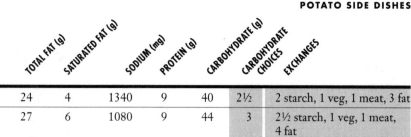

| TOTAL FAT (g) | SATURATED FAT (g) | SODIUM (mg) | PROTEIN (g) | CARBOHYDRATE (g) | CARBOHYDRATE CHOICES | EXCHANGES |
|---|---|---|---|---|---|---|
| 24 | 4 | 1340 | 9 | 40 | 2½ | 2 starch, 1 veg, 1 meat, 3 fat |
| 27 | 6 | 1080 | 9 | 44 | 3 | 2½ starch, 1 veg, 1 meat, 4 fat |
| 39 | 8 | 950 | 19 | 53 | 3½ | 3 starch, 1 veg, 2 meat, 5 fat |
| 44 | 10 | 1390 | 16 | 57 | 4 | 3½ starch, 1 veg, 1 meat, 7 fat |
| | | | | | | |
| 3 | 1 | 580 | 3 | 22 | 1½ | 1½ starch |
| 1.5 | 0.5 | 600 | 2 | 23 | 1½ | 1½ starch |
| 2.5 | 0.5 | 510 | 3 | 21 | 1½ | 1½ starch |
| 3 | 1 | 630 | 3 | 21 | 1½ | 1½ starch |
| 3 | 1 | 580 | 3 | 25 | 1½ | 1½ starch |
| 11 | 3 | 610 | 6 | 22 | 1½ | 1½ starch, 2 fat |
| | | | | | | |
| 2.5 | 1 | 600 | 3 | 21 | 1½ | 1½ starch |
| 10 | 2 | 580 | 3 | 23 | 1½ | 1½ starch, 2 fat |
| 3 | 1 | 520 | 3 | 20 | 1 | 1 starch, ½ fat |
| 2 | 1.5 | 390 | 2 | 19 | 1 | 1 starch |
| | | | | | | |
| 8 | 1.5 | 590 | 3 | 31 | 2 | 2 starch, 1 fat |
| 4 | 0.5 | 460 | 3 | 23 | 1½ | 1½ starch, ½ fat |
| 2.5 | 1 | 600 | 3 | 20 | 1 | 1 starch, ½ fat |
| 2 | 0.5 | 310 | 2 | 19 | 1 | 1 starch |
| 1 | 0 | 270 | 2 | 17 | 1 | 1 starch |
| 2 | NA | NA | 2 | 14 | 1 | 1 starch |
| 4 | 0.5 | 560 | 3 | 23 | 1½ | 1½ starch, ½ fat |
| 8 | 1.5 | 460 | 3 | 19 | 1 | 1 starch, 1 fat |
| 2.5 | 1 | 600 | 3 | 25 | 1½ | 1½ starch |
| 3 | 1 | 540 | 3 | 21 | 1½ | 1½ starch |
| 3 | 1 | 600 | 3 | 23 | 1½ | 1½ starch |

1 Carbohydrate Choice = 1 starch or 1 fruit or 1 milk exchange

## PRODUCTS

| PRODUCTS | SERVING SIZE | CALORIES | CALORIES FROM FAT |
|---|---|---|---|
| ❶ Scalloped, Idahoan® | ⅓ cup | 110 | 15 |
| Seasoned Fries, Potato Shakers® | 7 fries | 120 | 40 |
| ❶ Smokey Cheddar, Betty Crocker® | ½ cup | 120 | 20 |
| ❶ Sour Cream 'n Chive, Betty Crocker® | ½ cup | 120 | 25 |
| Sour Cream 'n Chive Potato Buds®, Betty Crocker® | ⅔ cup | 190 | 100 |
| ❶ Three Cheese, Betty Crocker® | ½ cup | 120 | 25 |
| ❶ Western Style, Idahoan® | ¼ cup | 100 | 5 |
| ❶ White Cheddar, Betty Crocker® | ½ cup | 120 | 25 |
| Zesty Cheddar, Potato Shakers® | ⅔ cup | 140 | 45 |

### POTATO SIDE DISHES (FROZEN)
see also French Fries, Hash Browns/Home Fries

| | SERVING SIZE | CALORIES | CALORIES FROM FAT |
|---|---|---|---|
| Bacon Artificial Flavor Tater Tots®, Ore-Ida® | ~9 pieces | 150 | 63 |
| Broccoli and Cheese Topped Baked Potato, Ore-Ida® | ½ baker (½ pkg) | 150 | 36 |
| Butter Flavor Twice Baked Potato, Ore-Ida® | 1 piece (½ pkg) | 200 | 81 |
| Cheddar Cheese Twice Baked Potato, Ore-Ida® | 1 piece (½ pkg) | 190 | 72 |
| Hot Tots™, Ore-Ida® | 84 g | 150 | 63 |
| Microwave Tater Tots®, Ore-Ida® | 1 pkg | 105 | 90 |
| Onion Tater Tots®, Ore-Ida® | 9 pieces | 150 | 63 |
| Potatoes au Gratin, Stouffer's® | ½ cup | 130 | 60 |
| Ranch Flavor Twice Baked Potato, Ore-Ida® | 1 piece (½ pkg) | 180 | 54 |
| Salsa and Cheese Topped Baked Potato, Ore-Ida® | 1 piece (½ pkg) | 160 | 40.5 |
| Scalloped Potatoes, Stouffer's® | ½ cup | 140 | 50 |
| Sour Cream & Chives Twice Baked Potato, Ore-Ida® | 1 piece (½ pkg) | 180 | 54 |
| Tater Tots®, Ore-Ida® | 9 pieces | 160 | 72 |

❶   Meets Low-Fat Guidelines

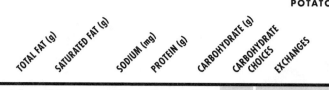

| TOTAL FAT (g) | SATURATED FAT (g) | SODIUM (mg) | PROTEIN (g) | CARBOHYDRATE (g) | CARBOHYDRATE CHOICES | EXCHANGES |
|---|---|---|---|---|---|---|
| 1.5 | 0.5 | 430 | 2 | 23 | 1½ | 1½ starch |
| 4 | 0.5 | 420 | 2 | 20 | 1 | 1 starch, ½ fat |
| 2.5 | 1 | 570 | 3 | 22 | 1½ | 1½ starch |
| 3 | 1 | 530 | 3 | 22 | 1½ | 1½ starch |
| 11 | 2.5 | 560 | 3 | 23 | 1½ | 1½ starch, 2 fat |
| 2.5 | 1 | 580 | 3 | 23 | 1½ | 1½ starch |
| 1 | 0 | 380 | 2 | 20 | 1 | 1 starch |
| 3 | 1 | 540 | 3 | 22 | 1½ | 1½ starch |
| 5 | 1 | 590 | 3 | 22 | 1½ | 1½ starch, ½ fat |
| 7 | NA | NA | 2 | 20 | 1 | 1 starch, 1 fat |
| 4 | NA | NA | 5 | 24 | 1½ | 1½ starch, ½ fat |
| 9 | NA | NA | 4 | 27 | 2 | 2 starch, 1 fat |
| 8 | NA | NA | 4 | 27 | 2 | 2 starch, 1 fat |
| 7 | NA | NA | 2 | 21 | 1½ | 1½ starch, 1 fat |
| 10 | NA | NA | 2 | 26 | 2 | 2 starch, 2 fat |
| 7 | NA | NA | 2 | 20 | 1 | 1 starch, 1 fat |
| 6 | 2.5 | 590 | 4 | 15 | 1 | 1 starch, 1 fat |
| 6 | NA | NA | 5 | 27 | 2 | 2 starch, 1 fat |
| 4.5 | NA | NA | 5 | 25 | 1½ | 1½ starch, ½ fat |
| 6 | 1 | 450 | 4 | 17 | 1 | 1 starch, 1 fat |
| 6 | NA | NA | 4 | 28 | 2 | 2 starch, 1 fat |
| 8 | NA | NA | 2 | 21 | 1½ | 1½ starch, 1 fat |

1 Carbohydrate Choice = 1 starch or 1 fruit or 1 milk exchange

## PRODUCTS

| | SERVING SIZE | CALORIES | CALORIES FROM FAT |
|---|---|---|---|
| **POTATO SIDE DISHES (REFRIGERATED)** | | | |
| Country Mashed Potatoes with Skins & Butter, Simply Potatoes® | ⅔ cup | 140 | 45 |
| ❶ Mashed Potatoes, Simply Potatoes® | ⅔ cup | 110 | 20 |
| **PRETZELS** | | | |
| ***Eagle® Pretzels*** | | | |
| ❶ Mini Bites, Low in Fat | ¾ cup | 110 | 10 |
| ❶ Sourdough Bavarian, No Fat | 2 pretzels | 110 | 0 |
| ❶ Sourdough Bavarian, No Salt Added No Fat | 2 pretzels | 110 | 0 |
| ❶ Sticks, Low in Fat | 46 sticks | 110 | 10 |
| ❶ Thin Twists, Low in Fat | 10 pretzels | 110 | 10 |
| ❶ Thin Twists, No Fat | 10 pretzels | 100 | 0 |
| ***Estee® Pretzels*** | | | |
| ❶ Nuggets | 30 pretzels | 120 | 10 |
| ❶ Ranch Nuggets | 23 pretzels | 130 | 20 |
| ❶ Unsalted | 23 pretzels | 120 | 10 |
| ❶ Unsalted Dutch | 2 pretzels | 130 | 10 |
| ***Keebler® Pretzels*** | | | |
| ❶ Butter Braids® | 22 pretzels | 100 | 10 |
| ❶ Butter Knots® | 7 pretzels | 100 | 10 |
| ❶ Mini Butter Knots® | 18 pretzels | 100 | 10 |
| ❶ Traditional Bavarian | 1 pretzel | 120 | 15 |
| ❶ Traditional Knots | 7 pretzels | 120 | 15 |
| ***Nabisco® Mister Salty® Pretzels*** | | | |
| ❶ Dutch | 2 pretzels | 120 | 10 |
| ❶ Mini | 22 pretzels | 110 | 10 |
| ❶ Sticks | 47 pretzels | 110 | 0 |
| ❶ Twists | 9 pretzels | 110 | 0 |

 Meets Low-Fat Guidelines

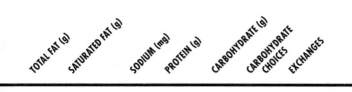

| TOTAL FAT (g) | SATURATED FAT (g) | SODIUM (mg) | PROTEIN (g) | CARBOHYDRATE (g) | CARBOHYDRATE CHOICES | EXCHANGES |
|---|---|---|---|---|---|---|
| 5 | 4 | 330 | 3 | 20 | 1 | 1 starch, 1 fat |
| 2 | 0 | 210 | 3 | 19 | 1 | 1 starch |
| 1 | 0 | 470 | 3 | 22 | 1½ | 1½ starch |
| 0 | 0 | 430 | 3 | 24 | 1½ | 1½ starch |
| 0 | 0 | 60 | 3 | 24 | 1½ | 1½ starch |
| 1 | 0 | 470 | 3 | 24 | 1½ | 1½ starch |
| 1 | 0 | 470 | 3 | 22 | 1½ | 1½ starch |
| 0 | 0 | 470 | 3 | 22 | 1½ | 1½ starch |
| 1.5 | 0 | 180 | 3 | 24 | 1½ | 1½ starch |
| 2 | 0.5 | 240 | 3 | 24 | 1½ | 1½ starch |
| 1 | 0 | 30 | 3 | 25 | 1½ | 1½ starch |
| 1 | 0 | 40 | 3 | 26 | 2 | 2 starch |
| 1 | 0 | 680 | 3 | 21 | 1½ | 1½ starch |
| 1 | 0 | 600 | 3 | 21 | 1½ | 1½ starch |
| 1 | 0 | 770 | 3 | 22 | 1½ | 1½ starch |
| 2 | 0.5 | 600 | 4 | 23 | 1½ | 1½ starch |
| 1 | 0 | 530 | 3 | 20 | 1 | 1 starch |
| 1 | 0 | 580 | 3 | 25 | 1½ | 1½ starch |
| 1 | 0 | 440 | 3 | 22 | 1½ | 1½ starch |
| 0 | 0 | 370 | 3 | 23 | 1½ | 1½ starch |
| 0 | 0 | 380 | 3 | 23 | 1½ | 1½ starch |

1 Carbohydrate Choice = 1 starch or 1 fruit or 1 milk exchange

## PRODUCTS

| | SERVING SIZE | CALORIES | CALORIES FROM FAT |
|---|---|---|---|
| **Old Dutch® Pretzels** | | | |
| Honey Mustard & Onion | ½ cup | 140 | 40 |
| ❶ Rods | 3 pieces | 130 | 15 |
| ❶ Sticks | 32 pieces | 110 | 15 |
| ❶ Thins | 13 pieces | 110 | 0 |
| ❶ Tiny Twist | 17 chips | 110 | 15 |
| ❶ Twists | 7 pieces | 110 | 10 |
| **Pepperidge Farm® Pretzels** | | | |
| ❶ Pretzel Snack Sticks | 9 sticks | 130 | 25 |
| ❶ Pretzel Tiny Goldfish Crackers | 45 pieces | 120 | 25 |
| **Rold Gold® Pretzels** | | | |
| ❶ Bavarian | 3 pretzels | 110 | 15 |
| ❶ Rods | 3 pretzels | 110 | 10 |
| ❶ Sourdough, Fat Free | 1 pretzel | 80 | 0 |
| ❶ Sticks | 48 pretzels | 110 | 10 |
| ❶ Sticks, Fat Free | 48 pretzels | 110 | 0 |
| ❶ Thin Twist | 10 pretzels | 110 | 10 |
| ❶ Thins, Fat Free Less Sodium | 10 pretzels | 110 | 0 |
| ❶ Tiny Twist | 18 pretzels | 110 | 10 |
| ❶ Tinys, Fat Free | 18 pretzels | 100 | 0 |
| **Other Pretzel Brands** | | | |
| ❶ Oat Bran Pretzel Nuggets, Smart Snackers® | 1 bag | 170 | 25 |
| ❶ Multigrain, Cape Cod® No Fat | 30 pretzels | 110 | 0 |
| ❶ Twists, Planters® | 1 oz | 100 | 5 |
| **PUDDING MIX (AS PREPARED)** | | | |
| ❶ Cook & Serve Pudding & Pie Filling, Jell-O®, all varieties (as prepared with 2% milk, avg) | ½ cup | 150 | 25 |
| ❶ Cook & Serve, Jell-O® Sugar Free Reduced Calorie, all varieties (as prepared with 2% milk, avg) | ½ cup | 85 | 25 |

❶ Meets Low-Fat Guidelines

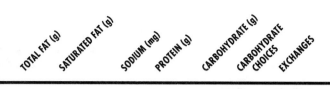

| TOTAL FAT (g) | SATURATED FAT (g) | SODIUM (mg) | PROTEIN (g) | CARBOHYDRATE (g) | CARBOHYDRATE CHOICES | EXCHANGES |
|---|---|---|---|---|---|---|
| 5 | 0.5 | 240 | 2 | 21 | 1½ | 1½ starch, ½ fat |
| 1.5 | 0 | 440 | 4 | 26 | 2 | 2 starch |
| 1.5 | 0 | 280 | 3 | 22 | 1½ | 1½ starch |
| 0 | 0 | 280 | 3 | 24 | 1½ | 1½ starch |
| 2 | 0 | 260 | 3 | 23 | 1½ | 1½ starch |
| 1.5 | 0 | 260 | 3 | 22 | 1½ | 1½ starch |
| 3 | 0 | 440 | 3 | 23 | 1½ | 1½ starch |
| 2.5 | 0.5 | 430 | 3 | 22 | 1½ | 1½ starch |
| 2 | 0.5 | 440 | 3 | 21 | 1½ | 1½ starch |
| 1.5 | 0.5 | 370 | 3 | 22 | 1½ | 1½ starch |
| 0 | 0 | 300 | 2 | 17 | 1 | 1 starch |
| 1 | 0 | 430 | 3 | 23 | 1½ | 1½ starch |
| 0 | 0 | 530 | 3 | 23 | 1½ | 1½ starch |
| 1 | 0 | 510 | 3 | 22 | 1½ | 1½ starch |
| 0 | 0 | 340 | 3 | 23 | 1½ | 1½ starch |
| 1 | 0 | 420 | 3 | 22 | 1½ | 1½ starch |
| 0 | 0 | 420 | 3 | 23 | 1½ | 1½ starch |
| 2.5 | 0 | 250 | 4 | 33 | 2 | 2 starch |
| 0 | 0 | 310 | 3 | 25 | 1½ | 1½ starch |
| 0.5 | 0 | 420 | 3 | 23 | 1½ | 1½ starch |
| 3 | 2 | 75–240 | 4 | 26 | 2 | 2 starch |
| 2.5 | 1.5 | 190–330 | 5 | 12 | 1 | 1 starch |

1 Carbohydrate Choice = 1 starch or 1 fruit or 1 milk exchange

## PRODUCTS

| | SERVING SIZE | CALORIES | CALORIES FROM FAT |
|---|---|---|---|
| ❶ Instant Pudding & Pie Filling, Jell-O®, all varieties (as prepared with 2% milk, avg) | ½ cup | 155 | 25 |
| ❶ Instant Pudding, Jell-O® Fat Free Sugar Free, all varieties (as prepared with skim milk, avg) | ½ cup | 75 | 0 |

### PUDDING SNACKS

| | | | |
|---|---|---|---|
| Pudding Snacks, Hunt's®, all varieties except lemon (avg) | 1 snack | 160 | 55 |
| ❶ Pudding Snacks, Hunt's®, lemon | 1 snack | 160 | 30 |
| ❶ Pudding Snacks, Hunt's® Fat Free, all varieties (avg) | 1 snack | 95 | 0 |
| Pudding Snacks, Jell-O®, all varieties (avg) | 1 snack | 165 | 45 |
| ❶ Pudding Snacks, Jell-O® Free, all varieties (avg) | 1 snack | 100 | 0 |
| Pudding Snacks, Swiss Miss®, all varieties (avg) | 1 snack | 165 | 55 |
| ❶ Pudding Snacks, Swiss Miss® Fat Free, all varieties (avg) | 1 snack | 100 | 0 |

### PUDDING, NON-DAIRY

| | | | |
|---|---|---|---|
| ❶ Pudding Snacks, Imagine®, all varieties (avg) | 1 pudding cup | 155 | 30 |

### QUICHE FILLING

| | | | |
|---|---|---|---|
| Broccoli & Cheddar, Pour a Quiche® | ⅙ carton | 180 | 130 |
| Ham, Pour a Quiche® | ⅙ carton | 190 | 130 |
| Three Cheese, Pour a Quiche® | ⅙ carton | 200 | 140 |

### RAMEN NOODLES
see Noodles

### RICE

| | | | |
|---|---|---|---|
| ❶ Boil-in-Bag Converted® Brand, Uncle Ben's® | 1 cup cooked | 170 | 0 |
| ❶ Boil-in-Bag, Minute® Rice | 1 cup cooked | 190 | 0 |
| ❶ Converted® Brand, Uncle Ben's® | 1 cup cooked | 170 | 0 |

❶   Meets Low-Fat Guidelines

| TOTAL FAT (g) | SATURATED FAT (g) | SODIUM (mg) | PROTEIN (g) | CARBOHYDRATE (g) | CARBOHYDRATE CHOICES | EXCHANGES |
|---|---|---|---|---|---|---|
| 3 | 2 | 320–470 | 4 | 30 | 2 | 2 starch |
| 0 | 0 | 395 | 5 | 13 | 1 | 1 starch |
| 6 | 2 | 124–211 | 2 | 24 | 1½ | 1½ starch |
| 3 | 1 | 100 | 0 | 33 | 2 | 2 starch |
| 0 | 0 | 167–212 | 2 | 21 | 1½ | 1½ starch |
| 5 | 1 | 175 | 3 | 26 | 2 | 2 starch, ½ fat |
| 0 | 0 | 190–240 | 3 | 23 | 1½ | 1½ starch |
| 6 | 2 | 160–195 | 3 | 25 | 1½ | 1½ starch, 1 fat |
| 0 | 0 | 160 | 2 | 22 | 1½ | 1½ starch |
| 3 | 0 | 50 | 1 | 33 | 2 | 2 starch |
| 14 | 8 | 270 | 10 | 4 | 0 | 1 meat, 2 fat |
| 15 | 11 | 330 | 12 | 4 | 0 | 2 meat, 1 fat |
| 16 | 12 | 310 | 13 | 4 | 0 | 2 meat, 1 fat |
| 0.5 | 0 | 15 | 4 | 40 | 2½ | 2½ starch |
| 0 | 0 | 10 | 4 | 42 | 3 | 3 starch |
| 0 | 0 | 0 | 4 | 38 | 2½ | 2½ starch |

1 Carbohydrate Choice = 1 starch or 1 fruit or 1 milk exchange

## PRODUCTS

| | | SERVING SIZE | CALORIES | CALORIES FROM FAT |
|---|---|---|---|---|
| ❶ | Fast Cook Converted® Brand, Uncle Ben's® | 1 cup cooked | 190 | 5 |
| ❶ | Instant Whole Grain Brown, Minute® Rice | ⅔ cup cooked | 170 | 15 |
| ❶ | Original, Minute® Rice | ¾ cup cooked | 170 | 0 |
| ❶ | Original Brown, Uncle Ben's® | 1 cup cooked | 170 | 10 |
| ❶ | Premium Long Grain, Minute® Rice | 1 cup cooked | 170 | 0 |

### RICE SIDE DISHES (DRY, AS PREPARED)

#### Beef Flavor Rice Side Dishes

| | | | | |
|---|---|---|---|---|
| | Beef, Lipton® Golden Sauté | 1 cup | 230 | 35 |
| | Beef, Rice-A-Roni® | 1 cup | 320 | 90 |
| | Beef, Rice-A-Roni® ⅓ less salt | 1 cup | 280 | 45 |
| | Beef & Mushroom, Rice-A-Roni® | 1 cup | 290 | 60 |
| ❶ | Beef Broccoli, Lipton® Rice & Sauce | 1 cup | 230 | 10 |

#### Cheese Rice Side Dishes

| | | | | |
|---|---|---|---|---|
| | Alfredo Broccoli, Lipton® Rice & Sauce | 1 cup | 250 | 40 |
| | Broccoli & White Cheddar, Uncle Ben's® Country Inn Recipes™ | 1 cup | 270 | 45 |
| | Broccoli Au Gratin, Rice-A-Roni® | 1 cup | 370 | 150 |
| | Broccoli Au Gratin, Rice-A-Roni® ⅓ less salt | 1 cup | 320 | 100 |
| | Broccoli Rice au Gratin, Uncle Ben's® Country Inn Recipes™ | 1 cup | 260 | 35 |
| ❶ | Cheddar Broccoli, Lipton® Rice & Sauce | 1 cup | 250 | 25 |
| | Herbed Rice au Gratin, Uncle Ben's® Country Inn Recipes™ | 1 cup | 260 | 30 |
| | White Cheddar & Herbs, Rice-A-Roni® | 1 cup | 340 | 120 |

#### Chicken Flavor Rice Side Dishes

| | | | | |
|---|---|---|---|---|
| ❶ | Chicken, Lipton® Rice & Sauce | 1 cup | 240 | 20 |
| | Chicken, Rice-A-Roni® | 1 cup | 310 | 80 |

❶ Meets Low-Fat Guidelines

| TOTAL FAT (g) | SATURATED FAT (g) | SODIUM (mg) | PROTEIN (g) | CARBOHYDRATE (g) | CARBOHYDRATE CHOICES | EXCHANGES |
|---|---|---|---|---|---|---|
| 0.5 | 0 | 15 | 3 | 43 | 3 | 3 starch |
| 1.5 | 0 | 10 | 4 | 34 | 2 | 2 starch |
| 0 | 0 | 10 | 3 | 36 | 2½ | 2½ starch |
| 1.5 | 0 | 0 | 4 | 37 | 2½ | 2½ starch |
| 0 | 0 | 10 | 3 | 36 | 2½ | 2½ starch |
| 4 | 1.5 | 930 | 6 | 43 | 3 | 3 starch |
| 9.5 | 1 | 1170 | 7 | 51 | 3½ | 3½ starch, 1 fat |
| 5 | 1 | 750 | 7 | 53 | 3½ | 3½ starch |
| 7 | 1.5 | 1210 | 7 | 51 | 3½ | 3½ starch, 1 fat |
| 1 | 0 | 940 | 6 | 46 | 3 | 3 starch |
| 4.5 | 2 | 860 | 7 | 44 | 3 | 3 starch |
| 5 | 3 | 580 | 8 | 48 | 3 | 3 starch, 1 fat |
| 17 | 4.5 | 890 | 8 | 47 | 3 | 3 starch, 3 fat |
| 11 | 3 | 590 | 8 | 49 | 3 | 3 starch, 2 fat |
| 4 | 2 | 740 | 8 | 49 | 3 | 3 starch |
| 3 | 1 | 940 | 6 | 48 | 3 | 3 starch |
| 3.5 | 1.5 | 770 | 7 | 51 | 3½ | 3½ starch |
| 14 | 4 | 980 | 7 | 49 | 3 | 3 starch, 2 fat |
| 2 | 0.5 | 900 | 7 | 48 | 3 | 3 starch |
| 9 | 2 | 1080 | 7 | 52 | 3½ | 3½ starch, 1 fat |

1 Carbohydrate Choice = 1 starch or 1 fruit or 1 milk exchange

| PRODUCTS | SERVING SIZE | CALORIES | CALORIES FROM FAT |
|---|---|---|---|
| Chicken, Rice-A-Roni® ⅓ less salt | 1 cup | 280 | 45 |
| Chicken & Broccoli, Rice-A-Roni® | 1 cup | 290 | 60 |
| Chicken & Broccoli, Uncle Ben's® Country Inn Recipes™ | 1 cup cooked | 270 | 60 |
| Chicken & Mushroom, Rice-A-Roni® | 1 cup | 360 | 120 |
| Chicken & Vegetables, Rice-A-Roni® | 1 cup | 290 | 60 |
| ❶ Chicken Broccoli, Lipton® Rice & Sauce | 1 cup | 250 | 20 |
| Chicken Broccoli Rice, Lipton® Golden Sauté | 1 cup | 260 | 40 |
| Chicken Flavored Rice, Lipton® Golden Sauté | 1 cup | 240 | 50 |
| Chicken Rice Pilaf, Knorr® | 1 cup | 260 | 60 |
| ❶ Chicken with Wild Rice, Uncle Ben's® Country Inn Recipes™ | 1 cup cooked | 200 | 10 |
| Creamy Chicken, Lipton® Rice & Sauce | 1 cup | 260 | 40 |
| Homestyle Chicken and Vegetable, Uncle Ben's® Country Inn Recipes™ | 1 cup cooked | 270 | 60 |

**Long Grain and Wild Rice Side Dishes**

| | | | |
|---|---|---|---|
| ❶ Creamy Mushroom and Wild Rice, Uncle Ben's® Country Inn Recipes™ | 1 cup cooked | 250 | 25 |
| ❶ Fast Cook Long Grain & Wild, Uncle Ben's® | 1 cup cooked | 200 | 10 |
| ❶ Long Grain & Wild Chicken Stock Sauce, Uncle Ben's® | ¾ cup cooked | 200 | 15 |
| ❶ Long Grain & Wild Garden Vegetable Blend, Uncle Ben's® | ¾ cup cooked | 200 | 15 |
| Long Grain & Wild Pilaf, Rice-A-Roni® | 1 cup | 240 | 50 |
| Long Grain & Wild Rice Chicken with Almonds, Rice-A-Roni® | 1 cup | 290 | 80 |
| ❶ Long Grain & Wild Rice Mix, Minute® | 1 cup cooked | 230 | 5 |
| Long Grain & Wild Rice Original, Rice-A-Roni® | 1 cup | 240 | 50 |
| ❶ Long Grain Mushroom, Lipton® Rice & Sauce | 1 cup | 250 | 10 |
| ❶ Natural Long Grain & Wild Original, Uncle Ben's® | 1 cup cooked | 190 | 5 |

 Meets Low-Fat Guidelines

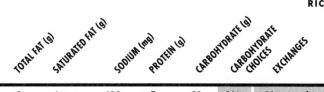

| TOTAL FAT (g) | SATURATED FAT (g) | SODIUM (mg) | PROTEIN (g) | CARBOHYDRATE (g) | CARBOHYDRATE CHOICES | EXCHANGES |
|---|---|---|---|---|---|---|
| 5 | 1 | 690 | 7 | 53 | 3½ | 3½ starch |
| 7 | 1.5 | 1410 | 7 | 51 | 3½ | 3½ starch, 1 fat |
| 7 | 3.5 | 580 | 8 | 47 | 3 | 3 starch, 1 fat |
| 14 | 2.5 | 1480 | 8 | 52 | 3½ | 3½ starch, 2 fat |
| 7 | 1.5 | 1470 | 6 | 52 | 3½ | 3½ starch, 1 fat |
| 2 | 1 | 940 | 6 | 48 | 3 | 3 starch |
| 4.5 | 1.5 | 800 | 8 | 47 | 3 | 3 starch |
| 5 | 2 | 920 | 6 | 44 | 3 | 3 starch |
| 7 | 1 | 1055 | 5 | 45 | 3 | 3 starch, 1 fat |
| 1 | 0 | 570 | 6 | 42 | 3 | 3 starch |
| 5 | 1 | 770 | 7 | 46 | 3 | 3 starch |
| 6 | 3 | 590 | 8 | 47 | 3 | 3 starch, 1 fat |
| 2.5 | 1.5 | 700 | 8 | 50 | 3 | 3 starch |
| 1 | 0 | 850 | 6 | 42 | 3 | 3 starch |
| 1.5 | 0 | 410 | 7 | 40 | 2½ | 2½ starch |
| 1.5 | 0 | 750 | 6 | 41 | 3 | 3 starch |
| 6 | 1.5 | 920 | 5 | 51 | 3½ | 3½ starch, ½ fat |
| 9 | 1.5 | 1240 | 7 | 51 | 3½ | 3½ starch, 1 fat |
| 0.5 | 0 | 960 | 6 | 50 | 3 | 3 starch |
| 6 | 1 | 1170 | 5 | 43 | 3 | 3 starch, ½ fat |
| 1.5 | 0.5 | 550 | 6 | 50 | 3 | 3 starch |
| .5 | 0 | 630 | 6 | 42 | 3 | 3 starch |

1 Carbohydrate Choice = 1 starch or 1 fruit or 1 milk exchange

| PRODUCTS | SERVING SIZE | CALORIES | CALORIES FROM FAT |
|---|---|---|---|
| ❶ Original Long Grain, Lipton® Rice & Sauce | 1 cup | 250 | 5 |
| White & Wild Rice, Green Giant® | 1 pkg | 250 | 45 |
| **Oriental Rice Side Dishes** | | | |
| ❶ Fried Rice, Lipton® Golden Sauté | 1 cup | 240 | 10 |
| Fried Rice, Rice-A-Roni® | 1 cup | 320 | 100 |
| Fried Rice, Rice-A-Roni® ⅓ less salt | 1 cup | 260 | 30 |
| Oriental, Lipton® Golden Sauté | 1 cup | 240 | 40 |
| ❶ Oriental, Lipton® Rice & Sauce | 1 cup | 230 | 10 |
| Oriental Stir Fry, Rice-A-Roni® | 1 cup | 290 | 60 |
| **Spanish Rice Side Dishes** | | | |
| Spanish Rice, Lipton® Golden Sauté | 1 cup | 250 | 40 |
| ❶ Spanish Rice, Lipton® Rice & Sauce | 1 cup | 230 | 5 |
| Spanish Rice, Rice-A-Roni® | 1 cup | 270 | 70 |
| ❶ Spanish Rice, Zapata® Low Fat | 1 cup | 240 | 25 |
| Spanish Rice Pilaf, Knorr® | 1 cup | 280 | 60 |
| **Other Rice Side Dish Flavors** | | | |
| ❶ Brown & Wild Mushroom Flavor, Uncle Ben's® | ⅔ cup cooked | 140 | 10 |
| ❶ Cajun, Lipton® Rice & Beans | 1 cup | 260 | 10 |
| ❶ Cajun, Lipton® Rice & Sauce | 1 cup | 230 | 10 |
| Herb & Butter, Lipton® Golden Sauté | 1 cup | 240 | 45 |
| Herb & Butter, Lipton® Rice & Sauce | 1 cup | 240 | 35 |
| Herb & Butter, Rice-A-Roni® | 1 cup | 310 | 80 |
| Lemon Herb with Jasmine Rice Pilaf, Knorr® | 1 cup | 320 | 70 |
| ❶ Medley, Lipton® Rice & Sauce | 1 cup | 240 | 15 |
| ❶ Mushroom, Lipton® Rice & Sauce | 1 cup | 220 | 10 |
| Onion Mushroom Rice, Lipton® Golden Sauté | 1 cup | 240 | 35 |
| ❶ Pilaf, Lipton® Rice & Sauce | 1 cup | 230 | 10 |
| Red Beans & Rice, Rice-A-Roni® | 1 cup | 280 | 60 |
| Rice Pilaf, Knorr® | 1 cup | 270 | 55 |

❶  Meets Low-Fat Guidelines

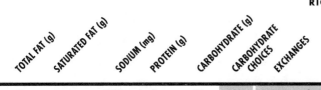

| TOTAL FAT (g) | SATURATED FAT (g) | SODIUM (mg) | PROTEIN (g) | CARBOHYDRATE (g) | CARBOHYDRATE CHOICES | EXCHANGES |
|---|---|---|---|---|---|---|
| 1 | 0 | 890 | 7 | 51 | 3½ | 3½ starch |
| 5 | 0.5 | 1000 | 6 | 45 | 3 | 3 starch |
| | | | | | | |
| 1 | 0 | 900 | 4 | 47 | 3 | 3 starch |
| 11 | 2 | 1590 | 6 | 52 | 3½ | 3½ starch, 1 fat |
| 3.5 | 0.5 | 930 | 6 | 52 | 3½ | 3½ starch |
| 4.5 | 1.5 | 910 | 6 | 43 | 3 | 3 starch |
| 1 | 0 | 750 | 6 | 46 | 3 | 3 starch |
| 6 | 1 | 1220 | 6 | 54 | 3½ | 3½ starch, ½ fat |
| | | | | | | |
| 4.5 | 1.5 | 910 | 6 | 46 | 3 | 3 starch |
| 1 | 0 | 940 | 6 | 47 | 3 | 3 starch |
| 8 | 1 | 1210 | 6 | 46 | 3 | 3 starch, 1 fat |
| 2.5 | 0.5 | 620 | 4 | 50 | 3 | 3 starch |
| 7 | 1 | 1175 | 5 | 50 | 3 | 3 starch, 1 fat |
| | | | | | | |
| 1 | 0 | 460 | 5 | 31 | 2 | 2 starch |
| | | | | | | |
| 1 | 0 | 540 | 10 | 53 | 3½ | 3½ starch |
| 1 | 0 | 930 | 6 | 49 | 3 | 3 starch |
| 5 | 2 | 870 | 6 | 42 | 3 | 3 starch |
| 4 | 2 | 920 | 5 | 43 | 3 | 3 starch |
| 9 | 1.5 | 1160 | 6 | 53 | 3½ | 3½ starch, 1 fat |
| 8 | 1.5 | 825 | 5 | 56 | 4 | 4 starch, 1 fat |
| 2 | 0.5 | 810 | 7 | 46 | 3 | 3 starch |
| 1 | 1 | 890 | 6 | 45 | 3 | 3 starch |
| 4 | 1.5 | 850 | 6 | 45 | 3 | 3 starch |
| 1 | 0 | 850 | 6 | 46 | 3 | 3 starch |
| 7 | 1 | 1200 | 8 | 51 | 3½ | 3½ starch, ½ fat |
| 6.5 | 1 | 955 | 5 | 47 | 3 | 3 starch, 1 fat |

1 Carbohydrate Choice = 1 starch or 1 fruit or 1 milk exchange

| PRODUCTS | SERVING SIZE | CALORIES | CALORIES FROM FAT |
|---|---|---|---|
| Rice Pilaf, Rice-A-Roni® | 1 cup | 310 | 80 |
| Savory Herb Rice, Lipton® Golden Sauté | 1 cup | 240 | 40 |
| ❶ Specialty Blends, Uncle Ben's®, all varieties (avg) | 1 cup cooked | 160 | 10 |
| Stroganoff, Rice-A-Roni® | 1 cup | 360 | 130 |
| ❶ Tomato & Herb, Uncle Ben's® Country Inn Recipes™ | 1 cup cooked | 240 | 10 |
| ❶ Vegetable Pilaf, Uncle Ben's® Country Inn Recipes™ | 1 cup cooked | 200 | 10 |

### RICE SIDE DISHES (FROZEN)

| | | | |
|---|---|---|---|
| ❶ Brown Rice with Pacific Vegetables, Norpac® | 1 cup | 70 | 5 |
| ❶ Oriental Style, Green Giant® International Mixtures | 8 oz | 180 | 5 |
| ❶ Orzo and Wild Rice with Vegetables, Norpac® | 1 cup | 90 | 0 |
| Rice & Broccoli, Green Giant® | 1 pkg | 320 | 110 |
| ❶ Rice Medley, Green Giant® | 1 pkg | 240 | 25 |
| ❶ Rice Pilaf, Green Giant® | 1 pkg | 230 | 25 |
| White & Wild Rice, Green Giant® | 1 pkg | 250 | 45 |

### RICOTTA CHEESE

| | | | |
|---|---|---|---|
| ❶ Ricotta, all light varieties (avg) | ¼ cup | 60 | 20 |
| Ricotta, all part-skim varieties (avg) | ¼ cup | 110 | 70 |
| Ricotta, all regular varieties (avg) | ¼ cup | 110 | 70 |

### RISOTTO (DRY, AS PREPARED)

| | | | |
|---|---|---|---|
| Broccoli au Gratin, Knorr® | 1 cup | 310 | 70 |
| ❶ Chicken, Lipton® Rice & Sauce | 1 cup | 230 | 20 |
| Milanese, Knorr® | 1 cup | 330 | 60 |
| Mushroom, Knorr® | 1 cup | 350 | 60 |
| Onion Herb, Knorr® | 1 cup | 360 | 60 |
| Primavera, Knorr® | 1 cup | 340 | 60 |

❶  Meets Low-Fat Guidelines

| TOTAL FAT (g) | SATURATED FAT (g) | SODIUM (mg) | PROTEIN (g) | CARBOHYDRATE (g) | CARBOHYDRATE CHOICES | EXCHANGES |
|---|---|---|---|---|---|---|
| 9 | 1 | 1100 | 6 | 53 | 3½ | 3½ starch, 1 fat |
| 4.5 | 1.5 | 900 | 6 | 43 | 3 | 3 starch |
| 1 | 0 | 0 | 4 | 35 | 2 | 2 starch |
| 14 | 3.5 | 1040 | 8 | 50 | 3 | 3 starch, 2 fat |
| 1 | 0 | 900 | 6 | 52 | 3 | 3 starch |
| 1 | 0 | 610 | 5 | 43 | 3 | 3 starch |
| 0.5 | 0 | 15 | 2 | 14 | 1 | 1 starch |
| 0.5 | 0 | 980 | 7 | 37 | 2½ | 2 starch, 1 veg |
| 0 | 0 | 25 | 4 | 18 | 1 | 1 starch |
| 12 | 3.5 | 1000 | 8 | 44 | 3 | 3 starch, 2 fat |
| 3 | 1.5 | 880 | 6 | 46 | 3 | 3 starch |
| 3 | 1.5 | 1020 | 6 | 44 | 3 | 3 starch |
| 5 | 0.5 | 1000 | 6 | 45 | 3 | 3 starch |
| 2.5 | 1.5 | 55 | 5 | 3 | 0 | 1 lean meat |
| 8 | 5 | 105 | 7 | 3 | 0 | 1 high fat meat |
| 8 | 5 | 105 | 7 | 3 | 0 | 1 high fat meat |
| 9 | 2 | 975 | 6 | 54 | 3½ | 3 starch, 1 veg, 1 fat |
| 2 | 0.5 | 740 | 7 | 44 | 3 | 3 starch |
| 7 | 1 | 1115 | 6 | 61 | 4 | 4 starch, ½ fat |
| 7 | 1 | 1195 | 7 | 66 | 4½ | 4½ starch, ½ fat |
| 7 | 1 | 1395 | 7 | 66 | 4½ | 4½ starch, ½ fat |
| 7 | 1 | 1125 | 6 | 61 | 4 | 4 starch, ½ fat |

1 Carbohydrate Choice = 1 starch or 1 fruit or 1 milk exchange

## PRODUCTS

| | SERVING SIZE | CALORIES | CALORIES FROM FAT |
|---|---|---|---|
| **RISOTTO (FROZEN)** | | | |
| Risotto Parmesano, Michelina's® | 1 pkg | 360 | 180 |
| Risotto with Cheese and Mushrooms, Weight Watchers® International Selections | 1 entree | 290 | 80 |
| **ROLLS, DINNER (REFRIGERATED)** | | | |
| Butterflake, Pillsbury® | 1 roll | 130 | 45 |
| Cheese Crescents, Pillsbury® | 2 crescents | 210 | 110 |
| Cornbread Twists, Pillsbury® | 1 twist | 130 | 50 |
| **SALAD DRESSING** | | | |
| ***Bacon and Tomato Salad Dressing*** | | | |
| Bacon & Tomato, Henri's® | 2 Tb | 140 | 108 |
| Bacon & Tomato, Kraft® | 2 Tb | 140 | 130 |
| Bacon & Tomato, Kraft® Deliciously Right® | 2 Tb | 60 | 45 |
| ***Blue Cheese Salad Dressing*** | | | |
| ❶ Blue Cheese Flavor, Kraft® Free® | 2 Tb | 50 | 0 |
| ❶ Blue Cheese, Estee® | 2 Tb | 15 | 5 |
| ❶ Blue Cheese, Henri's® Light | 2 Tb | 60 | 20 |
| Blue Cheese, Hidden Valley Ranch® | 2 Tb | 120 | 108 |
| ❶ Blue Cheese, Hidden Valley Ranch® Low Fat | 2 Tb | 20 | 0 |
| Chunky Blue Cheese, Seven Seas® | 2 Tb | 90 | 70 |
| Chunky Blue Cheese, Wish-Bone® | 2 Tb | 170 | 150 |
| ❶ Chunky Blue Cheese, Wish-Bone® Fat-Free | 2 Tb | 35 | 0 |
| Chunky Blue Cheese, Wish-Bone® Lite | 2 Tb | 80 | 70 |
| ❶ Creamy Blue Cheese, Marie's® Low-Fat | 2 Tb | 45 | 18 |
| Roka® Brand Blue Cheese, Kraft® Regular | 2 Tb | 90 | 70 |
| ***Caesar Salad Dressing*** | | | |
| Caesar, Kraft® | 2 Tb | 130 | 120 |
| Caesar, Kraft® Deliciously Right® | 2 Tb | 60 | 50 |

❶  Meets Low-Fat Guidelines

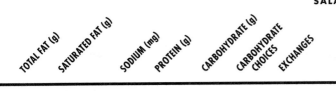

| TOTAL FAT (g) | SATURATED FAT (g) | SODIUM (mg) | PROTEIN (g) | CARBOHYDRATE (g) | CARBOHYDRATE CHOICES | EXCHANGES |
|---|---|---|---|---|---|---|
| 20 | 6 | 740 | 14 | 30 | 2 | 2 starch, 1 meat, 3 fat |
| 8 | 4 | 540 | 11 | 44 | 3 | 3 starch, 1 meat |
| | | | | | | |
| 5 | 1 | 530 | 3 | 19 | 1 | 1 starch, 1 fat |
| 12 | 3 | 600 | 4 | 21 | 1½ | 1½ starch, 2 fat |
| 6 | 1.5 | 320 | 3 | 17 | 1 | 1 starch, 1 fat |
| | | | | | | |
| 12 | 1.5 | 290 | 0 | 8 | ½ | ½ starch or fruit, 2 fat |
| 14 | 2.5 | 260 | <1 | 2 | 0 | 3 fat |
| 5 | 1 | 300 | <1 | 3 | 0 | 1 fat |
| | | | | | | |
| 0 | 0 | 340 | <1 | 12 | 1 | 1 starch |
| 0.5 | 0 | 80 | <1 | 1 | 0 | free |
| 2 | 0.5 | 430 | 1 | 9 | ½ | ½ starch or fruit |
| 12 | NA | 200 | <1 | 2 | 0 | 2 fat |
| 0 | NA | 240 | 0 | 4 | 0 | free |
| 7 | 4 | 470 | 1 | 5 | 0 | 1½ fat |
| 17 | 3 | 280 | <1 | 2 | 0 | 3 fat |
| 0 | 0 | 310 | 1 | 7 | ½ | ½ starch or fruit |
| 7 | 1.5 | 380 | 1 | 2 | 0 | 1 fat |
| 2 | NA | NA | 0 | 7 | ½ | ½ starch or fruit |
| 7 | 4 | 470 | 1 | 5 | 0 | 1½ fat |
| | | | | | | |
| 13 | 2.5 | 370 | <1 | 2 | 0 | 3 fat |
| 5 | 1 | 560 | <1 | 2 | 0 | 1 fat |

1 Carbohydrate Choice = 1 starch or 1 fruit or 1 milk exchange

## PRODUCTS

| PRODUCTS | SERVING SIZE | CALORIES | CALORIES FROM FAT |
|---|---|---|---|
| ❶ Caesar, Maple Grove Farms of Vermont® Fat Free | 2 Tb | 20 | 0 |
| Caesar, Maple Grove Farms of Vermont® Lite | 2 Tb | 70 | 50 |
| Caesar, Newman's Own® | 2 Tb | 150 | 140 |
| ❶ Caesar, Salad Celebrations® Fat Free | 2 Tb | 10 | 0 |
| Caesar, Seven Seas Viva® | 2 Tb | 120 | 110 |
| Caesar with Olive Oil, Wish-Bone® | 2 Tb | 100 | 90 |
| Caesar with Olive Oil, Wish-Bone® Lite | 2 Tb | 60 | 45 |
| Creamy Caesar, Seven Seas® | 2 Tb | 140 | 130 |
| Gourmet Caesar, Good Seasons (as prepared from mix) | 2 Tb | 150 | 140 |

### French Salad Dressing

| PRODUCTS | SERVING SIZE | CALORIES | CALORIES FROM FAT |
|---|---|---|---|
| ❶ Catalina, Kraft® Free® | 2 Tb | 45 | 0 |
| Catalina, Kraft® | 2 Tb | 140 | 100 |
| Catalina, Kraft® Deliciously Right® | 2 Tb | 80 | 40 |
| Catalina with Honey, Kraft® | 2 Tb | 140 | 110 |
| Deluxe French, Wish-Bone® | 2 Tb | 120 | 100 |
| ❶ French, Estee® | 2 Tb | 10 | 0 |
| ❶ French, Henri's® Fat Free | 2 Tb | 45 | 0 |
| ❶ French, Hidden Valley Ranch® Low Fat | 2 Tb | 35 | 9 |
| French, Kraft® | 2 Tb | 120 | 100 |
| ❶ French, Kraft® Deliciously Right® | 2 Tb | 50 | 30 |
| French, Western® | 2 Tb | 150 | 108 |
| ❶ French, Western® Fat Free | 2 Tb | 45 | 0 |
| ❶ French, Western® Light | 2 Tb | 70 | 22.5 |
| ❶ French, Wish-Bone® Fat Free | 2 Tb | 40 | 0 |
| ❶ French Style, Kraft® Free® | 2 Tb | 50 | 0 |
| ❶ French Style, Salad Celebrations® Fat Free | 2 Tb | 40 | 0 |
| ❶ French Style, Wish-Bone® Lite | 2 Tb | 50 | 20 |
| French with Bacon, Western® | 2 Tb | 140 | 99 |
| French with Blue Cheese, Western® | 2 Tb | 140 | 99 |

❶  Meets Low-Fat Guidelines

| TOTAL FAT (g) | SATURATED FAT (g) | SODIUM (mg) | PROTEIN (g) | CARBOHYDRATE (g) | CARBOHYDRATE CHOICES | EXCHANGES |
|---|---|---|---|---|---|---|
| 0 | 0 | 280 | 0 | 5 | 0 | free |
| 5 | 1 | 310 | 0 | 5 | 0 | 1 fat |
| 16 | 1.5 | 450 | 1 | 1 | 0 | 3 fat |
| 0 | 0 | 390 | 0 | 1 | 0 | free |
| 12 | 2 | 500 | <1 | 2 | 0 | 2 fat |
| 9.5 | 1.5 | 400 | 0 | 2 | 0 | 2 fat |
| 5 | 1 | 380 | <1 | 2 | 0 | 1 fat |
| 15 | 2.5 | 300 | <1 | 1 | 0 | 3 fat |
| 16 | 2.5 | 300 | 0 | 3 | 0 | 3 fat |
| 0 | 0 | 360 | 0 | 11 | 1 | 1 starch or fruit |
| 11 | 2 | 390 | 0 | 8 | ½ | ½ starch or fruit, 2 fat |
| 4 | 0.5 | 400 | 0 | 9 | ½ | ½ starch or fruit, ½ fat |
| 12 | 2 | 310 | 0 | 8 | ½ | ½ starch or fruit, 2 fat |
| 11 | 1.5 | 170 | 0 | 5 | 0 | 2 fat |
| 0 | 0 | 80 | 0 | 2 | 0 | free |
| 0 | 0 | 240 | 0 | 11 | 1 | 1 starch or fruit |
| 1 | NA | 210 | 0 | 7 | ½ | ½ starch or fruit |
| 12 | 2 | 260 | 0 | 4 | 0 | 2 fat |
| 3 | .5 | 260 | 0 | 6 | ½ | ½ starch or fruit, ½ fat |
| 12 | 1.5 | 230 | 0 | 12 | 1 | 1 starch or fruit, 2 fat |
| 0 | 0 | 250 | 0 | 11 | 1 | 1 starch or fruit |
| 2.5 | 0 | 240 | 0 | 11 | 1 | 1 starch or fruit |
| 0 | 0 | 270 | 0 | 9 | ½ | ½ starch or fruit |
| 0 | 0 | 300 | 0 | 12 | 1 | 1 starch or fruit |
| 0 | 0 | 200 | 0 | 9 | ½ | ½ starch or fruit |
| 2 | 0.5 | 250 | 0 | 9 | ½ | ½ starch or fruit |
| 11 | 1.5 | 210 | 0 | 10 | ½ | ½ starch or fruit, 2 fat |
| 11 | 1.5 | 230 | 0 | 9 | ½ | ½ starch or fruit, 2 fat |

1 Carbohydrate Choice = 1 starch or 1 fruit or 1 milk exchange

## PRODUCTS

| | SERVING SIZE | CALORIES | CALORIES FROM FAT |
|---|---|---|---|
| Hearty French, Henri's® | 2 Tb | 140 | 99 |
| Original French, Henri's® | 2 Tb | 120 | 99 |
| ❶ Original French, Henri's® Light | 2 Tb | 70 | 27 |
| ❶ Sweet & Spicy French, Wish Bone® Fat-Free | 2 Tb | 30 | 0 |
| Sweet 'N Spicy French, Wish-Bone® | 2 Tb | 130 | 110 |

### Honey Mustard Salad Dressing

| | SERVING SIZE | CALORIES | CALORIES FROM FAT |
|---|---|---|---|
| Honey Dijon, Hidden Valley Ranch® | 2 Tb | 120 | 108 |
| ❶ Honey Dijon, Hidden Valley Ranch® Low Fat | 2 Tb | 35 | 0 |
| Honey Dijon, Kraft® | 2 Tb | 150 | 130 |
| ❶ Honey Dijon, Kraft® Free® | 2 Tb | 50 | 0 |
| ❶ Honey Dijon, Maple Grove Farms of Vermont® Fat Free | 2 Tb | 45 | 0 |
| ❶ Honey Dijon, Salad Celebrations® Fat Free | 2 Tb | 45 | 0 |
| Honey Dijon, Wish-Bone® | 2 Tb | 130 | 90 |
| ❶ Honey Dijon, Wish-Bone® Fat-Free | 2 Tb | 45 | 0 |
| Honey Mustard, Good Seasons® (as prepared from mix) | 2 Tb | 150 | 140 |
| ❶ Honey Mustard, Good Seasons® Fat Free (as prepared from mix) | 2 Tb | 20 | 0 |
| Honey Mustard, Henri's® | 2 Tb | 100 | 54 |
| ❶ Honey Mustard, Henry's Fat Free | 2 Tb | 50 | 0 |
| Honey Mustard, Maple Grove Farms of Vermont® | 2 Tb | 120 | 80 |
| Honey Mustard, Maple Grove Farms of Vermont® Lite | 2 Tb | 80 | 45 |

### Italian Salad Dressing

| | SERVING SIZE | CALORIES | CALORIES FROM FAT |
|---|---|---|---|
| Classic House Italian, Wish-Bone® | 2 Tb | 140 | 130 |
| Classic Olive Oil Italian, Wish-Bone® | 2 Tb | 70 | 60 |
| Creamy Garlic Italian, Henri's® | 2 Tb | 110 | 90 |
| ❶ Creamy Italian, Estee® | 2 Tb | 15 | 5 |
| ❶ Creamy Italian, Good Seasons® Fat-Free (as prepared from mix) | 2 Tb | 20 | 0 |

❶  Meets Low-Fat Guidelines

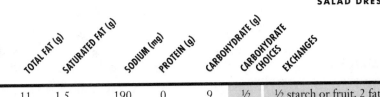

| TOTAL FAT (g) | SATURATED FAT (g) | SODIUM (mg) | PROTEIN (g) | CARBOHYDRATE (g) | CARBOHYDRATE CHOICES | EXCHANGES |
|---|---|---|---|---|---|---|
| 11 | 1.5 | 190 | 0 | 9 | ½ | ½ starch or fruit, 2 fat |
| 11 | 1.5 | 210 | 0 | 6 | ½ | ½ starch or fruit, 2 fat |
| 3 | 0 | 280 | 0 | 13 | 1 | 1 starch or fruit |
| 0 | 0 | 220 | 0 | 7 | ½ | ½ starch or fruit |
| 12 | 2 | 330 | 0 | 6 | ½ | ½ starch or fruit, 2 fat |
| | | | | | | |
| 12 | NA | 210 | <1 | 4 | 0 | 2 fat |
| 0 | 0 | 270 | 0 | 7 | ½ | ½ starch or fruit |
| 15 | 2 | 200 | 0 | 4 | 0 | 3 fat |
| 0 | 0 | 330 | <1 | 11 | 1 | 1 starch or fruit |
| 0 | 0 | 190 | 0 | 10 | ½ | ½ starch or fruit |
| 0 | 0 | 150 | 0 | 11 | 1 | 1 starch or fruit |
| 10 | 1.5 | 390 | <1 | 9 | ½ | ½ starch or fruit, 2 fat |
| 0 | 0 | 270 | 1 | 10 | ½ | ½ starch or fruit |
| 15 | 2 | 240 | 0 | 3 | 0 | 3 fat |
| 0 | 0 | 280 | 0 | 5 | 0 | free |
| 6 | 1 | 230 | 0 | 10 | ½ | ½ starch or fruit, 1 fat |
| 0 | 0 | 180 | 0 | 12 | 1 | 1 starch or fruit |
| 9 | 1.5 | 280 | <1 | 9 | ½ | ½ starch or fruit, 2 fat |
| 5 | <1 | 300 | <1 | 9 | ½ | ½ starch or fruit, 1 fat |
| | | | | | | |
| 14 | 2 | 360 | 0 | 2 | 0 | 3 fat |
| 10 | 1 | 400 | 0 | 4 | 0 | 2 fat |
| 9 | 1.5 | 290 | 0 | 6 | ½ | ½ starch or fruit, 2 fat |
| 0.5 | 0 | 80 | 0 | 2 | 0 | free |
| 0 | 0 | 280 | <1 | 3 | 0 | free |

1 Carbohydrate Choice = 1 starch or 1 fruit or 1 milk exchange

| PRODUCTS | SERVING SIZE | CALORIES | CALORIES FROM FAT |
|---|---|---|---|
| ❶ Creamy Italian, Henri's® Light | 2 Tb | 50 | 20 |
| Creamy Italian, Kraft® | 2 Tb | 110 | 100 |
| Creamy Italian, Kraft® Deliciously Right® | 2 Tb | 50 | 40 |
| ❶ Creamy Italian, Salad Celebrations® Fat Free | 2 Tb | 30 | 0 |
| Creamy Italian, Seven Seas® | 2 Tb | 110 | 110 |
| Creamy Italian, Seven Seas® Reduced Calorie | 2 Tb | 60 | 45 |
| Creamy Italian, Wish-Bone® | 2 Tb | 100 | 90 |
| Creamy Italian, Wish-Bone® Lite | 2 Tb | 60 | 35 |
| House Italian, Kraft® | 2 Tb | 120 | 110 |
| ❶ Italian, Estee® | 2 Tb | 5 | 0 |
| Italian, Good Seasons® (as prepared from mix) | 2 Tb | 140 | 140 |
| ❶ Italian, Good Seasons® Fat Free (as prepared from mix) | 2 Tb | 10 | 0 |
| Italian, Good Seasons® Reduced Calorie (as prepared from mix) | 2 Tb | 50 | 45 |
| ❶ Italian, Henri's® Fat Free | 2 Tb | 15 | 0 |
| Italian, Kraft® Deliciously Right® | 2 Tb | 70 | 60 |
| ❶ Italian, Kraft® Free® | 2 Tb | 10 | 0 |
| ❶ Italian, Newman's Own® Light | 2 Tb | 20 | 5 |
| ❶ Italian, Salad Celebrations® Fat Free | 2 Tb | 10 | 0 |
| ❶ Italian, Seven Seas Free® | 2 Tb | 10 | 0 |
| Italian, Wish-Bone® | 2 Tb | 100 | 80 |
| ❶ Italian, Wish-Bone® Fat Free | 2 Tb | 15 | 0 |
| ❶ Italian, Wish-Bone® Lite | 2 Tb | 15 | 5 |
| Italian Herb, Henri's® | 2 Tb | 110 | 100 |
| ❶ Italian Parmesan, Hidden Valley Ranch® Low Fat | 2 Tb | 20 | 0 |
| ❶ Italian Vinaigrette, Marie's® Fat Free | 2 Tb | 35 | 0 |
| Italian Wine & Cheese, Maple Grove Farms of Vermont® Lite | 2 Tb | 50 | 40 |
| Italian with Olive Oil, Oil Blend, Seven Seas® Reduced Calorie | 2 Tb | 50 | 40 |

❶ Meets Low-Fat Guidelines

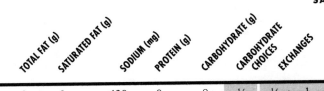

| TOTAL FAT (g) | SATURATED FAT (g) | SODIUM (mg) | PROTEIN (g) | CARBOHYDRATE (g) | CARBOHYDRATE CHOICES | EXCHANGES |
|---|---|---|---|---|---|---|
| 2 | 0 | 420 | 0 | 8 | ½ | ½ starch or fruit |
| 11 | 4 | 230 | 0 | 3 | 0 | 2 fat |
| 5 | 1 | 250 | 0 | 3 | 0 | 1 fat |
| 0 | 0 | 360 | 0 | 7 | ½ | ½ starch or fruit |
| 12 | 2 | 510 | 0 | 2 | 0 | 2 fat |
| 5 | 1 | 490 | 0 | 2 | 0 | 1 fat |
| 10 | 2 | 310 | 0 | 3 | 0 | 2 fat |
| 3.5 | 1 | 240 | 0 | 7 | ½ | ½ starch or fruit |
| 12 | 2 | 240 | 0 | 3 | 0 | 2 fat |
| 0 | 0 | 80 | 0 | 1 | 0 | free |
| 15 | 2 | 320 | 0 | 1 | 0 | 3 fat |
| 0 | 0 | 290 | 0 | 3 | 0 | free |
| 5 | 1 | 280 | 0 | 2 | 0 | 1 fat |
| 0 | 0 | 320 | 0 | 2 | 0 | free |
| 7 | 1 | 240 | 0 | 3 | 0 | 1 fat |
| 0 | 0 | 290 | 0 | 2 | 0 | free |
| 0.5 | 0 | 380 | 0 | 3 | 0 | free |
| 0 | 0 | 360 | 0 | 2 | 0 | free |
| 0 | 0 | 480 | 0 | 2 | 0 | free |
| 9 | 1.5 | 590 | 0 | 3 | 0 | 2 fat |
| 0 | 0 | 280 | 0 | 2 | 0 | free |
| 0.5 | 0 | 380 | 0 | 2 | 0 | free |
| 11 | 1.5 | 410 | 0 | 2 | 0 | 2 fat |
| 0 | 0 | 270 | 0 | 4 | 0 | free |
| 0 | 0 | NA | 0 | 8 | ½ | ½ starch or fruit |
| 4.5 | 1 | 280 | 0 | 3 | 0 | 1 fat |
| 5 | 1 | 450 | 0 | 2 | 0 | 1 fat |

1 Carbohydrate Choice = 1 starch *or* 1 fruit *or* 1 milk exchange

| PRODUCTS | SERVING SIZE | CALORIES | CALORIES FROM FAT |
|---|---|---|---|
| Mild Italian, Good Seasons® (as prepared from mix) | 2 Tb | 150 | 140 |
| ❶ Oil-Free Italian, Kraft® | 2 Tb | 5 | 0 |
| Olive Oil and Vinegar, Newman's Own® | 2 Tb | 150 | 150 |
| Presto Italian, Kraft® | 2 Tb | 140 | 130 |
| Robusto Italian, Wish-Bone® | 2 Tb | 100 | 90 |
| Traditional Italian, Henri's® | 2 Tb | 110 | 100 |
| Two Cheese Italian, Seven Seas® | 2 Tb | 70 | 60 |
| Viva Italian, Seven Seas® | 2 Tb | 110 | 100 |
| Viva Italian, Seven Seas® Reduced Calorie | 2 Tb | 45 | 35 |
| Zesty Italian, Good Seasons® (as prepared from mix) | 2 Tb | 140 | 140 |
| Zesty Italian, Good Seasons® Reduced Calorie (as prepared from mix) | 2 Tb | 50 | 45 |
| Zesty Italian, Kraft® | 2 Tb | 110 | 100 |

### Ranch Salad Dressing

| | | | |
|---|---|---|---|
| All Natural Ranch, Newman's Own® | 2 Tb | 180 | 170 |
| Bacon, Hidden Valley Ranch® | 2 Tb | 120 | 108 |
| Buttermilk Ranch, Kraft® | 2 Tb | 150 | 140 |
| Caesar Ranch, Henri's® | 2 Tb | 170 | 162 |
| Caesar Ranch, Kraft® | 2 Tb | 140 | 130 |
| Cucumber Ranch, Kraft® | 2 Tb | 150 | 140 |
| Cucumber Ranch, Kraft® Deliciously Right® | 2 Tb | 60 | 45 |
| Honey Ranch, Maple Grove Farms of Vermont® Lite | 2 Tb | 50 | 35 |
| Original (Buttermilk), Hidden Valley Ranch® | 2 Tb | 110 | 54 |
| Original (Milk), Hidden Valley Ranch® | 2 Tb | 120 | 108 |
| Original Ranch, Hidden Valley Ranch® Reduced Calorie (as prepared from mix) | 2 Tb | 80 | 63 |
| ❶ Original, Hidden Valley Ranch® Low Fat | 2 Tb | 40 | 27 |
| ❶ Original, Hidden Valley Ranch® Low Fat (as prepared from mix) | 2 Tb | 30 | 9 |

❶  Meets Low-Fat Guidelines

| TOTAL FAT (g) | SATURATED FAT (g) | SODIUM (mg) | PROTEIN (g) | CARBOHYDRATE (g) | CARBOHYDRATE CHOICES | EXCHANGES |
|---|---|---|---|---|---|---|
| 15 | 2.5 | 370 | 0 | 2 | 0 | 3 fat |
| 0 | 0 | 450 | 0 | 2 | 0 | free |
| 16 | 2.5 | 150 | 0 | 1 | 0 | 3 fat |
| 15 | 2.5 | 290 | 0 | 2 | 0 | 3 fat |
| 10 | 1.5 | 610 | 0 | 4 | 0 | 2 fat |
| 11 | 1.5 | 560 | 0 | 3 | 0 | 2 fat |
| 7 | 1 | 240 | 0 | 3 | 0 | 1 fat |
| 11 | 1.5 | 580 | 0 | 2 | 0 | 2 fat |
| 4 | 1 | 390 | 0 | 2 | 0 | 1 fat |
| 15 | 2 | 220 | 0 | 1 | 0 | 3 fat |
| 5 | 1 | 260 | 0 | 2 | 0 | 1 fat |
| 11 | 1.5 | 530 | 0 | 2 | 0 | 2 fat |
| 19 | 3 | 170 | 1 | 2 | 0 | 4 fat |
| 12 | NA | 220 | 1 | 2 | 0 | 2 fat |
| 16 | 3 | 230 | 0 | 2 | 0 | 3 fat |
| 18 | 3 | 290 | 1 | 2 | 0 | 4 fat |
| 15 | 2.5 | 300 | <1 | 1 | 0 | 3 fat |
| 15 | 2.5 | 220 | 0 | 2 | 0 | 3 fat |
| 5 | 1 | 450 | 0 | 2 | 0 | 1 fat |
| 4 | 1 | 260 | <1 | 4 | 0 | 1 fat |
| 6 | NA | 240 | <1 | 1 | 0 | 1 fat |
| 12 | NA | 210 | <1 | 2 | 0 | 2 fat |
| 7 | NA | 270 | 0 | 2 | 0 | 1 fat |
| 3 | NA | 270 | 0 | 5 | 0 | ½ fat |
| 1 | NA | 240 | 1 | 4 | 0 | free |

1 Carbohydrate Choice = 1 starch or 1 fruit or 1 milk exchange

## PRODUCTS

| | SERVING SIZE | CALORIES | CALORIES FROM FAT |
|---|---|---|---|
| Original, Hidden Valley Ranch® Reduced Calorie | 2 Tb | 70 | 54 |
| Parmesan Ranch, Henri's® | 2 Tb | 160 | 144 |
| ❶ Parmesan Ranch, Henri's® Light | 2 Tb | 60 | 18 |
| Peppercorn Ranch, Kraft® | 2 Tb | 170 | 160 |
| ❶ Peppercorn Ranch, Kraft® Free® | 2 Tb | 50 | 0 |
| Ranch, Good Seasons® (as prepared from mix) | 2 Tb | 120 | 110 |
| Ranch, Good Seasons® Reduced Calorie (as prepared from mix) | 2 Tb | 60 | 40 |
| Ranch, Henri's® | 2 Tb | 170 | 153 |
| ❶ Ranch, Henri's® Fat Free | 2 Tb | 40 | 0 |
| ❶ Ranch, Henri's® Light | 2 Tb | 60 | 18 |
| Ranch, Kraft® | 2 Tb | 170 | 170 |
| Ranch, Kraft® Deliciously Right® | 2 Tb | 110 | 100 |
| ❶ Ranch, Kraft® Free® | 2 Tb | 50 | 0 |
| ❶ Ranch, Salad Celebrations® Fat Free | 2 Tb | 35 | 0 |
| Ranch, Seven Seas® | 2 Tb | 150 | 140 |
| ❶ Ranch, Seven Seas Free® | 2 Tb | 50 | 0 |
| Ranch, Seven Seas® Reduced Calorie | 2 Tb | 100 | 80 |
| Ranch, Wish-Bone® | 2 Tb | 160 | 150 |
| ❶ Ranch, Wish-Bone® Fat-Free | 2 Tb | 40 | 0 |
| Ranch Italian, Hidden Valley Ranch® | 2 Tb | 140 | 126 |
| Ranch Italian, Hidden Valley Ranch® Reduced Calorie (as prepared from mix) | 2 Tb | 50 | 45 |
| Ranch Lite, Wish-Bone® | 2 Tb | 100 | 80 |
| Salsa® Ranch, Kraft® | 2 Tb | 130 | 120 |
| Sour Cream & Onion Ranch, Kraft® | 2 Tb | 170 | 160 |

### Russian Salad Dressing

| | SERVING SIZE | CALORIES | CALORIES FROM FAT |
|---|---|---|---|
| Russian, Henri's® | 2 Tb | 120 | 90 |
| Russian, Kraft® | 2 Tb | 130 | 90 |
| Russian, Seven Seas Viva® | 2 Tb | 150 | 140 |
| Russian, Wish-Bone® | 2 Tb | 110 | 50 |

❶ Meets Low-Fat Guidelines

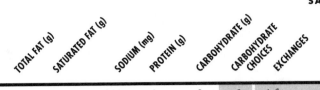

| TOTAL FAT (g) | SATURATED FAT (g) | SODIUM (mg) | PROTEIN (g) | CARBOHYDRATE (g) | CARBOHYDRATE CHOICES | EXCHANGES |
|---|---|---|---|---|---|---|
| 6 | NA | 240 | 1 | 2 | 0 | 1 fat |
| 16 | 2.5 | 290 | 1 | 4 | 0 | 3 fat |
| 2 | .5 | 310 | 1 | 10 | ½ | 1 starch or fruit |
| 18 | 3 | 340 | <1 | 1 | 0 | 4 fat |
| 0 | 0 | 360 | <1 | 11 | 1 | 1 starch or fruit |
| 12 | 2 | 220 | 1 | 2 | 0 | 2 fat |
| 4.5 | 1 | 240 | 1 | 3 | 0 | 1 fat |
| 17 | 2.5 | 270 | 0 | 4 | 0 | 3½ fat |
| 0 | 0 | 340 | 1 | 9 | ½ | ½ starch or fruit |
| 2 | 0 | 290 | 0 | 11 | 1 | 1 starch or fruit |
| 18 | 3 | 270 | 0 | 2 | 0 | 4 fat |
| 11 | 2 | 310 | 0 | 2 | 0 | 2 fat |
| 0 | 0 | 310 | <1 | 11 | 1 | 1 starch or fruit |
| 0 | 0 | 270 | 0 | 7 | ½ | ½ starch or fruit |
| 16 | 2.5 | 250 | 0 | 2 | 0 | 3 fat |
| 0 | 0 | 330 | <1 | 12 | 1 | 1 starch or fruit |
| 9 | 1.5 | 320 | 0 | 5 | 0 | 2 fat |
| 17 | 2.5 | 210 | 0 | 1 | 0 | 3 fat |
| 0 | 0 | 270 | 0 | 9 | ½ | ½ starch or fruit |
| 14 | NA | 250 | <1 | 3 | 0 | 3 fat |
| 5 | NA | 240 | 0 | 2 | 0 | 1 fat |
| 8 | 1.5 | 240 | 0 | 5 | 0 | 2 fat |
| 13 | 2 | 320 | 0 | 1 | 0 | 3 fat |
| 18 | 3 | 240 | 0 | 1 | 0 | 4 fat |
| 10 | 1.5 | 190 | 0 | 9 | ½ | ½ starch or fruit, 2 fat |
| 10 | 1.5 | 280 | 0 | 10 | ½ | ½ starch or fruit, 2 fat |
| 16 | 2.5 | 230 | 0 | 3 | 0 | 3 fat |
| 6 | 1 | 350 | 0 | 15 | 1 | 1 starch or fruit, 1 fat |

1 Carbohydrate Choice = 1 starch *or* 1 fruit *or* 1 milk exchange

| PRODUCTS | SERVING SIZE | CALORIES | CALORIES FROM FAT |
|---|---|---|---|
| **Thousand Island Salad Dressing** | | | |
| 1000 Island, Western® | 2 Tb | 120 | 100 |
| ❶ Thousand Island, Estee® | 2 Tb | 10 | 0 |
| Thousand Island, Henri's® | 2 Tb | 100 | 80 |
| ❶ Thousand Island, Henri's Fat Free | 2 Tb | 40 | 0 |
| ❶ Thousand Island, Henri's® Light | 2 Tb | 50 | 20 |
| ❶ Thousand Island, Hidden Valley Ranch® Low Fat | 2 Tb | 35 | 9 |
| Thousand Island, Kraft® | 2 Tb | 110 | 90 |
| Thousand Island, Kraft® Deliciously Right® | 2 Tb | 70 | 40 |
| ❶ Thousand Island, Kraft® Free® | 2 Tb | 45 | 0 |
| Thousand Island, Wish-Bone® | 2 Tb | 130 | 110 |
| ❶ Thousand Island, Wish-Bone® Fat-Free | 2 Tb | 35 | 0 |
| Thousand Island, Wish-Bone® Lite | 2 Tb | 80 | 45 |
| Thousand Island with Bacon, Kraft® | 2 Tb | 120 | 100 |
| **Vinaigrette Salad Dressing** | | | |
| ❶ Balsamic Vinegar Dressing, S&W® Vintage Lites | 2 Tb | 35 | 0 |
| Dijon Vinaigrette Classic, Wish-Bone® Lite | 2 Tb | 60 | 50 |
| ❶ Mango Key Lime Vinegar Dressing, S&W® Vintage Lites | 2 Tb | 30 | 0 |
| Olive Oil Vinaigrette, Wish-Bone® | 2 Tb | 60 | 45 |
| ❶ Raspberry Blush Vinegar Dressing, S&W® Vintage Lites | 2 Tb | 40 | 0 |
| ❶ Raspberry Vinaigrette, Maple Grove Farms of Vermont® Fat Free | 2 Tb | 35 | 0 |
| ❶ Red Wine Vinaigrette, Marie's® Fat Free | 2 Tb | 40 | 0 |
| Red Wine Vinegar & Oil, Seven Seas® Reduced Calorie | 2 Tb | 60 | 45 |
| Red Wine Vinegar & Oil, Seven Seas® Regular | 2 Tb | 110 | 100 |
| ❶ Red Wine Vinegar with Herbs Dressing, S&W® Vintage Lites | 2 Tb | 40 | 0 |

❶ Meets Low-Fat Guidelines

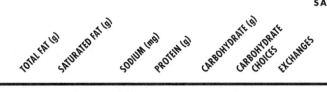

| TOTAL FAT (g) | SATURATED FAT (g) | SODIUM (mg) | PROTEIN (g) | CARBOHYDRATE (g) | CARBOHYDRATE CHOICES | EXCHANGES |
|---|---|---|---|---|---|---|
| 11 | 1.5 | 300 | 0 | 7 | ½ | ½ starch or fruit, 2 fat |
| 0 | 0 | 80 | 0 | 2 | 0 | free |
| 9 | 1.5 | 230 | 0 | 5 | 0 | 2 fat |
| 0 | 0 | 260 | 0 | 9 | ½ | ½ starch or fruit |
| 2 | 0 | 310 | 1 | 8 | ½ | ½ starch or fruit |
| 1 | NA | 240 | 0 | 6 | ½ | ½ starch or fruit |
| 10 | 1.5 | 310 | 0 | 5 | 0 | 2 fat |
| 4 | 1 | 320 | 0 | 8 | ½ | ½ starch or fruit, 1 fat |
| 0 | 0 | 300 | 0 | 11 | 1 | 1 starch or fruit |
| 12 | 2 | 340 | 0 | 7 | ½ | ½ starch or fruit, 2 fat |
| 0 | 0 | 290 | 0 | 8 | ½ | ½ starch or fruit |
| 5 | 1 | 250 | 0 | 7 | ½ | ½ starch or fruit, 1 fat |
| 11 | 2 | 190 | 0 | 5 | 0 | 2 fat |
| 0 | 0 | 460 | 0 | 8 | ½ | ½ starch or fruit |
| 5 | 1 | 400 | 0 | 3 | 0 | 1 fat |
| 0 | 0 | 390 | 0 | 7 | ½ | ½ starch or fruit |
| 5 | 0.5 | 250 | 0 | 4 | 0 | 1 fat |
| 0 | 0 | 410 | 0 | 10 | ½ | ½ starch or fruit |
| 0 | 0 | 180 | 0 | 9 | ½ | ½ starch or fruit |
| 0 | 0 | NA | 0 | 10 | ½ | ½ starch or fruit |
| 5 | 1 | 310 | 0 | 2 | 0 | 1 fat |
| 11 | 2 | 510 | 0 | 2 | 0 | 2 fat |
| 0 | 0 | 440 | 0 | 8 | ½ | ½ starch or fruit |

1 Carbohydrate Choice = 1 starch or 1 fruit or 1 milk exchange

## PRODUCTS

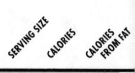

| PRODUCTS | SERVING SIZE | CALORIES | CALORIES FROM FAT |
|---|---|---|---|
| ❶ Red Wine Vinegar, Kraft® Free® | 2 Tb | 15 | 0 |
| ❶ Red Wine Vinegar, Seven Seas Free® | 2 Tb | 15 | 0 |
| ❶ White Wine Vinegar with Herbs Dressing, S&W® Vintage Lites | 2 Tb | 40 | 0 |

### Other Salad Dressings

| PRODUCTS | SERVING SIZE | CALORIES | CALORIES FROM FAT |
|---|---|---|---|
| Buttermilk Farm Style, Good Seasons® (as prepared from mix) | 2 Tb | 120 | 110 |
| Cheese Garlic, Good Seasons® (as prepared from mix) | 2 Tb | 140 | 140 |
| ❶ Coleslaw Dressing, Hidden Valley Ranch® Low Fat | 2 Tb | 35 | 0 |
| Coleslaw Dressing, Kraft® | 2 Tb | 150 | 110 |
| ❶ Creamy Cucumber, Henri's® Light | 2 Tb | 60 | 18 |
| ❶ Creamy Garlic, Estee® | 2 Tb | 10 | 0 |
| Creamy Garlic, Kraft® | 2 Tb | 110 | 100 |
| ❶ Creamy Parmesan, Hidden Valley Ranch® Low Fat | 2 Tb | 30 | 0 |
| Creamy Roasted Garlic, Wish-Bone® | 2 Tb | 140 | 120 |
| ❶ Creamy Roasted Garlic, Wish-Bone® Fat-Free | 2 Tb | 40 | 0 |
| Deluxe Cole Slaw Dressing, Western® | 2 Tb | 130 | 108 |
| Deluxe Salad Dressing, Western® | 2 Tb | 120 | 99 |
| Garlic and Herbs, Good Seasons® (as prepared from mix) | 2 Tb | 140 | 140 |
| Green Goddess, Seven Seas® | 2 Tb | 120 | 110 |
| Herbs & Spices, Seven Seas® | 2 Tb | 120 | 110 |
| Lemon 'N Dill, Maple Grove Farms of Vermont® Lite | 2 Tb | 80 | 45 |
| ❶ Mexican, Western® | 2 Tb | 60 | 27 |
| Mexican Spice, Good Seasons® (as prepared from mix) | 2 Tb | 140 | 140 |
| ❶ Oriental Rice Wine Vinegar Dressing, S&W® Vintage Lites | 2 Tb | 30 | 0 |

❶  Meets Low-Fat Guidelines

| TOTAL FAT (g) | SATURATED FAT (g) | SODIUM (mg) | PROTEIN (g) | CARBOHYDRATE (g) | CARBOHYDRATE CHOICES | EXCHANGES |
|---|---|---|---|---|---|---|
| 0 | 0 | 400 | 0 | 3 | 0 | free |
| 0 | 0 | 400 | 0 | 3 | 0 | free |
| 0 | 0 | 450 | 0 | 10 | ½ | ½ starch or fruit |
| 12 | 2 | 260 | 1 | 2 | 0 | 2 fat |
| 16 | 2.5 | 330 | 0 | 1 | 0 | 3 fat |
| 0 | 0 | 200 | 0 | 9 | ½ | ½ starch or fruit |
| 12 | 2 | 420 | 0 | 8 | ½ | ½ starch or fruit, 2 fat |
| 2 | 0 | 430 | 0 | 11 | 1 | 1 starch or fruit |
| 0 | 0 | 80 | 0 | 2 | 0 | free |
| 11 | 2 | 350 | 0 | 2 | 0 | 2 fat |
| 0 | 0 | 250 | 1 | 5 | 0 | free |
| 13 | 2 | 240 | 0 | 3 | 0 | 3 fat |
| 0 | 0 | 280 | 0 | 9 | ½ | ½ starch or fruit |
| 12 | 2 | 300 | 0 | 7 | ½ | ½ starch or fruit, 2 fat |
| 11 | 1.5 | 210 | 0 | 5 | 0 | 2 fat |
| 15 | 2 | 340 | 0 | 1 | 0 | 3 fat |
| 13 | 2 | 260 | 0 | 1 | 0 | 3 fat |
| 12 | 2 | 320 | 0 | 1 | 0 | 2 fat |
| 5 | 1 | 260 | <1 | 7 | ½ | ½ starch or fruit, 1 fat |
| 3 | 0.5 | 270 | 0 | 8 | ½ | ½ starch or fruit |
| 15 | 2.5 | 310 | 0 | 2 | 0 | 3 fat |
| 0 | 0 | 280 | 0 | 8 | ½ | ½ starch or fruit |

1 Carbohydrate Choice = 1 starch or 1 fruit or 1 milk exchange

## PRODUCTS

| | SERVING SIZE | CALORIES | CALORIES FROM FAT |
|---|---|---|---|
| Oriental Sesame, Good Seasons® (as prepared from mix) | 2 Tb | 150 | 140 |
| Parmesan & Cracked Pepper, Maple Grove Farms of Vermont® | 2 Tb | 120 | 100 |
| Pesto Parmesan, Maple Grove Farms of Vermont® Lite | 2 Tb | 70 | 45 |
| ❶ Poppyseed, Maple Grove Farms of Vermont® Fat Free | 2 Tb | 45 | 0 |
| Poppy Seed Dressing, Western® | 2 Tb | 100 | 72 |
| Salsa® Zesty Garden, Kraft® | 2 Tb | 70 | 60 |
| Santa Fe, Wish-Bone® | 2 Tb | 150 | 140 |
| Sierra, Wish-Bone® | 2 Tb | 150 | 140 |
| Sweet 'N Sour, Maple Grove Farms of Vermont® | 2 Tb | 110 | 60 |
| Tas-Tee®, Henri's® | 2 Tb | 110 | 81 |
| ❶ Tas-Tee®, Henri's® Light | 2 Tb | 60 | 18 |
| ❶ Zesty Herb, Good Seasons® Fat Free (as prepared from mix) | 2 Tb | 10 | 0 |

### SALSA
*see also* Sauces

| | | | |
|---|---|---|---|
| ❶ Salsa, all brands (avg) | 1 Tb | 10 | 0 |

### SARDINES

| | | | |
|---|---|---|---|
| Sardines in Mustard Sauce, Underwood® | 1 can | 180 | 100 |
| Sardines in Soy Oil, Underwood® | 1 can | 220 | 150 |
| Sardines in Tomato Sauce, Underwood® | 1 can | 180 | 100 |

### SAUCES

#### Mexican Sauces

| | | | |
|---|---|---|---|
| ❶ Chili Hot Dog, Gephardt® | ¼ cup | 57 | 27 |
| ❶ Enchilada, all varieties (avg) | 2 Tb | 10 | 0 |
| ❶ Enchilada, Gephardt® | ¼ cup | 35 | 18 |
| ❶ Enchilada, Old El Paso®, hot | ¼ cup | 30 | 10 |

 Meets Low-Fat Guidelines

| TOTAL FAT (g) | SATURATED FAT (g) | SODIUM (mg) | PROTEIN (g) | CARBOHYDRATE (g) | CARBOHYDRATE CHOICES | EXCHANGES |
|---|---|---|---|---|---|---|
| 16 | 2.5 | 360 | 0 | 3 | 0 | 3 fat |
| 11 | 2 | 360 | <1 | 4 | 0 | 2 fat |
| 5 | 1 | 310 | 0 | 5 | 0 | 1 fat |
| 0 | 0 | 90 | 0 | 9 | ½ | ½ starch or fruit |
| 8 | 1 | 230 | 0 | 8 | ½ | ½ starch or fruit, 1 fat |
| 6 | 1 | 280 | 0 | 3 | 0 | 1 fat |
| 15 | 2.5 | 220 | 0 | 3 | 0 | 3 fat |
| 16 | 2.5 | 260 | 0 | 2 | 0 | 3 fat |
| 7 | 1 | 150 | 1 | 12 | 1 | 1 starch or fruit, 1 fat |
| 9 | 1.5 | 200 | 0 | 8 | ½ | ½ starch or fruit, 2 fat |
| 2 | 0 | 220 | 0 | 11 | 1 | 1 starch or fruit |
| 0 | 0 | 260 | 0 | 2 | 0 | free |
| 0 | 0 | 95–300 | 0 | 2 | 0 | free |
| 12 | 3 | 820 | 17 | 2 | 0 | 2 meat |
| 16 | 3.5 | 310 | 18 | 1 | 0 | 3 meat |
| 11 | 3 | 960 | 16 | 4 | 0 | 2 meat |
| 3 | 1.5 | 262 | 3 | 6 | ½ | ½ starch, ½ fat |
| 0 | 0 | 200–400 | 0 | 2 | 0 | free |
| 2 | 1 | 218 | 0.5 | 4 | 0 | free |
| 1.5 | NA | 190 | 0 | 4 | 0 | free |

1 Carbohydrate Choice = 1 starch *or* 1 fruit *or* 1 milk exchange

| PRODUCTS | SERVING SIZE | CALORIES | CALORIES FROM FAT |
|---|---|---|---|
| ❶ Enchilada, Old El Paso®, mild | ¼ cup | 25 | 10 |
| ❶ Enchilada, Zapata® | 2 Tb | 10 | 0 |
| ❶ Extra Chunky, Old El Paso®, all varieties (avg) | 2 Tb | 5 | 0 |
| ❶ Green Chili Enchilada, Old El Paso®, hot | ¼ cup | 30 | 15 |
| ❶ Hot Sauce, Gephardt® | 1 tsp | 1 | 0 |
| ❶ Hot Sauce, Zapata® | 1 tsp | 0 | 0 |
| ❶ Jalapeno Relish, Old El Paso®, hot | 1 Tb | 5 | 0 |
| ❶ Taco, Old El Paso® | 1 Tb | 5 | 0 |
| ❶ Taco, Old El Paso®, all varieties (avg) | 1 Tb | 5 | 0 |
| ❶ Tomatoes and Green Chilies, Old El Paso®, hot | ¼ cup | 10 | 0 |
| ❶ Tomatoes and Jalapenos, Old El Paso®, hot | ¼ cup | 15 | 0 |
| **Oriental Sauces** | | | |
| ❶ Bangkok Padang™ Peanut Sauce, House of Tsang® | 1 Tb | 45 | 20 |
| ❶ Bead Molasses, La Choy® | 1 Tb | 49 | 0 |
| ❶ Brown Gravy Sauce, La Choy® | ¼ cup | 275 | 0 |
| Chun King Hot Teriyaki Sauce, La Choy® | 1 Tb | 17 | 4 |
| ❶ Classic Stir Fry Sauce, House of Tsang® | 1 Tb | 25 | 5 |
| ❶ Ginger Flavored Soy Sauce, House of Tsang® | 1 Tb | 20 | 0 |
| ❶ Ginger Flavored Soy Sauce, House of Tsang® Less Sodium | 1 Tb | 10 | 0 |
| ❶ Mandarin Marinade, House of Tsang® | 1 Tb | 25 | 0 |
| ❶ Mandarin Soy Sauce, La Choy® | ½ cup | 71 | 2 |
| ❶ Mushroom Flavored Soy Sauce, House of Tsang® Less Sodium | 1 Tb | 10 | 0 |
| ❶ Plum Sauce, La Choy® | 1 Tb | 25 | 1 |
| ❶ Saigon Sizzle™ Stir Fry Sauce, House of Tsang® | 1 Tb | 40 | 5 |
| ❶ Soy Sauce, La Choy® | 1 Tb | 11 | 0 |
| ❶ Soy Sauce, La Choy® Lite | 1 Tb | 15 | 0 |
| ❶ Spicy Sweet & Sour Sauce, La Choy® | ½ cup | 137 | 0 |
| ❶ Spicy Szechuan Sauce, La Choy® | ½ cup | 84 | 2 |
| ❶ Sweet & Sour Stir Fry Sauce, House of Tsang® | 1 Tb | 35 | 0 |

❶  Meets Low-Fat Guidelines

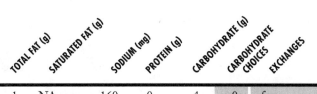

| TOTAL FAT (g) | SATURATED FAT (g) | SODIUM (mg) | PROTEIN (g) | CARBOHYDRATE (g) | CARBOHYDRATE CHOICES | EXCHANGES |
|---|---|---|---|---|---|---|
| 1 | NA | 160 | 0 | 4 | 0 | free |
| 0 | 0 | 180 | 0 | 2 | 0 | free |
| 0 | 0 | 80 | 0 | 1 | 0 | free |
| 1.5 | NA | 330 | <1 | 3 | 0 | free |
| 0 | 0 | 89 | 0 | 0 | 0 | free |
| 0 | 0 | 100 | 0 | 0 | 0 | free |
| 0 | 0 | 110 | 0 | 1 | 0 | free |
| 0 | 0 | 85 | 0 | 1 | 0 | free |
| 0 | 0 | 75 | 0 | 1 | 0 | free |
| 0 | 0 | 310 | 0 | 2 | 0 | free |
| 0 | 0 | 290 | 1 | 3 | 0 | free |
| 2.5 | 0.5 | 240 | 1 | 4 | 0 | ½ fat |
| 0 | 0 | 47 | <1 | 11 | 1 | 1 fruit |
| 0 | 0 | 320 | 3 | 66 | 4½ | 1 starch, 3½ fruit |
| <1 | 0 | 994 | 2 | 3 | 0 | free |
| 1 | 0 | 570 | 0 | 4 | 0 | free |
| 0 | 0 | 730 | 1 | 4 | 0 | free |
| 0 | 0 | 280 | 0 | 2 | 0 | free |
| 0 | 0 | 680 | 0 | 6 | ½ | ½ fruit |
| <1 | 0 | 852 | 2 | 16 | 1 | 1 starch |
| 0 | 0 | 280 | 0 | 2 | 0 | free |
| <1 | 0 | 4 | <1 | 6 | ½ | ½ fruit |
| 1 | 0 | 350 | 0 | 8 | ½ | ½ fruit |
| <1 | 0 | 1227 | 2 | 1 | 0 | free |
| <1 | 0 | 542 | 2 | 2 | 0 | free |
| 0 | 0 | 754 | 2 | 36 | 2½ | ½ starch, 2 fruit |
| <1 | 0 | 624 | 3 | 18 | 1 | 1 starch |
| 0 | 0 | 50 | 0 | 8 | ½ | ½ fruit |

1 Carbohydrate Choice = 1 starch or 1 fruit or 1 milk exchange

| PRODUCTS | SERVING SIZE | CALORIES | CALORIES FROM FAT |
|---|---|---|---|
| ❶ Sweet and Sour Sauce, Kraft® | 2 Tb | 80 | 5 |
| ❶ Sweet and Sour Sauce, Kraft® Sauceworks® | 2 Tb | 60 | 0 |
| ❶ Sweet and Sour Sauce, La Choy® | 2 Tb | 58 | 2 |
| ❶ Sweet and Sour Duck Sauce, La Choy® | 2 Tb | 61 | 2 |
| ❶ Teriyaki Sauce, La Choy® | 1 Tb | 17 | 1 |
| ❶ Teriyaki Sauce, La Choy® | ½ cup | 95 | 1 |
| ❶ Teriyaki Sauce, La Choy® Lite | 1 Tb | 18 | 0 |
| Wok Oil, House of Tsang® | 1 Tb | 130 | 130 |

### Sloppy Joe Sauces

| | | | |
|---|---|---|---|
| ❶ Manwich® Barbeque, Hunt's® | ¼ cup | 57 | 0 |
| ❶ Manwich® Bold, Hunt's® | ¼ cup | 62 | 9 |
| ❶ Manwich® Burrito Sauce, Hunt's® | ¼ cup | 25 | 0 |
| ❶ Manwich® Dry Mix, Hunt's® | ¼ oz | 22 | 0 |
| ❶ Manwich® Mexican Sauce, Hunt's® | ¼ cup | 27 | 0 |
| ❶ Manwich® Original Sauce, Hunt's® | ¼ cup | 32 | 4.5 |
| ❶ Manwich® Taco Sauce, Hunt's® | ¼ cup | 31 | 0 |
| ❶ Manwich® Thick & Chunky, Hunt's® | ¼ cup | 44 | 4.5 |
| Sandwich Spread & Burger Sauce, Kraft® | 1 Tb | 50 | 45 |
| ❶ Sloppy Joe Sandwich Sauce, Green Giant® | ¼ cup | 50 | 0 |

### Other Sauces

| | | | |
|---|---|---|---|
| ❶ Chicken Sensations, Hunt's®, all varieties (avg) | 1 Tb | 31 | 20 |
| ❶ Chicken Tonight® Chicken Cacciatore, Ragu® | ½ cup | 80 | 15 |
| Chicken Tonight® Country French Chicken, Ragu® | ½ cup | 130 | 100 |
| Chicken Tonight® Creamy Chicken Primavera, Ragu® | ½ cup | 90 | 60 |
| Chicken Tonight® Creamy Chicken with Mushrooms, Ragu® | ½ cup | 110 | 80 |
| Chicken Tonight® Herbed Chicken with Wine, Ragu® | ½ cup | 80 | 50 |
| Chicken with Mushroom, Hunt's® Homestyle Separates | 1 cup | 199 | 36 |

❶  Meets Low-Fat Guidelines

| TOTAL FAT (g) | SATURATED FAT (g) | SODIUM (mg) | PROTEIN (g) | CARBOHYDRATE (g) | CARBOHYDRATE CHOICES | EXCHANGES |
|---|---|---|---|---|---|---|
| 0.5 | 0 | 180 | 0 | 19 | 1 | 1 fruit |
| 0 | 0 | 125 | 0 | 14 | 1 | 1 fruit |
| <1 | 0 | 104 | <1 | 14 | 1 | 1 fruit |
| <1 | 0 | 128 | <1 | 15 | 1 | 1 fruit |
| <1 | 0 | 917 | 1 | 3 | 0 | free |
| <1 | 0 | 1154 | 3 | 22 | 1½ | 1½ starch |
| <1 | 0 | 439 | 1 | 4 | 0 | free |
| 14 | 3 | 0 | 0 | 0 | 0 | 3 fat |
| 0 | 0 | 887 | 1 | 14 | 1 | 1 starch |
| 1 | 0 | 802 | 0.5 | 13 | 1 | 1 starch |
| 0 | 0 | 559 | 1 | 6 | ½ | ½ starch |
| 0 | 0 | 351 | 0 | 5 | 0 | free |
| 0 | 0 | 552 | 1 | 5 | 0 | free |
| 0.5 | 0 | 365 | 1 | 6 | ½ | ½ starch |
| 0 | 0 | 587 | 1 | 7 | ½ | ½ starch |
| 0.5 | 0 | 737 | 1.5 | 9 | ½ | ½ starch |
| 5 | 0.5 | 100 | 0 | 3 | 0 | 1 fat |
| 0 | 0 | 420 | 2 | 11 | 1 | 1 starch |
| 2.5 | 0 | 300 | 0 | 2 | 0 | ½ fat |
| 1.5 | 0 | 530 | 2 | 14 | 1 | 1 starch |
| 11 | 2 | 860 | <1 | 6 | ½ | ½ starch, 2 fat |
| 6 | 1 | 750 | <1 | 7 | ½ | ½ starch, 1 fat |
| 9 | 1.5 | 750 | <1 | 5 | 0 | 2 fat |
| 6 | 1.5 | 670 | <1 | 6 | ½ | ½ starch, 1 fat |
| 4 | 2 | 908 | 10 | 32 | 2 | 2 starch, 1 lean meat |

1 Carbohydrate Choice = 1 starch *or* 1 fruit *or* 1 milk exchange

| PRODUCTS | SERVING SIZE | CALORIES | CALORIES FROM FAT |
|---|---|---|---|
| Chili Hot Dog Sauce, Open Range® | ¼ cup | 61 | 31.5 |
| ❶ Ham Glaze, Western® | 2 Tb | 50 | 0 |
| ❶ Honey Mustard, Maple Grove Farms of Vermont® | 1 Tb | 40 | 9 |
| ❶ Hot Dog Sauce, Just Rite® | ¼ cup | 50 | 27 |
| ❶ Spicy Simmer Sauce, Newman's Own® | ½ cup | 70 | 25 |
| ❶ Steak Sauce, Maple Grove Farms of Vermont® | 1 Tb | 20 | 0 |
| ❶ Sweet & Sour Chicken, Ragu® Chicken Tonight | ½ cup | 120 | 0 |
| Welsh Rarebit, Stouffer's® | ¼ cup | 120 | 80 |

### SAUERKRAUT

| | | | |
|---|---|---|---|
| ❶ All varieties (avg) | ¼ cup | 5 | 0 |

### SAUSAGE

| | | | |
|---|---|---|---|
| Bratwurst, Hillshire Farm®, all varieties (avg) | 2 oz | 185 | 150 |
| Breakfast Links, The Turkey Store®, all varieties (avg) | 2 oz | 140 | 100 |
| Breakfast Patties, The Turkey Store®, all varieties (avg) | 2.3 oz | 150 | 110 |
| ❶ Breakfast Sausage, Healthy Choice®, all varieties (avg) | 2 links or 2 patties | 50 | 10 |
| Bratwurst, Johnsonville™ (Cooked, Smoked, or Beef, avg) | 1 link | 250 | 200 |
| Lite Links, Hillshire Farms®, all varieties (avg) | 2.7 oz | 190 | 135 |
| Lit'l Links, Hillshire Farms®, all varieties (avg) | 2 oz | 180 | 144 |
| Polish Sausage or Smoked Sausage, Johnsonville™ (avg) | 1 link | 240 | 200 |
| ❶ Polska Kielbasa, Healthy Choice® Lowfat | 2 oz | 70 | 15 |
| Polska Kielbasa, Hillshire Farms® Flavorseal, all varieties (avg) | 2 oz | 190 | 150 |
| Pork Sausage, Oscar Meyer® | 2 links | 180 | 140 |
| Sausage, Hillshire Farms®, all varieties (avg) | 2 oz | 190 | 150 |
| Sausage, Johnsonville™ Beddar with Cheddar™ | 1 link | 240 | 200 |

❶  Meets Low-Fat Guidelines

| TOTAL FAT (g) | SATURATED FAT (g) | SODIUM (mg) | PROTEIN (g) | CARBOHYDRATE (g) | CARBOHYDRATE CHOICES | EXCHANGES |
|---|---|---|---|---|---|---|
| 3.5 | 1.5 | 255 | 3 | 6 | ½ | ½ starch, ½ fat |
| 0 | 0 | 25 | 0 | 13 | 1 | 1 fruit |
| 1 | 0 | 30 | <1 | 8 | ½ | ½ fruit |
| 3 | 1 | 265 | 2 | 5 | 0 | ½ fat |
| 3 | 0 | 510 | 0 | 10 | ½ | ½ fruit |
| 0 | 0 | 130 | <1 | 4 | 0 | free |
| 0 | 0 | 320 | <1 | 30 | 2 | 2 fruit |
| 9 | 4 | 280 | 5 | 5 | 0 | 1 veg, 2 fat |
| 0 | 0 | 210 | 0 | 1 | 0 | free |
| 17 | NA | 410–500 | 7 | 1 | 0 | 1 high fat meat, 2 fat |
| 11 | 3 | 360–430 | 9 | 1 | 0 | 1 meat, 1 fat |
| 12 | 3 | 410–490 | 10 | 1 | 0 | 1 high fat meat, 1 fat |
| 1.5 | 0.5 | 300 | 7 | 3 | 0 | 1 lean meat |
| 22 | 9 | 650–770 | 9 | 2 | 0 | 1 high fat meat, 3 fat |
| 15 | NA | 610–690 | 11 | 2 | 0 | 2 meat, 1 fat |
| 16 | NA | 600 | 8 | 2 | 0 | 1 high fat meat, 2 fat |
| 22 | 9 | 650 | 9 | 2 | 0 | 1 high fat meat, 3 fat |
| 1.5 | 0.5 | 480 | 9 | 5 | 0 | 1 lean meat |
| 17 | NA | 540 | 8 | 2 | 0 | 1 high fat meat, 2 fat |
| 16 | 6 | 450 | 9 | 1 | 0 | 1 meat, 2 fat |
| 17 | NA | 620 | 7 | 1 | 0 | 1 high fat meat, 2 fat |
| 22 | 8 | 650 | 9 | 2 | 0 | 1 high fat meat, 3 fat |

1 Carbohydrate Choice = 1 starch or 1 fruit or 1 milk exchange

| PRODUCTS | SERVING SIZE | CALORIES | CALORIES FROM FAT |
|---|---|---|---|
| Sausage, Johnsonville™ Beddar with Cheddar™ Light | 1 link | 140 | 80 |
| Sausage, Hillshire Farms® Lower Fat and Light, all varieties (avg) | 2 oz | 150 | 100 |
| Smoked Sausage, Hillshire Farms® Flavorseal, all varieties (avg) | 2 oz | 190 | 153 |
| ❶ Smoked Sausage or Kielbasa, Low-Fat, all varieties (avg) | 2 oz | 709 | 15 |
| Smokies (link sausage), Oscar Meyer®, all varieties (avg) | 1 link | 130 | 100 |
| Turkey Sausage, The Turkey Store®, all varieties (avg) | 3 oz | 140 | 80 |
| Turkey Smoked Sausage or Polska Kielbasa, Louis Rich® (avg) | 2 oz | 85 | 45 |

### SEAFOOD (FROZEN); SEE ALSO FISH

| PRODUCTS | SERVING SIZE | CALORIES | CALORIES FROM FAT |
|---|---|---|---|
| Breaded Butterfly Shrimp, Van de Kamp's® | 7 shrimp | 280 | 120 |
| Breaded Whole Popcorn Shrimp, Van de Kamp's® | 20 shrimp | 270 | 110 |
| Breaded Whole Shrimp, Van de Kamp's® | 7 shrimp | 240 | 90 |
| Oven Crunchy Jumbo Butterfly Shrimp, Sea Pak® | 4 shrimp | 200 | 80 |
| Oven Crunchy Popcorn Shrimp, Sea Pak® | 15 shrimp | 210 | 110 |
| Oven Crunchy Shrimp Poppers, Sea Pak® | 20 pieces | 210 | 110 |
| Popcorn Shrimp, Singleton® | 9 shrimp | 260 | 110 |

### SEAFOOD, IMITATION (REFRIGERATED)

| PRODUCTS | SERVING SIZE | CALORIES | CALORIES FROM FAT |
|---|---|---|---|
| ❶ Crab Delight, Louis Rich® | 3 oz | 70 | 0 |
| ❶ Lobster Delight, Louis Rich® | 3 oz | 80 | 0 |
| ❶ Scallop Delight, Louis Rich® | ½ cup | 80 | 0 |

### SEAFOOD MEALS/ENTREES (FROZEN)
see also Fish Meals/Entrees

| PRODUCTS | SERVING SIZE | CALORIES | CALORIES FROM FAT |
|---|---|---|---|
| ❶ Baked Fish with Cheddar Shells, Stouffer's® Lean Cuisine® | 1 pkg | 260 | 70 |

❶  Meets Low-Fat Guidelines

| TOTAL FAT (g) | SATURATED FAT (g) | SODIUM (mg) | PROTEIN (g) | CARBOHYDRATE (g) | CARBOHYDRATE CHOICES | EXCHANGES |
|---|---|---|---|---|---|---|
| 9 | 3.5 | 640 | 10 | 3 | 0 | 1 meat, 1 fat |
| 11 | NA | 410 | 7 | 2 | 0 | 1 meat, 1 fat |
| 17 | NA | 500 | 7 | 2 | 0 | 1 high fat meat, 2 fat |
| 1.5 | 0.5 | 480 | 9 | 5 | 0 | 1 lean meat |
| 11 | 6 | 440 | 6 | 1 | 0 | 1 meat, 1 fat |
| 9 | 3.5 | 530–680 | 14.5 | 2 | 0 | 2 meat |
| 5 | 1.5 | 500–540 | 9 | 2 | 0 | 1 meat |
| 14 | 2.5 | 580 | 12 | 28 | 2 | 2 starch, 1 meat, 1 fat |
| 13 | 2 | 610 | 11 | 28 | 2 | 2 starch, 1 meat, 1 fat |
| 10 | 1.5 | 520 | 13 | 26 | 2 | 2 starch, 1 meat, ½ fat |
| 9 | 1 | 770 | 10 | 20 | 1 | 1 starch, 1 meat, 1 fat |
| 12 | 2 | 720 | 9 | 18 | 1 | 1 starch, 1 meat, 1 fat |
| 12 | 2 | 530 | 8 | 19 | 1 | 1 starch, 1 meat, 1 fat |
| 13 | 1.5 | 130 | 10 | 27 | 2 | 2 starch, 1 meat, 1 fat |
| 0 | 0 | 560 | 8 | 10 | ½ | ½ starch, 1 very lean meat |
| 0 | 0 | 660 | 8 | 11 | 1 | 1 starch, 1 very lean meat |
| 0.5 | 0 | 560 | 9 | 11 | 1 | 1 starch, 1 very lean meat |
| 8 | 2 | 580 | 19 | 28 | 2 | 2 starch, 2 lean meat |

1 Carbohydrate Choice = 1 starch *or* 1 fruit *or* 1 milk exchange

## PRODUCTS

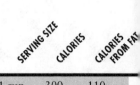

| | SERVING SIZE | CALORIES | CALORIES FROM FAT |
|---|---|---|---|
| Breaded Shrimp Over Angel Hair Pasta, Marie Callender's® | 1 cup | 300 | 110 |
| Linguini with Bay Shrimp and Clams Marinara, Budget Gourmet® | 1 entree | 270 | 80 |
| ❶ Shrimp and Vegetables Maria, Healthy Choice® | 1 meal | 270 | 25 |
| ❶ Shrimp Lo Mein, Yu Sing® | 1 pkg | 220 | 20 |
| ❶ Shrimp Marinara, Healthy Choice® | 1 meal | 220 | 5 |
| ❶ Shrimp Marinara, Smart Ones® | 1 meal | 200 | 15 |

### SNACK CAKES

| | SERVING SIZE | CALORIES | CALORIES FROM FAT |
|---|---|---|---|
| ❶ Angel Cakes (Low Fat Raspberry), Little Debbie® | 1 ind. pkg | 120 | 10 |
| Banana Nut Muffin Loaves™, Little Debbie® | 1 ind. pkg | 220 | 90 |
| Banana Twins Cakes, Little Debbie® | 1 ind. pkg | 250 | 90 |
| Caramel Cookie Bars, Little Debbie® | 1 ind. pkg | 160 | 70 |
| Chocolate Chip Cakes, Little Debbie® | 1 ind. pkg | 290 | 120 |
| Chocolate Snack Cakes, Little Debbie® | 1 ind. pkg | 310 | 130 |
| Chocolate Twins Cakes, Little Debbie® | 1 ind. pkg | 240 | 80 |
| Coffee Cakes (Apple Streusel), Little Debbie® | 1 ind. pkg | 230 | 60 |
| Creme-filled Chocolate Cupcakes, Little Debbie® | 1 ind. pkg | 180 | 80 |
| Cupcakes, Hostess® | 1 cake | 180 | 50 |
| Devil Cremes Cakes, Little Debbie® | 1 ind. pkg | 190 | 70 |
| Devil Square Cakes, Little Debbie® | 1 ind. pkg | 270 | 110 |
| Ding Dongs™, Hostess® | 2 cakes | 370 | 170 |
| Donut Sticks, Little Debbie® | 1 ind. pkg | 210 | 110 |
| ❶ Figaroos Snack Squares, Little Debbie® | 1 ind. pkg | 150 | 25 |
| ❶ Fruit Boosters Snack Bars, Sunbelt® | 1 pkg | 190 | 30 |
| Fudge Macaroo, Little Debbie® | 1 ind. pkg · | 140 | 70 |
| Golden Cremes Cakes, Little Debbie® | 1 ind. pkg | 170 | 70 |
| Ho Ho's®, Hostess® | 3 cakes | 380 | 160 |
| Marshmallow Pies (Banana or Chocolate), Little Debbie® | 1 ind. pkg | 160 | 50 |

❶  Meets Low-Fat Guidelines

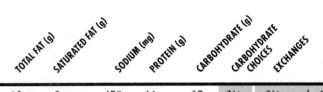

| TOTAL FAT (g) | SATURATED FAT (g) | SODIUM (mg) | PROTEIN (g) | CARBOHYDRATE (g) | CARBOHYDRATE CHOICES | EXCHANGES |
|---|---|---|---|---|---|---|
| 12 | 2 | 470 | 11 | 37 | 2½ | 2½ starch, 1 meat, 1 fat |
| 9 | 5 | 660 | 12 | 36 | 2½ | 2½ starch, 1 very lean meat, 1 fat |
| 3 | 1 | 540 | 15 | 46 | 3 | 3 starch, 1 very lean meat |
| 2 | 0 | 950 | 11 | 38 | 2½ | 2½ starch, 1 very lean meat |
| 0.5 | 0 | 220 | 10 | 44 | 3 | 2½ starch, 1 veg |
| 2 | 0 | 590 | 8 | 37 | 2½ | 2½ starch |
| 1 | 0 | 120 | 2 | 28 | 2 | 2 starch |
| 10 | 1.5 | 230 | 2 | 31 | 2 | 2 starch, 2 fat |
| 10 | 2.5 | 170 | 2 | 39 | 2½ | 2½ starch, 1 fat |
| 8 | 1.5 | 85 | 1 | 22 | 1½ | 1½ starch, 1 fat |
| 14 | 3.5 | 210 | 2 | 42 | 3 | 3 starch, 2 fat |
| 15 | 3.5 | 190 | 2 | 44 | 3 | 3 starch, 2 fat |
| 8 | 2 | 240 | 2 | 42 | 3 | 3 starch, 1 fat |
| 7 | 1.5 | 190 | 2 | 39 | 2½ | 2½ starch, 1 fat |
| 9 | 2 | 130 | 2 | 25 | 1½ | 1½ starch, 1 fat |
| 6 | 2.5 | 280 | 2 | 30 | 2 | 2 starch, 1 fat |
| 8 | 2 | 170 | 1 | 29 | 2 | 2 starch, 1 fat |
| 13 | 3 | 180 | 2 | 39 | 2½ | 2½ starch, 2 fat |
| 19 | 12 | 240 | 3 | 45 | 3 | 3 starch, 3 fat |
| 13 | 3 | 210 | 2 | 25 | 1½ | 1½ starch, 2 fat |
| 2.5 | 0.5 | 115 | 1 | 32 | 2 | 2 starch |
| 3 | 1 | 120 | 2 | 42 | 3 | 3 starch |
| 8 | 4 | 65 | 1 | 18 | 1 | 1 starch, 1 fat |
| 7 | 2 | 180 | 2 | 25 | 1½ | 1½ starch, 1 fat |
| 18 | 12 | 210 | 3 | 50 | 3 | 3 starch, 3 fat |
| 5 | 3 | 95 | 1 | 27 | 2 | 2 starch, ½ fat |

1 Carbohydrate Choice = 1 starch or 1 fruit or 1 milk exchange

## PRODUCTS

| | SERVING SIZE | CALORIES | CALORIES FROM FAT |
|---|---|---|---|
| Nutty Bars, Little Debbie® | 1 ind. pkg | 290 | 150 |
| Oatmeal Creme Pies, Little Debbie® | 1 ind. pkg | 170 | 60 |
| ❶ Oatmeal Lights™, Little Debbie® | 1 ind. pkg | 130 | 20 |
| Peanut Butter Bars, Little Debbie® | 1 ind. pkg | 270 | 130 |
| Pecan Spinwheels, Little Debbie® | 1 ind. pkg | 110 | 40 |
| Sno Balls, Hostess® | 2 cakes | 350 | 100 |
| Spice Cakes, Little Debbie® | 1 ind. pkg | 300 | 130 |
| Star Crunch Snacks, Little Debbie® | 1 ind. pkg | 140 | 60 |
| Strawberry Shortcake Rolls, Little Debbie® | 1 ind. pkg | 230 | 70 |
| Swiss Cake Rolls, Little Debbie® | 1 ind. pkg | 260 | 110 |
| Tiger Cakes, Little Debbie® | 1 ind. pkg | 310 | 140 |
| Twinkies®, Hostess® | 1 cake | 150 | 40 |
| ❶ Twinkies®, Hostess® Lights | 1 cake | 130 | 15 |
| Zebra Cakes, Little Debbie® | 1 ind. pkg | 320 | 140 |

### SNACK MIXES

| | | | |
|---|---|---|---|
| Cheez-It Party Mix, Sunshine® | ½ cup | 140 | 45 |
| Extra Nutty Snack Mix, Pepperidge Farm® | ½ cup | 180 | 80 |
| Honey Mustard & Onion Snack Mix, Pepperidge Farm® | ½ cup | 180 | 90 |
| Lightly Seasoned Snack Mix, Pepperidge Farm® | ½ cup | 170 | 70 |
| Original Goldfish Snack Mix, Pepperidge Farm® | ½ cup | 170 | 70 |
| Party Mix, Old Dutch® | ⅔ cup | 150 | 65 |
| Snack Mix, Eagle® | ½ cup | 150 | 70 |
| Snack Mix, Frito-Lay® | 27 pieces | 140 | 70 |
| Zesty Cheddar Goldfish Snack Mix, Pepperidge Farm® | ½ cup | 180 | 90 |

### SODA POP

| | | | |
|---|---|---|---|
| ❶ Diet soda, all brands, all varieties (avg) | 8 oz | 0 | 0 |
| ❶ Regular soda, all brands, all varieties (avg) | 8 oz | 115 | 0 |
| ❶ Regular soda, cans, all brands, all varieties (avg) | 12 oz can | 155 | 0 |

❶ Meets Low-Fat Guidelines

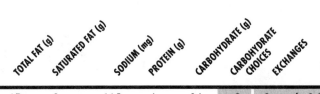

| TOTAL FAT (g) | SATURATED FAT (g) | SODIUM (mg) | PROTEIN (g) | CARBOHYDRATE (g) | CARBOHYDRATE CHOICES | EXCHANGES |
|---|---|---|---|---|---|---|
| 17 | 3 | 115 | 4 | 34 | 2 | 2 starch, 3 fat |
| 7 | 1.5 | 170 | 1 | 25 | 1½ | 1½ starch, 1 fat |
| 2.5 | 0 | 190 | 2 | 28 | 2 | 2 starch |
| 15 | 2.5 | 200 | 4 | 33 | 2 | 2 starch, 3 fat |
| 4 | 0.5 | 100 | 1 | 16 | 1 | 1 starch, ½ fat |
| 11 | 5 | 370 | 3 | 61 | 4 | 4 starch, 1 fat |
| 14 | 3.5 | 230 | 2 | 44 | 3 | 3 starch, 2 fat |
| 6 | 1.5 | 90 | 1 | 21 | 1½ | 1½ starch, 1 fat |
| 8 | 2 | 160 | 1 | 40 | 2½ | 2½ starch, 1 fat |
| 12 | 3 | 180 | 1 | 39 | 2½ | 2½ starch, 2 fat |
| 15 | 3.5 | 190 | 2 | 44 | 3 | 3 starch, 2 fat |
| 5 | 2 | 190 | 1 | 25 | 1½ | 1½ starch, ½ fat |
| 1.5 | 0 | 220 | 2 | 27 | 2 | 2 starch |
| 16 | 3.5 | 180 | 2 | 46 | 3 | 3 starch, 3 fat |
| | | | | | | |
| 5 | 1 | 270 | 4 | 19 | 1 | 1 starch, 1 fat |
| 9 | 1.5 | 330 | 5 | 20 | 1 | 1 starch, 2 fat |
| 10 | 1.5 | 390 | 4 | 19 | 1 | 1 starch, 2 fat |
| | | | | | | |
| 8 | 1 | 400 | 4 | 22 | 1½ | 1½ starch, 1 fat |
| 8 | 1.5 | 360 | 5 | 21 | 1½ | 1½ starch, 1 fat |
| 7 | 1 | 248 | 3 | 19 | 1 | 1 starch, 1½ fat |
| 7 | 1 | 270 | 4 | 17 | 1 | 1 starch, 1 fat |
| 8 | 1.5 | 230 | 2 | 17 | 1 | 1 starch, 1 fat |
| 10 | 1.5 | 390 | 1 | 19 | 1 | 1 starch, 2 fat |
| | | | | | | |
| 0 | 0 | 25–50 | 0 | 0 | 0 | free |
| 0 | 0 | 15–45 | 0 | 27–35 | 2 | 2 fruit |
| 0 | 0 | 75 | 0 | 39–47 | 2½–3 | 2½–3 fruit |

1 Carbohydrate Choice = 1 starch *or* 1 fruit *or* 1 milk exchange

| PRODUCTS | SERVING SIZE | CALORIES | CALORIES FROM FAT |
|---|---|---|---|

### SOUP (CANNED)
*see also* Chili; Stew

#### Bean and Ham Soup

| | | | |
|---|---|---|---|
| ❶ Bean & Ham, Campbell's® Home Cookin'® | 1 cup | 180 | 15 |
| ❶ Bean & Ham, Healthy Choice® | 1 cup | 170 | 10 |
| ❶ Bean & Ham, Progresso® | 1 cup | 160 | 20 |
| ❶ Old Fashioned Bean 'n Ham, Campbell's® Chunky | 1 cup | 190 | 18 |

#### Beef Soup

| | | | |
|---|---|---|---|
| ❶ Beef, Campbell's® | 1 cup | 80 | 20 |
| ❶ Beef & Potato, Healthy Choice® | 1 cup | 120 | 10 |
| Beef Barley, Progresso® | 1 cup | 130 | 35 |
| ❶ Beef Barley, Progresso® Healthy Classics | 1 cup | 140 | 20 |
| ❶ Beef Noodle, Campbell's® | 1 cup | 70 | 25 |
| Beef Noodle, Progresso® | 1 cup | 140 | 30 |
| ❶ Beef Vegetable, Progresso® Healthy Classics | 1 cup | 150 | 15 |
| Beef Vegetable & Rotini, Progresso® | 1 cup | 120 | 30 |
| Old Fashioned Vegetable Beef, Campbell's® Chunky | 1 cup | 150 | 45 |
| Sirloin Burger With Vegetables, Campbell's® Chunky | 1 cup | 190 | 81 |
| ❶ Vegetable Beef, Campbell's® | 1 cup | 80 | 18 |
| ❶ Vegetable Beef, Campbell's® Home Cookin'® | 1 cup | 120 | 20 |
| ❶ Vegetable Beef, Healthy Choice® | 1 cup | 130 | 10 |

#### Black Bean Soup

| | | | |
|---|---|---|---|
| ❶ Black Bean, Health Valley® Organic | 1 cup | 110 | 0 |
| ❶ Black Bean, Health Valley® Organic No Salt | 1 cup | 110 | 0 |
| ❶ Black Bean Vegetable, Health Valley® Fat-Free | 1 cup | 110 | 0 |
| ❶ Black Bean with Bacon, Old El Paso® | 1 cup | 160 | 15 |
| ❶ Hearty Black Bean, Progresso® | 1 cup | 170 | 15 |
| ❶ Spicy Black Bean with Couscous, Health Valley® | 1 cup | 130 | 0 |

 Meets Low-Fat Guidelines

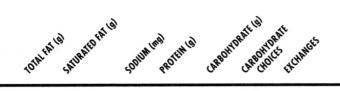

| TOTAL FAT (g) | SATURATED FAT (g) | SODIUM (mg) | PROTEIN (g) | CARBOHYDRATE (g) | CARBOHYDRATE CHOICES | EXCHANGES |
|---|---|---|---|---|---|---|
| 1.5 | 0.5 | 720 | 9 | 33 | 1½ | 1½ starch, 1 very lean meat |
| 1.5 | 0 | 480 | 9 | 31 | 2 | 2 starch |
| 2 | 0.5 | 870 | 10 | 25 | 1½ | 1½ starch, 1 very lean meat |
| 2 | NA | NA | 13 | 29 | 2 | 2 starch, 1 very lean meat |
| | | | | | | |
| 2 | 1 | 920 | 5 | 11 | 1 | 1 starch |
| 1 | 0.5 | 450 | 11 | 16 | 1 | 1 starch, 1 very lean meat |
| 4 | 1.5 | 780 | 10 | 13 | 1 | 1 starch, 1 very lean meat |
| 2 | 1 | 490 | 11 | 20 | 1 | 1 starch, 1 lean meat |
| 2.5 | 1 | 920 | 5 | 8 | ½ | ½ starch, ½ fat |
| 3.5 | 1.5 | 950 | 13 | 15 | 1 | 1 starch, 1 lean meat |
| 1.5 | 0.5 | 410 | 10 | 25 | 1½ | 1½ starch, 1 very lean meat |
| 3.5 | 1.5 | 830 | 11 | 10 | ½ | ½ starch, 1 meat |
| 5 | NA | NA | 10 | 17 | 1 | 1 starch, 1 meat |
| | | | | | | |
| 9 | NA | NA | 11 | 20 | 1 | 1 starch, 1 veg, 1 lean meat, 1 fat |
| 2 | NA | NA | 5 | 10 | ½ | ½ starch |
| 2 | 1 | 1010 | 7 | 18 | 1 | 1 starch, 1 very lean meat |
| 1 | 0 | 420 | 10 | 22 | 1½ | 1½ starch |
| | | | | | | |
| 0 | 0 | 290 | 8 | 28 | 2 | 2 starch |
| 0 | 0 | 45 | 8 | 28 | 2 | 2 starch |
| 0 | 0 | 280 | 11 | 24 | 1½ | 1½ starch, 1 very lean meat |
| 1.5 | <1 | 960 | 11 | 26 | 2 | 2 starch, 1 very lean meat |
| 1.5 | 0 | 730 | 8 | 30 | 2 | 2 starch, 1 very lean meat |
| 0 | 0 | 190 | 6 | 29 | 2 | 2 starch |

1 Carbohydrate Choice = 1 starch or 1 fruit or 1 milk exchange

## PRODUCTS

| | SERVING SIZE | CALORIES | CALORIES FROM FAT |
|---|---|---|---|
| ❶ Zesty Black Bean with Rice, Health Valley® | 1 cup | 100 | 0 |
| **Cheese Soup** | | | |
| Cheddar Cheese, Campbell's® | 1 cup | 130 | 70 |
| Chicken Broccoli Cheese, Campbell's® Chunky | 1 cup | 200 | 108 |
| Fiesta Nacho Cheese, Campbell's® | 1 cup | 140 | 70 |
| **Chicken Noodle Soup** | | | |
| ❶ Chicken Flavored Noodles with Vegetables, Health Valley® | 1 cup | 110 | 0 |
| ❶ Chicken Noodle, Campbell's® | 1 cup | 70 | 27 |
| ❶ Chicken Noodle, Campbell's® Healthy Request® | 1 cup | 70 | 27 |
| Chicken Noodle, Campbell's® Home Cookin'® | 1 cup | 120 | 36 |
| ❶ Chicken Noodle, Campbell's® Low Sodium | 1 cup | 80 | 27 |
| ❶ Chicken Noodle, Healthy Choice® | 1 cup | 140 | 25 |
| ❶ Chicken Noodle, Progresso® (10.5 oz) | 1 can | 110 | 20 |
| ❶ Chicken Noodle, Progresso® (19 oz) | 1 cup | 80 | 15 |
| ❶ Chicken Noodle, Progresso® Healthy Classics | 1 cup | 80 | 15 |
| ❶ Chicken Noodle, Weight Watchers® | 1 can | 150 | 15 |
| Chicken Noodle with Mushrooms, Campbell's® Chunky | 1 cup | 140 | 45 |
| Chicken with Noodles, Campbell's® Low Sodium Ready-to-Serve | 1 can | 170 | 45 |
| Classic Chicken Noodle, Campbell's® Chunky | 1 cup | 130 | 36 |
| ❶ Hearty Chicken Noodle, Old El Paso® | 1 cup | 110 | 30 |
| ❶ Homestyle Chicken Noodle, Campbell's® | 1 cup | 70 | 25 |
| **Chicken and Rice Soup** | | | |
| ❶ Chicken & Rice, Weight Watchers® | 1 can | 110 | 10 |
| ❶ Chicken & Wild Rice, Progresso® | 1 cup | 100 | 20 |
| Chicken Rice, Campbell's® Chunky | 1 cup | 130 | 36 |
| ❶ Chicken Rice with Vegetables, Progresso® Healthy Classics | 1 cup | 90 | 15 |
| ❶ Chicken with Rice, Campbell's® | 1 cup | 70 | 27 |

❶ Meets Low-Fat Guidelines

| TOTAL FAT (g) | SATURATED FAT (g) | SODIUM (mg) | PROTEIN (g) | CARBOHYDRATE (g) | CARBOHYDRATE CHOICES | EXCHANGES |
|---|---|---|---|---|---|---|
| 0 | 0 | 190 | 5 | 22 | 1½ | 1½ starch |
| | | | | | | |
| 8 | 3.5 | 1080 | 4 | 11 | 1 | 1 starch, 1 fat |
| 12 | NA | NA | 9 | 14 | 1 | 1 starch, 1 meat, 1 fat |
| 8 | 4 | 810 | 5 | 11 | 1 | 1 starch, 1 fat |
| | | | | | | |
| 0 | 0 | 190 | 5 | 24 | 1½ | 1½ starch |
| | | | | | | |
| 3 | NA | NA | 3 | 9 | ½ | ½ starch, ½ fat |
| 3 | NA | NA | 3 | 8 | ½ | ½ starch, ½ fat |
| 4 | NA | NA | 9 | 14 | 1 | 1 starch, 1 lean meat |
| 3 | NA | NA | 4 | 9 | ½ | ½ starch, 1 lean meat |
| 3 | 1 | 400 | 9 | 20 | 1 | 1 starch, 1 lean meat |
| 2.5 | 0.5 | 910 | 11 | 10 | ½ | ½ starch, 1 meat |
| 2 | 0.5 | 730 | 9 | 8 | ½ | ½ starch, 1 lean meat |
| 2 | 0.5 | 480 | 7 | 10 | ½ | ½ starch, 1 very lean meat |
| 2 | 0.5 | 740 | 9 | 25 | 1½ | 1½ starch, 1 very lean meat |
| 5 | NA | NA | 11 | 15 | 1 | 1 starch, 1 lean meat |
| | | | | | | |
| 5 | 1.5 | 120 | 14 | 18 | 1 | 1 starch, 2 lean meat |
| | | | | | | |
| 4 | NA | NA | 10 | 15 | 1 | 1 starch, 1 lean meat |
| 3 | 1 | 720 | 9 | 10 | ½ | ½ starch, 1 lean meat |
| 2.5 | 1.5 | 970 | 4 | 9 | ½ | ½ starch, ½ fat |
| | | | | | | |
| 1.5 | 0 | 720 | 6 | 17 | 1 | 1 starch, 1 very lean meat |
| 2 | 0.5 | 820 | 6 | 15 | 1 | 1 starch, 1 very lean meat |
| 4 | NA | NA | 8 | 15 | 1 | 1 starch, 1 lean meat |
| 1.5 | 0 | 450 | 7 | 12 | 1 | 1 starch, 1 very lean meat |
| | | | | | | |
| 3 | NA | NA | 3 | 9 | ½ | ½ starch, ½ fat |

1 Carbohydrate Choice = 1 starch or 1 fruit or 1 milk exchange

| PRODUCTS | SERVING SIZE | CALORIES | CALORIES FROM FAT |
|---|---|---|---|
| ● Chicken with Rice, Healthy Choice® | 1 cup | 110 | 25 |
| ● Chicken with Rice, Old El Paso® | 1 cup | 90 | 20 |
| Chicken with Rice and Vegetables, Progresso® (10.5 oz) | 1 cup | 130 | 35 |
| ● Chicken with Rice and Vegetables, Progresso® (19 oz) | 1 cup | 110 | 30 |
| ● Chicken with Wild Rice, Campbell's® | 1 cup | 70 | 18 |
| ● Hearty Chicken Rice, Campbell's® Healthy Request® | 1 cup | 120 | 27 |

### Chicken Soups, other

| | | | |
|---|---|---|---|
| Chickarina, Progresso® | 1 cup | 120 | 45 |
| ● Chicken Barley, Progresso® | 1 cup | 110 | 20 |
| ● Chicken Corn Chowder, Healthy Choice® | 1 cup | 150 | 25 |
| ● Chicken Gumbo, Campbell's® | 1 cup | 60 | 15 |
| Chicken Mushroom Chowder, Campbell's® Chunky | 1 cup | 210 | 110 |
| ● Chicken Vegetable, Campbell's® | 1 cup | 80 | 20 |
| Chicken Vegetable, Campbell's® Chunky | 1 cup | 150 | 45 |
| Chicken Vegetable, Campbell's® Home Cookin'® | 1 cup | 130 | 35 |
| ● Chicken Vegetable, Old El Paso® | 1 cup | 110 | 25 |
| ● Chicken Vegetable & Penne, Progresso® | 1 cup | 100 | 25 |
| ● Chicken with Pasta, Healthy Choice® | 1 cup | 120 | 25 |
| ● Hearty Chicken, Healthy Choice® | 1 cup | 130 | 25 |
| ● Hearty Chicken, Progresso® (10.5 oz) | 1 can | 120 | 25 |
| ● Hearty Chicken & Rotini, Progresso® | 1 cup | 90 | 20 |
| ● Hearty Chicken Vegetable, Campbell's® Healthy Request® | 1 cup | 120 | 27 |
| ● Homestyle Chicken/Vegetable, Progresso® | 1 cup | 100 | 20 |
| ● Old Fashioned Chicken, Campbell's® Chunky | 1 cup | 130 | 27 |
| ● Southern Style Chicken Vegetable, Campbell's® | 1 cup | 110 | 15 |
| Spicy Chicken & Penne, Progresso® | 1 cup | 120 | 35 |

● Meets Low-Fat Guidelines

| TOTAL FAT (g) | SATURATED FAT (g) | SODIUM (mg) | PROTEIN (g) | CARBOHYDRATE (g) | CARBOHYDRATE CHOICES | EXCHANGES |
|---|---|---|---|---|---|---|
| 3 | 1 | 430 | 7 | 15 | 1 | 1 starch, 1 very lean meat |
| 2.5 | <1 | 680 | 8 | 10 | ½ | ½ starch, 1 lean meat |
| 4 | 1 | 940 | 9 | 15 | 1 | 1 starch, 1 lean meat |
| 3 | 1 | 750 | 7 | 12 | 1 | 1 starch, 1 very lean meat |
| 2 | NA | NA | 3 | 9 | ½ | ½ starch |
| 3 | NA | NA | 6 | 17 | 1 | 1 starch, 1 lean meat |
| 5 | 2 | 710 | 8 | 10 | ½ | ½ starch, 1 meat |
| 2.5 | 0.5 | 720 | 10 | 14 | 1 | 1 starch, 1 very lean meat |
| 3 | 1 | 430 | 7 | 27 | 2 | 2 starch |
| 1.5 | 0.5 | 990 | 2 | 9 | ½ | ½ starch |
| 12 | 4 | 970 | 10 | 15 | 1 | 1 starch, 1 meat, 1 fat |
| 2 | 0.5 | 940 | 3 | 12 | 1 | 1 starch |
| 5 | NA | NA | 9 | 18 | 1 | 1 starch, 1 lean meat |
| 3.5 | 1 | 820 | 6 | 20 | 1 | 1 starch, 1 lean meat |
| 2.5 | <1 | 620 | 9 | 13 | 1 | 1 starch, 1 lean meat |
| 2.5 | 0.5 | 780 | 7 | 11 | 1 | 1 starch, 1 very lean meat |
| 2.5 | 1 | 470 | 8 | 17 | 1 | 1 starch, 1 very lean meat |
| 2.5 | 1 | 460 | 8 | 20 | 1 | 1 starch, 1 very lean meat |
| 2.5 | 0.5 | 1070 | 13 | 10 | ½ | ½ starch, 2 very lean meat |
| 2 | 0.5 | 860 | 10 | 8 | ½ | ½ starch, 1 lean meat |
| 3 | NA | NA | 7 | 17 | 1 | 1 starch, 1 lean meat |
| 2.5 | 0.5 | 680 | 9 | 10 | ½ | ½ starch, 1 lean meat |
| 3 | NA | NA | 9 | 12 | 1 | 1 starch, 1 lean meat |
| 1.5 | 0.5 | 900 | 7 | 18 | 1 | 1 starch, 1 very lean meat |
| 4 | 1 | 680 | 8 | 13 | 1 | 1 starch, 1 lean meat |

1 Carbohydrate Choice = 1 starch or 1 fruit or 1 milk exchange

## PRODUCTS

| | SERVING SIZE | CALORIES | CALORIES FROM FAT |
|---|---|---|---|
| **Clam Chowder** | | | |
| Manhattan Clam Chowder, Campbell's® Chunky | 1 cup | 130 | 36 |
| ❶ Manhattan Clam Chowder, Progresso® | 1 cup | 110 | 20 |
| New England Clam Chowder, Campbell's® Healthy Request® | 1 cup | 110 | 36 |
| New England Clam Chowder, Campbell's® Chunky | 1 cup | 250 | 135 |
| New England Clam Chowder, Campbell's® Home Cookin'® | 1 cup | 210 | 140 |
| ❶ New England Clam Chowder, Healthy Choice® | 1 cup | 130 | 25 |
| New England Clam Chowder, Progresso® (10.5 oz) | 1 can | 220 | 110 |
| New England Clam Chowder, Progresso® (18.5 oz) | 1 cup | 180 | 90 |
| **Cream Soup** | | | |
| ❶ Cream of Broccoli, Progresso® Healthy Classics | 1 cup | 90 | 25 |
| Cream of Celery, Campbell's® | 1 cup | 110 | 63 |
| Cream of Chicken, Progresso® | 1 cup | 170 | 90 |
| ❶ Cream of Chicken & Broccoli, Campbell's® Healthy Request® | 1 cup | 80 | 25 |
| ❶ Cream of Chicken with Mushroom, Healthy Choice® | 1 cup | 127 | 18 |
| ❶ Cream of Chicken with Vegetable, Healthy Choice® | 1 cup | 127 | 18 |
| Cream of Mushroom, Campbell's® | 1 cup | 110 | 63 |
| ❶ Cream of Mushroom, Campbell's® Healthy Request® | 1 cup | 70 | 27 |
| Cream of Mushroom, Campbell's® Low Sodium Ready-to-Serve | 1 can | 200 | 130 |
| ❶ Cream of Mushroom, Healthy Choice® | 1 cup | 77 | 9 |
| Cream of Mushroom, Progresso® | 1 cup | 140 | 80 |
| ❶ Cream of Potato, Campbell's® | 1 cup | 90 | 25 |

❶  Meets Low-Fat Guidelines

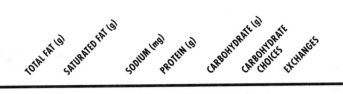

| TOTAL FAT (g) | SATURATED FAT (g) | SODIUM (mg) | PROTEIN (g) | CARBOHYDRATE (g) | CARBOHYDRATE CHOICES | EXCHANGES |
|---|---|---|---|---|---|---|
| 4 | NA | NA | 6 | 20 | 1 | 1 starch, 1 lean meat |
| 2 | 0 | 710 | 12 | 11 | 1 | 1 starch, 1 very lean meat |
| 4 | NA | NA | 5 | 15 | 1 | 1 starch, ½ fat |
| 15 | NA | NA | 8 | 21 | 1½ | 1½ starch, 1 meat, 1 fat |
| 16 | 5 | 1120 | 4 | 12 | 1 | 1 starch, 3 fat |
| 2.5 | 2 | 480 | 9 | 19 | 1 | 1 starch, 1 lean meat |
| 12 | 3.5 | 1050 | 7 | 21 | 1½ | 1½ starch, 1 meat, 1 fat |
| 10 | 3 | 850 | 6 | 17 | 1 | 1 starch, 1 meat, 1 fat |
| 3 | 0.5 | 580 | 2 | 13 | 1 | 1 starch |
| 7 | NA | NA | 2 | 9 | ½ | ½ starch, 1 fat |
| 10 | 3.5 | 880 | 8 | 11 | 1 | 1 starch, 1 meat, 1 fat |
| 2.5 | 1 | 480 | 3 | 10 | ½ | ½ starch, ½ fat |
| 2 | 1 | 421 | 7 | 20 | 1 | 1 starch, 1 very lean meat |
| 2 | 1 | 384 | 7 | 21 | 1½ | 1½ starch, 1 very lean meat |
| 7 | NA | NA | 2 | 9 | ½ | ½ starch, 1 fat |
| 3 | NA | NA | 2 | 9 | ½ | ½ starch, ½ fat |
| 14 | 4 | 50 | 3 | 18 | 1 | 1 starch, 2½ fat |
| 1 | 0.5 | 450 | 4 | 14 | 1 | 1 starch |
| 8 | 3.5 | 920 | 3 | 12 | 1 | 1 starch, 1 fat |
| 3 | 1.5 | 890 | 2 | 14 | 1 | 1 starch, ½ fat |

1 Carbohydrate Choice = 1 starch *or* 1 fruit *or* 1 milk exchange

| PRODUCTS | 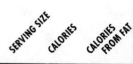 SERVING SIZE | CALORIES | CALORIES FROM FAT |
|---|---|---|---|
| Cream Soups (Chicken, Celery, Mushroom), Campbell's® Reduced Fat | 1 cup | 80 | 30 |
| ❶ Creamy Potato with Broccoli, Health Valley® | 1 cup | 80 | 0 |
| Creamy Tortellini, Progresso® | 1 cup | 210 | 140 |

### Lentil Soup

| | | | |
|---|---|---|---|
| ❶ Lentil & Carrot, Health Valley® Fat-Free | 1 cup | 90 | 0 |
| ❶ Lentil & Shells, Progresso® | 1 cup | 130 | 15 |
| ❶ Lentil, Health Valley® Organic | 1 cup | 90 | 0 |
| ❶ Lentil, Healthy Choice® | 1 cup | 150 | 10 |
| ❶ Lentil, Progresso® (10.5 oz) | 1 can | 170 | 25 |
| ❶ Lentil, Progresso® (19 oz) | 1 cup | 140 | 20 |
| ❶ Lentil, Progresso® Healthy Classics | 1 cup | 130 | 15 |
| ❶ Lentil with Couscous, Health Valley® | 1 cup | 130 | 0 |
| Lentil with Sausage, Progresso® | 1 cup | 170 | 60 |
| ❶ Savory Lentil, Campbell's® Home Cookin'® | 1 cup | 130 | 5 |

### Minestrone Soup

| | | | |
|---|---|---|---|
| Beef Minestrone, Progresso® | 1 cup | 140 | 40 |
| Chicken Minestrone, Progresso® | 1 cup | 120 | 30 |
| ❶ Hearty Minestrone/Shells, Progresso® | 1 cup | 120 | 15 |
| Minestrone, Campbell's® Chunky | 1 cup | 140 | 45 |
| ❶ Minestrone, Campbell's® Healthy Request® | 1 cup | 90 | 10 |
| ❶ Minestrone, Campbell's® Home Cookin'® | 1 cup | 120 | 20 |
| ❶ Minestrone, Health Valley® Fat-Free | 1 cup | 80 | 0 |
| ❶ Minestrone, Health Valley® Organic | 1 cup | 90 | 0 |
| ❶ Minestrone, Health Valley® Organic No-Salt | 1 cup | 90 | 0 |
| ❶ Minestrone, Healthy Choice® | 1 cup | 110 | 10 |
| ❶ Minestrone, Weight Watchers® | 1 can | 130 | 20 |
| ❶ Minestrone, Progresso® (19 oz) | 1 cup | 130 | 25 |
| ❶ Minestrone, Progresso® Healthy Classics | 1 can | 120 | 25 |
| Zesty Minestrone, Progresso® | 1 cup | 150 | 60 |

❶  Meets Low-Fat Guidelines

| TOTAL FAT (g) | SATURATED FAT (g) | SODIUM (mg) | PROTEIN (g) | CARBOHYDRATE (g) | CARBOHYDRATE CHOICES | EXCHANGES |
|---|---|---|---|---|---|---|
| 3.5 | 1 | 925 | 2 | 10 | ½ | ½ starch, ½ fat |
| 0 | 0 | 190 | 4 | 17 | 1 | 1 starch |
| 15 | 8 | 830 | 5 | 15 | 1 | 1 starch, 3 fat |
| | | | | | | |
| 0 | 0 | 220 | 10 | 25 | 1½ | 1 starch, 1 veg, 1 very lean meat |
| 1.5 | 0 | 840 | 7 | 22 | 1½ | 1½ starch |
| 0 | 0 | 240 | 9 | 20 | 1 | 1 starch, 1 very lean meat |
| 1 | 0.5 | 420 | 9 | 29 | 2 | 2 starch, 1 very lean meat |
| 2.5 | 0 | 930 | 11 | 27 | 2 | 2 starch, 1 very lean meat |
| 2 | 0 | 750 | 9 | 22 | 1½ | 1½ starch, 1 very lean meat |
| 1.5 | 0 | 440 | 8 | 20 | 1 | 1 starch, 1 very lean meat |
| 0 | 0 | 190 | 7 | 28 | 2 | 2 starch |
| 7 | 2 | 780 | 8 | 19 | 1 | 1 starch, 1 meat |
| 0.5 | 0 | 860 | 7 | 24 | 1 | 1 starch, ½ very lean meat |
| | | | | | | |
| 4 | 1.5 | 850 | 12 | 14 | 1 | 1 starch, 1 lean meat |
| 3.5 | 1 | 790 | 12 | 10 | ½ | ½ starch, 1 lean meat |
| 1.5 | 0 | 700 | 5 | 20 | 1 | 1 starch, 1 veg |
| 5 | NA | NA | 5 | 22 | 1½ | 1 starch, 1 veg, 1 fat |
| 1 | 0.5 | 480 | 4 | 17 | 1 | 1 starch |
| 2 | 1 | 990 | 4 | 19 | 1 | 1 starch |
| 0 | 0 | 210 | 8 | 21 | 1½ | 1½ starch, 1 very lean meat |
| 0 | 0 | 190 | 8 | 23 | 1½ | 1½ starch |
| 0 | 0 | 115 | 8 | 23 | 1½ | 1½ starch |
| 1 | 0 | 390 | 6 | 23 | 1½ | 1½ starch |
| 2 | 0.5 | 760 | 5 | 23 | 1½ | 1½ starch |
| 2.5 | 0.5 | 960 | 6 | 22 | 1½ | 1½ starch |
| 2.5 | 0 | 510 | 5 | 20 | 1 | 1 starch |
| 6 | 2.5 | 790 | 6 | 17 | 1 | 1 starch, 1 meat |

1 Carbohydrate Choice = 1 starch or 1 fruit or 1 milk exchange

## PRODUCTS

| | SERVING SIZE | CALORIES | CALORIES FROM FAT |
|---|---|---|---|
| **Split Pea Soup** | | | |
| ❶ Garden Split Pea with Carrots, Health Valley® | ⅓ cup | 110 | 0 |
| ❶ Green Split Pea, Progresso® | 1 cup | 170 | 25 |
| Split Pea, Campbell's® Low Sodium Ready-to-Serve | 1 can | 240 | 35 |
| ❶ Split Pea, Health Valley® Organic | 1 cup | 110 | 0 |
| ❶ Split Pea, Health Valley® Organic No Salt | 1 cup | 110 | 0 |
| ❶ Split Pea, Progresso® Healthy Classics | 1 cup | 180 | 20 |
| ❶ Split Pea & Carrot, Health Valley® Fat-Free | 1 cup | 110 | 0 |
| ❶ Split Pea with Ham, Campbell's® Home Cookin'® | 1 cup | 170 | 15 |
| ❶ Split Pea with Ham, Healthy Choice® | 1 cup | 160 | 20 |
| Split Pea with Ham, Progresso® | 1 cup | 160 | 35 |
| **Tomato Soup** | | | |
| ❶ Hearty Tomato & Rotini, Progresso® | 1 cup | 90 | 10 |
| ❶ Old Fashioned Tomato Rice, Campbell's® | 1 cup | 120 | 20 |
| Tomato Beef & Rotini, Progresso® | 1 cup | 140 | 40 |
| ❶ Tomato, Campbell's® | 1 cup | 100 | 18 |
| ❶ Tomato, Campbell's® Healthy Request® | 1 cup | 90 | 18 |
| ❶ Tomato, Health Valley® Organic | 1 cup | 90 | 0 |
| ❶ Tomato, Health Valley® Organic No Salt | 1 cup | 90 | 0 |
| ❶ Tomato, Progresso® | 1 cup | 90 | 20 |
| ❶ Tomato Garden, Campbell's® Home Cookin'® | 1 cup | 130 | 30 |
| ❶ Tomato Garden, Healthy Choice® | 1 cup | 110 | 15 |
| ❶ Tomato Garden Vegetable, Progresso® Healthy Classics | 1 cup | 100 | 10 |
| Tomato Tortellini, Progresso® | 1 cup | 120 | 45 |
| ❶ Tomato Vegetable, Health Valley® Fat-Free | 1 cup | 80 | 0 |
| **Vegetable Soup** | | | |
| ❶ 5 Bean Vegetable, Health Valley® | 1 cup | 140 | 0 |

❶ Meets Low-Fat Guidelines

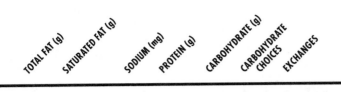

| TOTAL FAT (g) | SATURATED FAT (g) | SODIUM (mg) | PROTEIN (g) | CARBOHYDRATE (g) | CARBOHYDRATE CHOICES | EXCHANGES |
|---|---|---|---|---|---|---|
| 0 | 0 | 190 | 7 | 22 | 1½ | 1½ starch |
| 3 | 1 | 870 | 10 | 25 | 1½ | 1½ starch, 1 lean meat |
| 4 | 3 | 40 | 12 | 38 | 2 | 2 starch, 1 lean meat |
| 0 | 0 | 160 | 10 | 23 | 1½ | 1½ starch, 1 very lean meat |
| 0 | 0 | 115 | 10 | 23 | 1½ | 1½ starch, 1 very lean meat |
| 2.5 | 1 | 420 | 10 | 30 | 2 | 2 starch, 1 very lean meat |
| 0 | 0 | 230 | 8 | 17 | 1 | 1 starch, 1 very lean meat |
| 1.5 | 0.5 | 880 | 10 | 30 | 1½ | 1½ starch, 1 very lean meat |
| 2 | 1 | 400 | 9 | 19 | 1 | 1 starch, 1 lean meat |
| 4 | 1.5 | 830 | 9 | 20 | 1 | 1 starch, 1 meat |
| 1 | 0 | 820 | 4 | 16 | 1 | 1 starch |
| 2 | 0.5 | 790 | 2 | 23 | 1½ | 1½ starch |
| 4.5 | 1.5 | 750 | 11 | 15 | 1 | 1 starch, 1 lean meat |
| 2 | NA | NA | 2 | 18 | 1 | 1 starch |
| 2 | NA | NA | 2 | 18 | 1 | 1 starch |
| 0 | 0 | 250 | 4 | 22 | 1½ | 1½ starch |
| 0 | 0 | 25 | 4 | 22 | 1½ | 1½ starch |
| 2 | 0 | 990 | 3 | 15 | 1 | 1 starch |
| 3 | 1 | 720 | 4 | 21 | 1½ | 1½ starch |
| 1.5 | 0.5 | 420 | 5 | 21 | 1 | 1 starch, 1 veg |
| 1 | 0 | 480 | 3 | 19 | 1 | 1 starch |
| 5 | 1.5 | 910 | 5 | 13 | 1 | 1 starch, 1 fat |
| 0 | 0 | 240 | 6 | 17 | 1 | 1 starch |
| 0 | 0 | 250 | 10 | 32 | 2 | 2 starch |

1 Carbohydrate Choice = 1 starch *or* 1 fruit *or* 1 milk exchange

## PRODUCTS

| PRODUCTS | SERVING SIZE | CALORIES | CALORIES FROM FAT |
|---|---|---|---|
| ❶ Carotene Vegetable Power, Health Valley® Fat-Free | 1 cup | 70 | 0 |
| ❶ Country Corn & Vegetable, Health Valley® Fat-Free | 1 cup | 70 | 0 |
| ❶ Country Vegetable, Healthy Choice® | 1 cup | 100 | 5 |
| ❶ Garden Vegetable, Health Valley® Fat-Free | 1 cup | 80 | 0 |
| ❶ Garden Vegetable, Healthy Choice® | 1 cup | 120 | 10 |
| ❶ Garden Vegetable, Old El Paso® | 1 cup | 110 | 20 |
| ❶ Hearty Vegetable/Rotini, Progresso® | 1 cup | 110 | 10 |
| ❶ Vegetable, Campbell's® | 1 cup | 90 | 9 |
| ❶ Vegetable, Campbell's® Chunky | 1 cup | 130 | 30 |
| ❶ Vegetable, Health Valley® Organic | 1 cup | 80 | 0 |
| ❶ Vegetable, Progresso® | 1 cup | 90 | 15 |
| ❶ Vegetable, Progresso® Healthy Classics | 1 cup | 80 | 10 |
| ❶ Vegetable, Weight Watchers® | 1 can | 130 | 10 |
| ❶ Vegetable Barley, Health Valley® Fat-Free | 1 cup | 90 | 0 |

### Other Soups

| | | | |
|---|---|---|---|
| ❶ Broccoli & Shells, Progresso® | 1 cup | 70 | 5 |
| Clam & Rotini Chowder, Progresso® | 1 cup | 200 | 80 |
| ❶ Corn Chowder with Tomatoes, Health Valley® | ½ cup | 100 | 0 |
| Corn Chowder, Progresso® | 1 cup | 180 | 90 |
| ❶ Country Mushroom Rice, Campbell's® Home Cookin'® | 1 cup | 80 | 5 |
| ❶ Escarole in Chicken Broth, Progresso® | 1 cup | 25 | 10 |
| ❶ Fiesta Soup, Campbell's® Home Cookin'® | 1 cup | 130 | 25 |
| ❶ French Onion, Campbell's® | 1 cup | 70 | 25 |
| ❶ Garlic & Pasta, Progresso® Healthy Classics | 1 cup | 100 | 10 |
| ❶ Healthy Pasta Soup, Health Valley®, all varieties (avg) | 1 cup | 105 | 0 |
| ❶ Hearty Beef, Old El Paso® | 1 cup | 120 | 25 |
| ❶ Hearty Pasta & Vegetables, Campbell's® Healthy Request® | 1 cup | 90 | 10 |

❶  Meets Low-Fat Guidelines

| TOTAL FAT (g) | SATURATED FAT (g) | SODIUM (mg) | PROTEIN (g) | CARBOHYDRATE (g) | CARBOHYDRATE CHOICES | EXCHANGES |
|---|---|---|---|---|---|---|
| 0 | 0 | 240 | 5 | 17 | 1 | 1 starch |
| 0 | 0 | 135 | 5 | 17 | 1 | 1 starch |
| 0.5 | 0 | 430 | 4 | 23 | 1½ | 1 starch, 1 veg |
| 0 | 0 | 250 | 6 | 17 | 1 | 1 starch |
| 1 | 0 | 400 | 5 | 26 | 2 | 1½ starch, 1 veg |
| 2.5 | <1 | 710 | 5 | 17 | 1 | 1 starch |
| 1 | 0 | 720 | 4 | 20 | 1 | 1 starch, 1 veg |
| 1 | NA | NA | 3 | 17 | 1 | 1 starch |
| 3 | 1 | 870 | 3 | 22 | 1½ | 1½ starch |
| 0 | 0 | 230 | 5 | 18 | 1 | 1 starch |
| 2 | 0.5 | 850 | 4 | 15 | 1 | 1 starch |
| 1.5 | 0 | 470 | 4 | 13 | 1 | 1 starch |
| 1 | 0 | 680 | 4 | 27 | 2 | 2 starch |
| 0 | 0 | 210 | 6 | 19 | 1 | 1 starch |
| 1 | 0 | 720 | 3 | 14 | 1 | 1 starch |
| 9 | 2 | 800 | 7 | 21 | 1½ | 1½ starch, 1 meat |
| 0 | 0 | 190 | 5 | 21 | 1½ | 1½ starch |
| 10 | 4 | 780 | 5 | 20 | 1 | 1 starch, 2 fat |
| 0.5 | 0 | 820 | 3 | 16 | 1 | 1 starch |
| 1 | 0 | 980 | 2 | 2 | 0 | free |
| 2.5 | 0.5 | 750 | 3 | 24 | 1½ | 1½ starch |
| 2.5 | 0 | 980 | 2 | 10 | ½ | ½ starch, ½ fat |
| 1.5 | 0 | 450 | 4 | 18 | 1 | 1 starch |
| 0 | 0 | 290 | 4 | 21 | 1½ | 1½ starch |
| 2.5 | 1.5 | 690 | 10 | 14 | 1 | 1 starch, 1 lean meat |
| 1 | 0 | 480 | 3 | 16 | 1 | 1 starch |

1 Carbohydrate Choice = 1 starch or 1 fruit or 1 milk exchange

| PRODUCTS | SERVING SIZE | CALORIES | CALORIES FROM FAT |
|---|---|---|---|
| ❶ Hearty Penne & Chicken Broth, Progresso® | 1 cup | 70 | 10 |
| ❶ Italian Plus Carotene, Health Valley® Fat-Free | 1 cup | 80 | 0 |
| Macaroni and Bean, Progresso® | 1 cup | 160 | 40 |
| Meatballs & Pasta Pearls, Progresso® | 1 cup | 140 | 60 |
| ❶ Mushroom Barley, Health Valley® Organic | 1 cup | 60 | 0 |
| ❶ Mushroom Barley, Health Valley® Organic No Salt | 1 cup | 60 | 0 |
| Old Fashioned Potato Ham Chowder, Campbell's® Chunky | 1 cup | 220 | 130 |
| Oyster Stew, Campbell's® | 1 cup | 90 | 50 |
| ❶ Pasta Italiano, Health Valley® | ½ cup | 140 | 0 |
| Pepper Pot, Campbell's® | 1 cup | 100 | 45 |
| ❶ Potato Leek, Health Valley® Organic | 1 cup | 70 | 0 |
| ❶ Potato Leek, Health Valley® Organic No Salt | 1 cup | 70 | 0 |
| ❶ Salsa Bean, Campbell's® Home Cookin'® | 1 cup | 190 | 10 |
| ❶ Super Broccoli Carotene, Health Valley® | 1 cup | 70 | 0 |
| ❶ Tortellini/Chicken Broth, Progresso® | 1 cup | 80 | 20 |
| ❶ Turkey Vegetable, Campbell's® | 1 cup | 80 | 25 |
| ❶ Turkey with White and Wild Rice, Healthy Choice® | 1 cup | 90 | 20 |

## SOUP MIX (AS PREPARED)

### Chicken Noodle Soup Mix

| | | | |
|---|---|---|---|
| ❶ Chicken Flavor Noodle, Knorr® | 1 cup | 90 | 9 |
| ❶ Chicken Noodle, Lipton® Soup Secrets | 1 cup | 80 | 20 |
| ❶ Giggle Noodle with Chicken, Lipton® Soup Secrets | 1 cup | 80 | 20 |
| ❶ Noodle with Chicken Broth, Lipton® Soup Secrets | 1 cup | 60 | 15 |
| ❶ Ring-O-Noodle with Chicken, Lipton® | 1 cup | 70 | 15 |

❶  Meets Low-Fat Guidelines

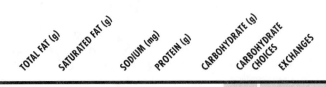

| TOTAL FAT (g) | SATURATED FAT (g) | SODIUM (mg) | PROTEIN (g) | CARBOHYDRATE (g) | CARBOHYDRATE CHOICES | EXCHANGES |
|---|---|---|---|---|---|---|
| 1 | 0 | 930 | 5 | 12 | 1 | 1 starch |
| 0 | 0 | 240 | 7 | 19 | 1 | 1 starch, 1 very lean meat |
| 4 | 1 | 800 | 7 | 23 | 1½ | 1½ starch, 1 lean meat |
| 7 | 3 | 700 | 7 | 13 | 1 | 1 starch, 1 meat |
| 0 | 0 | 220 | 5 | 15 | 1 | 1 starch |
| 0 | 0 | 95 | 5 | 15 | 1 | 1 starch |
| 14 | 8 | 840 | 6 | 16 | 1 | 1 starch, 1 meat, 1 fat |
| 6 | 3.5 | 940 | 2 | 6 | ½ | ½ starch, 1 fat |
| 0 | 0 | 190 | 5 | 31 | 2 | 2 starch |
| 5 | 2 | 1020 | 4 | 9 | ½ | ½ starch, 1 fat |
| 0 | 0 | 230 | 4 | 15 | 1 | 1 starch |
| 0 | 0 | 35 | 4 | 15 | 1 | 1 starch |
| 1 | 0.5 | 850 | 7 | 38 | 2 | 2 starch |
| 0 | 0 | 240 | 6 | 16 | 1 | 1 starch |
| 2 | 0.5 | 750 | 4 | 10 | ½ | ½ starch |
| 2.5 | 1 | 840 | 3 | 11 | 1 | 1 starch |
| 2.5 | 1 | 360 | 6 | 13 | 1 | 1 starch |
| 1 | 0.5 | 800 | 3 | 17 | 1 | 1 starch |
| 2.5 | 1 | 650 | 3 | 12 | 1 | 1 starch |
| 2 | 1 | 730 | 3 | 11 | 1 | 1 starch |
| 2 | 1 | 710 | 2 | 9 | ½ | ½ starch |
| 2 | 1 | 710 | 2 | 10 | ½ | ½ starch |

1 Carbohydrate Choice = 1 starch or 1 fruit or 1 milk exchange

## PRODUCTS

| | | SERVING SIZE | CALORIES | CALORIES FROM FAT |
|---|---|---|---|---|
| **Vegetable Soup Mix** | | | | |
| ❶ | Hearty Noodle with Vegetables, Lipton® Soup Secrets | 1 cup | 70 | 15 |
| ❶ | Spring Vegetable Soup and Recipe Mix, Knorr® | 1 cup | 25 | 0 |
| ❶ | Vegetable, Lipton® Recipe Secrets | 1 cup | 30 | 0 |
| ❶ | Vegetable Soup and Recipe Mix, Knorr® | 1 cup | 30 | 0 |
| **Other Soup Mixes** | | | | |
| ❶ | Beefy Mushroom, Lipton® Recipe Secrets | 1 cup | 35 | 0 |
| ❶ | Beefy Onion, Lipton® Recipe Secrets | 1 cup | 25 | 5 |
| ❶ | Black Bean & Rice, Uncle Ben's® Hearty Soups | 1 cup | 150 | 10 |
| ❶ | Broccoli Cheese & Rice, Uncle Ben's® Hearty Soups | 1 cup | 160 | 25 |
| ❶ | Chicken with Onion & Rice, Lipton® Kettle Creations | 1 cup | 120 | 10 |
| ❶ | Chicken with Pasta & Beans, Lipton® Kettle Creations | 1 cup | 110 | 10 |
| ❶ | Cream of Broccoli, Knorr® Chef's Collection | 1 cup | 60 | 14 |
| ❶ | Cream of Snow Pea, Knorr® | 1 cup | 70 | 18 |
| ❶ | Cream of Spinach Soup and Recipe Mix, Knorr® | 1 cup | 70 | 23 |
| ❶ | Extra Noodle, Lipton® Soup Secrets | 1 cup | 90 | 15 |
| ❶ | Fine Herb Soup and Recipe Mix, Knorr® | 1 cup | 100 | 45 |
| ❶ | Golden Herb with Lemon, Lipton® Recipe Secrets | 1 cup | 35 | 5 |
| ❶ | Golden Onion, Lipton® Recipe Secrets | 1 cup | 60 | 15 |
| ❶ | Hearty Chicken, Lipton® Soup Secrets | 1 cup | 80 | 15 |
| ❶ | Hot and Sour, Knorr® | 1 cup | 45 | 14 |
| ❶ | Italian Herb with Tomato, Lipton® Recipe Secrets | 1 cup | 40 | 5 |
| ❶ | Leek Soup and Recipe Mix, Knorr® | 1 cup | 70 | 27 |
| ❶ | Minestrone, Lipton® Kettle Creations | 1 cup | 110 | 10 |
| ❶ | New England Clam Chowder, Knorr® | 1 cup | 90 | 27 |
| ❶ | Noodle, Lipton® Soup Secrets | 1 cup | 60 | 15 |

❶ Meets Low-Fat Guidelines

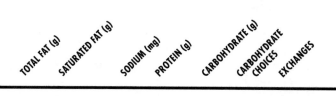

| TOTAL FAT (g) | SATURATED FAT (g) | SODIUM (mg) | PROTEIN (g) | CARBOHYDRATE (g) | CARBOHYDRATE CHOICES | EXCHANGES |
|---|---|---|---|---|---|---|
| 2 | 1 | 710 | 2 | 11 | 1 | 1 starch |
| 0 | 0 | 550 | 1 | 5 | 0 | 1 veg |
| 0 | 0 | 580 | <1 | 7 | ½ | ½ starch or veg |
| 0 | 0 | 730 | 1 | 6 | ½ | 1 veg |
| 0 | 0 | 650 | <1 | 7 | ½ | ½ starch |
| 0.5 | 0 | 610 | <1 | 5 | 0 | free |
| 1.5 | 0 | 430 | 7 | 28 | 2 | 2 starch |
| 3 | 1.5 | 870 | 7 | 26 | 2 | 2 starch |
| 1 | 0 | 690 | 4 | 24 | 1½ | 1½ starch |
| 1.5 | 0 | 690 | 5 | 20 | 1 | 1 starch |
| 1.5 | 0.5 | 660 | 2 | 9 | ½ | ½ starch |
| 2 | 0.5 | 700 | 2 | 10 | ½ | ½ starch or 2 veg |
| 2.5 | 1 | 600 | 2 | 9 | ½ | ½ starch |
| 1.5 | 0.5 | 680 | 3 | 15 | 1 | 1 starch |
| 5 | 1.5 | 1010 | 3 | 13 | 1 | 1 starch, 1 fat |
| 0.5 | 0 | 510 | <1 | 7 | ½ | ½ starch |
| 1.5 | 0 | 650 | 1 | 10 | ½ | ½ starch |
| 2 | 0.5 | 670 | 4 | 14 | 1 | 1 starch |
| 1.5 | 0.5 | 810 | <1 | 8 | ½ | ½ starch |
| 0.5 | 0 | 520 | 1 | 9 | ½ | ½ starch |
| 3 | 1 | 780 | 2 | 9 | ½ | ½ starch, ½ fat |
| 2 | 0 | 750 | 4 | 22 | 1½ | 1½ starch |
| 3 | 1 | 970 | 4 | 12 | 1 | 1 starch |
| 2 | 1 | 710 | 2 | 9 | ½ | ½ starch |

1 Carbohydrate Choice = 1 starch *or* 1 fruit *or* 1 milk exchange

| PRODUCTS | SERVING SIZE | CALORIES | CALORIES FROM FAT |
|---|---|---|---|
| ❶ Onion, Lipton® Recipe Secrets | 1 cup | 20 | 0 |
| ❶ Onion Mushroom, Lipton® Recipe Secrets | 1 cup | 35 | 5 |
| ❶ Onion Soup and Recipe Mix, Knorr® | 1 cup | 45 | 9 |
| ❶ Oxtail Soup and Recipe Mix, Knorr® | 1 cup | 60 | 23 |
| ❶ Pasta & Bean, Lipton® Kettle Creations | 1 cup | 130 | 15 |
| ❶ Ruffle Pasta, Lipton® Soup Secrets | 1 cup | 60 | 10 |
| ❶ Savory Herb with Garlic, Lipton® Recipe Secrets | 1 Tb | 35 | 5 |
| ❶ Tomato with Basil Soup and Recipe Mix, Knorr® | 1 cup | 80 | 18 |

## SOUP MIX, SINGLE-SERVING (AS PREPARED)

### Beans and Rice Soup Mix, single-serving

| | | | |
|---|---|---|---|
| ❶ Red Beans & Rice, Nile Spice® | 1 container | 170 | 9 |
| ❶ Red Beans and Rice, Spice Islands® | 1 container | 180 | 10 |
| ❶ Rice & Spicy Black Beans, Spice Islands® | 1 container | 190 | 10 |
| ❶ Rice & Spicy Red Beans, Spice Islands® | 1 container | 180 | 10 |
| ❶ Spanish Rice and Beans, Fantastic Foods® Low Sodium | 1 container | 210 | 15 |

### Black Bean Soup Mix, single-serving

| | | | |
|---|---|---|---|
| ❶ Black Bean, Knorr® | 1 container | 190 | 10 |
| ❶ Black Bean, Nile Spice® | 1 container | 170 | 14 |
| ❶ Black Bean, Spice Islands® | 1 container | 190 | 10 |
| ❶ Black Bean Salsa, Nile Spice® Organic | 1 container | 190 | 10 |
| ❶ Black Bean Salsa Couscous, Fantastic Foods® | 1 container | 240 | 15 |
| ❶ Jumpin' Black Beans, Fantastic Foods® | 1 container | 210 | 10 |

### Chicken Soup Mix, single-serving

| | | | |
|---|---|---|---|
| ❶ Chicken Flavor Vegetable, Knorr® | 1 container | 100 | 10 |
| ❶ Chicken Flavor Vegetable, Lipton® Cup-A-Soup | 1 envelope | 50 | 10 |
| ❶ Chicken Flavored Vegetable, Nile Spice® | 1 container | 110 | 13 |
| ❶ Chicken Free, Fantastic Foods® | 1 container | 140 | 5 |
| ❶ Chicken Noodle, Campbell's® | 1 can | 60 | 18 |
| ❶ Chicken Noodle, Lipton® Cup-A-Soup | 1 envelope | 50 | 10 |

❶ Meets Low-Fat Guidelines

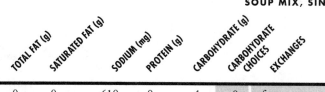

| TOTAL FAT (g) | SATURATED FAT (g) | SODIUM (mg) | PROTEIN (g) | CARBOHYDRATE (g) | CARBOHYDRATE CHOICES | EXCHANGES |
|---|---|---|---|---|---|---|
| 0 | 0 | 610 | 0 | 4 | 0 | free |
| 1 | 0 | 620 | 1 | 6 | ½ | ½ starch |
| 1 | 0.5 | 980 | 1 | 8 | ½ | ½ starch or 2 veg |
| 2.5 | 1 | 910 | 2 | 9 | ½ | ½ starch or 2 veg |
| 1.5 | 0.5 | 690 | 6 | 23 | 1½ | 1½ starch |
| 1 | 0 | 670 | 2 | 10 | ½ | ½ starch |
| 0.5 | 0 | 460 | 1 | 6 | ½ | ½ starch |
| 2 | 0.5 | 970 | 2 | 14 | 1 | 1 starch |
| 1 | 0 | 650 | 10 | 36 | 2½ | 2½ starch |
| 1 | 0 | 460 | 8 | 35 | 2 | 2 starch |
| 1 | 0 | 550 | 7 | 35 | 2 | 2 starch |
| 1.5 | 0 | 520 | 6 | 35 | 2 | 2 starch |
| 1.5 | 0 | 140 | 9 | 49 | 3 | 3 starch |
| 1 | 0 | 590 | 10 | 36 | 2½ | 2½ starch, 1 very lean meat |
| 1.5 | 0 | 600 | 11 | 35 | 2 | 2 starch, 1 very lean meat |
| 1.5 | 0 | 560 | 10 | 32 | 2 | 2 starch, 1 very lean meat |
| 1 | 0 | 630 | 9 | 34 | 2 | 2 starch, 1 very lean meat |
| 1.5 | 0 | 450 | 11 | 46 | 3 | 3 starch, 1 very lean meat |
| 1 | 0 | 470 | 12 | 39 | 2½ | 2½ starch, 1 very lean meat |
| 1 | 0.5 | 770 | 3 | 19 | 1 | 1 starch |
| 1 | 0 | 520 | 1 | 10 | ½ | ½ starch |
| 1.5 | 1 | 650 | 4 | 21 | 1½ | 1½ starch |
| 0.5 | 0 | 540 | 8 | 26 | 2 | 2 starch |
| 2 | NA | NA | 3 | 8 | ½ | ½ starch |
| 1 | 0.5 | 550 | 2 | 8 | ½ | ½ starch |

1 Carbohydrate Choice = 1 starch or 1 fruit or 1 milk exchange

## PRODUCTS

| | PRODUCTS | SERVING SIZE | CALORIES | CALORIES FROM FAT |
|---|---|---|---|---|
| ❶ | Chicken Rice Pilaf, Spice Islands® | 1 container | 180 | 10 |
| ❶ | Chicken Vegetable, Spice Islands® | 1 container | 130 | 15 |
| ❶ | Chicken with Rice, Campbell's® | 1 can | 50 | 18 |
| ❶ | Cream of Chicken, Lipton® Cup-A-Soup | 1 envelope | 70 | 20 |
| | Creamy Chicken Flavored Vegetable, Lipton® Cup-A-Soup | 1 envelope | 90 | 40 |
| ❶ | Hearty Chicken Flavored Noodle, Knorr® | 1 container | 110 | 20 |
| ❶ | Hearty Chicken Noodle, Lipton® Cup-A-Soup | 1 envelope | 60 | 10 |
| | Hearty Chicken Supper, Lipton® Cup-A-Soup | 1 envelope | 90 | 40 |

### Chili Soup Mix, single-serving

| | | | | |
|---|---|---|---|---|
| ❶ | Cha-Cha Chili, Fantastic Foods® | 1 container | 220 | 10 |
| ❶ | Chili & Corn, Nile Spice® | 1 container | 160 | 27 |
| ❶ | Four Bean Chili, Knorr® | 1 container | 230 | 10 |
| ❶ | Spicy Three Bean Chili, Spice Islands® | 1 container | 180 | 10 |
| ❶ | Three Bean Chili, Spice Islands® | 1 container | 180 | 10 |
| ❶ | Vegetarian Chili, Spice Islands® | 1 container | 180 | 20 |

### Corn Chowder Soup Mix, single-serving

| | | | | |
|---|---|---|---|---|
| ❶ | Corn and Potato Chowder, Fantastic Foods® | 1 container | 170 | 10 |
| ❶ | Corn Chowder, Knorr® | 1 container | 140 | 30 |
| ❶ | Corn Chowder, Spice Islands® | 1 container | 100 | 10 |
| ❶ | Sweet Corn Chowder, Nile Spice® | 1 container | 110 | 18 |

### Couscous Soup Mix, single-serving

| | | | | |
|---|---|---|---|---|
| ❶ | Couscous Almondine, Nile Spice® | 1 container | 200 | 22 |
| ❶ | Couscous Garbanzo, Nile Spice® | 1 container | 220 | 22 |
| ❶ | Couscous Lentil Curry, Nile Spice® | 1 container | 200 | 14 |
| ❶ | Couscous Minestrone, Nile Spice® | 1 container | 180 | 14 |
| ❶ | Couscous Parmesan, Nile Spice® | 1 container | 200 | 28 |
| ❶ | Couscous with Lentils, Fantastic Foods® | 1 container | 230 | 10 |
| ❶ | Couscous with Lentils, Fantastic Foods® Low Sodium | 1 container | 220 | 10 |

 Meets Low-Fat Guidelines

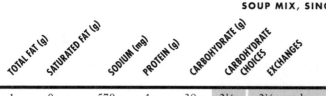

| TOTAL FAT (g) | SATURATED FAT (g) | SODIUM (mg) | PROTEIN (g) | CARBOHYDRATE (g) | CARBOHYDRATE CHOICES | EXCHANGES |
|---|---|---|---|---|---|---|
| 1 | 0 | 570 | 4 | 38 | 2½ | 2½ starch |
| 1.5 | 0 | 590 | 6 | 24 | 1½ | 1½ starch |
| 2 | NA | NA | 2 | 5 | 0 | free |
| 2 | 0 | 640 | <1 | 12 | 1 | 1 starch |
| 4 | 1.5 | 590 | 2 | 10 | ½ | ½ starch, 1 fat |
| 2 | 0.5 | 800 | 4 | 19 | 1 | 1 starch |
| 1 | 0 | 590 | 3 | 10 | ½ | ½ starch |
| 4 | 2 | 650 | 1 | 13 | 1 | 1 starch, ½ fat |
| 1 | 0 | 470 | 18 | 37 | 2½ | 2½ starch, 2 very lean meat |
| 3 | 0.5 | 730 | 7 | 25 | 1½ | 1½ starch, 1 very lean meat |
| 1.5 | 0 | 970 | 7 | 53 | 3½ | 3½ starch |
| 1.5 | 0 | 670 | 10 | 34 | 2 | 2 starch, 1 very lean meat |
| 1 | 0 | 640 | 9 | 34 | 2 | 2 starch, 1 very lean meat |
| 2 | 0 | 500 | 9 | 32 | 2 | 2 starch, 1 very lean meat |
| 1 | 0 | 580 | 7 | 34 | 2 | 2 starch |
| 3 | 2 | 700 | 3 | 26 | 2 | 2 starch |
| 1 | 0 | 300 | 4 | 23 | 1½ | 1½ starch |
| 2 | 1 | 420 | 3 | 23 | 1½ | 1½ starch |
| 2.5 | 0 | 490 | 7 | 37 | 2½ | 2½ starch |
| 2.5 | 0 | 500 | 9 | 39 | 2½ | 2½ starch |
| 1.5 | 0 | 730 | 10 | 36 | 2½ | 2½ starch |
| 1.5 | 0 | 590 | 8 | 34 | 2 | 2 starch |
| 3 | 1.5 | 570 | 8 | 34 | 2 | 2 starch, ½ fat |
| 1 | 0 | 480 | 12 | 44 | 3 | 3 starch, 1 very lean meat |
| 1 | 0 | 140 | 12 | 47 | 3 | 3 starch, 1 very lean meat |

1 Carbohydrate Choice = 1 starch *or* 1 fruit *or* 1 milk exchange

| PRODUCTS | SERVING SIZE | CALORIES | CALORIES FROM FAT |
|---|---|---|---|
| ❶ Creole Vegetable Couscous, Fantastic Foods® | 1 container | 220 | 15 |
| ❶ Nacho Cheddar Couscous, Fantastic Foods® | 1 container | 200 | 30 |
| ❶ Sweet Corn Couscous, Fantastic Foods® | 1 container | 180 | 10 |
| **Lentil Soup Mix, single-serving** | | | |
| ❶ Country Lentil, Fantastic Foods® | 1 container | 230 | 10 |
| ❶ Curry Lentil & Rice, Nile Spice® Organic | 1 container | 180 | 9 |
| ❶ Hearty Lentil, Knorr® | 1 container | 220 | 5 |
| ❶ Hearty Lentils & Wild Rice, Spice Islands® | 1 container | 190 | 10 |
| ❶ Lentil, Nile Spice® | 1 container | 180 | 14 |
| ❶ Lentil, Spice Islands® | 1 container | 190 | 5 |
| ❶ Lentil Almond Pilaf, Spice Islands® | 1 container | 190 | 20 |
| **Minestrone Soup Mix, single-serving** | | | |
| ❶ Hearty Minestrone, Knorr® | 1 container | 120 | 10 |
| ❶ Minestrone, Fantastic Foods® | 1 container | 150 | 10 |
| ❶ Minestrone, Nile Spice® | 1 container | 140 | 8 |
| ❶ Minestrone, Spice Islands® | 1 container | 120 | 5 |
| **Pasta Soup Mix, single-serving** | | | |
| Fettucine with Creamy Basil Sauce, Knorr® | 1 container | 220 | 35 |
| ❶ Garlic & Herb Pasta, Spice Islands® | 1 container | 160 | 10 |
| ❶ Mediterranean Pasta, Nile Spice® | 1 container | 180 | 23 |
| ❶ Parmesan Pasta, Nile Spice® | 1 container | 190 | 27 |
| ❶ Pasta Cup of Soups, Health Valley® Fat-Free | ½ cup | 100 | 0 |
| Pasta Primavera, Knorr® | 1 container | 210 | 40 |
| ❶ Pasta Primavera, Spice Islands® | 1 container | 170 | 20 |
| Pasta Twists with Creamy Tomato Sauce, Knorr® | 1 container | 230 | 35 |
| **Pea Soup Mix, single-serving** | | | |
| Green Pea, Lipton® Cup-A-Soup | 1 envelope | 110 | 35 |
| ❶ Split Pea, Fantastic Foods® | 1 container | 190 | 10 |
| ❶ Split Pea, Knorr® | 1 container | 150 | 5 |

❶ Meets Low-Fat Guidelines

| TOTAL FAT (g) | SATURATED FAT (g) | SODIUM (mg) | PROTEIN (g) | CARBOHYDRATE (g) | CARBOHYDRATE CHOICES | EXCHANGES |
|---|---|---|---|---|---|---|
| 1.5 | 0 | 590 | 10 | 41 | 3 | 3 starch |
| 3 | 0 | 590 | 8 | 36 | 2½ | 2½ starch |
| 1 | 0 | 510 | 7 | 36 | 2½ | 2½ starch |
| | | | | | | |
| 1 | 0 | 480 | 15 | 41 | 3 | 3 starch, 1 very lean meat |
| 1 | 0 | 570 | 10 | 33 | 2 | 2 starch, 1 very lean meat |
| 0.5 | 0 | 590 | 13 | 42 | 3 | 3 starch, 1 very lean meat |
| 1 | 0 | 500 | 6 | 37 | 2½ | 2½ starch |
| 1.5 | 0 | 520 | 12 | 31 | 2 | 2 starch, 1 very lean meat |
| 1 | 0 | 490 | 9 | 35 | 2 | 2 starch, 1 very lean meat |
| 2 | 0 | 490 | 6 | 37 | 2½ | 2½ starch |
| | | | | | | |
| 1 | 0.5 | 580 | 4 | 28 | 2 | 2 starch |
| 1 | 0 | 480 | 6 | 29 | 2 | 2 starch |
| 1 | 0 | 590 | 8 | 30 | 2 | 2 starch |
| 0 | 0.5 | 590 | 4 | 24 | 1½ | 1½ starch |
| | | | | | | |
| 4 | 2 | 810 | 6 | 41 | 3 | 3 starch |
| 1.5 | 0 | 420 | 6 | 32 | 2 | 2 starch |
| 2.5 | 1 | 350 | 7 | 33 | 2 | 2 starch |
| 3 | 1.5 | 470 | 8 | 32 | 2 | 2 starch |
| 0 | 0 | 190 | 5 | 20 | 1 | 1 starch |
| 4.5 | 1.5 | 840 | 6 | 36 | 2½ | 2½ starch |
| 2 | 0.5 | 470 | 7 | 30 | 2 | 2 starch |
| 4 | 2.5 | 800 | 8 | 41 | 3 | 3 starch |
| | | | | | | |
| 3.5 | 1 | 620 | 3 | 17 | 1 | 1 starch, ½ fat |
| 1 | 0 | 470 | 12 | 33 | 2 | 2 starch, 1 very lean meat |
| 0.5 | 0 | 690 | 8 | 29 | 2 | 2 starch |

1 Carbohydrate Choice = 1 starch *or* 1 fruit *or* 1 milk exchange

## PRODUCTS

| | SERVING SIZE | CALORIES | CALORIES FROM FAT |
|---|---|---|---|
| ❶ Split Pea, Nile Spice® | 1 container | 200 | 10 |
| ❶ Split Pea, Spice Islands® | 1 container | 150 | 5 |
| **Potato Leek Soup Mix, single-serving** | | | |
| ❶ Potato Leek, Knorr® | 1 container | 120 | 0 |
| ❶ Potato Leek, Nile Spice® | 1 container | 110 | 22 |
| Potato Leek, Nile Spice® Organic | 1 container | 160 | 54 |
| ❶ Potato Leek, Spice Islands® | 1 container | 120 | 10 |
| **Tomato Soup Mix, single-serving** | | | |
| Italian Tomato, Nissin® | 1 container | 320 | 130 |
| ❶ Tomato, Campbell's® | 1 can | 110 | 18 |
| ❶ Tomato, Lipton® Cup-A-Soup | 1 envelope | 90 | 10 |
| ❶ Tomato & Rice, Nile Spice® | 1 container | 130 | 27 |
| ❶ Tomato Herb, Nile Spice® Organic | 1 container | 120 | 28 |
| ❶ Tomato Rice Parmesano, Fantastic Foods® | 1 container | 200 | 15 |
| ❶ Vegetable Tomato, Fantastic Foods® | 1 container | 150 | 10 |
| **Vegetable Soup Mix, single-serving** | | | |
| ❶ Harvest Vegetable, Nile Spice® Organic | 1 container | 110 | 13 |
| ❶ Oriental Rice & Vegetables, Spice Islands® | 1 container | 180 | 10 |
| ❶ Rice & Country Vegetables, Spice Islands® | 1 container | 180 | 10 |
| ❶ Spring Vegetable, Lipton® Cup-A-Soup | 1 envelope | 45 | 10 |
| ❶ Vegetable, Campbell's® | 1 can | 70 | 18 |
| ❶ Vegetable Barley, Fantastic Foods® | 1 container | 150 | 5 |
| ❶ Vegetable Barley, Nile Spice® Organic | 1 container | 130 | 13 |
| ❶ Vegetable Beef, Campbell's® | 1 can | 60 | 27 |
| ❶ Vegetable Curry, Fantastic Foods® | 1 container | 140 | 10 |
| ❶ Vegetable Miso, Fantastic Foods® | 1 container | 130 | 10 |
| ❶ Vegetable Stew, Knorr® | 1 container | 160 | 15 |
| ❶ Wild Rice & Vegetables, Spice Islands® | 1 container | 170 | 10 |

❶ Meets Low-Fat Guidelines

| TOTAL FAT (g) | SATURATED FAT (g) | SODIUM (mg) | PROTEIN (g) | CARBOHYDRATE (g) | CARBOHYDRATE CHOICES | EXCHANGES |
|---|---|---|---|---|---|---|
| 1 | 0 | 700 | 13 | 35 | 2 | 2 starch, 1 very lean meat |
| 0.5 | 0 | 460 | 8 | 28 | 2 | 2 starch, 1 very lean meat |
| | | | | | | |
| 0 | 0 | 970 | 4 | 24 | 1½ | 1½ starch |
| 2.5 | 1.5 | 570 | 5 | 18 | 1 | 1 starch |
| 6 | 4 | 490 | 4 | 21 | 1½ | 1½ starch, 1 fat |
| 1 | 0 | 590 | 6 | 23 | 1½ | 1½ starch |
| | | | | | | |
| 14 | 7 | 940 | 7 | 42 | 3 | 3 starch, 2 fat |
| 2 | NA | NA | 2 | 21 | 1½ | 1½ starch |
| 1 | 0 | 510 | 2 | 20 | 1 | 1 starch |
| 3 | 1.5 | 550 | 5 | 23 | 1½ | 1½ starch |
| 3 | 1 | 420 | 4 | 19 | 1 | 1 starch, ½ fat |
| 2 | 0 | 550 | 6 | 41 | 3 | 3 starch |
| 1 | 0 | 490 | 5 | 31 | 2 | 2 starch |
| | | | | | | |
| 1.5 | 0 | 600 | 3 | 21 | 1½ | 1½ starch |
| 1.5 | 0 | 590 | 4 | 39 | 2½ | 2½ starch |
| 1 | 0 | 570 | 5 | 38 | 2½ | 2½ starch |
| 1 | 0 | 500 | 2 | 8 | ½ | ½ starch |
| 2 | NA | NA | 2 | 12 | 1 | 1 starch |
| 0.5 | 0 | 470 | 6 | 29 | 2 | 2 starch |
| 1.5 | 0.5 | 460 | 5 | 29 | 2 | 2 starch |
| 3 | NA | NA | 4 | 7 | ½ | ½ starch |
| 1 | 0 | 490 | 6 | 28 | 2 | 2 starch |
| 1 | 0 | 540 | 5 | 25 | 1½ | 1½ starch |
| 2 | 0 | 760 | 4 | 32 | 2 | 2 starch |
| 1 | 0 | 530 | 4 | 35 | 2 | 2 starch |

1 Carbohydrate Choice = 1 starch *or* 1 fruit *or* 1 milk exchange

## PRODUCTS

| | SERVING SIZE | CALORIES | CALORIES FROM FAT |
|---|---|---|---|
| **Other Soup Mixes, single-serving** | | | |
| ❶ Bombay Curry Rice, Fantastic Foods® | 1 container | 260 | 30 |
| ❶ Broccoli and Cheddar, Fantastic Foods® | 1 container | 130 | 15 |
| ❶ Cajun Rice, Fantastic Foods® | 1 container | 240 | 15 |
| ❶ Caribbean, Fantastic Foods® | 1 container | 230 | 15 |
| ❶ Caribbean Sweet Potato, Nile Spice® Organic | 1 container | 150 | 9 |
| ❶ Carrot Dill, Nile Spice® | 1 container | 100 | 18 |
| ❶ Country Mushroom, Nile Spice® | 1 container | 140 | 22 |
| Cream of Mushroom, Campbell's® | 1 can | 100 | 72 |
| ❶ Cream of Mushroom, Lipton® Cup-A-Soup | 1 envelope | 60 | 20 |
| ❶ Creamy Broccoli & Cheese, Lipton® Cup-A-Soup | 1 envelope | 70 | 25 |
| ❶ Creamy Tomato Basil Pasta, Spice Islands® | 1 container | 190 | 5 |
| ❶ Five Bean, Fantastic Foods® | 1 container | 230 | 10 |
| ❶ Italian Beans, Knorr® | 1 container | 230 | 20 |
| ❶ Mushroom, Fantastic Foods® | 1 container | 120 | 0 |
| ❶ Navy Bean, Knorr® | 1 container | 130 | 5 |
| ❶ Northern Italian Rice, Fantastic Foods® | 1 container | 240 | 15 |
| ❶ Primavera Pasta, Nile Spice® | 1 container | 190 | 23 |
| ❶ Ring Noodle, Lipton® Cup-A-Soup | 1 envelope | 50 | 10 |
| ❶ Spinach & Mushroom Pasta, Spice Islands® | 1 container | 160 | 15 |
| ❶ Szechuan Rice, Fantastic Foods® | 1 container | 210 | 20 |
| ❶ Tex-Mex Rice, Fantastic Foods® | 1 container | 270 | 20 |
| Three Cheese Macaroni, Knorr® | 1 container | 240 | 45 |
| **SOUR CREAM** | | | |
| ❶ Light sour cream, all varieties (avg) | 2 Tb | 40 | 20 |
| Regular sour cream, all varieties (avg) | 2 Tb | 60 | 50 |

❶  Meets Low-Fat Guidelines

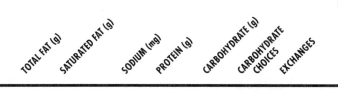

| TOTAL FAT (g) | SATURATED FAT (g) | SODIUM (mg) | PROTEIN (g) | CARBOHYDRATE (g) | CARBOHYDRATE CHOICES | EXCHANGES |
|---|---|---|---|---|---|---|
| 3 | 1.5 | 470 | 12 | 46 | 3 | 3 starch |
| 1.5 | 1 | 480 | 6 | 23 | 1½ | 1½ starch |
| 1.5 | 0 | 480 | 10 | 47 | 3 | 3 starch |
| 1.5 | 0 | 480 | 10 | 44 | 3 | 3 starch |
| 1 | 0 | 570 | 4 | 32 | 2 | 2 starch |
| 2 | 1 | 550 | 3 | 18 | 1 | 1 starch |
| 2.5 | 1 | 580 | 3 | 26 | 2 | 2 starch |
| 8 | NA | NA | 2 | 8 | ½ | ½ starch, 1 fat |
| 2 | 0 | 610 | 1 | 10 | ½ | ½ starch |
| 2 | 1.5 | 550 | 2 | 8 | ½ | ½ starch |
| 1 | 0 | 520 | 6 | 40 | 2½ | 2½ starch |
| 1 | 0 | 480 | 12 | 43 | 3 | 3 starch, 1 very lean meat |
| 2 | 0 | 920 | 9 | 50 | 3 | 3 starch |
| 0 | 0 | 570 | 6 | 24 | 1½ | 1½ starch |
| 0.5 | 0 | 660 | 7 | 26 | 2 | 2 starch, 1 very lean meat |
| 1.5 | 0 | 460 | 8 | 49 | 3 | 3 starch |
| 2.5 | 2 | 350 | 7 | 35 | 2 | 2 starch |
| 1 | 0 | 560 | 2 | 9 | ½ | ½ starch |
| 2 | 1 | 490 | 6 | 29 | 2 | 2 starch |
| 2 | 0 | 480 | 7 | 41 | 3 | 3 starch |
| 2 | 0 | 540 | 10 | 53 | 3½ | 3½ starch |
| 5 | 3.5 | 810 | 8 | 40 | 2½ | 2½ starch, ½ fat |
| 2.5 | 2 | 30 | 1.5 | 2.5 | 0 | ½ fat |
| 5.5 | 3.5 | 15–35 | 1 | 1.5 | 0 | 1 fat |

1 Carbohydrate Choice = 1 starch *or* 1 fruit *or* 1 milk exchange

## PRODUCTS

| | SERVING SIZE | CALORIES | CALORIES FROM FAT |
|---|---|---|---|

**SPAGHETTI SAUCE**
*see* Pasta Sauce

**STEW (CANNED)**
*see also* Soup

| | | | |
|---|---|---|---|
| Beef Stew, Cassleberry's® Original | 1 cup | 340 | 240 |
| Beef Stew, Cassleberry's® Premium | 1 cup | 340 | 230 |
| Beef Stew, Dinty Moore® | 1 cup | 230 | 120 |
| Beef Stew, Hunt's® Homestyle Separates | 1 cup | 155 | 41 |
| Chicken Stew, Dinty Moore® | 1 cup | 220 | 100 |
| Country Stew, Worthington® | 1 cup | 210 | 80 |

**STUFFING MIX (AS PREPARED WITH MARGARINE)**

| | | | |
|---|---|---|---|
| Apple & Raisin, Pepperidge Farm® | ⅕ pkg | 220 | 75 |
| Chicken Flavor, Stove Top® | ½ cup | 170 | 80 |
| Chicken Flavor, Stove Top® Flexible Serving | ½ cup | 170 | 80 |
| Chicken Flavor, Stove Top® Lower Sodium | ½ cup | 180 | 80 |
| Chicken Flavor, Stove Top® Microwave | ½ cup | 160 | 70 |
| Classic Chicken, Pepperidge Farm® | ⅕ pkg | 210 | 95 |
| Cornbread Flavor, Stove Top® | ½ cup | 160 | 70 |
| Cornbread, Stove Top® | ½ cup | 170 | 80 |
| Country Garden & Herb, Pepperidge Farm® | ⅕ pkg | 230 | 125 |
| Croutettes, Kellogg's | ⅕ pkg | 220 | 100 |
| For Beef, Stove Top® | ½ cup | 180 | 80 |
| For Pork, Stove Top® | ½ cup | 170 | 80 |
| For Turkey, Stove Top® | ½ cup | 170 | 80 |
| Harvest Vegetable & Almond, Pepperidge Farm® | ⅕ pkg | 320 | 105 |
| Homestyle Cornbread, Stove Top® | ½ cup | 160 | 60 |
| Homestyle Herb, Stove Top® | ½ cup | 170 | 80 |
| Honey Pecan Cornbread, Pepperidge Farm® | ⅕ pkg | 220 | 125 |
| Long Grain & Wild Rice, Stove Top® | ½ cup | 180 | 80 |
| Mushroom & Onion, Stove Top® | ½ cup | 180 | 80 |

 Meets Low-Fat Guidelines

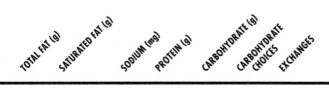

| TOTAL FAT (g) | SATURATED FAT (g) | SODIUM (mg) | PROTEIN (g) | CARBOHYDRATE (g) | CARBOHYDRATE CHOICES | EXCHANGES |
|---|---|---|---|---|---|---|
| 26 | 12 | 950 | 11 | 14 | 1 | 1 starch, 1 meat, 4 fat |
| 25 | 11 | 1130 | 15 | 12 | 1 | 1 starch, 2 meat, 3 fat |
| 14 | 7 | 950 | 11 | 16 | 1 | 1 starch, 1 meat, 2 fat |
| 4.5 | 2 | 1140 | 14 | 20 | 1 | 1 starch, 2 lean meat |
| 11 | 3 | 980 | 12 | 16 | 1 | 1 starch, 1 meat, 1 fat |
| 9 | 1.5 | 830 | 13 | 20 | 1 | 1 starch, 2 lean meat |
| | | | | | | |
| 10.5 | 1.5 | 605 | 4 | 27 | 2 | 2 starch, 2 fat |
| 9 | 1.5 | 510 | 4 | 20 | 1 | 1 starch, 2 fat |
| 8 | 1.5 | 520 | 3 | 19 | 1 | 1 starch, 1 fat |
| 9 | 1.5 | 340 | 4 | 21 | 1½ | 1½ starch, 1½ fat |
| 7 | 1.5 | 480 | 4 | 20 | 1 | 1 starch, 1 fat |
| 10.5 | 1.5 | 575 | 5 | 24 | 1½ | 1½ starch, 2 fat |
| 8 | 1.5 | 560 | 3 | 19 | 1 | 1 starch, 1 fat |
| 8 | 1.5 | 580 | 3 | 21 | 1½ | 1½ starch, 1½ fat |
| 14 | 1.5 | 445 | 4 | 22 | 1½ | 1½ starch, 3 fat |
| 11 | 2 | NA | 5 | 25 | 1½ | 1½ starch, 2 fat |
| 9 | 1.5 | 600 | 4 | 22 | 1½ | 1½ starch, 2 fat |
| 9 | 1.5 | 570 | 4 | 20 | 1 | 1 starch, 2 fat |
| 9 | 1.5 | 560 | 4 | 20 | 1 | 1 starch, 2 fat |
| 12 | 2 | 385 | 5 | 23 | 1½ | 1½ starch, 2 fat |
| | | | | | | |
| 7 | 1.5 | 480 | 3 | 20 | 1 | 1 starch, 1 fat |
| 8 | 1.5 | 500 | 3 | 19 | 1 | 1 starch, 1 fat |
| 14 | 2 | 485 | 3 | 23 | 1½ | 1½ starch, 3 fat |
| 9 | 1.5 | 560 | 4 | 22 | 1½ | 1½ starch, 1½ fat |
| 9 | 1.5 | 490 | 4 | 20 | 1 | 1 starch, 2 fat |

1 Carbohydrate Choice = 1 starch or 1 fruit or 1 milk exchange

| PRODUCTS | SERVING SIZE | CALORIES | CALORIES FROM FAT |
|---|---|---|---|
| San Francisco Style, Stove Top® | ½ cup | 170 | 80 |
| Savory Herbs, Stove Top® | ½ cup | 170 | 80 |
| Wild Rice & Mushroom, Pepperidge Farm® | ⅕ pkg | 250 | 130 |
| **SWEET ROLLS (FROZEN)** | | | |
| Cinnamon Rolls, Pepperidge Farm® | 1 roll | 250 | 100 |
| Deluxe Cinnamon Rolls, Sara Lee® | 1 roll | 320 | 140 |
| Glazed Cinnamon Rolls, Weight Watchers® | 1 roll | 200 | 45 |
| Honey Buns, Morton® | 1 bun | 250 | 90 |
| Mini Honey Buns, Morton® | 1 bun | 160 | 70 |
| **SWEET ROLLS (REFRIGERATED)** | | | |
| Apple Cinnamon Rolls with Icing, Pillsbury® | 1 roll | 140 | 45 |
| Caramel Rolls, Pillsbury® | 1 roll | 170 | 60 |
| Cinnamon Raisin Rolls with Icing, Pillsbury® | 1 roll | 180 | 60 |
| Cinnamon Rolls with Icing, Pillsbury® | 1 roll | 140 | 45 |
| Orange Sweet Rolls with Icing, Pillsbury® | 1 roll | 170 | 60 |
| **SYRUP** | | | |
| ❶ Corn syrup, light or dark, all brands (avg) | 2 Tb | 120 | 0 |
| ❶ Light syrup, all brands (avg) | ¼ cup | 100 | 0 |
| ❶ Sugar-free syrup, all brands (avg) | ¼ cup | 35 | 0 |
| ❶ Syrup, regular, all brands (avg) | ¼ cup | 200 | 0 |
| **TACO SHELLS** *see also* Tortillas | | | |
| Mini Taco Shells, Old El Paso® | 7 shells | 160 | 90 |
| Regular Taco Shells, Old El Paso® | 3 shells | 170 | 90 |
| Super Taco Shells, Old El Paso® | 2 shells | 190 | 100 |
| Taco Shells, Gephardt® | 3 shells | 155 | 76.5 |
| Tostaco Shells, Old El Paso® | 1 shell | 130 | 60 |
| Tostada Shells, Old El Paso® | 3 shells | 160 | 90 |
| White Corn Taco Shells, Old El Paso® | 3 shells | 170 | 90 |

❶  Meets Low-Fat Guidelines

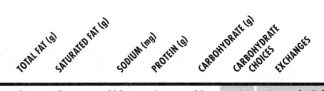

| TOTAL FAT (g) | SATURATED FAT (g) | SODIUM (mg) | PROTEIN (g) | CARBOHYDRATE (g) | CARBOHYDRATE CHOICES | EXCHANGES |
|---|---|---|---|---|---|---|
| 9 | 1.5 | 580 | 4 | 20 | 1 | 1 starch, 2 fat |
| 9 | 1.5 | 590 | 4 | 20 | 1 | 1 starch, 2 fat |
| 15 | 3 | 495 | 5 | 22 | 1½ | 1½ starch, 3 fat |
| | | | | | | |
| 12 | 2.5 | 220 | 4 | 33 | 2 | 2 starch, 2 fat |
| 15 | 9 | 300 | 5 | 41 | 3 | 3 starch, 2 fat |
| 5 | 1.5 | 200 | 4 | 33 | 2 | 2 starch, ½ fat |
| 10 | 2.5 | 160 | 3 | 35 | 2 | 2 starch, 2 fat |
| 8 | 2 | 100 | 2 | 19 | 1 | 1 starch, 1½ fat |
| | | | | | | |
| 5 | 1.5 | 310 | 2 | 21 | 1½ | 1½ starch, ½ fat |
| 7 | 1.5 | 330 | 2 | 25 | 1½ | 1½ starch, 1 fat |
| 7 | 1.5 | 310 | 2 | 26 | 2 | 2 starch, 1 fat |
| 5 | 1.5 | 330 | 2 | 21 | 1½ | 1½ starch, ½ fat |
| 7 | 1.5 | 330 | 2 | 25 | 1½ | 1½ starch, 1 fat |
| | | | | | | |
| 0 | 0 | 35 | 0 | 30 | 2 | 2 fruit |
| 0 | 0 | 100–230 | 0 | 26 | 2 | 2 fruit |
| 0 | 0 | 135 | 0 | 9 | ½ | ½ fruit |
| 0 | 0 | 15–135 | 0 | 53 | 3½ | 3½ fruit |
| | | | | | | |
| 10 | 1.5 | 130 | 2 | 18 | 1 | 1 starch, 2 fat |
| 10 | 1.5 | 130 | 2 | 18 | 1 | 1 starch, 2 fat |
| 12 | 2 | 150 | 2 | 21 | 1½ | 1½ starch, 2 fat |
| 8.5 | 2.5 | 7 | 2 | 19 | 1 | 1 starch, 2 fat |
| 7 | 1 | 10 | 2 | 14 | 1 | 1 starch, 1 fat |
| 10 | 2 | 220 | 2 | 19 | 1 | 1 starch, 2 fat |
| 10 | 1.5 | 30 | 2 | 18 | 1 | 1 starch, 2 fat |

1 Carbohydrate Choice = 1 starch *or* 1 fruit *or* 1 milk exchange

## PRODUCTS

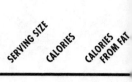

| | SERVING SIZE | CALORIES | CALORIES FROM FAT |
|---|---|---|---|
| **TARTAR SAUCE** | | | |
| Deluxe Tartar Sauce, Western® | 2 Tb | 160 | 144 |
| Natural Lemon & Herb Flavor Tartar Sauce, Kraft® SauceWorks® | 2 Tb | 150 | 140 |
| ❶ Tartar Sauce, Kraft® Nonfat | 2 Tb | 25 | 0 |
| Tartar Sauce, Kraft® SauceWorks® | 2 Tb | 100 | 90 |
| **TEMPEH** | | | |
| 5-Grain, White Wave® Tempeh | ⅓ block | 140 | 35 |
| Organic Wild Rice, White Wave® | ⅓ block | 140 | 40 |
| Original Soy, White Wave® | ⅓ block | 150 | 50 |
| Sea Veggie, White Wave® | ⅓ block | 140 | 40 |
| **TOASTER PASTRIES** | | | |
| ❶ Chocolate Healthy Tarts, Health Valley® Fat-Free | 1 tart | 150 | 0 |
| ❶ Fruit Healthy Tarts, Health Valley® Fat-Free, all varieties (avg) | 1 tart | 150 | 0 |
| Pop-Tarts®, Kellogg's®, all regular varieties (avg) | 1 pastry | 205 | 50 |
| ❶ Pop-Tarts®, Kellogg's® Low Fat, all varieties (avg) | 1 pastry | 190 | 25 |
| Pop-Tarts Minis®, Kellogg's®, all varieties (avg) | 1 pouch | 170 | 35 |
| Toaster Strudel™, Pillsbury®, cream cheese and fruit varieties (avg) | 1 pastry | 190 | 80 |
| Toaster Strudel™, Pillsbury®, French Toast Style | 1 pastry | 190 | 60 |
| Toaster Strudel™, Pillsbury®, fruit varieties (avg) | 1 pastry | 180 | 60 |
| Toastettes®, Nabisco®, all varieties (avg) | 1 tart | 190 | 45 |
| **TOFU** | | | |
| Italian Garlic Herb Tofu, White Wave® | 1 piece | 120 | 50 |
| Mexican Jalapeno Tofu, White Wave® | 1 piece | 120 | 50 |
| Organic Tofu, White Wave®, all varieties (avg) | ⅓ block | 90 | 50 |

❶  Meets Low-Fat Guidelines

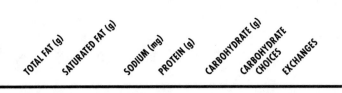

| TOTAL FAT (g) | SATURATED FAT (g) | SODIUM (mg) | PROTEIN (g) | CARBOHYDRATE (g) | CARBOHYDRATE CHOICES | EXCHANGES |
|---|---|---|---|---|---|---|
| 16 | 2.5 | 240 | 0 | 2 | 0 | 3 fat |
| 16 | 2.5 | 170 | 0 | <1 | 0 | 3 fat |
| 0 | 0 | 210 | 0 | 5 | 0 | free |
| 10 | 4 | 180 | 0 | 4 | 0 | 2 fat |
| 4 | 0.5 | 0 | 12 | 15 | 1 | 1 starch, 1 lean meat |
| 4 | 0.5 | 10 | 13 | 12 | 1 | 1 starch, 1 lean meat |
| 6 | 1 | 0 | 16 | 10 | ½ | ½ starch, 2 lean meat |
| 5 | 0.5 | 0 | 12 | 13 | 1 | 1 starch, 1 meat |
| 0 | 0 | 30 | 3 | 35 | 2 | 2 starch |
| 0 | 0 | 30 | 3 | 35 | 2 | 2 starch |
| 5.5 | 1 | 200 | 2.5 | 36 | 2½ | 2½ starch |
| 3 | 0.5 | 220 | 2 | 40 | 2½ | 2½ starch |
| 4 | 1 | 185 | 2 | 31 | 2 | 2 starch |
| 9 | 3 | 220 | 3 | 24 | 1½ | 1½ starch, 2 fat |
| 7 | 1.5 | 200 | 3 | 28 | 2 | 2 starch, 1 fat |
| 7 | 1.5 | 200 | 3 | 26 | 2 | 2 starch, 1 fat |
| 5 | 1.5 | 205 | 2 | 35 | 2 | 2 starch, ½ fat |
| 6 | 1 | 240 | 13 | 3 | 0 | 2 lean meat |
| 6 | 1 | 240 | 13 | 3 | 0 | 2 lean meat |
| 6 | 1 | 10 | 10 | 1 | 0 | 1 meat |

1 Carbohydrate Choice = 1 starch or 1 fruit or 1 milk exchange

## PRODUCTS

| | SERVING SIZE | CALORIES | CALORIES FROM FAT |
|---|---|---|---|
| Oriental Teriyaki Tofu, White Wave® | 1 piece | 120 | 50 |
| Reduced Fat Tofu, White Wave® | ⅕ block | 90 | 35 |
| ❶ Regular Tofu, Hiniochi® | 3 oz | 60 | 25 |
| ❶ Silken Tofu, Mori-Nu®, all varieties (avg) | 3 oz | 50 | 20 |
| ❶ Soft Tofu, Hinoichi® | 3 oz | 45 | 20 |
| Thai Sesame Peanut Tofu, White Wave® | 1 piece | 120 | 50 |
| Tidal Wave Tofu, White Wave® | ⅕ block | 90 | 50 |

### TOMATO PRODUCTS (CANNED)

| | SERVING SIZE | CALORIES | CALORIES FROM FAT |
|---|---|---|---|
| ❶ Stewed tomatoes, all brands (avg) | ½ cup | 40 | 0 |
| ❶ Tomato paste, all brands (avg) | 2 Tb | 30 | 0 |
| ❶ Tomato puree, all brands (avg) | ¼ cup | 25 | 0 |
| ❶ Tomato sauce, all brands (avg) | ¼ cup | 20 | 0 |
| ❶ Whole peeled tomatoes | ½ cup | 25 | 0 |
| ❶ Whole peeled tomatoes, no salt added, all varieties (avg) | ½ cup | 25 | 0 |

### TORTILLAS

| | SERVING SIZE | CALORIES | CALORIES FROM FAT |
|---|---|---|---|
| ❶ Apple/Cinnamon Flour Tortillas, Zapata® | 1 tortilla | 182 | 22.5 |
| ❶ Flour Tortillas (7"), Zapata® | 1 tortilla | 100 | 18 |
| Flour Tortillas (8"), Zapata® | 1 tortilla | 160 | 31.5 |
| Flour Tortillas (large), Tyson® Mexican Original® | 1 tortilla | 170 | 35 |
| ❶ Flour Tortillas (small), Tyson® Mexican Original® | 1 tortilla | 120 | 25 |
| Flour Tortillas, Old El Paso® | 1 tortilla | 150 | 25 |
| Heat Pressed Flour Tortillas, Tyson® Mexican Original® | 2 tortillas | 180 | 40 |
| ❶ Jalapeno & Cilantro Flour Tortillas, Zapata® | 1 tortilla | 140 | 9 |
| ❶ Onion & Garlic Flour Tortillas, Zapata® | 1 tortilla | 150 | 9 |
| Soft Taco Tortillas, Old El Paso® | 2 tortillas | 180 | 30 |
| ❶ Whole Wheat Tortillas, Zapata® | 1 tortilla | 100 | 18 |
| ❶ Yellow Corn Tortillas, Tyson® Mexican Original® | 3 pieces | 140 | 10 |

❶  Meets Low-Fat Guidelines

| TOTAL FAT (g) | SATURATED FAT (g) | SODIUM (mg) | PROTEIN (g) | CARBOHYDRATE (g) | CARBOHYDRATE CHOICES | EXCHANGES |
|---|---|---|---|---|---|---|
| 6 | 1 | 240 | 13 | 3 | 0 | 2 lean meat |
| 4 | 0 | 5 | 10 | 4 | 0 | 1 meat |
| 3 | 0 | 10 | 6 | 2 | 0 | 1 lean meat |
| 2.5 | 0 | 45 | 6.5 | 2 | 0 | 1 lean meat |
| 2.5 | 0 | 15 | 5 | 1 | 0 | 1 lean meat |
| 6 | 1 | 240 | 13 | 3 | 0 | 2 lean meat |
| 6 | 1 | 10 | 10 | 1 | 0 | 1 meat |
| 0 | 0 | 250–350 | 1 | 8 | ½ | ½ starch or 2 veg |
| 0 | 0 | 20 | 2 | 6 | ½ | 1 veg |
| 0 | 0 | 15 | 1 | 5 | 0 | 1 veg |
| 0 | 0 | 300 | 1 | 4 | 0 | 1 veg |
| 0 | 0 | 200–300 | 1 | 4 | 0 | 1 veg |
| 0 | 0 | 90 | 2 | 4 | 0 | 1 veg |
| 2.5 | 1 | 330 | 5 | 33 | 2 | 2 starch |
| 2 | 0.5 | 290 | 3 | 18 | 1 | 1 starch |
| 3.5 | 0.5 | 360 | 5 | 29 | 2 | 2 starch |
| 4 | 1 | 410 | 4 | 30 | 2 | 2 starch |
| 3 | 0.5 | 290 | 3 | 21 | 1½ | 1½ starch |
| 3 | <1 | 340 | 4 | 27 | 2 | 2 starch |
| 4.5 | 1 | 420 | 4 | 30 | 2 | 2 starch, ½ fat |
| 1 | 0.5 | 350 | 11 | 28 | 2 | 2 starch |
| 1 | 0.5 | 350 | 11 | 29 | 2 | 2 starch |
| 3.5 | <1 | 410 | 5 | 33 | 2 | 2 starch |
| 2 | 0.5 | 230 | 3 | 17 | 1 | 1 starch |
| 1 | 0 | 0 | 3 | 31 | 2 | 2 starch |

1 Carbohydrate Choice = 1 starch *or* 1 fruit *or* 1 milk exchange

## PRODUCTS

| | SERVING SIZE | CALORIES | CALORIES FROM FAT |
|---|---|---|---|

### TUNA (CANNED)

| | | | |
|---|---|---|---|
| Chunk light, in oil, all brands (avg) | 2 oz (¼ cup) | 110 | 50 |
| ❶ Chunk light, in water, all brands (avg) | 2 oz (¼ cup) | 60 | 5 |
| ❶ Chunk white, in water, all brands (avg) | 2 oz (¼ cup) | 60 | 10 |
| ❶ Solid white, in oil, all brands (avg) | 2 oz (¼ cup) | 90 | 30 |
| ❶ Solid white, in water, all brands (avg) | 2 oz (¼ cup) | 70 | 10 |

### TUNA NOODLE CASSEROLE
*see* Pasta Meals/Entrees

### TURKEY (FROZEN)

| | | | |
|---|---|---|---|
| Breaded Turkey Nuggets, Louis Rich® | 4 nuggets | 260 | 150 |
| Breaded Turkey Patties, Louis Rich® | 1 patty | 220 | 120 |
| Breaded Turkey Sticks, Louis Rich® | 3 sticks | 230 | 130 |
| ❶ Hickory Barbecue, Turkey By George® | 5 oz | 190 | 45 |
| ❶ Italian Parmesan, Turkey By George® | 5 oz | 170 | 45 |
| ❶ Lemon Pepper, Turkey By George® | 5 oz | 160 | 36 |
| Mustard Tarragon, Turkey By George® | 5 oz | 180 | 54 |

### TURKEY MEALS/ENTREES (FROZEN)

#### *Turkey with Dressing Meals/Entrees*

| | | | |
|---|---|---|---|
| Gravy and Turkey with Dressing, Morton® | 1 meal | 230 | 70 |
| Gravy with Turkey & Dressing, Michelina's® | 1 pkg | 260 | 120 |
| Roast Turkey and Homestyle Stuffing, Stouffer's® Homestyle | 1 pkg | 280 | 100 |
| ❶ Roasted Turkey Breast & Stuffing and Cinnamon Apples, Lean Cuisine® | 1 pkg | 290 | 35 |
| ❶ Stuffed Turkey Breast, Weight Watchers® | 1 entree | 230 | 45 |
| Turkey & Gravy with Dressing Dinner, Banquet® Extra Helping | 1 meal | 560 | 180 |

❶ Meets Low-Fat Guidelines

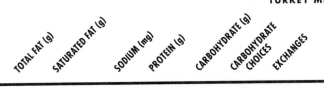

| TOTAL FAT (g) | SATURATED FAT (g) | SODIUM (mg) | PROTEIN (g) | CARBOHYDRATE (g) | CARBOHYDRATE CHOICES | EXCHANGES |
|---|---|---|---|---|---|---|
| 6 | 0.5 | 250 | 13 | 0 | 0 | 2 lean meat |
| 0.5 | 0 | 250 | 13 | 0 | 0 | 2 very lean meat |
| 1 | 0 | 250 | 13 | 0 | 0 | 2 very lean meat |
| 3 | 0.5 | 250 | 15 | 0 | 0 | 2 very lean meat |
| 1 | 0 | 250 | 15 | 0 | 0 | 2 very lean meat |
| | | | | | | |
| 16 | 3 | 640 | 13 | 15 | 1 | 1 starch, 2 meat, 1 fat |
| 13 | 2.5 | 550 | 12 | 13 | 1 | 1 starch, 1 meat, 1 fat |
| 15 | 3 | 580 | 12 | 12 | 1 | 1 starch, 1 meat, 2 fat |
| 5 | NA | 840 | 28 | 8 | ½ | ½ starch, 4 very lean meat |
| 5 | NA | 860 | 28 | 3 | 0 | 4 very lean meat |
| 4 | 1 | 830 | 28 | 4 | 0 | 4 very lean meat |
| 6 | NA | 830 | 29 | 3 | 0 | 4 very lean meat |
| | | | | | | |
| 8 | 3 | 1090 | 14 | 27 | 2 | 2 starch, 1 meat |
| 14 | 3.5 | 1270 | 11 | 22 | 1½ | 1½ starch, 1 meat, 1½ fat |
| 11 | 3 | 950 | 19 | 25 | 1½ | 1½ starch 2 meat |
| 4 | 1 | 530 | 16 | 48 | 3 | 3 starch, 1 lean meat |
| 5 | 1 | 680 | 17 | 28 | 2 | 2 starch, 2 very lean meat |
| 20 | 5 | 1910 | 32 | 63 | 4 | 4 starch, 3 meat |

1 Carbohydrate Choice = 1 starch or 1 fruit or 1 milk exchange

## PRODUCTS

| | SERVING SIZE | CALORIES | CALORIES FROM FAT |
|---|---|---|---|
| Turkey & Gravy with Dressing Meal, Banquet® Homestyle Menu | 1 meal | 270 | 90 |
| Turkey White Meat in Gravy with Dressing, Swanson® Homestyle | 1 pkg | 280 | 90 |
| Turkey with Gravy & Dressing, Marie Callender's® | 1 meal | 530 | 150 |
| **Other Turkey Meals/Entrees** | | | |
| ❶ Country Inn Roast Turkey, Healthy Choice® | 1 meal | 250 | 30 |
| ❶ Country Roast Turkey with Mushrooms, Healthy Choice® | 1 meal | 220 | 35 |
| Escalloped Noodles & Turkey, Budget Gourmet® | 1 entree | 430 | 190 |
| ❶ Glazed Turkey, Budget Gourmet® Light | 1 entree | 250 | 35 |
| ❶ Glazed Turkey, Stouffer's® Lean Cuisine® Cafe Classics | 1 pkg | 250 | 50 |
| Gravy and Sliced Turkey, Banquet® Family Size | 2 slices | 120 | 70 |
| Gravy and Sliced Turkey, Banquet® Toppers | 1 bag | 90 | 35 |
| ❶ Pasta and Turkey Dijon, Stouffer's® Lean Cuisine® Lunch Express® | 1 pkg | 270 | 60 |
| ❶ Roast Turkey Medallions, Weight Watchers® Smart Ones® | 1 entree | 190 | 15 |
| ❶ Traditional Breast of Turkey, Healthy Choice® | 1 meal | 280 | 25 |
| ❶ Turkey, Stouffer's® Lean Cuisine® Homestyle | 1 pkg | 230 | 50 |
| ❶ Turkey Fettuccini alla Crema, Healthy Choice® | 1 meal | 350 | 35 |
| Turkey Mostly White Meat, Swanson® | 1 pkg | 310 | 63 |
| Turkey Mostly White Meat, Swanson® Hungry-Man® | 1 pkg | 490 | 117 |
| Turkey Tetrazzini, Stouffer's® | 1 pkg | 360 | 150 |
| **VEAL MEALS/ENTREES (FROZEN)** | | | |
| Veal Parmigiana, Banquet® | 1 meal | 320 | 130 |
| Veal Parmigiana Patties (6), Banquet® Family Size | 1 patty | 230 | 120 |

❶  Meets Low-Fat Guidelines

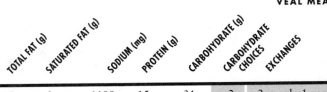

| TOTAL FAT (g) | SATURATED FAT (g) | SODIUM (mg) | PROTEIN (g) | CARBOHYDRATE (g) | CARBOHYDRATE CHOICES | EXCHANGES |
|---|---|---|---|---|---|---|
| 10 | 3 | 1100 | 15 | 31 | 2 | 2 starch, 1 veg, 1 meat |
| 10 | NA | NA | 17 | 30 | 2 | 1½ starch, 1 veg, 2 meat |
| 17 | 7 | 2030 | 33 | 51 | 3½ | 3 starch, 1 veg, 3 meat |
| 4 | 1 | 530 | 26 | 29 | 2 | 2 starch, 3 very lean meat |
| 4 | 1 | 440 | 19 | 28 | 2 | 2 starch, 2 very lean meat |
| 21 | 11 | 810 | 16 | 43 | 3 | 3 starch, 1 meat, 3 fat |
| 4 | 2 | 730 | 15 | 38 | 2½ | 2½ starch, 1 lean meat |
| 6 | 1.5 | 590 | 14 | 36 | 2½ | 2 starch, 1 veg, 1 lean meat |
| 9 | 3 | 670 | 8 | 5 | 0 | 1 meat, 1 fat |
| 4 | 1.5 | 670 | 8 | 7 | ½ | ½ starch, 1 lean meat |
| 6 | 1.5 | 570 | 16 | 37 | 2½ | 2½ starch, 2 lean meat |
| 2 | 0.5 | 530 | 10 | 34 | 2 | 2 starch, 1 very lean meat |
| 3 | 1 | 460 | 22 | 40 | 2½ | 2½ starch, 2 very lean meat |
| 6 | 1.5 | 590 | 18 | 26 | 2 | 2 starch, 1 meat |
| 4 | 1.5 | 370 | 28 | 50 | 3 | 3 starch, 3 very lean meat |
| 7 | NA | NA | 20 | 42 | 3 | 2½ starch, 1 veg, 2 lean meat |
| 13 | NA | NA | 35 | 59 | 4 | 3½ starch, 1 veg, 3 lean meat |
| 17 | 7 | 1060 | 19 | 33 | 2 | 2 starch, 2 meat, 1 fat |
| 14 | 5 | 960 | 13 | 35 | 2 | 2 starch, 1 veg, 1 meat, 1 fat |
| 14 | 4 | 740 | 9 | 19 | 1 | 1 starch, 1 meat, 2 fat |

1 Carbohydrate Choice = 1 starch or 1 fruit or 1 milk exchange

## PRODUCTS

| | SERVING SIZE | CALORIES | CALORIES FROM FAT |
|---|---|---|---|
| Veal Parmigiana with Spaghetti, Stouffer's® Homestyle | 1 pkg | 420 | 170 |
| Veal Parmigiana with Tomato Sauce, Morton® | 1 meal | 280 | 120 |

### VEGETABLE BURGERS
*see also* Vegetarian Meat Substitutes

| | | SERVING SIZE | CALORIES | CALORIES FROM FAT |
|---|---|---|---|---|
| ❶ | Better'n Burgers, Morningstar Farms® | 1 patty | 70 | 0 |
| ❶ | Chick'n Burger, White Wave® | 1 patty | 215 | 0 |
| ❶ | Garden Grain Pattie, Morningstar Farms® | 1 patty | 120 | 25 |
| | Garden Vege Pattie, Natural Touch® | 1 patty | 110 | 35 |
| ❶ | Garden Vege Patties, Morningstar Farms® | 1 patty | 100 | 25 |
| | Grillers, Morningstar Farms® | 1 patty | 140 | 60 |
| ❶ | Ground Meatless Vegetarian Beef, Worthington® | ½ cup | 80 | 25 |
| | Harvest Burgers®, Green Giant®, all varieties (avg) | 1 patty | 140 | 40 |
| | Hempeh™ Burger | 3 oz | 140 | 55 |
| | Lemon Broil Tempeh, White Wave® | 1 patty | 130 | 50 |
| ❶ | Prime Burger, White Wave® | 1 patty | 110 | 0 |
| | Prime Patties, Morningstar Farms® | 1 patty | 130 | 50 |
| | Redi-Burger, Loma Linda® | ⅝" slice | 170 | 90 |
| ❶ | Spicy Black Bean Burger, Morningstar Farms® | 1 patty | 100 | 10 |
| ❶ | Tempeh Burger, White Wave® | 1 patty | 110 | 25 |
| ❶ | Teriyaki Tempeh Burger, White Wave® | 1 patty | 110 | 20 |
| ❶ | Vegan Burger, Natural Touch® | 1 patty | 70 | 0 |
| ❶ | Vegetarian Burger, Worthington® | ¼ cup | 60 | 15 |
| ❶ | Vege-Burger, Loma Linda® | ¼ cup | 70 | 15 |
| | Vege Burger, Natural Touch® | 1 patty | 140 | 60 |
| ❶ | Veggie Burger, Ken & Robert's® | 1 patty | 130 | 10 |
| | Veggie Life Burger, White Wave® | 1 patty | 130 | 35 |
| ❶ | Vita-Burger Chunks, Loma Linda® | ¼ cup dry | 70 | 10 |
| ❶ | Vita-Burger Granules, Loma Linda® | 3 Tb | 70 | 10 |

❶  Meets Low-Fat Guidelines

| TOTAL FAT (g) | SATURATED FAT (g) | SODIUM (mg) | PROTEIN (g) | CARBOHYDRATE (g) | CARBOHYDRATE CHOICES | EXCHANGES |
|---|---|---|---|---|---|---|
| 19 | 4 | 1200 | 20 | 43 | 3 | 3 starch, 2 meat, 1 fat |
| 13 | 4 | 950 | 8 | 30 | 2 | 2 starch, 1 meat, 1 fat |
| 0 | 0 | 360 | 11 | 6 | ½ | ½ starch, 1 very lean meat |
| 0 | 0 | 480 | 30 | 25 | 1½ | 1½ starch, 3 very lean meat |
| 2.5 | 1 | 280 | 6 | 18 | 1 | 1 starch, 1 lean meat |
| 4 | 1 | 280 | 10 | 8 | ½ | ½ starch, 1 meat |
| 2.5 | 0.5 | 350 | 10 | 9 | ½ | ½ starch, 1 lean meat |
| 7 | 1.5 | 260 | 14 | 5 | 0 | 2 lean meat |
| 2.5 | 0.5 | 270 | 11 | 3 | 0 | 2 very lean meat |
| 4.5 | 1.5 | 370 | 17 | 8 | ½ | ½ starch, 2 lean meat |
| 6 | 1 | 110 | 10 | 12 | 1 | 1 starch, 1 meat |
| 6 | 1 | 340 | 8 | 11 | 1 | 1 starch, 1 meat |
| 0 | 0 | 350 | 24 | 4 | 0 | 3 lean meat |
| 5 | 1.5 | 240 | 16 | 4 | 0 | 2 lean meat |
| 10 | 1.5 | 460 | 16 | 5 | 0 | 2 meat |
| 1 | 0 | 470 | 8 | 16 | 1 | 1 starch, 1 very lean meat |
| 2.5 | 0 | 270 | 12 | 10 | ½ | ½ starch, 1 lean meat |
| 2 | 0 | 340 | 10 | 11 | 1 | 1 starch, 1 very lean meat |
| 0 | 0 | 370 | 11 | 6 | ½ | ½ starch, 1 very lean meat |
| 2 | 0 | 270 | 9 | 2 | 0 | 1 lean meat |
| 1.5 | 0.5 | 115 | 11 | 2 | 0 | 2 very lean meat |
| 6 | 1 | 320 | 15 | 4 | 0 | 2 lean meat |
| 1 | 0 | 260 | 5 | 26 | 2 | 2 starch |
| 3.5 | 0 | 250 | 6 | 20 | 1 | 1 starch, 1 lean meat |
| 1 | 0 | 350 | 10 | 6 | ½ | ½ starch, 1 very lean meat |
| 1 | 0 | 350 | 10 | 6 | ½ | ½ starch, 1 very lean meat |

1 Carbohydrate Choice = 1 starch or 1 fruit or 1 milk exchange

## PRODUCTS

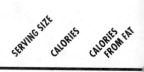

| | SERVING SIZE | CALORIES | CALORIES FROM FAT |
|---|---|---|---|
| **VEGETABLE MEALS/ENTREES (FROZEN)** | | | |
| Broccoli & Cheddar Cheese Sauce over Baked Potato, Stouffer's® Lean Cuisine® Lunch Express® | 10 oz | 220 | 50 |
| ❶ Broccoli and Cheese Baked Potato, Weight Watchers® | 1 entree | 250 | 60 |
| ❶ Cheddar Broccoli Potatoes, Healthy Choice® | 1 meal | 310 | 40 |
| ❶ Deluxe Cheddar Potato, Stouffer's® Lean Cuisine® | 1 pkg | 230 | 50 |
| ❶ Garden Potato Casserole, Healthy Choice® | 1 meal | 200 | 35 |
| ❶ Garden Potato Casserole, Life Choice® | 1 meal | 160 | 5 |
| ❶ Paella Rice and Vegetables, Weight Watchers® International Selections | 1 entree | 280 | 60 |
| Parisian Style White Beans/Vegetables, Weight Watchers® International Selections | 1 entree | 220 | 80 |
| ❶ Pilaf Florentine, Weight Watchers® International Selections | 1 entree | 290 | 60 |
| Santa Fe Style Rice and Beans, Weight Watchers® International Selections | 1 entree | 290 | 80 |
| ❶ Stuffed Cabbage with Whipped Potatoes, Stouffer's® Lean Cuisine® | 1 pkg | 220 | 60 |
| Stuffed Pepper, Stouffer's® | 1 pkg | 200 | 70 |
| Stuffed Peppers, Stouffer's®, two-serving size | ½ pkg | 180 | 70 |
| **VEGETABLE SIDE DISHES (FROZEN)** | | | |
| ***Broccoli Side Dishes*** | | | |
| ❶ Broccoli in Cheese Flavored Sauce, Green Giant® | ⅔ cup | 70 | 25 |
| ❶ Broccoli Spears in Butter Sauce, Green Giant® | 4 oz | 50 | 15 |
| ***Brussels Sprouts Side Dishes*** | | | |
| ❶ Baby Brussels Sprouts in Butter Sauce, Green Giant® | ⅔ cup | 60 | 15 |

❶  Meets Low-Fat Guidelines

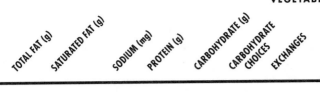

| TOTAL FAT (g) | SATURATED FAT (g) | SODIUM (mg) | PROTEIN (g) | CARBOHYDRATE (g) | CARBOHYDRATE CHOICES | EXCHANGES |
|---|---|---|---|---|---|---|
| 6 | 5 | 580 | 12 | 30 | 2 | 2 starch, 1 lean meat |
| 7 | 2 | 590 | 12 | 35 | 2 | 2 starch, 1 veg, 1 meat |
| 5 | 2 | 550 | 13 | 53 | 3½ | 3½ starch, 1 very lean meat |
| 6 | 2.5 | 570 | 13 | 32 | 2 | 2 starch, 1 meat |
| 4 | 1.5 | 520 | 11 | 30 | 2 | 2 starch, 1 very lean meat |
| 0.5 | 0 | 590 | 8 | 37 | 2 | 1½ starch, 1 veg |
| 7 | 1 | 680 | 7 | 48 | 3 | 3 starch, 1 fat |
| 9 | 3 | 690 | 13 | 23 | 1½ | 1½ starch, 1 meat, ½ fat |
| 7 | 2 | 550 | 9 | 47 | 3 | 3 starch, 1 veg, 1 fat |
| 9 | 4 | 670 | 12 | 41 | 3 | 3 starch, 1 meat |
| 7 | 1.5 | 460 | 11 | 27 | 2 | 1½ starch, 1 veg, 1 meat |
| 8 | 1.5 | 900 | 9 | 24 | 1½ | 1 starch, 1 veg, 1 meat |
| 7 | 1 | 590 | 8 | 20 | 1 | 1 starch, 1 veg, 1 meat |
| 2.5 | 1 | 520 | 3 | 9 | ½ | 2 veg, ½ fat |
| 1.5 | 1 | 330 | 2 | 7 | ½ | 2 veg |
| 1.5 | 1.5 | 270 | 3 | 9 | ½ | 2 veg |

1 Carbohydrate Choice = 1 starch or 1 fruit or 1 milk exchange

## PRODUCTS

| | SERVING SIZE | CALORIES | CALORIES FROM FAT |
|---|---|---|---|
| **Cauliflower Side Dishes** | | | |
| ❶ Cauliflower in Cheese Flavored Sauce, Green Giant® | ½ cup | 60 | 25 |
| **Corn Side Dishes** | | | |
| ❶ Corn in Butter Sauce, Green Giant® Niblets® | ⅔ cup | 130 | 25 |
| Corn Souffle, Stouffer's® | ½ cup | 170 | 60 |
| ❶ Cream Style Corn, Green Giant® | ½ cup | 110 | 10 |
| ❶ Shoepeg White Corn in Butter Sauce, Green Giant® | ¾ cup | 120 | 25 |
| **Lima Bean Side Dishes** | | | |
| ❶ Baby Lima Beans in Butter Sauce, Green Giant® | ⅔ cup | 120 | 25 |
| **Pea Side Dishes** | | | |
| ❶ Baby Early Peas in Butter Sauce, Green Giant® LeSueur® | ¾ cup | 100 | 20 |
| ❶ Sweet Peas in Butter Sauce, Green Giant® | ¾ cup | 100 | 20 |
| **Spinach Side Dishes** | | | |
| ❶ Creamed Spinach, Green Giant® | ½ cup | 80 | 25 |
| ❶ Creamed Spinach, PictSweet® | ¾ cup | 45 | 22.5 |
| Creamed Spinach, Stouffer's® | ½ cup | 160 | 100 |
| ❶ Cut Leaf Spinach in Butter Sauce, Green Giant® | ½ cup | 40 | 15 |
| Spinach Souffle, Stouffer's® | ½ cup | 150 | 90 |
| **Vegetable Mix Side Dishes** | | | |
| ❶ Broccoli, Cauliflower, Carrots, Corn & Sweet Peas in Butter Sauce, Green Giant® | ¾ cup | 60 | 20 |
| ❶ Broccoli, Cauliflower & Carrots in Cheese Flavored Sauce, Green Giant® | ⅔ cup | 80 | 25 |
| ❶ Broccoli, Pasta, Sweet Peas, Corn & Red Peppers in Butter Sauce, Green Giant® | ¾ cup | 70 | 20 |
| ❶ Cajun Gumbo with Seasoning, PictSweet® | ⅔ cup | 40 | 0 |
| ❶ Chinese Stir-Fry with Seasoning, PictSweet® | ¾ cup | 30 | 0 |

❶  Meets Low-Fat Guidelines

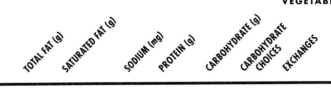

| TOTAL FAT (g) | SATURATED FAT (g) | SODIUM (mg) | PROTEIN (g) | CARBOHYDRATE (g) | CARBOHYDRATE CHOICES | EXCHANGES |
|---|---|---|---|---|---|---|
| 2.5 | 0.5 | 510 | 2 | 8 | ½ | 2 veg, ½ fat |
| 3 | 1.5 | 350 | 3 | 23 | 1½ | 1½ starch |
| 7 | 2 | 490 | 5 | 21 | 1½ | 1½ starch, 1 fat |
| 1 | 0 | 330 | 2 | 23 | 1½ | 1½ starch |
| 2.5 | 1.5 | 320 | 3 | 21 | 1½ | 1½ starch |
| 2.5 | 2 | 330 | 6 | 18 | 1 | 1 starch, 1 very lean meat |
| 2 | 1.5 | 370 | 5 | 16 | 1 | 1 starch |
| 2 | 1.5 | 400 | 4 | 16 | 1 | 1 starch |
| 3 | 1.5 | 520 | 4 | 10 | ½ | 2 veg, ½ fat |
| 2.5 | 1.5 | 260 | 3 | 4 | 0 | 1 veg, ½ fat |
| 12 | 4 | 380 | 4 | 8 | ½ | 1 veg, 2½ fat |
| 1.5 | 1 | 280 | 2 | 5 | 0 | 1 veg |
| 10 | 2 | 480 | 6 | 9 | ½ | 2 veg, 2 fat |
| 2 | 1.5 | 300 | 2 | 8 | ½ | ½ starch or 2 veg |
| 2.5 | 1.5 | 560 | 2 | 11 | 1 | 2 veg, ½ fat |
| 2 | 1.5 | 280 | 3 | 11 | 1 | 1 starch or 2 veg |
| 0 | 0 | 50 | 2 | 9 | ½ | 2 veg |
| 0 | 0 | 200 | 1 | 5 | 0 | 1 veg |

1 Carbohydrate Choice = 1 starch or 1 fruit or 1 milk exchange

| PRODUCTS | SERVING SIZE | CALORIES | CALORIES FROM FAT |
|---|---|---|---|
| English Style Cheddar, Green Giant® International Mixtures | 4 oz | 120 | 45 |
| ❶ French Style Garlic Dijon, Green Giant® International Mixtures | 4 oz | 60 | 25 |
| Green Bean Mushroom Casserole, Stouffer's® | ½ cup | 140 | 70 |
| ❶ Italian Style Parmesan, Green Giant® International Mixtures | 4 oz | 70 | 25 |
| ❶ Japanese Style Teriyaki, Green Giant® International Mixtures | 4 oz | 50 | 0 |
| ❶ Mexicali Mix, Flav-R-Pac® | ⅔ cup | 80 | 5 |
| ❶ Mixed Vegetables in Butter Sauce, Green Giant® | ¾ cup | 70 | 20 |
| ❶ New England Style, Green Giant® American Mixtures® | ⅔ cup | 70 | 15 |
| ❶ Normandy Style Mushroom, Green Giant® International Mixtures | 4 oz | 80 | 25 |
| ❶ Oriental Stir-Fry with Seasoning, PictSweet® | ¾ cup | 30 | 0 |
| ❶ Pasta Primavera with Garlic Sauce, PictSweet® | ¾ cup | 60 | 27 |
| ❶ Stir Fry Vegetables with Noodles, Flav-R-Pac® | 1 cup | 80 | 0 |
| ❶ Stir Fry Vegetables with Noodles, Westpac® | 1 cup | 80 | 0 |
| ❶ Western Style, Green Giant® American Mixtures® | ¾ cup | 50 | 15 |
| ❶ Vegetable Chow Mein Stir Fry, Flav-R-Pac® | 1 cup | 50 | 0 |
| ❶ Vegetable Chow Mein Stir Fry, Westpac® | 1 cup | 50 | 0 |
| ❶ Vegetable Stir Fry with Rice, Flav-R-Pac® | 1 cup | 80 | 0 |
| ❶ Vegetable Stir Fry with Rice, Westpac® | 1 cup | 80 | 0 |

## VEGETABLES

### Oriental Vegetables (canned)

| | | | |
|---|---|---|---|
| ❶ Bamboo Shoots, La Choy® | 2 Tb | 3 | 0 |
| ❶ Bean Sprouts, La Choy® | 1 cup | 11 | 1 |
| ❶ Chinese Mixed Vegetables, La Choy® | ⅔ cup | 9 | 1 |
| ❶ Chop Suey Vegetables, La Choy® | ½ cup | 14 | 1 |

❶  Meets Low-Fat Guidelines

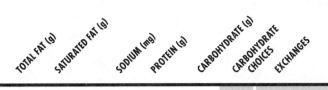

| TOTAL FAT (g) | SATURATED FAT (g) | SODIUM (mg) | PROTEIN (g) | CARBOHYDRATE (g) | CARBOHYDRATE CHOICES | EXCHANGES |
|---|---|---|---|---|---|---|
| 5 | 2 | 390 | 4 | 15 | 1 | 1 starch, 1 fat |
| 3 | 2 | 380 | 2 | 6 | ½ | ½ starch, ½ fat or 1 veg, ½ fat |
| 8 | 2 | 530 | 3 | 13 | 1 | 1 starch, 1½ fat or 2 veg, 2 fat |
| 2.5 | 1.5 | 250 | 4 | 8 | ½ | ½ starch, ½ fat or 2 veg, ½ fat |
| 0 | 0 | 400 | 3 | 9 | ½ | ½ starch or 2 veg |
| 0.5 | 0 | 75 | 3 | 18 | 1 | 1 starch |
| 2 | 1 | 240 | 2 | 11 | 1 | 1 starch |
| 1.5 | 0 | 70 | 2 | 13 | 1 | 1 starch |
| 3 | 2 | 270 | 2 | 11 | 1 | 1 starch |
| 0 | 0 | 310 | 1 | 5 | 0 | 1 veg |
| 3 | 1.5 | 105 | 2 | 7 | ½ | ½ starch, ½ fat |
| 0.5 | 0 | 15 | 4 | 14 | 1 | 1 starch |
| 0.5 | 0 | 15 | 4 | 14 | 1 | 1 starch |
| 1.5 | 0 | 10 | 1 | 9 | ½ | ½ starch or 2 veg |
| 0 | 0 | 40 | 3 | 10 | ½ | ½ starch or 2 veg |
| 0 | 0 | 40 | 3 | 10 | ½ | ½ starch or 2 veg |
| 0 | 0 | 15 | 3 | 18 | 1 | 1 starch |
| 0 | 0 | 15 | 3 | 18 | 1 | 1 starch |
| <1 | 0 | 0 | <1 | <1 | 0 | free |
| <1 | 0 | 17 | 1 | 1 | 0 | free |
| <1 | 0 | 32 | 1 | 1 | 0 | free |
| <1 | 0 | 323 | 1 | 3 | 0 | free |

1 Carbohydrate Choice = 1 starch or 1 fruit or 1 milk exchange

## PRODUCTS

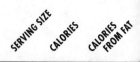

| | SERVING SIZE | CALORIES | CALORIES FROM FAT |
|---|---|---|---|
| ❶ Water Chestnuts, sliced, La Choy® | 2 Tb | 11 | 1 |
| ❶ Water Chestnuts, whole, La Choy® | 2 whole | 10 | 1 |

### Plain Vegetables (canned or frozen)

| | | | |
|---|---|---|---|
| ❶ Asparagus | ½–⅔ cup | 20 | 0 |
| ❶ Beets | ½ cup | 30–35 | 0 |
| ❶ Carrots | ½ cup | 25 | 5 |
| ❶ Corn, cream style | ½ cup | 100 | 10 |
| ❶ Corn, whole kernal | ½ cup | 90 | 10 |
| ❶ Corn on the Cob, frozen | 1 short ear | 75 | 10 |
| | 1 long ear | 135 | 15 |
| ❶ Green Beans | ½ cup | 20 | 0 |
| ❶ Mixed vegetables | ½ cup | 35 | 0 |
| ❶ Peas | ½ cup | 65 | 0 |
| ❶ Pimentos | 2¼ oz | 20 | 0 |
| ❶ Potatoes | ½ cup | 60 | 0 |
| ❶ Spinach | ½ cup | 30 | 0 |
| ❶ Succotash (corn, lima beans) | ½ cup | 100 | 10 |

### VEGETARIAN MEAT SUBSTITUTES
see also Vegetable Burgers; Tempeh; Tofu

### Green Giant® Vegetarian Meat Substitutes (frozen)

| | | | |
|---|---|---|---|
| Breakfast Links | 3 links | 110 | 45 |
| Breakfast Patties | 2 patties | 100 | 35 |

### Loma Linda® Vegetarian Meat Substitutes (canned)

| | | | |
|---|---|---|---|
| Big Franks | 1 link | 110 | 60 |
| ❶ Dinner Cuts | 1 slices | 80 | 15 |
| Fried Chik'n/Gravy | 2 pieces | 390 | 280 |
| Linketts | 1 link | 70 | 40 |
| Little Links | 2 link | 90 | 50 |
| Nuteena | ⅜" slice | 160 | 120 |
| Sandwich Spread | ¼ cup | 80 | 40 |

❶ Meets Low-Fat Guidelines

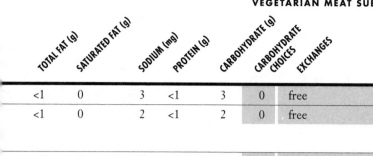

| TOTAL FAT (g) | SATURATED FAT (g) | SODIUM (mg) | PROTEIN (g) | CARBOHYDRATE (g) | CARBOHYDRATE CHOICES | EXCHANGES |
|---|---|---|---|---|---|---|
| <1 | 0 | 3 | <1 | 3 | 0 | free |
| <1 | 0 | 2 | <1 | 2 | 0 | free |
| 0 | 0 | 85–260 | 2 | 4 | 0 | 1 veg |
| 0 | 0 | 60–270 | 1 | 7 | ½ | 1 veg |
| 0.5 | 0 | 250 | 1 | 6 | ½ | 1 veg |
| 1 | 0 | 340–430 | 2 | 24 | 1½ | 1½ starch |
| 1 | 0 | 340 | 2 | 14 | 1 | 1 starch |
| 1 | 0 | 10 | 3 | 18 | 1 | 1 starch |
| 1.5 | 0 | 10 | 4.5 | 30 | 2 | 2 starch |
| 0 | 0 | 135–400 | 1 | 4 | 0 | 1 veg |
| 0 | 0 | 370 | 1 | 7 | ½ | 1 veg |
| 0 | 0 | 195–520 | 4 | 12 | 1 | 1 starch |
| 0 | 0 | 180 | 1 | 3 | 0 | free |
| 0 | 0 | 160 | 1 | 14 | 1 | 1 starch |
| 0 | 0 | 440 | 3 | 4 | 0 | 1 veg |
| 1 | 0 | 340 | 3 | 19 | 1 | 1 starch |
| 5 | 0.5 | 340 | 12 | 5 | 0 | 2 lean meat |
| 4 | 0.5 | 280 | 10 | 5 | 0 | 2 lean meat |
| 7 | 1 | 240 | 10 | 2 | 0 | 1 meat, ½ fat |
| 1.5 | 0.5 | 350 | 12 | 3 | 0 | 2 very lean meat |
| 31 | 4.5 | 810 | 21 | 6 | ½ | ½ starch, 3 meat, 3 fat |
| 4.5 | 0.5 | 160 | 7 | 1 | 0 | 1 meat |
| 6 | 1 | 230 | 8 | 2 | 0 | 1 meat |
| 13 | 5 | 120 | 6 | 6 | ½ | ½ starch, 1 meat, 1 fat |
| 4.5 | 1 | 260 | 4 | 7 | ½ | ½ starch, 1 fat |

1 Carbohydrate Choice = 1 starch or 1 fruit or 1 milk exchange

## PRODUCTS

| | SERVING SIZE | CALORIES | CALORIES FROM FAT |
|---|---|---|---|
| Swiss Steak | 1 piece | 120 | 50 |
| Tender Bits | 6 pieces | 110 | 40 |
| Tender Rounds | 8 pieces | 120 | 45 |
| **Loma Linda® Vegetarian Meat Substitutes (frozen)** | | | |
| Chik Nuggets | 5 pieces | 240 | 140 |
| Corn Dogs | 1 corn dog | 200 | 90 |
| Fried Chik'n | 1 piece | 180 | 130 |
| Griddle Steaks | 1 piece | 130 | 60 |
| Sizzle Burger | 1 patty | 100 | 110 |
| **Morningstar Farms® Vegetarian Meat Substitutes (frozen)** | | | |
| ❶ Breakfast Links | 2 link | 60 | 20 |
| ❶ Breakfast Patties | 1 patty | 70 | 25 |
| Breakfast Strips | 2 strips | 60 | 40 |
| Chick Patties | 1 patty | 170 | 80 |
| Deli Franks | 1 link | 110 | 60 |
| **Natural Touch® Vegetarian Meat Substitutes (canned)** | | | |
| Vegetarian Chili | 1 cup | 270 | 110 |
| **Natural Touch® Vegetarian Meat Substitutes (frozen)** | | | |
| Dinner Entree | 1 patty | 220 | 130 |
| Lentil Rice Loaf | 1" slice | 170 | 80 |
| Nine Bean Loaf | 1" slice | 160 | 70 |
| Okara Patty | 1 patty | 110 | 45 |
| Vege-Frank | 1 link | 100 | 50 |
| **White Wave® Vegetarian Meat Substitutes (refrigerated)** | | | |
| ❶ Beef Style Meatless Sandwich Slices | 2 slices | 90 | 0 |
| Bologna Style Meatless Sandwich Slices | 2 slices | 120 | 50 |
| ❶ Chicken Style Meatless Sandwich Slices | 2 slices | 80 | 0 |
| ❶ Meatless Healthy Franks | 1 frank | 90 | 15 |
| Meatless Healthy Links | 2 links | 140 | 90 |

❶ Meets Low-Fat Guidelines

| TOTAL FAT (g) | SATURATED FAT (g) | SODIUM (mg) | PROTEIN (g) | CARBOHYDRATE (g) | CARBOHYDRATE CHOICES | EXCHANGES |
|---|---|---|---|---|---|---|
| 6 | 1 | 430 | 9 | 8 | ½ | ½ starch, 1 meat |
| 4.5 | 0.5 | 440 | 11 | 7 | ½ | ½ starch, 1 meat |
| 5 | 1 | 330 | 14 | 5 | 0 | 2 lean meat |
| 16 | 2.5 | 710 | 12 | 13 | 1 | 1 starch, 1 meat, 2 fat |
| 9 | 1.5 | 240 | 10 | 18 | 1 | 1 starch, 1 meat, 1 fat |
| 15 | 2 | 500 | 11 | <1 | 0 | 2 meat, 1 fat |
| 7 | 1 | 410 | 13 | 4 | 0 | 2 lean meat |
| 12 | 1.5 | 540 | 13 | 10 | ½ | ½ starch, 2 meat |
| 2.5 | 0.5 | 340 | 8 | 2 | 0 | 1 lean meat |
| 3 | 0.5 | 270 | 8 | 2 | 0 | 1 lean meat |
| 4.5 | 0.5 | 220 | 2 | 2 | 0 | 1 fat |
| 10 | 1.5 | 570 | 7 | 13 | 1 | 1 starch, 1 meat, 1 fat |
| 7 | 1 | 520 | 10 | 3 | 0 | 1 meat, ½ fat |
| 12 | 2 | 1330 | 18 | 21 | 1½ | 1½ starch, 2 meat |
| 15 | 2.5 | 380 | 19 | 2 | 0 | 3 meat |
| 9 | 2.5 | 370 | 8 | 14 | 1 | 1 starch, 1 meat, ½ fat |
| 8 | 1.5 | 350 | 8 | 13 | 1 | 1 starch, 1 meat, ½ fat |
| 5 | 1 | 360 | 11 | 4 | 0 | 2 lean meat |
| 6 | 1 | 470 | 10 | 2 | 0 | 1 meat |
| 0 | 0 | 270 | 14 | 8 | ½ | ½ starch, 2 very lean meat |
| 8 | 1.5 | 370 | 8 | 5 | 0 | 1 meat, ½ fat |
| 0 | 0 | 260 | 12 | 8 | ½ | ½ starch, 1 very lean meat |
| 1.5 | 0 | 350 | 13 | 6 | ½ | ½ starch, 2 very lean meat |
| 10 | 1.5 | 450 | 8 | 5 | 0 | 1 meat, 1 fat |

1 Carbohydrate Choice = 1 starch or 1 fruit or 1 milk exchange

## PRODUCTS

| | | SERVING SIZE | CALORIES | CALORIES FROM FAT |
|---|---|---|---|---|
| ❶ | Meatless Jumbo Franks | 1 frank | 170 | 25 |
| ❶ | Pastrami Style Meatless Sandwich Slices | 2 slices | 90 | 0 |
| ❶ | Traditional Seasoned Seitan | 1 piece | 140 | 0 |
| ❶ | Turkey Style Meatless Sandwich Slices | 2 slices | 80 | 0 |
| ❶ | Vegetable Philly Steak Slices | 3 slices | 60 | 0 |
| | Vegetable Sloppy Joe | 1 cup | 320 | 90 |
| ❶ | Vegetarian Fajita Strips | ⅓ cup | 60 | 0 |

### Worthington® Vegetarian Meat Substitutes (canned)

| | | | | |
|---|---|---|---|---|
| | Chili | 1 cup | 290 | 140 |
| ❶ | Choplets | 2 slices | 90 | 15 |
| ❶ | Cutlets | 1 slice | 70 | 10 |
| | Diced Chik | ¼ cup | 60 | 30 |
| | FriChik | 2 pieces | 120 | 70 |
| ❶ | Multigrain cutlet | 2 slices | 100 | 15 |
| | Numete | ⅜" slice | 130 | 90 |
| | Prime Stakes | 1 piece | 140 | 80 |
| | Protose | ⅜" slice | 130 | 60 |
| | Saucettes | 1 link | 90 | 60 |
| | Savory Slices | 3 slices | 150 | 80 |
| | Sliced Chik | 3 slices | 90 | 50 |
| | Super-Links | 1 link | 110 | 70 |
| | Turkee Slices® | 3 slices | 190 | 130 |
| ❶ | Vegetable Skallops | ½ cup | 90 | 15 |
| ❶ | Vegetable Steaks | 2 pieces | 80 | 10 |
| ❶ | Veja-Links | 1 link | 50 | 25 |

### Worthington® Vegetarian Meat Substitutes (frozen)

| | | | | |
|---|---|---|---|---|
| | Beef Style Meatless | ⅜" slice | 110 | 60 |
| | Bolono | 3 slices | 80 | 30 |
| | Chic-ketts | 2 (⅜") slices | 120 | 60 |
| | Chicken, Sliced | 2 slices | 80 | 40 |

 Meets Low-Fat Guidelines

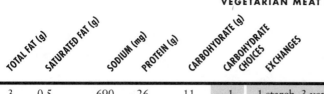

| TOTAL FAT (g) | SATURATED FAT (g) | SODIUM (mg) | PROTEIN (g) | CARBOHYDRATE (g) | CARBOHYDRATE CHOICES | EXCHANGES |
|---|---|---|---|---|---|---|
| 3 | 0.5 | 690 | 26 | 11 | 1 | 1 starch, 3 very lean meat |
| 0 | 0 | 270 | 14 | 8 | ½ | ½ starch, 2 very lean meat |
| 0 | 0 | 240 | 31 | 4 | 0 | 4 very lean meat |
| 0 | 0 | 400 | 13 | 7 | ½ | ½ starch, 2 very lean meat |
| 0 | 0 | 105 | 14 | 2 | 0 | 2 very lean meat |
| 10 | 0 | 810 | 36 | 21 | 1½ | 1½ starch, 4 lean meat |
| 0 | 0 | 105 | 14 | 2 | 0 | 2 very lean meat |
| 15 | 2.5 | 1130 | 19 | 21 | 1½ | 1½ starch, 2 meat, ½ fat |
| 1.5 | 1 | 500 | 17 | 3 | 0 | 2 very lean meat |
| 1 | 0 | 340 | 11 | 3 | 0 | 2 very lean meat |
| 3.5 | 0.5 | 240 | 5 | 1 | 0 | 1 lean meat |
| 8 | 1 | 430 | 10 | 1 | 0 | 1 meat, 1 fat |
| 2 | 0.5 | 390 | 15 | 5 | 0 | 2 very lean meat |
| 10 | 2.5 | 270 | 6 | 5 | 0 | 1 meat, 1 fat |
| 9 | 1.5 | 440 | 9 | 4 | 0 | 1 meat, 1 fat |
| 7 | 1 | 280 | 13 | 5 | 0 | 2 lean meat |
| 6 | 1 | 200 | 6 | 1 | 0 | 1 high fat meat |
| 9 | 3.5 | 540 | 10 | 6 | ½ | ½ starch, 1 high fat meat |
| 6 | 1 | 390 | 9 | 1 | 0 | 1 meat |
| 8 | 1 | 350 | 7 | 2 | 0 | 1 high fat meat |
| 14 | 2.5 | 580 | 13 | 3 | 0 | 2 meat, 1 fat |
| 1.5 | 0.5 | 410 | 15 | 3 | 0 | 2 very lean meat |
| 1.5 | 0.5 | 300 | 15 | 3 | 0 | 2 very lean meat |
| 3 | 0.5 | 190 | 5 | 1 | 0 | 1 lean meat |
| 7 | 1 | 620 | 9 | 4 | 0 | 1 meat, ½ fat |
| 3.5 | 1 | 720 | 10 | 2 | 0 | 1 meat |
| 7 | 1 | 390 | 13 | 2 | 0 | 2 lean meat |
| 4.5 | 1 | 370 | 9 | 1 | 0 | 1 meat |

1 Carbohydrate Choice = 1 starch or 1 fruit or 1 milk exchange

## PRODUCTS

| | SERVING SIZE | CALORIES | CALORIES FROM FAT |
|---|---|---|---|
| ChikStiks | 1 piece | 110 | 60 |
| Corned Beef, Sliced | 4 slices | 140 | 80 |
| Diced Chik, Meatless | ¼ cup | 80 | 40 |
| Dinner Roast | ¾" slice | 190 | 110 |
| Fillets | 2 pieces | 180 | 90 |
| FriPats | 1 patty | 130 | 60 |
| Golden Croquettes | 4 pieces | 210 | 90 |
| Ground Meatless Vegetarian Sausage | ½ cup | 110 | 50 |
| Leanies | 1 link | 110 | 70 |
| ❶ Prosage Links | 2 links | 60 | 20 |
| Prosage Patties | 1 patty | 100 | 60 |
| Prosage Roll | ⅝" slice | 140 | 90 |
| Salami, Meatless | 3 slices | 130 | 70 |
| Smoked Beef Slices | 6 slices | 120 | 60 |
| Smoked Turkey Slices | 3 slices | 140 | 90 |
| Staklets | 1 piece | 140 | 70 |
| Stripples | 2 strips | 60 | 40 |
| Tuno (drained) | ½ cup | 80 | 50 |
| Veelets | 1 patty | 180 | 80 |
| Wham | 2 slices | 80 | 45 |

### WAFFLE MIX (AS PREPARED)

| | SERVING SIZE | CALORIES | CALORIES FROM FAT |
|---|---|---|---|
| Belgian Waffle Mix, Krusteaz® | ½ cup mix | 440 | 170 |

### WAFFLES (FROZEN)

| | SERVING SIZE | CALORIES | CALORIES FROM FAT |
|---|---|---|---|
| Apple Cinnamon Eggo®, Kellogg's® | 2 waffles | 220 | 70 |
| Blueberry, Krusteaz® | 2 waffles | 230 | 70 |
| Blueberry Eggo®, Kellogg's® | 2 waffles | 220 | 70 |
| Blueberry Eggo Minis®, Kellogg's® | 3 sets of 4 waffles | 240 | 70 |
| Buttermilk, Krusteaz® | 2 waffles | 220 | 70 |
| Buttermilk Eggo®, Kellogg's® | 2 waffles | 220 | 70 |

❶  Meets Low-Fat Guidelines

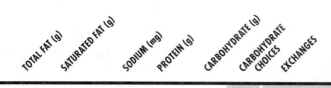

| TOTAL FAT (g) | SATURATED FAT (g) | SODIUM (mg) | PROTEIN (g) | CARBOHYDRATE (g) | CARBOHYDRATE CHOICES | EXCHANGES |
|---|---|---|---|---|---|---|
| 7 | 1 | 360 | 9 | 3 | 0 | 1 meat, ½ fat |
| 9 | 2 | 520 | 10 | 5 | 0 | 1 meat, 1 fat |
| 4.5 | 1 | 360 | 9 | 1 | 0 | 1 meat |
| 12 | 2 | 580 | 12 | 5 | 0 | 2 meat, ½ fat |
| 10 | 2 | 750 | 16 | 8 | ½ | ½ starch, 2 meat |
| 6 | 1 | 320 | 14 | 4 | 0 | 2 meat |
| 10 | 1.5 | 600 | 14 | 14 | 1 | 1 starch, 2 meat |
| 6 | 1.5 | 330 | 11 | 3 | 0 | 2 lean meat |
| 8 | 1.5 | 430 | 7 | 2 | 0 | 1 high fat meat |
| 2.5 | 0.5 | 340 | 8 | 2 | 0 | 1 lean meat |
| 7 | 2 | 370 | 9 | 1 | 0 | 1 meat |
| 10 | 2 | 390 | 10 | 2 | 0 | 1 meat, 1 fat |
| 8 | 1 | 930 | 12 | 2 | 0 | 2 meat |
| 6 | 1 | 730 | 11 | 6 | ½ | ½ starch, 1 meat |
| 10 | 2 | 620 | 10 | 3 | 0 | 1 meat, 1 fat |
| 8 | 1.5 | 480 | 12 | 6 | ½ | ½ starch, 2 lean meat |
| 4.5 | 0.5 | 220 | 1 | 1 | 0 | 1 fat |
| 6 | 1 | 290 | 6 | 2 | 0 | 1 meat |
| 9 | 1.5 | 390 | 14 | 10 | ½ | ½ starch, 2 meat |
| 5 | 1 | 430 | 7 | 1 | 0 | 1 meat |
| 19 | 3.5 | 1050 | 12 | 56 | 4 | 4 starch, 3 fat |
| 8 | 1.5 | 450 | 5 | 33 | 2 | 2 starch, 1 fat |
| 8 | 1 | 420 | 4 | 35 | 2 | 2 starch, 1 fat |
| 8 | 1.5 | 450 | 5 | 33 | 2 | 2 starch, 1 fat |
| 8 | 1.5 | 510 | 6 | 37 | 2½ | 2½ starch, 1 fat |
| 8 | 1 | 420 | 5 | 33 | 2 | 2 starch, 1 fat |
| 8 | 1.5 | 480 | 5 | 30 | 2 | 2 starch, 1 fat |

1 Carbohydrate Choice = 1 starch *or* 1 fruit *or* 1 milk exchange

## PRODUCTS

| | SERVING SIZE | CALORIES | CALORIES FROM FAT |
|---|---|---|---|
| Cinnamon Toast Eggo Minis®, Kellogg's® | 3 sets of 4 waffles | 290 | 90 |
| Eggo® Common Sense® Oat Bran, Kellogg's® | 2 waffles | 200 | 60 |
| Eggo® Common Sense® Oat Bran with Fruit & Nut, Kellogg's® | 2 waffles | 220 | 70 |
| Eggo® Nut & Honey, Kellogg's® | 2 waffles | 240 | 90 |
| Eggo® Nutri-Grain®, Kellogg's® | 2 waffles | 190 | 60 |
| Eggo® Nutri-Grain® Multi-Bran, Kellogg's® | 2 waffles | 180 | 50 |
| Eggo® Nutri-Grain® Raisin & Bran, Kellogg's® | 2 waffles | 210 | 50 |
| ❶ Eggo® Special K, Kellogg's® | 2 waffles | 140 | 0 |
| Eggo® Strawberry, Kellogg's® | 2 waffles | 220 | 70 |
| Homestyle, Krusteaz® | 2 waffles | 220 | 70 |
| Homestyle Eggo®, Kellogg's® | 2 waffles | 220 | 70 |
| Homestyle Eggo Minis®, Kellogg's® | 3 sets of 4 waffles | 240 | 70 |
| Waffles, Aunt Jemima® (Original, Buttermilk, and Blueberry, avg) | 2 waffles | 200 | 60 |
| ❶ Waffles, Aunt Jemima® Lowfat | 2 waffles | 160 | 10 |
| ❶ Waffles, Belgian Chef® | 2 waffles | 140 | 25 |
| Waffles, Downyflake® (Homestyle, Buttermilk, and Blueberry, avg) | 2 waffles | 170 | 40 |

### WHIPPED TOPPINGS

| | | | |
|---|---|---|---|
| ❶ Whipped toppings, all brands (avg) | 2 Tb | 20 | 15 |

### YOGURT

#### Breyers® Yogurt

| | | | |
|---|---|---|---|
| ❶ 1.0% Milkfat Yogurt, all varieties (avg) | 8 oz | 250 | 25 |
| ❶ 1.5% Milkfat Yogurt, all varieties (avg) | 8 oz | 220 | 25 |
| ❶ 1.5% Milkfat Yogurt, plain | 8 oz | 130 | 30 |

#### Columbo® Yogurt

| | | | |
|---|---|---|---|
| ❶ Banana/Strawberry Yogurt, Fat Free | 8 oz | 220 | 0 |
| ❶ Cappuccino Yogurt, Fat Free | 8 oz | 170 | 0 |

❶ Meets Low-Fat Guidelines

| TOTAL FAT (g) | SATURATED FAT (g) | SODIUM (mg) | PROTEIN (g) | CARBOHYDRATE (g) | CARBOHYDRATE CHOICES | EXCHANGES |
|---|---|---|---|---|---|---|
| 10 | 2 | 470 | 5 | 45 | 3 | 3 starch, 1 fat |
| 7 | 1.5 | 350 | 6 | 27 | 2 | 2 starch, 1 fat |
| 8 | 1.5 | 340 | 6 | 32 | 2 | 2 starch, 1 fat |
| 10 | 2 | 480 | 6 | 32 | 2 | 2 starch, 2 fat |
| 6 | 1 | 430 | 5 | 30 | 2 | 2 starch, 1 fat |
| 6 | 1 | 400 | 5 | 32 | 2 | 2 starch, 1 fat |
| 6 | 1 | 390 | 5 | 36 | 2½ | 2½ starch, ½ fat |
| 0 | 0 | 250 | 6 | 29 | 2 | 2 starch |
| 8 | 1.5 | 460 | 5 | 32 | 2 | 2 starch, 1 fat |
| 8 | 1 | 420 | 4 | 34 | 2 | 2 starch, 1 fat |
| 8 | 1.5 | 470 | 5 | 30 | 2 | 2 starch, 1 fat |
| 8 | 1.5 | 520 | 6 | 34 | 2 | 2 starch, 1 fat |
| 7 | 1 | 550 | 5 | 28 | 2 | 2 starch, 1 fat |
| 1 | 0 | 540 | 5 | 33 | 2 | 2 starch |
| 2.5 | 0.5 | 340 | 3 | 24 | 1½ | 1½ starch |
| 4 | 1 | 465 | 4 | 29 | 2 | 2 starch |
| 1.5 | 1 | 5 | 0 | 1.5 | 0 | free |
| 2.5 | 1.5 | 110 | 8 | 49 | 3 | 2½ fruit, 1 milk |
| 3 | 2 | 135 | 10 | 38 | 2½ | 2 fruit, 1 milk |
| 3 | 2 | 150 | 11 | 15 | 1 | 1 milk |
| 0 | 0 | 120 | 8 | 45 | 3 | 2 fruit, 1 milk |
| 0 | 0 | 140 | 9 | 32 | 2 | 1 fruit, 1 milk |

1 Carbohydrate Choice = 1 starch or 1 fruit or 1 milk exchange

| PRODUCTS | SERVING SIZE | CALORIES | CALORIES FROM FAT |
|---|---|---|---|
| ❶ Fruited Flavors Yogurt, Fat Free | 8 oz | 200 | 0 |
| Fruit Flavors Yogurt, Lowfat | 8 oz | 200 | 30 |
| ❶ Light Flavors Yogurt | 8 oz | 100 | 0 |
| Vanilla, Lowfat | 8 oz | 180 | 35 |
| **Dannon® Yogurt** | | | |
| ❶ Fat Free Chunky Fruit™ Yogurt, all varieties (avg) | 6 oz | 160 | 0 |
| ❶ Nonfat Tropifruita™ Yogurt, all varieties (avg) | 6 oz | 150 | 0 |
| **Knudsen® Yogurt** | | | |
| ❶ Cal 70® Yogurt, all varieties (avg) | 6 oz | 70 | 0 |
| ❶ Knudsen Free® Yogurt, all varieties (avg) | 6 oz | 165 | 0 |
| **Light 'N Lively® Yogurt** | | | |
| ❶ 1.5% Milkfat Yogurt, Multipack, all varieties (avg) | 4.4 oz | 140 | 10 |
| ❶ 50 Calories® Yogurt, all varieties (avg) | 4.4 oz | 50 | 0 |
| ❶ 70 Calories® Yogurt, all varieties (avg) | 6 oz | 70 | 0 |
| ❶ Kidpack Yogurt, all varieties (avg) | 8 oz | 140 | 10 |
| ❶ Light 'N Lively Free® Yogurt, all varieties (avg) | 6 oz | 175 | 0 |
| **Yoplait® Yogurt** | | | |
| ❶ Crunch 'n Yogurt™ Light, all varieties (avg) | 7 oz | 140 | 15 |
| ❶ Custard Style™ Yogurt, fruit varieties (avg) | 6 oz | 190 | 30 |
| ❶ Custard Style™ Yogurt, Vanilla | 6 oz | 190 | 30 |
| ❶ Extra Creamy Non-Fat Plain Yogurt | 8 oz | 130 | 0 |
| ❶ Extra Creamy Non-Fat Vanilla Yogurt | 8 oz | 210 | 0 |
| ❶ Fat Free Fruit-on-the-Bottom Yogurt, all varieties (avg) | 6 oz | 160 | 0 |
| ❶ Light Yogurt, all varieties (avg) | 6 oz | 90 | 0 |
| ❶ Original Yogurt, all varieties except coconut (avg) | 6 oz | 180 | 15 |
| ❶ Original Yogurt, fruit varieties, 99% Fat Free (avg) | 4 oz | 120 | 10 |

❶ Meets Low-Fat Guidelines

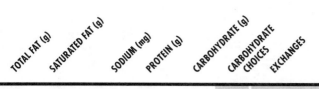

| TOTAL FAT (g) | SATURATED FAT (g) | SODIUM (mg) | PROTEIN (g) | CARBOHYDRATE (g) | CARBOHYDRATE CHOICES | EXCHANGES |
|---|---|---|---|---|---|---|
| 0 | 0 | 120 | 8 | 41 | 3 | 2 fruit, 1 milk |
| 3.5 | 2 | 110 | 6 | 36 | 2½ | 1½ fruit, 1 milk, ½ fat |
| 0 | 0 | 110 | 7 | 16 | 1 | 1 milk |
| 4 | 2.5 | 130 | 7 | 29 | 2 | 1 fruit, 1 milk, ½ fat |
| 0 | 0 | 100 | 7 | 33 | 2 | 1½ starch, 1 milk |
| 0 | 0 | 105 | 7 | 31 | 2 | 1 starch, 1 milk |
| 0 | 0 | 84 | 7 | 11 | 1 | 1 milk |
| 0 | 0 | 105 | 8 | 32 | 2 | 1 fruit, 1 milk |
| 1 | 0.5 | 65 | 5 | 27 | 2 | 1 fruit, 1 milk |
| 0 | 0 | 60 | 5 | 8 | ½ | ½ milk |
| 0 | 0 | 87 | 7 | 11 | 1 | 1 milk |
| 1 | 0.5 | 65 | 5 | 27 | 2 | 1 fruit, 1 milk |
| 0 | 0 | 105 | 8 | 35 | 2 | 1½ fruit, 1 milk |
| 1.5 | 0 | 130 | 7.5 | 23 | 1½ | 1 fruit, 1 milk |
| 3 | 2 | 100 | 8 | 32 | 2 | 1 fruit, 1 milk, ½ fat |
| 3 | 2 | 95 | 8 | 32 | 2 | 1 fruit, 1 milk, ½ fat |
| 0 | 0 | 170 | 13 | 19 | 1 | 1½ milk |
| 0 | 0 | 140 | 11 | 41 | 3 | 2 fruit, 1 milk |
| 0 | 0 | 95 | 7 | 34 | 2 | 1 fruit, 1 milk |
| 0 | 0 | 88 | 6 | 16 | 1 | 1 milk |
| 1.5 | 1 | 125 | 7 | 33 | 2 | 1½ fruit, 1 milk |
| 1 | 0.5 | 80 | 4 | 22 | 1½ | 1 fruit, ½ milk |

1 Carbohydrate Choice = 1 starch or 1 fruit or 1 milk exchange

| PRODUCTS | SERVING SIZE | CALORIES | CALORIES FROM FAT |
|---|---|---|---|
|  Original Coconut Cream Pie Yogurt | 6 oz | 200 | 25 |
|  Original Plain Yogurt, Nonfat | 6 oz | 100 | 0 |
|  Trix® Fruit Flavors Yogurt (avg) | 6 oz | 160 | 15 |

### YOGURT, FROZEN

#### Ben & Jerry's® Frozen Yogurt

| | | | |
|---|---|---|---|
|  Lowfat Frozen Yogurt, all varieties (avg) | ½ cup | 180 | 30 |
|  Nonfat Frozen Yogurt, all varieties (avg) | ½ cup | 140 | 0 |
| Regular Frozen Yogurt, all varieties (avg) | ½ cup | 210 | 35 |

#### Breyers® Frozen Yogurt

| | | | |
|---|---|---|---|
|  Chocolate Frozen Yogurt, Lowfat | ½ cup | 130 | 25 |
|  Strawberry Frozen Yogurt, Fat Free | ½ cup | 100 | 0 |

#### Columbo® Frozen Yogurt

| | | | |
|---|---|---|---|
|  Butter Nut Toffee & Butter Pecan Frozen Yogurt, Nonfat | ½ cup | 100 | 0 |
|  Chocolate Frozen Yogurt, Slender Sensations | ½ cup | 70 | 0 |
|  German Chocolate Fudge Frozen Yogurt, Nonfat | ½ cup | 110 | 0 |
|  Old World Chocolate Frozen Yogurt, Lowfat | ½ cup | 110 | 15 |
|  Other Chocolate Flavors Frozen Yogurt, Nonfat | ½ cup | 100 | 0 |
|  Other Flavors Frozen Yogurt, Nonfat | ½ cup | 100 | 0 |
|  Peanut Butter Frozen Yogurt, Lowfat | ½ cup | 120 | 25 |
|  Vanilla Frozen Yogurt, Nonfat | ½ cup | 100 | 0 |
|  Vanilla/Fruit Flavors Frozen Yogurt, Lowfat | ½ cup | 110 | 15 |
|  Vanilla/Fruit Flavors Frozen Yogurt, Slender Sensations | ½ cup | 60 | 0 |

#### Kemp's® Frozen Yogurt

| | | | |
|---|---|---|---|
| Apple Cinnamon or Pralines & Caramel Frozen Yogurt, low-fat (avg) | ½ cup | 145 | 35 |
|  Chocolate or Vanilla Frozen Yogurt, low-fat (avg) | ½ cup | 110 | 20 |

 Meets Low-Fat Guidelines

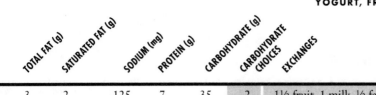

| TOTAL FAT (g) | SATURATED FAT (g) | SODIUM (mg) | PROTEIN (g) | CARBOHYDRATE (g) | CARBOHYDRATE CHOICES | EXCHANGES |
|---|---|---|---|---|---|---|
| 3 | 2 | 125 | 7 | 35 | 2 | 1½ fruit, 1 milk, ½ fat |
| 0 | 0 | 130 | 10 | 14 | 1 | 1 milk |
| 2 | 1 | 95 | 7 | 28 | 2 | 1 fruit, 1 milk |
| 3 | 2 | 70–115 | 5 | 34 | 2 | 2 starch |
| 0 | 0 | 55 | 4 | 31 | 2 | 2 starch |
| 3.5 | 2.5 | 110 | 5 | 39 | 2½ | 2½ starch |
| 2.5 | 2 | 40 | 3 | 24 | 1½ | 1½ starch |
| 0 | 0 | 40 | 2 | 22 | 1½ | 1½ starch |
| 0 | 0 | 140 | 3 | 20 | 1 | 1 starch |
| 0 | 0 | 70 | 4 | 11 | 1 | 1 starch |
| 0 | 0 | 60 | 4 | 23 | 1½ | 1½ starch |
| 2 | 1 | 65 | 3 | 22 | 1½ | 1½ starch |
| 0 | 0 | 65 | 3 | 22 | 1½ | 1½ starch |
| 0 | 0 | 55 | 3 | 20 | 1 | 1 starch |
| 2.5 | 0.5 | 75 | 4 | 20 | 1 | 1 starch, ½ fat |
| 0 | 0 | 60 | 3 | 22 | 1½ | 1½ starch |
| 1.5 | 1 | 55 | 3 | 21 | 1½ | 1½ starch |
| 0 | 0 | 60 | 4 | 11 | 1 | 1 starch |
| 4 | 2 | 80 | 3 | 25 | 1½ | 1½ starch ½ fat |
| 2 | 1.5 | 50 | 3 | 21 | 1½ | 1½ starch |

1 Carbohydrate Choice = 1 starch or 1 fruit or 1 milk exchange

## PRODUCTS

| | SERVING SIZE | CALORIES | CALORIES FROM FAT |
|---|---|---|---|
| ❶ Fat-Free Frozen Yogurt, all varieties (avg) | ½ cup | 110 | 0 |

### TCBY® Frozen Yogurt

| | | | |
|---|---|---|---|
| ❶ Classic Vanilla Frozen Yogurt | ½ cup | 110 | 10 |
| ❶ Cookies 'n Cream Frozen Yogurt | ½ cup | 120 | 20 |
| ❶ Crispie Cone Crunch Frozen Yogurt | ½ cup | 130 | 25 |
| ❶ Homestyle Banana Pudding Frozen Yogurt | ½ cup | 120 | 20 |
| ❶ Peach Frozen Yogurt | ½ cup | 110 | 10 |
| ❶ Peanut Butter Fudge Sundae Frozen Yogurt | ½ cup | 110 | 15 |
| ❶ Pecan Praline Crisp Frozen Yogurt | ½ cup | 120 | 20 |
| ❶ Summertime Strawberry Frozen Yogurt | ½ cup | 100 | 10 |

### Other Frozen Yogurt Brands

| | | | |
|---|---|---|---|
| ❶ Dannon Light® Frozen Yogurt, all varieties (avg) | ½ cup | 85 | 0 |
| ❶ Edy's Frozen Yogurt, all varieties (avg) | ½ cup | 100 | 30 |
| ❶ Haagen-Daz® Frozen Yogurt, Fat-Free, all varieties (avg) | ½ cup | 130 | 0 |
| ❶ Wells® Dairy Frozen Yogurt, all varieties (avg) | ½ cup | 85 | 20 |

### YOGURT BEVERAGES

| | | | |
|---|---|---|---|
| Drinkable Lowfat Yogurt, Lifeway™, all varieties (avg) | 8 oz | 175 | 45 |
| ❶ Yo-J™ Fat-Free Yogurt & Juice Blend, Kemps® (avg) | 8 oz | 150 | 0 |

 Meets Low-Fat Guidelines

| TOTAL FAT (g) | SATURATED FAT (g) | SODIUM (mg) | PROTEIN (g) | CARBOHYDRATE (g) | CARBOHYDRATE CHOICES | EXCHANGES |
|---|---|---|---|---|---|---|
| 0 | 0 | 85 | 3 | 24 | 1½ | 1½ starch |
| 1.5 | 1 | 50 | 3 | 21 | 1½ | 1½ starch |
| 2.5 | 1 | 80 | 3 | 23 | 1½ | 1½ starch |
| 3 | 2 | 55 | 3 | 22 | 1½ | 1½ starch |
| 2 | 1 | 55 | 3 | 22 | 1½ | 1½ starch |
| 1 | 1 | 45 | 3 | 21 | 1½ | 1½ starch |
| 1.5 | 1 | 50 | 3 | 23 | 1½ | 1½ starch |
| 2.5 | 1 | 70 | 3 | 23 | 1½ | 1½ starch |
| 1 | 1 | 40 | 3 | 20 | 1 | 1 starch |
| 0 | 0 | 0 | 4 | 21 | 1½ | 1½ starch |
| 3 | 1.5 | 50 | 3 | 18 | 1 | 1 starch, ½ fat |
| 0 | 0 | 40 | 5 | 28 | 2 | 2 starch |
| 2.5 | 1.5 | 60 | 3 | 20 | 1 | 1 starch |
| 5 | NA | 120 | 9 | 23 | 1½ | 1 fruit, 1 milk, 1 fat |
| 0 | 0 | 55 | 3 | 35 | 2 | 2 starch or ½ milk, 2 fruit |

1 Carbohydrate Choice = 1 starch or 1 fruit or 1 milk exchange

# Brand-Name Guide to Frozen Meals/Entrees

## Banquet®

## Yu Sing®

# Brand-Name Guide to Frozen Pizza

Mexican-Style, Krisp 'n Flaky Crust,
single-serving ............................276
Pepperoni Krisp 'n Flaky Crust,
single-serving ............................278
Sausage, Krisp 'n Flaky Crust,
single-serving ............................280
Supreme, Krisp 'n Flaky Crust,
single-serving ............................278

## Pappalo's®
Pepperoni, Deep Dish....................272
Pepperoni, Pizzeria Style ..............272
Pepperoni, Pizzeria Style (9") ........272
Pepperoni Deep Dish, single-
serving ...................................278
Pepperoni, single-serving ..............278
Sausage, Deep Dish.......................274
Sausage, Pizzeria Style ..................274
Sausage, Pizzeria Style (9") ...........274
Sausage & Pepperoni, Deep
Dish.......................................270
Sausage & Pepperoni, Pizzeria
Style.......................................270
Sausage & Pepperoni, Pizzeria Style
(9")........................................270
Sausage & Pepperoni Deep Dish,
single-serving ............................278
Sausage & Pepperoni, single-
serving ...................................276
Supreme, Deep Dish......................270
Supreme, Pizzeria Style..................270
Supreme, Pizzeria Style (9")...........270
Supreme Deep Dish, single-
serving ...................................278
Supreme, single-serving................278
Three Cheese Deep Dish...............266
Three Cheese Deep Dish, single-
serving ...................................276
Three Cheese Pizzeria Style ..........266
Three Cheese, single-serving ........276

## Pepperidge Farm®
Cheese Croissant Crust Pizza,
single-serving ............................276
Deluxe Croissant Crust Pizza,
single-serving ............................276
Pepperoni Croissant Crust Pizza,
single-serving ............................278

## Red Baron®
Canadian Style Bacon ...................266
4 Cheese ......................................266
Mexican Style, Supreme................268
Pepperoni .....................................272
Sausage .......................................274
Sausage & Mushroom...................268
Sausage & Pepperoni ...................270
Special Deluxe..............................270
Supreme ......................................270

## Stouffer's®
Bacon Cheddar French Bread Pizza,
single-serving ............................276
Cheeseburger French Bread Pizza,
single-serving ............................276
Cheese French Bread Pizza, single-
serving ...................................276
Cheese French Bread Pizza, Lean
Cuisine, single-serving..............276
Deluxe French Bread Pizza, single-
serving ...................................276
Deluxe French Bread Pizza, Lean
Cuisine, single-serving..............276
Double Cheese French Bread Pizza,
single-serving ............................276
Pepperoni French Bread Pizza,
single-serving ............................278
Pepperoni French Bread Pizza, Lean
Cuisine, single-serving..............278
Pepperoni & Mushroom, French
Bread Pizza, single-serving .......276
Sausage French Bread Pizza,
single-serving ............................280
Sausage & Pepperoni French Bread
Pizza, single-serving..................278
Vegetable Deluxe French Bread
Pizza, single-serving..................280
White French Bread Pizza,
single-serving ............................276

## Tombstone®
Canadian Style Bacon, Original.....266
Cheese, for One 1/2 Less Fat,
single-serving ............................276
Cheese, Sausage and Mushroom,
Original....................................268

## Totino's®

# Brand-Name Guide to Ready-to-Eat Cereals

## Estee®

## General Mills®

## Health Valley®

## Heartland®

# Index